TREATISE

ON

CLOCK AND WATCH MAKING,

THEORETICAL AND PRACTICAL.

BY THOMAS REID,
EDINBURGH,
HONORARY MEMBER OF THE WORSHIPFUL COMPANY OF CLOCKMAKERS, LONDON.

" TEMPUS IMPERATOR RERUM."

ILLUSTRATED BY PLATES.

1826.

TO

HIS ROYAL HIGHNESS,

Prince Augustus Frederick,

DUKE OF SUSSEX,

EARL OF INVERNESS AND BARON OF ARKLOW, K. G.
PRESIDENT OF THE SOCIETY FOR THE ENCOURAGEMENT OF ARTS,
MANUFACTURES, AND COMMERCE.

SIR,

The great attention and zeal with which your Royal Highness has on all occasions fostered, and patronized every attempt towards the improvement of the Arts and Sciences, and which have so eminently conduced to their rapid progress, suggested to me the propriety of soliciting the honour of dedicating the following Treatise to your Royal Highness.

I beg to return my most grateful acknowledgment for the distinction of having been permitted to inscribe, to so Illustrious a Personage, a Work which contains the result of my practical experience of many years labour in my more active days.

The chief object which I have had in view, and which has not hitherto, that I am aware of, been attempted in the English Language, is to give to the Philosopher, and scientific Artist, an account of the Art, from the earliest period to the present enlightened age, and to endeavour to abridge the labour, and accelerate the dexterity of the practical and operative artizan.

I have the distinguished honour to be,

SIR,

Your Royal Highness's

Most devoted,

And obliged humble Servant,

THOMAS REID.

EDINBURGH,
27th January, 1826.

PREFACE.

THE Article HOROLOGY, which I contributed to the *Edinburgh Encyclopædia*, abridged and imperfect as it is, from the limits to which I was necessarily confined, attracted the attention, and met the approbation of several scientific and practical Clock and Watchmakers; and a separate publication, in a more extended form, was called for by some, whose opinions I am bound to respect.

Retired from the active pursuit of a profession, to which my whole life has been devoted, I have endeavoured to combine my own observations with those of the best practical writers, and to give the operative Clock and Watchmaker a condensed view of the Art in Great Britain and on the Continent of Europe. I am sensible the work still labours under many defects, and that I require the indulgence of the Critical Reader; yet I am unconscious of omitting, or slightly passing over any subject of essential importance.

At the advanced age of *Fourscore*, I have now completed a work, which will, with all its imperfections, I am willing to believe, prove a useful *vade mecum* to the Mechanic, for whose use chiefly it was written, and who, I doubt not, will consider the solid information it may contain, of more value to him than the blandishments of a fine style; at the same time, it illustrates, by historical and biographical details, subjects which might otherwise prove dry and uninteresting to the young Artist. I am not without hope also, that my labours may meet that candid reception from the Professors and Lecturers on Mechanical Philosophy, at our Universities, Provincial Academies, and Mechanics' Institutions, to which such attempts for the advancement of useful knowledge are justly entitled.

My not having complied with the wish of the late lamented Professor Robison of this city, may perhaps be received as an apology for the absence of those theoretical and philosophical discussions which might otherwise have formed a prominent feature in the Work now submitted to the public. That learned gentleman, so early as 1793, had projected a work on the Theory and practice of Horology,[*] a subject which he had studied with particular attention; and, in a letter addressed to me, requested my assistance and participation in the composition and publication of the proposed work. The active duties of an extensive business forbade my acceptance of so very flattering and apparently profitable proposition: I have, however, endeavoured, to the best of my abilities, to sup-

---

[*] See Robison's *Mechanical Philosophy*, edited by Dr. Brewster, vol. iv. page 609, under the head "WATCHWORK."

ply the want of such a publication, unaccompanied indeed with those spirited and scientific views of Mechanical Philosophy, which it would have derived from the aid of Professor Robison, yet, I flatter myself, not the less calculated for the practical Clock and Watchmaker, nor for the student and amateur in those branches of minute mechanism,—the wonderful results of which are every day unfolding themselves to the world.

I have entrusted the publication and future revision of this Work to my friend and late partner, Mr. WILLIAM AULD, a gentleman who is practically acquainted with the Art; and I have no doubt the subsequent editions, should the publication ever acquire that circulation, will be found to keep pace with the march of general improvement.

ERRATA.

Page 106, bottom line, *for* " see top of page 105," *read* " see 2d Table, page 105."
266, beginning of last paragraph, *for* " Lodi," *read* " Locle."
274, 5th line of end of Chap. *for* " Tome," *read* " Dome."
292, line 28, *for* " Plate IV." *read* " Plate XIV."
348, line 11 from bottom, *for* " Muschenbroeck's," *read* " Musschenbroeck's."
363, line 6 from bottom, *for* " view of section," *read* " view, or section."
401, line 5 from top, *for* " a strong tight collet," *read* " a strong spring tight collet."
407, line 10 from bottom, *for* " 7.436," *read* " .7436"
407, line 10 from bottom, *for* " 1.322," *read* " 1.522"
440, top line, *for* " poin," *read* " point."

CONTENTS.

CHAPTER I.—Introductory and historical remarks, Vick's clock, &c. 1

II.—To find the number of vibrations in a minute or in an hour, having the number of wheel teeth and of the pinion leaves; and also to find the numbers for the wheel-teeth, having assumed numbers for the pinions, for the swing or balance wheel, and the number of vibrations required in an hour . . . 12

III.—On dial-wheels or motion work, length of time of going without winding up; and of the trains for three-part-clocks, such as those which strike quarters of themselves, or give chimes or tunes, as musical clocks do, &c. 31

IV.—On finding numbers for the wheels and pinions of orreries, planetariums, &c. . 49

V.—On wheel-teeth, their shape; the proportional sizes of wheels to pinions, and of pinions to wheels, with the distances which their centres ought to have, so as to form proper pitchings 82

VI.—On pendulums; the influence of gravity on them at different parts of the globe, compared with the influence of their suspension springs, by changes of temperature, &c. . 121

VII.—Having the length of a pendulum, to find the number of vibrations it must make in an hour and *vice versa*, knowing the number of vibrations that a pendulum makes in an hour, to find its length, &c. . 140

VIII.—On the Escapement or 'scapement, and the discovery of the pendulum, with its application to a clock 172

IX.—On compensation curbs and balances 257

X.—On the balance spring of watches and chronometers, commonly called the pendulum spring 263

CONTENTS.

	Page
CHAPTER XI.—On the jewelling of pivot holes in watches, chronometers, and clocks	269
XII.—On the various sorts of machinery for going in time of winding	274
XIII.—On the force of main-springs in box chronometers and how to calculate it	280
XIV.—On the dividing and cutting engine, and on the methods of dividing circles into various numbers for the plates of dividing and wheel-cutting engines	284
XV.—On equation clocks, equation of time, and lunar motions	295
Table of the equation of time	318
mean time at true noon	320
the acceleration of the fixed stars for 32 days	323
For other Tables, See Index T.	
XVI.—On repeating clocks and watches,	328
XVII.—On thermometers, pyrometers, and the expansive ratio of metals	345
XVIII.—On compensation pendulums	357
XIX.—Sympathy, or mutual action of pendulums of clocks	387
XX.—On Turret-clocks	389
XXI.—On the method of fitting up astronomical clocks	405
XXII.—On Church bells and gongs	408
XXIII.—On clock chimes and bell music, mode of pricking barrels, construction of organ clocks, &c.	412
TABLE of Prime Numbers, up to 10,000	426
APPENDIX A. Letters,—Smeaton, Ludlam, and Holmes, on the subject of turret-clock work	429
B. Description of Plate IX. 48, Dutertre's clock escapement	453
C. Description of Plate IX. 51, Arnold's detached ditto	453
D. Description of Plate IX. 52, Earnshaw's ditto	555
E. Description of Plate IX. 53, Robinson's ditto	457
F. Description of Plate XI. 61, Le Roy's marine time-keeper	458
G. Further particulars regarding month clocks	461

A

TREATISE

ON

CLOCK AND WATCH-MAKING,

THEORETICAL AND PRACTICAL.

CHAPTER I.

Introductory and Historical Remarks—Vick's Clock, &c.

THE art of constructing machines for measuring time has sometimes been denominated *Horology*. This word is derived from the Greek Ὡρολογιον, (through the Latin *Horologium*) compounded of ὥρα, *an hour*, and λόγω, *to read or point out*; hence ὡρολόγιον, a machine for indicating the hours of the day.

Long before sun-dials were invented, Clepsydræ, or water clocks, had been made in the most remote periods of antiquity, and were used in Asia, China, India, Chaldea, Egypt, and Greece, where Plato introduced them. Julius Cæsar found them even in Britain when he carried his arms thither, and it was by them he observed that the nights in this climate were shorter than those in Italy; (see his *Commentaries*, lib. v. xiii.) Clepsydræ had been known at Rome about an hundred years before this, and it is probable, they may have been as long known in Britain, seeing the early intercourse the Phoenicians had with our ancestors in quest of tin. See a description of a very curious Clepsydra given by Mr. Hamilton in No. 479 of the Phil. Trans.

Toothed wheels, although known a considerable time before, were first applied to Clepsydræ by Ctesibius, a native of Alexandria, who lived 145 years before the Christian æra. But at what time, or by whom, the clock with toothed wheels, crown-wheel scapement, and the regulator in form of a cross suspended by a cord, with two weights

B

to shift on it when regulating the clock, was invented, can now only be guessed at, as no positive information on this subject has been handed down to us. It was this kind of clock, a large turret one, which Charles V. King of France, surnamed the Wise, caused to be made at Paris by Henry Vick, who was sent for from Germany for the express purpose, and which was put up in the tower of his palace about the year 1370. Julien Le Roy, who had seen this clock, has given some account of it in his edition of Sully's *Règle artificielle de temps*, Paris, 1737. See this ancient clock by Vick, in Plate I. No. 1, a description of which shall be given afterwards.

Before a clock could be brought even to the state of the one made by Vick, there must have been many alterations and progressive improvements upon that which had first been projected, so that it must have been invented at least two or three centuries before Vick's time.

As the same word for a sun-dial among the Greeks and Romans, was also that for a clock, disputes have arisen, whether the *horologia* of Pacificus and of Gerbert, were sun-dials or clocks. Father Alexander asserts, that the horologium of Gerbert was a clock; while Hamberger supposes it to have been a sun-dial, from the pole star having been employed in setting it. Pacificus was Archdeacon of Verona about the year 850. Gerbert was Pope, under the name of Silvester II. and made his clock at Magdeburg about the year 996.

Richard of Wallingford, Abbot of St. Alban's in England, who flourished in 1326, by a miracle of art constructed a clock, which had not its equal in all Europe, according to the testimony of Gesner. Leland too, an old English author, informs us, that it was a clock which shewed the course of the sun, moon, and stars, and the rise and fall of the tides; that it continued to go in his own time, which was about the latter end of Henry the Seventh's reign; and that according to tradition, this famous piece of mechanism was called *Albion* by the inventor.

"In 1382," says Father Alexander, "the Duke of Burgundy ordered to be taken away from the city of Courtray, on the French army entering it, a clock which struck the hours, and which was the best at that time known, either on this side or beyond seas, and made it to be brought to Dijon, his capital, where it still is in the tower of Notre Dame. These are the three most ancient clocks that I find after that of Gerbert."

"We know no person," continues this author, "more ancient, and to whom we can more justly attribute the invention of clocks with toothed wheels than to Gerbert. He was born in Auvergne, and was a Monk in the Abbey of St. Gerard D'Orillac, of the order of St.

Bennet. His abbot sent him into Spain, where he learned astrology and the mathematics, in which he became so great a proficient, that, in an age when these sciences were little known, he passed for a magician, as well as the Abbot Trithemius. (*It may have been for the crime of magic imputed to Gerbert, that he was afterwards banished from France.*) From Spain he came to Rome, and being a man much superior to the times in which he lived, he was there appointed to superintend the monastic studies in the Abbacy of Bobio, situated among the Appenines in Liguria, founded by St. Columbanus in the year 613; but the low state of its funds compelled him to return to France. The reputation of his learning and uncommon genius induced Adalberon, Archbishop of Rheims, to establish him in 970, as rector of the schools there, and at the same time to make him his private secretary.

It was near the end of the tenth century, about the year 996, when he made at Magdeburg this clock so wonderful and surprising, as to go *by means of weights and wheels*. He was Archbishop of Rheims in 992, a situation which he held during three years, then Archbishop of Ravenna in 997, and at last, Sovereign Pontiff, under the name of Silvester II. in 999; he died at the beginning of the fifth year of his pontificate, in 1003.* The clock constructed by Gerbert seems to have been made after he left Rheims, and before his appointment to Ravenna; and, it is highly probable, that this was the period when clock-making was introduced into Germany.

"William Marlot, to show how wonderful this piece of work was, makes use of an expression which can hardly be suffered in our language: *Admirabile horologium fabricavit per instrumentum diabolica arte inventum.*"

The western Christians were particularly indebted to Gerbert for having transmitted to them the arithmetic which we make use of at the present day. *Abacum certe primus a Saracenis rapiens regulas dedit quaea sudantibus Abacistis vix intelliguntur,* says the historian, William of Malmesbury, ad annum 999. Gerbert had also a great taste for mechanics. William of Malmesbury says, *ibid.* "that in his time" (that is to say, some time or long before the year 1142, the year in which he died,) "there was to be seen in the church at Rheims, a mechanical clock which Gerbert had made, and hydraulic organs, where," says he, "the wind, pushed in a wonderful manner by water, made them give *des sons modulés à des flutes d'airain.*"

"Les horloges à roues sont une invention du moyen age, dont on ignore la datte et l'auteur. Dans les usages de Citeaux vers 1120, il

pose the balance clock, have only been made after a long train of research and time, and that clocks were not known in France till the middle of the fourteenth century."

The art of horology might be going slowly on in Germany, though the balance clock was unknown in France till 1370, previous to which Vick had been sent for by Charles V. of France. Had this not taken place, it might perhaps have remained still longer unknown. It must be allowed, that there is something inconsistent in Father Alexander's argument for giving the clock to Gerbert, and refusing it to Pacificus, " because it was not known in France till 250 years after. The discovery was of too great utility not to be spread abroad, particularly in monasteries, where it was so much required to regulate the religious duties of the night. In the famous monastery of Cluny, however, the Sacristan, in 1108, went out to observe the stars, to know the time when to awaken the monks to prayer." In the early stages of the art, very few clocks could have been made, and those which were constructed must have been very imperfect.

" As all arts are at first imperfect," says Hamberger, " it is observed of these clocks, that they sometimes deceived; and hence in the *Ordo Cluniacensis Bernardi Monasterii*, the person who regulated the clock is ordered, in case it should go wrong, " ut notet in cœlo, et in cursu Stellarum vel etiam Lunæ, ut fratres surgere faciat ad horam competentem : The same admonition is given in the *Constitutiones Hirsaugienses.*" From what is said here, it may be inferred that those who had clocks in the earliest periods, could not place much dependance on their keeping time; and with great probability we may suppose, that many a palace, castle, and monastery, might long continue unprovided with such a machine. It was near the end of the fifteenth century before they came to be in use in private families.

The art of clock-making seems to have been introduced into Europe by some one or other of the Romish clergy. They were, in general, especially the higher orders, possessed of wealth, and had leisure to cultivate such of the arts and sciences as were then to be attained ; and if the art of horology did not originate with them, they certainly were among the first who did every thing in their power to promote and encourage it. Time-measuring being so desirable for the regulation of the stated services required by the Church, which took place at all hours of the day and night, their attention was naturally called to a subject in which they were so much interested. Those who wish for farther information on the origin of clocks, are referred to *The Artificial Clock-Maker*, by Wm. Derham. D. D.

London, 1698—*Traité général des Horloges, par le R. P. Dom. Jacque Alexandre, Religieux Benedictin de la Congregation de Saint Maur*, à Paris, 1734—A Dissertation by Hamberger in Beckmann's *History of Inventions*, vol. iii. Lond. 1797—*Histoire de la Mesure du Temps par les Horloges, par Ferdinand Berthoud, Mechanicien de la Marine*, &c. &c. à Paris, 1802. This last is a very interesting work for an amateur in horology, and was the result of seven year's labour, when the author was at a very advanced period of life. To these may be added, *Histoire de l'Astronomie Moderne*, tom. i. p. 60, edition de 1785; and *Histoire de l'Astronomie Ancienne Eclaircissemens*, liv. iv. § 34. liv. ix. § 5—*Vitruvius's Architecture.*

Pollius Vitruvius lived 40 years before Christ, and was architect to Augustus. In a triumph of Pompey, among the spoils brought from the east, was a water-clock, the case of which was strung round with pearls, *Pliny*, lib. xxxvii. cap. i. *Mémoires de l'Academie des Inscriptions*, tom. xx. p. 446.

It would be a waste of time to describe the nature of wheels and pinions, as this kind of machinery is now so generally known. It may be sufficient to remark, that a clock or watch movement is an assemblage of wheels and pinions, contained in a frame of two brass plates, connected by means of pillars; the first, or great wheel, in an eight day movement, has, concentric with it, a cylindrical barrel, having a spiral groove cut on it. To this cylinder is attached one end of a cord, which is wrapped round in the groove, for any determined number of turns, and to the other end of the cord is hung a weight, which constitutes a power or force to set the whole in motion. Their time of continuing in motion will depend on the height through which the weight has to descend, on the number of teeth in the first or great wheel, and on the number of teeth or leaves of the pinion upon which this wheel acts, &c.

The wheels in spring clocks and in watches are urged on by the force of a spiral spring, contained in a hollow cylindrical barrel or box, to which one end of a chain or cord is fixed, and, lapping it round the barrel for several turns outside, the other end is fixed to the bottom of a solid, shaped like the frustrum of a cone, known by the name of the *fusee*, having a spiral groove cut on it. On the bottom of this cone, or fusee, the first or great wheel is put. The arbor on which the spring barrel turns, is so fixed in the frame that it cannot turn when the fusee is winding up; the inner end of the spring hooks on by an eye to the barrel arbor, and the outer end hooks by the same way to the inside of the barrel. Now, if the fusee is turned round in the proper direction, it will take on the cord or chain, and consequently take it off from the barrel. This bends up the spring, and, if the fusee and great wheel are left to themselves, the force exerted by the spring in the barrel to unbend itself, will make the barrel turn in a contrary direction to that by which it was bent up. This force of the spring unbending itself, being communicated to the wheels, will set them in motion, and they will move with considerable velocity. Their time of continuing in motion will depend on the number of turns in the spiral groove on the fusee, the number of teeth in the first or great wheel, and on the number of leaves in the pinion upon which the great wheel acts, &c. The wheels in any sort of movement, when at liberty or free to turn, and when impelled by a force, whether it is that of a weight or a spring, would soon allow this force to terminate; for as the action of the force is constant from its first commencement, the wheels would be greatly accelerated in their course, and it would be an improper machine to register time or its parts; the necessity of checking this acceleration, and making the wheels move with an uniform motion, gave rise to the invention of the escapement, or 'scapement, as it is commonly called. To effect this, an alternate motion was necessary, which required no small effort of human ingenuity to produce.

To a professional artist, a description of all the parts of Vick's clock is quite unnecessary, as a mere view of it in the plate would to him be sufficient; but, as it is handed down to us as one of the most ancient balance clocks, and having been seen almost in our own time, or very near to it, a description of the going part may be given.

A is a weight suspended by a cord, which is wrapped round a cylinder or barrel B, keyed spring tight on an axis or arbor *aa*, whose smaller parts *b b*, called the *pivots*, enter into holes made in the plates CC, DD, in which they turn: These plates in the ancient clocks were made of iron, and put together by the kneed parts EE, which are formed from the ends of the plate CC; a screwed part at the extremity of the knees connects this plate by nuts to the plate DD; this assemblage of the plates and kneed parts is called *the frame*.

The action of the weight A, necessarily tends to turn the cylinder B; so that, if it was not restrained, its descent would be by an accelerated motion, like to that of a body which falls freely; but the cylinder has at one end a ratchet toothed wheel F, the face of the ratchet teeth strike or butt on the end of the click *c*, the click is pressed by a spring *d*, which forces it to enter into the ratchet, when it has been set aside from them. It is this mechanism which is called the *click and ratchet work*, and by means of which, the weight, when wound up, is prevented from turning back. It may then be conceived that the action of the weight is transmitted to the toothed wheel GG; the teeth of this wheel enter within the spaces of the teeth, or trundles, which are formed on the small wheel, or lantern pinion e, and so that they oblige or force it to turn on its pivots ff. This communication of the teeth of one wheel with those of another, or with a pinion of any kind, is, in technical language, called *pitching*.

The wheel HH is fixed on the arbor of the lantern pinion e; thus the motion communicated by the weight to the wheel GG is transmitted to the pinion e, and consequently to the wheel HH, (and causes it to turn on its pivots ff); this pitches into the lantern pinion g, whose axis carries the crown wheel II, which is named the scapement wheel, or *wheel of rencounter*; at last, the motion impressed by the weight A, is transmitted from the crown wheel II to the levers or pallets $h\ i$, which are formed on the vertical axis KK, moveable on its two pivots $K\ l$; it is on this axis that the regulator, or balance LL is fixed; this balance is suspended by a cord M, and can describe round its pivots, arcs of a circle going and returning alternately on itself, making *vibrations*.

The alternate motion or vibration of the balance is produced by the action of the wheel II, on the pallets which project from the axis of the balance, the angle formed between them is about 90 degrees; so that when a tooth of the wheel has drawn aside the pallet h, and escapes or gets past it, the other pallet i presents itself to a tooth of the wheel nearly diametrically opposite, which in its turn is drawn aside; so that the wheel turning always the same way, the balance goes and comes on itself, forming vibrations which moderate and regulate the velocity of the wheel II, and consequently the wheels H, and G, whose revolutions serve to measure time. The balance here, in place of being like the fly of a kitchen jack, as they sometimes were, is formed of two thin arms projecting from the verge or axis of the balance, making a sort of cross; on these arms several concentric notches are made; a small weight m is appended to each arm; by carrying the weights mm, more or less from the centre, will make the clock go slow or fast.

The reciprocal action of the wheel II, on the pallets $h\ i$, carried by the axis of the balance, and of the pallets themselves on the wheel to regulate the motion of it, is what is called the *Scapement* or *Scaping*.

The wheel GG, makes a revolution in an hour, the pivot *b b* of this wheel is prolonged beyond the outside of the plate CC; it carries a pinion, *u*, which pitches in, or leads the wheel NN, and causes it to make a turn in 12 hours; the axis of this wheel carries the index or hand, O, which points out the hours on the dial. It must be explained what determines the wheel GG to make one revolution precisely in an hour; for this purpose it must be known, that the vibrations of the regulator or balance are so much the slower the heavier it is, or is of a great diameter. Suppose that the balance LL can make vibrations whose time is exactly that of one second, and this is come at by bringing nearer or farther from the centre the weights *m m*, as has been already noticed; that being understood, it may be shown how, by means of the number of the teeth of the wheels and pinions, we determine the wheel GG to make a revolution exactly in an hour. In giving 30 teeth to the crown wheel II, then, during the time it takes to make one turn, the balance will make 60 vibrations, for at each turn of the wheel the same tooth acts once on the pallet A, and once on that of *i*, which produces two vibrations for each tooth, so thus the wheel having 30 teeth, it must cause twice 30 vibrations to be made; it then makes its revolution in a minute of time; it is also necessary that this wheel makes 60 turns during the time that the wheel GG makes one. Now to determine the number of the teeth in the wheels GG and HH and their pinions, it is proper to observe, that a wheel gives as many more turns to its pinion, whilst it makes one, as the number of the teeth of the pinion is contained a greater number of times in that of the teeth of the wheel; for, supposing the wheel GG has 64 teeth, and the lantern pinion *e* 8, this pinion will make 8 turns during the time that the wheel will make one: which is evident, for each tooth of the wheel moves forward one tooth of the pinion; so thus, when the pinion has advanced forward 8 teeth, which makes its revolution, the wheel GG has only advanced 8 teeth: now, for the wheel to complete its revolution, it must yet advance 56 teeth more, which will make 7 times 8 of the pinion; that is to say, it shall cause it to make 7 turns, which, joined to the one which it has made, gives 8 revolutions of the pinion for one of the wheel. By the like means, the wheel HH having 60 teeth, and the pinion *g* 8, it will cause the pinion to make $7\frac{1}{2}$ turns; but the wheel HH carries the pinion *e*, making 8 turns for one of the wheel GG; the pinion *g* makes then 8 times $7\frac{1}{2}$ turns, that is to say, 60 during the time that the wheel GG makes one turn: and having seen that the wheel II, carried by the pinion *g*, makes a revolution in a minute, the wheel GG makes then a turn in an hour. By the same reasoning, we see that the pinion *n*, carried by the axis of the wheel GG, must make 12 turns during the time that the wheel NN makes one. This wheel ought to have 12 times more teeth than the pinion; and if it has 8 teeth, the wheel NN must have 96. From the side of the wheel NN, twelve pins project, which serve to discharge the striking part.

When the cord which suspends the weight A is wholly run off from the cylinder, a handled key is used, whose canon has a square hole in it so as to enter upon the square P, on the arbor of the lantern pinion *n*, which pitches in with the wheel R, fixed on the end of the barrel B; and in turning this key the weight is again wound up. The wheel R, and that of F, can turn separately from that of GG, which keeps its place. This retrograde motion of the cylinder or barrel is obtained by means of the click and ratchet work F, *c*, *d*. The teeth of the ratchet are inclined on one side, which raise up the click *c*, so that during the time of winding up the weight, the ratchet F turns separately from the wheel GG; but, upon ceasing to wind up the weight, it acts upon the cylinder and ratchet, the faces of whose teeth butt or come anew against the end of the click *c*, which forces the wheel GG to turn with the cylinder; the spring *d* serves, as has been already mentioned, to bring the click back into the space of the ratchet teeth. Of the striking part of Henry Vick's clock we have only to remark, that it must have raised a very massy hammer, considering the enormous weight applied to it, being above 500 pounds to each part.

It was thought nowise necessary to give either a representation or description of the striking part; suffice it to say, that, like the old clocks, it locked against an interrupted hoop, fixed on what was called the hoop wheel; and eleven notches on the circumference or edge of a plate wheel, commonly called the count wheel, determined the hours or number of blows which the hammer should give.

Either Julien Le Roy, or Berthoud, must have made a mistake, in making the crown wheel in Vick's clock to have 30 teeth, unless it may have been merely for the purpose of showing in a clearer point of view, that the time of a revolution should be equal to one minute. It is well known, that the crown wheel 'scapement cannot admit the wheel to have an even number, no other than an odd number will 'scape with the pallets on the verge. Had the number been 29, and the time of one vibration about equal, or nearly so, to one second, then one revolution of the crown wheel, or 58 vibrations, would have been nearly one minute, or somewhat thereabouts.

12   FINDING NUMBERS FOR

Before giving an account of the first 'scapement, and the improvements on it, which subsequently followed, it may be more in order, first to enter into the calculation of the numbers for wheels and pinions, their proportional sizes, trains, length of pendulum, &c. &c.

CHAPTER II.

To find the Number of Vibrations in a Minute, or in an Hour, having the numbers of the wheel teeth and of the pinion leaves; and also to find the numbers for the wheel teeth, having assumed numbers for the pinions, for the swing or balance wheel, and the number of Vibrations required in an Hour, &c. &c.

THE beats given by the alternate motion of the 'scapement, are a determined number in a minute, or in an hour, called the train, which depend on the number of wheels in the movement, their number of teeth, on the number of the pinions, and the number of their teeth or leaves: the beats in an hour of a common seconds clock are 3600, and 17280 are the number of beats given by a common watch.

In a combination of two or more wheels and their pinions, the ratio of the pinions to their wheels being given, the number of revolutions of the last wheel, for one of the first, can be deduced. The first wheel being supposed to make a revolution in an hour, during which time let it drive a pinion eight times round, concentric with the pinion is a wheel which drives another pinion seven and a half times round; on the arbor of this pinion is a wheel that may at pleasure, or rather *must* be cut into such a number of teeth as to make up the required number of vibrations. The wheels and their pinions may be represented thus: $\frac{\text{wheels}}{\text{pinions}} \frac{8 \times 7\frac{1}{2}}{1 \times 1} = 60$, which is the number of revolutions that the last pinion must make for one of the first wheel. If the pinions have eight leaves each, then it follows that one of the wheels must have eight times this number of teeth, which will be 64, and the other seven and a half times equal to 60. The revolutions will be the same to the last wheel or its pinion, in whatever order the two wheels are taken.

A fraction does not lose its value whether it is divided or multiplied by a like number. The wheels being 64 and 60, their pinions 8, they may stand thus: $\frac{64 \times 60}{8 \times 8} = 60$; if we were to double the numbers of the pinion leaves, they would become 16, the wheels would then be 128 and 120. By taking a fourth part from them, they become pinions of 6, in this case the wheels would be 48 and 45, as 6×8=48, and 6×7½=45. The revolutions of the last pinion may be found without the use of fractions. Let the product of the wheel teeth, when multiplied into one another, be divided by the product of the pinions, the quotient will be the number of revolutions of the last pinion, which here will be evident, for 64×60=3040÷64=60. Whatever number of teeth is cut in the last or swing wheel, it will give double the number of vibrations for every revolution; then, if the number of teeth is 30, the vibrations will be 60; and, as it makes 60 revolutions in an hour, it must make 3600 vibrations in an hour, for 60×60=3600. If the pinions here, in place of being driven, were made the drivers, or, more properly, the leaders, as in orreries, or planetariums, and what was the last pinion before, to be placed as the first leader, making its revolution in an hour, then the first wheel before, being now last in the order, would take 3660 hours, or 150 days, to make one revolution.

The number of vibrations in an hour being given, likewise the numbers of the wheel teeth, and of the pinion leaves, to know what must be the number to cut for the swing wheel teeth. The product of the numbers of the wheel teeth multiplied into one another, divided by the product of the pinions, the quotient will give the number of the revolutions which the swing wheel must make in an hour; the given number of vibrations in an hour being divided by this quotient, will give double the number of the swing wheel teeth.

Examples.—Given 7200 as the number of vibrations required in an hour, the wheels having 80 teeth each, and the pinions 8 leaves each; required the number of teeth to be cut in the swing wheel, so as to give this number of vibrations in an hour?

Here 80×80=6400÷64=100 and 7200÷100=72, the half of this is 36, being the number for the swing wheel teeth. Let the required number of vibrations be 7560, the wheels 90 and 84, and the pinions 8 each; what must be the number of teeth in the swing wheel?—90×84=7560÷64=118.125, and 7560÷118.125=64; the number of teeth in the swing wheel must then be 32. The number of vibrations being 6720, the wheels 84 and 80, the pinions 8

each, what number is required for the swing wheel teeth?—
84×80=6720÷64=105. and 6720÷105=64, the swing wheel teeth are then 32. It might happen that the number of vibrations required, and the numbers of the wheel teeth, and of the pinion leaves, may be so incommensurate, that the quotient obtained, besides being a whole number, may have some decimal parts annexed to it, which would in this case be improper, and could not be used.

In order to ascertain what the numbers for the wheel teeth of a clock or watch movement should be, three things are requisite to be known or fixed upon; First, the number of beats to be given in a minute or in an hour; Second, the number of the pinions and of their leaves; and, Third, the number of teeth it is intended for the swing or balance wheel to have.

Rule.—The number of vibrations or beats in an hour, being multiplied by the number of leaves in each pinion, or, what is the same thing, each pinion being multiplied into one another, and with the product multiply the number of vibrations in an hour, this last product being divided by double the number intended for the swing, or balance wheel, will give for the quotient such a number, that when divided by prime numbers, first by two, as often as it will divide by two, without leaving a remainder; then by three, as often as it will divide by it; by five, as often as it will; and by 7, 11, 13, &c. until no remainder is left; and afterwards arranging the divisors, they may be made out so, as to have sets of them, which when multiplied into one another, will give the proper numbers for the wheel teeth required. A few examples will make the matter so plain and easy, that few can fail to comprehend them; and the numbers in a common clock movement being known to almost every clock maker, an example of it shall be taken for the first, in order that the beauty and facility of the rule may the more readily be seen.

The vibrations or beats of a common seconds pendulum clock are 60 in a minute, or 3600 in an hour; the pinions are commonly two of 8 leaves each, and the swing wheel having 30 teeth: Required the number of teeth that must be put into the second and third wheels?

The two pinions of 8, multiplied together, make 64, and 3600 being multiplied by 64, gives for the product 230400, which, divided by 60, the double of the number of teeth in the swing wheel, we obtain a quotient of 3840; and this last being divided by 2, 3, and 5, will, by the divisors, when taken in separate sets and multiplied into one another, give two numbers, which will be those of the teeth for the second and third wheels.

$3600\times8\times8+60=$ 3840 | 2   Here the divisors are eight 2^s,
                   1920 | 2   one 3, and a 5, which, when arran-
                   960 | 2   ged into proper sets, will give the
                   480 | 2   numbers for the teeth of each wheel.
                   240 | 2 $2\times2=4\times2=8\times2=16\times2=32\times2=64$
                   120 | 2 $2\times2=4\times3=12\times5=60$
                   60 | 2
                   30 | 2   The number 64 is given for the
                   15 | 3   teeth of the second wheel, and 60 for
                   5 | 5   those on the third wheel; or the num-
                   1 | bers for the wheels may be *vice versa*.

The vibrations being 1800 in an hour, two pinions of 10 leaves each, and the swing wheel 30 teeth: Required the numbers for the teeth of the second and third wheels?

$1800\times10\times10+60=$ 3000 | 2   This gives for the divisors three
                    1500 | 2 2^s, one 3, and three 5^s, and, when
                    750 | 2   arranged into two sets, give the
                    375 | 3   numbers 60 and 50 for the teeth
                    125 | 5   of the second and third wheels.
                    25 | 5 $2\times2=4\times3=12\times5=60$
                    5 | 5 $2\times5=10\times5=50$.
                    1 |

Having two pinions of 12 each, and the swing wheel with 32 teeth: Required the numbers for the teeth of the two wheels, so as to give 100 vibrations in a minute?

$100\times60\times12\times12=864000$.$\div64=135000$ | 2   Here are two 2^s, three 3^s, and
                                           6750 | 2   three 5^s, which, made into pro-
                                           3375 | 3   per sets, will give the numbers for
                                           1125 | 3   the teeth of the wheels.
                                           375 | 3
                                           125 | 5
                                           25 | 5 $5\times5=25\times5=125$
                                           5 | 5 $2\times2=4\times3=12\times3=36\times3=108$
                                           1 |

By this is shewn, that a second wheel of 125 teeth, and a third wheel of 108, the swing wheel 32, and two pinions of 12 each, will give 100 vibrations in a minute.

Two pinions of 10 each, and the swing wheel 30: Required the numbers for the teeth of the two wheels, so as to give 100 vibrations in a minute?

16   FINDING NUMBERS FOR

$100 \times 60 \times 10 \times 10 \div 60 =$ 10000 | 2   The divisors of this being
                          5000 | 2   four 2^s, and four 5^s, when put
                          2500 | 2   into sets, will give 100 for
                          1250 | 2   the teeth of each wheel.
                           625 | 5
                           125 | 5
                             25 | 5 $2 \times 2 = 4 \times 5 = 20 \times 5 = 100$
                              5 | 5 $2 \times 2 = 4 \times 5 = 20 \times 5 = 100$.
                                  1

Two pinions of 8 leaves each, and the swing wheel 30: Required the numbers of the second and third wheels, so as to give 120 vibrations in a minute?

$120 \times 60 \times 8 \times 8 \div 60 =$ 7680 | 2
                         3840 | 2
                         1920 | 2   Nine 2^s, one 3, and a 5, when
                          960 | 2   properly arranged, will give the
                          480 | 2   numbers 96 and 80 for the teeth
                          240 | 2   of the two wheels.
                          120 | 2 $2 \times 2 = 4 \times 2 = 8 \times 2 = 16 \times 2 = 32 \times 3 = 96$
                            60 | 2 $2 \times 2 = 4 \times 2 = 8 \times 2 = 16 \times 5 = 80$
                            30 | 2
                            15 | 3
                             5 | 5
                             1

There are some cases where the double of the number of the swing wheel teeth, will not divide the product of the vibrations in an hour multiplied by the pinions, without leaving a remainder; and, even where no remainder is left, there are sometimes such disproportionate and prime numbers given for the wheel teeth, as could not well be adopted in practice; assuming 118 for the number of vibrations in a minute is one of those cases.

The swing wheel having 32 teeth, a pinion of 9, and one of 8, the vibrations 102 in a minute: Required the numbers for the teeth of the second and third wheels?

$102 \times 60 \times 9 \times 8 \div 64 =$ 6885 | 3   The divisors are four 3^s, one 5, and a 17,
                       2295 | 3   which last being a prime number, cannot be
                        765 | 3   farther divided; taking it therefore with the
                        255 | 3   5, will give 85 for the second wheel, the
                         85 | 5   four 3^s will give the other.
                         17 | 17 $5 \times 17 = 85$ second wheel
                          1       $3 \times 3 = 9 \times 3 = 27 \times 3 = 81$ third wheel.

The vibrations being 115 in a minute, the pinions 6 each, and the swing wheel 30: What must be the numbers for the teeth of the wheels?

115×60×8×8÷60= 7360
2×2=   4×23= 92
2×2=4×2=8×2=16× 5= 80

The divisors are six 2^s, one 5, and a 23. The wheels 92, 80, and 30, and 2 pinions of 8 each; will give 115 vibrations in a minute.

The two foregoing examples, although they are within the limits of practice, may serve to shew that larger prime numbers may occur, and, consequently, be unfit for use, as is the case in assuming 118 for the beats in a minute, as noticed above, where the prime number 59 is the constant result of the division, and which number is quite incommensurate with the other divisors to make proper sets for the numbers of the wheel teeth.

The vibrations 108 in a minute, the pinions 8 and 7, the swing wheel 30: What must be the numbers for the wheel teeth?

108×60×8×7÷60= 6048
2×2=4×3=12×7= 84
2×2=4×2=8×3=24×3= 72

The divisors are five 2^s, three 3^s, and a 7; the wheels 84, 72, and 30; the pinions 8 and 7; will give 108 vibrations in a minute.

The number of examples given, is in order that the rule may become the more familiar and easy. Those who wish to prosecute this subject, and would require to have rules for finding not only the numbers for the wheel teeth, but to find at the same time the numbers for the pinion leaves, and the numbers for the teeth of swing or balance wheels, are referred to *Élémens de Mechanique Statique, tome second, troisième edition, par M. Camus, à Paris, de l'Imprimerie de Prault,* 1767, or an English translation of this part of it, for J. Taylor, at the Architectural Library, No. 59, High Holborn, London, 1806. These problems by *Camus,* are more requisite for the finding of such numbers for wheels and pinions, as will give the nearest times for the revolutions of the planets, in planetariums or orreries, than for any motion wanted in clock or watch-work simply.

The preceding rule applies equally to the finding of numbers for the wheel teeth in watch movements; and, for the sake of the watch-movement maker, some examples shall be given.

c

For the first example, let that of a common watch be taken, where the balance wheel has 15 teeth, three pinions, having six leaves each, and the beats, train, or vibrations in an hour is 17280: Required the numbers for the teeth of the second, third, and fourth, (or contrate) wheels?

Vibrations per minute 288×60×6×6×6÷30=124416

$$2\times3=6\times3=18\times3=54$$
$$2\times2=4\times2=8\times2=16\times3=48$$
$$2\times2=4\times2=8\times2=16\times3=48.$$

The divisors here will be found to consist of nine 2^s, and five 3^s, which, when properly arranged, will give for the numbers of the wheel teeth, 54, 48, and 48, with a balance wheel of 15 teeth, and three pinions of 6 each, will give a train of 17280, the beats in an hour.

The train is 18000 in an hour, the balance wheel 15 teeth, and three pinions of 6 leaves each: Required the numbers for the second, third, and fourth wheels?

Vibrations per minute 300×60×6×6×6÷30=129600. The divisors of which are six 2^s, four 3^s, and two 5^s.

$$3\times3=9\times3=27\times2=54$$
$$2\times5=10\times5=50$$
$$2\times2=4\times2=8\times2=16\times3=48.$$
} The numbers for the wheel teeth.

These divisors can be arranged into another set of numbers, should it be thought necessary, as thus:

$$2\times2=4\times3=12\times5=60$$
$$2\times2=4\times2=8\times2=16\times3=48$$
$$3\times3=9\times5=45.$$
} Numbers given for the teeth of the wheels.

Taking the train 17280, the balance wheel 14, two pinions of 8, and one of 7, what must be the numbers for the teeth of the three wheels?

17280×8×8×7÷28=276480. The divisors are eleven 2^s, three 3^s, and one 5.

$$2\times2=4\times2=\ 8\times3=24\times3=72$$
$$2\times2=4\times2=8\times2=16\times2=32\times2=64$$
$$2\times2=\ 4\times3=12\times5=60.$$
} Numbers given for the wheel teeth.

If the number 72 is taken for the fourth wheel, then this will be a fourth wheel seconds movement.

The beats in an hour 17920, two pinions of 8, and one of 7, the balance wheel 14: Required the numbers for the teeth of the second, third, and fourth wheels?

17920×8×8×7÷28=286720, whose divisors are thirteen 2°, one 5, and a 7.

$$2\times5=10\times7=70$$
$$2\times2=4\times2=8\times2=16\times2=30\times2=64$$
$$2\times2=4\times2=8\times2=16\times2=32\times2=64$$
} Numbers given for the teeth of the wheels.

The beats in an hour being assumed at 16000, two pinions of 10, and one of 8, the balance wheel 15 teeth: Required the numbers for the teeth of the second, third, and fourth wheels?

16000×10×10×8÷30=480000. The divisors are eight 2°, one 3, and four 5°.

$$2\times2=4\times2=8\times2=16\times5=80$$
$$2\times2=4\times2=8\times2=16\times5=80$$
$$3\times5=15\times5=75.$$
} Numbers for the wheel teeth.

If the fourth wheel in this is made 80, that is changing places and numbers with the third wheel, it will then become a fourth wheel seconds movement.

Given 18432 for the beats in an hour, the pinions 8 each, and the balance wheel 16: Required the numbers for the teeth of the three wheels?

18432×8×8×8÷32=294912. The divisors are fifteen 2°, and two 3°; (or one 9, which is the same thing; yet, properly speaking, 9 should never in these cases be expressed, although it may be implied, as it is not itself a prime number.)

$$2\times2=4\times2=8\times9=72$$
$$2\times2=4\times2=8\times2=16\times2=32\times2=64$$
$$2\times2=4\times2=8\times2=16\times2=32\times2=64$$
} Numbers for the wheel teeth.

Given 360 beats in a minute, or 21600 in an hour, the pinions 8 each, and the balance wheel 15: What numbers will be required for the teeth of the wheels?

21600×8×8×8÷30=368640. The divisors are thirteen 2°, two 3°, and a 5.

$$2\times2=4\times2=8\times2=16\times5=80$$
$$2\times2=4\times2=8\times3=24\times3=72$$
$$2\times2=4\times2=8\times2=16\times2=32\times2=64$$
} The numbers for the wheel teeth.

Given 18000 beats in an hour, the pinions 8, and the balance wheel 15: What numbers will be required for the teeth of the wheels?

18000×8×8×8÷30=307200. The divisors are twelve 2', one 3, and two 5'.

$$3\times5=15\times5=75$$
$$2\times2=4\times2=8\times2=16\times2=32\times2=64$$
$$2\times2=4\times2=8\times2=16\times2=32\times2=64.$$
} The numbers for the wheel teeth.

Given the same as the preceding example, only the balance wheel 16 in place of 15: To find the numbers for the wheel teeth?

18000×8×8×8÷32=288000. The divisors are eight 2', two 3', and three 5'.

$$5\times5=25\times3=75$$
$$2\times2=4\times2=8\times2=16\times2=32\times2=64$$
$$2\times2=4\times5=20\times3=60.$$
} The numbers for the wheel teeth.

Given 20250 for the train, pinions of 6, and the balance wheel 15: To find the numbers for the wheel teeth?

20250×6×6×6÷30=145800. The divisors are three 2', six 3', and two 5'.

$$3\times3=9\times3=27\times2=54$$
$$3\times3=9\times3=27\times2=54$$
$$5\times5=25\times2=50$$
} The numbers found for the wheel teeth.

Given 7200 beats in an hour, the pinions 8, and the balance wheel 15: To find the numbers for the teeth of the wheels?

7200×8×8×8÷30=122880. The divisors are thirteen 2', one 3, and a 5.

$$2\times2=4\times2=8\times2=16\times2=32\times2=64$$
$$2\times2=4\times2=8\times2=16\times3=48$$
$$2\times2=4\times2=8\times5=40.$$
} Numbers for the wheel teeth.

Given 14400 beats in an hour, the pinions 8 each, and the balance wheel 15: To find the numbers for the teeth of the wheels?

14400×8×8×8÷30=245760. The divisors are fourteen 2', one 3, and a 5.

$$2\times2=4\times2=8\times2=16\times2=32\times2=64$$
$$2\times2=4\times2=8\times2=16\times2=32\times2=64$$
$$2\times2=4\times3=12\times5=60.$$
} Numbers for the wheel teeth.

Making the third wheel 60, and the fourth wheel 64, it becomes a fourth wheel seconds movement.

The beats in an hour being 14400, the pinions 10 each, and the balance wheel 15: Required the numbers for the wheel teeth?
Vibrations in a minute 240×60×10×10×10÷30=480000. The divisors are eight 2', one 3, and four 5'.

$$\left.\begin{array}{l} 2\times 2=4\times 2=8\times 2=16\times 5=80 \\ 3\times 5=15\times 5=75 \\ 2\times 2=4\times 2=8\times 2=16\times 5=80 \end{array}\right\} \text{Numbers for the wheel teeth.}$$

The beats in an hour 14400, two pinions of 12, and one of 10, the balance wheel 16: What must be the numbers for the wheel teeth?
14400×12×12×10÷32=648000. The divisors are six 2', four 3', and three 5'.

$$\left.\begin{array}{l} 2\times 2=4\times 2=8\times 2=16\times 2=32\times 3=96 \\ 2\times 3= 6\times 3=18\times 5=90 \\ 3\times 5=15\times 5=75. \end{array}\right\} \text{Numbers for the wheel teeth.}$$

The same as the preceding, only the pinions here are all 12.
14400×12×12×12÷32=777600. The divisors are seven 2', five 3', and two 3'.

$$\left.\begin{array}{l} 2\times 2=4\times 2=8\times 2=16\times 2=32\times 3=96 \\ 2\times 3= 6\times 3=18\times 5=90 \\ 2\times 3= 6\times 3=18\times 5=90. \end{array}\right\} \text{Numbers for the wheel teeth.}$$

Slow trains are suited only for box chronometers; 14400 has been generally adopted; and where the balance wheels have 12, 14, 15, or 16 teeth, numbers for the teeth of the other wheels may easily be obtained. But with common numbers for the teeth of the wheels and leaves of the pinions, and a balance wheel of 13, the seconds hand cannot point in a regular order to the seconds, on the seconds circle. The nearest approximation to this is by making the fourth wheel 74, and the balance wheel pinion 8, the train would then be 14430, being 240.5 beats in a minute in place of 240. If we take numbers such as are not altogether impracticable for the fourth wheel, and balance wheel pinion, the balance wheel being 13, we can get 14400 exactly: a fourth wheel of 120, and a balance wheel pinion of 13, will do this.

The following shews the train of 14400, with fourth wheels and balance wheels, with their pinions of different numbers. The fourth wheel is divided by the balance wheel pinion; the quotient, multiplied by double of the number in the balance wheel teeth, gives the beats in a minute.

8)80(10 ×24 double the number of the balance wheel=240×60=14400.
13)120(9 1/1 ×26 - - - - - - 240×60=14400.
*14)120(8 4/7 ×28 - - - - - - 240×60=14400.
10) 80 (8 ×30 - - - - - - 240×60=14400.
10) 75 (7½ ×32 - - - - - - 240×60=14400.

The beats 18000 in an hour, two pinions of 8, and one of 7, the balance wheel being 15: Required the numbers for the teeth of the wheels.

Vibrations in a minute 300×60×8×8×7÷30=268800. The divisors are nine 2's, one 3, two 5's, and a 7.

$$\left. \begin{array}{r} 2\times5=10\times7=70 \\ 2\times2=4\times2=8\times2=16\times2=32\times2=64 \\ 2\times2=4\times3=12\times5=60. \end{array} \right\} \text{Numbers for the wheel teeth.}$$

These numbers are suitable for a fourth wheel seconds movement by putting 70 for the fourth wheel, but this makes the teeth to be rather fine; and where fourth wheel seconds are not intended, it is in favour of the movement to have the wheels in the order of 70, 64, and 60.

Although there are more examples given for finding numbers for the teeth of wheels than might be thought necessary, it was judged proper not to set any of them aside that have been given.

When the numbers of the wheel teeth, and of the pinion leaves, are known, the train or beats in an hour in either a clock or watch, is obtained by multiplying the wheels into one another, and the product by the double of the number of teeth in the swing or balance wheel, and this last product, divided by the amount of the pinions multiplied into one another, will give for the quotient the number of beats in an hour.

Take for example the wheels 72, 64, 64, and 16, three pinions of 8 each to find the train?

72×64×64×32=9437184÷8×8×8=512 gives the train 18432.

When the movement is for a fourth wheel seconds, then the train is got by dividing the fourth wheel by the balance wheel pinion, the

---

* The numbers here can be 7 and 60, which is dividing the fraction $\frac{14}{7}$ by 2.

quotient, multiplied by double of the number of teeth in the balance wheel, and then by 60, will give the beats or train in an hour.

Let the fourth wheel be 80, the balance wheel 15, and its pinion 8.

Then $80 \div 8 = 10 \times 30 \times 60 = 18000$, the train required.

It may be observed, that the rule for finding the train is nearly the converse of that for finding the teeth of the wheels. And as the number which is decomposed into divisors is the product of the wheel teeth multiplied into one another; so this again being multiplied by double of the number of the balance wheel teeth, and divided by the train, the quotient will be that number, which when resolved into divisors and properly arranged, will become numbers for the pinion leaves.

It is evident, that if the number 9437184 be divided by the train 18432, that the quotient 512 must be the product of the pinions multiplied into one another. The divisors of 512 are nine 2's, making three sets of $2 \times 2 = 4 \times 2 = 8$, all the pinions being 8.

The product of the wheels 96, 90, 75, and 32, the double of the balance wheel, being divided by the train 14400, the quotient will be 1440, whose divisors are five 2's, two 3's, and a 5; arranging them will shew the pinions.

$$\left. \begin{array}{l} 2 \times 2 = 4 \times 3 = 12 \\ 2 \times 2 = 4 \times 3 = 12 \\ 2 \times 5 = 10. \end{array} \right\} \text{Numbers for the pinion leaves.}$$

It deserves to be remarked, that it has been frequently the practice, to put an odd number of teeth into the balance wheel, although the nature of the scapement would have allowed one of an even number, all other circumstances being made to accord; this seems to have arisen from the old crown wheels, whose scapement would admit no other number but an odd one, (as has already been mentioned in page 11.)

In movements intended to give seconds by the fourth wheel in a watch or chronometer of any kind, having assumed the train, and the number of teeth in the balance wheel, nothing more is wanting than to find the number of turns, (and parts of a turn when there are any) that the balance wheel must make in a minute, from which is derived the number for the balance wheel pinion, and by it is obtained that for the teeth of the fourth wheel.

The numbers for the teeth of the second and third wheels, and for the third and fourth wheel pinions, whatever they are, ought always to give the revolutions of the fourth wheel, to those of the second wheel in the constant ratio of 60 to 1.

It may be thought unnecessary to mention here, that for this purpose the number of teeth in the second wheel should be eight times that of the third wheel pinion, and those in the third wheel seven and a half times that of the fourth wheel pinion. Indeed it will be the same thing whether the greater number is put into the second or third wheel, provided the pinions be contained in these numbers 8 times and $7\frac{1}{2}$ times. If the number of teeth in the second wheel, when multiplied by those in the third wheel, and the product divided by that of the third and fourth wheel pinions multiplied into one another, have 60 for the quotient, they will then be in their proper ratio.

Now to find the numbers for the balance wheel pinion, and the fourth wheel, in a fourth wheel seconds watch. As *a first example in this way*, we may take the train of a common watch, which in general is 17280, the number of teeth in the balance wheel 15, and let the fourth or contrate wheel be supposed to make a revolution in a minute : It is required to find the numbers for the balance wheel pinion, and for the teeth of the fourth wheel ?

Rule.—Divide the train by 60, the quotient will be the train or beats in a minute, which being subdivided by double the number of teeth in the balance wheel, will give the number of revolutions, (and fractional parts of a revolution when there are any,) made by the balance wheel in a minute. If the revolutions are composed of a whole number, then the pinion may at pleasure be any number, which when multiplied by the whole number in the quotient, will give the number for the fourth wheel teeth. But should the revolutions of the balance wheel be in whole numbers, and fractional parts of another, the denominator of the fraction determines the number of the pinion ; and the number for the fourth wheel teeth is obtained by multiplying the denominator by the whole number, to which the numerator must be added, making what is called an improper fraction, the numerator of which will represent the number for the fourth wheel teeth, and the denominator that for the pinion, as has been observed. The train 17280 being divided by 60, will give 288 in the quotient for the train or number of beats in a minute, and this subdivided by 30, the double of the number of teeth in the balance wheel will give the number of revolutions and parts of a revolution, made by the balance wheel in a minute, which in this case will give $9\frac{18}{30}$ for the quotient, as thus, $30)288(9\frac{18}{30}$, which is the same with $9\frac{6}{10}$, the denominator 10 of the fraction represents the number for the pinion, and the whole number 9 being multiplied by it, and the number 6 added, will give the improper fraction $\frac{96}{10}$, of which the numerator 96 represents the number for the fourth wheel teeth. The fraction $\frac{96}{10}$ may be reduced to $\frac{48}{5}$, where 5 represents the pinion, and 48 the fourth wheel. *Ten* for the pinion may be thought too *high*, and if we take 48 for the wheel, and 5 for the pinion, *five* may be thought too *low* a number.

There is, however, nothing impracticable here, whether the pinion 10 or 5 be taken.

Example 2d. Let 17400 be assumed for the train, and 15 for the balance wheel teeth, what must be the numbers for the balance wheel pinion, and for the fourth wheel teeth?

$17400 \div 60 = 290 \div 30 = 9\frac{20}{30}$, or $9\frac{2}{3}$, for the revolutions of the balance wheel in a minute; the mixed number, $9\frac{2}{3}$, as it is called when reduced to an improper fraction, will be $\frac{29}{3}$; the numerator 58 being the number for the fourth wheel teeth, and the denominator 6 for that of the pinion,

Example 3d. Take the train 18000, and the balance wheel 15: to find the numbers for the fourth wheel and balance wheel pinion?

$18000 \div 60 = 300 \div 30 = 10$, the number of revolutions made by the balance wheel in a minute, which being a whole number, any number may be taken for the pinion; if 7 is taken, then the fourth wheel must be 70; if 8 is taken, then the fourth wheel must be 80.

Example 4th. Let 18432 be assumed for the train, and 16 for the balance wheel: Required the numbers for the balance wheel pinion, and for the fourth wheel?

$18432 \div 60 = 307.\frac{12}{15}$, or $307.2 \div 32 = 9.6$, the number and decimal parts of the revolutions, which would be made by the balance wheel in a minute; the pinion here must be 10, and the wheel 96, as represented in the improper fraction obtained from 9.6 or $9\frac{6}{10} = \frac{96}{10}$.

Example 5th. The train 18000, the wheel 14?

$18000 \div 60 = 300 \div 28 = 10\frac{20}{28}$, or $10\frac{5}{7} = \frac{75}{7}$. With the same train, and a balance wheel of 16, the fraction would be $\frac{75}{7}$. The wheel being 18, the fraction would be $\frac{75}{7}$.

Example 6th. The train 21600, the wheel 15.

$21600 \div 60 = 360 \div 30 = 12$, and 12×7 taken here for the pinion, will give 84 for the fourth wheel.

Example 7th. The train 14400, the wheel 15.

14400÷60=240÷30=8, taking 10 for the pinion, and multiplying it by 8, gives 80 for the wheel.

Example 8th. The train 14400, the wheel 14?
14400÷60=240÷28=8$\frac{4}{7}$, or $8\frac{4}{7}=\frac{120}{14}$, or $\frac{60}{7}$; for 18000, $\frac{150}{7}$.

Example 9th. The same train as the preceding, with a balance wheel of 13?

14400÷60=240÷26=9$\frac{6}{13}$, or $9\frac{6}{13}=\frac{120}{13}$. This is the only fraction that in this case can be obtained for a balance wheel of 13 teeth; and although the numbers are rather high, they are not quite impracticable.

It has been alleged by some, that with a balance wheel of 13 teeth, it was impossible to constitute a box chronometer, and to have a train of 14400. An eminent maker has said that 18000 was the best train for them, at the same time giving 13 teeth to the balance wheel in box chronometers, and 15 teeth to pocket ones: now a train of 18000, with a balance wheel of 13 teeth, cannot possibly be obtained, unless by using very high numbers for the fourth wheel, and also for the balance wheel pinion. What the numbers were which he adopted, we have not been favoured with, and are of the opinion that no other can give the train 18000 but the following. The beats in a minute are 300, this divided by the double of 13, will give the revolutions and parts of a revolution which the balance wheel must make in a minute. 300÷26=11$\frac{14}{26}$, or $11\frac{7}{13}$; this reduced to an improper fraction gives it $\frac{150}{13}$. So that the fourth wheel must have 150 teeth, and the balance wheel pinion 13 leaves; and without these numbers, it is impossible to obtain 18000 for the train, the balance wheel having 13 teeth.

Example 10th. The train 7200, the balance wheel 12?

7200÷60=120÷24=5. Taking 12 as the number for the balance wheel pinion, it will require 60 for the fourth wheel; a pinion of 14 requires 70.

The foregoing examples apply wholly to such movements as are intended for fourth wheel seconds; but even in movements where there are no fourth wheel seconds, numbers for the balance wheel pinion, and fourth wheel teeth, may be obtained, provided we have those in the second, third, and balance wheels, and in the third and fourth wheel pinions, along with the assumed train. Let the common train of 17280 be assumed, the second wheel 72, the third 64, the balance wheel 15, and the third and fourth wheel pinions 8 each: Required the number for the balance wheel pinion, and that for the fourth wheel?

Rule.—Find how many seconds the fourth wheel pinion takes to make a revolution; from this number of seconds, calculate the train or number of beats given by the balance wheel during that time, the beats being divided by the double of the number of the balance wheel teeth, the quotient will give the number of turns (and fractional parts of a turn when there are any,) made by the balance wheel in that time. $72 \times 64 \div 8 \times 8 = 72$, the fourth wheel then makes 72 revolutions in an hour; the seconds in an hour are $3600 \div 72 = 50$, which is the number of seconds for every revolution of the fourth wheel or its pinion; the train in a minute, or 60 seconds, is 288.

Then $60 : 288 : : 50 : 240$, and $240 \div 30 = 8$, the turns made in 50 seconds by the balance wheel or its pinion; the fourth wheel must be 64, and the balance wheel pinion 8, which will be turned round 8 times in 50 seconds. If the balance wheel was 14, then the pinion would be 7, and the fourth wheel 60, as $240 \div 28 = 8\frac{4}{7} = \frac{60}{7}$.

Let the train assumed be 18000, the balance wheel 15, the second and third wheels 54 and 50, the third and fourth wheel pinions 6 each: It is required to find the numbers for the balance wheel pinion, and for the teeth of the fourth wheel.

The fourth wheel, or its pinion, takes 48 seconds to make a revolution. Then as $60 : 300 : : 48 : 240 \div 30 = 8$, the number of revolutions which the balance wheel takes to give 240 beats. If we take 6 for the pinion, the wheel will be 48, as $8 \times 6 = 48$.

Take as the last example: The train 18000, the balance wheel 15, the second and third wheels 80 each, the third and fourth wheel pinions 10 each: Required the numbers for the balance wheel pinion and fourth wheel teeth?

The fourth wheel pinion takes 56.25 seconds to make a revolution; then, as $60 : 300 : : 56.25 : 281.25 \div 30 = 9.375$, or $9\frac{3}{8} = \frac{75}{8}$.— 75 is the number for the fourth wheel, and 8 for the balance wheel pinion.

Trains for common watch movements, with balance wheels of 13 or 11 teeth, are not readily made out, from the frequent recurrence of prime numbers, which are so high as to be unfit for the number of teeth in any wheel. The following, however, are trains and numbers for the wheel teeth, where the balance wheels have 11 and 13 teeth.

The train assumed is 17160, the pinions 6 leaves each, and the balance wheel 11 teeth: Required the numbers for the second, third, and contrate wheels?

17160×6×6×6÷22=168480. The divisors are five 2^s, four 3^s, one 5, and a 13; when they are arranged, may stand thus:

$$\left.\begin{array}{l} 2\times2=4\times3=12\times5=60 \\ 2\times3=6\times3=18\times3=54 \\ 2\times2=4\times13=52 \end{array}\right\} \text{Numbers for the wheel teeth.}$$

or the divisors can be so disposed as to give the numbers 65, 54, and 48.

Should the train 17160 be thought too slow, then take 17732, with pinions of 6 each, and the balance wheel 11, and the wheel teeth will be 62, 54, and 52.

Required the numbers for the wheel teeth, where the pinions are 8, 7, and 6, the balance wheel 13, and the train 17160?
17160×8×7×6÷26=221760. The divisors give 64, 63, and 55 for the numbers of the wheel teeth.

With the same pinion and balance wheel, the train fixed at 17732, what must be the numbers for the wheel teeth?
17732×8×7×6÷26=229152. From the divisors here are obtained the numbers 66, 62, and 56, for the wheel teeth.

The pinions 8 each, the balance wheel 13, and 17732 the train: the wheels required for this are 88, 64, and 62.

The pinions 7 each, balance wheel 13, and the same train as in the last two cases: the wheels required are 77, 62, and 49.

Numbers may be got that are nearer in proportion to one another than those in the last two examples: there would then be a fraction in the train; but this might be considered as a thing of little or no consequence.

The following are a few sets of wheels and pinions, whose trains might be very admissible in practice.

CONTRATE OR FOURTH WHEELS.

Wheels.	Pinions.	Trains.
72, 60, 56, 13.	7, 7, 7.	18337$\frac{4}{7}$
70, 60, 54, 13.	ditto	17191$\frac{2}{7}$
70, 60, 55, 13.	ditto	17513$\frac{4}{7\cdot 7}$
74, 56, 56, 13.	ditto	17590$\frac{5}{7}$
74, 56, 55, 13.	ditto	17276$\frac{1}{7}$
74, 56, 54, 13.	8, 7, 6.	17316

A balance wheel of 9 is rather an uncommon thing, but, if a very flat verge watch was wanted, the train 17160 may be taken, the pinions being 6 each; then, in this case, the wheels 66, 60, 52, and 9, will give the train here assumed.

When a watch movement does not shew seconds by the fourth wheel, it is requisite to know the time that the fourth or contrate wheel takes to make one revolution; for, knowing this, the watch can be more speedily regulated or brought to time.

Having the numbers of the teeth in the second and third wheels, and the number of leaves in the third and fourth, or contrate wheel pinions, it is easy to find the number of turns that the contrate wheel must make for one turn of the second or center wheel; and the time that the center wheel takes to make one revolution being an hour, from this can be found the time that the contrate wheel takes to make one revolution.

The numbers of the second and third wheel teeth, in a common watch movement, are 54 and 48, the third and contrate pinions are 6 each; then to find the revolutions that the contrate wheel or its pinion must make for one revolution of the second wheel:—*Rule,* Multiply the numbers of the second and third wheels into one another, the product divided by that of the third and contrate wheel pinions will give, for quotient, the number of turns that the contrate wheel or its pinion must make for one turn of the second wheel.— 54×48=(2592)÷6×6=(36)=72, the number of revolutions which the contrate wheel must make in an hour; if 3600, the number of seconds in an hour, be divided by 72, it will give in the quotient 50 for the number of seconds that the contrate wheel takes to make one revolution.

The wheels 72, and 64, the pinions 8 each; how many revolutions does the contrate or fourth wheel make in an hour, and how many seconds are taken in each revolution?

72×64=(4608)÷8×8=(64)=72. the number of turns in an hour; and 3600÷72=50, the number of seconds that each revolution takes?

—The wheels 70, and 64, the pinions 8, give 70 for the number of turns in an hour, and 51.43 seconds, the time taken for one revolution.—The wheels 54, and 50, the pinion 6; the revolutions 75, the time 48 seconds to each.—The wheels 75 and 64, the pinions 8, give 75 revolutions, and the time 48 seconds.—The wheels 75 and 64, the pinions 10 and 8, give 60 revolutions each in a minute.—The wheels 54 and 52, the pinions 6, give 75.22 revolutions; 47.86 seconds in time.—The wheels 80, and 64, the pinions 8, give 80 revolutions; the time 45 seconds each. A watch movement may come from the maker with its wheels and pinions properly adapted for the train intended; but this may be rendered of no avail, unless the finisher takes the trouble to compute what number of teeth the balance wheel should have. It has happened (though rarely) from a want of attention to this, that a balance wheel has been cut 13, in place of 15, making the train 15600 instead of 18000.

A center seconds watch whose train was 14400, which is by far too slow for a pocket watch, and therefore it was necessary to have it altered, and made quicker; and here there lay some difficulty, owing to its having center seconds, and more particularly so when a pinion of 7, and a balance wheel of 14 is wanted: by the former method, this process required to be frequently gone over in consequence of which we took a process by analysis.

1st, Supposing the balance wheel to have 14 teeth, and to make 10.5 turns in a minute, then,

$14 \times 2 = 28 \times 10.5 = 294$ the beats in a minute.

This multiplied by - 60 the minutes in an hour,

gives - - - 17640 the train or beats in an hour
Again, multiply by the pinions 448 that is $8 \times 8 \times 7 = 448$,

gives for product - 7902720 From this deduce numbers for the wheels,

64 63
70)7902720(112996(1764(28

Then with the wheels 70, 64, 63, 14, the pinions 8, 8, and 7, the train will be 17640; and if the leading pinion on the balance wheel pinion arbor be 8, this, multiplied by 10.5, will give 84 for the teeth of the center seconds wheel, which will be carried round once in a minute; or the leading pinion may be 6 if the wheel is 63.

2d. Wheels 70, 64, 60, 15; pinions 8, 8, 7; train 18000; leading pinion being 6, 7, or 8. The seconds wheel will be accordingly 60, 70, or 80.

Ten turns of the balance wheel in a minute gives 300 beats, and this multiplied by 60, the minutes in an hour, gives 18000, the beats in an hour.

$$30 \times 10 = 300 \times 60 = 18000$$

Multiplied by the product of the pinions - $448 = 8 \times 8 \times 7$

$$\overline{8064000}$$

$$\overline{6460}$$
$$80)8064000(115200(1800(30.$$ Here the wheels are as above, and 30, the double of 15, the number of the balance wheel teeth.

3d, $28 \times 11 = 308 \times 60 = 18480$
Multiplied by the product of the pinions - $448 = 8 \times 8 \times 7 = 448$

$$\overline{8279040}$$

$$\overline{6664}$$
$$70)8279040(118272(1792(28.$$ Here the wheels are 70, 66, 64, and 28, the double of 14, the number of the balance wheel teeth; then a pinion of 7, leading a wheel of 77, will turn it round in a minute.

CHAPTER III.

Of Dial Wheels or Motion Work, Length of Time of Going without Winding Up; and of the Trains for Three Part Clocks, such as those which strike Quarters of themselves, or give Chimes or Tunes as Musical Clocks do, &c. &c.

To show how to compute numbers for the teeth of those wheels and pinions, which constitute what is commonly called the Dial or Motion Work of a clock or watch, may seem unnecessary, yet to assist those who may not have had practice in this way, a few examples shall be given. The canon pinion which goes spring tight on the arbor of the center or second wheel, prolonged a little above the surface of the dial, carries the minute hand round the dial in an hour.

If the number of teeth or leaves that it contains be multiplied by the number of teeth or leaves in the minute wheel pinion, and with the product, divide the product of the hour and minute wheels multiplied into one another; the quotient should then be 12, equal to 12 revolutions of the canon pinion and minute hand, or one revolution of the hour wheel, and hour hand.

Suppose the canon pinion to have 10 leaves, and the minute pinion 12, these multiplied into one another will be 120; in this case the hour wheel must have 36 teeth, and the minute wheel 40, which multiplied into one another produce 1440, and this divided by 120 gives 12 for the quotient, equal to 12 revolutions of the minute hand, and one of the hour hand. Taking four times the number of the canon pinion, will give that of the minute wheel, and three times the minute pinion, will give that of the hour wheel. If the numbers of the two pinions are assumed, they will lead to the numbers of the two wheels, unless they are such as to bring in fractional parts into the numbers of the two wheels. In the case where the canon pinion is 10, and the minute pinion 12, their product 120, multiplied by 12, will give 1440; this divided by prime numbers, as was done in the case of finding numbers for the wheel teeth in movements, will give divisors when right arranged; to produce numbers for the teeth in the dial wheels. The divisors of 1440, are five 2's, two 3's, and a 5.

$$2\times2=4\times2=8\times5=40$$
$$2\times2=4\times3=12\times3=36$$
Numbers for the teeth of the dial wheeels.

Twelve being the number of revolutions of the canon pinion and minute hand, for one revolution of the hour wheel and hour hand, becomes the constant number, by which the product of the canon and minute pinions is multiplied, in order to ascertain numbers for the teeth of the hour and minute wheels.

Let the numbers assumed for the canon and minute pinions be 12 and 14, these multiplied into one another will produce 168, and this again multiplied by 12, the constant number, will give 2016, whose divisors are five 2's, two 3's, and a 7.

$$2\times2=4\times2=8\times2=16\times3=48$$
$$2\times3=6\times7=42$$
The number of teeth for the { Minute wheel. Hour ditto.

If 14 was taken for the canon pinion, 42 and 12 for the minute wheel and pinion, the hour wheel 48, the ratio would be the same—that is, 12 to 1.

DIAL WHEELS, &c.

Let the canon pinion be 14, and the minute wheel pinion 16: Required the numbers for the teeth of the minute and hour wheels?

$14 \times 16 \times 12 = 2688$, whose divisors are seven 2's, one 3, and a 7.

$2 \times 2 = 4 \times 2 = 8 \times 7 = 56.$
$2 \times 2 = 4 \times 2 = 8 \times 2 = 16 \times 3 = 48.$ } The number for the teeth of the { Minute wheel. Hour ditto.

Although not so direct a method as breaking the number down by divisors, it may be seen that 2688 is divisible by 48 into 56, or vice versa. When this is obvious, recourse need not be had to getting the number of the teeth by divisors.

In the case of a common eight-day seconds clock, it may be seen that the number 3840 is divisible by 60 into 64, which were the numbers got for the wheel teeth from the divisors in breaking it down. But where a number is high, such as 124416, got from a train of 17280, it requires to be made into divisors: The wheels here are 54, 48, and 48, which, when multiplied into one another, will give 124416, and this, if divided by 54, 48, and 48, will leave no remainder.

Let another example be taken for dial wheels, where the canon pinion is 18, and the minute wheel pinion is 20: What must be the numbers for the teeth of the minute and hour wheels?

$18 \times 20 \times 12 = 4320$. The divisors are five 2's, three 3's, and a five.

$2 \times 2 = 4 \times 2 = 8 \times 3 = 24 \times 3 = 72$
$2 \times 2 = 4 \times 3 = 12 \times 5 = 60$ } The number of teeth for the { Minute wheel. Hour ditto.

The dial wheels which are used in the Stogden repeating motion work of a repeating watch, consist of a lantern or canon pinion of 4, leading a wheel of 48, on which is the hour snail; concentric with them is a wheel driving the hour wheel, both being of the same diameter and number, which is usually 35 or 36. The dial wheels of a common eight-day clock are somewhat similar to those in Stogden motions, only put in a reverse order. Two wheels, of equal diameter and number, one of which is called the minute pipe wheel, and has place of that of the canon pinion, the other is the minute wheel, having usually a pinion of 6, 7, or 8, leading the hour wheel, of 12 times the number of teeth to that of the pinion leading it, which number may be 72, 84, or 96, according as the minute pinion is 6, 7, or 8; the minute wheels have usually 42 teeth each.

To find how long a clock or watch will continue to go, before requiring to be wound up, the number of teeth in the first or great

D

wheel, and the number of the pinion which it drives, must be known. The number of teeth in the great wheel of the going part of a common clock is for the most part 96, and the number of leaves in the center or second wheel pinion which it acts in, is 8, and makes one revolution in an hour; so, consequently, it must make 12 revolutions for one of the great wheel, as 96, divided by 8, is equal to 12. Two revolutions of the great wheel is then equal to 24 hours, and 16 turns or revolutions of the great wheel and barrel will be equal to 8 days. The diameter of the barrel must depend on the inside length or height of the case where the weight falls.

In a common watch, the number of leaves in the second or center wheel pinion is 12, and makes one revolution in an hour, the number of the great wheel teeth which drives it being 48; for one revolution of which the second wheel pinion must make four, equal to four hours, the great wheel turning with the fusee having seven and a half turns of a spiral groove cut on it; $7\frac{1}{2}$ being multiplied by 4, will give the length of time which the watch will go before it requires to be wound up. 7, multiplied by 4, is equal to 28, the half turn is equal to two more, making in all 30 hours that the watch will go before it can be run down, or require to be wound up; but the winding up of a watch is done regularly, or as nearly so as may be, at the end of every twenty-four hours, being a more regular kind of period, and, at the same time, taking the power of the main spring more at an equality of force.

Hours.

For the clock the ratio may be put thus $96 \div 8 = 12 \times 16 = 192$ } The time it will go.
For the watch the ratio may be put thus $48 \div 12 = 4 \times 7.5 = 30$

When a clock is required to go a month, or 32 days, it must have an additional wheel and pinion to that of the eight-day clock. The center wheel, (or second in ordinary,) becomes the third wheel in the movement. In 32 days there are 768 hours, and to find the numbers for the teeth of the great and second wheels for a clock to go that time, the numbers for the pinions of the second and center wheels must be known, and the number of revolutions to be made by the great wheel, which must always be equal to the number of turns cut on the barrel. If we assume 20 and 16 as the numbers for the pinions, and 16 for the revolutions of the great wheel and barrel, each turn is then equal to 48 hours, we can from these get such a number, that, when decomposed into factors or divisors, will give sets to produce the numbers for the teeth of the two wheels. The rule to find the number to be decomposed, is: Multiply the pinions into one anopher, and the product by the number of hours that the first or great wheel takes to make one revolution; this last product will be the number which is to be decomposed.

20×16×48=15360. The divisors are ten 2's, one 3, and a 5.
2×2=4×2=8×2=16×2=32×2=64×2=128
2×2= 4×2= 8×3=24×5=120

The number 120 may be taken for the teeth of the great wheel, and 128 for those in the second wheel: as a proof, let the number 15360 be divided by any one of the numbers 128 or 120, it will shew itself. 15360÷128=120.

Let the numbers assumed of the two pinions be 24 and 20, the revolutions of the great wheel and barrel 16, each being equal to 48 hours, the time which the clock must go is then 32 days: hence to find the numbers for the teeth of the great and second wheels?

24×20×48=23040. The divisors are nine 2's, two 3's, and a 5.
2×2=4×2=8×2=16×3=48×3=144 } The number for the teeth of the { Great wheel.
2×2=4×2=8×2=16×2=32×5=160 }   { Second wheel.

No clock ought to go longer than a month, or 32 days; yet, if it is required to make one go for six months, or 200 days, the center wheel, in a movement fit for this purpose, will become the fourth wheel. To find the number for the teeth of the three wheels, assume 20, 16, and 12, for the numbers of the three pinions, the barrel having 16 turns, to find the time for one revolution of it and the great wheel: 200 days, divided by 16, the turns on the barrel, will give twelve days and a half for each revolution of the great wheel; twelve and a half days, reduced to hours, will give 300 hours for each revolution of the first or great wheel; 300 hours being multiplied by the product of the pinions multiplied into one another, will give such a number, when decomposed into factors or divisors, that sets of them may be obtained to represent the numbers required for the teeth of the three wheels?

20×16×12×300=1152000. The divisors are ten 2's, two 3's, and three 5's.
2×2=4×2=8×2=16×5= 80)   (Great wheel.
2×2=4×2=8×3=24×5=120 } The number for the teeth of the { Second wheel.
2×2=4×2=8×3=24×5=120)   (Third wheel.

As a proof of the operation, divide 1152000 by 80, and the quotient by 120, the next quotient will be 120.

As in the last example: a clock with three wheels, going 200 days, and the barrel making a revolution in 300 hours. Suppose it was resolved to have this performed by two wheels and two pinions, one of 12, and the other of 10: Required the numbers for the teeth of the two wheels?

$12 \times 10 \times 300 = 36000$. The divisors are five $2'$, two $3'$, and three $5'$.
$2 \times 2 = 4 \times 3 = 12 \times 3 = 36 \times 5 = 180$ } The number for the teeth of the { Great wheel.
$2 \times 2 = 4 \times 2 = 8 \times 5 = 40 \times 5 = 200$ } { Second wheel.

What are called month clocks, are supposed to be wound up on the first day of every month, for which reason they are commonly made to go 32 days, or a very little longer. It may be said that it is not easy to remember or attend to the first day of every month, by this day having (or falling on) no regular or fixed day of the week, and that it would be better if the clock was made to go so as the winding up could be done on the first Saturday, Sunday, or Monday of the month, which at first sight seems to have some sort of order in it; but the intervals in this way are of very different lengths: four of these would consist of 35 days each, and eight of them of 28 days each; therefore, in order that the clock may suit this time of winding up, it would require to be made to go, at the shortest, 36 days; this however would be lessening the force in the inverse ratio of 36 to 32. An astronomical clock, or regulator, to go 32 days, will be afterwards described. In making one to go 36 days, we must have a great wheel of a higher number, and the barrel a little less in diameter. To make a clock go 36 days, many ways may be adopted: the following is perhaps as good a plan as any: Suppose the case for this clock to be in length, from the inside of the bottom to the center of the dial, 5 feet 4.7 inches, the pulley, if the seatboard is of cast iron, will come within 4.5 inches of the center of the dial, (one of the sides of its square being 12 inches,) and allowing 8 inches for the length of weight and pulley, will make 12.5 inches to be taken from 5 feet 4.7 inches, leaving 4 feet 4.2 inches; and, as the clock goes with a pulley, the double of this is 8 feet 8.4 inches, or 104.4 inches. If we divide 104.4 by 17.5, the number of turns proposed to be cut on the barrel, it will give 5.96 inches for each turn, which is so near to 6 inches, that we may take it for the circumference of the barrel, the diameter by the common proportion; 355 to 113 will then be found to be as near as possible 1.91 inch. In rigid calculation, the diameter 1.91 must be lessened by the diameter of the gut, supposed here to be .050 of an inch; this, taken from 1.91, leaves 1.860; but as the groove or screw which is cut on the barrel for the gut to lap round on it, diminishes the diameter, whatever this is must be added to 1.860; take one-third of the diameter of the gut for this, which is .016, and this, added to 1.860, makes 1.876. The difference between 1.91 and 1.876, is so little as to be of no consideration; it is now however on the safer side.

The length of the barrel between the ends may be determined thus: The diameter of the gut being taken at .050, multiplied by 17.5, the number of turns proposed to be cut on the barrel, will give .875 of an inch; this allows no freedom for the gut to lay on the barrel; therefore, to have some degree of freedom, let the diameter or room which the gut ought to have, be taken at .070; this being multiplied by 17.5, the product will be 1.225 inch for the length of the barrel between the ends, which is so near 1.25 inch, that it may be taken for the length. If the great wheel is to have 150 teeth, and that they should have the same strength as those in the wheel 144 teeth in the first plan, the diameter must be 3667, say 3 inches 6 tenths, and .67 of one-tenth of an inch; the great wheel here, in place of going round in 48 hours, as by the wheel of 144, will require 50 hours; and 50, multiplied by 17.5, the number of turns on the barrel, will give 875 hours, or 36 days 11 hours, for the weight to fall before it can be wholly run down in the case. 17.3 turns is equal to 36 days; the pinions being 24 and 20, and the time of one revolution of the barrel being 50 hours, from these may be deduced numbers for the wheel teeth.

$24 \times 20 \times 50 = 24000$. The divisors are six 2^s, one 3, and three 5^s.

$$\begin{array}{l} 2 \times 3 = 6 \times 5 = 30 \times 5 = 150 \\ 2 \times 2 = 4 \times 2 = 8 \times 2 = 16 \times 2 = 32 \times 5 = 160 \end{array}\Big\} \text{The number for the teeth of the} \begin{cases} \text{Great wheel.} \\ \text{Second wheel.} \end{cases}$$

Spring clocks have seldom been made to go longer than eight days, yet, by judicious arrangement of the wheels, they could be made to go a month, or longer, if such a thing was wanted. The great wheels are commonly made smaller in diameter than what they ought to be, (consequently the teeth are too fine,) having 96 teeth acting into a pinion of 8; enlarging the diameter would no doubt require larger frame plates, which might easily be adopted. The disadvantages attending first or great wheels of a small diameter, are, the force of the main spring acting strongly or forcibly in pitching, where the teeth have no great depth of hold on the pinion; and in cases of the fusee chain, gut, or spring breaking, the sudden jerk backwards of the great wheel is frequently apt to break not only the second wheel pinion, but also to strip the great wheel of some of its teeth. The force of the spring in a spring-clock barrel, is greater than that of the weight usually hung on at common eight-day clocks, whose great wheel teeth are stronger than those of the great wheels in spring clocks, which are, however, commonly made a little thicker than the others, for the purpose of giving strength to the teeth; yet this is not altogether adequate to the end required. The length of chain, or gut, which, measured or lapped round a fusee of 16 turns, when applied round the barrel, measures six turns and three quarters on it, shews that the spring ought to make about nine turns and a quarter in the barrel, which will allow to set up (or bend up the spring as it is called,) one turn, or one turn and a half, leaving, what is little enough, one turn unbent, in order not to strain the spring, which might cause risk of breaking it.

In flat watches, the movement cannot admit the height of the fusee to have seven turns and a half on it, as in the common sort, because this would require the fusee chain to be so thin, that it would not have strength to resist the force of the main spring, and, therefore, liable to be broke, a circumstance which from this cause very frequently takes place; therefore, to prevent such accidents, a less number of turns, such as five or six, should be cut on the fusee, so as to allow as strong a chain as may be. The second wheel pinion, in place of being one of 12, might be of a less number, and that of the great wheel increased, in order that the watch may go 30 hours before being run down; or, if the pinion is required to be one of 12, this will require the number of the great wheel teeth to be still more increased.

Suppose the second or center wheel pinion to be 12, and the fusee to have six turns and a half cut on it: Required the number of teeth for the great wheel, so as the watch will go 30 hours? Take the proportion of the common watch, where the fusee has seven turns and a half, the great wheel 48 teeth, and the pinion 12, which is the same as in the example taken, and say, as 6.5 : 7.5 : : 48 to the number of teeth required, it is evident that a greater number than 48 is required, so that 48 must be multiplied by 7.5, and divided by 6.5, the quotient will be found to be nearly 55.4, as a number for the teeth of the great wheel; but this being a fractional number, and impracticable in wheel teeth, the great wheel may be made 56; this, divided by the pinion 12, will give for quotient 4.66 hours for one revolution of the great wheel; when this is multiplied by 6.5 turns made by the great wheel and fusee, it will give 30.29 hours for the time that the watch will go.

The number for the great wheel teeth may be found by another way. Whatever is the number of turns proposed for the fusee to have, by it divide 30, the number of hours which it is intended the watch shall run, the quotient will be such a number, that when the number of the second wheel pinion is multiplied by it, the product will be the number for the teeth of the great wheel. For example, let the number of turns on the fusee be 6, and the number of the second wheel pinion 14: to find the number of teeth that the great wheel must have, so as the watch shall go thirty hours?
$30 \div 6 = 5 \times 14 = 70$, the number of teeth which the great wheel must have.

If it is proposed for the second wheel pinion to be 10, and the fusee to have 6 turns: What is the number of teeth that the great wheel ought to have, so as the watch shall go 30 hours?
$30 \div 6 = 5 \times 10 = 50$. The number of teeth for the great wheel.

The fusee to have 5 turns, the second wheel pinion 10: Required the number for the great wheel teeth?
$30 \div 5 = 6 \times 10 = 60$. The number for the teeth of the great wheel.

When flat watches have been required, the movement is sometimes made without a fusee, and in its place is introduced a *large* toothed barrel, in order to admit of a thick and sufficiently strong spring, the barrel having a great number of teeth, and the center wheel pinion a small number; so as that the spring, the barrel teeth, and the second or center wheel pinion, may contribute as much as possible to give the watch an equable power during the time of running out the 30 hours or a little more. There is an economy (if the expression may be used,) made with the main spring, by means of a fusee, which makes every part of the spring more effective, than where a fusee is wanting.

A few more examples may be given to find the numbers for the great wheel teeth.

It is proposed that the fusee is to have 7 turns, the second wheel pinion 16, and that the watch shall go 30 hours: Required the number of the teeth for the great wheel?

The hours 30, being divided by 7, the proposed number of turns for the fusee, the quotient is 4.3 nearly; 16, the number of the second wheel pinion, being multiplied by it, gives 68.8 as the number for the great wheel teeth; but, being a fractional number, it cannot be used as a number for wheel teeth. The wheel, however, may be cut 68, 69, or 70, as either of them will be near enough. $30 \div 7 = 4.3 \times 16 = 68.8$, which may be called 69, for the number of the great wheel teeth.

The fusee to have $6\frac{1}{2}$ turns, the second wheel pinion to be 14, and the watch to go 30 hours: Required the number for the great wheel teeth?

30 hours, divided by 6.5, the turns, the quotient is 4.616 nearly, which, being multiplied by 14, the pinion, gives 64.624 for the wheel teeth; 65, or 66, may then be taken, as 64.624 is a fractional number. $30 \div 6.5 = 4.616 \times 14 = 64.624$.

In a box chronometer, where depth of room, and great height of fusee can be easily got, let the fusee have 10 turns, a second wheel pinion of 20, and the time required it should go before being run down, 40 hours: Required the number of teeth for the great wheel?
$40 \div 10 = 4 \times 20 = 80$. The number of teeth.

In a box chronometer, the fusee to have 8 turns, the second wheel pinion 18 leaves, and the time it must go, 40 hours: Required the number of teeth for the great wheel?
$40 \div 8 = 5 \times 18 = 90$. The number required.

Box chronometers are sometimes required to go eight days, a length of time by no means in their favour; and some address is required to plan out a movement of this sort, so as it shall be well suited for the purpose. As in an eight day spring-clock, the fusee may have 16 turns, the great wheel 96 teeth, and the second wheel pinion 8 leaves, which will make it run eight days; but it would be better to have two wheels in place of one, and two pinions, each of a greater number than that of 8. The hours in eight days are 192, which, divided by 12, the proposed number of turns for the fusee and great wheel to make, will give 16 hours for each revolution; the pinions being assumed at 24 and 20: Required the numbers for the teeth of the great and intermediate wheels?—Observe, that the intermediate wheel is the second, the center or second wheel in common now becomes the third.

The product of the pinions multiplied into one another, being multiplied by 16, the hours for one revolution will give such a number, that, when decomposed, the divisors can be formed into sets for the numbers of the teeth required in the two wheels.

$24 \times 20 \times 16 = 7680$. The divisors are nine 2's, one 3, and a 5.

$$\left.\begin{array}{l}2\times2=4\times2=8\times2=16\times5=80\\ 2\times2=4\times2=8\times2=16\times2=32\times3=96\end{array}\right\} \text{The number for the teeth of the } \left\{\begin{array}{l}\text{Great wheel.}\\ \text{Intermediate}\\ \text{ditto.}\end{array}\right.$$

The preceding Rules, and examples given of them, it is presumed, may be of some use to either the clock or watch movement maker. When movements come into the hands of the *finisher*, the wheels and pinions are made; therefore, a few examples, although very simple, shall be given, in order to know what are the numbers required to be cut on a watch or clock, fusee, or barrel. In a watch movement, the great wheel having 60 teeth, and the second wheel pinion 10: Required the number of turns to be cut on the fusee, so as the watch may run 30 hours? The great wheel 60, divided by the pinion 10, the quotient is 6; and 30, divided by 6, gives 5 for the number of turns requred. For $60 \div 10 = 6$, and $30 \div 6 = 5$.

The number of turns which a spring should make in the barrel, depends on the number of turns made on the outside of the barrel, measured by the length of chain which fills the groove on the fusee.

Suppose a chain which fills the fusee measures four turns on the barrel, then the spring ought not to make less than six turns in the barrel. If the chain which fills the fusee measures three and a half turns on the barrel, the spring should make about five turns in the barrel. Having met with some who were bred to the business, *as they said*, yet did not know even this plain and simple rule, which may stand as an apology for its insertion here.

The train of the striking and quarter parts of clocks may now be taken into consideration, as well as that of the *runners*, as they are called by the movement makers, that is, the wheels in the repeating parts of watch and clock repeaters.

The striking part in an ordinary eight-day clock, has 84 teeth in the great wheel, 56 in the pin wheel, 48 in the tumbler wheel, and 42 in the fly wheel; the pinions are one of 8 for the pin wheel, one of 7 for the tumbler wheel, and two of 6 each for the fly wheel and fly. The fly here makes 56 revolutions for every blow of the hammer, and eight blows for every revolution of the pin wheel, which has eight lifting pins in it, while the tumbler wheel makes one for every blow. The tumbler and fly wheels being multiplied together, and the product divided by the product of the fly and fly wheel pinions multiplied into one another, the quotient will be 56, for $\frac{48\times42}{6\times6}=56$, the number of turns which the fly makes for every blow of the hammer.

In common, the great wheels have been made with 84 teeth, in case of the clock when made to repeat or strike the hour which it last struck; and this was done to prevent the striking part from running sooner down than the going part. But when the clock is allowed to strike only of itself, a wheel of 84 is not necessary, providing the barrels in both the going and striking parts are made of equal diameters. The number of blows given in 12 hours is 78, for if the first blow 1 at the one o'clock hour, is added to 12, the number of blows given at the twelve o'clock hour, the sum will be 13, and this multiplied by 12, the number of times the hours are struck, the half of this sum will be the number of blows struck by the hammer in twelve hours. For $12+1=13\times12=156\div2=78$. or $6\frac{1}{2}$ taken as a mean term to 1 and 13; then 12 multiplied by $6\frac{1}{2}$ will give 78.

The great wheel then may have 78 teeth, the pin wheel pinion which it drives being 8, the wheel having 8 pins for raising the hammer tail, it will be seen, that the pin wheel must raise the hammer tail 78 times for one revolution of the great wheel. The great wheel 78 being divided by the pin wheel pinion 8, the quotient will be $9\frac{3}{4}$, the number of turns and parts of a turn, which the pin wheel makes for one revolution of the great wheel, which multiplied by 8, the number of pins in the pin wheel, the sum will be 78: For $\frac{78}{8}=9.75$, and $9.75\times8=78$. The advantage, though not very great, is on the side of the wheel of 78, in the inverse ratio of 84 to 78.

The wings or vanes of the fly by resisting the air in its revolutions, tend to regulate the motion of striking wheels when lifting the hammer, otherwise there would be an acceleration when striking the long hour, (twelve,) as it is called, which would easily be perceived by the ear. The wings of the fly are commonly made too thin; were they to be made thicker, it would give the fly a degree of momentum to carry forward the wheels a little, in case of any temporary resistance from thick oil or such like; and, in order that the fly should act both in resisting the air, and, at the same time, to have a tendency to carry the wheels forward; the fly pinion in its size should be made a mean, to that of driving and being driven. When nicety is aimed at, the train of the wheels should be reduced, and the wings of the fly a good deal extended, making its revolutions outside of the frame, placed com-

mostly behind the pillar plate, as is sometimes done with the fly, to music or quarter parts, limiting the number of revolutions to ten, or a dozen, or a very little more, (in place of 56) for every blow of the hammer. In turret clocks, we have reduced the revolutions of the fly to three or four for every blow of the hammer.

Striking parts can be regulated by means of an escapement and a pendulum, the teeth of the wheel which lifts the hammer tail serving for scaping with the pallets, no train of wheels and pinions being beyond that of the lifting wheel. A lifter, having at one of its ends a spring jointed piece (or nags-head joint,) which locks the pendulum by the end of the rod, when the lifter is discharged at the hour, and falling down, it gives liberty for the pendulum to vibrate while the clock is striking; at the last blow of the hammer, the lifter being raised up when the pendulum is very near the extremity of its vibration, it passes the nags-head joint, but in returning it is locked and cannot pass, until the hour is again at the discharging of the lifter.

The mechanism required here may be greater perhaps than any advantage that can be gained by it. Reducing the train of the wheels as much as may be, and giving extension and momentum to the fly, appear to be the best means to regulate the striking parts, and lessen the influence of oil on the pivots; where the train is great, and cold weather thickening the oil, clocks and repeating watches are very apt to strike so slow, that it becomes tiresome to attend to the number of blows which are to be made. Adopting in common eight-day clocks a principle very proper for a hammer-head in steeple clocks, but very improper in the former, (as has been found by experience,) that is, by giving a massy head to the hammer, the consequence of this is, that in cold weather, common clocks are found to strike very slow; on reducing the weight of the hammer-head one half, the effect of this on the striking, particularly in cold weather, is greatly to its advantage.

Since the old locking plate and count wheel method was given up, the locking of the striking of a common eight-day clock has generally been done by means of a tumbler tail, pressing on a pin fixed behind the rack on one end of its arch, the tumbler being put on by means of a square, on a thick pivot of the tumbler wheel pinion squared for this purpose, and when not well fitted, the tumbler was apt to get loose and sometimes drop from its place. There was even some nicety required to make the pressure of the tumbler on the pin in the rack, so that the force of the striking weight on the tumbler wheel, should not make the tumbler bear too hard on the rack pin, and consequently make the rack tooth bear equally so on the nose of the rack catch. When the tumbler pressed in this way, it made the discharge of the striking require more force than was proper. On the other hand, if the tumbler rested in such a manner on the rack pin as not to press it, as it were in some degree from it, in this case the rack sometimes did not fall, and then no striking took place, or, if any did, it was only by giving a single blow.

To prevent such occurrences in future, we made the pivot of the tumbler wheel smaller, and fitted the tumbler on by a round in place of a square, having no tail to it, the locking now being by a pin in the fly wheel, pressing very gently on a piece fixed to the inside of the arm of the rack catch; a like piece was fixed to one end of an arm of the discharging lifter, a little behind the other, so as to give some room for warning when at this; on the lifting arm dropping off from the pin in the minute wheel, the pin in the fly wheel at this instant got free or discharged, and the striking went on till the locking of the fly wheel again took place. The first opening, or space for teeth in the rack, was made somewhat deeper than the rest, so as the rack catch when falling into it at the close of the striking, might get down enough with its piece to catch the pin in the fly wheel and lock it; the other spaces between the rack teeth being less in depth, kept the rack catch and its locking piece so much up during the striking, as prevented the pin in the fly wheel from interfering with it. This mode of locking a striking part will, on the whole, be found safe, sure, and easy. Reducing the train of striking parts, we have long insisted on and practised, having brought the train of repeaters down from above 6000 (at which many were made) to 2000, and even to 1200, or 1000 with success. What a labour the fly pinion had to perform in those high trains? making above 300 revolutions for every blow of the hammer, which might have been effected with one third of the number. Julien le Roy had good reason for reducing the train so low in number, as to find it was necessary at last to bridle it by means of a scapement; this was certainly an ingenious contrivance, and from which there is no doubt that M. Berthoud took the idea of bridling the striking part of a clock also by means of such an escapement and pendulum as has just now been described.

The train of the runnings, (that is the wheels and pinions which serve for the repeating part of a repeating watch) when carried to a high number, must necessarily require a considerable portion of the force of the repeating main spring to turn the wheels and pinions, independent of that required to lift the hour and quarter hammers: hence the feeble blows given by many of our repeating watches. Compare the 6050 revolutions made by the fly pinion for one turn of the first wheel, with that of another, where the last wheel which is a scapement one, makes only $147\frac{44}{147}$ revolutions. The runnings of the one were $\dfrac{40\times 36\times 33\times 33\times 30}{6\times 6\times 6\times 6\times 6} = 6050$, the number of turns made by the fly pinion. The runnings of the other were $\dfrac{44\times 36\times 32}{7\times 7\times 7} =$ $147\frac{44}{147}$, the number of revolutions made by the scapement wheel which had 15 teeth, the double of which is 30, and $30\times 147\frac{44}{147} =$ $5433\frac{111}{147}$, the number of beats made by the pallets.

Our repeating movement makers have of late got into the way of making the ratchet teeth of the arbor of the first wheel of the runnings, in the reverse order to what they ought to be, and this seems to have caused the repeating motion maker to introduce an intermediate pinion or wheel between the rack and the pinion, which is on a square on the arbor of the first wheel in the Stogden motions, which takes away from the good effect, which the rack would otherwise have did it operate solely with the pinion on the ratchet arbor.

In repeating movements, where the repeating barrel is made with a ratchet edge on the lower end (as it may be called,) the barrel let through the potence plate from outside, the ratchet edge being sunk in it, having a click and spring fixed on the potence plate so as to act with the ratchet edge, a bar across the barrel, and its ratchet edge is screwed on the potence plate and keeps the barrel in its place, just allowing it to have freedom to be set about by means of the ratchet edge. This is a contrivance which is neat, ingenious, and convenient, as by it the repeating spring can be set up any part of a turn that should be requisite without interfering with the motion work. Where a pinion, or a pulley, is put on the ratchet arbor with a square, they require to be taken from off the square, and besides interfering with the motion work this way, a turn is the least quantity that the repeating spring can be set up.

The following are trains for a three part spring clock, or quarter clock, as it is called. For the great wheel of the going part, 120 teeth, second wheel 100, and the pinion 10, third wheel 100, and the pinion 10, the swing wheel 30 teeth, and a pinion of 10. The vibrations will be found to be 100 in a minute, and the pendulum (by a rule to be given afterwards for finding the lengths of pendulums,) will require to be 14.112 inches in length. The great wheel of the striking part 100 teeth, the pin wheel 64 teeth, 8 pins, and a pinion of 10, the tumbler wheel 56, and a pinion of 8, the fly wheel 46, and a pi-

pion of 8, the fly pinion 12. The revolutions then made by the fly for every turn or revolution of the tumbler wheel will be 26.833. For 56×46+8×12=26.833, the number of turns made by the fly and its pinion. The great wheel of the quarter part has 120 teeth, the second wheel 80, and a pinion of 10, the tumbler wheel 56, and a pinion of 8, the fly wheel 46, and a pinion of 8, and the fly pinion 12. The fly and fly pinion in this part make also 26.833 revolutions for every turn made by the tumbler wheel, which is one for every quarter, each quarter being 8 blows of as many hammers, each on its own bell. The second wheel of 80 turns, a wheel of 40 which is on one of the ends of the quarter barrel, having five rows of pins put on it for the same number of quarters, making two revolutions in the hour, it gives ten quarters in that time, as 1+2+3+4=10. The length over all in the flys used in the striking and quarter parts may be about three inches and a half. If the tumbler wheels were made 56, the fly wheel 42, their pinions 8, and the fly pinion 14, the revolutions of the fly would then be 21 for every blow of the hammer. For 56×42+8×14=21. A fly to bridle this would require to be in length, over all, four inches and a half, or a little more. The numbers for the teeth of the tumbler and fly wheels may be deduced from assuming the number of the revolutions the fly is required to make, and knowing the numbers for fly and fly wheel pinions. Suppose the pinions are 8 and 14, the number of revolutions the fly is required to make is 20, then to find the numbers for the tumbler and fly wheel teeth. The pinions multiplied into one another, and the product by the number of revolutions of the fly pinion, will give such a number, that when made into divisors, will give sets for the two wheels.

8×14×20=2240. The divisors are six 2, one 5, and a 7.

$$\begin{matrix}2\times 2=4\times 2=8\times 5=40\\ 2\times 2=4\times 2=8\times 7=56\end{matrix}\Bigg\}\text{ The number for the teeth of the }\begin{cases}\text{Fly wheel.}\\ \text{Tumbler wheel.}\end{cases}$$

The great wheels of the going and quarter parts make one revolution in 12 hours, the fusee must then have 16 turns. In the quarter part, the tumbler wheel making one revolution every quarter, 80 the number of the second wheel, being divided by 8, the tumbler wheel pinion will give 10 for the number of quarters struck in an hour. The second wheel 80, makes 12 revolutions for one of the great wheel, as 10, the second wheel pinion, will divide the great wheel of 120 into 12, therefore the great wheel of the quarter part will make a revolution every 12 hours. By the striking part, there are 80 blows given by the hammer for one revolution of the great wheel, so that the number of turns given to the fusee may rather be less than 16. For if 78 blows require 16 turns on the fusee, so as to keep up the striking for eight days, then 80 blows for one turn of the fusee will require only 15.6 turns to keep up the striking for the same time. In an inverse ratio, say as 78 is to 16, so is 80 to 15.6, that is 78×16÷80=15.6. If the number of teeth in the striking great wheel had been 96, then the blows given in one revolution would have been 76.4. For 100 : 80 : : 96 : 76.4, and the number of turns required for the fusee 15.91, or 15.92 nearly : For as 76 : 16 : : 76.4 : 15.91 + taken as above in an inverse ratio.

Music, or chime parts in clocks, have their trains regulated sometimes much in the same way, as has been described for the spring quarter part, and sometimes they have the fly turning with the upper end of an upright arbor on the lower end, of which is formed an endless screw, either of a single, double, triple, or quadruple thread, into which the last wheel in the train works. In a single threaded endless screw, one tooth of the wheel must pass for every turn or revolution of the fly, two for the double, three for the triple, and four teeth of the wheel must pass for every turn of the fly, having an endless screw of four threads on its arbor. The number of threads in the endless screw, and the position of its arbor, for it may be placed either horizontally or upright, are things which may be determined according to the fancy of the movement maker, or to the plan he may have designed for the clock. A fly having an upright arbor, and a quadruple threaded endless screw, will turn easily and with great velocity: hence it will require to have the wings or vanes of considerable extent so as to bridle the train. The *wheel* on the end of the music barrel which is turned by part of the train of wheels and pinions, has sometimes no connection with the regulating part of it, which is formed by the fly wheel and pinion, and the fly having either a pinion or an endless screw for its arbor. But this *wheel* is made to pitch nicely in with another wheel of the same number and diameter, which may be considered rather as a kind of an imperfection, as in this way the music barrel wheel will have some degree of liberty by the shake of the teeth (however little) in the two wheels. The barrel cannot turn so steadily as it would have done when placed between the fly wheel and fly, but to have this, three wheels of the same number and diameter are required, the barrel wheel is driven by one, and it drives the other which turns the fly wheel pinion, and the fly wheel turns either a fly pinion or an endless screw. Sometimes there is a wheel more in the train, the pinion of which is driven by the wheel that is driven by the barrel wheel, and the wheel which is on this pinion drives the fly wheel, and so on. The first or great wheel of a music part being 96, on the pinion of 8, which it turns, is a wheel of 72, pitching with the music barrel wheel of 72, each being of the same diameter; the second wheel of 72 also turns the fly wheel pinion of 12, on whose arbor is the fly wheel of 32 teeth working into a single threaded endless screw, on the arbor of which the fly is carried. The music barrel is made to turn three times round, at the end of every three hours, and the tune which is on it is played three times over; during the time of one revolution or tune, the fly makes 108 turns and two thirds of a turn. For 72×32÷12=108⅔, being the second wheel of 72, multiplied by 32 the fly wheel, and the product divided by the fly wheel pinion of 12, gives the number of turns which the fly must make. The pinion of 8 being taken to divide the great wheel of 96, the quotient will be 12, the number of tunes played in 12 hours, the threes in 12 are four, and three the number of times the tune is played every third hour. For 3×4=12, a revolution of the second wheel is made in the same time as one of the music barrel and its wheel. In this example the music barrel is out of the power of the regulating fly.

The example of a music part now to be given, shall be of that kind where the music barrel is placed as it were within the control of the regulating fly. The first or great wheel is 96, the second wheel pinion is 8, and the wheel 84, which turns the music barrel and its wheel of 84; this, again, turns another wheel of 84; these three wheels being of the same number, must consequently be of the same diameter. The last of the three turns a pinion of 8, whose wheel is 64, which turns the fly-wheel pinion of 8; the fly wheel of 48 turns the fly pinion of 10, it must then make 403.2 revolutions for one of the music barrel; the three wheels which are between the barrel wheel and fly pinion being multiplied into one another, and the product divided by the product of the two pinions of 8, and the fly pinion multiplied into one another, will give 403.2 for the quotient. For 84×64×48÷8×8×10=403.2; the number of revolutions made by the fly and its pinion for one turn of the music barrel. The music part, by the going of the clock, is discharged every three hours, and plays the tune three times over as in the first example, consequently the tune is played 12 times over, for every revolution of the great wheel. The length of the vanes of the fly over all, must be about 3.65 inches, and breadth half an inch.

CHAPTER IV.

On Finding Numbers for the Wheels and Pinions of Orreries, Planetariums, &c. &c.

HAVING given a sufficient number of examples how to obtain numbers fit for the wheel teeth of any watch, time-keeper, or clock of any description, it may not now be out of the sphere of practical horology to select a few numbers, such as are properly suited for the motions requisite for orreries or planetariums. The business of making planetariums or orreries, is so closely connected with that of the clockmaker, that a sort of Table shall be given of most of the numbers that can be adopted for such machines. The greater part of them are those of Janvier, taken or copied from *Histoire de la mesure du temps, tom.* ii. *chap.* vi. *Des horologes à Sphere Mouvante,* pp. 238, 239, 240, *and* 241. *Par Ferdinand Berthoud. Paris,* 1802. A description of the *Sphere Mouvante* by Janvier, with the numbers of its wheel teeth and pinions, had been given by him to the National Institute; and Berthoud, as one of the commissioners appointed to examine it, got the opportunity of seeing these numbers, which he soon afterwards published, and, as we suspect, without Janvier's consent. We are led to suppose this from Janvier himself declining to make them public, as seems evident from his own work published, and entitled, " *Des Revolutions des corps Célestes, par le mechanism des Rouages,*" Paris 1812; which see.

The first planetary machine or orrery made in this country, was by the celebrated George Graham, clock-maker, (so he is styled in a print engraved by Faber, from his picture by Hudson, in the possession of the noble family of Macclesfield,) who was well skilled in the various branches of speculative and practical philosophy. Orrery was a name given afterwards to it, but not by Graham.

What follows, is intended to show, how to find the numbers for the teeth of wheels and the leaves of pinions, that shall give a revolution to a wheel, or figure representing the motion of a planet, in a clock, orrery, or in any planetary machine; which must be performed in a determined or certain period of time. It has already been shewn, *when* in the train of a clock or watch, the number of the pinions and their leaves, and the number of teeth in the swing, or balance wheel, *are fixed upon,* that it is an easy matter to find numbers for the teeth of the other wheels. But to find such numbers for the

E

wheels and pinions in a planetary machine, as shall cause a revolution to be made by a wheel, which must give the mean synodical revolution of a planet, that of the moon for instance, in a period of time consisting of 29 days, 12 hours, 44 minutes, 2.8283 seconds, will be, at least to some, rather an intricate and difficult operation to make out; being confined to have this revolution performed within, or exactly to an almost infinitely small portion of space or time. Formerly, calculations to find numbers for the teeth of wheels and pinions, suited to give the revolution of a planet tolerably near, seems to have been the work of years, and that not very long ago, a thing which may now be done in a few minutes. The clock which was made by Dauthieu for Louis XIV. king of France, about the year 1749, moved a small sphere, or rather more properly in our language, an orrery, representing the solar system, according to Copernicus. The construction and arrangement of it, and the calculation of the wheel teeth, were made out by M. Passemant, in which *it is said*, that he had been employed for such a length of time as twenty years. The motions in this sphere, or planetary machine, were allowed to be very exact by the report of M. M. Camus, and Deparcieux, delegated by the Royal Academy of Sciences to examine them. And even still nearer to our own day, much time and labour seems to have been spent, not less than eleven years, as is related, if not in the calculation of numbers for the wheel teeth, and leaves of the pinions, it must at least have been in the construction and execution of one of the finest planetariums, by M. Antide Janvier, that has as yet been any where exhibited: it was purchased by the then existing government of France. This planetarium is kept constantly going by an excellent chronometer, or time-piece. The numbers of the wheel teeth and of the pinion leaves in it, certainly approximate as nearly as it is possible to give the periodical revolutions of the planets, and other circumstances attending them, to the greatest nicety, such as their states of retrogradation, progression, and when stationary, also their phases, place of the nodes, eclipses, &c. There are two plates of this planetarium, and a detailed description of it, besides the numbers of the wheel teeth and pinion leaves, given in the *Histoire de la Mesure*, &c.

We have seen no account of that magnificent planetarium, sent some years ago by our government to China, as a present, among many other fine things, to the good old Emperor Kien Lung, along with the splendid embassy under Lord Macartney. It is said to have been made at Erfurt in Germany; for in the year 1791, a pamphlet was published in London, giving a description of this planetarium or astronomical machine, invented and partly executed by Phil. Mat.

Hahn, member of the Academy of Sciences at Erfurt, and completed by Albert Mylins.

We were informed by the late Dr. Dinwiddie, who was astronomer and mathematician in that embassy, and had charge of this planetarium, and who of course had to explain the various motions and uses of it, to those who were appointed to receive it for the Emperor, but as they seemed to set little or no value on it, perhaps they did not understand it, or were unable to appreciate the merits of a machine calculated to give such a correct representation of the motions of the heavenly bodies as it did. At this the Doctor was so indignant and provoked, that he was induced to bring away some parts of the machinery, which after all we may suppose could be of little or no use to any one, when detached from the principal to which they were adapted.

M. Camus, in his *Cours de Mathématiques*, Paris, 1767, third edition, has given a few cases for finding the numbers for the teeth of wheels, and the leaves of pinions, two in particular, by way of problems; that shall give the annual revolution of the earth, or the apparent revolution of the sun, and also that of a synodical revolution of the moon, when represented in a planetary machine: the solutions of these problems are done in a very ingenious manner by algebraic equations. But algebraic equations not being so generally known among those of our profession, as the arithmetic of decimal or vulgar fractions may be, we shall attempt to show, by means of these fractions, how the numbers of wheel teeth and pinion leaves may be obtained, so as to produce a revolution in a given time for any planetary motion. Since the time of *Camus*, modern mathematicians appear to have brought this subject, if not to a greater degree of perfection, they have certainly shewn how it may be done, and that in a very simple manner, so as it may be more easily acquired, by those who are not in the daily practice of seeing, what it is in the power of figures or numbers to do. None have displayed such a knowledge of this subject as has been done by the Rev. Dr. Pearson, who certainly has taken uncommon pains, in which he has completely succeeded, by having the motions of the planets to be more correctly represented in an orrery or planetarium than has hitherto been done. The numbers he gave for the motions of Jupiter's satellites were published 10th March, 1798, in Nicholson's Journal, vol ii. 4to edition, p. 122, *et seq*. which was somewhile before we had any account of Janvier's *Sphere Mouvante*, whose numbers for the same motions were so nearly similar to those of Dr. Pearson's, that we could hardly be restrained from suspecting at first sight, some degree of plagiarism on the part of M. Antide Janvier; but having taken, as we are led to suppose, the same way to find numbers for the teeth of the wheels, &c. in his planetary machine, as Dr. Pearson did, and the principle being a general one, the results would and must naturally be the same. Janvier appears, however, from his works, to be master of this subject, had got a liberal education, and of that rank in life, of being the son of one who was a general, second in command of the French army at the battle of Fontenoy.

To the practical astronomer, an orrery can be of little use, unless in the hands of those who may give public lectures on Astronomy, where it is very well calculated to show the motions of the heavenly bodies, and the beauty and order of the solar system, in such a familiar way, as to impress the subject readily on the minds of young students. As there is some ingenuity required to find the numbers for the wheel teeth, as well as to construct and arrange the wheels in an orrery, so as to show the motions of the planets in their natural time and order, it is for these reasons that we have been induced to enter a little into the subject, that the practical artist may derive some small assistance from it, yet without any pretensions of making him an adept. He will acquire much useful information by consulting the articles *Orrery, Planetary Numbers, Planetary and Satellitian Machines*, in Dr. Rees' new Cyclopædia.

The method to be now shewn, is founded on what is called by arithmeticians the reduction of ratios, that is, reducing what is expressed in large numbers to their equivalents nearly; and so as they may be represented in lower terms; as shall be illustrated by the following examples:—

PROBLEM.

Any ratio between two given numbers, consisting of many places of figures, being proposed, to find a set of integral numbers that shall be the nearest to that given ratio?

Divide the consequent by the antecedent, and the divisor by the remainder, and the last divisor by the last remainder, till nothing shall remain, in the same way as finding the greatest common measure for any two numbers: then, for the terms of the first ratio, unity will always be the first antecedent, and the first quotient, the first consequent; for the second ratio, multiply the first antecedent and consequent, by the second quotient, and to the product of the antecedent add 0, and to the consequent add 1, and the sum shall be the terms of the second ratio. For the following ratios, multiply the last antecedent and consequent by the next quotient, and to the pro-

ALTERNATE RATIOS.   53

duct add the last antecedent and consequent but one, and the sum shall be the present antecedent and consequent. It is necessary to remark, that if the terms of the given ratio are not prime to each other, they must be made so, before the operations proposed above are performed.

EXAMPLE.

Let the ratio of 7988 to 163704 be proposed, and to find smaller integral numbers in the same proportion as near as can be found. The ratio expressed in the usual form is $\frac{7988}{163704}$; and it is easily seen that the terms are not prime to each other, for $\frac{7988}{163704} = \frac{3994}{81852} = \frac{1997}{40926}$, which are prime to each other, that is, where no other number except unity will divide both without a remainder.

```
1997)40926(20
     3994
     ─────
      986)1997(2
          1972
          ─────
           25)986(39
              75
              ───
              236
              225
              ───
               11)25(2
                  22
                  ──
                   3)11(3
                      9
                      ─
                      2)3(1
                        2
                        ─
                        1)2(2
                          2
```

The quotients found in this operation are 20, 2, 39, 2, 3, 1, and 2.

The first quotient $20 \times 0 + \dfrac{1}{0} = \dfrac{1}{20}$ or first ratio.

$\dfrac{1}{20} \times 2 + \dfrac{0}{1} = \dfrac{2}{41}$ second ratio.

$\dfrac{2}{41} \times 39 + \dfrac{1}{20} = \dfrac{79}{1619}$ third ratio.

$\dfrac{79}{1619} \times 2 + \dfrac{2}{41} = \dfrac{160}{3279}$ fourth ratio.

$\dfrac{160}{3279} \times 3 + \dfrac{79}{1619} = \dfrac{559}{11456}$ fifth ratio.

$\dfrac{559}{11456} \times 1 + \dfrac{160}{3270} = \dfrac{719}{14735}$ sixth ratio.

$\dfrac{719}{14735} \times 2 + \dfrac{559}{11456} = \dfrac{1997}{40926}$ seventh ratio.

The last ratio is, that, where the numbers are prime to each other, and, therefore, a proof of the operation. It is necessary to observe, that the first ratio of 1 to 20 is farther from the truth than the second, which is 2 to 41; and the third, 79 to 1619, is still nearer to the given ratio, and all of them are the nearest that can be found in round numbers, where the antecedent and consequent is one of the numbers above. Thus, the ratio of 7988 to 163704, may be expressed by six different ratios, all of them in smaller whole numbers, that constantly approach nearer and nearer to the truth, till the seventh ratio above, which is the same with it, as well as the ratio $\dfrac{3994}{81852}$.

The application or use of the foregoing problem will be seen in the following example:—

A lunation, or synodical revolution of the moon, consists of 29 days, 12 hours, 44 minutes, 2 seconds, and 52 thirds: It is required to find such numbers for the teeth of the wheels, and leaves of the pinions, as shall cause the last wheel in the train to make one turn in the above period of time?

Reduce the 12 hours, 44 minutes, 2 seconds, 52 thirds, to the decimal of a day; the number of thirds here, is 2750572: this, divided by 518400, the thirds in a day or 24 hours, the quotient .5305887 will be the decimal part of a day; the lunation is then 29.5305887 days, and this being divided by 1.0000000, and so on, reducing it to get a few quotients, as in the preceding operation. The quotients

PLANETARY NUMBERS.

obtained by these operations, are, 29, 1, 1, 7, 1, 2, 17, 2; with these quotients we proceed to obtain a ratio somewhat near to $\frac{1.0000000}{29.5305887}$, but represented in lower terms; now, 29 being the first quotient, will be represented in the first ratio as 1 to 29, or $\frac{1}{29}$. The numbers of the fraction $\frac{1.0000000}{29.5305887}$ are prime to each other, 1 being the common divisor, and the quotients, in addition to the above, 1, 11, 1, 1, 1, 1, 1, 2, 2, 1, 1, and 2.

$$29 \times 0 + \frac{1}{0} = \frac{1}{29} \quad \text{first ratio.}$$

$$\frac{1}{29} \times 1 + \frac{0}{1} = \frac{1}{30} \quad \text{second ratio.}$$

$$\frac{1}{30} \times 1 + \frac{1}{29} = \frac{2}{59} \quad \text{third ratio.}$$

$$\frac{2}{59} \times 7 + \frac{1}{30} = \frac{15}{443} \quad \text{fourth ratio.}$$

$$\frac{15}{443} \times 1 + \frac{2}{59} = \frac{17}{502} \quad \text{fifth ratio.}$$

$$\frac{17}{502} \times 2 + \frac{15}{443} = \frac{49}{1447} \quad \text{sixth ratio.}$$

$$\frac{49}{1447} \times 17 + \frac{17}{502} = \frac{850}{25101} \quad \text{seventh ratio.}$$

$$\frac{850}{25101} \times 2 + \frac{49}{1447} = \frac{1749}{51649} \quad \text{eighth ratio.}$$

If we take the eighth ratio, and divide the consequent by the antecedent, we shall have 29 days for the quotient; the remainder being multiplied by 24, and the sum again divided by the antecedent 1749, the quotient will be 12 hours, and so on, as seen in the following operation:—

PLANETARY NUMBERS.

```
1749)51649(29 days.
     3498
     ─────
     16669
     15741
     ─────
       928
        24
     ─────
      3712
      1856
```

```
1749)22272(12 hours.
     1749
     ────
     4782
     3498
     ────
     1284
       60
     ────
```

```
1749)77040(44 minutes.
     6996
     ────
     7080
     6996
     ────
       84
       60
     ────
```

```
1749)5040(2 seconds.
     3498
     ────
     1542
       60
     ────
```

1749)92520(52 thirds $\frac{524}{583}$ or $\frac{9}{10}$ nearly.
    8745
    ────
    5070
    3498

$3)\frac{1572}{1749} = \frac{524}{583}$, or $\frac{9}{10}$ nearly

If the antecedent of the fraction $\frac{1749}{51649}$ is divided by prime numbers, we shall get numbers for the pinions, and numbers for the wheel teeth will be got in the same manner, by dividing the consequent with the like kind of numbers.

1749	3		51649	13
583	11		3973	29
53	53		137	137
1			1	

The fractions then are $\frac{3}{13} \times \frac{11}{29} \times \frac{53}{137} = 29$ days, 12 hours, 44 minutes, 2 seconds, $52\frac{144}{137}$ thirds; or they can be made $\frac{15}{65} \times \frac{22}{58} \times \frac{53}{137} =$ to the above.

If a cipher is added to both parts of the fraction $\frac{1749}{51649}$, they will then decompose into such numbers, as are better suited for the teeth of the wheels and leaves of the pinions, as may here be seen, but differing nothing from the fractions already stated.

516490	2		17490	2	
258245	5	Wheels.	8745	3	Pinions.
51649	13	- 2×29= 58	2915	5	3× 5=15
3973	29	- 5×13= 65	583	11	2×11=22
137	137	- 137=137	53	53	53=53

If the ratio had been carried on to the ninth or tenth quotient, they would have been represented by so great a number of places of figures, that before they could have been divided into such small numbers as were practicable for wheel teeth, we should have been prevented by meeting with prime numbers of too great extent, an inconvenience that frequently occurs in this method of finding numbers.

The numbers that have been obtained here for the teeth of wheels, and leaves of pinions, are the same which give the synodical revolution of the moon in Janvier's *Sphere Mouvante*.

The earth is computed to perform its annual revolution for a tropical year, in 365 days, 5 hours, 48 minutes, 48 seconds. A train of wheels and pinions to represent this motion of the earth, may be obtained by a process like that of the preceding; and a neat scheme of it, by Dr. Pearson, may be seen in Rees's new Cyclopædia, under the article Planetary Numbers. Reduce 5 hours, 48 minutes, 48 seconds, to the decimal of a day, which becomes .242̇, making the time of the earth's annual motion to be 365.242̇ days. To reduce this decimal part to a vulgar fraction, being a repeater, it cannot be reduced in the common way; the finite part being subtracted from the whole decimal, will give the numerator of the fraction; the denominator must be 9 for each figure of the infinite part, (that with a dot on the top of the last figure 2,) and having as many ciphers added to it as there are integers in the finite part, which in this case are two; as thus:

$$\frac{242̇-24}{218} = \frac{218}{900} = \frac{109}{450}.$$

Or it may be represented thus, $\frac{242̇-24}{900} = \frac{218}{900} = \frac{109}{450}$. And $365\frac{109}{450}$, reduced, becomes the improper fraction $\frac{164359}{450}$, this, when inverted, will be the fraction $\frac{450}{164359}$, the same as produced by the process of reduction in the seventh ratio in the scheme alluded to.

```
450 | 2      Pinions.              | Wheels.
225 | 3      2×5=10          164359 | 13
 75 | 3      3×3= 9           12643 | 47
 25 | 5        5= 5             269 | 269
  5 | 5
```

$\frac{10}{269} \times \frac{9}{47} \times \frac{5}{13}$ or $\frac{10}{269} \times \frac{9}{47} \times \frac{10}{26} = 365$ days, 5 hours, 48 minutes, 48 seconds.

Or thus, $\frac{9}{26} \times \frac{10}{47} \times \frac{10}{269}$, giving the same result as above. These are the same numbers as are in Janvier's *Sphere Mouvante*.

The first pinion 9 in this train, and 15 in that of the moon's synodical revolution, are supposed to turn round once in 24 hours; the time of the revolutions of the last wheel in each is respectively given.

A solar or tropical year being computed to consist of 365 days, 5 hours, 48 minutes, 48 seconds, the siderial revolutions in that time are 366 days, 5 hours, 49 minutes, 47 seconds, 9¹⁵⁵⁄₁₇₇ thirds. To find numbers for the wheels and pinions to produce a siderial motion, reduce 5 hours, 49 minutes, 47 seconds, $9\tfrac{111}{117}$ thirds, to the decimal of a day, and it will be represented by the fraction $\frac{1.0000000}{366.2429068}$, whose greatest common measure is 4, consequently the numbers are not prime to each other, neither are $\frac{5000000}{183.4214534}$, which is the half of the first fraction, but this last, when again divided by 2, becomes so; as $\frac{2500000}{91.5607267}$; and from this we obtain the following nineteen quotients, viz. 366, 4, 8, 1, 1, 3, 1, 1, 2, 1, 1, 2, 1, 2, 1, 4, 1, 2, 3, and the last ratio produced from them will be $\frac{2500000}{91.5607267}$, which, multiplied by 4, gives the original $\frac{1.0000000}{366.2429068}$. The same quotients can be got from any of the three fractions, and, of course, the same ratio will be the result. The tenth ratio, $\frac{2009}{735782}$, may be decomposed into numbers for the wheels and pinions, though, by itself, it is not so well suited as other numbers would be, the divisors of the numerator being two 7's, and a 41; those of the denominator, one 2, a 37, a 61, and 163, which give for $\frac{\text{pinions}}{\text{wheels}} \frac{7 \times 7 \times 41}{61 \times 74 \times 163} = \frac{2009}{735782}$; and if the denominator be divided by the numerator, and the reduction carried on, it will give 366 days, 5 hours, 49 minutes, 47 seconds, $9\tfrac{111}{117}$ thirds. It is, however, from the ratio $\frac{2009}{735782}$ that the fraction $\frac{96432}{35317536}$ is derived; and this, when divided by prime numbers, gives for the numerator four 2's, one 3, two 7's, and a 41; and for the denominator, five 2's, one 3, a 37, 61, and 163, making the numbers for the $\frac{\text{pinions}}{\text{wheels}} \frac{12 \times 14 \times 14 \times 41}{48 \times 61 \times 74 \times 163} = \frac{96432}{35317536}$; and these are the actual numbers that Janvier had in his *Sphere Mouvante*, of a new and simple construction, to produce in it, an annual siderial revolution. He has not given us the process by which the fraction $\frac{96432}{35317536}$ was obtained, nor even the fraction itself, though, from his numbers, it is evident that they are derived from this fraction: he only mentions that the numbers were derived from the solids 2009 and 735782. We observe that the fraction $\frac{96432}{35317536}$ may be obtained by multiplying the tenth ratio $\frac{2009}{735782}$ by 48, which is half of the product of the remaining nine quotients multiplied into one another; or it may be found by the simple addition of several of the ratios together; such, for example, as that of the 4th, 7th, 8th, 9th, 10th, 11th, 12th, 13th, and the double of the 14th ratio; or otherwise by that of the 4th, 7th, 8th, 9th, 10th, and the double of the 15th, as may easily be seen, for

$$\frac{37}{13551} + \frac{317}{116099} + \frac{564}{206561} + \frac{1445}{529221} + \frac{2009}{735782} + \frac{3454}{1265003} + \frac{8917}{3265788} +$$

$$\frac{12371}{4530791} + \frac{33659}{12327370} + \frac{33659}{12327370} = \frac{96432}{35317536},$$ the fraction required;

or, secondly, $\frac{37}{13551} + \frac{317}{116099} + \frac{564}{206561} + \frac{1445}{529221} + \frac{2009}{735782} + \frac{46030}{16858161}$

$$+ \frac{46030}{16858161} = \frac{96432}{35317536}$$ as before; but in order that the addition may appear more clear, we shall place all the numerators in one column, and all the denominators in another, thus:

37	-	4th	-	13551				
317	-	7th	-	116099				
564	-	8th	-	206561				
1445	-	9th	-	529221	37	-	4th -	13551
2009	-	10th	-	735782	317	-	7th -	116099
3454	-	11th	-	1265003	564	-	8th -	206561
8917	-	12th	-	3265788	1445	-	9th -	529221
12371	-	13th	-	4530791	2009	-	10th -	735782
33659 } 33659 }	-	14th	- {	12327370 12327370	46030 } 46030 }	-	15th - {	16858161 16858161
96432				35317536	96432			35317536

It is unnecessary here to put down the whole ratios in detail, as any one may at pleasure find them with the assistance of the nineteen quotients before mentioned, viz. 366, 4, 8, 1, 1, &c. &c. proceeding in the same manner as in pages 54 and 55.

The two following problems are from *Cours de Mathématiques*, par M. Camus.

PROBLEM.

To find the numbers of the teeth of wheels, and leaves of pinions, in a machine, which being led by a pinion placed on the hour wheel of a clock, shall cause a wheel to make a revolution in a mean year, supposed to consist of 365 days, 5 hours, 49 minutes.

Solution.

Let A (No. 5, Plate I.) be the wheel which ought to make a revolution in 365 days, 5 hours, 49 minutes; h, the pinion, to be placed on the hour wheel, and like it make a revolution in 12 hours; and

BC, fg, two other wheels and two other pinions, by means of which the motion of the pinion h will be communicated to the wheel A.

As the pinion h makes a revolution in 12 hours, or two revolutions in a day, it will make 730 revolutions in 365 days, and $\frac{1}{12}$ or $\frac{100}{720}$ of a revolution in five hours; and as a minute is equal to $\frac{1}{60}$ of an hour, or $\frac{1}{720}$ of 12 hours, the same pinion will perform $\frac{49}{720}$ of a revolution in 49 minutes. This pinion therefore will make $730\frac{149}{720}$ revolutions in 365 days, 5 hours, 49 minutes; that is to say, during the time that the wheel A ought to perform its revolution. But the product of the wheels ABC is equal to the product of the pinions $f g h$, multiplied by the number of the revolutions made by the pinion h during a revolution of the wheel A. We shall therefore have this equation $A \times B \times C = 730\frac{149}{720} \times f \times g \times h$; and as the numbers of the teeth of the wheels ought not to contain fractions, the value $730\frac{149}{720} \times f \times g \times h$ must be a whole number. Therefore, if the number $730\frac{149}{720}$ be multiplied by the product of the pinions $f \times g \times h$, the fraction which has 720 for denominator must become a whole number, consequently the product of the pinions $f \times g \times h$ must be equal to 720, or be a multiple of 720.

If the product of the pinions $f \times g \times h$ were made equal to 720, it might be decomposed into the three factors 8, 9, 10, which could be taken as the numbers for the leaves of these pinions; the equation $A \times B \times C = 730\frac{149}{720} \times f \times g \times h$, would then become $A \times B \times C = 525949$, as $730 \times 720 + 349 = 525949$. But this number found as the product of the numbers of the teeth of the three wheels A B C, cannot be decomposed into three factors, which could be the numbers for the teeth of these wheels; it must then be concluded, that it is not possible for it, to cause the wheel A to make a revolution in 365^d 5^h 49^m.

If a multiple of 720 were taken as the product of the pinions, nothing would be gained, as we should find for the product of the wheels ABC, a number, a multiple of 525949; and this multiple could not be better decomposed than 525949. As the number $730\frac{149}{720}$, multiplied by any other product of the pinions than 720, or than a multiple of 720, would not give a product without fractions for that of the wheels; and as the fractions must be neglected in the product of the wheels ABC, it is necessary to find for the product of the pinions $f \times g \times h$, a whole number, which, being multiplied by $730\frac{149}{720}$, may give a product as near as possible to a whole number. In general, this is done by repeated trials; but as this method is defective, we shall here propose another, by which the problem may be solved with more certainty. When, in searching for the value of the product of the wheels $A \times B \times C$, or to approach as near to it as possible, we have multiplied $730\frac{4}{7}\frac{9}{2}\frac{9}{0}$ by the product of the pinions $f \times g \times h$, which will be a whole number; the product found will be composed of these two parts $730 \times f \times g \times h$ and $\frac{349 \times f \times g \times h}{720}$. But the first part $730 \times f \times g \times h$ is a whole number, since its two factors, 730 and $f \times g \times h$, are whole numbers. We must therefore proceed in such a manner that the second part $\frac{349 \times f \times g \times h}{720}$ may approach as near as possible to a whole number. That this may be the case, it is necessary that its numerator, which is a whole number, should be too great or too little, only by unity, to be divided by its denominator 720. But, if we suppose that this numerator is too great by unity, and if we lesson it by that unity, we shall have $\frac{349 \times f \times g \times h}{720}$ equal to a whole number. If this whole number then be represented by S, we shall have $\frac{349 \times f \times g \times h - 1}{720} =$ S.

If each member of this equation be multiplied by 720, we shall have $349 \times f \times g \times h - 1 = 720$ S. Then adding 1 to each member of the last equation, and afterwards dividing each of its new members by 349, it will be reduced to the following, $f \times g \times h = \frac{720 +}{349}$.

As the product of $f \times g \times h$, which forms the first member of the last equation, is a whole number, so the second member $\frac{720 \, S + 1}{349}$ of the same equation will also be a whole number. But this whole number $\frac{720 \, S + 1}{349}$ is composed of two parts,

$\frac{698 \, S}{349}$ which is equal to 2 S, and $\frac{22 \, S + 1}{349}$. Put then $\frac{22 \, S + 1}{349} = t$

therefore $22 \, S + 1 = 349 \, t$

$22 \, S = 349 \, t - 1$

$S = \frac{349 \, t - 1}{22}$ which is composed of $\frac{330 \, t}{22} = 15 \, t$ and $\frac{19 \, t - 1}{22}$

Putting then $\frac{19 \, t - 1}{22} = v$, we shall have

$19 \, t - 1 = 22 \, v$

$19 \, t = 22 \, v + 1$

$t = \frac{22 \, v + 1}{19}$ which is composed of $\frac{19 \, v}{19} = v$, and $\frac{3 \, v + 1}{19}$.

Say now $\frac{3v+1}{19} = s$ we have

$3v+1 = 19 s$

$3v = 19 s - 1$

$v = \frac{19 s - 1}{3}$ which is composed of $\frac{18 s}{3} = 6 s$ and $\frac{s-1}{3}$.

Then put $\frac{s-1}{3} = y$, then

$s - 1 = 3 y$

$s = 3 y + 1$

Then if we make $y = 0$
we shall have $s = 1$, and we may find the product of $f \times g \times h$ by simple substitutions, for putting 1 for s in the equation $v = \frac{19 s - 1}{3}$, we find $v = 6$, and putting 6 for v in the equation $t = \frac{22 v + 1}{19}$, we obtain $t = 7$; and 7 for t in $S = \frac{349 t - 1}{22}$ we get $S = 111$; lastly, putting 111 for S in the equation $f \times g \times h = \frac{720 S + 1}{349}$ we find the product of the pinions to be 229, for $720 \times 111 + 1 \div 349 = 229$.

As the number 229 found for the value of the product of the pinions $f \times g \times h$, is a prime number, which cannot be decomposed into several factors; and, as it exceeds the number of leaves that can be given to a pinion, it will be necessary to seek for another more convenient. If, instead of making $\frac{s-1}{3} = y$, it had been made successively equal to 1, to 2, to 3, &c., we should have, as the product of $f \times g \times h$ other numbers, 949, 1669, 2389, &c., formed by the continual addition of 720 to 229; but as these new products are prime numbers, or composed of factors too great, to be the numbers of the leaves of pinions, or give, as the product of the wheels, numbers composed of factors too great, they cannot be employed. In a word, this article is not demonstrated, because there are no rules to enable us to determine whether a number resulting from these compositions will be a prime number, or composed of several factors of a certain quantity.

As the number 229 cannot be the product of the several pinions f, g, h, we must search for another, which, being multiplied by 349, shall give a product too great by 2 or 3, to be divisible by 720; that is to say, we must make $\frac{349 \times f \times g \times h - 2}{720}$ or $\frac{349 \times f \times g \times h - 3}{720}$ equal to a whole number, represented by S, repeating the operations above explained, in the case where it was required, that $\frac{349 \times f \times g \times h - 1}{720}$ should be a whole number; and we shall have the following equations, which will differ from the first only in this, that they will contain +2 and —2, or +3 and —3, instead of +1 and —1, which were in the first.

$$\left. \begin{array}{l} f \times g \times h = \frac{720\,S + 2}{349} \\ S = \frac{349\,t - 2}{22} \\ t = \frac{22\,v + 2}{19} \\ v = \frac{19\,x - 2}{3} \\ x = 2 \end{array} \right\} \text{ or } \left\{ \begin{array}{l} f \times g \times h = \frac{720\,S + 3}{349} \\ S = \frac{349\,t - 3}{22} \\ t = \frac{22\,v + 3}{19} \\ v = \frac{19\,x - 3}{3} \\ x = 3 \end{array} \right.$$

But if to find the value of the product of the pinions $f \times g \times h$, we substitute in these two new series of equations 2 or 3, in the place of x, in the value of v, then the value of v in the room of t, and that of t in the room of S, and the value of S in that of the product of the pinions $f \times g \times h$, we shall find for that product 458, which is the double of 229, or 687, which is the triple of 229: and as we rejected 229, because it was indecomposable, and too great to be the number of the leaves of a pinion, we must reject also the two numbers 458 and 687, which both have the same number 229 as one of their factors. But, if we endeavour to find for the product of the pinions $f \times g \times h$, a number, which, being multiplied by 349, shall give a product too great by 4 units, to be divisable by 720, that is to say, if it be required that $\frac{349 \times f \times g \times h - 4}{720}$ should be a whole number, we shall have the following equations, which will differ from the former only in this, that they will contain +4, or —4, whereas the first contained +1, or —1.

$$f \times g \times h = \frac{720\,S + 4}{349}$$
$$S = \frac{349\,t - 4}{22}$$
$$t = \frac{22\,v + 4}{19}$$
$$v = \frac{19\,x - 4}{3}$$

And as the value $\frac{19z-4}{3}$ of the whole number v, is composed of these two parts, $\frac{18z-3}{3}$, $\frac{z-1}{3}$, and as the first of these two parts, $\frac{18z-3}{3}$ is a whole number, the second part, $\frac{z-1}{3}$, will also be a whole number, or equal to y or zero. Now, if it is known that $\frac{z-1}{3}=0$, we shall have $z=1$

Substituting 1 for z in $\frac{19z-4}{3}$ value of v, we shall have $v=5$.

Putting 5 for v in $\frac{22v+4}{19}$ value of t, we shall find $t=6$.

Putting 6 for t in $\frac{349t-4}{22}$, value of S, we shall have $S=95$.

Finally, putting 95 for S in $\frac{720S+4}{349}$ value of $f\times g\times h$, we shall have $f\times g\times h = 196$: because $720\times95+4+349 = 196$. Now, the number 196, found as the value of the product of the pinions $f\times g\times h$, is decomposible into the three factors 4, 7, 7, which can be the numbers of the leaves of these three pinions, therefore these pinions are determined.

To determine the numbers for the teeth of the three wheels ABC, we shall resume the equation $A\times B\times C = 730\frac{11}{12}\times f\times g\times h$, which we found at the beginning of the solution; and putting 196 for the product of $f\times g\times h$, we shall find $A\times B\times C = 143175\frac{4}{15}$; for $730\times720+349\times196+720 = 143175\frac{1}{15}$. Neglecting the fraction $\frac{1}{15}$ that we proposed to reject, we shall have for the product of the wheels ABC, the number 143175, which will decompose easily into these three factors, 25, 69, 83, that can be the numbers for the teeth of the three wheels ABC.

Therefore, to cause the wheel A make one turn in 365 days, 5 hours, 49 minutes, or nearly so, by means of a wheel-work led by a pinion h, placed on the hour-wheel, *(as it is commonly called by clock-makers, although its revolution takes 12 hours,)* of a clock, we may make use of three wheels ABC, the numbers of whose teeth must be 83, 69, and 25, and three pinions f, g, h, the number of whose leaves will be 4, 7, 7.

In place of the pinion h turning round in 12 hours, let us suppose it to go round every 24 hours; 196, the number found for the pinions, must now be doubled also, that is, it must be 392; the pinions will then be 8, 7, 7, and the wheels, as before, 83, 69, 25, which may thus be represented, $\frac{392}{143175} = \frac{8\times7\times7}{25\times69\times83} \frac{\text{pinions}}{\text{wheels}} = 365$ days, 5

F

hours, 48 minutes, 58 seconds, $46\frac{16}{19}$ thirds, being the time that the wheel A will take to make one revolution, and less than the proposed time by 1 second, $13\frac{11}{19}$ thirds. Hence, we remark, that the fraction $\frac{4}{119}$, which has been neglected in the product of the wheels, will not cause, (on the time of the revolution required,) an error of more than 1 second, $13\frac{11}{19}$ thirds, and that it would take near 2940 years before this error, in being multiplied into itself, could mount up to an hour, or 49 years before it would come to 1 minute.

PROBLEM.

To find the numbers of the teeth of the wheels, and leaves of pinions of a machine, which, being moved by a pinion (in a clock) that makes a revolution in an hour, shall cause the last wheel in the machine to make a revolution in 29 days, 12 hours, 44 minutes, 3 seconds, and 12 thirds, being the time of a mean synodical revolution of the moon.

SOLUTION.

Let A (No. 5. Plate I.) be the wheel which it is proposed shall make a revolution in 29 days, 12 hours, 44 minutes, 3 seconds, and 12 thirds; h, the pinion, which placed on the arbor of the center wheel of a clock, like it shall make a turn in an hour; and BC, two other wheels, and f, g; two other pinions, by whose means the motion of the pinion h will be communicated to the wheel A.

The pinion h making one turn in an hour, or 24 turns in a day, it will make 696 turns in 29 days, and 708 turns in 29 days, 12 hours.

A minute being $\frac{1}{60}$ or $\frac{1600}{113000}$ of an hour, the pinion h will make $\frac{118400}{113000}$ turns in 44 minutes.

A second, being $\frac{1}{3600}$ or $\frac{60}{113000}$ of an hour, the pinion h will make $\frac{180}{113000}$ turns in 3 seconds.

A third, being $\frac{1}{113000}$ of an hour, the pinion h will make $\frac{12}{113000}$ turns in 12 thirds.

So, while the wheel A makes one turn, the pinion h will make $708\frac{118592}{113000}$ turns, or $708\frac{126}{192}$ turns, in dividing the two terms of the fraction by 192. But the product of the wheels A×B×C, is equal to the product of the pinions $f \times g \times h$, multiplied by the number of the turns that the pinion h makes during one turn of the wheel A. We shall then have $A \times B \times C = f \times g \times h \times 708\frac{126}{192}$.

Therefore when it is required that the wheel A should make a turn, exactly in 29 days, 12 hours, 44 minutes, 3 seconds, 12 thirds, we must take for the product of the pinions $f \times g \times h$, a number which may be equal to the denominator of the fraction $\frac{116}{1125}$, or which may be a multiple of that denominator.

But, in taking the number 1125 for the value of the product of the pinions $f \times g \times h$, and substituting it in the place of this product in the equation $A \times B \times C = f \times g \times h \times 708 \frac{116}{1125}$, we shall have for the value of the product of the wheels $A \times B \times C$, the number 797326, which cannot be decomposed into factors fit to be the numbers of the teeth of two or three wheels. The wheel A therefore cannot be made to perform a revolution in 29 days, 12 hours, 44 minutes, 3 seconds, and 12 thirds; and it will be requisite to find, as the product of the pinions $f \times g \times h$, a whole number, which, being multiplied by $708 \frac{116}{1125}$, may give a product approaching as near as possible to a whole number.

In searching for the product of the wheels, or endeavouring to approach it, when we have multiplied $708 \frac{116}{1125}$ by the product of the pinions $f \times g \times h$, the product will be composed of these two parts, $708 \times f \times g \times h$, and $\frac{826 \times f \times g \times h}{1125}$. But, as the first part $708 \times f \times g \times h$ will be a whole number, and as the sum of these two parts ought to approach as near as possible to a whole number, it will be necessary to proceed in such a manner, that the second part $\frac{826 \times f \times g \times h}{1125}$, may approach as near as possible to a whole number.

That the fraction $\frac{826 \times f \times g \times h}{1125}$ may differ as little as possible from a whole number, its numerator must be too large or too small, only by unity, to be divisible by 1125. But by making the numerator greater or less by unity, or even by 2, or 3, or 4, or 5, or 6, or 7, or 8 units, than a number divisible by 1125, we shall find, as the product of the wheels $A \times B \times C$, numbers, some factors of which will be too great to be the numbers of some of the wheels; and therefore it will be necessary to proceed in such a manner, that the numerator of the fraction may be 9 units too small to be divisible by 1125; that is to say, having added 9 to the numerator $826 \times f \times g \times h$, we shall suppose the new fraction $\frac{826 \times f \times g \times h + 9}{1125}$ equal to a whole number represented by S, which will give this equation, $\frac{826 \times f \times g \times h + 9}{1125} = S$.

Proceeding now in this problem as we did in the former, and multiplying both members of this last equation by 1125, then taking 9 from each, and dividing the remainder by 826, we obtain the equation $f \times g \times h = \frac{1125 S - 9}{826}$, which is composed of

NUMBERS FOR A LUNATION.

$\frac{826\,S}{826} = S$, and $\frac{299\,S-9}{826}$: put this last part of the equation, $\frac{299\,S-9}{826} = t$, we then have $299\,S - 9 = 826\,t$

$$299\,S = 826\,t + 9$$

$$S = \frac{826\,t+9}{299}, \text{ which is composed of } \frac{598\,t}{299} = 2\,t, \text{ and } \frac{228\,t+9}{299}. \text{ Put then}$$

$\frac{228\,t+9}{299} = v$, and we have $228\,t + 9 = 299\,v$.

$$228\,t = 299\,v - 9$$
$$t = \frac{299\,v-9}{228}, \text{ which is composed of } \frac{228\,v}{228} = v$$

and $\frac{71\,v-9}{228}$ which say $= x$. Then $71\,v - 9 = 228\,x$

$$71\,v = 228\,x + 9$$
$$v = \frac{228\,x+9}{71}, \text{which is composed of} \frac{213\,x}{71} = 3\,x$$

and $\frac{15\,x+9}{71}$ which say $= y$. Then $15\,x + 9 = 71\,y$

$$15\,x = 71\,y - 9$$
$$x = \frac{71\,y-9}{15}, \text{which is composed of} \frac{60\,y}{15} = 4\,y$$

and $\frac{11\,y-9}{15}$ which say $= z$. Then $11\,y - 9 = 15\,z$

$$11\,y = 15\,z + 9$$
$$y = \frac{15\,z+9}{11}, \text{which is composed of} \frac{11\,z}{11} = z$$

and $\frac{4\,z+9}{11}$ which say $= \&$. Then $4\,z + 9 = 11\,\&$

$$4\,z = 11\,\& - 9$$
$$z = \frac{11\,\&-9}{4}, \text{which is composed of} \frac{8\,\&-8}{4}$$

and $\frac{3\,\&-1}{4}$ which say $= \Delta$. Then $3\,\& - 1 = 4\,\Delta$

$$3\,\& = 4\,\Delta + 1$$
$$\& = \frac{4\,\Delta+1}{3}, \text{ putting then } \Delta = 2, \text{ we}$$

obtain the nine following equations:

1st, $\& = 3$

2d, $z = \frac{11\,\&-9}{4}$

3d, $y = \frac{15\,z+9}{11}$

4th, $x = \frac{71\,y-9}{15}$

5th, $v = \frac{228\,x+9}{71}$

6th, $t = \frac{299\,v-9}{228}$

7th, $S = \frac{826\,t+9}{299}$

8th, $f \times g \times h = \frac{1125\,S-9}{826}$

9th, $A \times B \times C = f \times g \times h \times 706\,\frac{826}{1125}$

NUMBERS FOR A LUNATION. 69

As the 1st equation gave $k=3$, if we put 3 for k, in the 2d, we shall have $z=6$, for $11\times3-9=24+4=6$.

Putting 6 for z, in the 3d, we get $y=9$, for $15\times6+9=99+11=9$.

Putting 9 for y, in the 4th, we find $x=42$, for $71\times9-9=630+15=42$.

Putting 42 for x, in the 5th, we obtain $v=135$, for $228\times42+9=9585+71=135$.

Putting 135 for v, in the 6th, we have $t=177$, for $299\times135-9=43056+228=177$.

Putting 177 for t, in the 7th, we get $s=489$, for $826\times177+9=146211+299=489$.

Putting 489 for s, in the 8th, we find $f\times g\times h=666$, for $1125\times489-9=550116+826=666$.

Lastly, putting 666 for $f\times g\times h$, in the 9th, we have $A\times B\times C=472017-\frac{8}{1111}$, for $708\frac{816}{1111}\times666=472017-\frac{9}{1111}$.

The number 666, found as the value of the product of the pinions $f\times g\times h$, being reducible to these four factors, 2, 3, 3, 37, they may be compounded into these three, 3, 6, 37, which may be the numbers of the leaves of three pinions; and the number 472017, which has been found for the product of the wheels, neglecting the negative fraction $-\frac{9}{1111}$, being composed of these factors 3, 7, 7, 13, 13, 19, they may be divided into these three sets, (3×19), (7×13), (7×13), equal to these three factors, 57, 91, 91, which may be the numbers of the teeth of the three wheels: it is therefore proved that the problem is solved.

It is to be remarked, that the negative fraction $-\frac{9}{1111}$, neglected in the product of the wheels, and by which this product is rendered greater than it ought to be, to cause the wheel A make one revolution in 29 days, 12 hours, 44 minutes, 3 seconds, 12 thirds, will not produce, *(in the time of the revolution of that wheel)* an error of more than $2\frac{11}{37}$ thirds. For if we seek for the number of revolutions which the pinion h will make during a revolution of the wheel A, dividing the product of the wheels 472017, by the product of the pinions 666, it will be found that this pinion h, which makes a revolution in an hour, will make 708 revolutions, which correspond to 708 hours, or to 29 days, 12 hours, and there will remain 489 revolutions, or 489 hours, which being divided by 666, will give 44 minutes, 3 seconds, and $14\frac{11}{37}$ thirds.

The time, therefore, which the wheel A will take to make a revolution, will be 29 days, 12 hours, 44 minutes, 3 seconds, $14\frac{11}{37}$ thirds; consequently will exceed the proposed time only by $2\frac{11}{37}$ thirds.

The pinion h, which is three here, being rather too low a number or practice, it would be as well to make it three times that, which will be 9; consequently *both* parts of the fraction $\frac{666}{472017}$ must be multiplied by 3, the fraction now will be $\frac{1998}{1416051}$, representing the wheels and pinions multiplied into one another, and this when decomposed will give for $\begin{cases} \text{pinions} & \frac{6}{91} \times \frac{9}{91} \times \frac{37}{171} \end{cases}$, producing the same result as above, 29 days, 12 hours, 44 minutes, 3 seconds, $14\frac{13}{17}$ thirds.

The late James Ferguson, who was equally eminent as a writer as well as a lecturer on Natural Philosophy, being in Edinburgh about the year 1767, was so obliging as to communicate to us a description of the wheels, pinions, and endless screws, in a train of wheel work to produce a mean synodical revolution of the moon, mentioning that they were, (as he supposed) computed and invented by Mudge, but at that time no account of them had been published, nor was so till long afterwards. The effect of this train makes the revolution equal to 29 days, 12 hours, 44 minutes, and 3 seconds. It is perhaps as ingenious a mechanical contrivance as can well be imagined, and was executed, and put to a clock by Mudge himself, for his sincere noble friend and patron, his Excellency the late Count Bruhl. A particular description, and a drawing of this contrivance, may be seen in a book published in the year 1799, by Mudge's son, chiefly intended for giving an account of the merits of his father's time-keepers. This lunation of Mudge's being so very curious a piece of clock-work for showing the moon's age, we shall give an account of it, taking the description from the publication now alluded to.

" There are no numbers, nor method that I have seen," says Mr. Mudge, " by which the mean motion of the moon can be represented more correctly than by those in No. 2. Plate I. or a multiple of them, where A is a wheel that goes round in 24 hours.
B a pinion with 8 leaves.
C a wheel with 45 teeth.
D a pinion with 8 leaves.
E a wheel with 42 teeth, which carries the moon on its axis in 29 days, 12 hours, and 45 minutes. But, as from these numbers there is an error of 57 seconds in one revolution of the moon, I propose to correct that error by the method in the scheme represented in Plate I. No. 3 and 4. the latter of which is a la-

teral view of the former, said in both, the same parts are represented by the same letters. F, No. 4. is a stud fixed in the plate, at the bottom of which is fixed the pinion 8 immoveably. The wheel A moves freely round on the stud F, once in 24 hours. On the wheel A moves the wheel b, and is carried along with the wheel A, round the stud F. The teeth of the wheel b run in the pinion a, on the axis of which there is an endless screw c, that runs in the teeth of the wheel d, which wheel is also fixed to the wheel A, to the plane of which its axis is parallel. On the axis of the wheel d is another endless screw e, which runs into the wheel f: This wheel is also fixed to the wheel A, and its axis goes through it, and has on the upper side of it a pinion of 3 leaves, or pins g, which runs in the wheel h, which wheel h moves round the same stud that the wheel A does, and has fixed to it the pinion B. The pinion B in No. 2. is fixed to the wheel A that goes round once in 24 hours. The pinion B in No. 3. and 4, is fixed to the wheel h, and has a relative motion to the wheel A $\frac{1}{1515\frac{11}{44}}$ of a revolution, in the space of 29 days, 12 hours, 45 minutes, which is equal to 57 seconds, the error that was to be removed.

"The other wheels that are moved by the pinion B are the same as in No. 2. The numbers for effecting the motion of the pinion B on the wheel A, are as follows:

Pinion a - - - 19
Wheel b - - - 45
Endless screw c - 1
Wheel d - - - 21
Endless screw e - 1
Wheel f - - - 45
Pinion g - - - 3
Wheel h - - - 60 on which is fixed the pinion B.

The mean motion of the moon from this contrivance will be exceedingly near the truth, as one revolution will be completed in 29 days, 12 hours, 44 minutes, 3 seconds."*

All this correcting work hangs on the 24 hour wheel A, and is carried round with it; both the endless screws are right handed.

In 1321912 days, the correcting wheels cause the lunation wheel to turn once more round than it would do without them; then, as 1321912 is to 29.53 days, the time of one lunation, so is 2551443,

* The MS. note of Ferguson's, in possession of the Editor of Mudge's Lunation Work, is what we gave him many years before the above work was given to the public.

the number of seconds in a lunation, to 56.996, which may be reckoned 57 seconds, as it is within the hundredth part of a second.

The product of all the pinions and screws multiplied into one another is 3648, and the product of the wheels multiplied into one another is 48223355000, and $\frac{48223355000}{3648} = 1321912$.

Finding that a mean lunation could be given by three pinions, and three wheels simply, as given by Camus, we sent them to Count Bruhl, to show how it differed from Mudge's, and seeing it could be easier made. His Excellency had some doubt as to the correctness of Camus's numbers, and was not satisfied till he got the calculation made out by another. He appears, either on this or a former occasion, to have made application to Mr. Mudge himself on the subject, if we may judge by a letter of Mr. Mudge's to him, of which the following is an extract:

——————" But totally had forgot the process you wished to be informed of, and find I cannot so easily recover any particular train of thinking as I could formerly; and, indeed, I almost despair of finding the meaning of the fraction $\frac{4}{182250}$. However, after having gone over the same ground I did, when I first contrived this approximation, I think I have perfectly recovered it, and will explain it in the best manner I can, though I fear, not so intelligibly as I could wish. The first mover is a wheel that goes once round in 24 hours, on which is supposed to be fixed a pinion of 8, which runs in a wheel of 45 teeth, to which is fixed a pinion of 8 or 4, which runs into a wheel of 42 or 21, which wheel will go round once in 29 days, 12 hours, 45 minutes, or $29\frac{17}{32}$ days: this is the imperfect lunation, but the most perfect that can be produced by simple numbers. In order to approximate it still nearer to the truth, I considered, that if instead of fixing the pinion to the wheel, which goes once round in 24 hours, it was made to move round the wheel very slowly the same way that the wheel moved, it would accelerate all the wheels in the train that was moved by the pinion; and the time in which it is to make one complete revolution on the wheel, (which is equal to 24 hours) is found by dividing the seconds that are in 24 hours, by the error of the imperfect lunation, viz. $86400 \div 57 = 1515\frac{15}{57}$, or $86400 \div 56 = 1542\frac{6}{7}$, in which number of lunations, the error of 57 or 56 seconds will amount to 24 hours. If then you divide $1515\frac{15}{57}$ into two quotients, as suppose $1515 \div 90 = 16\frac{5}{6}$, these two quotients multiplied by the two quotients that produce the imperfect lunation, viz. $5\frac{5}{8}$, and $5\frac{1}{4}$, (or if reduced to one quotient $29\frac{17}{32}$) will give the number of days, or revolutions the first wheel must make, to increase the error, 57 seconds to one complete day, in which time the pinions move once round on the wheel: The approximating numbers then, in the first supposition, will stand thus: 8 pinion, wheel 15, 8 — 42, 1 — 90, 19 — 320; these reduced to their lowest denominations, the ratio of the pinions to the wheels remaining the same, will be 1 — 45, and 1 — 21, 1 — 45, 19—20; all the pinions or endless screws (which is the same thing) multiplied by each other, will produce 19, and all the wheels multiplied also by one another, will produce 850500, and the denominator, divided by the numerator, will give the number of days, in which 57 seconds in *one lunation* will amount to 24 hours, the time employed by one revolution of the first wheel. I shall only just add the numbers necessary to correct the error of 56 seconds, leaving the process to your Excellency."

Pinion 4, wheel 45, 1 — 15, 1 — 45, 1—6.
19)850500(=44763$\frac{3}{19}$ for 57 seconds.
4)122250(=30562$\frac{1}{2}$ for 56 seconds."

TABLE I.

The Periodical Revolutions of the Planets, or of their return to the Equinox, taken from Lalande's Astronomy. Edition 1792.

	Days	h.	m.	s.
Mercury - - - -	87	23	14	32.7
Venus - - - -	224	16	41	27.7
The Earth - - - -	365	5	48	48.
Mars - - - -	686	22	18	27.4
Jupiter - - - -	4330	14	39	2.3
Saturn - - - -	10746	19	16	15.5

The Georgium Sidus is purposely omitted being taken from Lalande.

	Days	h.	m.	s.
Periodical revolution of the Moon	27	7	43	4.6795
Synodical revolution of do. -	29	12	44	2.8283

Synodical Revolutions of the Satellites of Jupiter.

	Days.	h.	m.	s.
1st	1	18	28	36
2d	3	13	17	54
3d	7	3	59	36
4th	16	18	5	7

	Days.	h.	m.	s.
Synodical revolution of Jupiter	398	19	12	54.15

TABLE II.

Wheel Work employed by A. Janvier *in his Sphere Mouvante, and calculated by him to imitate the periodical revolutions of the Planets.*

Mercury.

Pinions 10 43 53 ⎫
Wheels 80 140 179 ⎭ = 87 days 23 h. 14 m. 30 s. 22 th.

Venus.

Pinions 7 17 37 ⎫
Wheels 62 81 197 ⎭ = 224 16 41 25

The Earth.

Pinions 7 13 23 ⎫
Wheels 52 61 241 ⎭ = 365 5 48 $49\tfrac{11}{101}$

Mars.

Pinions 6 6 71 ⎫
Wheels 89 137 144 ⎭ = 686 22 18 35

Jupiter.

Pinions 6 6 6 41 ⎫
Wheels 57 72 89 105 ⎭ = 4330 14 38 2

PLANETARY NUMBERS.

Saturn.

		Days.	h.	m.	s.
Pinions	4 6 8 37 } =	10746	19	14	35
Wheels	82 92 92 110 }				

The wheel of the clock which acts as a mover to these wheels and pinions makes a revolution in 24 hours = 86400 seconds.

TABLE III.

Wheel Work serving to imitate the synodical revolutions of the Satellites of Jupiter, (conducted by a wheel whose revolution is made in 24 hours = 86400 seconds.)

			Days	h.	m.	s.	th.
First Satellite	{ Pinions 3 31 181 } =		1	18	28	35	37
	{ Wheels 4 76 98 }						
Second Satellite	{ Pinions 6 6 19 } =		3	13	17	53	41
	{ Wheels 11 13 17 }						
Third Satellite	{ Pinions 19 31 } =		7	3	59	35	33.1
	{ Wheels 63 67 }						
Fourth Satellite	{ Pinions 4 71 } =		16	18	5	4	13
	{ Wheels 61 78 }						

Synodical revolution of Jupiter from a mover of 7 days.

Pinions	6 61 } =	396	19	12	54
Wheels	132 158 }				

TABLE IV.

Wheel Work employed to produce the different motions and revolutions of the Moon.

			Days	h.	m.	s.	th.
Periodical revolution from a mover of 24 hours	{ Pinions 3 20 19 } =		27	7	43	4	25¼
	{ Wheels 23 37 61 }						
Synodical Revolution	{ Pinions 15 22 53 } =		29	12	44	2	52¼¼
	{ Wheels 56 65 137 }						

Wheel work for the revolution of the apogee of the moon, mover of 24 hours $\begin{cases} \text{Pinions} & 6 & 8 & 10 \\ \text{Wheels} & 69 & 127 & 177 \end{cases} = 3231$ Days 8 h. 39 m.

Mover of 27 d. 7 h. 43 m. $\begin{cases} \text{Pinions} & 10 & 13 & 31 \\ \text{Wheels} & 57 & 74 & 113 \end{cases} = 3231$ 8 44

Revolution of the nodes by a wheel N = $\begin{cases} \text{Pinions} & 25 & 59 \\ \text{Wheels} & 106 & 259 \end{cases} = 6798$ 5

Wheel work calculated (as the preceding was) by A. Janvier, to obtain an annual revolution of the Earth, exactly conformable to that of the present Astronomical Tables.

$$\begin{matrix}\text{Pinions} & 10 & 12 & 15 \\ \text{Wheels} & 47 & 52 & 269\end{matrix} \bigg\} = 365 \text{ Days } 5 \text{ h. } 48 \text{ m. } 48 \text{ s.}$$

TABLE V.

A set of Numbers for Wheels and Pinions, as given by Dr. Pearson, to produce the time of the Revolutions of Jupiter's Satellites, from a mover of 24 hours.

Sat.	Wheels and Pinions.	Periods.	Errors in 24 Hours.
		Days. h. m. s.	m. s.
1st.	$\frac{39}{69}$ of 24 hours.	1 18 27 41	— 0 30.7
2d.	$\frac{27}{96}$ of ditto.	3 13 20 0	+ 0 36.9
3d.	$\frac{18}{129}$ of ditto.	7 4 0 0	+ 0 3.4
4th.	$\frac{8}{194}$ of ditto.	16 18 0 0	— 0 18.0

The seconds in a day are 86400, and $86400 \times 69 \div 39 = 152861.54$ seconds = 1 day, 18 hours, 27 minutes, $41\frac{7}{10}$ seconds.

The following are the numbers which have already been given of Janvier's, only differently arranged.

Sat.	Trains.	Periods produced.
		D. h. m. s. th.
1st.	$\frac{4}{3} \times \frac{76}{31} \times \frac{181}{98}$ of 24 hours.	1 18 28 35 37
2d.	$\frac{11}{6} \times \frac{13}{6} \times \frac{19}{17}$ of ditto.	3 13 17 53 41
3d.	$\frac{63}{19} \times \frac{67}{31}$ of ditto.	7 3 59 35 33
4th.	$\frac{61}{4} \times \frac{78}{71}$ of ditto.	16 18 5 4 13

A Table of the numbers of the wheels and pinions to give the revolutions of Jupiter's Satellites, as calculated by Dr. Pearson, the 9th April, 1805, from a mover of seven days.

Sat.	Trains.	Synodic Periods.
		D. h. m. s.
1st.	$\frac{49}{57} \times \frac{25}{85}$ of 7 days.	1 18 28 36.4066
2d.	$\frac{61}{29} \times \frac{21}{87}$ of ditto.	3 13 17 54.4352
3d.	$\frac{139}{29} \times \frac{22}{103}$ of ditto.	7 3 59 35.8955
4th.	$\frac{75}{83} \times \frac{98}{37}$ of ditto.	16 18 5 2.4422

The periods produced by the numbers in the above Table approach so nearly to those given as the result of a great many observations, that they may be depended upon as the nearest approximation to truth.

Let the train for the first satellite in the last table be taken as an example, where the pinions are 49 and 25, and the wheels 57 and 85. The wheels 57 and 85, multiplied into one another, give for product 4845, and the product of the pinions, multiplied together, is

1225, by which they become the fraction $\frac{1225}{4845}$ of seven days. Multiply then the numerator 1225 by 7, the days, divide the product by the denominator 4845, the quotient will be 1 day; the remainder, multiplied by 24, the hours in a day, this product, divided again by 4845, the quotient, will be 18 hours. Multiply the next remainder by 60, for minutes, and divide the product by the former divisor, and the quotient will be 28 minutes, the last remainder being multiplied by 60, for seconds, and this, divided as before, will be 36.4086 seconds. The first wheel making only one revolution in seven days, makes it necessary to multiply the numerator by seven.

We shall conclude this chapter by taking the liberty of giving Dr. Pearson's valuable process for obtaining numbers to give the revolution of the Georgian.

Dr. Pearson says, "We come lastly to the tropical revolution of the Georgian planet, which we have seen revolves through the ecliptic in 30589.35208 days, and its numbers may be ascertained by the following process:

Divisors.	Dividends.	Quotients.	Formulæ.	Ratios.
				$\frac{0}{1}$
				$\frac{1}{0}$
365.2422	30589.35208 2921937777 136997431 109572666	83	$\frac{83 \times 1 + 0}{83 \times 0 + 1}$	$\frac{83}{1}$
27424764	36524222 27424764	1	$\frac{1 \times 83 + 1}{1 \times 1 + 0}$	$\frac{84}{1}$
9099457	27424764 27298373	3	$\frac{3 \times 84 + 83}{3 \times 1 + 1}$	$\frac{335}{4}$
126391	9099457 884737 252087 126391	71	$\frac{71 \times 335 + 84}{71 \times 4 + 1}$	$\frac{23869}{285}$
125696	126391 125696	1	$\frac{1 \times 23869 + 335}{1 \times 285 + 4}$	$\frac{24204}{289}$
694	125696	181		

"The value of the last ratio of this series is equal to 83.7509650 tropical years, which differs from the exact truth only unity in the seventh place of decimals, but unfortunately it is not reducible into lower numbers than $\frac{2017 \times 12}{17 \times 17}$; and the numerator of the next preceding ratio is a prime number, so that we must either use $\frac{335}{4}$, which has been before determined, or otherwise substitute another quotient for 71. The most convenient, we find from a few trials, will be 66, which gives the ratio $\frac{22194}{265}$, the value of which is a revolution in 83.750943 tropical years, or 30589 days, 9 hours, 8 minutes, 10.7 seconds, and is capable of forming the train $\frac{162 \times 137}{5 \times 53}$."

These examples of all the primary planets given at full length, and accompanied by our remarks on them, will enable any well educated instrument-maker to ascertain wheel work from any other data, which he may have occasion to employ, and will serve, at the same time, to show that the two methods of approximating towards the truth, where the original numbers run too high for construction in practice, supply the defects of each other in particular cases, but generally come, by different results, to the same mark."

In this subject, it may contribute greatly to assist the artist with the management of figures, by giving an example from the same eminent master before quoted, which we shall also take the liberty of transcribing :

"When a simple motion is produced by means of one wheel and a corresponding pinion, let the number of teeth which each contains, be carefully counted and noted down, and also which of the two is the *driver* ; the numbers of the wheel and pinion will constitute a ratio, which is a fraction of that time, proper or improper, according as the *driver* is the greater or smaller number, which *driver* must be in all instances the *denominator*. The value of the fraction thus constituted, it will be superfluous to scientific readers to say, is found by multiplying the assumed time of a revolution of the first mover by the numerator, and dividing by the denominator, the remainders being reduced to their next lowest denomination of time, after every successful division.

"An example will render this simple case intelligible by every reader.

"Suppose that a wheel, consisting of 75 teeth, and revolving once in a tropical year, drives a pinion of 6 ; and that it be required to

FINDING THE TIME OF A REVOLUTION.

know in what time the latter revolves? the work at full length will stand thus:

       D. h. m. s.
   365.24222 = 365 5 48 48
     6

75)2191.45333(29 days.
 150
 ———
  691
  675
  ———
   16.45333
     24
   ———
   6581333
   32906666
   ———
   75)394.87999(5 hours.
   375
   ———
    19.87999
      60
    ———
    75)1192.79999(15 minutes.
    75
    ———
     442
     375
     ———
      67.79999
        60
      ———
      75)4067.99999(54.24 seconds.
      375
      ———
       317
       300
       ———
        17.9
        150
        ———
         299
         30
         ===

"Hence it appears, that $\frac{6}{75}$ths of 365.24222 days is equal to 29 days, 5 hours, 15 minutes, 54.24 seconds. The computation may be sometimes abridged, by converting the vulgar fraction into a decimal, where there is no remainder, and then multiplying thereby instead of dividing. Thus:

$$75)6.00(.08$$
$$600$$

$$365.24222$$
$$.08$$
$$\overline{29.2193777 \text{ days.}}$$
$$24$$
$$\overline{8775111}$$
$$43875555$$
$$\overline{5.2650666 \text{ hours}}$$
$$60$$
$$\overline{15.9040000 \text{ minutes.}}$$
$$60$$
$$\overline{54.2400000 \text{ seconds.}}$$

"Either of these methods may be used with a like result.

"If, instead of the wheel, we make the pinion the driver or denominator of the fraction, the motion of the second mover will be retarded, for $\frac{75}{6}$ths of 365.24222 days is equal to 4565 days, 12 hours, 40 minutes. This difference in the two revolutions, when the parts of the fraction are reversed, points out the necessity of attending very accurately to the circumstance of the *driver* being made the *denominator* of the *fraction*."

G

CHAPTER V.

On Wheel Teeth, their Shape; the Proportional Sizes of Wheels to Pinions, and of Pinions to Wheels, with the Distances which their Centres ought to have, so as to form proper Pitchings, partly from Berthoud's ESSAI.

OF THE LEVER.

Definition.

A B (Plate II. No. 6.) is supposed an inflexible rod, to the ends of which are attached two bodies P and p without gravity, and that the rod is made to turn on a fixed point H, the body P describing the arc A a, the body p will describe the arc B b; it is evident that the arcs A a, B b, are in the proportion of the distances H A, H B; for example, that is, if B H is double, triple, &c. of A H, B b will be double, triple, &c. of A a; then the body p will turn with a velocity double, triple, &c. of that of the body P: then if these bodies are equal, to stop suddenly the body p, would require a force double, triple, &c. of that which would be necessary to stop suddenly the body P. If the body p is triple of the body P, it is evident that P always describing A a, and p, B b, we might, in place of the body p, suppose three masses equal to P, each impressed with the velocity B b, and then the force required to stop p, will be triple of what it ought to have been in the preceding case; but if the mass p, in place of being triple of P, is, on the contrary, only a third, the force required to stop it, must be three times less than in the same case preceding, and it will be equal to that which would stop the body P, the distance H B being triple of the distance A H; if the mass p, on the other hand, is the third of the mass P, these masses can each be stopped by the same force, then each could stop the other. If we imagine these two masses to have weight, their efforts to turn being now directly opposite and equal, they will mutually be in equilibrium. For a like reason, it will be seen, that if the distance B H is quadruple, quintuple, &c. of the distance A H, and the mass p, the fourth, the fifth, &c. of the mass P, they will make an equilibrium, from whence is deduced, in general, this principle. If two masses P and p, attached to the ends of an inflexible rod A B, are such that the mass P contains as many times the mass p as the arm of the lever H B contains the arm A H, they will be in equilibrium.

Of Wheels and Pinions.

If round a point H, (No. 8.) are described two circles A a, B b, which have for radius the lengths A H, and H B, as levers, (H B is supposed triple of A H,) and on whose circumferences are wrapped round as on pulleys, whose centre is at H, two threads charged with the weights P and p; these weights will remain in equlibrium if the mass p is to that of P, as H A is to H B; and if it is required to impress on the weight P, a force capable of making it fall in a given time from P to C, so that the point A comes to a, then must the weight p rise to d, and the point B comes to b; the weight p, would consequently go through three times more space than the weight P. From whence it follows, that any motion which should be impressed on the weight P, would be exactly compensated by that which would result from it in the weight p, and that thus these two weights cannot fail to maintain an equilibrium, or restore themselves to it, if after being put in motion they are left at liberty; since according to the supposition, A a and B b are pulleys; and consequently H A is equal to H a, and H B is equal to H b.

It again follows, that when two bodies are in equilibrium, the velocity which they acquire by any motion being communicated to them, are in the inverse ratio of their masses. Now, if the weight p is taken away, the weight P will pull the lever and the circumference A, and make the point b turn with a force capable of communicating an action of one pound (the supposed weight of the body p) so in place of the circumference B b, let us imagine the radii, or levers H B, H b, &c. (No. 9.) and equally distant from one another, each of these levers will act with a force of one pound. It is in considering the levers under this point of view, that this circumference becomes a wheel, and each radius, or lever, will be a tooth; if we make a second wheel, or pinion C, which has radii, or teeth, equally distant from one another, as those of the wheel B; that is to say, that the number of the teeth of C, is to those of B as the circumference of C is to that of B, and that the pinion is placed so, that the teeth of the wheel can act on those of the pinion, (as in the figure,) the teeth of the wheel will communicate to the teeth of the pinion the force which they have;[*] so that if a weight of one pound is applied to

---

[*] There is no account taken in here, of the decomposition of the force in the pitching and the friction which arises from it, which always diminishes a part of the weight P: it is sufficient for the present, to view the wheels as if they were without weight, and without friction, as was done with the simple lever, supposed to be without gravity. In the sequel will be seen, what the curve ought to be, which terminates the teeth of wheels and leaves of pinions.

the circumference, it will be in equilibrium with that of P, nothing having been done to change the equilibrium which formerly existed; and if the wheel and pinion are made to move, the circumference of the pinion will describe the same space as that of the wheel, since each of its teeth are equally distant among themselves as those of the wheel; and the number of the revolutions of the pinion, will be to those of the wheel, as the circumference of the pinion is to that of the wheel; but the circumferences of circles being to one another as their diameters, or radii, the number of the revolutions of the pinion C, will be to that of the wheel B, as $C\,d$ is to B H.

Having seen that a wheel which drives a pinion, communicates to the circumference of the pinion the same force which *it* has; let there then be a wheel and a pinion, that we have supposed to have the force of one pound at their circumferences; if to the centre C of this pinion, is fixed a wheel D, three times larger than the pinion, it will describe three times more space, and will have three times more velocity than the pinion; to make equilibrium with the weight P, there must be applied at the point D of the wheel, a weight only three times lighter than *p*, and consequently nine times lighter than P. The point D goes then nine times quicker, and describes a space nine times greater than the point A. Let us now proceed to the way of finding this force, in wheel work composed of several wheels, and in a general way.

Remarks.

It has just now been shewn, that the diameters, or the circumferences of a wheel, and of a pinion pitched into this wheel being given, the number of the revolutions of the pinion for one of the wheel, is determined by that which expresses, how many times the diameter of the pinion is contained in that of the wheel. That being done, the number of the teeth of one of these two, that is, either of the wheel, or of the pinion, is arbitrary; and we can at pleasure give to a wheel 100, 200, &c. teeth, or any other number whatever; but then, the number of the teeth of the pinion must be contained in the number of the teeth of the wheel, as many times as the circumference of the wheel contains that of the pinion; for example, on a pinion which is ten times smaller than the wheel which drives it, may be put indifferently six, eight, ten, twelve, fifteen, twenty teeth, &c. provided that the wheel has always ten times as many; from which it follows, that a wheel and its diameter being given, as also the number of the turns of the pinion which it conducts, the diameter of the pinion is determined. The following proposition will serve to show, how the force transmitted *(by any power or weight applied)* to the last wheel of any wheel-work ought to be calculated.

Proposition.

The space described by D (No. 9) is to the space described by B, as the length C D is to C d; which is a consequence of what has been shewn, that the space described by the pinion C is the same as that of the wheel B; and if D C = B H, the space described by D will be to the space decribed by B, as C d is to B H, and the number of the revolutions of the pinion C, is to that of the wheel B, as C d is to B H : So in order that the velocity of D may be to the velocity of B, as the number of the revolutions of the pinion C is to that of B, the wheel D must have the same diameter as the wheel B, to which the weight is applied; and, in this case, the force transmitted to the wheel D by the weight p, is to the weight p as the number of the revolutions of the pinion C is to that of the wheel B.

We have seen that when two bodies are in equilibrium, their velocities must be in the inverse ratio of their masses: now, when it is wanted to have the velocity of any wheel whatever, in an assemblage of wheels, we must not only compare its revolutions with the wheel where the weight is applied, but must compare the diameters of both wheels: For it is plain, that if the wheel D is supposed greater than B, the space described by D will no longer be in the proportion of the revolution of the pinion C, and consequently there will no longer be an equilibrium, the gravity of the weight q will be too much, and will not be to that of p, as the number of the revolutions of the pinion C is to that of the wheel; and, on the contrary, if the wheel D is smaller than B, the weight q will be too little to make equilibrium with p; for the space described by D will no longer be to the space described by B, as the number of the revolutions of C is to B.

It will in like manner be shewn, that whatever be the number of wheels and pinions, to find the force transmitted to the last wheel, the revolutions must not only be compared, but also the diameters of the first and last wheels, in order to know the spaces described, seeing the revolutions do not suffice to give the velocity.

We shall then draw from this, a rule, to find the force transmitted to the circumference of a wheel, and shall suppose the last wheel of the same diameter as the first : we then will make the proportion : The weight P, applied to the circumference of the first wheel, is to the weight p, which must be applied to the circumference of the last wheel to make equilibrinm, as the number of revolutions of this last wheel in a given time, is to the number of revolutions of the first in the same time. The weight p being found, that, required to make equilibrium will easily be deduced, when the last wheel shall be either of a greater or smaller diameter than that of the first, because, if the last wheel of a wheel-work was five times smaller than the first, it would describe five times less space than if it had been of an equal diameter, and consequently the weight required, must be five times heavier.

Remarks.

We have supposed, that the weight P was applied to the circumference of the first wheel; but it frequently happens, that it acts only on the circumference of a cylinder concentric with the first wheel, and smaller; then it is seen that the weight or force applied to the circumference of the cylinder, is to the force communicated to the circumference of the wheel, as the diameter of the wheel is to the diameter of the cylinder; that is to say, if the diameter of the cylinder is only half of that of the wheel, the force transmitted to the circumference of the wheel B, will only be the half of that of the weight P, and so of others.

Let this principle be now applied to find the force transmitted to the last wheel E, of an assemblage of wheels for a clock movement, giving seconds, which is represented in No. 7. And first, to calculate the number of the revolutions of the pinion d, which carries the wheel E, for one of the wheel A.

The wheel A of 84 teeth, pitches with the pinion a of twelve leaves, which makes 7 turns for one of the wheel A.

The wheel B of 80 teeth, pitches with the pinion b of 10, which makes 8 turns for one of B, and 7 multiplied by 8, gives 56, the number of turns made by the pinion b of 10 for one of the wheel A.

The wheel C of 80, pitches with the pinion c of 10, making 8 turns for one of the wheel C, and 56 multiplied by 8, gives 448 turns to the pinion c for one of the wheel A.

The wheel D of 75, pitches with the pinion d of 10, making 7½ turns for one of the wheel D, and 448, multiplied by 7.5, gives 3360 turns to the pinion d for one of the wheel A.

The pinion d, and the wheel E which it carries, make 3360 turns in the time that the wheel A makes one, which is easily seen; for the wheel B makes 7 turns for one of the wheel A, and the pinion b makes 8 turns for one of the wheel B; this pinion b, as well as the wheel C which it carries, make then 56 turns in the time that the wheel A makes one, since 7 turns of the wheel B, multiplied by 8 of the pinion b, make 56 ; moreover, the pinion c makes 8 turns for one of the pinion b and of the wheel C ; so, multiplying the 56 turns of the wheel C by the 8 turns of the pinion c, will give 448 turns of the pinion c and of the wheel D, during one of the wheel A ; and, at each turn of the wheel D, the pinion d makes 7 turns and a half; and 448 turns of the wheel D must be multiplied by 7½, the turns which it gives to the pinion d, and we shall have 3360, the number of turns of the pinion d, (and of the wheel E which it carries) for one of the first wheel.

If it is wanted to know the time, which the first wheel takes to make one turn, this will depend on that, which the last wheel E takes to make one revolution ; for the wheel A will always be 3360 times longer, in making one turn than the wheel E, since this last makes 3360 times more turns ; if then, the wheel E is supposed to make one turn in a minute, the wheel A will make one in 3360 minutes. To know how many hours this makes, we must divide it by 60, *(the number of minutes in an hour,)* and we find 56 hours for the quotient, which is 2 days and 8 hours to make one revolution.

To find how much force the weight P will transmit to the circumference of the wheel E, let it be supposed to weigh 12 pounds, and that the diameter of the cylinder F is to that of the wheel A as 8 is to 12, or 2 to 3. In this supposition, the weight will act at the circumference of the wheel A with 8 pounds, which make 128 ounces = 1024 gros, or 73728 grains. Make then the following proportion: The force which is exerted at the circumference of the wheel A, is to the force which it communicates to the wheel E, (call this force x,) supposed of the same diameter, as the number of the revolutions of the wheel E, is to the number of the revolutions of the wheel A, or 73728 : x : : 3360 : 1, multiplying the extremes, and dividing by the mean term known, the value of x is found to be $21\frac{1168}{3360}$ grains, and the fraction being reduced, we have $21\frac{11}{35}$ grains ; this is then the force, which would be transmitted to the wheel E, if it was of the same diameter as the wheel A : but, in supposing it three times smaller, the weight p which is applied to it, describes then three times less space, so as to make it in equilibrium with the weight P ; it must be triple of that which has been found in the preceding calculation ; it must then be $65\frac{3}{35}$ grains.

We shall insert what has been done in this way by a very ingenious friend. The clock was a month one, having the same number of wheels as in No. 7. The semi-diameter of the barrel being .9834 inch, has one half of the power of the weight applied to its circumference, (the gut passing below the pulley of the weight, and being brought up, is supposed to be fastened to the seat-board of the clock,) the whole weight being 24 lb. = 168000 grains; the quantity acting on the circumference of the barrel, is there stated at 84000 grains, which, at the extremity of the great wheel of $1.662\frac{1}{4}$ inch semi-diameter, becomes = 49642.1 grains. This force being communicated to the circumference of the second wheel pinion of $.293\frac{1}{4}$ inch semi-diameter, and thence to the circumference of the second wheel of 1.299 inch semi-diameter, becomes = 11216.3 grains; and in like manner this too, and from the third wheel pinion of .182 semi-diameter, to the extremity of the third wheel of 1.171 inch semi-diameter, is reduced to = 1743.2 grains; and so by the fourth wheel pinion of .166 semi-diameter, to the circumference of the fourth wheel of $1.006\frac{1}{4}$ inch semi-diameter, becomes = 287.5 grains; and, lastly, through the swing wheel pinion of $.153\frac{1}{4}$ semi-diameter, to the circumference of that wheel which has $.972\frac{1}{4}$ inch in semi-diameter, it becomes equal to 45.4 grains nearly. This seems to be the calculated power transmitted, without any allowance for friction, or any other retarding cause; and say, that we should deduct on these accounts about one third of the calculated force, the 45.4 grains may then be estimated about 30 grains. He adopted the plan of calculating the force transmitted from the lengths of the levers, in preference to the mode used of multiplying the numbers of the pinions together, and with their product, dividing the amount of the wheel teeth, whereby, to get at once a divisor, with which to divide the power at the circumference of the great wheel. After having made the foregoing calculation, he set to try how far they would agree. It was somewhat flattering to see their exact similarity.

Pinions 135.5× 166 × 182×293.5 = 1361118577.
Wheels 972.5×1006.5×1171×1299 = 1488913400191.25.
1488913400191.25÷1361118577 = 1093.9.

Now, if we divide the power of 49642.1 grains, being that which is at the circumference of the great wheel, by the above quotient 1093.9 obtained by dividing the product of the numbers of the wheels, by the product of the numbers of the pinions, we get the exact same result, as was got by treating the wheels as levers, viz. 45.4 grains nearly, for the power transmitted to the circumference of the swing wheel, which should, in the same manner, be reduced on account of friction; so, we may conclude, the actual force transmitted will be nearly 30 grains at the extremity of the swing wheel teeth.

Remarks.

It is not enough to have calculated the force transmitted by the mover to the last wheel of any wheel-work; there must also be deduction made for the friction, and the resistance caused by the inertia or inactivity of the wheels. This last consideration is very essential; for, previous to, and even after the termination of each vibration of the pendulum, the wheels have an instant of rest,* so that the force which puts them in motion, is renewed at every vibration, and draws the wheels from a state of rest. The friction caused by the weight of the wheels and their inertia, then, requires a surplus of force beyond the quantity which has been calculated.

These two quantities, the force necessary to overcome the resistance caused by the inertia, and the force to overcome friction, increase so much the more, as the wheels are heavy, and have more velocity. It is then very essential to reduce the wheels to their least weight; for this purpose they ought to be made very small, which is possible, particularly with the last wheels, which have little effort to overcome; and, as high numbered pinions require, that the wheels which drive them should be of the greatest diameter, it is better, with the latter wheels, to use pinions of six or eight only, *(in regard to the pitchings, by forming good curves to the teeth, they may be made as perfect as if the pinions were of a higher number.)* Thus the wheels may be reduced to their smallest diameters, and consequently to the least weight; the motive force will then become more constant, and be reduced to the smallest quantity. If it is required to make the wheels large, they must have the greatest numbers possible, without, however, having weak teeth; and making them pitch only with pinions of a low number, diminishes their revolutions, or rather the spaces in which the wheels revolve.

Of the Pitchings of Wheels and Pinions.

The perfection of Pitchings is a part so essential in machines, particularly in those which measure time, such as clocks and watches, that too much care and attention cannot be given to them. It has been thought necessary to mention here the effects, which result in watches from bad pitchings, and to give afterwards, the principles on which the theory of pitching is founded, and, finally, to shew the practical means of making good pitchings.

* This case is chiefly with the dead beat 'scapement; with the recoiling one, if the wheels have any rest, it may be said to be momentary indeed.

Inquiry into the effects which arise from bad Pitchings.

When the curves of the teeth are badly made, the wheel drives the pinion with different degrees of force, from whence it happens: 1st, (if this wheel communicates its force to a balance,) that the balance loses its isochronism, or, which is the same thing, that it vibrates with different degrees of velocity, and that the time of the vibration changes according to the different actions of the wheel on the pinion. 2d, That the force of the mover to turn the pinion ought to be greater, than it would be requisite if the wheel made the pinion to turn in an uniform manner: this excess of motive force, of itself alone, tends (*independently of other variations,*) to destroy the machine by the friction which it causes, and these at length produce variations to the regulator. If a wheel drives a pinion which is too large, or, which is the same, whose teeth or leaves are more distant from one another, than those of the wheel, the force communicated by the wheel, will in part be destroyed by the leaves of the pinion, which butt against the wheel teeth; this force so destroyed will require that a greater motive force be used, to keep up the motion of the machine, from which will result friction, wearing, variations, &c.

If a wheel drives a pinion which is too small, or whose teeth or leaves are less distant than those in the wheel, it will happen that a tooth of the wheel acting on a lever or tooth too short, the pinion will turn with less force, and more velocity, as will be seen afterwards: It will again follow from this, that a part of the force of the wheel is lost, by the drop or fall of the tooth driving, to that of the next which it is to drive; the pinion will then turn with a part only of the force of the wheel: thus the mover will require to have a greater power, than it would have required, if the wheel drove the pinion uniformly; this excess of force, and inequalities of the pitchings, will tend to destroy the machine, and to make it vary, &c. as stated above.

And, *lastly*, wheel-work being composed of wheels and pinions, whose pitchings are bad, in certain movements, each wheel will act on its pinion with the greatest advantage, then, the force transmitted to the regulator will be the greatest possible: and in other instances, each wheel acting on its pinion with the least advantage, the force of the mover will be, as it were almost annihilated: the regulator (*pendulum,* or *balance,*) will receive only small impulsions: now, the force of the mover ought to be sufficient for the least favourable case in the pitchings; it is then too great in the most favourable case;

from whence arises the inconveniencies which have been already remarked.

Upon the whole, this is what results from badly made pitchings; the next will show how wheels ought to act on their pinions, and to determine the form of the teeth of wheels, so as they shall drive the pinion uniformly, in such a way as to communicate to it all the power of the mover.

Demonstration of Pitching. Of the proper curves of the teeth of Wheels, and leaves of Pinions, and the manner of tracing them.

Let it be supposed that two angular levers,* b A D and b a C, (Plate II. No. 10.) moveable on two fixed points A a, having each a constant arm A D, a C, drawn on the line A a, which joins the points of support, and loaded at their extremities with the constant weights P p, and each a variable arm, A b, a b, so that their extremities act always reciprocally one on the other; we say that the two weights P p, which make equilibrium in the case, where the two variable arms have their point of contact in O, situated in the right line A O, a O, will also be in equilibrium when the point b, where they butt on one another, is found in the circumference of a circle, of which A O, or a O, will be the diameter.

Demonstration.

Let b n, a perpendicular on b A, (*and which represents the small arc that the lever b A tends to describe in an instant, in turning upon A,*) express the absolute force which is exerted at the extremity b of the angular lever b A D, by the action of the weight P; if we suppose this force, b n, decomposed into two others, b m and b i, one of which, viz. b m, is perpendicular to a c, and the direction of which passes through the point of contact, s, (since the angle b, which has its summit at the circumference a b s, is a right one;) and the other, b i, is directed towards b A: it is seen that b m expresses part of the force b n, which is employed to push the point b of the lever a c from b towards o, and, consequently, to turn the lever a c,

---

* The simple levers, b A D, b a C, for the present, shall be considered only as such, in order not to make the matter too complicated, when it shall be shown how they ought to drive uniformly, whether that the great lever drives the small one after the line of the centers, or that the small drives the great after the line of centers, or indeed, whether the great or the small lever drives before and after the line of centers: all this being well established for simple levers, will be easily applicable to wheels and pinions, which are in truth only an assemblage of levers.

whilst bi expresses that part of the force bn, which tends to push the point b towards A, and which is destroyed by the resistance of the fixed point A: Now, we say that bn expresses also the absolute force, which is exerted at the extremity, b, of the angular lever, C ab, to oppose the rotation of the point b round the point a; for, on account of the right lines, D P and bn, being perpendicular to the arms of the levers A D, A b, the weight P is to the force bn, as A b is to A D; and, in drawing A B perpendicular on bs prolonged, the similar triangles, nbm, and A b B, give $bn : bm :: $ A B : A b, then (*in multiplying with order,*) P : $bm :: $ A B : A D; moreover, let x be called the absolute force, with which the weight p tends to turn the point b in a direction opposite to bo, and we shall have $p : x :: ab : ac$, or, on account of the similar triangles $a b$ O, A B O, as A B to A O; but, in the supposition that the two weights p and P can be in equilibrium, when they communicate their actions by the point O, we can, on account of the arms of the equal levers a C, a O, suppose that the weight p is suspended at the point O : so then, P : $p :: $ A O : A D; then, by multiplying in order, P : $x :: $ A B : A D; now it has been proved that P : $mb :: $ A B : A D; then $bm = x$: then will there be an equilibrium, since the force bm is equal to the force, with which the point b is urged to turn by the weight P; it is likewise shown that there will be an equilibrium there, since the levers A b, ab, will communicate their forces by another point u of the circumference $a b u$ O.

Corollary I.

If by the points O (No. 10. and 11.) from the centers A a of motion, we describe the circles R, X, and suppose that one of the circles acts with the other, by a pitching of infinitely small teeth, the weights P, p, will remain in equilibrium; and if the circle R, for example, goes uniformly, the circle X will also move uniformly : for, 1st, the teeth being infinitely small, the radii A O, a O, by which these teeth act, will be always of the same length, and the action of the weights p and P will always be applied in the same manner, hence there will be always an equilibrium. 2d, If one of these circles is moved with an uniform force, so will the other be: for each point of one circle will apply itself successively to all the points of the other, so that the space described by a point O, situated in the circumference of one, will be equal to that of O, situated in the circumference of the other; and this space being the same, as well as the time of motion, the velocities of the circles R, X, will also be the same, from whence follows uniformity of motion.

The radii A O, a O, of the circles R, X, which express the ratio of the revolutions, are called the *primitive radii*.

Corollary II.

The point b (No. 10.) by which the lever b A D conducts the lever b A C, being always supposed in the circumference a b O, the primitive circles tend to turn with the same force and the same velocity; for, 1st, Let F, f, be the forces with which in this case they tend to turn the circumference of the circle R, and that of X, we shall have $bn : F :: AO : Ab$, and $f : bm :: ab : ac$, or aO; besides, it has been seen above, that $bm : bn :: Ab : AB$; then $f : F :: AO \times ab : aO \times AB$: and the similar triangles, abO, and ABO, give $aO : AO :: ab : AB$; then $aO \times AB = AO \times ab$; then $f = F$: and the circle R being moved with an uniform motion, the circle X will also be moved with an uniform motion. 2d, Whatever be the velocity at the point b of the lever D A b, that which it will communicate to the lever b a C, following the perpendicular b m to the point of contact, must be the same as that of the point b in the same direction; and if we let fall the perpendicular a o, the velocity following b n will be represented by b n, and the velocity following b m will be represented by b o. Moreover, let V be the velocity of the circumference R of the wheel, and u that of the circumference X of the pinion, it is evident that $V : bn :: AO : Ab$ and $bo : u :: ab : ac$, or aO; besides the similar triangles bno, and AbB give $bn : bo :: Ab : AB$; then $V : u :: AO \times ab : aO \times AB$; and these two last products are equal, as hath already been seen; then $u = F$.

Corollary III.

If the point b (No. 11.) where the lever D A b acts on the lever a b c, is not situated in the circumference of a circle described on a O, or on A O; if it was, for example, placed within, as at g, or without, as at h, the weights P p will no longer be in equilibrium: to prove it, draw the line n h perpendicular to the lever a b c; then, according to what has been said above, we have

$$P : hn :: Ah : AD$$
$$hn : hm :: Ax : Ah$$
$$p : P :: AD : AO$$
$$x : p :: aO : ah$$

In calling x the force with which the weight p tends to turn the point h in the opposite direction to ah, we have $x : hm :: A x \times aO : AO \times ah$: now, it is easy to show, that if the point h is not on the circle abO, the product $Ax \times aO$ can never be equal to the product $AO \times ah$; then x can never (*in the same supposition,*) be equal to hm; hence there can be no equilibrium.

Corollary IV.—No. 11.

Things remaining the same as in the preceding Corollary, it will be shown, in a manner analagous to that which has been used in the Second Corollary, that the forces with which the primitive circumferences tend to move one another, cannot be equal; and, as the velocity of one being uniform, that of the other cannot be so; then the point h, (No. 11.) by which the lever Ah pushes the lever ao, cannot be at a distance from A, which is always the same, since there would be an infinity of cases where this point would not be in the circumference abO, which is, however, necessary for uniformity of motion; then the figure which ought to be given to the teeth of a wheel, to conduct uniformly the right lined leaf of a pinion, cannot be a right line.

Corollary V.—Plate II. (A.) Fig. 1.

Finally, if the lever prolonged AOb, is formed by a curve $b\ t''\ t''\ N$, which is such, that when a fixed point, N, of the circle R, shall have described any space $O\acute{N}$, the lever ac touches this curve in a point b, which is on the circumference abO, and so placed, that the arc Ob may be equal to the arc ON; then this lever will conduct the pinion with an uniform velocity and force; for the arc Ob being equal to the arc Oc, as is easy to be proved, it will also be equal to the arc ON; and, consequently, this point N, and the point c, will have described equal spaces in equal times; from whence naturally results the following method to trace the figure of the teeth of wheels, when they must conduct a pinion whose leaves are right lines.

Problem I.

A lever, AO, (Fig. 1.) acting on a lever aO, on the point O' in the line of centers, and the weights Pp, being in equilibrium, it is wanted to trace on the end prolonged of the lever AO, such a curve, $O\ t'\ r'\ s'\ b'$: 1st, That it shall cause the circle X describe a space equal to that of the primitive circle R: 2d, That at all the points of motion, the weights, Pp, remain in equilibrium.

Solution.

With the points A *a* of the centers of motion of the levers A O, *a* O, and through their point of touching at O, must be drawn the primitive circles R and X, to divide the circumference of the circle X in setting out from the point O, at pleasure into any number of equal arcs, to divide likewise the circle R, in setting out from the point O into a number of equal arcs, which are to the number of those of the circle X, as the radius A O is to the radius *a* O; in this example, the radii being to one another as 3 to 1, and the circle X being divided into six equal parts, we divide the circle R into 18; if then these two circles turn one another by simply touching, the circle X will make three turns in the time that the circle R will make one; and when the point O of the primitive circle X shall have described an arc of 60 degrees, as O *c*, the point O of the primitive circle R will have described the space O N, or the arc of 20 degrees: these two quantities, O *c*, O N, are then equal, and express the unfolding of the two circles; we then divide each space O N, O *c*, into the same number of equal parts, as into 5, so when the two circles R, X, turn one another round by simply touching, each division, 1, 2, 3, 4, and 1', 2', 3', 4', meet in O, division after division. From the center *a*, let the lines *a c*, *a* 1, *a* 2, *a* 3, *a* 4, be drawn, which will mark the different positions of the lever *a* O, while it turns from O to *c*; and the points *b*, *r*, *s*, *t*, *o*, express the overplus lengths of the lever A O, when it acts on that of *a* O, in its different positions, *a* 4, *a* 3, *a* 2, *a* 1; if we then draw through these points of intersection, *b*, *r*, *s*, *t*, of the semicircle *a* O, portions of a circle, *b' b*, *r' r*, *s' s*, *t' t*, &c. these portions of a circle will mark the different lengths, that the lever A O must have, to drive that of *a* O uniformly, and we will carry these lengths, O *b*, O *r*, O *s*, O *t*, &c. to 5" *b'*, 4" *r'*, 3" *s'*, 2" *t'*, 1" *u'*, and describe portions of circles, *b'*, *r'*, *s'*, *t'*, which cut those of *b' b*, *r' r*, *s' s*, *t' t*, &c. If these intersections are joined by small curve lines, we shall have the curve, *b'*, *r'*, *s'*, *t'*, *u'*, O, which will fulfil the conditions required; for when the point O of the primitive circle R shall have described the space O N, the line 5" *b'* will fall in with that of O *b*; thus the weights P *p* will be in equilibrium, and the primitive circle X will have described the similar space O *c*. Moreover, when the point O shall have described the space O *s*, the line 4" *r'*, will apply itself on that of O *r*, and the lever *a* O will have come to *a r* 1, the weights will be in equilibrium, and the spaces O 1, O 1', of the primitive circles X, R, will be alike, and so on, &c.

We shall determine (Fig. 2.) the curve O t' s' r' b', that the lever a O ought to have, to lead uniformly the right lined lever A O, by making use of the same method, and in applying the same reasonings, &c. which served in the case where the great lever drove the small one : we shall operate on the great primitive circle R, as was done on the circle X ; trace on A O a semi-circle A B O; divide the circle X into six equal parts, for example, and the circle R into 18; divide likewise the spaces O c, O N, into similar parts 1, 2, 3, 4; 1', 2', 3', 4' ; and draw, as in the preceding example, the radii A c, A 1, A 2, &c. and draw through the points of intersection of the semi-circle A B O, portions of circles b b', r r', s s', t t', &c. which will serve to form the curve, by describing from the points 5", 4", 3", 2", &c. portions of circles b' r' s' t' u', which cut those of b' b, in such a manner, that 5" b' is equal to o b; 4" r' to o r; 3" s' to o s, &c., and drawing through these points a line, we shall have the curve b', r', s', t', O' ; and by the same operations its like, b r'' s'' t'' N ; by these means in all the points of motion, the weights P p will be in equilibrium, and the spaces described by the primitive circles X and R will be alike.

Remarks.

The same things will take place, whether the curve O u' t' s' r' b' (Fig. 2.) drives the lever A O from O to B, or that the lever A B drives the curve b r'' s'' t'' N, from B to O ; or whether (Fig. 1.) the curve O u' t' s' r' b' drives the lever a O, from O to c, or that the lever a b c drives the curve b r'' s'' t'' N, from c to O : but although in these different cases, the spaces described by the primitive circles are equal, and that the weights P p are always in equilibrium, it does not follow from thence, that it should be indifferent to cause the levers drive before or after the line of their centres ;* on the contrary, it is always preferable to make them drive *after the line of the centres*, as when the curve O t' s' r' b', (Fig. 1.) drives the lever a O from O to c; for in this case, if the curve is not of an extreme precision, there will only follow from this, inequality of force and of motion ; on the contrary, if the lever drives the curve before the line of the centres, there may result from this, butting and friction capable

---

* The right line a O A, which goes from the centre of the wheel to the centre of the pinion, is called the line of the centres : it is said, the wheel drives before the line of the centres, when a tooth R (Fig. 4.) which advances from R to N, begins to act on the leaf s of the pinion, before that the point s has come into the right line a O A. The wheel drives after the line of the centres, after that the point s is come into the right line a O A, and that the tooth continues to drive the leaf in turning from R to N.

to prevent the levers from turning; the reason of it is, that the force of the lever which drives before the line of the centres is decomposed, in so much that one part tends to drive, and the other is destroyed by the centre of the lever, to where a part of the force is directed, and so much the more so, that as in figure 1, the lever *a b c* will drive the curve *b r s t* N in a point which is more distant from the line of the centres of motion. The line *b* B expresses the direction of the force which tends to move, and *b* A the direction of the force which is destroyed by the centre A.

Problem II.

The number of the teeth of a wheel being given, as well as that of the pinion which it must drive, to trace the curve of the teeth of the wheel and of the pinion, and to determine the driving before and after the line of the centres: Let R N (Plate II. A. Fig. 3.) be the primitive circle of the wheel, which shall have 18 teeth, and X that of the pinion, which shall have 6; divide the circle R into 18 parts, setting out from the line of the centres *a* O A, and the circle X into 6 parts, setting out from the same line; subdivide into several like parts, as into 5, for example, the divisions O N, O *c*, of the wheel, and of the pinion; these subdivisions will serve to form, by the method given in the first Problem, the curve N *u' t' s' r' d*; supposing then, the leaf, or tooth of the pinion, must be of the thickness O *u*, divide the arc N 4 remaining of the division of the wheel, into two parts N *m*, *n m*, leaving a small distance between *n* and *u* for the play or freedom of the pitching; from the point *m*, and centre A of the wheel, draw the line A *m d*, which will cut the curve *b s t u* N in a point *d*; so the curve *d r' s' t' u'* N will be that of the teeth of this wheel, and *m d*, the surplus of the teeth on the primitive radius, and then *n* N will be the arc of driving after the line of the centres, and *n* O, that which ought to be described before the line of the centres.

Now to construct the wheel and pinion, we draw again (Fig. 4.) the primitive radii of the wheel and pinion; and in the line of the centers A *a* draw the semicircle O *d a* on the radius of the pinion, then from the centre A, (Fig. 3.) and top of the tooth N *u' t' s' d' n*, take the distance A *d*, which carry to (Fig. 4.) from the centre A, describe a portion of a circle, which shall cut the semicircle *a d* O in a point *d*; this point will mark the top of the tooth; so in drawing from the centre *a* of the primitive circle X, the radius *a d c*, this radius will represent the flank, or side of the leaf of the pinion; and setting out from this point, divide the circle X into 6 parts, through

H

which draw radii to the centre a; make the thickness of the leaves of the size O u (Fig. 3.) and the sides of the pinion leaves will be formed.

Finally, to form the teeth of the wheel, draw from the centre A to the point d, the line A m d, and setting out from the point m, divide the circle R into 18 parts, and draw the lines A R n, which mark the distance of the teeth; and on the sides of these lines from the curves traced (Fig. 3.) we shall have[*] by this means a wheel, which will make the pinion turn as uniformly as if the circle R carried round that of X by simply touching it. The curves of the leaves of the pinion are traced in the way which has been shewn before; but as in the proposed example, they become very small, having for length only the interval which is between the point r of the primitive circle X, and the point s of the semicircle A B s O, (Fig. 4.) in taking this greatest length r s of the pinion, and applying it (Fig. 2.) in such a way, that from the centre a we cut the curve N, t, the small section v will determine the length o v of this curve of the pinion; if the driving began rather before the line of the centres, we could determine the curve of the pinion, by working as has been done in figure 2, and applying the same method which was used for the teeth of the wheel; but we ought to avoid as far as possible having much to drive before the line of the centres.

"To render a pitching the most perfect possible, and to avoid the inequalities of the curves of the teeth, in the case even of the driving after the line of the centres, pinions should be made with the greatest number of teeth or leaves, as of 8, 10, or 12, &c.; by this means we reduce to the least quantity, the obstacles which arise from the driving before and after the line of the centres, and the curves of the teeth becoming insensible, there results the least inequality, should they even be badly formed; for the pitching of pinions of 6, requires care to have them well made, not only in determining the size, *which varies*, but in forming the curves exactly, and to avoid at the same time inequalities, butting, friction, &c.

The example which has been given, will suffice to explain how we might trace the form of the teeth of wheels and pinions for large work, and thus to form pitchings which will drive uniformly.

---

[*] To form teeth similar to those of N d n (Fig. 3.) without beginning again the preceding operations, take from the centre A to the top d of this tooth, and carry it to any line whatever A d (Fig. 9.); describe from the same centre A the portions t' s, t' t, u' u, N n, which mark on the line A d, and take the lengths m N, o u, p t, i s, and describe small portions of circles which cut those of s' s, &c.; and leading through the points of intersection a line N u' t' d s t n, we shall have two curves, and consequently, a tooth similar to that N t' d n (Fig. 3.)

It is to be observed, that the driving before and after the line of the centres, differs according to the number of the teeth of the wheels and of the pinions; and, according to the proportion of the leaves of the pinions to the number of the teeth of the wheel; so it would be proper, that for each different number we made figures of teeth in large size, that thereby we could determine in all cases, the driving before and after the line of the centres, the sizes of the pinions, and the excess of the teeth of the wheel beyond the primitive radius; for it is again necessary to remark, that the sizes of pinions of 6, for example, or any other, differ, according as they make a greater or less number of turns, with regard to the wheel; thus a pinion of 6 which is driven by a wheel of 60, is of a different size from the pinion of 6 which is driven by a wheel of 30, even when the wheels should be of a size proportioned to their number of teeth, and the driving in both cases, not made equally before and after the line of their centres; having fixed such principles, workmen, in following them attentively, will make good pitchings. See *Essai sur l'Horlogerie, tom.* ii. pp. 2 to 24, *par M. Ferdinand Berthoud, Horloger. Paris* 1763. Those who wish for more particulars on this subject, are referred to *Cours de Mathematique, troisième partie. Elémens de Méchanique Statique, tom. i. par M. Camus, Paris* 1767; *or a translation of that part of it, regarding the Numbers and Forms of Wheel Teeth, for J. Taylor, of the Architectural Library,* 59, *High Holborn, London,* 1806.

M. de la Hire seems to have been the first who shewed how to trace the curve, that was best adapted for the teeth of wheels and pinions, so as they might turn with an uniform motion.—When a wheel turns a pinion, it may be said to *drive* it, and when a pinion turns a wheel, it may be said to be *leading* the wheel; the one being a quick, the other a slow motion.

To have a good or safe pitching, much depends on the proper size, or diameter of the pinion, on the figure of the wheel teeth, and of the pinion leaves: if the pinions are high numbered, that is, not less than eight or ten, any small deviation from a true figure may not be of so much consequence as some have attached to it. With such small teeth as are in clocks and watches, in practice, the figure of the teeth cannot well be drawn, nevertheless, our workmen, and wheel teeth finishers, make the nearest approximation they can to the shape required; where this is well attained, it is wonderful how it prevents rubbing, or wearing in the pinions. A strong instance of this is in a Regulator, which we made upwards of thirty years ago, where no impression whatever, is to be seen on the pinion leaves. Much of this will also depend on the goodness of the qualities of the brass and steel from which the wheels and pinions are made. Lepine, a watch-maker of considerable eminence in Paris, had in some of his watches the wheel teeth and pinion leaves of a saw-teeth, or ratchet-like form, having a very small rounding off to wards the point of the acting sides to prevent any catching taking place; these kind of teeth have a great appearance of strength.

In the sizing of pinions, it is no doubt desirable to have them as large in diameter as they can safely be admitted, and rules for this purpose have been given by several artists, which from longer and more experience have afterwards been given up. An instance of this with Berthoud shall be given, by taking his Table for getting the diameters, and comparing it, as we shall afterwards do, with the diameters of the pinions, in one of his first-rate marine time-keepers. The best method to determine with the greatest precision, the size of a pinion for any wheel whatever, (he says) is, before hardening and tempering it, to put it with its wheel into the pitching tool; for this purpose, some of the wheel teeth must be rounded off, when it will be seen by its pitching, if it is of a right diameter and figure; if it is too large, reduce it, till it comes so as to have the pitching made to move in as uniform a manner as possible; if it is too small, another must be made, or the wheel reduced.

But to prevent this inconvenience, make use of the following methods, which serve to give the size as nearly as may be, to which a clock pinion ought to be turned before cutting it. Cut a slip of paper whose breadth should be about that of the thickness of the wheel, for which a pinion is required to be made; apply this slip of paper on the circumference of the wheel teeth, supposed cut, but not rounded off, and clip it to such a length as to take over as many teeth of the wheel, and two more than the pinion is to have leaves, the length of the slip of paper will be the measure for the circumference of the pinion. If we have, for example, a pinion of 16 to make, cut the slip so as it shall lay over 18 teeth of the wheel, then apply it round the pinion, which reduce in turning, till such time as the two ends of the paper slip meet on lapping it round. The pinion being afterwards cut and rounded up, (but before tempering it,) let some of the wheel teeth be rounded off, and fixing it on a smooth arbor, put the wheel and pinion into the pitching tool, and see if it is of such a diameter as will, with the teeth of the wheel, produce a regular pitching. With small pinions for clocks, and in those for watches, slips of paper cannot readily be made use of, but here are rules founded, as well as the preceding, on experience, and agreeable to the practice of the best workmen.

When the teeth of wheels are cut, and the diameter of pinions are required to be taken from them, callipers, or spring pinion gages, are used. If, for example, it is required to make a pinion of 16 teeth, or leaves, give an extent or opening to the callipers, or gage, so as to take in 6 teeth of the wheel, taken from the outer flank of the first tooth to the outer flank of the sixth; this is what is called six full teeth.

For a pinion of
- 15, the callipers must extend not quite to the flank of the sixth tooth.
- 14, take 6 teeth on the points, or middle of their tops.
- 12, five full teeth when it is for a large wheel of a clock, and when it is for a watch, take five teeth fully on the points.
- 10, four full teeth.
- 9, a little less than four full teeth.
- 8, for a clock, four teeth on the points, for watches, take four teeth on the points, less the fourth of a space of one tooth.
- 7, in a clock, three full teeth, and a fourth of a space of one tooth; for watches, take a little less than three teeth of the wheel, when finished by forcing the callipers over them.
- 6, for clocks, take three full teeth; for watches, a little more than three teeth on the points.
- 5, three teeth on the points.
- 4, take two square and full teeth. When the pinion leads, take two square teeth of the wheel, and a half of a space of one of the teeth more: in general, all pinions which lead, ought to be somewhat larger than those which are driven.

The pitching tool which Berthoud recommends for trying the pitching of a wheel and pinion, is that which, with us, is called the Geneva pitching tool, and has been long known and used in this country. He has given a drawing and description of it in the first volume of his *Essai sur l'Horlogerie*, pp. 169, 170, 171. Where, after describing it, he says, " The great facility which this tool gives of seeing pitchings, repairing them, carrying them in a correct state to the frame-plates of a clock or watch, renders this instrument very necessary to the workman; it can be made use of even in setting off various 'scapements, such as the anchor, cylinder, or horizontal one, &c. But, notwithstanding its utility, there are few workmen who have it, or who even know it. It is, however, not new, seeing that Thiout has described it in his *Traité d'Horlogerie*; but the extreme indolence of the most part of workmen, has made the use of it to be very limited, for they seek more to gain money than to make good things."

It has the advantage over the sector kind of pitching tools, which do not take in the wheels and pinions, by allowing the working of the pitching to be seen, and serves to check any pinion of an improper diameter, which may at times, by mischance, have been overlooked, both by the movement-maker and by the watch-maker.

In the year 1778 or 79, having got rather an imperfect description of a sector or kind of pitching tool, made up in some degree on the principle of proportional compasses, but having an objection to the points standing always in an angular position, by which they were not fitted to draw truly off the pitching, from one hole to another, as can be done by the Geneva tool, we made a sector having thick and broad brass limbs, with a strong and true joint, so as it might be always stiff, firm, and easy, at the time when using it. On the line where the legs meet, when the sector is close shut, and about three inches from the centre of the joint, were placed two small cylindrical steel pins, about one-tenth of an inch in diameter, and two inches long, having conical points; one of the pins had at the middle a sole made from the solid, by which it was screwed on to the upper side of one of the legs; the other had a socket fixed on the opposite leg, through which the other cylindrical steel pin passed, and could at pleasure be set and fixed so as to make the plane of the sector legs stand parallel to the plane of the frame-plate of any movement when setting off a pitching. The manner of making and using the cylindrical steel pins, and the apparatus for fixing them on the legs of the sector, are the same which the late Mr. Pennington afterwards adopted for his sector, a drawing of which is seen in Plate VII. No. 37.

These steel pins were placed perpendicularly to the plane of the legs of the sector, and so as the points of both would coincide in the inside line of the sector edges, when the legs are supposed to be shut. On the side of one of these legs, three inches in length from the end and near to the inner edge, a small groove was sunk, having a square bottom, to receive a part of a straight toothed rack fitted to it, and made to slide backward and forward in it. The rack was a small slip of brass, about three inches long, and three-tenths of an inch broad, the outer edge of which was toothed; from the inner projected a nose-piece, bearing on the inner edge of the leg of the sector, and which served as a guide to set the wheel on, when taking its diameter across between the edges of the legs of the sector; about an inch from the end of one of the legs, a pinion of 16 or 18 leaves was made to pitch with the toothed edge of the rack, and fixed to the under side of a small circular plate of brass two inches in diameter; on the upper side were traced a few concentric circles, the lower pivot of the pinion turned in a hole made in the leg of the sector, the upper one turned in a cock, which was screwed to the leg of the sector, and served to keep the pinion and its plate in their place. From the cock was formed, on the opposite end to that by which it was screwed to the sector leg, an index which lay across the semi-diameter of the circular plate. The rack had two small cocks which lay on it, pressing spring tight, and which were screwed on the leg of the sector, keeping the rack steady to its place or groove on the sector leg. The spaces on the plate between the concentric circles, served for pinions of different numbers, from 12 to 6 inclusively. On turning round the plate in either direction, the rack moved backward and forward, carrying the nose-piece with it. Taking a wheel of 64, and a pinion of 8, for example, and setting them to their proper depth in the Geneva pitching tool, which, being set off on any plane or plate of brass, the steel points of the sector pitching tool were made to stand at the same distance as those of the Geneva putting the wheel of 64 so as its diameter might stand across between the edges of the legs, and bringing the nose-piece to this place, a small line was made across one of the spaces between the concentric circles, appropriated for pinions of 8, and wheels of different numbers, so that wheels of 64, and of any other diameter, could be set to their pitching. And, in like manner, were pinions and wheels of various numbers and diameters, marked with their places on the plate, having their proper depths previously made by the Geneva tool. No tool could be so easily and safely used as this sector pitching tool, which gave such dispatch, as made it extremely useful in repairing or examining the depth or pitchings of new or old work.

Soon after this sector pitching tool was finished, a more improved one from it, was made by Mr Pennington, and during the making of it, we had with him a great many trials with pitchings, so as to make it as complete as possible; notwithstanding the great utility which it possessed, it is perhaps the only one of the kind that ever was made, except a large one made many years ago for our clock-makers, who, like the greater part of workmen, were neither anxious to use it, nor to acquire a knowledge how to use it.

The sector made by Pennington was purchased from him by Mr. Auld when in London, and the one for clock-makers, are at present in our possession. Having thought this sector deserving of a place, a description herewith is given, as taken from the original pamphlet, published in London, 1780. For its figures, see Plate VII.

" This sector is composed of the legs A and B, and the joint C; it is divided into 100 (as appears by the figure) on one side, and on the other side into 150, in the manner shown at No. 38. At the 50th division, and having its centre exactly on the edge of the leg A, is fixed the piece D; and on the same part of the leg B is fixed the socket E, with the moveable cylinder F going through it, and which may be fastened at any place required by the screw G. No. 39. is another view of the socket, &c. the same letters refer to each. H and I (No. 37.) are pieces screwed upon the leg A, having their edges next each other shelving so as to form a dovetail groove, in which the pieces K and L slide; the piece L has a notch through it from one end to the other to admit the piece a, which goes through both it and the leg of the sector, and has a nut screwed on the other side to fasten it at any place; the pieces K and L are connected together by the screw M, the use of which is to set the piece K exactly to the place required. On this piece is screwed the piece N, which lies over the edge of the leg A; it has likewise on it a nonius of 10. O is an arch fixed to the leg A, and on which the end of the leg B moves. P is a piece fitted upon the arch O, and moveable upon it, and which may be fastened at any place by the piece b going through it, and having a nut screwed upon it on the other side. The piece P and the leg B are connected together by the screw Q, the use of which is to set the leg B exactly to the place required.

THE USE OF THE SECTOR.

I.—*To find the proportional sizes of Wheels and Pinions.*

Look for the number of the wheel on the sector, then open it till the diameter of the wheel just reaches from one leg to the other even with the number: the diameter of the pinion will be even with the number in the small table annexed, as near as I have been able to come at by a great many experiments.

Pinions.	Numbers on the Sector.
6	7.2
7	8.1
8	9.0
9	9.9
10	10.8
11	11.7
12	12.6

II.—*To draw circles the proportionable sizes of Wheels and Pinions.*

The line drawn from the center of the joint, and which is called the line of lines, or equal parts, and divided into 150, (No. 38.) is for the convenience of setting the compasses, to take the sizes, and answers the same purpose for circles, as the edges of the sector does for wheels and pinions.

III.—*To set the centers of circles at a proper distance from each other in drawing callipers.*

Having the numbers of the wheel and pinion, and the diameter of the wheel, look for the number opposite that of the pinion in the the small table annexed, and subtract that from the wheel.

Pinions.	Numbers on the Sectors.
6	3.8
7	4.6
8	5.7
9	6.4
10	7.0
11	7.7
12	8.3

This table is constructed by experiments with wheels and pinions, as appears by No. 40. of the Plate for pinions of six. The wheel 48 and the pinion of 6 being at a proper distance, and having their centres even with the 24th division, the diameter of the wheel touches the lines just 3 divisions and 8-10ths from the 48 division. The same rule will do for every other wheel.

For example, suppose a wheel of 48 teeth, and a pinion of 6 leaves, in the table, opposite 6, you find 3.8, which you subtract decimally from

48; thus, $\frac{48.0}{44.2}$, which produces 44 and 2-10ths; then take the diameter of the wheel in your compasses, set one foot on 44.2 on one leg, and open the sector till the other falls on the same number on the other leg, the distance then between half 48 on each leg, will be the distance of the two centres for the wheel to carry the pinion, as appears by No. 40. A and B are the supposed lines, drawn apart from the sector, for the convenience of having the wheel and pinion larger. G, a wheel of 48, and D, a pinion of 6.

IV.—*To set Wheels and Pinions the proper depth in each other, by only having the Wheels given.*

At H (No. 37.) are divisions corresponding with those on the sector, only numbered the contrary way, beginning at the 100th; and these are the divisions to be observed in this case: By means of the nonius on the piece K, the edge of the piece N may be set the 10th part of one of the divisions, and answers the same purpose as if every single one were actually divided into 10: so that, in using it for this purpose, every single division must be called 10, the 10 a 100, &c. Suppose a wheel of 48 teeth, and a pinion of 6 leaves, to be set a proper depth, look in the table for pinions of 6, and opposite 48 you will find 79.1, which is 79, and 1-10th of the small imaginary divisions before mentioned; so that you set the cipher on the nonius as far beyond the 7th division, as till the 9th, corresponds with one of the other divisions, (the fractional part in this case need not be taken notice of;) then, if the wheel be applied to the edge of the sector, close to the piece N, and the legs be brought together until it reaches the same part on each leg, the points at D and F will then give the proper distance.

The method of constructing the following tables is thus: divide 1000 (which is the number the sector is supposed to be divided into) by the number of the wheel, and multiply this product by the number opposite to that of the pinion in the table, and this will be the number for that wheel. The sector may be divided into any number which may be judged most convenient, and the same rule will continue to answer in the construction of the tables, or rather multiply 1000 by the number in the table, and divide by the number of the wheel.

Mr. Pennington has said, multiply the product, whereas he should have said, multiply the quotient, by the number opposite that of the pinion in the Table, p. 9. of his pamphlet. See top of page 105.

A better way is to multiply 1000 by the number in the table, and divide by the number of the wheel teeth. For example, a pinion of 8, and a wheel of 96. 1000×5.7÷96 = 59.48 nearly. The numbers in the tables here, were made according to the last rule.

TABLE I.

Pinions of Six Leaves.

Number of teeth in the wheel.	Numbers on the Sector.	Number of teeth in the wheel.	Numbers on the Sector.	Number of teeth in the wheel.	Numbers on the Sector.	Number of teeth in the wheel.	Numbers on the Sector.	Number of teeth in the wheel.	Numbers on the Sector.
24	158.3	40	95.0	56	67.8	72	52.7	96	39.5
25	152.0	41	92.6	57	66.6	73	52.0	98	38.7
26	146.1	42	90.4	58	65.5	74	51.3	100	38.0
27	140.7	43	88.3	59	64.4	75	50.6	102	37.2
28	135.7	44	86.3	60	63.3	76	50.0	104	36.5
29	131.0	45	84.4	61	62.2	77	49.3	106	35.8
30	126.6	46	82.6	62	61.2	78	48.7	108	35.1
31	122.5	47	90.8	63	60 3	79	48.1	110	34.5
32	118.7	48	79.1	64	59.3	80	47.5	112	33.9
33	115.1	49	77.5	65	58.4	82	46.3	114	33.3
34	111.7	50	76.0	66	57.5	84	45.2	116	32.7
35	108.5	51	74.5	67	56.7	86	44.1	118	32.2
36	105 5	52	73.0	68	55.8	88	43.1	120	31.6
37	102.7	53	71.7	69	55.0	90	42.2	—	—
38	100.0	54	70.3	70	54.2	92	41.3	—	—
39	97.4	55	69.0	71	53.6	94	40.4	—	—

TABLE II.

Pinions of Seven Leaves.

Number of teeth in the wheel.	Numbers on the Sector.	Number of teeth in the wheel.	Numbers on the Sector.	Number of teeth in the wheel.	Numbers on the Sector.	Number of teeth in the wheel.	Numbers on the Sector.	Number of teeth in the wheel.	Numbers on the Sector.
28	164.2	41	112.1	54	85.1	67	68.6	80	57.5	106	43.3
29	158.6	42	109.5	55	83.6	68	67.6	82	56.0	108	42.5
30	153.3	43	106.9	56	82.1	69	66.6	84	54.7	110	41.8
31	148.3	44	104.5	57	80.7	70	65.7	86	53.4	112	41.0
32	143.7	45	102.2	58	79.3	71	64.7	88	52.2	114	40.3
33	139.3	46	100.0	59	77.9	72	63.8	90	51.1	116	39.6
34	135.2	47	97 8	60	76.6	73	63.0	92	50.0	118	38.9
35	131.4	48	95.8	61	75.4	74	62.1	94	48.9	120	38.3
36	127.7	49	93.8	62	74.1	75	61.3	96	47.9	122	37.7
37	124 3	50	92.0	63	73.0	76	60.5	98	46.9	124	37.0
38	121.0	51	90.1	64	71.8	77	59.7	100	46.0	—	—
39	117.9	52	88.4	65	70.7	78	58.9	102	45.0	—	—
40	115.0	53	86.7	66	69.6	79	58.2	104	44.2	—	—

TABLE III.
Pinions of Eight Leaves.

Number of teeth in the Wheel	Numbers on the Sector.	Number of Teeth in the Wheel.	Numbers on the Sector.	Number of Teeth in the Wheel.	Numbers on the Sector.	Number of Teeth in the Wheel.	Numbers on the Sector.	Number of Teeth in the Wheel.	Numbers on the Sector.	Number of Teeth in the Wheel.	Numbers on the Sector.
32	178.1	45	126.6	58	98.2	71	80.2	88	64.7	114	50.0
33	172.7	46	123.9	59	96.6	72	79.1	90	63.3	116	49.1
34	167.6	47	121.2	60	95.0	73	78.0	92	61.9	118	48.3
35	162.8	48	118.7	61	93.4	74	77.0	94	60.6	120	47.5
36	158.3	49	116.3	62	91.9	75	76.0	96	59.3	122	46.7
37	154.0	50	114.0	63	90.4	76	75.0	98	58.1	124	45.9
38	150.0	51	111.7	64	89.0	77	74.0	100	57.0	126	45.2
39	146.1	52	109.6	65	87.6	78	73.0	102	55.8	128	44.5
40	142.5	53	107.5	66	86.3	79	72.1	104	54.8	130	43.8
41	139.0	54	105.5	67	85.0	80	71.2	106	53.7	132	43.1
42	135.7	55	103.6	68	83.8	82	69.5	108	52.7	134	42.5
43	132.5	56	101.7	69	82.6	84	67.8	110	51.8	136	41.9
44	129.5	57	100.0	70	81.4	86	66.2	112	50.8	—	—

TABLE IV.
Pinions of Ten Leaves.

Number of teeth in the wheel	Numbers on the Sector.	Number of teeth in the wheel.	Numbers on the Sector.	Number of teeth in the wheel.	Numbers on the Sector.	Number of teeth in the wheel.	Numbers on the Sector.	Number of teeth in the wheel.	Numbers on the Sector.	Number of teeth in the wheel.	Numbers on the Sector.
40	175.0	52	134.6	64	109.3	76	92.1	96	72.9	120	58.3
41	170.7	53	132.0	65	107.6	77	90.9	98	71.4	122	57.3
42	166.6	54	129.6	66	106.0	78	89.7	100	70.0	124	56.4
43	162.7	55	127.2	67	104.4	79	88.6	102	68.6	126	55.5
44	159.0	56	125.0	68	102.9	80	87.5	104	67.3	128	54.6
45	155.5	57	122.8	69	101.4	82	85.3	106	66.0	130	53.8
46	152.1	58	120.6	70	100.0	84	83.3	108	64.8	132	53.0
47	148.9	59	118.6	71	98.5	86	81.3	110	63.6	134	52.2
48	145.8	60	116.6	72	97.2	88	79.5	112	62.5	136	51.4
49	142.8	61	114.7	73	95.8	90	77.7	114	61.4	—	—
50	140.0	62	112.9	74	94.5	92	76.0	116	60.3	—	—
51	137.2	63	111.1	75	93.3	94	74.4	118	59.3	—	—

TABLE V.
Pinions of Twelve Leaves.

Number of teeth in the wheel	Numbers on the Sector.	Number of teeth in the wheel.	Numbers on the Sector.	Number of teeth in the wheel.	Numbers on the Sector.	Number of teeth in the wheel.	Numbers on the Sector.	Number of teeth in the wheel.	Numbers on the Sector.	Number of teeth in the wheel.	Numbers on the Sector.
48	172.9	59	140.6	70	118.5	82	101.2	104	79.8	126	65.8
49	169.3	60	138.3	71	116.9	84	98.8	106	78.3	128	64.8
50	166.0	61	136.0	72	115.2	86	96.5	108	76.8	130	63.8
51	162.7	62	133.8	73	113.6	88	94.3	110	75.4	132	62.8
52	159.6	63	131.7	74	112.1	90	92.2	112	74.1	134	61.9
53	156.6	64	129.6	75	110.6	92	90.2	114	72.8	136	61.0
54	153.7	65	127.6	76	109.2	94	88.2	116	71.5	138	60.1
55	150.9	66	125.7	77	107.7	96	86.4	118	70.3	140	59.2
56	148.2	67	123.8	78	106.4	98	84.6	120	69.1	142	58.4
57	145.6	68	122.0	79	105.0	100	83.0	122	68.0	144	57.6
58	143.1	69	120.2	80	103.7	102	81.3	124	66.9	—	—

Those who might have occasion to have wheels and pinions of such numbers as are not in these Tables, may easily by analogy compute where to set the sector, to give the pitching for a number of any pinion and wheel whatever.

The sector can be made useful in another way, in giving the sizes of wheels and pinions, their pitchings, &c.

Supposing the distance of the centres of a wheel and pinion is two inches, and eight tenths of an inch, and it is required to find the diameters of the wheel and pinion, the wheel to have 120 teeth, and the pinion 20 leaves. To find the acting semi-diameters, say, as the sum of the wheel and pinion, is to the distance of their centres, so is the number of teeth which the wheel is to have, to its acting semi-diameter 120+20=140, and as 140 : 2800 : : 120 to a fourth term which is found to be 2400, or 2.4 inches for the acting semi-diameter of the wheel. To get the semi-diameter of the acting part of the pinion, say, as 140, the sum of the teeth of the wheel and of the pinion, is to the distance of their centres, so is the number of the pinion to its acting semi-diameter, which will be found to be 400, or four tenths of an inch. The inch is here supposed to be divided into a thousand, which is the reason of the distance of the centres being expressed by 2800. Taking a radius of 2400, and from the centre of the wheel's place, describe a circle, then, with a radius of 400, describe from the centre of the pinion's place another circle; these circles will touch or coincide with each other on the line joining their centres, and this place of touching is, in mill machinery, called the pitch line, and by Camus the circles are called the primitive circles. Taking these diameters as they are now given, that is, the pinion at .8 of an inch, and the wheel at 4.8 inches, these being set to their respective places on the sector, that is, to 120 and to 20; then 122.25 taken from the sector will be the true diameter of the wheel, and 21.5 taken also from the sector, that of the pinion, which are what was required.

The converse of this rule is obvious. Let it be required to find the distance of the centres of a wheel and pinion, so as they can be set to a proper pitching. It is supposed to be a settled point, that two and a quarter may be taken on the sector, or line of equal parts, over and above the number of the wheel teeth, when the wheel drives the pinion; and the pinion's place on the sector, at one and a half more than the number of leaves which it contains. But when the pinion leads the wheel, the addenda for it must be two and a quarter, and that for the wheel one and a half.

The wheel having 120 teeth, and the pinion 20 leaves, it is required to find the distance of their centres. Set the wheel to 122.25

on the sector, and from 120 to 120 across take the distance, the half of which take as a radius, and with it describe a circle from the centre of the wheel's place; let a straight line be drawn from the wheel's centre, towards the place where the centre of the pinion is required to be. The pinion 20 being set to 21.5 on the sector, let the distance 20 be taken from it, and with the half of this as radius, set one foot of the compasses at the place where the wheel's circle intersects the straight line, and with the other foot intersect this line; this intersection will then be the distance of the centres, where the wheel of 120, and the pinion of 20, will pitch properly together. The same opening of the sector must serve for both wheel and pinion, if they are duly proportioned to one another. If these operations are carefully gone about, the diameters of wheels and pinions, and their distance of centres, may be very accurately obtained, in work approaching nearly as small as that of watch-work, and in which too it even might be done, if required. An example of such may be taken: The distance of the centres of a wheel and pinion is .8 of an inch, which call 800, being 800 thousandths of an inch. The wheel is to have 84 teeth, and the pinion 16 leaves, it is required to find their diameters? The sum of the wheel and pinion is 100; then say, as 100 is to 800, so is 84, the number of the wheel teeth, to a fourth number, which will be the acting semi-diameter of the wheel. 100 : 800 : : 84 : 672, which is the acting semi-diameter, being 672 thousand parts of an inch. The acting semi-diameter of the pinion is found in the same way. 100 : 800 : : 16 : 128, the number of the thousand parts of an inch for the acting semi-diameter of the pinion. Then 672+128 = 800, the distance of their centres. With these numbers, 672 and 128, taken as radii, describe circles, take the diameter of each and apply them to their respective numbers on the sector, viz. 84 and 16, and with this opening take 86.25 from the sector for the diameter of the wheel, and 17.5 for that of the pinion, which will be their true diameters.

Having a wheel of 84 teeth and a pinion of 16, it is required to find the distance of their centres? Set the wheel to 86.25 on the sector, and from 84 to 84 across take the distance, with the half of which taken as radius, describe a circle whose centre is in some straight line or other; the pinion being set to 17.5 on the sector, take the distance between 16 and 16 on the legs of the sector, and with the half of this distance taken as radius, describe a circle on the same right line where the wheel circle is, whose circumference shall fall in with that of the wheel; the distance between their centres will be the distance where the wheel of 84, and the pinion of 16 will pitch properly together.

For such purposes as these, it is requisite to have very nice dividers, or compasses, and a scale having the inch divided into tenths and thousandths of an inch.

It is more than forty years since we urged the expediency of workmen in the different branches, making use of inches and parts of an inch, in whatever kind of gage was used; and from this would result much ease, convenience, and advantage, not only to themselves, but to those who employed them, or gave them orders for what might be wanted. To show how irregular they are in this part of their business, for example, one movement-maker had his pillars called 12, and his frame or pillar plate 8, as one of his movement sizes; another had also a way of expressing by numbers his sizes, but differing from those of his neighbour; and neither of them had the smallest analogy to any known measure, each having his gage made according to his own fancy. Were every size, either in height of pillars, or verges, diameters of plates, dials, glasses, &c. expressed by measures of inches and its parts, every one could then understand what he had ordered, and what he had to expect. The breadth of springs and their lengths, should be expressed in the same way, and even their weight in grains, or in ounces, pennyweights, and grains troy. There seems to be but little difficulty in adopting a plan of this sort; but it has not yet been done, and we regret to say we suspect it never will.

The following is a description of a sliding scale of equal parts, of such general utility, that no clock or watch-maker ought to be without having one of them, as it supplies the place of a sector, of a pitching tool, of calipers, or pinion gages; it may be used also as compasses, or dividers, and as a pivot gage for clock pivots; it might be rather heavy for watch pivots, which would require a very small sector, or micrometer spring gage, such as Berthoud used; the common pivot gage with holes not being readily reducible so as to give the diameter of the pivots to a known measure; the sliding scale may be made to various sizes, or according to what description of work it is intended chiefly to be applied:—Take a piece of plate brass well hammered, seven inches in length, three quarters of an inch in breadth, and about one tenth of an inch thick, made very straight and plain on the sides and edges, like to what may be called a plain scale or straight edge; let there be put on one of the sides, two slips of well hammered plate brass, whose sides and edges are truly filed, one of the edges on each must be filed a little bevelled, so as when the slips are fixed to the scale, these edges will form a dovetail; the slips are fully six inches long, one quarter of an inch broad, and one twentieth of an inch thick: the square edges of the slips must coincide with the outer or plain edges of the scale when fast pinned on it, the space then between the bevelled edges will be about three tenths of an inch in breadth; in this space, another piece of good and well hammered plate brass is fitted, being of the same thickness with the pinned on slips, and somewhat more than two inches long, having a small slit of half an inch long made in each end, and near to the side which is opposite to that, on which a nonius or vernier is to be put; the small slips at the end made by the slits are set out a little, so as to form or give a kind of spring tightness to this piece of brass when moving in the dovetail groove, and keep the side where the nonius is, close up against the slip fixed on the scale.. On this slip, at the line of the bevelled edge, is laid down six inches, numbered 0, 1, 2, 3, &c. to 6, each inch divided into ten, and each tenth divided into five, so that each inch is divided into fifty parts. On the piece of brass fitted into the dovetail groove, and at the line which corresponds with the inches and parts laid down on the scale, is the nonius laid down, consisting of 20 divisions of equal parts, and numbered into twice five and ten. These 20 divisions on the nonius correspond to 19 divisions, or nineteen fiftieths on the scale, and by this means the nonius can divide each fiftieth into twenty, consequently an inch can be divided into a thousand,—a measure so extremely small, that few could work nearer, or even up to it, in the very nicest parts of watch-making. The beginning of the nonius divisions is distinguished by a sort of lozenge, which corresponds to zero or O on the scale, when the dovetail piece is home to its place. On the outside of the slips on the scale are screwed two thin pieces of steel somewhat in the form of a square, one leg of the square being screwed on, the other projects beyond the edge of the scale about three-tenths of an inch, one at each side or edge; another thin and nearly straight piece of steel is screwed on to the dovetail piece, near to the end opposite to that on which the lozenge is engraved. When the line of the lozenge corresponds with O on the scale, then the edge of the steel square, (which is on that side of the scale opposite to that where the divisions are laid down,) and the piece of steel which is on the dovetail piece meet or coincide; between these edges, the diameters of wheels and pinions, &c. are taken, the lozenge, or some division of the nonius corresponding to the number on the scale, gives the diameter in inches, tenths, and thousands: between the edge of the other steel square and the corresponding end of the steel piece on the dovetail, a small opening is left, in space equal to the outside of the opposite steel ends, when home at 0 or zero ; this is for taking the outside diameter of any thing, the other for the inside of that, for which the other is intended to be fitted into. On the end of the dovetail piece, outside of the steel piece is fixed a small brass stud, another small stud somewhat larger, whose shoulder moves along the space of the scale, which is between the dovetail edges ; an opening is made in this space 4.5 inches long, and three twentieths of an inch wide ; a double shouldered screw, having a steel collet, and brass milled head ; the double shoulder comes from under the scale, and through the opening the screw is tapped, and works in a hole in the sole of the largest brass stud ; another milled headed screw turns in the largest brass stud, the head near the stud outside ; this part of the screw cannot move endways in the stud ; the tapped part turns in a screwed hole in the head of the smallest brass stud. The screw under the scale fixing the largest brass stud on the dovetail space, the other, on being turned, will, by means of the smallest stud, bring the nonius very accurately to the place wanted on the scale ; the long opening is for the double shoulder of the screw to move back and forward in, along with the dovetail piece and nonius on it. A very small and nice beam compass is requisite to accompany this sliding scale ; or two small and short cylindrical steel pins with conical points may be attached to the scale itself, as done in the one we use. When the lozenge is home and coinciding with 0, let a hole be made through the dovetail piece *near to the end where the nonius is laid*, and the scale truly opened, so as the steel points may stand perpendicular to the plane of the scale, and coincide in the same point ; but to this point they cannot be brought, when the one point is fixed to the scale, and the other to the sliding dovetail piece ; one of these points, the one which is attached to the sliding piece, will require to be unfixed or taken out of its place for the time, when very small diameters are to be taken. In making use of this sliding scale, a little knowledge of the rule of proportion, and of decimals, is necessary ; by it the size of the pinions may be had before the wheels are made, or give the diameter of a wheel to a given pinion. Clock-makers, before making their pinions, are in the practice of first having their wheels cut ; as it is from the teeth and spaces, they get the diameter of their pinions. By the proper use of this scale, the pinions may be made at any time, whether the wheels are made, cut or not cut. Clock and watch-makers have different methods for taking the diameters of pinions, as well as different sizes : some take more or less of teeth and space by the pinion gage than others do, and the greatest accuracy

114   DIAMETER OF WHEELS AND PINIONS BY S. S. P. TOOL.

by this way, is not quite attainable, unless having very extensive and nice practice. Some use a sector, having a line of equal parts laid down on the legs, and just at their inner edges; but if no mistake is made in calculation, the sliding scale appears to give these things with the greatest degree of precision. A few examples with it shall be given.

The great wheel of a turret clock being 12 inches in diameter, and having 120 teeth, the pinion which it is to drive to have 20 leaves: It is required to have the diameter of the pinion?

Say, as 120 teeth + 2.25 (the addenda for the driver) = 122.25 is to 12 inches, or 12000, the diameter of the wheel, so is 20 the pinion leaves + 1.5 (the addenda for the driven) = 21.5 to a fourth number, which will be that for the diameter required.

Then, as 122.25 : 12000 : : 21.5 : x.

```
            21.5
          _____
          60000
          12000
          24000
          _____
122.25)258000.0(2110.4.   The number required for the
       24450               diameter of the pinion. Say 2.1
       _____              inches, and $\frac{104}{1000}$ of an inch.
       13500
       12225
       _____
        12750
        12225
       _____
        52500
        48900
       _____
         3600
```

The diameter which is given here for the pinion, is greater than the projection of the steel edges of the sliding scale can take in, which was not intended for work quite so large; yet when it is set to 2110.4, the diameter may easily be transferred from the steel edges by means of a pair of calipers. In such large work as this, what cannot be done by the sliding scale, may be done very easily, and with the greatest exactness by the common Gunter's scale, where inches, tenths, and two hundredths of an inch, can be taken.

The great wheel of an astronomical clock having 96 teeth, the diameter 3.2 inches, and $\frac{20}{1000}$ of an inch more, or say 3220, the pinion which it is to drive is to have 30 leaves: What must the diameter of this pinion be?

96+2.25=98.25. The diameter 3220, and the pinion 30+1.5= 31.5.

Then, as 98.25 : 3220 : : 31.5 : x
```
      31.5
     ─────
     16100
     3220
     9660
```

98.25)101430.0(1032.3.   The diameter of the pinion must
      9825   be 1 inch, and 1¼¼/1000 of an inch.
      ─────
      31800
      29475
      ─────
      23250
      19650
      ─────
      36000
      29475
      ─────
      6525

The great wheel of a common eight-day clock having 96 teeth, and 3.2 inches in diameter, or 3200; the second wheel pinion 8, what should be the diameter of the pinion?

As 98.25 : 3200 : : 9.5 : 309.4. The diameter of the pinion must be .3 of an inch, and 9.4/1000 of an inch more.

The diameter of any wheel (by having the diameter of the pinion) may be found in the same way as that of the pinions.

The diameter of the centre, or second wheel pinion of a spring clock, being 2.8 tenths of an inch, or 280, and 8 leaves, the great wheel to have 96 teeth: Required the diameter?

Say, as 9.5 : 280 : : 98.25 : x, or 2895.8. The diameter which the great wheel ought to be, being 2.8 inches, and 95/1000 of an inch.

Having a wheel of 120 teeth, and whose diameter was 4.8 inches, to get the diameter of a pinion of 48, a slip of paper was extended over 50 teeth, according to a rule of *M. Berthoud's*, which measured in length 6200 as the circumference of the pinion. From this circumference to find the diameter, say 355 : 113 : : 6200 : 1973, this last number is the diameter of the pinion. By the same method, 1012 was given for the diameter of a pinion of 24; and for a pinion of 12, 538 for the diameter of it.

Calculating these numbers by the rule given when using the sliding scale, they were 1943, 1001, and 530; and comparing them with those given by Berthoud's rule, it will be seen that *it* gives the diameters rather too large. It may be observed here, that pinions of lesser numbers have a greater diameter in proportion than those of double or quadruple the number. For example, the pinion here of 12 has the diameter 530; this multiplied by 4, will be 2120, and the diameter of the pinion of 48, was only given 1943. But the more a pinion approximates in number to the wheel, the less will be the difference of the ratio of their diameters.

It would appear, as has already been hinted, that Berthoud had relinquished the rules for taking the diameters of pinions, as given in his *Essai*, by comparing them with the pinions in a very fine marine time-keeper, No. xxxiii. *Inventée par Ferdinand Berthoud*, 1785, being twenty-two years after the publication of his *Essai*. All the pinions in it had 16 leaves, and were all of the same diameter 148, as taken by the gage of the sliding scale, measuring ten teeth and spaces of the wheels, whereas they should have measured eleven teeth and spaces. The slip of paper method would have made their circumference 520; and the diameter 165.5, or 11.18 teeth and spaces, giving a much greater diameter than what he had afterwards adopted in his practice. The diameter of the great wheel 1751, and 192 teeth, driving a pinion of 16 leaves: Required the diameter of the pinion? Say, 194.25 : 1751 : : 17.5 : 157.7; this last number is then greater than 148 by $\frac{97}{1000}$ of an inch. All the pitchings in this time-keeper were, however, extremely good, the teeth apparently approached to that of having a drop, and yet it could not be confidently said that they had.

The rule which Mr. Hatton, (in his introduction to the mechanical part of clock and watch-making,) has given for finding the diameters of pinions, will make them too large: and that which is given in a very respectable work (Rees's Cyclopædia) will make them larger still. The rules are nearly the same in both, only Mr. Hatton's addenda is 1, and that of the other is 1.5. Multiply the number intended for the pinion by 2, then divide the product by 3, and to the quotient add 1, or 1.5, as they may apply, and this will be the diameter in teeth and spaces, taken from the wheel which is to drive the pinion. An example shall be taken in both cases for the diameter of a pinion of 8 leaves.

$8 \times 2 = 16 + 3 = 5\frac{1}{3} + 1 = 6\frac{1}{3}$
$8 \times 2 = 16 + 3 = 5\frac{1}{3} + 1.5 = 6.8.$

Although the rule now to be given, differs not very materially from the two last, yet it will be found to be a good one, and give such diameters to the pinions as will at all times and cases ensure safe pitching Multiply the given number of the pinion by 2, to the product add 1, and then divide by 3, the quotient will be the diameter required. Take the former as an example, $8 \times 2 = 16 + 1 = 17 + 3 = 5\frac{2}{3}$. Being three teeth, two spaces, and two thirds of a space, taken by the calipers from the teeth of a wheel not rounded up, and which will be a diameter sufficiently large. In taking the diameter for a leading pinion, it will make but a very small difference, whether the addenda is two, or two and a quarter. For a pinion of eight, the diameter in the one case is 6, and in the other 6.08.

In a very excellent clock, which was planned out by a very ingenious artist, and executed by another, who (it may truly be said) have perhaps not left their equals behind them, were two leading pinions so very accurately made, that it has been thought proper to give them a place here. One of them, a pinion of 8, leading a wheel of 96 teeth, and 3 inches in diameter; the diameter of the pinion by the sliding scale was 316. To find its diameter, say, as 97.5 : 3000 : : 10.25 : 315.6; this last is so near, that between it and the actual diameter 316, there is not $\frac{1}{1000}$ of an inch of difference. The other a pinion of 12, leading a wheel of 365 teeth, whose diameter was 7.9 inches, that of the pinion 307. To show what it ought to be, say, as 366.5 : 7900 : : 14.25 : 307.; such extreme accuracy is rarely to be met with. The diameter of the great wheel of a clock being 3.2 inches, having 96 teeth, and the pinion which it is to drive has 8 leaves: Required the distance their centres should have, so as they may pitch properly together? say, as 98.25 is to 3200, the diameter of the wheel, so is half the sum of the wheel and pinion added together, to a number which shall be the distance required. $96 + 8 = 104$, half of which is 52.; then 98.25 : 3200 : : 52 : 1693.6, the distance which the centres ought to have, which is 1.6 inch, and $\frac{916}{1000}$ of an inch more.

Having the distance of the centres, it is required to find the diameter of a wheel of 96 teeth, and the diameter of a pinion of 8, which it is to drive, so that they may pitch properly together? The half sum of the wheel and pinion is 52, the distance of the centres is 1693.6, and the wheel $96 + 2.25 = 98.25$; then say, as, 52 : 1693.6 : :

98.25 : 3199.9, which number is that for the diameter of the wheel 96, and is within $\frac{1}{10,000}$ part of an inch of 3200. To find the diameter of the pinion, say, as 52 : 1693.6 : : 9.5 : 309.4, the number for the diameter of the pinion being the same as was found in another case. The examples given here for the practical clockmaker, ought to be sufficient for the watchmaker also : but, in order to make the matter as familiar to the latter as possible, a few cases may be taken with watch wheels.

The fusee great wheel of a repeating watch, having 60 teeth, and 780 in diameter, the second wheel pinion (which it is to turn) to be 12: Required the diameter of the pinion ? Say, as 62.25 : 780 : : 13.5 : 169, the number of thousand parts of an inch on the sliding scale, taken from between the steel edges, for the diameter of the pinion. The second wheel of the same watch having 64 teeth, and the diameter 668, the pinion which it is to drive to have 8 leaves : Required the diameter of the pinion ?

as 66.25 : 668 : : 9.5 : 96.

The second wheel of a watch having 100 teeth, and in diameter 769, the pinion 10 which it is to drive : Required the diameter of the pinion ? As 102.25 : 769 : : 11.5 : 86.4, the diameter required.

A wheel of 64, and one inch in diameter, drives a pinion of 8 leaves : Required the diameter of the pinion ? As 66.25 : 1000 : : 9.5 : 143.4, the diameter required.

To find the diameter of a wheel, 64 being the number of teeth which it is to have, the diameter of the pinion 143.4, and 8 leaves, as in the last example ? As 9.5 : 143.4 : : 66.25 : 1000. The number 1000, or one inch, is the diameter required for the wheel.

The diameter of a fusee great wheel of 60 teeth is 780, the second wheel pinion which it is to drive is 12: it is required to find the distance of their centres ? The wheel 60, and the pinion 12, added together, make 72, the half of which is 36; then as 62.25 : 780 : : 36 : 451, the distance between the centres, being 4.5 tenths of an inch, and $\frac{1}{1000}$ part of an inch more.

The diameter of a second wheel of 64 is 668, the pinion of the third wheel which it drives is 8 : Required the distance of their centres ? 64 + 8 = 72 ÷ 2 = 36. Then as 66.25 : 668 : : 36 : 363, the distance between the centres; being three-tenths of an inch, and $\frac{63}{1000}$ parts of an inch more.

Supposing the fusee great wheel to be lost, as also the second wheel pinion, having the distance of their centres, to find what should be the diameter of each, so as they may be made to pitch properly together at the given distance of their centres ? The distance given is 451, the great wheel is to have 60 teeth, and the second wheel pinion to be 12. To find the diameter of the great wheel, say, as 36 (which is the half of the sum of the wheel 60, and the pinion 12, added together,) is to 451, so is 62.25 to the diameter required.

```
36 : 451 :: 62.25 : x              36 : 451 :: 13.5 : x
        451                                13.5

       6225                               2255
      31125                               1353
      24900                                451

36)28074.75(780 Dia. of the wheel.  36)6088.5(169.1 Dia. of the pinion.
   252                                 36

    287                                248
    288                                216

                                       328
                                       324

                                        45
                                        36
```

A wheel of twice the diameter of another will contain twice the number of teeth, but the area of the circle will be four times that of the other, so that if the weight is eight ounces, that of the other will be two, both being supposed of equal thickness,—the circumferences of circles being to each other as their diameters, their areas as the squares of their diameters.

Although high numbers have been very properly and frequently recommended, yet there is a danger in carrying this too far, because they require to have the size or diameter of the pinions a little less, than to those where common numbers are used, as the smallest deviation or wearing of the holes will alter them considerably in their pitchings; and this is what we conceive must have led Berthoud at last to have the diameters of his pinions smaller than what the common rules give.

A sector, and a sector depthening tool, were made by Mr. Joseph Ridley, for which the Society for the Encouragement of Arts, Commerce, &c. voted him a premium of twenty guineas. See an account of them published in 1788, in the sixth volume of the Transactions of that Society, page 188, accompanied with two plates of the sectors.

The description which is given of them is not so complete as could have been wished, nor do they appear to be so convenient as the one made by Pennington, which serves both as a sector for taking the proportional sizes of wheels and pinions, and as a depthening tool. In this of Ridley's, we have to adjust the sector to the half sum of the number of teeth in the wheel and leaves in the pinion, and then bring two legs of the depthening tool to be adjusted to this place: this is requiring two sectors, when one could do the business equally well. It is objectionable also, by the steel pins or cylinders for marking off, standing in an angular position to one another,—one of them, a pumping one, is held up in a perpendicular position, when marking off by the other leg, which is a fixed one, and thereby is made to mark off in an oblique position. In Pennington's, the two marking legs, or cylindrical pins with conical points, stand at all times parallel to each other, and they will set off at any opening the true places of wheels and pinions.

The plain sliding scale is much preferable to either Pennington's or Ridleys, only it requires a little more calculation to be made when using it.

Some few years ago, we had seen it stated somewhere, (so far as we recollect,) that a sector pitching tool had been invented by M. Le Cerf, watch-maker in Geneva, and that a description of it was given in the 68th vol. of the Philosophical Transactions. Lately, on turning up this volume, we were much disappointed to find *no description*, although a paper was given in by the inventor to Lord Viscount Mahon, then residing at Geneva, along with the two instruments, requesting his Lordship to present them to the Royal Society of London. The paper is entitled, " A Description of the Instruments ;" yet in reality there is no description given of the instruments, although a long detail is given of their properties and various uses, whereby they can be applied to the properly sizing of wheels and pinions in watch-making, &c. As the Reverend Secretary of the Royal Society had got these instruments in 1778, with the *said description*, to present to that honourable and learned body, it is to be regretted that a drawing or engraving had not been taken of *them*, as then a description of them might have been given, (though not in the inventor's words,) which might have conveyed some idea of the mechanism or construction of these *machines*. This term is used by the inventor, as well as *instruments*. We are, however, humbly of opinion, that from what has been said of Pennington's sector, and also of the sliding scale, that they come as near to the purpose as those of M. Le Cerf. And taking sizes even by the teeth and spaces on a wheel, for the size of a pinion, every intelligent workman knows what allowances are to be made, according as the wheel is to give a more or less number of revolutions to the pinion.

CHAPTER VI.

On Pendulums; the influence of gravity on them at different parts of the Globe, compared with the influence of their suspension-springs by changes of temperature, &c. &c.

THE motion of the pendulum is intimately connected with the law of falling bodies. Early in the seventeenth century, Gallileo observed, that a body, when left by itself to fall, the spaces it descends in equal times will increase as the odd numbers, 1, 3, 5, 7, 9, &c., and, when thrown up by any force, the spaces gone through in ascending, decrease in the same way, nor will it begin to fall back till it has completed *one*, the last number in the decreasing progression. Suppose the line A E, Plate III. No. 12. to be a perpendicular height divided into 16 equal parts, each of which to represent a space, equal to that which a falling body goes through in the first second of time when descending. From experience and demonstration, this is found to be 16 feet 1 inch, and a small fraction of an inch more: taking it for such as measured from A to B; in the next second of time it falls from B to C, a space three times that of A B; in the third second, it falls from C to D, which is five times that of A B; and from D it falls to E, seven times the length of A B, in the fourth second of time. The square of the times is proportional to the spaces descended by a falling body; for example, in falling from A to E, the time was four seconds, and the space descended 257.438 feet, being the product of 16 feet 1 inch, and .079 of an inch, multiplied by 16, the square of the time of falling. From A to C it falls in two seconds, the square of which is 4, and $16_{1_1}^{1} \times 4$ = 64 feet 4 inches, the length of the space descended.

It can be shown, that the square of the diameter of a circle is to the square of its circumference, as the length of a pendulum is to double the height from which a body falls during the time of one of its vibrations. A pendulum which vibrates seconds, being in length

39.126 inches, it can thence be deduced from what height a heavy body will fall in one second of time. Let 113 be taken for the diameter, and 355 for the circumference of a circle; then, as the square of 113 is to the square of 355, so is 39.126 inches, the length of a second's pendulum, to 386.158 inches, the half of which is 193.079 inches, or 16 feet 1.079 inch, the space which a falling body will descend in one second of time. By taking 19.563 inches, the half of the length of the second's pendulum, the same result is more directly obtained; that is, as 12769 : 19.563 : : 126025 : 193.079 — 193.079 inches is the height from which a heavy body will descend (or fall through), in the time of one vibration of a seconds pendulum; the length of this pendulum may be found by the following proportion, as 126025 : 12769 : : 193.079 : 19.563, and twice 19.563 = 39.126 inches, the required length of the pendulum. If a pendulum makes two vibrations in the time that a heavy body takes to fall 193.079 inches, its length may be known as thus: The square of two is four, by which divide the length of the second's pendulum, and 9.78 inches is given for the length of the other pendulum. The second's pendulum being shorter at the equator than in the latitude of London, a heavy body there will fall through a less space in a second of time; at the pole it will fall through a greater space, the length of a second's pendulum being greater there. The force of gravity at the equator being to that at the pole, as 144 to 145. As they apply to this subject, the following are some particulars of an astronomical clock made by Geo. Graham, and sent in the year 1731 out to Black River, in the island of Jamaica, in the latitude of 18° north: The clock weight that keeps the pendulum in motion is 12 lbs. 10¼ oz. and is to be wound up once a month. The weight of the pendulum itself is 17 lbs.; and during the time that the clock was compared with the transits of the star Lucida Aquilæ, it vibrated each way from the perpendicular 1° 45′. The magnitude of the vibrations was estimated by means of a brass arch, which was fixed just under the lower end of the pendulum rod, and divided into degrees, &c. August 31st, Mr. Graham took off the weight belonging to the clock, and hung on another of 6 lbs. 3 oz., and with this weight the pendulum vibrated only 1° 15′ on each side, and the clock went slower 1¼ seconds in 24 hours, than when its own weight of 12 lbs. 10¼ oz. was hung on. On comparing the vibrations, it appears, that in one apparent revolution of the stars, the clock went 2 minutes, 6¹ seconds, slower in Jamaica than in London; deducting therefore 8¼ seconds, on account of the greater heat in Jamaica, there remains a difference of 1 minute 58 seconds, which must necessarily arise. Without entering into the dispute about the figure of the earth, Mr. Bradley at present supposes, with Sir Isaac Newton, that the increase of gravity, as we recede from the equator, is nearly as the square of the sine of the latitude, and that the difference in the length of pendulums is proportional to the augmentation or diminution of gravity.

On these suppositions, Mr. Bradley collects from the above mentioned observations, that if the length of a simple pendulum that swings seconds at London, be 39.126 English inches, the length of one at the equator would be 39.00, and at the poles 39.206. And abstracting from the alteration, on account of different degrees of heat, a pendulum clock, that would go true under the equator, will gain 3 minutes, 48¼ seconds in a day at the poles; but the number of seconds that it would gain in any other latitude would be, to 3 minutes, 48¼ seconds, nearly as the square of the sine of that latitude, to the square of the radius; whence it follows, that the number of seconds a clock will lose in a day, on its removal to a place nearer to the equator, will be, to 3 minutes 48¼ seconds nearly, as the difference of the squares of the sines of the respective latitudes is to the square of the radius; for example, the latitude of London is 51° 31′, the sine of which is 7828, and the latitude of Black River 18°, the sine of which is 3090,—the difference of the squares of these sines is .5173; then, as 1.000 : .5173 : : 3 minutes, 48¼ seconds : 1 minute 58 seconds,—the number of seconds that the clock lost in a day at Black River. See *Philosophical Transactions*, anno 1734, No. 432. A pendulum keeping mean time at the equator, will go faster as the degrees of latitude increase, as exhibited in the following

TABLE.

Latitude.	Seconds gained by a clock in a day.	Additional length required to correct the error in parts of an English inch.
5	1.7	0.0016
10	6.9	0.0062
20	26.7	0.0246
30	57.1	0.0516
45	114.1	0.1033
50	134.0	0.1212
55	150.2	0.1386
60	171.2	0.1549
75	213.0	0.1927
90	228.5	0.2065

The latitude of Edinburgh being 55° 56', the sine of which is .8284, and the square .6862, the difference of the squares of the sines of the latitudes of London and Edinburgh is .0735, giving 16.79 seconds that a clock would lose in a day, on being removed from Edinburgh to London. As 1 : 0735 : : 228.5 : 16.79.

The rule given here may be an approximation to the time that a clock ought to keep according to the latitude of the place. To show that it is only an approximation; two clocks, one of which kept siderial time, the other kept mean time, each with great exactness at Edinburgh in the year 1818, on being sent to London, every precaution was used, that nothing should tend to affect or alter the pendulums; the siderial clock lost about 18 seconds a day there, and the mean time clock lost about 21 seconds. It has been stated by some, that the gain at the Pole would be 5 minutes a day. Captain Phipps, in his voyage towards the North Pole in 1772, tried the going of a seconds pendulum, which had been long before that fitted up by Mr. George Graham to vibrate seconds in London, at the temperature of 60°. The trial was made on a rocky island in latitude 79° 50' north. And *this pendulum* was found to accelerate from 72 to 73 seconds a day. The difference of the squares of the sines is .3559, and by the rule gives 81.23 seconds that should have been the gain in a day.

Captain Kater, who is eminently qualified to make experiments with the pendulum, went for that purpose, in 1819, to Unst, one of the most northerly of the Shetland isles, in latitude 60° 44', where he found it to have 36 seconds of acceleration in a day, on the mean time which it kept at London.

The sine of 60° 44' is .8723, the square is .7609, the difference is .1482, and 228.5 × .1482 = 33.86 seconds.

$$228.5 \quad \log. \quad 2.3588862$$
$$.1482 \quad \log. \quad 9.1708482$$
$$33.86 \text{ seconds. } \log. \quad 1.5297344$$

On this subject there is a very able and ingenious paper by Captain Warren, given in the eleventh volume of the *Asiatic Researches*, which see.

It is well known, that if a body P (Plate III. No. 13.) in place of descending vertically, is made to roll down on an inclined plane P S, when it arrives at S, it will have acquired the same velocity as if it had fallen in the perpendicular line P R, but after a longer time, and if from the point R a line is drawn perpendicular to the inclined plane P S, the space P T will be that which the body P will roll down in the same time that it would have taken to fall down the line P R.

In a semi-circle, such as A G C, No. 14. if from a point G or *g* wherever placed in the circumference, lines A G and G C, or A *g* and *g* C, are drawn from the extremities of the diameter A C, a body falling from A to G on the inclined plane A G, or from G to C on the inclined plane G C, will fall always exactly in the same space of time that it would have taken to fall along the vertical line or diameter A C; the same will be the case on the lines A *g* and *g* C.

The simple pendulum C M, No. 15. in its state of rest, takes the vertical line C E, because it cannot fall below the point E; when drawn aside from E to M it will be raised up to a height equal to H I, F M, or E D, called the versed sine of the arc E M; falling then from M to E, it will accelerate its motion according to the observed law of falling bodies; arriving at E, it will have acquired a velocity capable of raising it to the same height, it will then go as far as I, and will describe the arc E I; these two arcs, or two half oscillations, form one oscillation, or one whole vibration.

If the vibrations are very great, they will not be isochronal, that is, they will not be performed in equal times, should they be a little enlarged or diminished: for the oscillation which shall begin at K will be sooner completed, than that which shall begin at M, the arc being longer, more time will be required to describe it. But if the vibrations are very short, such as one or two degrees, the arcs will be almost equal to their chords, which must be easily seen. The chords G C, *g* C, No. 14. are always fallen through in equal times, and so will be their arcs, at least they will be somewhat very near to it.

A simple pendulum is understood to be a heavy body, conceived to be in one fixed point, M, No. 15. and suspended to a point C by an inflexible line C M, supposed to be without weight, and without resistance, either from the point of suspension C, or from the volume of the air through which it vibrates. The compound pendulum is that, where several bodies are considered to be fixed on the line C M; if, for example, in place of supposing the mass of the body M to be wholly in one point M, we suspend a heavy ball, whose semi-diameter is M G, or that the line C G has itself a certain weight, or that there are two weights A C, on the line S C, as in No. 16, the pendulum will be a compound one, because its weight is no longer in one point, but is found distributed on different parts of the rod, or on the diameter of the ball.

Although a simple pendulum, *(like mathematical lines and points may be defined,)* yet no such thing can exist in nature; on the contrary, all pendulums that are made use of, have a weight distributed on different points of their length; yet in calculation it becomes requisite to reduce them to the *simple kind*. The nearest approximation to it may be a small ball of lead, gold, or platinum, suspended by a thread of the finest silk, or by a filament of a species of aloe, which is extremely light, and not affected by drought or moisture. Suppose a pendulum S C loaded, not only with one weight, but with two, (or a greater number,) such as A and C, so that each of these weights is considered as reduced to a point; it may easily be seen, that this new pendulum will make its vibrations faster, than if it had only the weight C, because the weight at A tends to make its vibrations with the same precipitation as if the pendulum had only the length S A, which is much shorter; and it, on the other hand, is in part retarded by the weight C, which cannot make its vibrations, but with the slowness that the long pendulum S C requires; thus the compound pendulum will neither be isochrone with the pendulum S C, loaded with the weight C, nor with the pendulum S A, loaded with the weight A, and its velocity will hold a mean between both, and will be isochrone only with another simple pendulum S D, whose length must be sought.

The point D is called the centre of oscillation, or centre of percussion of the compound pendulum; thus the centre of oscillation D is the point where all the weight of the body which oscillates might be brought, without changing the time of the vibrations. It is also called the centre of percussion, because it is the point where the whole effort combines, where the percussion must be the strongest, and where all the parts would remain in equilibrium, if the pendulum should be stopped at this point; supposing that the point of suspension produced no resistance, and became free at the moment of percussion. As the weights A C are combined together, and cannot move one without the other, it follows that each of the weights will distribute its effort, and will communicate it to all the others in proportion to their mass, and to their distance from the point of suspension S. Thus the velocity of the entire body will keep a mean, between the velocities that the different parts would effect separately; consequently there will result from it a common effort, that will maintain the mean between all the others, and this effort will be exerted at the point D, as their common centre; so that, in any other point that should be higher up, the upper parts would act more than the under ones, and in any other point that should be below the centre of oscillation, the under parts C would act more than the former; the centre of oscillation is then the only point on which all the parts act equally, during the vibration of the pendulum, when going to mean time. And, therefore, to find the centre of oscillation

D, multiply each of the weights by the square of its distance from the point S, add all these products together, and also the products of each of the weights by their distance from the point S, and divide the first sum of the products by this new sum, the quotient will be the length sought S D. Suppose the length of the pendulum rod from S to the point C, 42 inches, and to the point A, 36 inches, the weights A and C 8 lb. each. Finding the length S D by this rule, it will be given a little more than 39.2 inches. The more elaborate calculations for this purpose, known only to those who have practised in the higher branches of mathematics, come not within the plan proposed for this work.

$$42 \times 42 \times 8 = 14112$$
$$36 \times 36 \times 8 = 10368$$

$$42 \times 8 = 336$$
$$36 \times 8 = 288$$

624)24480(39.2,$\frac{4}{7}$ inches.   624

It is well known that a clock, when going either too fast or too slow, is corrected by the letting down or raising up the ball of the pendulum, or, in common language, by the lengthening or shortening of the pendulum. At the time of this operation, few of the practical artists ever think of the determined or fixed point of the centre of oscillation, where mean time can only be produced; and touching the pendulum in this way, is actually no more than to arrange or bring all the parts which form its mass, to combine their efforts at this point, (or centre of oscillation,) so as to give the time required.

To mathematicians it is known, that the centre of gravity in a pendulum must be above the centre of oscillation, the latter being a fixed point, the other not so; but in common, both are above the centre of the ball; yet pendulums having a small or slender rod of metal, such as brass or iron, or of wood, like what is used in ordinary clocks, will come very near the clock-maker's purpose, when making his pendulum to a length, by setting off the centre of oscillation, then bringing near to it the centre of gravity. For this purpose the pendulum is laid across an edge, the edge of a knife for example, in order to bring it more readily to an equilibrium, which is done by means of the regulating nut and screw, setting the ball more or less distant from the edge; this determines the point or centre of gravity. The pendulum ball may thus be brought so near to its place, that when regulating the clock, little more will be afterwards required, as it will be found going at or very near to time. Were these things attended to, pendulums would be better formed, and much time saved.

The centre of oscillation is understood here, to be a point on the seconds pendulum rod or ball, measured off at 39.2 inches from the point of suspension, (or rather 39.126 inches, but the former is perhaps easier, and any of them is near enough for the purpose,) or from that point where the pendulum spring bends when the pendulum vibrates. With pendulums having heavy balls and compound rods, such as the Gridiron, or zinc tube pendulums, or even the mercurial one, with its slender rod, it becomes a very intricate calculation in the science of Dynamics, for which few are competent, to get the exact place or point for the ball, or that of the centre of gravity for the pendulum, as shall co-operate with the centre of oscillation; various and minute circumstances will contribute greatly to affect the relative situation of these points, and none more so than that of the pendulum spring, according to its strength or thickness; as will afterwards be shown.

On this subject, see *Montucla's Histoire des Mathématiques, tome second. Article III. p. 421.* The preceding was, however, written before we had an opportunity of seeing Montucla.

What the relative situation of these centres were in some of our pendulums, shall now be stated for the information of those who may take an interest in a subject so curious as this is.

A wooden rod pendulum, weighing 10 lbs. 10¼ oz. of which the ball was 10 lbs. the centre of gravity was .8 of an inch above the centre of the ball, and .7 of an inch above the centre of oscillation. Another pendulum of the same kind, the ball of which weighed 7 lbs. 13¼ oz. the rod, regulating nut, steel wires, brass mounting, and pendulum spring, 11¼ oz.; the centre of gravity was above the centre of the ball 1.5 inch, and above the centre of oscillation 1.35 inch. One of this sort, whose ball, regulating nut, and socket, weighed 9 lb. 2¼ oz.; the wooden rod, with the regulating screw fixed on it, the brass mounting on it, pendulum spring and top piece, 6 oz. 2 drs.; in all, 9 lbs. 8.875 oz., the thickness of the pendulum spring .006 of an inch, the centres of the ball, and that of oscillation nearly coincided at 39.2 inches, the centre of gravity was about .8 of an inch, or a very little higher *above them.*

A gridiron pendulum, the ball of which weighed 16 lbs. 3¼ oz., and in all, with the rods, 19 lbs. 9¼ oz. The centre of gravity was 4.75 inches above the centre of the ball, and 2.42 inches above the centre of oscillation. Another pendulum of this sort, the ball weighed 10 lbs. 8 oz., and the rods, &c. 5 lbs. 13 oz., the whole 16 lbs. 5 oz. The centre of gravity in it 7 inches above the centre of the ball, and 4 inches above the centre of oscillation. A zinc tube pendulum weighed 21 lbs. 15 oz., of which the ball was 18 lbs. 7¼ oz. The centre of gravity above the centre of the ball about 2.63 inches, and above the centre of oscillation 1.53 inch. A pendulum after *Ward's* plan, the zinc and steel bars, &c. weighed 2 lbs. 13¼ oz., the ball 12 lbs. 13 oz., in all 15 lbs. 10¼ oz. The centre of oscillation was above the centre of the ball 1.55 inch; the centre of gravity had been omitted to be taken.

A mercurial pendulum, which weighed in all about 14 lbs. 2 oz.; the centre of oscillation in it was 4.75 inches above the sole of the jar; the column of mercury was about 6.75 inches, of which near to four inches were below that centre.

Peter Le Roy thought it possible that the pendulum spring of a clock might be so formed, that the long and the short vibrations should be performed in equal times. See his *Memoire*, page 15, at the end of " *Voyage fait par Ordre du Roi, en* 1768, *pour eprouver les Montres Marines, inventées par M. Le Roy, Paris,* 1770." This is exactly what was suggested *long* ago by our countryman John Smith, C.M. See his *Horological Disquisitions*, p. 48. London, 1694. Berthoud appears to have sometime afterwards taken up the same opinion. In his *Supplément au Traité des Montres a Longitude*, Paris, 1807, he says, p. 38, " *Nous terminerons ces Notes en observant que la suspension à resort bien construite tend à rendre isochrones les oscillations de pendule.*"

We are humbly of opinion that this is not to be obtained by means of the pendulum spring, unless the pendulum is made to vibrate larger arcs than would be consistent with good time-keeping. But, by endeavouring to obtain isochronism in the way alluded to, it may be asked, whether the pendulum should be left in any degree under the influence of the pendulum spring, which in this case would of course take away somewhat of that influence which gravity must naturally have on the pendulum ball; or by keeping the pendulum spring no stronger than is requisite to sustain the pendulum properly, and to allow gravity to have its influence as freely and independently as possible, seems to be a question that appears should be decided in favour of allowing gravity to exert its utmost influence and force. This conclusion is founded on an experiment which we made a few years ago with a wooden rod pendulum, the ball of which weighed ten pounds, the pendulum spring was about .016 parts of an inch thick, three quarters of an inch long, and nearly half an inch broad. This pendulum, previous to the said spring being applied to it, had one which was a little thinner, and much about the same length and breadth, and with it, had been going for some time at a clock, which, after being regulated, kept very close, and extremely near mean time. The clock 'scapement was of the spring pallet kind, the same as represented in Plate VI. No. 35. During the time that the motion of the pendulum was kept up with the clock by the force of the pallet springs, the arc of vibration described on each side the point of rest, was very little more than two degrees. The pendulum remaining in its place, having the same length as before, (and the clock with its 'scapement being detached from it,) was then made to vibrate an arc of two degrees and a half on each side the point of rest, in eight minutes it lost one second; and on being made to describe an arc of one degree and twenty minutes on each side, it lost also one second in the same space of time: one second in eight minutes, would, in twenty-four hours, be equal to 180 seconds, or three minutes, slower (in that state of the pendulum) than when connected with the clock and 'scapement. Had the pendulum spring been made thinner, or of such a strength as properly to support the pendulum and a little more, the arc of vibration would have been greater, when the pendulum was impelled by the 'scapement or pallet springs, consequently, from the greater extent of the arc of vibration, the clock would go slow; to correct which, the ball* would require setting up: Hence the time in the detached state, and that when connected with the 'scapement, would have been more nearly equal, from which it appears that the pendulum should be more under the influence of gravitation, and less under that of the pendulum spring. When the thicker spring was put to the pendulum, the influence of it was such, that before the clock could be brought to time, the pendulum ball was obliged to be let down about an inch. There are some 'scapements which have a tendency to retard the vibrations of the pendulum, others to accelerate them; a moderate recoil, or a dead beat, are of the first sort; those which are composed of springs, or which have a considerable recoil, are of the last. It would be a good criterion of a clock and its 'scapement, if the pendulum, when tried in the detached state, should perform its vibrations in the same time as when attached to the clock; but it is a painful and tedious task to count the vibrations of a detached pendulum for an hour or two, and any artificial mode of ascertaining the number might ultimately prove an *unfair trial.* Calculation for the length of pendulums being founded on their vibrations, as exhibited in their most *simple state*, when strong springs

---

* Ball, or Bob, of a pendulum, is a general name for the mass or weight applied near to the lower end of the rod, without any regard to the figure, which is commonly lenticular; it may be globular, conical, two frustrums of cones, &c. &c.

are put to them, so much additional length of rod is required, that the clock-maker is often surprised, and put to some trouble, by the unforeseen consequences that result from them.

Berthoud made some experiments to see whether the knife pivot, or spring suspended pendulums in a detached state, would longest maintain their vibrations, and found them in favour of the former: hence he concluded that the edge or knife pivot was the better suspension; but this was not a fair inference, at least it was not an inference that perhaps time would have warranted. In time, the friction of the knife pivot gets so much increased by its wearing, and that of the groove in which it acts, particularly if the ball should be heavy, and the semi-arc of vibration more than a degree, or if even so much, that the former superiority of the knife pivot over that of the spring would soon be at an end. He did not afterwards acknowledge this openly, but his tacit acknowledgment is sufficiently strong, by adopting at last the pendulum spring as the better suspension, and Harrison's gridiron pendulum as the best mode of compensation. It must be observed, that Berthoud had compensation pendulums fitted up in various ways, some of them nearly like to that of Harrison's. Since these experiments of Berthoud's were made, a very beautiful contrivance has been adopted with the knife pivot, which is, by making the groove look downward, and the edge upward; this prevents dust, when falling, from lodging or getting to the inside of the groove.

It has been said by some ingenious philosophers, that the motion of a pendulum must be affected by different densities of the atmosphere, which certainly is a circumstance very reasonable to suppose, and future experience or observations may yet be brought forward to show the result or the effects of these on the pendulum. Indeed, this has already in some measure been done by Mr. Rittonhouse, an eminent Swiss residing in America, who says, " that a change in the barometer, from 28 to 31 inches, will make an alteration in the going of a good astronomical clock, to the amount of half a second in a day," an error or change of rate that cannot be called great, considering that the whole range of the barometer is required to produce it: therefore, any partial change, even that of an inch, we may suppose, cannot greatly alter the rate of the clock. To compensate these effects would be a very difficult matter, in whatever way it may be done, whether by the pendulum, or any sort of mechanism put to the 'scapement, because any difference in the extent of the arcs of vibration, arising solely from this cause, must nevertheless be extremely small, at least so we suspect; and this is greatly confirmed by the small difference that there is between the length of a pendulum vibrating seconds in vacuo and in common air, as late experiments

make the length of a pendulum vibrating seconds *in vacuo* in the
latitude of London to be - - - - - 39.1386 inches
Desagulier states the length of a seconds pendulum 39.128
Others have it - - - - - - 39.126
By trials at Edinburgh to get the length, we made it 39.192
In our calculations it was generally taken at - - 39.2
For the clock-maker's purpose, any of the lengths may be taken, and the results cannot materially differ.

Mr. Rittenhouse's contrivance for correcting the error caused by the different densities of the air, is a large, hollow, and light ball, placed on the upper end of the pendulum rod, in an opposite direction to that of the pendulum ball; of this we can say nothing, having had no experience of it. There are other causes which affect the extent of the arcs of vibration, of a more powerful nature than that of changes in the densities of the atmosphere, and these are, cold in winter, and heat in summer, which will operate on the pendulum spring in such a manner that the vibrations in summer will be longer than those in winter, making a difference perhaps of three or four minutes, or more, of a degree. Any changes, *however small*, on the strength of the pendulum spring, will be easily perceived on the extent of the arcs of vibration, whether arising from different temperatures or different thicknesses. Cold in winter will stiffen it or make it more rigid, and summer's heat will relax it. The same causes ought, and must inevitably produce the same effect on the pallet springs, but the body or mass of the pendulum spring being so much greater than that of the pallet springs, the impression or effect of heat and cold on *it*, is in a much greater ratio than it is on *them*. And this ratio will increase according to the thickness of the pendulum spring. The short arcs in winter must be attributed to the increased tensity of the pendulum spring from cold, and, when relaxed by the heat in summer, allows the pendulum to vibrate to a greater extent. A clock having the spring pallet 'scapement, or any 'scapement with a spring suspended pendulum; compensation pendulums for such, must be made not only to correct the lengthening or shortening of the rod from changes of temperature, but the compensation must be made so much in excess, as to correct the long vibrations of summer, and the short ones of winter.[*]

If, in place of a pendulum spring, we adopt the knife edge[†] for

---

[*] As platinum is less affected by changes of temperature than steel, it might be an improvement to have the suspension spring of that metal.

[†] Knife-edge implies a sharp instrument, but is here merely a technical term: when used to carry a heavy pendulum, it is formed like a short wedge with a long edge, the sharp angle of which is rounded off a little, or blunted in a small degree.

the pendulum to vibrate on, it will not have the same causes of error from changes of temperature which took place with the pendulum spring, but there still must be a small difference in the arcs of vibration, arising from the effects of heat and cold on the pallet springs, and which will be shown in a contrary way to those where a pendulum spring is used: nothing but heat and cold can operate on the length of the rod of a pendulum vibrating on an edge, yet the cold in winter will make the pallet springs a little stiffer; by this they will act more forcibly on the pendulum, and cause it to vibrate a little more out. On the other hand, the heat in summer will relax them, which consequently will lessen the arc of vibration. In the case of the spring suspended pendulum, the compensation was required to be in excess, as has already been mentioned; and in this of the pendulum acting on an edge, the compensation for heat and cold on the pendulum rod must be made a little deficient, the increased length of the arc in winter, and the decreased arc in summer, supplying what is wanted in the compensation. It would be a very difficult matter to determine that strength of pendulum spring which would support a pendulum properly; the strength should in some degree be proportionable to the weight of the ball, because, if they are too thin, and on getting a little relaxed by heat, the weight of the ball may be so great as to oppose the spring contracting on a return of cold; if they are too thick, then the bad consequences which have been previously shown will ensue. Yet there are artists who have said, that a pendulum spring might be made as thick as the twentieth part of an inch, or more, if you will; there was certainly no knowledge of the subject displayed in saying so. When the weight of a pendulum ball runs from ten to twenty pounds, the thickness of the pendulum spring may go from .008 to .016 parts of an inch; not that these are fixed points, and are by no means given here as such, but they are nearly about the thickness of those pendulum springs which we have been in the practice of making use of. It is a curious enough circumstance, that when a pendulum spring is polished down to any gage for its thickness, it will not go into the gage after being blued, getting on it, by this process, a coat of enamel, which adds both to its thickness and elasticity. It is well known to watch-makers, that after watch pendulum springs are blued, their elasticity is so much increased, that watches, when going at time with them in the white state, are now found to go much faster than before: there is no doubt a considerable difference in the time kept, would be seen between the white and blue state by such a change in the pendulum spring of a clock, was the experiment properly tried.

M. Le Roy, in his *Memoire*, which has been already quoted, mentions an experiment he made with a spring fitted up expressly for the purpose of seeing the effects of change of temperature, which he placed in a horizontal position : one end being fixed, on the other a weight was suspended, which fell or rose from the spring getting heat or cold, and the changes of temperature were seen and pointed out by a long index on a graduated arch ; for the first six months the changes were obvious, and became afterwards gradually less so ; the weight during cold being up a little way, then, on applying some degree of heat to the spring, the weight came down, and did not again return to its former position ; perhaps the heat applied may have been greater than the heat of our atmosphere in the warmest summer. This experiment, however, serves little for the purpose of clock pendulum springs, the circumstances being no way similar.

Having shown that the effects of temperature on spring pallets, and on the pendulum spring, may be compensated by an excess of compensation in the pendulum rod ; yet should this, to some, be unsatisfactory, other means shall be pointed out, where changes of temperature can have no place except on the pendulum rod. In those 'scapements, such as the common recoil, or dead beat, where the pendulums are suspended by a spring, still the effects of the change of temperature will take place on the pendulum spring, though this change does not appear to have been observed ; where a compensation pendulum is used, these changes might have been either compensated or overlooked, or the effects of them so little, that they could not be well ascertained.

Let then a pendulum be suspended, so as to act smoothly and freely with a groove, moveable upon a well-finished and fixed edge, the groove being uppermost, and in place of spring pallets to have small balls, that shall, *as in Mr. Cumming's way*, be impelled by *gravity alone* when giving impulse to the pendulum, *which* in the same latitude must constantly have the same force, and cannot be influenced by any change of temperature, (any influence on the arms of the balls is too trifling to take into account,) consequently, whatever errors were attributed to the clock, arising from changes of temperature on the spring pallets, and on the pendulum spring, would be completely done away by adopting the knife pivot, and making use of gravity to keep up the motion of the pendulum.

But it is very doubtful, if greater errors might not come in, and take place of the former, (nay, it is even probable they may,) arising from the friction, and wearing of the edge and the groove, and also from the slow progress or motion of the balls when falling ; or when raised, the swing wheel could not be so safely locked with a nib, or detent of that shortness which the spring pallets will allow; and, at all events, it would be requisite that the arc of vibration of the pendulum should be very limited, in order to lessen as much as possible the friction and wearing of the edge and groove; forty-five minutes of a degree on each side the point of rest, would perhaps be as much as the pendulum could be allowed to vibrate, and this might be even too much, if the ball was of a considerable weight.

Mr. Cumming, in his 'scapement, has the force of gravity applied directly to the regulator, or pendulum itself.* The balls where this force is generated, are raised up by the swing wheel teeth. When doing so, they raise the balls at once nearly up to their maximum of height, and at the time of unlocking, the force of the pendulum is so much gone, that little more is left than barely to unlock the wheel, any height given beyond that to which the wheel raised them being extremely trifling. In place of doing so, and although we propose likewise that the swing wheel teeth shall raise up the balls, yet our unlocking is to take place at a time when the force of the pendulum is at its greatest, which by this means will carry the balls on to a height still greater than that to which the wheel teeth had raised them, and *they will*, on the return of the pendulum, impel it with a *force* derived jointly from that of the pendulum itself, and from the swing wheel. A small number of grains, Troy, at any of the points of the swing wheel teeth, when in a horizontal position, would hold the wheel in equipoise, but the number will depend on the length of time the clock is made to go without requiring to be wound up. A very small force then appears to be sufficient to keep a pendulous body in motion when once put into it, but to bring it aside from a state of rest into this, requires comparatively a great force, which must at first be applied, as no clock can of itself begin, or give motion to, or set its pendulum a-going. In place of the balls being on projecting arms, let them be placed immediately behind the pallets; it is presumed that this will make the locking safe, and with detent nibs rather short as otherwise. The common arbors of the pallets and detents, though concentric with the verge pivots, and with the motion of the crutch and anchor, have *their* pivots to run in small cocks, which are fixed to strong ones, such as what the spring pallets were fixed to; by this means, the pressure of the swing wheel teeth on the detents, will have no *interference* with the motion of the verge

---

* The force of gravity, as well as of springs, was very early used in clocks, by way of an auxiliary to the 'scapement, but not in so direct a way as has since been done. This piece of mechanism is by some called a *Remontoir*.

and pendulum during the interval of rest, as is the case in Mr. Cumming's plan, which, however small or great the resistance may be arising from it, is here removed: a drawing, and a more detailed description of this 'scapement, will afterwards be given. Now, the whole of what has been pointed out, we are humbly of opinion, appears to be an improved kind of 'scapement, where the gravity of balls are to keep up the motion of the pendulum.

Although it has been proposed to remove the objections that may be made to the pendulum spring, and the pallet springs of a clock, by adopting the mode of making the pendulum to vibrate on an edge, this end may likewise be attained, by making the pendulum to vibrate on and between friction rollers, which is perhaps the preferable way of the two. Suppose two large rollers to be fixed on a strong steel arbor, the distance between them one inch, the large one three inches in diameter, thickness one quarter of an inch, two of which are fixed on the same arbor, placed about an inch from each other, that is, the space between them one inch; two arbors are run in the same frame, with that of the arbor of the large rollers, each of these arbors have also two rollers fixed on them, the diameters, two inches, and thickness two tenths of an inch, placed at such a distance from each other as to go outside of the large rollers, and all of them to have at the same time proper freedom. In a line perpendicularly up from the centre of the large rollers, the pivots of a strong and thick steel arbor, lie across on their edges, and the centre of the small rollers being placed in a line horizontal to the upper edge of the large rollers, or rather to that of the centre of the pivots of the strong arbor, the pivots of the strong arbor are kept to their places by means of the edges of the small rollers. Projecting from the middle of the strong arbor, and at right angles to it, are fixed two stout pivots, over which the upper end of the pendulum road, formed into two kinds of eyes or hooks, is hung, and when the pendulum vibrates, the pivots of the strong arbor move on the edges of the large rollers, and between the edges of the small ones; so that, by them, any resistance to the motion of the pendulum may easily be conceived to be done away, or at least, very much reduced. In the edges of the large rollers, a segment may be taken out for one eight part of the circumference, and hard pieces of stone, fitted in and formed into the same circle; on these, the pivots of the strong arbor turn, all the rollers may be crossed out, so as to be as light as possible, and yet have strength enough; the segment, where the stones are set, should be kept solid into the centre, and banking put in to prevent the rollers getting farther, so that some part of the stones shall always be under the pivots which lie across them; near to the ends of these pivots, cocks should be fixed, between which they should have freedom to move, and no more. In a line with the pivots on which the pendulum hangs, brass cocks should be fixed on the frame which contains the rollers: into these cocks run the pivots formed each at the end of strong screws, put into strong iron cocks, fixed to the iron bracket which supports the clock: it is on these screw pivots that the frame and rollers will freely turn, allowing the pendulum to hang freely, easily, and perpendicularly down. The brass cocks may be kneed and so formed, as to serve as pillars to the upper end of the roller frame; two common pillars being at the lower angles.

Length of pendulum is of advantage to the time keeping of a clock; a half seconds pendulum can never be equal to that whose vibrations are made in a second, nor will the seconds pendulum be equal to that which makes a vibration in two seconds, *particularly in turret clocks*. Hindley of York had pendulums put to some of his turret clocks, which gave a vibration only once in four seconds; but such a pendulum requiring a length of fifty-two feet, three inches, and two tenths of an inch, is not an easy matter to fit up; it will either be too flexible in the rod, or, if it is made stiff enough, it will be heavier than what the strongest or largest turret clock, that has hitherto been made, is well calculated to carry; but where ingenuity is exerted in constructing a pendulum of this length, it will have a *prodigious dominion* over the clock. Having never seen or met with a spring clock, where advantage was taken to have such a length of pendulum as the case would have admitted, showed, that either the value of length was not understood by clock-makers, or that the method was not known of computing numbers for the teeth of wheels and pinions, so as to give such a number of vibrations as to answer for that length of pendulum, which would have suited the case in which the spring clocks were fitted; hence, we are led to infer, that neither were known to them. The method of computation has already been shewn, the other will be so in the sequel.

The pendulum of a regulator, or astronomical clock, ought to swing in as free or open space as can, with propriety, be taken within the case. Cases are, in general, too confined, and when the weight comes down opposite to the pendulum ball, the vibratory motion it has, gives agitation to the air between it and the weight, which must influence the vibrations more or less, consequently must affect the time-keeping. In order to get the weight as much to a side as possible, let the great wheel be pretty large in diameter, and the centre of it on a line horizontal to the centre of the dial, the pulley for the weight should be large in diameter also, which will have the effect of leading the weight more to one side of the case. Where there are two wheels from or between the centre of the dial and that of the great wheel or barrel, they will allow a greater scope for this purpose, than where there is only one wheel. These are circumstances which have hitherto been unnoticed by clock-makers, and yet when they are pointed out, nothing can be more simple and obvious. The body of the case should be both wide and deep, not less than 14 inches wide, and 8 inches deep, inside measure ; a little more may still be better, and the pendulum hung in the middle of the space between the back of the case, and that side of the weight nearest to the pendulum ball ; perhaps openings made in the sides of the case opposite to the edges of the pendulum ball, and covered over outside with neat circular pieces of wood, would give additional freedom to the air.

A considerable part of the length of the fall for a clock weight, was commonly lost by our clock-makers, by making the pulley strap much longer than was necessary, to which was put a hook too long also ; to some of the clocks we have made, such defects as these were completely done away, in the method we took with pullies and weights.

To lead the going weight, as much as possible, to one side, might be done, so as to get 3 or 4 inches more of fall, which would be gaining something two ways, that is, more length of fall, and taking the weight at the same time out of the way of disturbing the pendulum ball. Let two rollers, or pullies, be put into a brass kind of frame, run apart, or at such a distance from each other as may be thought proper, the weight being hung at equal distances from the centre of the pullies, whose diameters may be one inch, or one inch and a quarter, or, in short, whatever diameter the artist may choose to give. To an arbor, whose pivots run in the frame, is fixed a kind of swivel, which comes no lower down than just to allow the barrel cord to pass freely through it. The frame may be composed of two bars of brass, about 5 or 6 inches long, three quarters of an inch broad, and a little more than one-eighth of an inch thick ; the ends of the bars are screwed to double kneed pieces of brass, an inch in height or thereabouts, by way of pillars, to keep the frame together. The clock-case will require to be a little wider than ordinary, to admit a pulley-frame of this kind, if 6 inches in length. In Plate VII. No. 41, a double pulley, like what has been proposed, is represented ; it will easily be seen how the barrel cord is applied, by referring to the letters a, b, c.

To show that room in the inside of a case is so necessary for a pendulum to swing through, we shall give a detail of an experiment made for this purpose. A clock with a spring pallet 'scapement, and zinc tube compensation pendulum, after being brought to mean time, the accumulated gain in 44 days, viz. from the 16th February to the 1st of April, 1819, amounted to one second only, and with little or no greater deviation in the interim; after this, it gained one second a day, and sometimes less. Suspecting that the pendulum ball might not have sufficient room, (what it had was, nevertheless, fully more than usual,) there was a piece taken out of the back of the case behind the pendulum ball, and from the sides opposite to the edges of the ball. The clock, when again set agoing, on the 24th of April, had the semi-arc of vibration of the pendulum increased 25', that is, from 1 12', the former arc to 1° 37' on each side of Zero, and from this circumstance alone, the clock ought to have gone much slower; whereas, it gained at the rate of 42 seconds a day, which showed the great liberty that the pendulum had acquired when swinging in less confined air. This is a thing we suppose nobody has hitherto seen or suspected, and becomes a very nice and valuable experiment, so far as regards the fitting up clocks for astronomical purposes. The edges of the openings made on the back and sides of the case, not being, as we thought, properly chamfered or shelved off, on this being afterwards done, it gave the air more freedom to pass readily over them, and the pendulum increased its semi-arc of vibration a little more, and swung out now to 1° 45'. The angle of 'scapement being 21' or 22'. A pendulum, swinging with a greater degree of freedom than before, ought to be less affected by the different densities of the atmosphere.

Many years ago, we gave an opinion to one or two, who were considered ingenious in the profession, that the balances of watches and chronometers, were made to vibrate in a too confined space: this they seemed to consider as a thing more imaginary than real. The experiment just now mentioned, with the freedom given, and the consequences it had on the pendulum, goes, however, a great way to corroborate this opinion. To make such experiments with watches or chronometers, would come to be so great an expense, both of time and money, that, probably, they never will be tried.

CHAPTER VII.

Having the length of a Pendulum, to find the number of vibrations it must make in an hour; and, vice versa, knowing the number of vibrations that a Pendulum makes in an hour, to find its length, &c. &c.

" IT is known that pendulums which describe any arc whatever, give their vibrations in the times which are to one another, as the square roots of the lengths of these pendulums, and that the lengths of pendulums are to one another as the squares of the times of vibration in each, and the longer a pendulum is, the more time it will take to give its vibrations; so that, if the lengths of two pendulums are to one another as *four is to one*, the times of their vibrations will be as *two is to one*, the square roots of their lengths; from whence it follows, that in the time the pendulum *four* makes one vibration, the pendulum *one* will make *two*. It also follows, that, if these pendulums vibrate during a certain time, the number of vibrations will be to one another as *one is to two*; that is, reciprocally as the square roots of their lengths. The lengths of two pendulums are reciprocally to one another, as the squares of the numbers of vibrations made in the same time. If then, the number of vibrations that a pendulum makes in a given time is known, and the length of the pendulum, we can deduce the length of any other pendulum if the number of vibrations which it must give in a certain time is known; and reciprocally the length of a pendulum being given, we can find the number of vibrations which it must give in a certain time.

To find the length of a pendulum, according to a given number of vibrations.

Rule.—Multiply the number of vibrations made in a minute by the standard, or second's pendulum, (viz. 60,) by itself, which is squaring it, and this being multiplied by the standard length of 39.2 inches, and the last product divided by the square of the number of vibrations given in a minute, by the pendulum whose length is required, the quotient will be the length of that pendulum, in inches and decimal parts of an inch.

FINDING LENGTH OF PENDULUM.

Example.—To find the length of a pendulum which shall make 120 vibrations in a minute.

```
   120            60
   120            60
  ─────         ─────
 14400 : 39.2 : : 3600
            3600
         ───────
         235200
          1176
         ───────
14400)141120.0(9.8 inches, the length of the pendulum which was
      129600              required.
      ───────
      115200
      115200
      ───────
```

The times of the vibrations of pendulums are in the direct ratio of the square roots of their lengths, and the number of vibrations made in a given time, are in the inverse ratio of the square roots of their lengths.

```
Vib.    Vib.    In.     In.
120² :  60² : : 39.2 : 9.8   direct ratio.
60²  : 39.2 : : 120² : 9.8   inverse ratio.
In.     In.     Vib.         Vib.
9.8  : 39.2 : : 60²  : 14400 | 120.
```

As the product 141120.0 is that which arises from the square of 60, the number of vibrations given in a minute, multiplied by 39.2 inches, the length of the standard pendulum, it will be unnecessary, in any future examples, to make the multiplication,—it will be enough to divide this number by the square of the given number of vibrations in a minute, to obtain the length of any pendulum required. We may take an example or two more, in order to make the rule as obvious as possible to those who may have had but little practice with figures.

It is required to have the length of a pendulum whose vibrations shall be 30 in a minute?

FINDING LENGTH OF PENDULUM.

```
    30
    30
    ─────
              Inches.    Feet.   Inches.
900)141120.0(156.8, or 13 - 0.8, the length of the pendulum required.
    900
    ─────
    5112
    4500
    ─────
     6120
     5400
     ─────
      7200
      7200
```

Let the vibrations be 80 in a minute, what is the length of the pendulum?

```
    80
    80
    ─────
              Inches.    Feet.   Inches.
6400)141120.0(22.05, or 1 - 10 5/100, the length required.
     12800
     ─────
     13120
     12800
     ─────
       32000
       32000
```

Vibrations 100 in a minute.	Vibrations 140 in a minute.
100	140
─────	─────
10000)141120.0(14.112 in.	5600
10000	140
─────	─────
41120	19600)141120.0(7.2 in.
40000	137200
─────	─────
11200	39200
10000	39200
─────	─────
12000	
10000	
─────	
20000	
20000	

Having the length of a pendulum,—to find the number of vibrations it will give in a minute.

FINDING NUMBER OF VIBRATIONS.

Rule.—Divide the constant number 141120.0 by the length of the given pendulum, the square root extracted from the quotient will be the number of vibrations in a minute.

Example.—The length of the pendulum given is 6.272 inches: Required the number of vibrations it must give in a minute?

```
Inches.
6.272)141120.000(22500        1|22.500(150 the number of vi-
       12544         •         1|1           brations in a mi-
       ─────                   ─────          nute required.
       15680                   25|125
       12544                   5|125
       ─────                   ─────
       31360                   30|000
       31360
       ─────
         000
```

The length of a pendulum being 156.8 inches: Required the number of vibrations it will give in a minute?

```
156.8)141120.0(900(30, the number of vibrations it will give in
      14112    9                a minute.
      ─────   ───
        00    00
```

Let the length of a pendulum be 9.03168 inches: Required the number of vibrations it will give in a minute?

```
9.03168)141120.00000(1,56,25(125 vibrations will be given in a minute.
         903168 · · · · 1
         ──────
         5080320          22|56
         4515840          2|44
         ───────          ─────
         5644800          245|1225
         5419008          5|1225
         ───────
         2257920
         1806336
         ───────
          4515840
          4515840
```

To those who can make use of logarithms in computing the lengths of pendulums, or the number of their vibrations in a minute, *they* will find them much neater and easier perhaps than in the foregoing examples, done by the common rules of multiplication, division, and the extracting the square root. In order to shew the difference, we shall give a few examples of each done by logarithms. It is not to be thought that every clock and watch-maker can apply these rules to serve his purpose, even if he should know as much of arithmetic or of logarithms as are requisite. It becomes necessary for many that their application should be shown, which are, however, of great advantage to those who know how to apply them. For instance, having a spring clock case of a given length or height, which should admit a pendulum of as much length as can with propriety be put into it, length of pendulum, as has already been observed, being always absolutely necessary to good time keeping; but, it so happens, that the cases of most spring clocks which are seen, would have allowed a much greater length of pendulum than was taken, arising solely from that want of knowledge, necessary in the calculation of the train, or of the numbers of teeth of the wheels and pinions requisite to produce any given length. We shall, in the course of this work, have occasion to make use of rules taken from conic sections, or mensuration of solids, in the calculating of several things connected with clock-making, such as the solid contents of the going and striking weights, of the solid contents of the pendulum ball, whether it may be composed of equal parts of a sphere, or lenticular form, or of two equal frustrums of cones, globular, or cylindrical, things requiring to be properly sized both as to shape and weight. And if the clock-maker is any way desirous of having his work as it ought to be, he will find these rules both easy and convenient, the more so by having *them inserted at the particular places of their application;* as it is distracting to be looking for rules elsewhere, sometimes not knowing them, or even where to look for them, but, by *this method,* both trouble and memory will be saved.

Having the number of vibrations given in a minute, to find (by logarithms) the length of the pendulum.

Rule.—Take the logarithm of the given number of vibrations in a minute, and double it; the sum subtracted from the constant logarithm 5.1495886, the remainder will be the logarithm of the length of the pendulum. The constant logarithm 5.1495886 is the logarithm of the constant and standard number 141120.0; in place of using *it,* we now make use of its logarithm.

FINDING LENGTH OF PENDULUM BY LOGARITHMS.   145

Example.—The number of vibrations given in a minute is 120: Required the length of the pendulum?

Standard number, 141120.0   -   -   log. 5.1495886
Vibrations given, 120, logarithm, 2.0791812, double
of which is,   :   -   -   -   log. 4.1583624

Length of pendulum, 9.8 inches, equal to - remaining log. 0.9912262

The number of vibrations in a minute is 30: Required the length of the pendulum?

Standard number, 141120.0   -   -   log. 5.1495886
Vibrations, 30, log. 1.4771213, double of which is   log. 2.9542426

Length of pendulum, 156.8 inches, equal to remaining log. 2.1953460

The number of vibrations in a minute is 80: Required the length of the pendulum?

Standard number, 141120.0   -   constant log. 5.1495886
Vibrations 80, log. 1.9030900, double of which is   log. 3.8061800

Pendulum 22.05 inches, equal to   -   remaining log. 1.3434086

The number of vibrations in a minute is 100: Required the length of the pendulum?

Standard number 141120.0   -   -   constant log. 5.1495886
Vibrations 100, log. 2.0000000, double of
which is   -   -   -   -   log. 4.0000000

Pendulum, 14.112 inches, equal to   -   remaining log. 1.1495886

Having the length of a pendulum in inches, and decimal parts of an inch, to find by logarithms the number of vibrations it will make in a minute?

Rule.—From the constant logarithm, 5.1495886, subtract the logarithm of the given length, half of the remainder will be the logarithm of the number of vibrations in a minute.

Example.—The length of the pendulum given, is 9.8 inches: Required the number of vibrations it will give in a minute?

Constant log. 5.1495886
Length of pendulum 9.8 inches, log. 0.9912261

2)4.1583625

Vibrations.
120   log. 2.0791812

L

146 FINDING LENGTH OF PENDULUM BY LOGARITHMS.

The length of pendulum 156.8 inches: Required the vibrations in a minute?

Constant log. 5.1495886
Inches.
Length of pendulum 156.8 log. 2.1953460

2)2.9542426

Vibrations.
30 - - log. 1.4771213

The length of pendulum is 9.01368 inches: Required the vibrations in a minute?	The length of pendulum 22.05 inches: Required the vibrations in a minute?
Constant log. 5.1495886	Constant log. - 5.1495886
Inches, 9.01368, log. 0.9549022	Inches, 22.05, log. 1.3434086
2)4.1946864	2)3.8061800
125 vibrations, log. 2.0973432	80 vibrations, log. 1.9030900

What has already been said on finding the lengths of pendulums, according to their number of vibrations in a minute, and *vice versa*, is sufficient for the clock-maker's purpose: Yet, for the sake of such as may wish to instruct themselves more in the subject, we shall exhibit it under a different view. *Heretofore*, we have taken the length of the standard pendulum at 39.2 inches, and the vibrations 60 in a minute; we shall now take the pendulum at 39.126 inches, and the vibrations 86400, which is the number of seconds in 24 hours. The square of 86400 is 7464960000, which being multiplied by 39.126 inches, the length of the standard pendulum, we shall have 292074024960.000; this being constantly divided by the square of any other number of vibrations made by a pendulum in 24 hours, the quotient will be the length of the pendulum. Likewise, if the constant number is divided by any given length of pendulum, the quotient will be the square of the number of vibrations it will give in 24 hours, which will be found by extracting the root. For example, if a clock gains a minute in a day, or goes at the rate of 86460 seconds in 24 hours; the square of which is, 7475331600, by this divide the constant number 292074024960.000, and the quotient will give, for the length of the pendulum, 39.071714, &c. inches, which, being subtracted from the standard length, will show how much the pendulum, which gains a minute in a day, must be lengthened; and, according to this example, it will be found to be .0542 of an inch. It is evident that, if the number 292074024960.000 was divided by the number 39.071714, &c., the length of the pendulum just now found, that the quotient must be the number 7475331600; and it is evident also, from this example, that the square root, when extracted, would be 86460, the number of vibrations produced by this length of pendulum.

The table which is given, to show how much a pendulum must be lengthened or shortened, according to the gain or loss in a day, is so far curious, seeing what an amazingly small quantity is required to make a pendulum gain or lose, even one second in a day, to say nothing of one tenth of a second in that time. The thousandth part of an inch is hardly visible, even to a very good eye; yet this is a greater quantity than is required to make a change on the length of a pendulum for one second in a day: it is then no wonder that it is so difficult to make astronomical clocks keep so near to time as they do, or that compensation pendulums should be brought to that state in which they are; much greater perfection can hardly be expected or attained.

Length of a Pendulum in Inches and Decimal parts of an Inch	Loss or Gain per day in Seconds and Decimal Parts.	Decimals of an Inch.
39.18639845	losing 60.	must be shortened 0.05439845
39.07171486	gaining 60.	lengthened 0.05428514
39.15318499	losing 30.	shortened 0.02718499
33.06682992	gaining 30.	lengthened 0.02717088
39.12690571	losing 1.	shortened 0.00090571
39.12509431	gaining 1.	lengthened 0.00090569
39.12645366	losing 0.5	shortened 0.00045365
39.12544213	gaining 0.5	lengthened 0.00045287
39.12609056098	losing 0.1	shortened 0.0000905690
39.12509007	gaining 0.1	lengthened 0.0000905693

We still may be allowed to take another view of the subject, regarding the length of pendulums, and the number of their vibrations, although it should be nearly on the same ground as has been gone over; because the practical artist requires to have it made quite familiar and easy, and there is no doing this, without giving a greater variety of examples, than might otherwise be thought necessary; but it is now meant to show how to deduce the lengthening and shortening of pendulums for their difference of vibrations; and thereby to ascertain how much they must be made longer or shorter, by means of the regulating screw and nut of the pendulum, which is determined by the number of the threads of the screw in an inch, and the divisions of the nut, where every prime division should be made equal to one second in twenty-four hours.

The length of pendulums are in the inverse ratio of the squares of their vibrations in a minute. The number of vibrations in a minute by the seconds pendulum, is 60, the square of which is 3600, which, multiplied by the length of what may be called the standard pendulum of 39.2 inches, gives 141120. A pendulum, gaining at the rate of one minute in a day, or vibrating 86460 seconds, will make 60.04166 vibrations in a minute, the square of which is 3605.0009355556; then inversely, as 3600 : 39.2 : : 3605.000935556 : 39.1456 inches, the length of the pendulum which gains at the rate of one minute in a day; and to keep mean time, it would require to be lengthened .05444 of an inch, the difference between this and the length of the standard pendulum. A screw having 36.75 turns in an inch, two turns of which would be equal to one minute; the nut divided into thirty, each division would be equal to one second, or as nearly so as possible; as .05444 × 36.75 = 2.0006700 turns, or .0544 × 36.75 = 1.999200 turns. In the calculation for this lengthening of a pendulum by Professor Ludlam, he makes it .0543877844, and .05438 × 36.8 = 2.001184. If a clock loses one minute in a day, or goes 86340 seconds in twenty-four hours, the vibrations in a minute will be 59.9583, the square of which is, 3594.99783889. Then inversely, as 3600 : 39.2 : : 3594.99783889 : 39.2548 inches, being the length of that pendulum, which will lose a minute in a day, and will require to be shortened .0548 of an inch. A screw, having 36.5 threads in an inch, two of which would be equal to one minute, .0548 × 36.5 = 2.00020. A pendulum being shortened an inch, or 38.2 in length, the vibrations in a minute will be 60.78, or 18.72 minutes fast in twenty-four hours, which call 18 minutes, 43.20 seconds. A pendulum being lengthened an inch, or 40.2 inches in length, the vibrations in a minute 59.2489, or 18 minutes, 1.584 seconds slow in twenty-four hours. To find the vibrations in a minute by a pendulum of 40.2 inches in length? 40.2)141120.(3510.447761194, the square root of which quotient is 59.24903 vibrations in a minute. To shorten the seconds pendulum the thousandth part of an inch, and find how much the clock would gain in twenty-four hours? Suppose the seconds pendulum 39.200 inches, and the other 39.199 inches, the square roots of these will be 6.260990337, and 6.260910477 : If we put them 6.260990337 : 6.260910477 : : x : 3600, we shall find the value of x, or the number of vibrations in an hour, by multiplying the extreme terms together, and dividing by the mean, the quotient will be 3600.0459, the number of vibrations in an hour, and .0459, the excess above 3600, being multiplied by 24, will give 1.1016 second gained in a day by shortening the pendulum the thousandth part of an inch. That pendulum, which makes 30 vibrations in a minute, is 156.8 inches in length; but, on its losing 30 seconds in twenty-four hours, what is its length, or how much must it be shortened? The vibrations of the first being 30 in a minute, we have 86400 : 30 : : 86370 : 29.989583, the vibrations in a minute made by the other, and the square of this is 899.375088513889, and the square of the first is 900 ; so, if we multiply the length, 156.8 inches, by 900, the square of the vibrations, and divide the product by 899.375088513889, we shall have the length for the other pendulum, 156.909 inches; so that, shortening it .109 of an inch, would correct the error of going slow 30 seconds in a day. A clock, with a half-seconds pendulum, which should be 9.8 inches in length, loses 30 seconds in a day. The vibrations of the half seconds pendulum are 120 in a minute, the vibrations of the losing pendulum will be 119.958333, the square of which is, 14390.001656138.889; the square of 120, the vibrations of a half-seconds pendulum in a minute, is 14400, which, multiplied by 9.8, the product will be 141120.0, and this, divided by 14390.001656138889, gives, for the length of the pendulum, 9.8068 inches, and being shortened .0068 of an inch, will correct the error of losing 30 seconds in a day. A pendulum, gaining one minute in 24 hours, must be lengthened as 719 is to 720, or $\frac{1}{720}$ of 39.2 inches = 0.0544 = $\frac{1}{18}$ of an inch nearly. A pendulum, gaining one second in 24 hours, must be lengthened, as 43199 is to 432000, or $\frac{1}{43200}$ of 39.2 = .0009, or $\frac{9}{10.000}$ of an inch. The length of a siderial pendulum is, 39.2 inches — 0.216 = 38.984 inches. A pendulum, of the standard length, which gains half a second a day, must be lengthened 0.00045 of an inch. A pendulum of ditto, which loses half a second a day, must be shortened 0.00059 of an inch. The standard taken in the two last cases, at 39.126 inches. The siderial pendulum, or that which keeps siderial time, being supposed 38.984 inches in length : Required the number of vibrations it would make in a minute? 38.984)141120.000(3619.9466. The square root of which is, 60.166 vibrations in a minute. The mean solar day is 24 hours, or 1440 minutes. A siderial day, or the mean solar time, which a star takes from one transit over the meridian to the next, is, 23 hours, 56 minutes, 4.1 seconds, or 1436.0683 minutes of mean solar time. The siderial pendulum is supposed to make 1440 siderial minutes in the siderial day ; hence its length must be shorter than that which keeps mean solar time. The difference in length of these two pendulums may be shown thus :

TOUCHING PENDULUM WHILE GOING FAST OR SLOW.

	1440.		1436.0683
log.	3.1583625	log.	3.1571750
square,	6.3167250	square,	6.3143500
a, c, of 1440²			3.6832740
inches,	39.2	log.	1.5932861
siderial length,	38.986	log.	1.5909101
Difference,	0.214		

Let it be required to find the length of a pendulum which will make 120 vibrations in a minute? *Rule.*—To the logarithm of the square of 60, (the standard taken), add the arithmetical complement of the logarithm of 120 square, and also the logarithm of 39.2 inches, the standard length, the sum will be the logarithm of the pendulum required.

	120		60
log.	2.0791812	log.	1.7781512
square,	4.1583624	square,	3.5563024
a, c, of 120²			5.8416376
39.2 inches.		log.	1.5932861
9.8 inches.		log.	0.9912261

Let it be required to find the number of vibrations given in a minute by a pendulum, whose length is 12.098 inches?

12.098 inches, log. 1.0827136, a, c, of which is, 8.9172864
39.2 inches,   -   -   -   log. 1.5932861
60²   -   -   log. 3.5563025
                                                             4.0668750
Vibrations in a minute, 108.   -   log. 2.0334375

These give the same result as in the former examples by k rithms.

A short and easy rule for touching a pendulum is given by fessor Bridge, in the following theorem, for ascertaining the qua to touch a pendulum according to its daily gain or loss. W] pendulum of a given length has been observed to gain or lose tain quantity daily, it is convenient in making adjustment for time to have some concise theorem as a guide to bring it to the point desired at one trial in all cases. "Multiply twice the length of the pendulum by the number of seconds gained or lost, and *divide* the result by the number of seconds in a day, the *quotient* will give the number of inches, or parts of an inch, by which the pendulum is to be lengthened or shortened. Suppose the *gain* of a second's pendulum to be three minutes, or 180 seconds in a solar day, then $\frac{39.2 \times 2 \times 180}{86400} = .1633$ parts of an inch, which is the quantity in this case, by which the pendulum must be *lengthened* to measure mean time. But, if the three minutes had been *loss* with a half second's pendulum, then $\frac{9.8 \times 2 \times 180}{86400} = .04083$ of an inch, or the fourth part of the former quantity that was to be lengthened, which, in this case, it requires to be *shortened.*"

The second's pendulum being 39.2 inches, and the daily loss or gain being supposed 18 minutes: Required the quantity by which this pendulum must be shortened or lengthened? $\frac{39.2 \times 2 \times 1080}{86400} = .980$ of an inch. 1102.05 seconds would be equal to one inch. The screw of a pendulum rod, having 54 turns in .98 parts of an inch, three turns of which would be equal to one minute, and the regulating nut divided into 20 prime divisions, each of which would be equal to one second in a day; but, in case 54 threads of a screw in such a space should be thought rather too fine, let us take a screw of 45 turns in the same space, two and a half turns would be equal to one minute, and the nut divided into 24 prime divisions, each would be equal to one second. A screw of 36 threads, in that space, would require two turns of the nut to be equal to a minute, and 30 prime divisions on it, each would be equal to one second.

The pendulum of a clock being 12.8 inches in length, and it loses one minute, or 60 seconds, in 24 hours: How much must the pendulum be shortened?

$\frac{12.8 \times 2 \times 60}{86400} = .018$ nearly of an inch. The number of turns which the regulating screw has in an inch is 34; then what turns, or parts of a turn, ought to be given to the regulating nut to shorten the pendulum, so as to correct the error? Suppose an inch to contain one thousand equal parts, the number 1000 being divided by 34, the number of threads on the screw in an inch, it will give nearly 30 of the thousand equal parts for every thread or turn of the screw;

then, if 60 seconds require .018 of an inch, .030 will be equal to 100 seconds, and 100 seconds requiring one turn, 60 seconds will require six-tenths of a turn. The following length of pendulums, to vibrate military pace time, may be easily made: Take a musket bullet, and attach it to the end of a very fine thread, from the centre of the bullet to the point of suspension where the thread is tied or fixed, measure off 25.04 inches, this will then be a simple pendulum, and from its length will, when vibrating, give 75 vibrations in a minute, or the number of paces when marching to slow time. When ordinary time is wanted, the thread can be shortened to 12.075 inches from the centre of the ball, and the vibrations given will be 108 in a minute, the number of steps required in ordinary time. For quick time, bring the length of the pendulum to 9.8, or 9.781 inches, the vibrations will be 120 in a minute, being the number of steps required for that kind of marching. An apparatus for this purpose might be easily made, and would be very useful to a field-officer when exercising troops to march to the different times required. One bullet, with the same thread, could at once be set to any of the lengths which are supposed to have been previously marked off; and by this means no time need be lost in adjusting the length for the different pendulums; or a small brass frame, containing a common 'scapement-work, to act or impel a pendulum of 9.8 inches long, having a small square rod above the centre of motion, and on the rod a sliding weight, adjusted so as set at places for slow and ordinary time. If the drum-major corps play the marches in their proper time, this will make the troop keep to the proper number of steps.

How a clock may be regulated, or made to keep mean time, or very near to it, in twenty-four hours. Knowing the number of turns in an inch, and parts of an inch, of the regulating screw of the pendulum, and having the nut so divided to answer the screw as that each division on it shall be equal to one second in twenty-four hours.

On setting the clock agoing, and comparing it very accurately with a well regulated time-piece or astronomical clock, at first for one hour, as we shall suppose, and in that time it is observed to have gained five seconds, then calculate how much this rate would be in twenty-four hours, which would be two minutes, or 120 seconds. The regulating nut being divided into thirty, each turn of it would then be equal to thirty seconds, and four turns would be equal to 120 seconds, give the regulating nut then four turns downwards, and the clock will be found very nearly at time. Let it be again set, and allowed to go on for the remaining twenty-three hours, and observe what it has gained or lost in that time; if the amount of error is two seconds slow, set the nut up about two divisions, and the clock will now be regulated, or nearly so. In twenty-four hours we have regulated a clock by this method, that at the end of twenty-three days afterwards, it was found to have lost only four seconds, or going at the daily rate of — 0.174 of a second.

In comparing a clock or chronometer with the regulating clock, when they are under regulation. There is in this, as well as in every other thing, a neat or proper method: Suppose the clock or watch under regulation is found to be faster than the regulating clock, count in your own mind the beats or seconds of the regulating clock by the ear, keeping, at the same time, your eye steadily on the seconds hand of the clock or chronometer under regulation, and when the beat of the regulator is on the sixtieth second, mark well where the seconds hand of the piece under regulation is, and you will have exactly what it has gained. On the other hand, should the piece under regulation be loosing, count the beats of the regulating clock in your own mind, knowing, at the same time, where the seconds hand of it is at, and keeping your eye on the seconds hand of the piece to be regulated, notice the instant when the seconds hand of it comes to the sixtieth second, and what beat or second the regulator is at, and you have the difference, or the number of seconds which the clock or chronometer may have lost. When addition or subtraction is used, with the differences between two clocks, where one of them is to be regulated, errors may take place; but, in the method we have just described, this is not likely to happen.

If a simple pendulum, vibrating seconds in a very small arc, is made to describe any of the arcs in the following Table, the daily loss will be according to the extent of the arc made on each side the point of rest, as shown there:

Arcs Described on each side.	Inches and Decimal Parts.	Daily loss.
0° 15′	0.168	0.1 sec.
0 30	0.337	0.4
1 0	0.674	1.6
2 0	1.349	6.6
3 0	2.024	14.8
4 0	2.699	26.3
5 0	3.374	41.1

To set off degrees and Minutes on the Pendulum Index Plate.

In clocks made for astronomical purposes, the lower end of the pendulum rod is sometimes formed into a small and sharp point, serving as an index to a plate of brass, (fixed to the inside back of the clock-case,) on which is graduated degrees, and parts of a degree, of a great circle. The length of the pendulum over all being given, thence to find the chord of one degree. Suppose the length to be 45 inches; then say, as the arc of 1′ is to 0.0002908, so is 45 inches to x.

$$1' : 0.0002908 :: 45 \text{ inches}$$

```
        0.0002908
             45
        ─────────
          14540
         11632
        ─────────
         .01308660
      ×      60  the minutes in a degree.
        ─────────
         0.7851600  parts of an inch, equal to one degree.
```

.78516 parts of an inch, must be taken for the length of every degree set off on the brass plate, and, subdividing each degree either into four or six, will shew the minutes.

It may not be uninteresting to some, to have directions how to lay off the degrees and minutes on the brass index plate. Provide a deal-board, about four feet in length, and seven or eight inches broad, and a thin piece of well hammered plate brass, six inches long, its breadth an inch and four-tenths; let it be pinned fast across the board, and near to one end of it; at the other end, fix a round pin of steel wire, (not less than a quarter of an inch in diameter,) having an inch or two above the surface of the board, to serve as a centre of motion, to a rectangular bar of wood, four feet in length, one and a half inch broad, and the thickness about an inch; near to one end of the bar, make a hole for the steel pin to go through, at the other end, taking a distance from the centre of motion, somewhat less than 45 inches, make a hole, into which is fixed a cutter, to trace two portions of circles on the brass plate; the first portion being traced, to get the other, the cutter must be shifted lower down, near to two-tenths of an inch, to give the space between the circles. On this space, at a distance of three inches or so, (supposed equi-distant,) from the ends of the brass plate, make a point for Zero, or O; from it, towards each end, mark points for the degrees, 1, 2, 3, or more, then subdivide each degree, to show either ten or fifteen minutes. The cutter may now be taken out of its place, and a flat thin piece of brass fixed to the lower end of the bar, projecting a little way beyond the bar, having one of its edges straight, in order to mark off the degrees and their subdivisions; another hole must be made at the upper end of the bar, (for the steel pin to go through,) at such place and distance as to bring the brass straight edge to lay across the index plate; stepping the different points, and holding the straight edge steady at them, with a sharp knife-edge, or such like, mark the degrees and their subdivisions.

The length of a degree can be determined also by rules in plain trigonometry.

A B = 45.
A C = 45.
B C = .78516
_____
Sum 90.78516

½ Sum 45.39258	= H =	45.39258	co. log.	8.3430258
	H — B C =	44.60742	co. log.	8.3505930
	H — A B =	.39258	log.	9.5939282
	H — A C =	.39258	log.	9.5939282
	30′ × 2 = 1°	Sum		15.8814752
	Tang^t. of 30 = ¼ Sum			7.9407376

Given two sides of a triangle, each 45 inches, and the angle contained one degree: To find the chord? Say, as radius is to twice the sine of 30′, so is 45 inches to x.

N. S. of 30′ is 87.265 × 2 = 174.530 N. S. of 1°
N. S. of 1° is 174.530, the log. sine of which is 8.2418553
The log. of 45 inches is - - - - 1.6532125
_____
.78536 parts of an inch - - = log. 9.8950678

Three sides given : Required the angle?

$$
\begin{array}{lr}
& \text{45. inches.} \\
& \text{45.} \\
& .78536 \\ \hline
\text{Sum} \quad - \ - \ - & 90.78536 \\
\text{Half sum} \ - \ - & 45.39268 \\
\text{— Opposite angle} \ .78536 \ - \ - \ - \ - \ \text{co. log.} & 8.3430192 \\ \hline
44.60732 \ - \ - \ - \ - \ \text{co. log.} & 8.3505938 \\
\tfrac{1}{2} \text{ Opposite angle} \quad .39268 \ - \ - \ - \ - \ - \ \text{log.} & 9.5940388 \\
\text{Ditto} \ - \ - \ .39268 \ - \ - \ - \ - \ - \ \text{log.} & 9.5940388 \\ \hline
\text{Tang}^t. \text{ of } 30' \times 2 \quad - \ - \ - & 15.8816906 \\
\end{array}
$$

The angle? $= 1° - 30'$ Tang^t. $= \tfrac{1}{2}$ sum 7.9408453

The Table which we are about to give, containing different lengths of pendulums, the number of their vibrations in a minute, and the numbers for the teeth of the wheels and pinions, to produce the vibrations, will be found very useful and convenient for the clock-maker, who having determined on his height of case, or length of pendulum, has only to inspect the Table to find what his wheels and pinions should be, which will save a great deal of trouble. For the like reason is added a Table of various trains of watches, and chronometers, and the numbers of their wheels and pinions calculated to produce them, and which may be useful to many a watch-maker, and watch-movement maker.

LENGTH OF PENDULUMS, &c.

A Table of the Lengths of Pendulums, their Vibrations in a Minute, and the Numbers for the Teeth of such Wheels and Pinions as are calculated to produce them.

Vibrations in a minute.	Length of Pendulums in inches, and decimal parts of an inch.	Numbers for the Wheel Teeth.				Number of Leaves in the Pinions.
188	3.928	47	36	36	20	6
180	4.355	45	36	36	20	6
175	4.608	128	105	25		8
175	4.608	36	36	35	25	6
170	4.883	128	102	25		8
165	5.183	132	100	27		9 & 8
160	5.512	128	80	30		8
160	5.512	120	96	30		9 & 8
156	5.797	104	96	30		8
152	6.108	96	95	32		8
151.2	6.172	84	72	27		6
150	6.272	100	96	30		8
145	6.712	120	87	30		9 & 8
145	6.712	100	87	32		8
144.9	6.720	92	84	36		12 & 8
142	7.001	128	71	30		8
142	7.001	120	71	32		8
141.75	7.023	90	84	36		8
140	7.200	96	80	35		8
140	7.200	84	80	40		8
137.8	7.430	90	84	36		8
135	7.745	96	90	30		8
135	7.745	90	90	32		8
133.8	7.874	90	84	34		8
132.3	8.062	84	84	36		8
130.3	8.320	90	88	40		9
130	8.350	100	78	32		8
129.9	8.362	90	84	3		8
129.1	8.465	84	83	45		9
128.6	8.577	84	84	35		8
128	8.610	100	96	40		10
126	8.880	90	84	36		9 & 8
126	8.880	90	84	32		8
126	8.880	108	100	35		10
125	9.031	100	80	30		8
122	9.471	90	84	31		8
120	9.800	90	80	32		8
120	9.800	90	80	36		9 & 8
120	9.800	80	72	40		8

(Table continued.)

Vibrations.	Length of Pendulums.	Wheel Teeth.			Pinion Leaves.
120	9.800	96	80	30	8
120	9.800	80	80	36	8
118.5	10.050	90	79	32	8
118	10.135	Numbers for this not easily to be got, unless very disproportionate.			
117.5	10.220	94	75	32	8
117.3	10.256	90	88	32	9 & 8
115	10.672	115	100	30	10
114	10.858	96	76	30	8
112	11.250	105	100	32	10
112	11.250	90	84	32	9 & 8
112	11.250	84	80	32	8
110.25	11.610	84	84	30	8
110	11.662	110	100	30	10
110	11.662	88	80	30	8
108	12.098	81	80	36	9 & 8
108	12.098	96	72	30	8
108	12.098	90	90	32	10 & 8
105	12.800	105	100	30	10
102	13.564	83	72	32	8
102	13.564	85	81	32	9 & 8
100	14.112	125	108	32	12
100	14.112	100	100	30	10
100	14.112	80	80	30	8
100	14.112	80	72	32	8
100	14.112	96	80	25	8
98	14.694	98	60	32	8
98	14.694	84	64	35	8
98	14.694	84	84	30	9 & 8
96	15.400	108	100	32	12 & 10
94	15.971	94	64	30	8
90	17.422	80	72	30	8
88	18.223	100	88	32	8
88	18.223	88	64	30	8
86	19.098	86	64	30	8
84	20.000	84	64	30	8
80	22.050	64	60	40	8
80	22.050	75	64	32	8
78	23.182	72	65	32	8
75	25.088	75	60	32	8
72	27.222	72	64	30	8
70	28.800	70	64	30	8
68	30.519	64	64	30	8

A Table of the Trains of Watches, Chronometers, &c. or their Beats in an Hour, with the Numbers for the Wheels and Pinions, as calculated to produce them.

Beats in an hour.	Numbers of the Wheel Teeth.				Numbers of the Pinion Leaves.		
16200	70	56	54	15	8	7	7
16489½	57	54	60	15	8	7	6
16800	70	64	64	15	8	8	8
16800	80	64	60	14	8	8	8
16800	70	64	60	16	8	8	8
16900	54	52	50	13	6	6	6
16925¼	52	52	52	13	6	6	6
16950 1/11	54	52	52	13	6	6	6
17010	72	64	63	15	8	8	8
17160	64	63	55	13	8	7	6
17325	64	63	55	15	8	8	6
17333¼	60	50	48	13	6	6	6

The above were chiefly the trains of old watches.

7200	64	48	40	15	8	8	8
14400	64	64	60	15	8	8	8
14400	96	90	90	16	12	12	12
14400	96	90	75	16	12	12	10
14400	80	75	80	15	10	10	10
17280	54	48	48	15	6	6	6
17280	63	56	56	15	7	7	7
17280	72	64	64	15	8	8	8
17280	72	64	60	14	8	8	7
17920	70	64	64	14	8	8	7
18000	54	50	48	15	6	6	6
18000	60	48	45	15	6	6	6
18000	80	80	75	15	10	10	8
18000	75	64	64	15	8	8	8
18000	75	64	60	16	8	8	8
18432	72	64	64	16	8	8	8
20250	54	54	50	16	6	6	6
21600	80	72	64	15	8	8	8

Should there be any trains required which are not in the Tables, the artist can supply this, by having recourse to the method which has been given to find numbers for wheel teeth, &c.

Between the weight of the pendulum ball of a clock, and that of the weight or moving force applied to it, there ought to be some sort of proportion; for, if the moving force is too great, it will tend to

160   DIMENSIONS OF HOLLOW CYLINDERS.

increase the friction, and wear the machine faster out; if it is too little, the clock will not get well through when the oil gets thick and foul: The arc of vibration should have the supplementary angle about equal to the angle of 'scapement, the nature of which may require more or less. The far greater number of clocks have the moving force much more powerful than what is necessary, arising in some degree from the trouble of getting weights to any specific number of pounds, or not having any rule to determine what the weight of any given cylinder, &c. of lead should be. It is for these reasons that we shall insert rules and examples for finding this, so as a clockmaker, when making trial with his clock, should give no more than the motive force requisite for the pendulum; he should hang on weights by degrees, until he sees that it has got the proper quantity, which he finds to be, *as we shall suppose*, 10 lbs., and he wants to have a hollow cylindrical brass or tin-plate shell, that shall hold exactly 10 lbs. weight of lead. Although, to find this, is a case in the mensuration of solids, it is nevertheless a subject requisite to the profession.

A cubic inch of lead is known to weigh 6 ounces, 9.08 drams avoirdupois; now, by the simple rule of three, we may find how many cubic inches will be required for 10 lbs. of lead. Say, if 6 oz. 9.08 drams is equal to one cubic inch, what number of cubic inches will 10 lbs. require?

```
   oz.    dr.    cub. in.        lbs.
    6    9.08  : 1   : :         10
   16                            16
  ─────                         ─────
 105.08                         160
                                 16
                                ─────
                                960
                                160
                                ─────
          105.08)2560.00(24.362 cubic inches.
```

Then, to find a hollow brass cylindrical shell of such a length and diameter, as to contain the given number of cubic inches, 24.362, or as near to it as may be; a little will depend on practice, but, to save the trouble of computing this, a table will be given of shells of different capacities, and, consequently, of different weights. To find the solidity of a cylinder in cubic inches, and decimal parts of a cubic inch: The rule is, multiply the area of the base of the cylinder by the perpendicular height; the product will be the solidity: Or, as 1 is to 0.7854, (or, rather 0.785399,) so is the square of the diameter of the cylinder, taken in inches, and parts of an inch, to the number of square inches, &c. contained in the area of the base, which number being multiplied by the height, taken in inches, and parts of an inch, will give the solid contents thereof in cubic inches, &c.

Suppose we have a cylinder, whose diameter is 2.25 inches, and the height or depth 6.25 inches: Required the solidity?

```
The diameter       -    -    2.25
Multiplied by itself  -    -  2.25
                              ─────
                              1125
                              450
                              450
                              ─────
The product        -    -    5.0625  the square of the diameter
Multiplied by      -    -    -  0.7854
                              ─────
                              202500
                              253125
                              405000
                              354375
                              ─────
                              3.97608750  area of the base.
Multiplied by      -          6.25  the height.
                              ─────
                              1988043750
                              795217500
                              2385652500
                              ─────
                              24.8505468750  solid contents in cub. inches
Multiplied by      -          105.08  drams in a cubic inch.
                              ─────
                              1988043750000
                              1242527343750
                              248505468750
                              ─────             lbs.  oz.
                              2611.295465625000  drams = 10  3
```

This cylinder appears then to have been taken too large in its dimensions. If we had taken one at 6.18 inches in height, and 2.24 inches in diameter, we would have come nearer to the required solidity and weight.

M

```
        2.24                       3.94082304 area of the base.
        2.24            multiplied by the height, 6.18

        ────                       ──────────
         896                        3152658432
         448                         394082304
         448                        2364493824
        ────                       ──────────
       5.0176                      24.3542863872 cubic inches.
       0.7854                              105.08 dr. in a cubic inch
       ──────
       200704                      1948342910976
       250880                      1217714319360
       401408                       243542863872
       351232                      ──────────────
       ──────                                                lbs.  oz.
                                   2559.148413566976 drs. = 9   15.9
    3.94082304 area of the base.
```

This is brought as near as may be to 10 lbs.

A cylinder, being 6 inches in height, and 2.5 in diameter: Required the solidity?

```
        2.5              0.7854
        2.5              6.25 square of base.
        ───              ──────
        125              39270
         50              15708
        ───              47124
        6.25             ──────
                         4.908750 area of base.
                         6 height.
                         ──────
                                                      lbs.
                         29.452500 contents in cubic in. = 12.08933, or
  lbs.  oz.  dr.
   12   1   6.86.
```

Two or three more examples shall be given, with oval, in place of cylindrical shells. The solidity of any body having an oval form, may be found by the following *Rule*:—Multiply the transverse, or long diameter, by the conjugate or short diameter, and the product by .7854; the product will be the area of the base, which, being multiplied by the height, will give the solidity or number of cubic inches. The transverse diameter being 3.5 inches, and the conjugate 1.5 inch, the height 6 inches: Required the cubic inches, and weight of lead, to fill such a shell?

Transverse diameter, 3.5   .7854
Conjugate ditto,   1.5   5.25

```
          175       39270
           35       15708
         ———       39270
          5.25     ————
                   4.123350 area of the base.
                   6 the height.
                   ————
                   24.740100 cubic inches.
                   105.08 drams in a cubic inch.
                   ————
                   197920800
                   123700500
                   24740100
                   ————————       lbs.  oz.  dr.
drams in a pound, 256)2599.689708(10   2    7
```

The transverse diameter being 4 inches, the conjugate 2, and the height 6.25 inches: Required the solid contents or number of cubic inches?

Transverse diameter, 4   drams in a cubic inch, 105.08
Conjugate ditto,   2   multiplied by the cubic in. 39.27

```
             8                        73556
           .7854                      21016
          ——————                      94572
area of base,  6.2832                 31524
height, -      6.25                  ————       lb.  oz.  dr.
          ——————        drams in a pound, 256)4126.4916(16   1   14
           314160
           125664
           376992
          ——————
cubic inches, 39.270000
```

If these examples were done by logarithms, they would be much easier. Having found the number of cubic inches, add their logarithm to the constant logarithm, 9.6134202, the sum will be the logarithm of the number of pounds in the cubical inches.

```
         The constant logarithm     9.6134202
         Cubic inches, 39.27,   log. 1.5940609
                                    ————————
         16.119 lb. =     -     log. 1.2074811
```

Pendulum balls are commonly composed of two equal segments of a sphere, forming a lens, or a sort of lenticular shape, and the workman, or those who may direct him, when making up the brass shells, or covers for the pendulum ball, which are to be filled with lead, should know exactly the quantity which will be required to fill them, otherwise they must make the pendulum either too light or too heavy for that which may be wanted: and, without knowing before hand, by calculation, to give the requisite dimensions for the covers, they must be labouring, in some degree, at random.

To find the solidity of the segment of a sphere.—*Rule.* To three times the square of the radius of its base, add the square of the height, and this sum, multiplied by the height, and the product again by .5236, will give the solidity.

The diameter of a pendulum ball being 6.2 inches, and thickness 2.1 inches: Required the solidity and weight of lead? Being composed of two equal segments of a sphere, if we get the solidity of one of them, doubling it will give the solidity of both. Here the radius of the segment base is 3.1 inches, and the height 1.05 inch: To find the solidity of such a segment?

```
Height, 1.05 inch.    radius of base, 3.1              31.429125
        1.05                          3.1   multiply by the dec. .5236
        ----                          ---              188574750
         525                          3.1
         105                           93              94287375
        ----                          ---              62858250
       1.1025 square of height     9.61 sq. of rad.   157145625
                                     3 times
                                                      16.4562898500  solidity of
                                    28.83                   2         one seg.
                              add  1.1025 sq. of height
                                   ------              32.91257970  the two segments
                                   29.9325
                       multiply by  1.05  the height.
                                   -------
                                   1496625
                                   299325
                                   -------
                                   31.429125
```

To the constant log.   -   -   -   9.6134202
Add the log. of the solidity, 32.91257   1.5173617

13.513 lbs. =   -   -   -   log. 1.1307819

Let the diameter of the base of the segment be 6 inches, and the height 1 inch: Required the solidity?

LENTICULAR PENDULUM BALLS, &c.

Radius of the base, 3 inches   height 1. Square is 1.
                           3

Square of radius,   9
                       3 times.

                       27
Add the square of height, 1

                       28
Multiply by height,   1

                       28
Multiply by the dec. .5236

                     41888
                     10472

               14.6606 solidity of one segment.
                      2

               29.3216 ditto of both segments.
     To the constant log. - 9.6134202
     Add solidity, 29.3216, log. 1.4671877

      12.04 lbs. = - - log. 1.0806079

The diameter of the base of the segment 6 inches, and the height .5 of an inch: Required the solidity?

     Radius of the base 3 inches.   height .5
                    3   .5

                  9   .25 sq. of height.
               3 times

                 27
Add the square of the height 0.25

               27.25
Multiply by the height -   .5

               13.625
Multiply by the decimal .5236

              81750
              40875
              27250
              68125

            7.1340500 solidity of one segment.
                 2

            14.2681 ditto of both segments.

Constant log.	-	9.6134202
Solidity 14.2681	log.	1.1543660
5.8585 lbs. =	- log.	0.7677862

A pendulum ball may very properly be formed of two equal frustums of cones, being a shape very fit for the purpose. An example or two may be taken, and the Rule given to find the solidity of the frustum of a cone.

To find the solid contents of the frustum of a cone.—*Rule*, Multiply the diameters at top and bottom into one another, to the product add a third part of the square of their difference; multiply this sum by .7854, and the product shall be a mean area, which being multiplied by the perpendicular height, the last product shall be the solid contents in cubical measures of the whole, in such parts, (as inches, feet, &c.) as the diameters and height were taken.

Example. Let the greater diameter of the frustum of a cone be 7 inches, the lesser 4 inches, and the height 0.5 of an inch: Required the solidity?

```
                  Greater diameter   7 inches.
                  Lesser ditto   -   4               7
                                 ———               4
                                  28               ———
Add the third of square of diff.   3              3 difference.
                                 ———              3
                                  31              ———
Multiply by the decimal    -    .7854           3)9 square of diff.
                                 ———              ———
                                 7854             3 third of sq. of diff.
                                23562
                                 ———
                                24.3474
Multiply by the height     -      0.5
                                 ———
Solidity of one        -    -   12.17370
                                     2
                                 ———
Solidity of both       -    -   24.34740
                          constant log.   -    9.6134202
                         24.3474 log.  -   -   1.3864526
                                 ———
                          9.997 lbs. = log.    0.9998728
```

Another example will make the rule sufficiently plain. Let the greater diameter be 7 inches, the lesser 3.5 inches, and the height .7 of an inch: Required the solidity?

```
            Greater diameter    7
            Lesser ditto   -   3.5           7
                              ─────         3 5
                               24.5         ─────
Add the third of square of diff. 4.083      3.5 difference.
                              ─────         3.5
                               28.583       ─────
Multiply by the decimal   -    .7854        175
                              ─────         105
                              114332        ─────
                              142915       3)12.25 square of diff.
                              228664       ─────
                              200081   -    4.083 third of sq. of diff.
                             ─────────
                             22.4490882
Multiply by the height         .7
                             ─────────
                             15.71436174 solidity of one.
                                   2
                             ─────────
Cubic inches    -    -    31.42872348 ditto of both.
                    Constant log.  -   9.6134202
                    31.4287 log. -   -  1.4973264
                                       ─────────
                    12.904 lbs. = log.  1.1107466
```

Although a sphere or globe is not a common figure for the ball of a pendulum, yet that shape is very proper for large turret clocks, where the pendulums are often exposed to currents of air or eddy winds blowing in, and up and down in the steeples. Suppose a pendulum ball or globe, 6.75 in diameter: Required the solidity, and weight in lead; to find the solid contents of a sphere or globe?

Rule.—Multiply the diameter of the sphere twice into itself, (which gives the cube,) and the product by .5236, the last product is the solidity required.

6.75
6.75
———
3375
4725
4050
———
45.5625
6.75
———
2278125
3189375
2733750
———
307.546875
.5236
———
1845281250
922640625
615093750
1537734375
———
161.0315437500 cubic inches in the sphere.

Constant logarithm - 9.6134202
161.03154 - log. 2.2069112
———
66.12 lbs. = - log. 1.8203314

All other things in a turret clock, according with a length of pendulum whose vibrations are one in two seconds, a ball of 66 lbs. is not too much. The figures required in finding the solidity of a globe are much abridged by the use of logarithms.

The diameter of a globe being 6.75 inches - log. 0.8293038
which, multiplied by 3, will give the log. of the cube   3

The cube of 6.75 is 307.546875, the log. of which is   2.4879114
.5236, the log. of which is, add   9.7189996
———
Cubic inches 161.03154, the log. of which is - - 2.2069110

The glass jar for a mercurial pendulum being 7 inches deep, and two inches in diameter, both inside measure, it is required to know what quantity of mercury will fill the jar or cylinder up to 6.4 inches?

GLASS JAR FOR MERCURIAL PENDULUM.

Find the solidity as directed in the case for clock cylindrical weight shells.

```
           The diameter 2 inches
                         2
                        ———
                         4 sq. of the dia.
Multiply the square of the diameter by the decimal  .7854
                                                     4
                                                    ———
              Area of the base      -    3.1416
              Multiply by the height      6.4
                                         ———
                                         125664
                                         188496
                                         ———
              Solidity in cubic inches  -  20.10624
```

To the constant logarithm for Mercury, add the logarithm of the cubic inches, the sum will be the logarithm for the weight of mercury required.

```
    Constant log. for mercury  -  9.6908553
    20.10624 cubic inches  -  log.  1.3033308
                                   ——————————
    9.867 lbs. =       -     log.  0.9941861
```

Seeing we have used one constant logarithm for lead, and another for mercury, to be added to the logarithm of the cubic inches, to find the logarithms of the weight of lead and of mercury, it may be proper to show how these constant logarithms are obtained. To the arithmetical complement of the logarithm of 1728, (the number of cubic inches in a cubic foot,) add the logarithm of 62.5 lbs. (the weight of a cubic foot of pure water,) together with the logarithm of the specific gravity of whatever metal or substance it is required.

```
1728 inches, log. 3.2375437   a. c. 6.7624563  -  -  -  -  6.7624563
Weight of a cubic foot of water 62.5 log. 1.7958800   -  -  -  -  1.7958800
Specific gravity of lead 11.3523  log. 1.0550839 s. g. of merc. 13.5681 log. 1.1325190
           Constant log. for lead 9.6134202  Constant log. for mercury 9.6908553
```

When any vessel is to be filled with lead, filling it first with pure water,* the weight of which being taken, and multiplied by 11.3523,

---

* Before pouring melted lead into a vessel which has been previously filled with water, it is requisite that the vessel be completely emptied of the water, and thoroughly dried.

the specific gravity of lead, will give the weight of the lead which the vessel will hold. If a glass jar for a mercurial pendulum be filled up with water to any required height, and the weight of the water multiplied by 13.5681, the specific gravity of mercury, it will give the weight of the mercury required. The foregoing rules, with the cases resolved by them, will appear not to be so neatly done as they might have been; but, had they been set out with such formulæ and characters as mathematicians are accustomed to make use of, they would have been wholly unintelligible to a great part of those for whom the rules are given.

For *Example*. To find the solidity of the frustum of a cone?

Put D = greater diameter.
    d = lesser diameter.
    m = .7854.
    h = height.
    S = solidity.

Theorem
$$\frac{m\,h}{3} \times : \overline{D+d}|^2 - D \times d = S$$
or rather
$$\frac{m \times h}{3} \times \overline{D+d}|^2 - D \times d = S$$

This to a mathematician is a very simple business, and yet with many a clock-maker nothing could be made of it.

A Table of various sizes of Clock weights Shells, their lengths and Diameters given in Inches and Decimal parts of an Inch, with their Solidity or Number of Cubic Inches, and the Number of Pounds and Decimal parts of a Pound, avoirdupois weight, of Lead required to fill them.

Length in Inches and Decimal Parts.	Diameter in Ditto.	Cubic Inches, &c.	Number of Pounds, Weight of Lead, &c.
4.	2.	12.576	5.151
4.25	2.	13.351	5.482
4.5	2.	14.137	5.804
4.75	2.	14.922	6.127
5.	2.	15.718	6.449
5.25	2.	16.493	6.772
5.5	2.	17.278	7.094
5.75	2.	18.064	7.589
6.	2.	18.849	7.739
6.25	2.	19.645	8.062
6.5	2.	20.420	8.384
6.75	2.	21.699	8.909
6.	2.25	23.856	9.795
6.25	2.25	24.851	10.203
6.5	2.25	25.844	10.611
6.75	2.25	26.838	11.029
6.	2.5	29.452	12.093
6.25	2.5	30.679	12.597
6.5	2.5	31.906	13.101
6.75	2.5	33.134	13.604
6.	2.75	35.637	14.632
6.25	2.75	37.122	15.252
6.5	2.75	38.607	15.852
6.75	2.75	40.090	16.461
6.	3.	42.411	17.414
6.25	3.	44.178	18.129
6.5	3.	45.945	18.865
6.75	3.	47.713	19.591
7.	3.	49.480	20.316
7.25	3.	51.347	21.042
7.5	3.	53.014	21.767
7.75	3.	54.781	22.503
8.	3.	56.548	23.219

CHAPTER VIII.

On the Escapement, or 'Scapement ; and the discovery of the Pendulum, with its application to a Clock.

THE escapement is that part of a clock or watch connected with the beats which we hear them give; and these beats are the effects of the moving power, carried forward by means of the wheels in the movement to the last one, which in a clock is called the *swing wheel,* and in a watch, the *balance wheel.* The teeth of these wheels act on the pallets or verge, which are of various shapes; and which form the most essential part in a 'scapement ; the drop from each tooth of the swing or balance wheels on their respective pallets, giving one beat or impulse to the pendulum or balance, in order to keep up or maintain their motion ; and were it not for the pallets, which alternately stop the teeth of the swing or balance wheels, the motive force would have no check. Hence it is, that, by this mechanism of the 'scapement, the wheels in the movement are prevented from having their revolutions accelerated, which would take place to such a degree, as to make the machine run down in a minute or two ; whereas, from the resistance opposed by the pallets, it is kept going for twenty-four or thirty hours, for a week, or a month, or even for twelve months. In such clocks or watches, however, which, as a matter of curiosity, have been made to go longer than a month, there is less reason to expect an accurate measure of time, unless great skill is displayed, not only in the execution, but also in their construction.

No part of a clock or watch requires so much skill and judgment in the contrivance, and so much care and nicety in its execution, as that of the 'scapement ; and none of the 'scapements of the present day require this more than the crown wheel and verge 'scapement, which, when nicely executed on proper principles, does extremely well for a common pocket watch: but this is a thing hardly now to be met with.

From the time of Dr. Hooke, and during the last century, many ingenious contrivances for 'scapements were suggested ; but the number of those adopted in practice is very limited. The crown wheel and verge 'scapement is represented in Plate III. No. 17. where V is the verge, and C the crown wheel, *p p* the pallets, and B B the balance. It is the oldest that is known, and must have been the only one used in clocks for several centuries previous to the middle of the seventeenth, or towards the end of it. Although it has been so long in use, and so well known to every clock and watch-maker, that its merits are now overlooked, and held in little estimation; yet, if it is duly considered, it will be found to have been a very masterly and ingenious device. The crown wheel and verge are of such an odd shape, that they resemble nothing that is familiar to us; yet some ancient artist had contrived it for the purpose, *(and it certainly was an ingenious thought,)* to give an alternate motion to a plain wheel or cross, which he had suspended from the upper end of its axis by a string, whereas formerly it rested on the lower end of the axis or *foot pivot*. This plain wheel was like the fly of our common kitchen-jack. In place of this circular rim or plain wheel on the axis, there were some of them that had two arms, forming something like a cross; on these were made notches, concentric to the axis, in which, on each arm, were hung a small weight; by shifting these more or less from the centre, the clock was made to go slow or fast. From the weightiness of this kind of balance, and the rude execution of the work, the friction on the end of the foot pivot would be so great, that it is probable there was some difficulty to make the clock keep going for any length of time. Recourse was then had to suspend the balance by a small cord, so that the end of the lower pivot should not rest on the foot of the potence. This ingenious idea has, in modern times, been adopted both by Berthoud and Le Roy, who have had the balances, in some of their marine time keepers, suspended by a piece of very small harpsichord wire, or by a very delicate piece of watch pendulum spring wire. The mechanism of the movement of these ancient clocks is exactly the same as has been frequently made for an alarm. To construct this, and apply it to a clock, there was hardly a step to go; and therefore, in all probability, the invention of the alarm part took place before that of the striking part, though some have thought otherwise. Berthoud thought so, as appears by his having put the striking part as the prior invention of the two.

In many parts of India, where public clocks are unknown at this day, they strike the hour upon a plate of silver, (or silver alloyed with some other metal,) of a lenticular shape, about 18 inches in diameter, and formed from the middle of a thin square plate of the same metal. The plate is hung by a double string, on a cross bar of wood, whose ends are supported on the tops of wooden posts fixed firmly in the ground; and when the hour is indicated either by their sand-glasses, clepsydræ, or water dropping instruments, which they sometimes use, they strike with a wooden mallet on the circular or lenticular part of the plate, and thus proclaim the hour of the day; the sound produced is strong, clear, and pleasant. This device is practised in many of the towns and camps throughout India.

The invention of the striking part to a clock was a more complex process than that of an alarm, and we have no doubt of the priority of the latter.

Plate IV. No. 19. represents, in profile, a clock with an alarm; No. 20. shows the dials of this machine, with the hours, minutes, and seconds, as seen in front. The small dial A is that of the alarm; the large dial concentric with the small one, is that of the hours and minutes; and the dial B is that of the seconds. The wheel work of the movement, No. 19. is composed of four wheels contained in the frame C D; H is the great wheel, which carries on its arbor a pulley, in whose groove are fixed several steel pins with sharp points, serving to enter into the texture of the cord carrying the weight F of the going part, and the counter weight G. This pulley carries the *encliquetage*, a kind of click and ratchet work, by means of a step spring, and the crosses of the great wheel, so that when the counter weight is drawn down, it winds up the weight F.

The first wheel H makes its revolution in an hour; its axis, which is also that of the pulley, carries the pivot *b* prolonged outside of the plate C. This pivot carries a cannon, (or socket,) on the end of which is fitted the minute hand, on the lower end is riveted the wheel *c*, which pitches into the wheel *d* of the same diameter and number of teeth; the axis of the wheel *d* carries the pinion *e*, which pitches in and leads the wheel *f*, that makes a turn in 12 hours, and its socket carries the hour hand.

The wheel H, which has 64 teeth, pitches into the pinion *g* of 8 leaves. The axis of this pinion carries the wheel I of 60 teeth, which pitches into the pinion *h* of 6 leaves; this makes 60 turns for one of the wheel H, and consequently one turn in a minute; and the hand *i*, carried by the long pivot of the axis *h*, points out the seconds on the dial B, No. 20.

The axis of the second's pinion *h* carries the contrate wheel K, which has 48 teeth; it pitches into the pinion *k* of 12 leaves. The axis of this pinion carries the wheel of rencounter, or crown wheel L of 15 teeth. This wheel makes 'scapement with the pallets *l, m*, carried by the axis of the balance M M, which is the regulator of the machine.

At each revolution of the crown wheel L, the balance makes twice

15 vibrations, that is to say, 30; and this wheel makes 4 turns for one of the wheel for seconds, so that the balance makes 120 vibrations in a minute, and 7200 in an hour; each of these vibrations, then, is half a second of time, and the second's hand makes two beats in a second.

The mechanism of the alarm part, which is very simple, is contained in the second frame N O, connected with that which encloses the wheel work or movement of the going part of the clock.

The crown wheel P, or that of the 'scapement, carries on its axis the pulley Q, (of the same kind as that on the going great wheel H) surrounded or overlapped with the cord which supports the weight R, the mover of the alarm, and its counterweight S. This pulley makes a kind of click and ratchet work, with that of the wheel P for the winding up of the weight R.

The teeth of the wheel P 'scape, with the pallets n, o, formed on the vertical axis T V, whose kneed arm p p, q q, forms in u the hammer of the alarm. This hammer is in form of a small cylinder, the two ends of which are shaped somewhat like a hemispherical button, or it is a cylinder of a larger diameter, with hemispherical ends, as seen at No. 19. and strikes alternately upon the opposite inside edges of a bell, which is not represented in the plate.

The alarm wheel P carries on its circumference a pin, which serves to stop the alarm after winding up the weight: this stop is made by means of the arm p of the detent p, q, r, put within the frame composed of the dial-plate, and that of the back plate O of the alarm part. To make the *detention* of the alarm, there is placed on the socket of the hour wheel, another socket which carries the dial of the alarm t, and a counter spring s, on which is fixed a pin, which serves to raise the arm r of the detent p, q, r; so that the arm p is drawn up from the wheel P, and disengages the pin which it carries; the alarm then sets off, and strikes rapidly on the bell.

In order that the alarm may set off at the precise hour at which one wants to be awakened, it is only turning the dial A of the alarm, No. 20. so that the cypher of the hour required is placed under the small end v of the hour hand. If it is wanted that it should give the alarm at four hours and a half, place the dial as it is seen, No. 20. between the ciphers 4 and 5, &c.

On comparing the alarm part of this clock, with the 'scapement-work in that of Vick's, the difference may be said to be very little; for a pulley, when put on the arbor of Vick's crown wheel, and into it a pin, along with the other apparatus which has just now been described, will truly constitute what may be called an alarm. The mechanism of an alarm part is greatly improved by making it in such a way as we sometimes have done, and here it is actuated by a spring, in place of a weight as in the former, not that this difference is considered as any part of the improvement. The wheels are 72, 64, and 60, three pinions of 8, eight semi-circular steel lifting pins, set alternately on each side of the wheel of 64, with two hammers and a bell to each, on separate and slender bell-studs; by this means, each bell retains the sound brought out of it by its own hammer, and no jarring or confused disagreeable sort of noise can take place as in the *old way*, from which, however, few or none of the modern alarms differ. The fly and its pinion will make 3.75 revolutions for the lifting of each of the hammers. A wheel of 48, in place of 60, would give 3 revolutions for the lift. The alarm barrel and spring is put on, and inside of the fore-plate, the great wheel of 72 lays near to the pillar plate, the fly turns behind the pillar-plate, and may be made somewhat like that which is frequently used for the quarter part of a clock; that is, so as at pleasure it can be set to moderate the velocity of the train of wheels, by extending the wings (or vanes) more or less. The length of the fly over all may be from 2.5 to 4 inches, the weight about 118 grains. If the main spring of the alarm makes four turns in the barrel, the time of the alarm running may be from a minute to two minutes, according to existing circumstances.

The opinion, viz. that the alarm part was a prior invention to the striking part in clocks, is strongly corroborated by the observations of Hamberger, in Beckman's *History of Inventions.* " These horologia," he remarks, " not only pointed out the hours by an index, but emitted also a sound. This we learn from *Primaria Instituta Canonicorum Præmonstatentium*, where it is ordered that the sacristan should regulate the horologium, and make it sound before matins to awaken him. I dare not, however, venture thence to infer, that these machines announced the number of the hour by their sound, as they seem only to have given an alarm at any proposed time of getting up from bed. I have indeed never yet found an author where it is mentioned that the number of the hour was expressed by them; and when we read of their emitting a sound, weare to understand, that it was for the purpose of awakening the sacristan to prayers. The expression *horologium cecidit*, which occurs frequently in the before quoted writers, I consider as allusive to this sounding of the machine. Du Fresne, in my opinion, under the word *horologium*, mistakes the expression, *de ponderibus in imum delapsis*, because the machine was then at rest, and could raise neither the sacristan, or any one else, whose business it was to beat the *scilla*."

When an alarm is set off, the weight which is the moving force of it very soon falls to the bottom, and then the alarm ceases.

In attempting to make the first 'scapement, there can be little doubt that something of the circular or cylindrical kind was contrived or discovered, and the only thing which could give *it* an alternate motion, was either a spiral spring or a pendulum; but these things being then unknown, the clock-maker was obliged to seek after other methods, and at last produced the crown wheel and verge 'scapement. How came it that means so complicated were taken, when those which were more simple and better were overlooked?

It is a very singular circumstance, that as a small ball or weight, when suspended by a slender thread, and drawn a little aside from the perpendicular, on being let go, continues to vibrate for a considerable time, and with the utmost regularity; and as many things in domestic life were hung up or suspended by strings, and were every day seen or observed: yet so long a time elapsed before any thing of this kind was ever thought of, or applied to regulate the motion of a clock! It is said that Galileo took his idea of a pendulum from the motion of a lamp suspended from the roof, or ceiling of a church, which had been accidentally set a vibrating. He used the simple pendulum, in his astronomical observations, long before it was applied to a clock. Some of the earlier astronomers, as well as Galileo, used a common string and ball, which they made to vibrate a little while during the time of an observation of any of the heavenly bodies; yet even these astronomers did not think of its application to clocks. Many watch-finishers, when their watch is finished, *for want of a pendulum clock*, regulate it by means of a ball and string, which will answer very well, by taking 50 vibrations of a pendulum, whose oscillations are made in a second, in the same time that the contrate wheel of a common watch ought to make one revolution.

As gravitation is the principle on which the isochronal motion of a pendulum is founded, it cannot properly be considered as an invention, as some have called it, whatever name may be given to it when applied to regulate the motion of a clock. The pendulum having before this been long known in its simple state, and used as a sort of time-measurer, it was no wonder that the idea of applying it to a clock was entertained by several persons nearly about the same period. The movement of the ancient balance clocks was not adapted for the application of the pendulum, so as readily to give motion to it. The wheels in them were all flat ones, except the crown wheel, and no other 'scapement at this time was known but that of the crown wheel and verge; so that, without considerable difficulty and invention, the pendulum could not well be applied to this construction of a clock movement. The pocket watch had been made a considerable time before this, and the construction of its movement, which had a contrate wheel in it, would naturally lead them to that of one which would adapt itself to the motion of a pendulum, as by means of the contrate wheel, the arbor of the crown wheel could be made to stand in a vertical position, whereas, in the old balance clocks, the position was horizontal. Galileo seems early to have discovered the properties of the pendulum; it has been said, as early as towards the end of the sixteenth century, and their investigation long after that was prosecuted with great success by Huyghens.

The son of Galileo applied the pendulum to a clock at Venice, in the year 1649; but to what sort of a movement we cannot pretend to say, though we suspect, from that want of success which seems to have attended his trials, that he had not adopted the contrate wheel movement, already mentioned, as the most proper for it. We know that Huyghens made use of this sort of movement, as the only one fit to be regulated by the motion of the pendulum, which he had also applied. Of late, another candidate for the application of the pendulum to a clock has been brought forward by such respectable authority, that leaves little or no room to doubt of its authenticity. Mr. Grignion informs us, " that a clock was made in 1642, by Richard Harris of London, for the church of St. Paul's, Covent Garden, and that this clock had a pendulum to it." It appears, from unquestionable evidence, that Galileo, mathematician to the Grand Duke of Tuscany, first discovered the properties of the pendulum, used it in his astronomical observations, as has been already mentioned, and wrote a tract explaining its principles. This tract was translated from the Italian into French at Paris, printed in 1639, in a duodecimo volume, and sold by Pierre Ricolet. Galileo intended to apply it to a clock, but this he never put in execution. Father Alexander says, " that they had nothing better than the balance clocks in France until the year 1660."

It may be observed, that the application of the pendulum to a clock, and of the spiral spring to the balance of a watch, were the greatest improvements that could possibly have been made in the machinery of time-measuring, and they both happened to have been brought into use nearly about the same period.

Seeing that Daniel and Thomas Grignion had been watch-makers in London as early as 1740, if not before, were long afterwards in great repute, men of integrity, and great ingenuity, especially Thomas, who has left us in such a positive manner this account of

Harris's pendulum clock, that a doubt of the fact cannot well be admitted; and although it had not till of late got any kind of publicity, yet this cannot be a sufficient reason to make us withhold our assent to it. Galileo had published an account of the nature and properties of the pendulum a few years before Harris's clock was made, who may have by some means got hold of it, and, being a clock-maker, might very readily fall on the way of applying a pendulum to his clock. Inigo Jones was the architect for the church of St Paul's, Covent Garden, he had been twice in Italy during the time that Galileo flourished, and possibly may have communicated to Harris what he might have heard in Italy of a pendulum.

Justus Borgen, or Byrgius, a Swiss, who was allowed to be an excellent mechanic, as well as a profound mathematician and astronomer, is said to have put a pendulum to a clock, and this at a considerable time before that of Harris's. Being much engaged in making philosophical and mathematical instruments of various kinds, he may probably have seen the nature of a swinging body or pendulum, and adapted it to his clock; or he may have heard of what had been done or published by Galileo, who was well on in the vigour of life somewhile before Tycho Brahe came to Prague.

The evidence for this, as will be seen in the sequel, surely carries along with it such a degree of respect, that there seems to be no rational ground to refuse or deny it.

Berthoud has a train of arguments against that of Borgen having applied the pendulum to a clock, yet says, " considering his great abilities, it is not improbable, but from not having published it, he is not entitled to the merit of it." The arguments used here against Borgen may come equally so to Harris. " That because a pendulum clock was not known in France before the year 1660, it is not likely that it could have been applied any where else, for any length of time, before this period,"—" that so great an improvement as this is to a clock could not fail to be soon and widely spread abroad." It may, however, be remarked, that there are many things of great utility that get diffused, but very slowly and gradually after the discovery. *Watch-jewelling, for instance,* was practised, as a trade, in London nearly an hundred years before it was introduced in Paris, or even Geneva, the native place of the invention. Indeed, this art was so long established in London, that most of the watch-makers there thought it an English invention, at least we found this to be their general opinion in the year 1797, when in that city, on a deputation from Edinburgh for effecting the repeal of the watch tax act. In corroboration of this, we shall insert what has been said on the subject by a very eminent *French* author. " Nous finirons, en annoncant que les Cit. Mole et Magnin, artistes de Genêve, qui avoient travaillé à Paris, chez le Cit. Berthoud, ont executée en 1798, une montre marine, qui a été eprouvée avec le plus grand succès dans l'observatoire de Genêve, (*Bibliothèque Britannique*, An. 7.) Ils y font usage de l'art de percer les rubis, anciennement porté de Genêve en Angleterre, et qu'ils ont apprit du Cit. Mallet, qui avoit travaillé à Londresc hez Harlay, possesseur de cet art; le Cit. Louis Berthoud se l'est aussi procuré." Voyez, *Histoire des Mathématiques*, par *J. E. Montucla.* Tome quatrième, p. 568. A Paris, Mai 1802. Which, in English, is this, " We shall conclude by mentioning, that the citizens Mole and Magnin, artists of Geneva, who had practised at Paris with citizen Berthoud, made, in 1798, a marine (time-keeper) watch, which has been tried in the Observatory at Geneva, where it gave satisfactory proofs of its great regularity. (*Bibliothèque Britannique*, An. 7.) In it they made use of the art of piercing rubies, formerly carried from Geneva into England, in which they had been taught by citizen Mallet, who had worked in London with *Harley*, a watch-jeweller there. Citizen Louis Berthoud is also a master in this branch of watch-making." See *The History of Mathematics*, by J. E. Montucla, vol. iv. p. 568. Paris, May, 1802.—*We knew Harley to be an excellent maker of ruby cylinders, having frequently employed him in that way.*

With regard to the pendulum clocks of Borgen, Harris, and even those of Huyghens, they all had the old crown wheel and verge 'scapement, and pendulums of no great length, consequently their precision of time-keeping was not so great as to attract, or much interest the attention of astronomers or of artists, unless in so far as the latter were professionally interested.

" Among them," says Derham, " that have claimed the merit of the invention, the great Galileo hath the most to be said on his side. Dr. John Joachim Becher, (who printed a book when he was in England, entitled, *De Nova temporis dimetiendi ratione Theoriæ*, &c. which he dedicated to the Royal Society, anno 1680,) he, I say, tells us, ' that Count Magalotti (the Great Duke of Tuscany's resident at the Emperor's court) told him the whole history of these pendulum clocks, and denied Mr. Zulichem to be the author of them. Also, that one Treffler (clock-maker to the father of the Great Duke of Tuscany) related to him the like history : and said, moreover, that he had made the first pendulum clock at *Florence*, by command of the Great Duke, and by the directions of his mathematician Galileus a Galileo, a pattern of which was brought to Holland. And farther he saith, that one *Caspar Doms*, a Fleming, and mathematician to *John Philip a Schonbern*, (the late Elector of Mentz), told him that he had seen at Prague, in the time of the Emperor Rudolphus, (who reigned from 1576 to 1612,) a pendulum clock made by the famous Justus Borgen, mechanic and clock-maker to the Emperor, which clock the great Tycho Brahe used in his astronomical observations."

An epitome of this celebrated astronomer's history shall be given, as it tends, in some degree, to confirm this account as given by Becher. Derham, after Sturmius, says, " that Riccioli first made use of pendulums to measure time." This seems to be incorrect, as Galileo knew the properties of the pendulum even before Riccioli was born. See *Derham's Artificial Clock-maker*. Having given a historical detail of the first pendulum clocks, it is left for the reader to judge for himself, who, it is hoped, will also excuse any repetitions that may have occurred, arising from causes which are nowise necessary to be explained here.

Tycho Brahe having attained, by his astronomical labours, so much honour and fame, as to draw upon him (during the minority of a young prince) the envy of a few illiberal courtiers of Denmark, who got him removed from his observatory and place of residence, which he had erected on the small island of Huen, in order to deprive him of the power of prosecuting his observations; he came then to Copenhagen, and had not been long there, when, persecuted by the same blind malignity, he was ordered by the minister to desist from his astronomical and chemical pursuits. It was these circumstances which led him to Prague in 1599, where Rudolphus, who well knew his merits, patronised him, and gave him a considerable pension, and a castle, at five miles distance, for himself and family to reside in. It must have been at this period that he used the pendulum clock, said to have been made by Justus Borgen. But he did not live long to enjoy the generous appointment of the Emperor Rudolphus, being very suddenly carried off by an acute disease, induced by an over delicacy in a retention of water, in the year 1601, and in the fifty-fifth year of his age.

Description of Huyghens' Clock.

Plate IV. No. 21, represents a view of it in profile; A A, B B, are two plates placed vertically. They are 6 inches in height, and 2 inches and a half broad, and connected together by four pillars placed at the angles. The height of these pillars is one inch and a half, the pivots of the arbors of the principal wheels run in these plates. The first wheel marked C has 80 teeth, and 2 inches and a half in diameter; it carries on its arbor a pulley D, whose convex edge is furnished with sharp steel points, to prevent the cord which laps over it from slipping, and to this cord two weights are attached, as shall afterwards be explained. The wheel C then receives its motion by one of the weights, and communicates it to the pinion E of 8 leaves, and consequently to the wheel F of 48 teeth, which has the same arbor as the pinion. The wheel F drives the pinion G, and the contrate wheel H on the same arbor with G, having 48 teeth. It is from the last wheel that the pinion I and the wheel K receive their motion; the pinion I is of 24 leaves, and the wheel K 15 teeth, inclined as represented in the figure. N Q and P are two cocks fixed on the plate B B. The extremities P and Q of the two cocks carry the pivots of the verge L M, and the projecting part of the cock Q is pierced with two holes, one for the traverse of the verge L M, the other which receives the upper pivot of the arbor of the wheel K. The arbor, or verge L M, (which also crosses the plate B B,) carries the two pallets L L, which must be alternately raised, in contrary directions, by the teeth of the wheel K. The part M of the verge L M, which goes outside of the frame, carries the fork S, between which passes the rod V V of the pendulum V X, suspended by means of two threads between the cycloidal cheeks, of which T is the profile, but seen moreover in perspective in No. y, both show sufficiently how the whole is connected.

Moreover, here is what regards the disposition and going of the hands; gg is a third plate, and parallel to the two first, distant a quarter of an inch from the plate A A. Through the centre of the dial, traced on this plate, the arbor of the wheel C is lengthened out. On the dial are traced two concentric circles, one divided into 12, the other into 60 parts. On the arbor of the wheel C, and outside of the plate A A, the canon or socket of the wheel a is put on spring tight, and goes as far as e through the plate gg, and can turn with the wheel C, or, independent of it, when thought proper to make it do so, it is at the point e, where the minute hand is put. With regard to the wheel a, it drives a wheel b of the same number of teeth, whose axis carries a pinion of 6 leaves, one of its pivots run in the plate A A, the other in the cock c, screwed on to the plate A A.

Lastly, this last pinion leads the wheel d of 72 teeth, whose socket goes on that of the wheel a, coming below e, and passes like it through the plate gg; the end of this socket carries the hour hand, which is a little shorter than the minute hand. With regard to the seconds, to avoid confusion, the arbor of the wheel H, which is prolonged as far as the plate gg, carries a dial ff divided into 60 parts, which turns in the same time as the wheel H, and an index g fixed to the upper part of the opening made on the plate gg, marks the seconds, according as the divisions pass.

It shall now be shown, in what way the going weight was applied by Huyghens, so as to keep the clock going during the time of winding up, a contrivance, says he, hitherto not thought of, and which deserved some consideration. The cord which is used here is continued, that is, its ends are joined together, and hence it may be called an endless cord. It is first passed over the pulley D, attached to the great wheel C, (or its representative A, No. 22), from whence it comes down, and takes in the pulley d, (of the main weight P) passing under it and carried upwards, it passes over and takes in the ratchet pulley H, which turns on a stud, fixed to the inside of the back plate of the clock frame. From this pulley the cord comes down, and goes under the pulley f, which carries the counter weight p, in order to prevent the main weight P from descending, (otherwise, than when making the pulley D, and the great wheel C to turn), and lastly, from the pulley f, the cord returns to the first pulley A or D. The ratchet pulley H, like D has jagged steel points inserted in the bottom of the groove, besides having a click and spring to prevent its turning backward; and can only turn one way, by pulling down the cord at m, when it is wanted to raise up the main weight P. It is clear by this way, that the main weight P, exerts only half of its force to turn the wheel work, and this effort is not suspended during the time that the going weight is brought up. This, we may observe, is the first application of a going work in time of winding. See *Horlogium Oscillatorium. Paris*, 1673, p. 5. Or *Histoire de la Mésure du Temps par les Horloges, par Ferdinand Berthoud.* Tome premier. *A Paris*, An X. (1802 *V. S.*)

In some of the old Dutch striking clocks of 30 hours going, an endless cord went over, not only the pulley of the going part, but also over that of the striking part, and one weight served for both; the winding up was, by pulling down the cord from the striking side, the pulley on the great wheel there having a circular steel step spring, the step butted against the crosses of the wheel, when the force of the weight was applied, but passed them freely when winding up.

Notwithstanding the application of the pendulum, and the ingenious contrivance of cycloidal cheeks by Huyghens, in order to make the long and short vibrations be performed in nearly as equal times as possible; yet these clocks did not keep time with that correctness which was expected. This arose from the great extent of the arc of vibration, the lightness of the pendulum ball, the great *dominion* which the clock had over the pendulum, and the bad effects produced by the cycloidal cheeks, which, however excellent in theory, were never found useful in practice.

This led artists and amateurs of the profession to think of farther means of improvement. Accordingly, about the year 1680, a clock was made by W. Clement, a clock-maker in London, having, in place of the crown wheel and verge 'scapement, a 'scapement which was nearly the same as the common recoiling one of the present day. The swing wheel S W, Plate IV. No. 23, was flat, having a sort of ratchet or saw-like teeth, and the pallets PP, had a remote resemblance to the head of an anchor, by which it acquired at that time the name of the *anchor 'scapement*. The ball of the pendulum was made much heavier than what formerly had been used, the arc of vibration much shorter, and the motive force much less. From the excellent time-keeping of the clock, this was found to be a great improvement, and hence this 'scapement was afterwards generally adopted. It passed into Holland, Germany, but was hardly known in France until the year 1695. See *Histoire de la Mésure du Temps*, tom. i. p. 100.

At the time this clock of Clement's appeared, Dr. Hooke claimed the invention of it as his, and affirmed, that after the great fire of London in 1666, he had shewn to the Royal Society, a clock with this very 'scapement. " Considering," says Sully in his *Histoire des Echappemens*, " the genius, and the great number of fine discoveries of this excellent man, I see no room to doubt that he was the first inventor of it." The pendulum with this 'scapement had received the name of the Royal Pendulum.

Robert Hooke came to Oxford as a poor scholar, and brought with him a number of mechanical nick-nacks, which he had made at home. His mechanical genius soon made him known to the members of the Invisible Society there, who employed him to work for them, making apparatus for their experiments. Dr. Ward, afterwards Bishop of Salisbury, took a liking for him, and instructed him in mathematics and astronomy. He urged him to try his mechanical genius in contriving a 'scapement for a pendulum. It would appear that they found that the 'scapement for a balance, which had long been in use, did not answer, probably because it required very wide vibrations, which were found to be not so equable as required ; and Hooke invented this some time before February 1656 ; for there are observations of a solar eclipse made in that month, at Oxford, by a pendulum clock.

Hooke's father was a watch-maker at Bayeswater, in the Isle of Wight, where he had probably been taught to work. The contrivances and inventions of Hooke are numerous, and all of them very ingenious. A catalogue of them has been selected from his works and others, by the late Professor Robison, who was a great admirer of his ingenuity, and is inserted in the Supplement to the third edition of the Encyclopædia Britannica, under the *article* Dr. ROBERT HOOKE. His researches were much the same as those afterwards pursued by the immortal Newton, whose prototype he seems to have been. He also proposed to make a clock to register the changes in the barometer. Cumming may have taken up this idea of Hooke's, having made a barometrical clock for his late Majesty King George the Third; though this is not mentioned in the Supplement, yet it is said to be one of Hooke's inventions, as stated in the Professor's manuscript Catalogue of them, in our possession.

Dr. Hooke's claim to the merit of the invention of the anchor pallet 'scapement appears to be completely confirmed by the silence of Smith in his *Horological Disquisitions*, which were published not very long afterwards, who then, and who is the *only* one that has mentioned several improvements applied to a clock made by *Clement*, but takes no notice of the anchor pallets, a thing at that time (1680) so new, and which, from their very construction or figure, could not be used without adopting the consequences to which they would naturally lead, viz. the pendulum rod to be longer, the ball much heavier than what was used before, the swing to be shorter, and the moving power much less. Mr. Smith must have known that the anchor pallets were the contrivance of Dr. Hooke, otherwise he would have described them, being the panegyrist of *Clement*, and, as a clock-maker, very capable of doing so, knowing well it was on them the whole improvement hinged. The following is an extract from his little book: " At length, in Holland, an ingenious and learned gentleman, Mr. Christian Hugens by name, found out the way to regulate the uncertainty of its motion, (that of a clock,) by the vibration of a pendulum. From Holland, the fame of the invention soon passed over into England, where several eminent and ingenious workmen applied themselves to rectify some defects which as yet were found therein; among which that eminent and well-known artist, *Mr. William Clement*, had at last the good fortune to give it the finishing stroke, he being the real contriver of that curious kind of long pendulum, which is at this day so universally in use among us; an invention that exceeds all others yet known as to the exactness and steadiness of its motion, which proceeds from two properties peculiar to this pendulum; the one is the weightiness of its bob, and the other the little compass in which it plays: The first of these makes it less apt to be commanded by the accidental differences of strength that may sometimes happen in the draught of the wheels; and the other renders the vibrations more equal and exact, as not being capable of altering so much in the distance of the swing as the other kind of pendulums are, which fetch a larger, and, by consequence, a less constant compass."

Lepaute is also of Sully's opinion, and thought that Dr. Hooke had the best title to the merit of the invention. That he invented the anchor pallets must now appear unquestionable; and there can be little or no doubt that he applied the long pendulum rod and heavy ball, whose short arcs required but a small force to keep them up.

Clement, being an ingenious clock-maker, may have been (of his profession) the first who made and sent a clock of this description abroad to the public: this was about fourteen years after Dr. Hooke had shown *his* to the Royal Society. It is singular that neither Smith nor Derham, who were contemporary with Clement, take the least notice of the pallets which were at his clock; mentioning the collateral circumstances only.

The *dead beat* 'scapement of Graham's next succeeded, which was invented some time before the beginning of the eighteenth century; the principle of it in the horizontal watch was adopted in the pallets of a clock 'scapement, which has continued to be the one generally used in regulators or astronomical clocks, with a very few exceptions.

About ten or fifteen years afterwards, it came to be known in France, where it was adopted as the best for clocks intended to measure time accurately. *Lepaute*, a very ingenious watch-maker in Paris, produced, about the year 1753, or some time thereabout, a 'scapement founded on that of Graham's *dead beat* one. In Lepaute's, the *rest* of the teeth on the pallets was always with the same effect, because it was on the same circle, whichsoever of the pallets it rested upon; and the impulse was always the same on whichsoever pallet it was given, the flanches of the pallets being planes equally inclined, or having the same angle. This was, no doubt, some improvement on *Graham's*; but the teeth of the swing wheel in Lepaute's consisted of sixty small steel pins, thirty being arranged on each side of the rim of the wheel; and where pin teeth are used, oil, which is in some degree necessary, cannot easily be kept on them, the attraction of the rim of the wheel constantly draining the oil from these pin sort of teeth, an evil which is perhaps not easily to be got the better of, unless by using stone pallets and hard tempered steel pins.

Description of Lepaute's 'Scapement. (Plate V. No. 27.)

On an arbor F, or what is called the verge in a clock, are fixed two pallet arms, of such a shape as represented in the figure; the arm G A e is behind the swing wheel, the other, H B d, is on the opposite side, and the acting parts are at such a distance from each other as just to allow a proper freedom for the plane of the wheel to pass between them; the arm G A must be filed away at G, so as to clear the tops of the pin teeth on that side of the wheel: one of the arms is riveted fast to the socket which connects them with the arbor, the other must be allowed to turn about, (though with difficulty,) so as the pallet flanches can be set or made to any angle required. The parts R I, L S, of the pallets, are arcs of a circle, whose centre is at F, and in the same plane with that of the wheel teeth, it is on them that they rest during a part of the times of ascending and descending of the pendulum; the acting parts are the inclined planes I e, L d, by means of which the teeth of the wheel give impulse to the pendulum. The white pins x y, are on this side of the wheel: the pins u n, are on the other side, placed alternately with each other: There are three faint traces of circles drawn on the rim of the wheel, for the purpose of arranging the pin teeth properly; the acting part of the white teeth are on the inside of the middle circle, that of the darker teeth are on the outside; by this way the impulses are given quite equal by all the teeth, in so far as regards their effect on the pendulum, and the effect during the time of rest may be said to be the same; the teeth have one half of their diameter or thickness taken away, so as to allow the pallets to get clear more instantly at the time of dropping from them, than they could otherwise do, were the pin teeth left wholly round.

The wheel turning from u towards x, by the force of the going weight, the teeth on this side of the wheel meet the inclined plane L d, and pushes it towards B; by this the pallet G A e, which is on the opposite side of the wheel, advances under the next coming on tooth u; at this time the point v having escaped from the point d, and the pallet arm G A continuing to go on that side, by the impulsion given to it by the pendulum, while the tooth u is on the concave circular part R, which is the arc of rest. The pallet arms being brought back towards the side A, by the descending oscillation of the pendulum, the pin u, which rubbed on the arc R I during the time of rest, immediately meets the inclined plane I e, on which it acts as the tooth *v* did on the plane L *d*, but in a contrary direction, in pushing the pallet arms from *e* towards A, until the following or next tooth finds itself on the constant arc L S, to re-descend from it upon the inclined plane L *d*, and so on. It may be remarked, that 60 teeth in the swing wheel are necessary in this 'scapement, whereas, in ordinary 'scapements, half of this number serves the same purpose, which is obvious, because in the ordinary way each tooth gives impulse to the pendulum on both sides; but in this of Lepaute's, 30 teeth give impulse only to the pendulum on one side, and 30 to the other side.

Notwithstanding the seeming superiority and great character which the dead beat 'scapement had long acquired over that of the *recoiling* one, represented Plate IV. No. 25, this last, however, had its partizans, and among them were artists and amateurs possessed of first-rate talents: Professor Ludlam of Cambridge, Berthoud, Smeaton, and others. Harrison, indeed, always rejected the dead beat 'scapement with a sort of indignation. The author of the Elements of Clock and Watch-making has said a great deal in favour of the dead beat, and as much against the recoiling 'scapement, without having shown in what the difference consisted, or what was the cause of the good properties in the one, or what were the defects in the other. It appears doubtful if these causes were known to him; indeed, from his book, it may fairly be presumed that they were not, at least at the time it was written; yet he was deservedly allowed to be a man of great talent in every respect, and of considerable genius. When pallets are intended to give a small recoil, their form, if properly made, differs very little from those made for the dead beat, as may be seen by the dotted curve lines on the dead beat pallets in No. 26. The circular parts of the dead beat pallets are drawn from their centre of motion *v*, those for recoiling pallets are drawn from points eccentric to that of *their* motion.

We shall endeavour to point out the properties and defects naturally inherent in each:—When the teeth of the swing wheel, in the recoiling 'scapement, drop or fall on either of the pallets, the pallets, from their form, make all the wheels have a retrograde motion, opposing, at the same time, the pendulum in its ascent, and the descent from the same cause being equally promoted. This recoil or retrograde motion of the wheels, which is imposed on them by the reaction of the pendulum, is sometimes nearly a third, sometimes nearly a half or more, of the step previously advanced by the movement. This is perhaps the greatest or the only defect that can properly be imputed to the recoiling 'scapement, and is the cause of the greater wearing in the holes, pivots, and pinions, than that which takes place in a clock or watch, having the dead beat or cylindrical 'scapement; but this defect may partly be removed by making the recoil small, or a little more than merely a dead beat. After a recoiling clock has been brought to time, any additional motive force that is put to it will not greatly increase the arc of vibration, yet the clock will be found to go considerably faster; and, it is known, that where the arc of vibration is a very small matter increased, the clock ought to go slower, as would be the case, in some small degree, even with the isolated and *simple pendulum*. The form of the recoiling pallets tends to accelerate and multiply the number of vibrations according to the increase of the motive force impressed upon them, and hence the clock will gain on the time to which it was before regulated. Professor Ludlam, who had four clocks in his house, three of them with the dead beat, and the other with a recoil, said, " that none of them kept time, fair or foul, like the last: this kind of 'scapement guages the pendulum, the dead beat leaves it at liberty." Were it necessary, many incontestible proofs could be adduced of the excellent performance of clocks which have the recoiling 'scapement.

Let us now make a similar comparative trial with the dead beat 'scapement. An additional motive force being put to it, we find that the arc of vibration is considerably increased, and the clock in consequence of this goes very slow. There are two causes which produce this: the one is, the greater pressure by the swing wheel teeth on the circular part of the pallets during the time of rest; the other is, the increase of the arc of vibration. It was observed in the case of recoil, that an additional motive force made the clock go fast; and the same cause is found to make the clock, having the dead beat, to go slow. As the causes are the same, and yet produce effects diametrically opposite, does not this evidently point out what is necessary to be done? The pallets should be so formed, as to have very little of a recoil, and as little of the dead beat; and here any small variation of the motive force, or in the arc of vibration, will produce no sensible deviation from its settled rate of time-keeping. Pallets of this description were early proposed by our ingenious countryman *Sully*, after having seen the inutility of Huyghen's cycloidal cheeks. See his *Histoire des Eschappemens*. We are informed that a clock was given by the late Mr. Thomas Grignion, to the Society for the Encouragement of Arts, Manufactures, &c., " which had a dead beat 'scapement, so constructed or drawn off, that any diminution or addition of motive force, would not alter the time-keeping of the clock." All the 'scapements of this kind which have been hitherto made, were commonly drawn off nearly in the same way as Mr. Grignion's, that is, the distance between the centre of the pallets and the centre of the swing wheel, is equal to one diameter of the wheel, taken on the line which joins these centres; and the acting parts of the pallets is a tangent taken from the centre of the pallets to the wheel, taking in ten teeth, and 'scaping on the eleventh; this is nearly the same as represented in Plate II. of Mr. Cumming's book. The only difference is, that Mr. Grignion's circle of rest is the same on each pallet; but whether it possesses the properties which have been ascribed to it, shall be left to the determination of those who may choose to try this experiment with it. The circle for the time of rest being the same, then the flanches should be made to give the angles alike on both sides; we suppose this to have been Graham's way of it.

Notwithstanding what has been said respecting the giving isochronal curves to the pallets of a clock, it appears doubtful if such a curve can possibly be given them, that shall make the long and short vibrations of the pendulum be all performed in the same time. Even in the best executed clock, whose 'scapement is equally so, having the same motive force constant, the arc of vibration will be seen in a state of continual change; and where this arc is not constant, there will be a small difference in the time-keeping, that is to say, if nicely observed. With the spring pallet 'scapement, whose motive force may be said to be very constant and uniform, yet the vibrations of the pendulum with it, will be found to have changes in a small degree. At all events, if the semi-angle of a dead beat 'scapement, is equal to one degree, and that of the additional, or arc of supplement as it may be called, is half a degree more, this should be more than sufficient to make the pendulum to escape even in the worst state of the oil. Pallets having so short a line of curve as this, must be of little or no consideration in regard to their possessing isochronal properties.

Clock-makers in general have an idea that in a 'scapement, the pallets ought to take in seven, nine, or eleven teeth, thinking that an even number could not answer. This opinion seems to have arisen (as has been before mentioned) from the old crown wheel having always an odd number of teeth, because an even number could not have been so fit for it; there seems to be no rules (*as some have imagined*) necessarily prescribed for drawing off either the recoiling or the dead beat 'scapement, for any particular distance which the centre of the pallets ought to have from that of the swing wheel. The nearer that the centres of the swing wheel and pallets are, the less will be the number of teeth required to be taken in by the pallets, when a tangent to them is drawn to the wheel.

It is very obvious, that when the arms of the pallets are long, the influence of the motive force on the pendulum will be great; and vice versa, that is, when the pallet arms are short, the influence of the motive force will be less, but the angle of the 'scapement will naturally be greater than may be required; but this can be easily remedied by making the flanches so as to give any angle required. In ordinary clocks, when this angle is not quite half a degree on each side, a very small motive force will keep a very heavy pendulum in motion. We have known a very good clock-maker, who thought that the flanch of a pallet was an arbitrary or fixed point, which could be made only in one way, and it was some little while before he could be convinced of the contrary. The flanches may be made so long as to act something like detents, so as to stop the wheel altogether by the teeth, or they may be made so short as to allow the wheel teeth to pass them altogether without even giving impulse to them. It is true there would be no 'scapement here; only it shews that the flanches of the pallets may be made to give any angle of 'scapement, from a few minutes of a degree to two or three degrees. Whatever the angle of the flanches may be taken at, all that is requisite is to make the wheel 'scape so, that the tooth, when it drops on the pallet, shall fall just beyond the corner of the flanch, and in on the circular part of the dead beat pallet; this rule will equally serve where a moderate recoil is intended. The common recoiling pallets may be made in various ways, according to the fancy of the maker. At No. 24, the dead beat 'scapement is represented: the wheel has ten teeth, taken in by the pallets, one of which is seen to have dropped off from the driving pallet, and another, at this instant, to have got in on the circular part of the leading pallet, where it rests during the time of the vibration, at the end of it, the tooth will have got further in on the circular part; when returning, it gets on the flanched part of the pallet, and gives new impulse to the pendulum, and so on. By making the pallets to agree with the dotted curve lines, in place of having a dead beat, they will make a small recoil. The arms of the pallets are not quite so long as in Graham's original dead beat 'scapement, yet they might with advantage be a little shorter, in order that the influence of the motive force on the pendulum may be lessened. Probably Graham's reason for having such long arms to his pallets, was to show the superiority of his 'scapement over that of the recoiling one, by the very heavy pendulums he put to his clocks, and moved by a very light weight; many of his regulators went a month, and even to these he put heavy pendulums.

In the Journal of Science, Literature, and the Arts, published by Mr. John Murray, London, in the Numbers XXVIII and XXXI, for January and October, 1823, there is an account or description of a very neat and ingenious mode of fitting up a dead beat 'scapement for a clock, given by Mr. Vulliamy, clock-maker to the King.

Harrison's clock pallets (which are sometimes made to act by means of very delicate springs, and sometimes by their own gravity) have a very considerable recoil; they certainly were a most ingenious contrivance to supersede the necessity of having oil put to them. Their construction seems to be but little known, and they have very rarely been adopted in practice. Indeed it is a 'scapement of such a nature, that very few would be competent to execute it properly. The circumstances which led to the invention of it, were mentioned by Mr. Harrison himself to Professor Robison. "Having been sent for to look at a turret clock, which had stopt, he went to it, though it was at a considerable distance from his home, and found that the pallets were very much in want of oil, which he then applied to them. On his returning, and ruminating by the way on the indifferent sort of treatment which he thought he had met with, after having come so far, he set himself to work to contrive such a 'scapement as should not give to others that trouble to which he had been put, in consequence of this turret clock." Hence the origin of his pallets. A drawing and description of them shall be given in the course of this work.

We have been informed that a 'scapement somewhat of the same nature as this of Harrison's, was contrived by Mudge, with this difference of its being a dead beat one.

The justly celebrated Mudge, in a small tract published in June 1763, relative to the best means of improving marine time-keepers, suggested, as a great advantage, that of making the moving power bend up at every vibration of the balance, a small spring whose returning force should be exerted in maintaining the motion of the balance. See Plate VI. No. 32. and 33, and this is the same principle which some years afterwards he adopted and practised in those timekeepers which he made.

About two or three years after the publication of this tract, Mr. Cumming contrived a clock 'scapement nearly on the same principle as that of Mudge's, where the motion of the pendulum was maintained by the force of gravity from two small balls, which acted upon it during the time of the descent. In this 'scapement the centre of motion of the pallets is independent of that of the pendulum and verge, although concentric with them; two detents were applied for locking the swing wheel teeth, one for each pallet; from each of the pallet arbors, a wire projected in a horizontal position, and on the ends of these wires the balls were fixed, which were alternately raised up at every vibration of the pendulum, by means of the action of the swing wheel teeth on the pallets. In a periodical philosophical journal, it is insinuated that Mudge had borrowed the idea of the 'scapement which he used in his time-keepers, from this of Cumming's. That Mudge's 'scapement was his own invention, is evident from the historical facts which have been stated: and although there is an apparent similarity between Cumming's and it, yet we are not inclined to be of opinion that either borrowed from the other. The 'scapement of the clock made by Cumming, for his Majesty King George the Third, in the year 1763, is of the free or detached kind, a name which was at that time not known. The improvement which he himself made upon *it* two or three years after, was to keep up the motion of the pendulum, by the gravity of two small balls, independent of the motive force through the wheels of the movement.

In this 'scapement, he insists on the adjustment between the pendulum screws and crutch being made so as precisely to unlock the swing wheel and no more. This can be only unlocked at the time, when the force of the pendulum in its ascent is nearly gone, and that the pendulum should then not only meet with the arm of the ball, but receive it just before the descent of the pendulum has commenced. The swing wheel must at all events be unlocked, and however small the force of the pendulum may be at this time to do that, the vibrations of it cannot be so restricted as *just to do so*; but they must do even a little more, otherwise the unlocking could not at all times be effectually done: and here a kind of recoil, an evil reprobated by Mr. Cumming, would in a small degree inevitably take place on the pendulum, though not on the wheels.

In that part of Mudge's 'scapement, each pallet and detent are formed in one, and the unlocking takes place a considerable while before the end of the vibration. Thus, the springs which maintain the motion of the balance are bent up, not only by means of the swing or balance wheels raising up the pallets so far at every vibration, till the wheel teeth are locked, but the springs are still a little more bent up afterwards, when the teeth are unlocked, and this by the sole exertion or momentum of the balance or pendulum, which is done with great force, soon after the ascending vibration begins: By this accumulated force, the descending vibration is greatly accelerated; and this is one of the greatest properties of the 'scapement, particularly where a balance and spiral spring is used; it may perhaps be more so with the pendulum, provided that the temperature of the atmosphere be kept as near as may be to the same degree.

No 'scapement appears to be better calculated than this is, to keep the balance or pendulum constantly up to the same arc of vibration, notwithstanding its having what some have been pleased to call a *defect* in the recoiling one, that of opposing the balance or pendulum in its ascent, and promoting its descent. In the spring pallet 'scapement, as in the recoiling one, the pendulum is opposed in its ascent, and has its descent equally promoted; but there is still a difference between them notwithstanding this similarity.

In the spring pallet 'scapement, no retrograde motion is given to the wheels, pinions, and pivots which produce the early wearing that takes place by the retrograde motion which is given to the wheels in the common recoiling 'scapement, strongly pointed out by the recoil which the seconds hand of the clock shows on the dial, and it is even obvious in that of the minute hand. These are circumstances which have no place in that of the other. In such 'scapements as Mudge's or Cumming's, it has been said by some, and even by Cumming himself, that it matters not what sort of work the clock movement is, or however ill it may be executed; since the motion of the pendulum is kept up by a force which in some degree is independent of the motive force produced through the wheels in the movement. This may be so far true; yet there is no 'scapement where any irregularity in the pitchings, pinions, &c. of the movement will be more readily discovered than in this; during the going of the clock, it will be very perceptible to the ear, at the time of raising up the balls, or of bending up the springs. We would therefore by no means advise that this sort of 'scapement should be put to a movement of indifferent execution: on the contrary, it seems to require one finished in the best possible manner.

The motive force put to it requires to be greater than that which is usually put to clocks having either the dead beat or the recoiling 'scapement. It may be asked, whether weights or springs are the best for these sort of 'scapements? This is perhaps a question not easy to be resolved. We confess that springs appear to be preferable; they seem to have an alertness or quickness of action, when compared to the apparent heavy dull motion of gravity in the balls. The pivots which are at the centre of motion of the pallets and balls would be regarded by many as objectionable, from the belief that oil is necessary to them. Oil does not seem to us in the least degree requisite, considering the very small angle of motion which they would have; and we have always thought, for the same reason, that oil was not necessary to the pivots of such detents as were sometimes used in the detached 'scapement. To shew, that so far from the nature of a 'scapement actuated by springs or by the gravity of balls, " allowing the movement to have imperfection in its pitchings or any other parts," as has been said by the author of the *Elements of Clock and Watch-making*, we, from experience, found it to be very much the reverse: In clocks where every degree of care was taken *throughout*, both in the sizing of the pinions and their pitchings, so much so, that the most experienced and critical workman could not have discovered any thing that would have led him to say they were in the least faulty: yet when set agoing, a circumstance which was very sensibly perceived by the ear, they showed that the pallets were not always raised up with the same force or velocity, having sometimes the appearance even of not getting fully up. If personification might have been allowed to the clock, in this case it would have said, " you are not a judge of pitchings, let me have a trial of them, and then I will show you whether they are faulty or not." There certainly could have been no tool or experiment better calculated or contrived to show what the pitchings were, than was done by this kind of 'scapement; and, by our experience with it, it seemed evident that the rules in general hitherto given for the size of pinions, will make them rather too large in diameter.

Such clocks as have recoiling or dead beat 'scapements, would continue to go on imperceptibly with pinions sized in the ordinary way, without leading to any discovery of this nature, unless the pitchings were faulty in the extreme, and the pinions very far out of size. Mr. Cumming must surely have applied an overpowering force, for the going weight of his clock, otherwise he would not have given those statements which he has in his *Elements*, &c. But the wide vibrations which he made the pendulums of his clocks to give, necessarily required a great force to keep them up, and this might prevent the ear from observing what we have here remarked.

We shall now proceed to give a description of a clock 'scapement' on the same principle as that of Mudge's in his marine time-keepers, which was put to a very excellent regulator or astronomical clock, made by us some years ago for the Right Honourable Lord Gray, and placed in his Lordship's observatory at Kinfauns Castle. It had a mercurial compensation pendulum, and its time of going *without winding* was forty-five days. The pivots of the great wheel, the second wheel, and the swing wheel, are run on rollers, three being put to each pivot; the pivots of the centre and of the fourth wheels run in holes, and are the only pivots in the clock to which oil is applied.

Friction-rollers were first applied by *Sully* to the balance pivot of his marine time-keeper, and have since been adopted for the same purpose in time-keepers, by Berthoud, by Mudge, and others. They have sometimes been used for clock pivots, but in such an injudicious manner, that in place of relieving the friction of the pivots, they have at last jambed them to such a degree, that the pivots could not at all turn or revolve upon them.

The pivots of the said centre and fourth wheels would have been run on rollers also, but not chusing to go farther, for even with those which were made to run so, the trial was new; besides, had these two been done so, it would have required such a number of additional pieces, as in the end would have been truly appalling and depressing; even as it is, there is about 500 individual pieces in the clock: The expense incurred would have been greatly augmented; yet this, however, would have been no bar with Lord Gray's liberality, had it so happened. The clock has been going about nine years, and with a close and steady rate of time-keeping, during which it has not required the smallest help, not even that of cleaning.

The clock made by us for the Edinburgh Astronomical Institution, or *Royal Observatory*, has the same kind of 'scapement and pendulum, goes eight days, but has no friction rollers in any part of it. It has been going upwards of ten years without requiring any help, or even cleaning.

In Plate VI. No. 35. S W is the 'scapement or swing wheel, whose teeth are cut not unlike those of the wheel for a dead beat, but not so deep; P P are the pallets, the upper ends of whose arms at *s s*, are made very thin, so as to form sort of springs, which must be made very delicate, for if they are any way stiff, the force of the swing wheel will not be able to bend them when raising up the pallets. In order that those springs may have a sufficiency of strength, and at the same time be as delicate as possible, they are cut open at the bending parts, as may be seen at No. 36. These springs come from a kneed sort of sole, formed from the same piece of steel; by which sole they are screwed on to cocks, which are attached to the back or pillar plate of the clock frame. The pallet arms must be made very light and stiff, in order that their weight may have the least possible load or burden on the springs; *a a* are the arms of the pallets, as represented in the front view, No. 35. and are fully as broad as is necessary; their thickness may be made much less than this. An edge view of the pallet arms is seen at a No. 36. The acting parts of the pallets at P P, No. 35. should be made of such a thickness as to allow an opening or room to be made in them for the insertion of a piece of ruby, saphire, agate, or any fine and hard sort of stone; the thickness of the stone being somewhat more than that of the 'scapement or swing wheel teeth, say twice or thrice as much so: Each of these stone pallets has a sort of nib, or *detent*, (for the stopping of the wheel teeth,) which is left at the end of the pallet flanches, as may easily be seen at the left hand pallet, No. 35. These nibs are made for the locking of the swing wheel teeth, and their use will be more particularly explained afterwards. On the back of the pallets are screwed to each, kneed light brass pieces, *c c*, as seen at No. 35. On the lower end of these kneed pieces, the screws, *d d*, are put through, serving the double purpose of adjusting the 'scapement, and setting the pendulum on beat. The upper part of the pendulum rod is composed of a kind of frame, whose steel plates, A A A A, No. 35. are represented as being contained within the dotted circular figure; the thickness of these ring sort of plates is seen at A A A A, No. 36. This frame has three pillars to keep the plates properly together; and though they are not represented in the drawing, yet any one may readily conceive where there places ought to be, and what should be their length or height. At *e e*, No. 36. is seen on each side the ends of a thin steel plate, or traverse bar, which goes from plate to plate, and is fixed in the frame. An oblique view of one of them is seen at *e e*, No. 36. In the steel frame plates, there is a circular opening, as represented by the dotted inner circle, No. 35. This opening must be of such a diameter or width as to allow the swing wheel, and the cock which supports it, to come freely through; a part of the cock is seen at *f f*, No. 36., the sole of which, F, is screwed to the back of the pillar plate of the clock; the knee, K, turns up, or is set to receive the pivot of the arbor of the swing wheel; the pivot at the other end of the arbor being supposed to run in the fore plate, or in a cock attached to it, and is the pivot which carries the seconds hand. This description of the manner by which the swing wheel is supported within the pendulum, it is to be hoped, will be sufficiently understood, notwithstanding the want of a proper drawing of that part,

The swing wheel S W, and part of its pinion arbor *g*, are seen edgewise at No. 36.; also the arm *a* of one of the pallets P, and its screw *d*, bearing on the steel bar *e e*: At the point of contact, between the end of the screw *d*, and the bar *e*, a small piece of fine stone may be inserted into each bar: This will prevent any wearing or magnetic attraction which might otherwise take place if the screws were left solely to act on the steel bars; as the smallest wearing here would in some degree alter the effects of the 'scapement. In

No. 35. B represents a part of the bar of the pendulum rod, which is fixed into the lower part of the steel frame; an edge view of this bar is seen at B, No. 36. At the upper part of the steel frame is inserted a piece, c c, No. 35. and 36.; in this piece the pendulum spring is fixed, whose top piece goes into a strong brass cock, which is firmly attached either to the back of the clock-case, to a wall, or to a large stone pier; the end of the projecting part of this cock is seen at D D, No. 35. and a side view of it at D D, No. 36. The top piece of the pendulum spring has a long and strong steel pin through it, which lies in a notch made across on the upper side and projecting part of the pendulum suspension cock: by this pin the pendulum is suspended. In the side of the pendulum spring top piece is a large hole, made so as to admit freely a strong screw, the head of which is seen at E, No. 36. This screw serves to pinch the top piece and cock firmly together, after the pendulum has been made to take a true vertical position. This strong pin and screw are not represented in the drawing, but the description which has been given, will, it is presumed, easily supply this want. In the pendulum spring, h h, No. 36. may be seen an opening, so as to have the appearance of a double spring. This opening is made to allow the spring parts of the pallets S S, to be brought very near together, and this at the bending part of the pendulum spring, so that it and the bending parts of the pallet springs should be in one common centre. A part only of the cocks on which the spring pallets are screwed is represented by k k, No. 35.; m m are the heads of the screws by which they are fixed to these cocks. It must be observed here, that the spring pallets are so placed, that they should act on the line of suspension and gravitation of the pendulum, which necessarily brings the swing wheel to the place where it is; no verge, crutch, or fork are required; the influence of the oil on the verge pivots, and the friction by the crutch or fork on the pendulum rod, are done away by this arrangement. The motion of the pendulum is kept up *entirely* by the force of the spring part of the pallets, independent of any impediment in the wheel work, so long as the wheels have force sufficient to raise up the pallets readily: This force may be considered as permanent and invariable, and so should be the arc decribed by the pendulum. If the length of the pendulum and of the arc it describes are invariable, so should be the time which is kept by the clock. Having described the parts which compose this 'scapement, it will now be requisite to show their mode of action, which is extremely simple.

When the pendulum is set in motion, it will, by means of either the one or the other of the screws d, unlock the swing wheel, which, in the drawing, is represented as being locked by one of its teeth on the nib or detent part of the right hand pallet, and the moment when the wheel is unlocked, the tooth at the left hand pallet is ready to press forward and raise up that pallet,—and, of course, it bends up the spring. Let the pendulum be now brought to the right hand side, the steel bar s will meet with the screw d, and, carrying or pushing it on, will by this means unlock the swing wheel, and allow it to escape. At this instant, the wheel teeth meeting with the pallet at the left hand side, will force its way on the flanch, and raise it up till it is stopped by the detent or pallet nib. Here the wheel is locked until the return of the pendulum to that side, when it will again be unlocked. From the time of the unlocking at the right hand pallet, till the same takes place at the left hand, the pendulum, during its excursion to the right, is opposed by the spring part of the pallet; and, on its return, it is assisted by the same part, until the pendulum comes in contact with the point of the screw d on the left hand. Here it is again opposed in its excursion as far as the arc it describes; and on its descent or return, it is assisted or impelled by the spring part of the pallet, in conjunction with the force of gravity. In this clock, all that the motive force through the wheels has to do, is to raise up the pallets, by bending up the springs, and these, (as has been already stated,) along with the force of gravity, maintain the motion of the pendulum.

When clocks of the common construction get foul in the oil, or dirty, the arc of vibration falls off, or is less than what it was when the clock was clean and free. In this 'scapement, however, when the clock gets foul, the force of the swing wheel teeth on the detent part of the pallets will be lessened, consequently the wheel will be more easily unlocked by the pendulum. Hence we may expect a small increase in the arc of vibration; but whether this will affect the time-keeping by making it slow, must be left to the experience of those who may think of prosecuting such trials It appears to us, that if any lengthening of the arc of vibration takes place, it will be equally accelerated on its return by the greater tension of the spring part of the pallets. A clock, with this kind of 'scapement, which went thirty-six days without requiring to be wound up, the going weight twenty pounds, and semi-arc of vibration one degree twelve minutes; on an addition of four pounds being put to the going weight, it brought the semi-arc of vibration to two minutes less than one degree, confirming so far the hypothesis which has been advanced.

Another clock, having the same kind of 'scapement, has since been made by us, where the adjustments for 'scapement and beat are transferred from the pallets to the pendulum itself. By this means these adjustments are not only easier made, but are effected without that danger to which the pallets are exposed when this is done by the screws. This mode is adopted in the pendulum at the clock made for the Edinburgh Astronomical Institution or *Royal Observatory* (formerly noticed), which was put up in the year 1813.

The spring pallet 'scapement, which has been described, having neither verge nor crutch, and these being necessary where the upper part of the pendulum is a simple bar or rod, it shall now be shown how to construct a 'scapement of this kind with a verge and crutch.

On the verge is screwed a thin piece of steel, of an anchor form, which has a kind of crank in the middle, in order to give freedom to the acting parts, or centre of motion of the pallet springs; to coincide with that of its arbor, against one of the kneed ends of the crank the anchor is screwed. The place of the swing wheel is with the frame in the usual way; the anchor lies pretty close behind it on that side next the pillar frame plate. On the ends of the circular arch part of the anchor, are screwed kneed pieces of steel which come outside; and at a little distance from the tops of the swing wheel teeth, in each of the kneed pieces, is inserted a flat piece of diamond, ruby, or any hard stone. These pieces are made or placed so as to be in a line drawn from the centre of the verge; and it is on these stones, which are in the plane of the swing wheel, that the point of the screws which are in the pallet tails *act* and give impulse to the pendulum, communicated to it by means of the crutch, whose socket is twisted firm on that end of the arbor of the verge whereon the anchor piece goes. Two kneed brass cocks are screwed on the inside of the pillar plate, the distance between them may be a quarter of an inch, or so; it is on their upper surface that the soles or palms of spring pallets are screwed. The arms of the pallets should be as light as possible, and the pallets, the tails, soles, and springs, may all be made out of one piece of steel. The extremity of the pallet springs coincide with the upper surface of the soles, and also with the centre of motion of the verge and anchor.

From the nature of the spring pallet 'scapement, there is a wonderful and beautiful variety in it; the distance between the points of the screws in the pallet tails is limited by the stones of the kneed pieces screwed on the ends of the anchor arch. If this distance is less than what it should be, it will give too much scope for the discharged pallet, when impelling the anchor, to fall more in between the teeth than it should do, and by this means give a small retrograde motion to the tooth which is to raise it up, just at the instant when the opposite pallet is discharged; and this, unless the motive force is sufficiently powerful, will be apt to prevent the pallet from being altogether quite raised up, and consequently stop the clock. If the distance between the screw points is greater than it should be, then the pallet which is to be raised up will not fall so much in between the teeth as it ought to do; hence the acting tooth will pass over a part of the inclined plane, or flanch of the pallet, without any action being exerted on it, by which a diminution of the motive force *takes place*. The great nicety in the distance of the screw points is to have it so, as, on the discharge of one pallet, the other shall come close in on the tooth which is to receive it, but only just so as not to touch it. The taking out or in of the screws by a very small part of a turn will have a great effect in putting the clock on beat; yet it seems more adviseable to do this first by the bending of the crutch, the 'scapement being supposed previously and properly adjusted in all its parts. In this operation, the discharge of the pallets should be made to take place, at equal distances, on each side of the point of rest; for example, suppose the discharge is made on the left hand, when the pendulum index is at forty minutes, and on the right hand at thirty minutes, bending the crutch the smallest matter to the right, will make the discharges each at thirty-five minutes; and here the clock will be exactly in beat.

The following is a scheme and description of another 'scapement, contrived by the Author, and executed about two and twenty years ago. In Plate VI. No. 34. S W is the swing wheel, whose diameter may be so large as to be sufficiently free of the arbor of the wheel which runs into its pinion: this, in eight-day clocks, is the third wheel. The teeth of this swing wheel are cut thus deep, in order that the wheel may be as light as possible; and the strength of the teeth little more than what is necessary to resist the action or force of a common clock weight through the wheels. They are what may be called the locking teeth, as will be more readily seen from the use of them, afterwards to be explained. Those called the impulse teeth, consist of very small tempered steel pins, inserted on the surface of the rim of the wheel on one side only. They are nearly two-tenths of an inch in height, and, the smaller they are, so much more room will be given to the thickness of the pallets. If they have strength to support about eighty or a hundred grains, they will be strong enough. There is no rule required for placing them relatively to the locking teeth, only they may as well be opposite these teeth as any where else. P P are the pallets whose centre of motion is the same with that of the verge at a. These pallets are formed so as to have the arms sufficiently strong, and at the same time as light as may be. That part where the arms meet at the angle at a, has a steel socket made out of the same piece as the arms, being forged together in this manner. The socket is made to fit well on the verge on which it is only twisted fast, and is turned pretty thin on the outside, in order to allow the arbors of the detents to be laid as close to the verge as may be, so that their centres of motion may coincide as nearly as possible. A perfect coincidence of the centres might be obtained, by using a hollow cylinder for the verge, with the detent arbors running in the middle of it; but this would have occasioned more trouble. Yet this non-coincidence of centres has its advantage here, by the wheel teeth, while resting on the detent nibbs, being prevented from having any opposing force to the motion of the pendulum, which they would have, were the detents placed otherwise, unless the method was taken which we propose in another scapement. That part of the pallet frame, in which is set the stone for receiving the action or impulse of the small pin teeth, is formed into a rectangular shape, so as to allow room for a dovetail groove, into which the stone pallets are fixed, as may be seen at P P, No. 84, and at P 2. which also gives a side view of the verge at a, and where the socket of the pallets is seen as fixed on the verge. At b 2. is seen the outer end of one of the stone pallets made flush with the steel. That part of the stone pallets upon which the pin teeth act, may be seen where they are represented in their respective positions relative to the pin teeth. Their shape or form is exactly that which gives the dead beat. In the figure are seen the detents $d\ d$, whose centre of motion is at $e\ e$; they are fixed on their arbors by a thin steel socket, made as forged with the detents, much in the same way as the pallets were, as may be seen at e 1. which gives a side view of one of the detents and its arbor. The screws $e\ e$, $f f$, in the arms of the detents, have places made to receive them, which are more readily seen in No. 34. than in 1. and 2. The screws $e\ e$, serve for the purpose of adjusting that part of the 'scapement connected with the pallets, pushing the detents put from locking the wheel by means of the locking teeth. The ends of the screws *e e*, on the unlocking, are met by the ends of the stone pallets, one of which is represented at *b* 2. The screws *f f* serve to adjust the locking of the wheel teeth on the detents. *g g* are brass rectangular pieces or studs, which are fixed to the inside of the pillar frame plate, and may be near an inch in height. The ends of the screws *f f* rest on the side of these studs, and according as they are more or less screwed through at the ends of the detents, so much less or more hold will the detent pieces have of the teeth. These holding pieces of the detents are not represented in the drawing, as they would have made other parts of it rather obscure. They are made of stone, and are fitted in by means of a dovetail, cut in a piece left for that purpose on the inside of the detent arms, as may easily be conceived from the drawing, where it is represented in part at *e* 2, and is in the line across the arm with the screw *e*, which is close by the edge of the detent stone-piece that projects a little beyond the end of the screw.

Having described the parts of the 'scapement, we shall now explain their mode of action. On the left hand side the pin tooth is represented as having just escaped its pallet, as may be seen; but previous to its having got on to the flanch of this pallet, let us conceive that the back or end part *b* of the pallet had come in consequence of the motion of the pendulum to that side, and opposing the screw *e*, which is in the detent arm, pushes or carries it on with it, and consequently unlocks the wheel, which then endeavours to get forward; but the pin tooth, at this instant of unlocking, meeting with the flanch of the pallet at the lower edge inside, and pushing forwards on the flanch, by this means impells the pendulum, and after having escaped the pallet, the next locking tooth is received by the detent on the right hand side, where the wheel is now again locked. In the meantime, while the pendulum is describing that part of its vibration towards the left hand, free and detached, as the pallets are now at liberty to move freely and independently of the small pin teeth; on the return of the pendulum to the right hand side, the detent, by means of the back of the pallet on that side, is pushed out from locking the wheel, and at the instant of unlocking, the wheel gets forward, and the pin tooth is at the same instant ready to get on the flanch of its pallet, and give new impulse to the pendulum, as is obvious by what is represented in the drawing. After the pin tooth has escaped the pallet, the wheel is again locked on the opposite or left hand side; the pendulum moves on to the right freely and independently till the next locking on the left takes place, and so on.

It may be observed, that the unlocking takes place when the pendulum is near the lowest point, or point of rest, and of course, where its force is nearly a maximum. Without attaching any thing to the merits of this 'scapement, we may remark, that the rate of the clock was observed from time to time by an excellent transit instrument, and during a period of eighty-three days it kept within the second, without any interim apparent deviation. This degree of time keeping seemed to be as much a matter of accident as otherwise, and cannot reasonably be expected from this, or any clock whatever, as a fixed or settled rate.

This 'scapement being a detached or free one, can at pleasure be converted either into a recoiling or a dead beat one, without so much as once disturbing or stopping the pendulum a single vibration. To make a dead beat of it, put in a peg of wood, or a small wire into each of the detents, so as to raise them free of the pallets, and the peg of wood keeping the detents in the required position, the pin teeth will now fall on the circular parts of the pallets, and so on to the flanch, and the 'scapement is then to all intents and purposes a dead beat one. To make a recoiling one of it, let there be fixed to each arbor of the detents, a wire to project horizontally from them, about 3¼ or 4 inches long, the outer ends of the wires must be tapped about half an inch in length, provide two small brass balls, half an ounce weight each, having a hole through them, and tapped so as to screw on to the wires, the balls can thus be put more or less home, and be adjusted proportionably to the force of the clock on the pendulum. No recoil will be seen by the seconds hand, yet these balls will alternately oppose and assist the motion of the pendulum as much as any recoiling pallets can possibly do, and as their effect on the pendulum will be exactly the same, it may be considered as a good recoiling 'scapement. This sort of detached 'scapement, as it may be so called, by becoming a dead beat, or a recoiling one, at any time when required, makes it convenient for trying various experiments with these kind of 'scapements. This 'scapement keeps its arc of vibration pretty steadily, as experience of it has shown.

We shall now proceed to the description of a clock 'scapement, whose pallets require no oil, invented by the late Mr. John Harrison, who received the parliamentary reward of £20,000 for his marine time-keeper, having kept the longitude at sea within the limits prescribed by the act of parliament, made in the reign of Queen Ann.

In Plate V. No. 28. S W is the swing wheel, whose teeth are shorter than usual; on the verge is a brass arm, of a sort of cross and flat pronged form, as may be seen at $e, e, e,$ and at $e, e,$ No. 29. and 30. upon this arm are screwed two brass cocks, marked $d, d,$ in No. 28. and $d,$ in No. 29. and 30. the upper pivots of the pallet arbors, as seen at $a,$ No. 29. and 30. run in these cocks, and the lower pivots in the end of the prongs. On the lower end of the pallet arbors is a brass socket to each, having freedom to move easily in them, and also a proper end-shake between the prongs and the pallet arms. On that end of each of the sockets next to the pallet arms, is rivetted a thin piece of brass, the piece on the socket of the driving pallet being shaped, as seen at $h\ h,$ No. 28. and 29. and having two holes in it, one of these holes has a range limited by a pin fixed to the brass arm from the verge; the other hole, which is at the outer end, allows range to a pin which is fixed to an arm on the pallet arbor, as may be seen at $h\ h,$ No. 28. and $h\ h,$ No. 29. The piece of brass on the socket of the leading pallet arbor is shaped, as seen at $k\ k,$ No. 28. and 30. having a tail which comes to rest on the outer edge of the cock $d,$ after being carried a little way by the motion of the pallet; at the outer end at $k,$ is a small brass screw, serving as a counterbalance to the opposite arm or pallet hook. In this pallet arm is an opening through which the swing wheel comes, as may be seen at $l,$ No. 30. the arm at the other end being filed thin down, having a sort of shoulder on it. A B, No. 28. is a stout piece of brass, rivetted or screwed to the verge collet; $c\ c,$ is the steel crutch having another arm which comes up on the inside of the piece of brass; the ball, or palm of the crutch is kept to the verge collet, by a sort of spring collet which has two screws outside, and through to the verge collet, the crutch having liberty to turn on the verge. The piece of brass A B has two short knees turned up, having a hole tapped into each to receive the two screws $s\ s,$ whose ends bear on the upper arm of the crutch, and serve to move the arm to one side or the other, so as to put the pendulum or clock on beat; $p\ p$ is a piece of hard wood, (such as lignumvitæ, or green ebony,) put on the lower end of the crutch, having an opening in it, to clip, or take in with the middle rod of a gridiron pendulum.

The parts of this 'scapement being described, it now remains to explain their action. The tooth of the swing wheel which has hold of the hook of the leading or right hand pallet, carries it on until ano-their tooth meets with the hook or notch at the end of the driving pallet arm. When this takes place, the wheel is made to recoil a little back, and at this instant the hook of the leading pallet gets free of the tooth, and is made to rise clear off the top of it, by means of the counterbalancing of the brass arm, and the screw is at the end of it. The tooth of the swing wheel which has now got into the notch, at the end of the driving pallet arm, carries it forward until another tooth, meeting with the hook of the leading pallet, causes the wheel again to recoil. This allows the notch of the driving pallet to get free of the tooth, and the brass piece which is on the pallet arbor falls down till it comes to rest on the pin, in the brass cross piece, making the pallet notch get quite clear of the top of the tooth, and so on. There is a great deal of ingenuity displayed in the contrivance of this 'scapement, yet the nice and ticklish balancing of the pallets occasions some degree of uncertainty in their operations; and whether the great recoil which it has may not be against the time-keeping of the clock, remains yet to be proved. Was it this 'scapement in a clock of Harrison's, at his house in Orange Street, of whose going, Mr. Short said, "That he could depend on it to one second in a month," and " that it had been going for fourteen years at this rate?"

No. 31. is a segment of a swing wheel, or part of one, where the teeth are made so as to keep the oil constantly to their points. It is well known that oil is very apt to run down from the points of swing wheel teeth, especially those in the common recoiling 'scapement, where they are for the most part rather thin and sharp.

The teeth proposed here, after being cut on the engine, have their points formed somewhat like an epicycloid, and close below is a small hole is drilled from back to front; with one of the smallest round files a hollow is made across the front of the tooth, keeping the hole rather on the upper part of the hollow; the hole should be chamfered a little at both ends, and a broach put through so as to clean it. Indeed, if a hole is made not far from the points of teeth in common swing wheels, it will keep the oil to them; they should have a gentle rounding off, which will be of advantage.

This scheme answers the end proposed extremely well; the teeth carries the oil along with them during their acting on the pallets, and on leaving them takes it away. It is above forty years since we suggested this, but had somehow overlooked it, till being lately reminded of it by one who had successfully put it in practice a considerable time ago, he having got the hint from some of our people.

Directions how to fit up a 'scapement for an astronomical clock, where gravity is made the impelling force to the pendulum, and where the influence of heat and cold can have no place, as in the case of spring pallets, and where the pendulum is suspended by a spring.

Let a piece of fine cast steel be prepared, from which a hollow cylinder can be made, the length three inches, or it may be near to a quarter of an inch more, the outside diameter four-tenths of an inch, the inside about three-tenths or so; being truly turned on the outside after it is well finished in the inside, it may then be hardened, and so far brought back or let down, that a good file may be used to open a part of it to admit the detent or pallet arbors: A short part of the cylinder is left whole at the ends for the purpose of having brass or copper plugs fixed in them; it is in these plugs that small pieces of steel are put, on the outer ends of which are turned the pivots of the verge, as it may be called. The cylinder, so far as it is described, may be seen in Plate VIII. No. 42. A 1, A 2, is an edge view of a cock which is screwed on the inside of the pillar plate, and A 1, A 2, is a flat view of it, as if the kneed part was made straight; on the upper surface or part A 1, are screwed two small cocks c, c, having each a jewelled hole in it; c 2 is an edge or side view of these small cocks, the pivots of the pallet arbor a run in these jewelled holes, b is a socket formed on one end of the pallet arm, serving to twist it on the arbor a. The main cock with the small cocks c c must be so placed as to have the line of the arbor to coincide with the dotted line represented in the cylinder as its centre. Another main cock, the same as A 1, A 2, is screwed on the inside of the foreplate of the clock frame, having small cocks on it, in which runs a pallet arbor, and pallet arm socket twisted on it; the line of this arbor must be made also to coincide with the line at the centre of the cylinder, taking up the vacant space as seen in the drawing of the cylinder. The small cocks which are at the extremes, must be free of the cylinder inside, and of the plugs in the ends of it; those in the middle may be placed as near to each other as may be; one of the plugs to have a round part outside of the cylinder, turned so as that the crutch may be twisted on it, and yet a small degree of rivetting, when brought to its position, should it be found necessary. S S represents the swing wheel; T T T is a sort of anchor having a hook to it for the purpose of twisting it on to the cylinder. This anchor is brought up pretty close to the plane of the swing wheel; there should be a screw in the upper part of the hook to fix it to the cylinder. At that part of the anchor represented by the segment of a circle, T T, are pieces kneed up, and screwed on at the ends, an edge view of them is seen at *k*, and extending equally on both edges or tops of the swing wheel teeth, and somewhat beyond them; in these kneed up pieces is set a diamond, or a bit of any hard stone, against which a screw in the tails of the pallets act; *p p* 1. represents one of the pallet arbors and its arm, and P, one of the pallets with a tail to it, in which is a screw, the end of which comes outside the anchor knee, acting occasionally on it; *p p*, and P 2, is a side view of one of the pallets and its arm. This part of the 'scapement and its pallets are a near representation of what has already been described; the action of which being understood, will easily be applied to this, as it is as nearly alike in both as may be. The pallet arbors being placed in this manner, are independent of the motion of the verge and pendulum; and in its vibrations, however much the teeth of the swing wheel may press on the detents or nibs of the pallets, the motion of the pendulum cannot be affected by it. The arms of the pallets, one of them particularly, will require a kind of crank part in it, in order to bring the pallets into the plane of the swing wheel; and with the acting part of the anchor, a hollow must be made in the upper part of the anchor, to give freedom to one of the pallet arbors. A small weight is put behind each of the pallets, and adjustable, so as to impress more or less force upon the pendulum.

The pendulum to this clock is proposed to be hung in a frame, containing friction rollers for the pendulum to vibrate on, such as have already been described; and, if all the pivot holes are made in plumbago, it will supersede the necessity of applying oil to the pivots: The pieces of plumbago should have a slight roasting, so as to dispel any sulphureous matter; otherwise it would show itself, by making the frame plates of a dull yellow or brownish colour, round where the plumbago pieces are inserted.

Having, in our proposed 'scapement, adopted gravity as the maintaining force to keep up the motion of the pendulum, it might be so modified as to do this and no more, allowing its natural influence to be as wholly on the pendulum ball as may be. If we use the verge and crutch with an anchor on the verge, the distance between the kneed parts at the ends of the anchor arch, which discharge the locking of the swing wheel, may be made so near to each other, that from the return of one pallet, after impelling to that of disengaging the other, the pendulum shall vibrate freely and independently of every thing for the space of two or three degrees, the whole arc being supposed to be four; that is, two degrees on each side of the point or rest. In this mode of the 'scapement, there must be limits or banking for the pallets to stay on, from the time of the pendulum leaving them, and during the interim, till the return; this might, with some propriety, be called a detached 'scapement. Perhaps, during the motion of the pendulum going through an arc of half a degree only, it might be giving too little time to discharge one pallet, and raise up the other; but this is the proportion required for such a modification. If no verge and crutch are used, the length of the segment, or piece fixed on the pendulum rod for discharging the swing wheel, may be made so as to discharge it, and even allow the pendulum to vibrate freely for the space of two or three degrees. Should thirty-five minutes of a degree be found too little, perhaps it may be practicable to *discharge* and *raise*, through an arc of forty or fifty minutes; but, even to do this, will require a considerable force. But, supposing the discharge of one pallet or detent, and the raising up of the other, could be done in the course of the pendulum swinging through one degree, the force required to do so cannot be little: this would give to every vibration an arc of two degrees to swing freely through, and while detached from every thing else. It may be observed, that the whole time given for the swing wheel tooth to raise a pallet up, may be taken from the discharge on the opposite side till its return there, which would be the double of one degree; and here a less force may be required to raise the pallets up with the small weights attached to them than it would otherwise do.

In a 'scapement of this kind, where an anchor on the verge is used, the discharging of the swing wheel from its locking takes place at 34 minutes of a degree beyond the point of rest; during the time that the pendulum swings through an arc of one degree and 26 minutes more, the swing wheel has got the pallet on the opposite side raised, and the time before it can be again unlocked, the pendulum, in returning, must swing through an arc of two degrees 34 minutes.

The force required to keep a pendulum in motion, will depend on the weight of the pendulum ball; half the force will keep a pendulum in motion, whose weight is only 12 lbs., that will be required to keep one in motion of 24 lbs. 'Scapements in general have more force than is necessary to keep the *pendulum* in motion: and where this is the case, *it* must, according to the nature of the 'scapement, be either retarded or accelerated,—of course, the pendulum will not be so much under the influence of gravity as we here wish to propose. Let the flanches of the pallets be made so as to subtend a small angle, they will then, with the small weights attached to them,

P

be easier raised up; and having a little way to descend and impel the pendulum, the force may be made sufficient to keep up the motion, and yet leave a great part of it free and detached, and, as it were, wholly under the force and influence of gravity,—a force that must be very uniform and constant.

Some idea of the expediency of allowing gravity to exert itself as much as possible on the pendulum, may be taken from what was observed in our operations with the spring kind of pallets, by showing the different effect which they had on the motion of the pendulum, according as the springs were set strong, or less so. When they had somewhat of strength, they made the pendulum to vibrate a semi-arc of about 2 degrees 10 minutes; and here the clock had a tendency to gain a few seconds in the day; setting the strength the smallest possible degree weaker, it gave a semi-arc of vibration of about 1 degree 50 minutes; with the shorter arc, the clock ought to have gone faster than it did before, whereas, on the contrary, it went slower,— the influence of gravity being more disturbed in the first case than in the last. It is probable, that where the motion of a pendulum is kept up by a force just sufficient to do so, and no more, that the pendulum, in this case, would be more readily affected by changes in the density of the atmosphere, than it would be were the case otherwise; yet there appears to be no reason here that we should interfere with the influence of gravity on that account.

When the ball of a gridiron pendulum rod should happen to be rather light, the performance here will not be so equal or so steady as with a heavier one. Indeed, the weight of the entire pendulum should lie as much as possible in the ball itself, that it alone may have all the momentum, or force of motion. Perhaps the regularity of some clocks, which have pendulums with a wooden rod, besides having little or no variation in length from change of temperature, may owe a great part of this to the small proportion which the weight of the rod bears to that of the ball,—these rods for a second's pendulum being seldom much heavier than an ounce or two; whereas, in some compound pendulums, the parts composing the rod will amount to two, three, four, or even five lbs.—In a *Treatise on Mechanics*, by Dr. Olinthus Gregory, Vol. II. p. 389. Plate XXIX. Fig. 8: a description is given of a very nice gravitating 'scapement of Mudge's contrivance.

The properties of a good 'scapement are, that the impelling force should be applied in the most uniform and direct way, and with the least friction and loss of motive power; that it requires little or no oil, and that the oscillations of the regulator, whether it is a pendulum or a balance, be made in as free and undisturbed a manner as possible. The nice execution required in a 'scapement, whether for a clock or a watch, formerly engrossed so much of the attention of workmen, that they, in some measure lost sight of the properties of the pendulum, as well as that of the spiral or balance spring, and thought that the time-keeping of their machines depended more on the 'scapement than on any other thing, without considering that the regularity in time-keeping lies wholly, or almost so, in the pendulum and in the spiral spring. Berthoud imputes a notion like this to Harrison, for attempting to make the 'scapement in his time-keeper, so, that the long and short vibrations should be made in equal times. Whereas he says, " he ought to have looked for this in the isochronous property of the spiral or balance spring. But this property (he adds) was unknown at that time to the English artists, and was a discovery of those in France, from whom the English artists afterwards obtained it." If this had been the case, how did it happen, *(and that too so long before the period when Le Roy and Berthoud disputed, each claiming the merit of having first made the discovery of this property in the spiral spring,)* that Mudge should have mentioned in his tract published in 1763, " that the pendulum, or balance spring, from physical principles, made the balance perform the long and short vibrations in equal times?" He learned this from Dr. Hooke's works, with which he was well acquainted ; for this property of springs was known to Dr. Hooke, and pointed out by him upwards of an hundred years before Mudge published his pamphlet. It is but too true that few or none of the English artists appear to have been acquainted with these properties till very lately, though Mr. Mudge had adverted to them so long before, *and though* they were contained in the works of Dr. Hooke. Lepaute's book was published at Paris in 1767 ; and it does not contain the most distant hint of these properties of the balance spring ; hence they were not known *there* at the time Lepaute wrote, otherwise he would have mentioned them, being a man of genius and of considerable research. It was about this time, or soon after, that the disputes commenced between Le Roy and Berthoud regarding this subject.

Watch-finishers always made the pendulum spring for the watches of their own finishing, while, at the same time, knowing nothing of its properties, the general practice was to taper them, so that the coils, while bending or unbending, should preserve an equal distance with one another ; and this method has been used ever since the application of the spiral spring. Those who finished watches for Mudge and Dutton were never employed to make the pendulum spring : this was always done at home by either Mudge or Dutton themselves, who, no doubt, endeavoured to make them as nearly isochronous as possible. This, among other causes, perhaps, gave their watches the celebrity which they at that time so deservedly acquired.

As we shall soon be on the subject of remontoirs, the following history of them may not be impertinent:—The pallets of the 'scapement at the turret clock in Greenwich Hospital are said to have been contrived by Mr. Smeaton, civil engineer. The following narrative will so far show how he came to be concerned in it. It may be observed that he was at this time one of the Commissioners of the said Hospital.

The turret clock which is in the cupola of Greenwich Hospital, was undertaken by the late Mr. John Holmes, watch-maker, London, and executed, under his directions, by Mr. Thwaites. But before any thing was done, Mr. Holmes consulted two gentlemen, very intimate friends of his; the one was the Rev. Professor Ludlam of Cambridge, the other Mr. Smeaton, both of whom were eminently qualified to give such advice as was wanted in this business, not only about the 'scapement, but how every part of the clock should be fitted up, so as to insure safety and utility in its performance. Several very long and masterly letters (of which we have copies, though none of the originals were ever published,) passed between them on this occasion, and evince much ingenuity. They agreed that the 'scapement should have a recoil. Mr. Smeaton recommended that the pallets, in place of having planes, as was common for their acting parts, should have curved surfaces,—the leading pallet being concave, and the driving one convex; and when the pendulum was at or near to the extremity of the vibration, the 'scapement should then be nearly dead. This was, he said, what "*old Father Hindley at York* had ultimately come into." Professor Ludlam advised that the swing wheel teeth should be thick and deep, and of such a shape as to roll on the pallets, and not to slide on them, which would prevent biting or wearing. The pallet arms were of brass, made so as to put it in the power of the clock-maker to take the pallets very easily out, when repairing was necessary. These methods had long before this been used by Harrison, and were adopted in a clock of his in Trinity College, Cambridge, as mentioned by the Professor. Broad rubbing surfaces were strongly advised by them. *Mr. Smeaton, at this period, took away gudgeons from a mill wheel, whose diameters were only two and a half inches, and put others in their place of eight inches, with great success, as it afterwards proved.* On the same principles which have just now been mentioned, was the 'scapement made for the clock which the author put up in St. Andrew's church,

Edinburgh; and although it has been going *well on to* forty years, there is not yet the smallest appearance of biting or wearing on the pallets.

'Scapements have been divided into classes, one of which has been called that of the *remontoir* kind. Now the mechanism of a remontoir may be applied to any 'scapement; and even then it can hardly be said to form a part of it, more than the wheels of the movement, or the weight which impels them.

The motive force, passing through the wheels, may at times be unequally impressed upon the 'scapement, either of a clock or a watch. This idea gave rise to the invention of what has been called *remontoirs*; that is, that the movement should at intervals be made to wind up either a small weight, or bend up a delicate spring, which alone should give its force to the 'scapement, by which means the pendulum or balance is supposed to be always impelled by an equal and uniform force. The earliest thing of this sort was used about the year 1600. Huygens applied it to some of his clocks, and gives a description of it in his *Horologium Oscillatorium*; and Harrison had one in the marine time-keeper, which gained him the great reward. We are of opinion that they are of no great use, either to a clock or to a spring time-piece; for if the pendulum of the one is well fixed, and the momentum of the ball is not too little, any small inequalities of the motive force through the wheels will hardly be perceptible; and in the spring time-keeper, the isochronism of the pendulum or balance spring is sufficient to correct any inequalities whatever in the motive force. As their mechanism, however, is curious, and has been rarely described, it may not be uninteresting to the reader to have an account of it, and also such as would enable the clock-maker to construct and adopt it, should he think proper.

The one which is proposed to be described, is that which we contrived for the clock in St. Andrew's Church, Edinburgh. Suppose a small frame, separate and independent of the clock frame, to contain two wheels, one of which is the swing wheel, the frame having within it the 'scapement work also. The other wheel is crossed out so as to be very light, the rim being left just so broad as to admit fixing on it seven kneed pieces or teeth, each about a quarter of an inch thick, and half an inch long, three of which are on one side of the rim, and four on the other side. Three on each side have the knees of different heights, corresponding each to each; the fourth is a little higher than either of the third highest. The wheel on which these are fixed has a tooth prolonged beyond the rim, of the same thickness and length as the others, making eight teeth in all, having a small space left between each. These teeth become as it were so many wheels, but in different planes, and are at equal distances from one another, with the same extent of radius coming to the centre of the swing wheel arbor, being just so much larger than that of the swing wheel, as to allow the swing wheel teeth to clear the arbor of it. The edges or sides of the teeth which rest on the swing wheel arbor are planes, and rounded off on the opposite sides to the point or angle formed by this plane. The arbor of the swing wheel has eight notches cut into it a little beyond the centre. These correspond to the eight teeth of the other wheel, and are sufficiently wide and deep to allow the teeth to pass freely through them. Each notch stands at an angle of 45 degrees to the one which is next it, which difference is continued along the arbor, through the whole, making 360 degrees for one revolution of the swing wheel. On each of the arbors of these wheels, is fixed a pulley, having a square bottom, in which were set ten hard tempered steel pins, a little tapered, something like the pulleys at the old thirty-hour clocks, but the bottom of which was a round groove in place of a square. The pendulum was fixed to the wall of the steeple, as well as the frame containing the 'scapement work, and with the apparatus which has been described. The arbor of the eight-toothed wheel had one of its pivots prolonged with a square made on the end outside. The clock frame containing the movement was in the middle or centre part of the steeple, and a pinion in it, which represented or had the place of the swing wheel pinion; had one of its pivots also prolonged and squared outside; these squared parts of the pivots were connected by a steel rod, and Hooke's joints. The main weight of the clock being put on, must urge not only the wheels to turn, but also that wheel having the kneed teeth; and some one or other of these teeth pressing on the arbor of the swing wheel, they cannot turn, consequently none of those in the large frame can turn, nor can the swing wheel turn here, unless some other means are used. An endless chain was provided, and passed over the two pulleys fixed on the wheel arbors, and through two common pulleys, to one of which is hung the small weight that is to turn round the swing wheel, and to the other a counter weight. The weight which turns the swing wheel has its force applied on that side, so as to make the wheel act properly with the pallets; now, while the swing wheel is turning, *the pendulum being supposed in motion*, one of the other wheel teeth is gently pressing on its arbor. Whenever this tooth meets with its own notch, it will, by means of the main weight, be made to pass quickly through it; *while passing*, the small weight is wound up a little by the main one; the succeeding tooth then meeting with the swing wheel arbor, rests on it for a quarter of a minute, till its notch comes about; it then passes in its turn, and so on. The swing wheel makes a revolution every two minutes, in which time the wheel with the eight teeth makes also one. The minute hand, by this mechanism, *at the time of any of the teeth passing through the notches,* makes a start every quarter of a minute; and at every such passing, the small weight, as has been stated, is wound up a little by the great or main one. After the clock had gone a considerable time with this, it was found that the kneed teeth got a little swelled, or staved up, on their parts of rest, by the force of the main weight, which made them fall too rapidly on the swing wheel arbor.

To remedy this, an endless screw wheel was put on the arbor of the remontoir wheel, *or wheel with the kneed teeth,* working into an upright endless screw, on the upper end of whose arbor was fixed a pretty large fly, in order to lessen the velocity of the remontoir wheel, and make the kneed teeth fall gently on the swing wheel arbor. This helped the swelling greatly, but did not entirely prevent it taking place, though it now came slowly on, and existed in a less degree. The endless chain had also a tendency to wear fast: in consequence of this, and no provision being made for the swelling of the kneed teeth, which might have been done in some degree, by making the notches on the swing wheel arbor much wider at first than was required for them when newly finished and first applied; this part of the remontoir was taken away, and the rod with Hooke's joints was put on the square of the pivot of the swing wheel arbor prolonged on the outside of its frame. These matters being previously guarded against, it might be well for some artist, in future, to try such a remontoir. During the four years it was in use, the clock went uncommonly well, and was the admiration of all, and particularly a gentleman who lived opposite the church, who was an amateur in horology. One of our men who took an interest in this clock, said it did not do so well after the remontoir was taken away. This, however, may have been more owing to a change in the position of the weights, than to any thing else, occasioned by a chime of eight bells being put up in the steeple. For the weights, in place of having their natural fall, were now carried a great way up in the steeple above the bells and clock, in order to fall down again; and here a complication of rollers and pulleys became requisite.

A scheme was made out, to make the rewinding by a spring, in order to get rid of pulleys and the endless chain, but being a thing that is nowise likely to be adopted, it becomes therefore unnecessary to describe it.

We observe a model, something like this, has lately been given in to the Society for the Encouragement of Arts, &c. by an old and excellent workman of our own bringing up. See Vol. XLII. of that Society's Transactions.

This clock was put up in the beginning of the year 1788; after going till August 1796, *being eight years and three quarters nearly*, it was taken down and cleaned; during the period it had been going, two sets of pins in the rewinding pulleys were nearly worn out. The endless chain seemed also to wear very fast; in short, the rewinding part seemed to promise much, but being liable to so many accidents, frequently causing the clock to stop, from these parts wearing so fast, it was thought proper to take it away, and to connect the swing wheel arbor with the pinion which ran within the main frame; for this purpose the swing wheel got another arbor, with one of the pivots thick and prolonged outside, so as to have part of it squared; between it and the square part of the pinion in the main frame, a connecting rod with Hooke's joints was put, by this means an immediate communication took place between the main frame and the swing wheel,—thus removing all the accidents continually attending the rewinding part. The clock nevertheless seemed to perform very well; the pendulum being firmly fixed to the wall of the steeple, certainly contributed not a little to this.

After this alteration had been made, the arc of the pendulum's vibration increased very much beyond what it was before; in order to bring it back to its former arc, it was found necessary to reduce the going weight considerably. Does not this say that much of the force of the main weight must have been taken up, in the rewinding of the small weight which carried the swing wheel forward? May not this be the same in all cases, where a rewinding part is introduced, such as in Harrison's, Mudge's, Haley's, &c.? They are all on the same principle, only differently modified.

It must be confessed, that in the apparatus of rewinders, there is an appearance of their giving an equal impulse at all times to the regulator of the machine, whether it is a pendulum or a balance; in our experience with them, they have always been found so far useless, that there seemed to be no possibility of keeping them constantly to their purpose. Having in one instance applied to a spring time-piece, a rewinder made after that of Haley's, and notwithstanding a continuance of repeated trials, and every thing done in order to make it do what was intended, yet, after all, it was at last found requisite to take it away.

It is singular, in all their correspondence with Mr. Holmes, neither Smeaton nor Ludlam ever once hinted of applying a rewinder to the turret clock, which at that time was in hands for the Royal Hospital at Greenwich, seeing the great anxiety they displayed to have it as complete as possible, they surely were not ignorant of the mechanism of such a thing; Ludlam in particular, who had been appointed by the Board of Longitude, as a man of talent, to take from Harrison an explanation of the mechanism of his time-keeper; they must have known something of the ticklishness or fallibility of a rewinder, or perhaps they thought it of little or no use, so far as regarded the making of a strong and sound clock. At the time we were making up the clock for St. Andrew's church, Mr. Holmes very kindly sent, for our information, the letters which Smeaton and Ludlam had written to him, when he was engaged with the clock for Greenwich Hospital: it must be allowed that they are invaluable, so far as regards the making up of turret clocks. The late Professor Robison having got a reading of them, was so highly pleased, that he took a kind of interest, and entered into such ideas as he thought might improve the clock for St. Andrew's church; among other things, he suggested that of a rewinder. He had been talking to the late Dr. John Hutton, and the celebrated *James Watt*, of our making up the clock, and in a note sent, says, " They have just been with me, and have assured me, that the transparent black *gun-flint* is of prodigious hardness, and takes an exquisite polish; the white flint is not near so hard, and the dull black flint is gritty. Mr. Watt advises to make the swing wheel of hard steel, or toughish bell metal; because, all sort of metals, such as brass, take hold of the dust and other grinding matters, it sticks fast on their surface, and hence will cut the pallets. He also disapproves of friction rollers in the dial-work, because, when out of order, they cannot easily be got at to be repaired. He recommended a slip of thin tanned leather, soaked in oil, *not linseed*, between the hour-hand socket, and the minute-hand rod; it keeps out all wet and dust, and will last forever, even under very great pressure, as he has experienced in *his Engines*."

Professor Robison was deservedly allowed to be a very able philosopher, and may be considered to have been more or less an adept in all the sciences, but perhaps had not that experience with clocks which Smeaton and Ludlam seem to have possessed; indeed Smeaton was bred a clockmaker with the celebrated Henry Hindley of York.

Notwithstanding Mr. Watt's Observations, the swing wheel was made of very fine brass, and the pallets of steel very hard tempered, and, after going nearly forty years, there is hardly any appearance of biting or wearing to be seen on them, as has already been stated; it is true that the 'scapement work and its frame, were inclosed in a wooden box, in order to prevent dust getting to it. It was never in our contemplation to use friction rollers to the dial wheels; they are however fitted up in such a manner, that neither the hour wheel socket, nor the rod of the minute hand wheel, can tend to pinch one another in their end shakes. A piece of leather, however thin, could not well be introduced into the hour wheel socket; leather might have been put into the socket at the centre of the dial where the hands bear, though with no great pressure, chiefly on the hour hand socket; but the motion is so very slow, making one revolution only in 12 hours, that even *here* leather was hardly necessary.

Having said so much about rewinders, we may give Berthoud's opinion of them, after giving the description of the 'scapement contrived by Mudge for his time-keepers. He says, " The combination of this 'scapement must appear seducing, yet it is to be suspected, that a mechanism so complicated, and whose effects are so nice, cannot be easily put in practice; for it requires an extreme precision of execution to make its performances sure, such as the stopping of the balance wheel teeth by the nibs of the *pallets*; also to make their *axis's* coincide exactly with that of the balance, the pallets in rewinding, increasing the friction of the regulator, two pivots of these pallets are constantly in action, during each vibration, which comes to be the same thing as if the balance had four pivots, &c."

" We shall observe, moreover, says Berthoud, that the regulator of Mr. Mudge is composed of four spiral springs, two for the pallets, that is, one for each pallet arbor, and two for the balance, and these ought to obtain isochronism; for it is indispensably necessary in a portable machine, that the oscillations of unequal extent of the balance should be isochrone; now, if they are so, the mechanism of the *remontoir*, or that of rewinding, is not of any use; and if they are not so, the chronometer will vary *notwithstanding the rewinder*, when by agitations or shocks the balance shall describe the greatest or the smallest arcs, and when these arcs shall vary, either from the friction of the pivots, or from a change of force in the spirals, produced by heat or by cold, &c. See *Histoire de la Mésure du Temps*, tom. ii. p. 50.

It is a great many years since Mr. Charles Haley took out a patent for a rewinder; and soon after this, Mr. Delafons contrived another, both of a very nice construction,—a description of which is given in the Transactions of the Society for the encouragement of Arts, Commerce, and Manufactures; how far they answered the end proposed we have not been able to learn, although our utmost endeavours were exerted to procure this information. A very ingenious thing of this kind has lately been put to a chronometer by Mr. Jardingour, watch-maker, Glasgow, an artist of considerable talent, and an enthusiast in his profession, which appears to promise well; and we sincerely wish that it may come up to meet his most sanguine expectations.

Harrison's remontoir was a very delicate spring, which was bent or wound up eight times in a minute. Were it necessary, a more particular description could be given of it than what is detailed in the description of his time-keeper. In Haley's, the remontoir is bent up 150 times in a minute. In the 'scapement of Mudge's marine time-keepers, what may be called the remontoir, was bent up 300 times in a minute; the 'scapement here became, in some degree, wholly the remontoir. A variety of clock 'scapements may be seen in Thiout, and in some of the modern periodical works; yet, for the purpose of common and ordinary sort of clocks, they are confined chiefly to those of the dead beat, and the recoil. Where accurate performance is required and expected, some may have recourse to 'scapements of a different description.

About the year 1752, Le Roy, Lepaute, and other clock-makers in Paris, were much engaged in making clocks having only one wheel in them, and some had not even a single wheel in the movement part. They were, however, more expensive in making, and performed much worse than those which were constructed in the ordinary way. Simplicity in the machinery seems to have been their chief object. It requires, however, experience to know what simplicity in machinery is; although apparently more simple, a clock having two wheels will not be equal to that having three or four; yet it does not follow, that, by having more wheels, the clock will be proportionally better. It has already been mentioned, that there are bounds which cannot be overstepped with impunity.

This subject cannot be better exemplified than by making a comparison of one of Hindley's clocks having two wheels, and the pendulum giving thirty vibrations in a minute, with a clock giving the same number of vibrations in the same time, and with three wheels.

The first or great wheel in one of Hindley's had 180 teeth, the second or swing wheel 120, and the pinion 8. The number of these teeth and pinion-leaves amounts to 308. In the other, the wheels were 48, 40, and 30, with two pinions of 8; the sum of these is 134; the difference is 174, being the number of teeth more in the one clock than in the other, and which is greater than the number of the teeth in the three-wheeled clock taken altogether.

We shall now proceed to give a short account of such watch 'scapements as have been thought worthy of notice, from the ancient crown wheel and verge one, to the modern free or detached 'scapement; but in order that the reader may be able to follow our descriptions, we have given from Berthoud a view of an assemblage of wheels and pinions, to represent something like the movement of a watch or small time-piece. They are contained in a frame made for the purpose of allowing them to be more readily seen. D E, Plate VIII. No. 43. is the pillar plate, or pillar frame plate; G F, the fore plate of the frame; A, is the balance; the arbor or axis on which it is fixed, is the verge, whose two pallets *p p*, 'scape with the teeth of the crown wheel C. The pivots of the balance turn or run in the frame; those of the crown wheel C, and of its pinion *d*, run in the potence I, and in the counter potence H, both of which are screwed on the inside of the pillar plate, the arbor of the pinion *d* being at right angles to the axis of the balance. The contrate wheel K, and its pinion *c*, turn also in the frame; the teeth of the contrate wheel pitch into the balance (or crown) wheel pinion, and can turn or drive it; the third wheel L, and its pinion *b*, run in the frame; the teeth of the third wheel pitch into the contrate wheel pinion and turn it. The centre or second wheel M, and its pinion *a*, have a long arbor going beyond the outside of the dial R S. The second wheel M pitches with the third wheel pinion *b*, which it likewise can turn. N is the first or great wheel pitching with the second wheel pinion *a*; X is the ratchet, *m* the click, and *n* its spring. On the arbor of the great wheel the ratchet is fixed, and on winding up the main-spring, the ratchet and arbor turn freely in the hole at the centre of the great wheel which keeps its place during the time of winding. O P is the main-spring deprived of its barrel, the inner end of it hooks on to the lower part of the great wheel arbor, and the outer end is hooked to the barrel, but is here fixed to a temporary stud. The force of the main-spring, after being wound up, sets all the wheels and pinions in motion, and would oblige the ratchet and arbor to turn round independent of the great wheel; by this the main spring would be instantly unbent, but is prevented from this by the click *m* being forced by its spring *n* to fall into the teeth of the ratchet, applying its end to the face of the ratchet teeth: by this means the main spring must unbend itself very slowly, the motion of the wheels being checked by the 'scaping of the verge with the crown-wheel teeth. Q is the canon pinion, put spring tight on the arbor of the second wheel, whose socket or canon goes outside or beyond the dial, where it is squared for the purpose of the minute-hand being put on it. T is the minute wheel, *g* its pinion; the canon pinion pitches into or leads the minute wheel; the hour wheel V, having a hollow arbor or socket, *t*, is put on the canon pinion, and is led by the minute pinion, which pitches into its teeth. It is on the socket of the hour wheel, which comes a little above the dial, that the hour-hand is put. When a wheel pitches with a pinion, and turns it, the pinion is said to be driven by the wheel; if the pinion turns the wheel, the wheel is then said to be led by the pinion. No pendulum or balance spring being at the movement, (No. 43.) yet we may suppose one to be so, having its inner end fixed to a collet, which goes spring tight on the axis of the balance; the outer end is fixed or pinned into a stud fixed on the inside of the fore-plate. In the action of the crown-wheel teeth on the pallets, the balance spring is either bent up or unbending; it is by the small force of it that the balance is made to give twice the number of vibrations in a given time than it would give without it. It should have been observed, that by putting a key on the square of the canon pinion, and turning it about, this will not only move the minute hand round, but will oblige the hour hand to follow slowly, in the ratio of one turn to twelve of the minute hand.

The first watches may readily be supposed to have been of rude execution. Having no pendulum spring, and only an hour hand, and being wound up twice a day, they could not be expected to keep time nearer than 15 or 20 minutes in the twelve hours. After the application of the pendulum spring, they would no doubt go considerably better, and may now be made to keep time sufficiently correct for the ordinary purposes of life. Indeed, when the crown wheel and verge 'scapement is executed with care, it will do uncommonly well. Let the angle of the verge be 95 degrees or upwards, the teeth of the crown wheel undercut to an angle of 28 or 30 degrees, and 'scaped as near to the body of the verge as just to be clear of it; (it is to be understood here that the verge holes are jewelled.) To carry the matter still farther, the body may so far be taken away as to admit the teeth near to the centre, which will tend to allow the vibrations of the balance to move more freely and independently; but this requires such nice execution *here*, and in other parts of the *'scapement*, that, from not having encouragement, few are fit to execute it, and therefore it may in general be safer not to bring the wheel teeth so near to the body of the verge. Care must also be taken to have the balance of a proper diameter and weight, which has of late been much neglected, since the old fashion of half-timeing has been left off; that is, making the watch go without the pendulum spring, —if it goes slow, 30, 32, or 33 minutes in an hour, the balance may be considered of such a weight, as to be in no danger of knocking on the banking, from any external motion the watch may meet with in fair wearing. When the pallets of the verge are banked on pins in the potence, they should, to prevent straining, both bank at the same time, alternately the face of one pallet on a pin, when the back of the other is on its pin, or the banking may be done in the rim of the balance, but not near the edge of it. Which of the two is preferable, we shall not stop to determine.

The verge watch, as has been already said, will perform extremely well. About 40 years ago nearly, we had some of them made up in such a way, that they went fully as well as any horizontal 'scapement, and for a longer time,—this last requiring oil to the cylinder after going ten or twelve months. Oil, however, should never be allowed to come near the wheel teeth or pallets of a verge. Verge or contrate wheel watches have, of late years, been very much overlooked and neglected in many respects, and in none more so than in the relative position of the balance wheel and contrate wheel arbors. They are rarely seen, but at a considerable distance from one another, which gives a very oblique direction in the pitching of the contrate wheel with the balance wheel pinion. It is well known, that where force is indirectly or obliquely applied, it will work under great disadvantage. These arbors ought to be placed as near to each other as can be. In order to obtain this, reduce the balance wheel pinion arbor *towards the end to the smallest size it will bear*; and, turning a hollow out of that of the contrate wheel arbor, this will allow them to come very near the line of their centres. To get this pitching to the greatest advantage, some place their counter-potence within the rim, and near the arbor of the contrate wheel, so as to have the line of the balance-wheel pinion direct to the centre of the *contrate wheel*, as may be seen in Plate VIII. No. 43.

It has been recommended by a very celebrated artist, that the movement wheels should be placed in such a manner as to act at equal distances from the pivots of those pinions which they drive, in order to divide the pressure or action of the wheel between the pivots, and that one pivot should not bear more than the other. This is apparently sound reasoning; but, having put it in execution, the pivots unexpectedly seemed to wear very fast, even more so than in the common barred movement,—the pivots, it is true, were small, and the motive force rather great. It is to be wished that a further trial should be made, to bring it completely to the test. No pivots have been found to stand so well as those in movements of the double barred sort.

A pendulum spring collet, made as it ought to be, is as seldom to be met with, as that which we have noticed regarding the *positions* of the contrate and balance wheel arbors. Yet, simple as the thing is, it seems to require a rule to show *how it should be done*, there appearing to be no such rule at present, if we may judge by the greater part of those which have hitherto been made. The ring of the collet should be no broader than to allow a hole to receive the pendulum spring and pin which fixes it. The *slit* made in the collet, for the purpose of its being always spring tight on the outside taper of a cylinder, or verge collet, tapered a little inwards, should be put close to where the small end of the pin comes, when the spring is pinned fast in. The pendulum spring in this case will have the first or inner coil at such a distance as to allow the point of a small screw-driver to get into the slit, without any danger to the spring, when it is wanted to set the collet and spring to any required place. If the slit is put at the other end of the pin, where it is oftener than any where else, it is evident that the workman cannot get into it without danger to the spring. The outer end of the pendulum spring ought to be pinned or fixed into a brass cock or stud ; in performing this operation, it goes easily on, whereas, with steel cocks or studs, there is a crossness or trouble, which shows that they should never be used, independent of other reasons that might be urged. These studs and cocks are in general very improperly placed, being put at a greater distance from the curb pins than is requisite. We have seen this distance so great, that the motion of the pendulum spring between the stud and the pins was such, as to take away a part from every vibration of the balance ; which is something like a pendulum when suspended to a vibratory or ill fixed cock, where it would not be allowed to have half the motion it would have otherwise acquired.

A few years ago, our modern improvers would have the joint transferred from the pillar-plate to the brass edge ; nothing worse could have been proposed. In the old way, the whole of the movement was kept in its place, by the united assistance of the joint, and of the bolt and its spring ; whereas, in the other way, the movement has its sole dependence on the pins of the brass edge feet, from which it frequently would be disengaged, by violent exercise on horseback, &c.

From what has been said of the imperfections in watches, it may be seen, that they inevitably arise from the want of that energy of mind in workmen, of which not one in a hundred is possessed. Can it then be supposed that every new watch which is purchased is complete and requires no assistance ? Whoever thinks so, must, and will be disappointed. On finding it not go as they expected, bring it to some watch-maker or other, many of whom cannot put it in a better state than that in which the workman or finisher gave it as complete. But it is brought to him, not with the view of having any thing done to it, *as it is supposed to require nothing*, but *merely to see* what is the *matter* with it, never considering that any irregular going, or stopping, must imply some fault or other, and is the very cause that brings them to the watch-maker. It does not follow, however, from this, that every watch which stops is badly executed; this will happen sometimes with those of the very best execution, and frequently from an *over-nicety* of the finisher. On the watch being left, he (the watch-maker) takes it down, examines it, and reports accordingly what is necessary to make it keep time. The owner, on being told afterwards, that it will cost so much to make it do what is required, frequently and strongly suspects, though he may be polite enough not to say so, that there must be some imposition on the part of the watch-maker. Much is the trouble many watch-makers have of rectifying the faults of work given in, and large sums paid for such alteration of work thought originally to have been complete. We have known four guineas paid to a workman for doing a particular branch: and it not being executed to the satisfaction of the watch-maker, he has given half as much more to another to have it corrected. There are as few who excel in this art, as in those of sculpture, painting, and engraving, which are called the fine arts, —a name to which watch-making, in every sense of the word, is equally entitled, but which labours under the great misfortune in not being properly seen, that few or none are enabled to appreciate the merits even of the finest executed piece. This will ultimately sink the profession to nothing, which, we are afraid, it is daily doing, and so much so, that no young man can now be found to go to it who has got the smallest degree of education, or of ingenuity; and when the provincial towns decline to give their quota in this way, the capitals will not be able to support the character that such a profession requires, from want of a supply of hands.

The old 'scapement, even after the application of the pendulum, and of the pendulum spring, not giving that satisfaction which was required or expected, induced both Hooke and Huyghens to think of other means of improving it, or to substitute a superior mechanism in its place. In this pursuit the mechanical talents of Hooke stood conspicuously eminent over those of the justly celebrated Huyghens. Some of the movements of Huyghens' watches, or time-keepers, were much larger than those of our box chronometers. The contrate wheel was cut into teeth of the same form as those of the common crown wheel, and made to 'scape with a verge of the usual kind. On the axis of this verge was a sort of contrate or crown wheel, having teeth like the ordinary contrate wheel, which drove a pinion fixed on the axis of the balance. The verge, when 'scaping with its wheel, caused the balance to make several revolutions from every impulse on the pallets; some of them had no pendulum spring, having been made perhaps before its application. When the balance made several revolutions in every vibration, each being two seconds, this 'scapement would be but ill suited for the coils of a pendulum spring. Those having the pendulum spring appeared about 1675. This was the origin of the half-timeing which we have alluded to, upon seeing, that when the pendulum spring was applied, it made the balance give two vibrations in the same time that it gave one without it; a particular reference to Plate VIII. No. 44. may tend to show the action of this mechanism still better than what has been given or said of it. In the frame A B is contained the contrate wheel E E, whose teeth, in place of being of the ordinary form, are like the common crown wheel teeth, and 'scape with the pallets on the verge $f e$; on it is rivetted an ordinary contrate wheel D D, whose teeth pitch in with the pinion $d c$; the pinion being the axis of the balance C C, kept in its place by a cock of the usual kind, the foot pivot turning in the lower frame plate; $a\ a$ represents the pendulum spring as seen edgewise

About the same period, Dr. Hooke brought into notice his watch with a new 'scapement, which, for seventeen years before, he had been privately endeavouring to improve. This was very different from the old crown wheel one, and as much so from that of Huygens'. It had two balances, on the axis of each was a toothed wheel pitching into one another; the verge or axis of these balances had each a pallet on it: The balance wheel was flat, having a few ratchet or sawlike teeth; its arbor run within the frame, parallel to those of the balances, at a point equally distant from their centres; the three points forming as it were the angles of an equilateral triangle. When a tooth of the balance wheel gave impulse on one pallet, the other, by the pitching of the two wheels, was brought about to meet another tooth, *after the wheel had escaped from the pallet on the opposite side*, in order to receive impulse in its turn. There was a pendulum spring on one of the balances, and the object of their being pitched together was to prevent the effect of external motion on them, while it served the double purpose of bringing alternately about the pal-

Q

lets, and still gave some little recoil to the wheels by the reaction of the balances. Although this was a very ingenious contrivance for a 'scapement, yet it appears not to have given that satisfaction which was expected, *probably from indifferent execution, as, from Sully's account, was the case,* and the old one was again resumed. However, some years afterwards, other artists, among whom was *Dutertre,* were attracted by this 'scapement of Dr. Hooke's, and were led from time to time to make improvements on it. From it, originated the duplex 'scapement, which has of late years been so much in repute. A large old German clock had a 'scapement on the same principle as the above, of which the maker's name is unknown; see Thiout, tom. 1. p. 110. and Plate XLIII. Fig. 31. Dr. Hooke's claim to his own 'scapement remains however undisputed.

The famous Tompion (who was upwards of sixty years in business, as a watch-maker, in London, and who, by his labours, contributed greatly to the reputation that the art had acquired in England) made a 'scapement about 1695, and flattered himself by its succeeding as an improvement. The verge, or axis of the balance, was a small solid steel cylinder, cut across at the middle, and nearly half way down; in the longitudinal direction of the cylinder, a deep angular notch was made, forming a sort of pallet on the left hand side; the balance wheel was flat, and much like Dr. Hooke's, the spaces between the teeth sufficiently wide to allow the cylinder to turn freely between them. When a tooth of the wheel had impelled the pallet on 'scaping from it, the following tooth dropped on the outside of th cylinder near the right edge, resting on the cylinder during this v bration of the balance; after passing the right edge, and meeting little recoil, it got again on the pallet and gave a new impulse, whi took place only at every second vibration. An excellent property observed in this 'scapement, that any inequalities in the motive fr made no deviation in its time-keeping; but the friction of the lance-wheel teeth on the cylinder and its edges, was so great and structive, that it was given up in consequence.

Knowing what Tompion had been doing, *being bred under* Graham, a good many years after, set to work with the cy 'scapement, and ultimately succeeded. Although this 'scape now pretty generally known, yet we may be allowed to give count of what he did. In place of Tompion's solid cylin made a hollow one, see Plate III. No. 18.: On the points pion's wheel teeth were raised something like small pins or the tops of which a sort of inclined or wedge-like teeth wer

of such a length as to have a very little freedom when in the inside of the cylinder, and the outside of the cylinder to have the same freedom between the point of one tooth and the heel of the other. A notch or opening was made across the cylinder not quite half way down the diameter; the edges of the cylinder made by this opening, were dressed so that the curved edge of the tooth might operate easily on them; the left hand edge was flanched outward, the right hand rounded; when the balance was at rest, and the wheel in its place to 'scape, the point of the tooth got them just in on the cylinder edges and no more; a second notch was made below the other, to allow the bottom of the wheel to pass, leaving hardly a fourth of the circumference of the cylinder, the other leaving more than a semicircle. The highest part of the wedge or curved teeth being in a circle, greater or beyond that on which the point was, it is evident, that if the wheel is urged forward, it will make the cylinder to turn, and the angle of 'scapement will be according to the height of the wedge: when a tooth of the wheel escapes from the right hand edge of the cylinder, the point of it falls into the inside; after reposing there, it then passes and impels the left hand edge; on escaping it, the point of the succeeding tooth drops on the outside of the cylinder where it reposes; on the return of the balance, it gets on the right hand edge, giving a new impulse, and so on; the teeth impel on both edges of the cylinder, giving, by each, a vibration to the balance. See Plate III. No. 18. B is the balance, A the cylinder, 1, 2, its pivots, F the cylinder or balance-wheel pinion, the curved part of the wheel teeth are particularly marked at *a*, *b*, and *c*.

This 'scapement being the best of any that had preceded it, *Debaufre's perhaps excepted*, procured for Graham's watches a very considerable reputation, as their performance was much superior to that of the old construction. However, on comparing the going of some of Graham's with those of a later date, we confess that none of his, though excellent, were ever equal to them in performance. The cylinders were rather large in diameter, the balances too light, the motive force too weak, and he had great difficulty in obtaining good pendulum spring-wire, meeting sometimes with iron where he expected steel-wire. Watches having the cylinder 'scapement were not known in France till 1728, when Julien Le Roy commissioned one of them from Graham: They were losing their character here sometime before the introduction of the duplex, which contributed afterwards still more to lessen their value: The duplex will, in its turn, be supplanted, for reasons which will be afterwards noticed. Flat movements, shallow balance wheels, steel and brass of bad quality, (from the difficulty of getting them good,) injudicious execution, and low prices, must have tended to make the cylinder 'scapement so bad as they have been of late; many of the cylinders were destroyed and cut to pieces in a few years, and some of them could not last so long. Let these be compared with the cylinder 'scapements of *old Hull, a cylinder 'scapement-maker in London*, many of which we have seen, after having been in use thirty years and upwards, with little or no impression *even* on their edges. In what did Hull's art consist? There must have been some causes for it, but what these are we shall not attempt to conjecture. Like Graham, with whom he was instructed, Hull soldered in the plugs of his cylinders with silver solder, which caused a very tedious process in the course of finishing the cylinder; but this is not offered as any reason, or the cause of his excelling in the art of cylinder 'scapement making. The acting edges of the teeth have hitherto been made too thin, *particularly for steel cylinders*, with the view of lessening the friction; but this was evidently going on an erroneous principle. The friction was increased by the rapid cutting of the cylinder, and was worse than if the teeth had had thicker working edges, which would have made the friction more constant, and, of course, less liable to cut the cylinder.

When the vibrations of the balance are at the lowest point, the resistance of the pendulum spring is at the least; but the more it is bent or unbent, the greater is the resistance; consequently, when at the height of the wedge or tooth, it is greater than when the tooth first begins to act. Two or three different curves for this purpose have been imagined; one approaching nearly to a right line, which is supposed to give the wheel time to acquire a velocity during the passing of two-thirds of the curve and the least resistance of the spring, by which the other third is more readily overcome, when the resistance to it, is greatest. This has been thought to give a greater extent to the arc of vibration, and has been adopted by the French artists. Another curve, where equal spaces make the balance describe equal portions of a circle, is thought to give the least wearing to the edges of the cylinder, and is that which is practised by our 'scapement makers. Arguments equally good for either, as it thus appears, might be given.

The weight and diameter of the balance, are circumstances very materially connected with the wearing of the cylinder edges. Whatever will prevent this wearing, should be carefully attended to. When the diameter is large, the balance must of consequence be less heavy a sort of sluggishness in its motion takes place, the pendulum spri making great resistance to the teeth passing the cylinder edges, causing rapid wearing. On the contrary, when the diameter is small, and the weight at a proper medium, there is an alertness in the vibration; the momentum of the balance has such force over the pendulum spring, that it allows the teeth to pass the edges quickly, and hence there is a less tendency to wear them. The diameter of the balance should be less than in a verge watch of equal size, and it should be no heavier than just to prevent setting, unless where a going in time of winding is used. The cylinder 'scapement, on the whole, must be allowed to be a very excellent one; and where care is taken to have it made as it ought to be, such watches will give very good performance. Provision for oil on the cylinder should be made as ample as can be admitted; that is, the part where the tooth acts should be as distant from the notch where the wheel bottom passes as possible, and, at the same time, more distant from the upper copper plug; the lower notch should not be longer than to give freedom for the wheel bottom to pass easily. When they are made long, as they frequently are, the cylinder will readily break there, if the watch receives any slight shock from falling. The acting part of the tooth, as has already been noticed, should not be too thin, nor the stems too short. If the diameter of the balance is too great, any addition of motive force will make the watch go slow; if too little, the watch will go fast; and if, of a proper weight and diameter, any addition of motive force will make little or no change on the time-keeping, whether the watch is hanging or lying: we have made the motive force more than double, and no change took place; the isochronism of the pendulm spring no doubt had its share in keeping up this uniformity. Balances, whose diameters are rather small, will have a natural tendency to cross farther; that is, the arcs of vibration will be greater than where the diameters are great. Their weight will be in the inverse ratio of the squares of their diameters; from which it follows, that if the balance is taken away from a watch which has been regulated, and another put in its place, having the diameter only one-half of the former; before the watch could be regulated with the same pendulum spring, the balance would require to be four times heavier than the first. One way of estimating the force of a body in motion, is to multiply the mass by the velocity. Let us then calculate the respective forces of two balances, whose diameters are to one another as two to four. The radii in this case express the velocity. According to this principle, we shall have, for the small balance, two for the radius multiplied by eight of the mass, equal to sixteen; and for the great one, four of the radius by two of the mass, equal to eight; sixteen and eight are then the products of the masses by the velocities; consequently they express the force at the centre of percussion of each balance: and as it is double in the small one, it is evident that the arcs of vibration will be greater, having the faculty of overcoming easily any resistance opposed to it by the pendulum spring, without requiring any additional motive force.

Let us take an example done in another way:—Which is the square of the product of the diameter, multiplied by the velocity or number of degrees in the vibration, and this again multiplied by the mass or weight, so as to compare the relative momentum of two balances of different diameters, &c.? Suppose one balance to be .8 of an inch in diameter, the degrees of vibration 240, and the weight 8 grains; the other .7 of an inch in diameter, the arc of vibration 280°, and the weight 10 grains:

$$240 \times .8 = 192 \times 192 = 36864 \times 8 = 294912$$
$$280 \times .7 = 196 \times 196 = 38416 \times 10 = 384160.$$

The balance having the smaller diameter, has its momentum to that of the greater, as 384160 is to 294912, or in smaller numbers, as 99 is to 76 very nearly. When the arcs of vibration are great, the nearer to isochronism will the long and short ones be.

If the balance of a watch has its arms and centre part rather a little heavy as otherwise, and these be made less so, the watch by this will be found to go slower than it did before, owing to the effect of the increased momentum of the balance. This unusual, *perhaps hitherto untried and very delicate* experiment, we made once or twice, and the result was that which has now been stated. The momentum of a watch balance should be as nearly in one point of the rim as possible, and is somewhat analagous to that which is required in the ball of a clock pendulum.

Berthoud, in his *Essai*, &c. insists much on the advantage of light balances, great diameters, and quick vibrations: principles, however well dressed up as a theory, will be found not to agree with sound practice and a little experience. M. Jodin, a very ingenious watchmaker, contemporary with Berthoud, in Paris, knowing what Berthoud had advanced on this subject in his *Essai*, took an opportunity of putting him to rights, by using such arguments as ought in our humble opinion to have convinced him; but in this interview *Jodin's* endeavours were to no purpose. Berthoud, indeed, seems not to have acted in conformity with the principles he wished to establish, if we may judge by what he did, seeing that he made the trains of his marine time-keepers in such various numbers, from that of giving one vibration in a second to that of giving six in the same time; and the performance of one of those which gave one vibration in a second, is mentioned as having maintained the best rate of going of all that he had made. Mr. Cumming got also into the system of quick trains, but was obliged at last to give it up, and was in the end put to a considerable expense in altering every one of these his quick trained watches, when he could lay his hands on them, because the cylinders were going so fast to ruin, that the watches gave no satisfaction.

It may be found very convenient, and sometimes of great utility, for the practical artist to have a little knowledge in the theory of the relative force of balances, according to their diameter, weight, and the number of vibrations given in a minute. An instance shall be given that tends in some degree to show this:—A small eight-day spring time-piece, of a size somewhat less than that of common spring clocks, which had a balance and a detached 'scapement; the train was rather slow, being 5400, but with such a train the force of the main-spring had so much power over the balance, as to make the vibrations at times go so far as to unlock the detent a second time in the course of one and the same excursion; the vibration being thus carried to such an extreme, and when nearly at the end of it; although a tooth of the balance wheel had for a second time dropped on the face of the pallet, it had no force to impel it farther on, that of the pendulum spring was greater from being now so much bent up; on its unbending, the balance was made to return a very little way back, which brought the circular part of the pallet into contact with one of the balance-wheel teeth, and by this means the tooth was now allowed to pass freely on the roller or circular part of the pallet, which had the effect of stopping the motion of the balance, and, consequently, stopped the going of the time-piece. It would have been a very inconvenient matter, at this time, *as we shall suppose*, either to have made the train quicker, or to have got a main-spring of less force, as any one of the two ways would have brought the vibrations of the balance within a shorter compass. Now, what device must be fallen on, in order to lessen the arc of vibration, so as the balance shall not go so far as to make a second unlocking, keeping still the same train of wheels, and the same force of main-spring? There is only one way to do this, and that is by increasing the diameter of the balance; which will then require a stronger pendulum spring, and this will of course give a little more opposition to the impelling force of the balance-wheel teeth on the face of the pallet. If we suppose the diameter of the balance to be one inch, or, what is the same thing, ten-tenths of an inch, and, to increase it, the three mean time screws which were in the edge of the rim of the balance, being brought out so far as to make the diameter one inch and a quarter, or 12.5 tenths of an inch; by this alteration the time-piece was found to lose an hour and a quarter in the 24 hours. It is evident that a stronger pendulum spring must then be applied, before the balance can be made to vibrate mean time, and that in the ratio of the squares of the diameter of the balances, the square of 10 is 100, and the square of 12.5 is 156.25, the difference between these numbers shows that a considerable difference will be required in the strength of the pendulum springs. The weight of the balance, including the three mean time screws, pendulum spring, and stud, balance arbor, and roller, was 137 grains.

How to remedy the converse of the preceding case should be very obvious, and to many it will appear unnecessary to say any thing about it. Yet there may be some few who may not so readily fall on it, and therefore one example in this way shall be given. Suppose the balance of a time-piece has its vibrations so short, that no good performance can be derived from it, notwithstanding the movement, the 'scapement, the main-spring, &c. are as correct as could be wished. The short vibrations must then arise from the balance being too large in diameter, and from having too strong a pendulum spring. Now, if a balance of the same weight, or nearly so, but less in diameter, and a weaker pendulum spring be applied, this will allow the vibrations of the balance to be carried to a greater extent, which was all that was required.

When a little expense in the cylinder or horizontal 'scapement is not grudged, a ruby cylinder is certainly a great acquisition, to prevent wearing on the edges. If it is wholly of stone, and not steel cased, as is usual, it will be so much the better, by giving a little more scope to extend the limits of the banking, the steel crank of the cased ruby cylinder confining the banking. There would no doubt be a greater risk of breaking than in the steel-cased stone cylinder; yet this might be considerably lessened, were some attention paid to make the notch, which frees the bottom of the wheel, no longer than is necessary, as has been proposed in the case of the steel cylinder. It would be desirable to have the cylinder formed with the strata of the sapphire or ruby, placed in a vertical position, instead of a horizontal one. This is surely attainable, when we know that diamond splitters can distinguish the strata or layers of the diamond,—a stone which may be supposed more compact than either the ruby or sapphire. We have seen a cylinder wholly of stone, in a watch belonging to a gentleman who was wearing it when between 70 and 80 years of age; he used frequently to let it fall without any accident happening to the cylinder. Three small griffs, or cocks, placed on the potence plate, so as to allow the edge of the balance to come into notches fitted for it, and having at the same time sufficient freedom, would prevent either the cylinder or the cock pivot from breaking. A little practice should make the stone cylinder easier made, and perhaps cheaper, than even the steel cased one; at all events, even on equal terms, it ought to be the preferable of the two. From what has already been said, it appears, that the weight and diameter of the balance are matters that cannot be said to be merely arbitrary; for, if the motive force is too great for that of the balance, the watch will go fast when in the lying or horizontal position, and slow when in the vertical or hanging position. By diminishing either the motive force, or making the balance heavier, the watch may be made to go alike in both positions. The properties of the pendulum spring may conduce a little to this. It is in some degree a desideratum for a pocket-watch to have the balance pivots and holes made so, that the balance with its spring, when in a state by itself, and free of any communication with the wheels, should vibrate the same length of time, whether it is in a vertical or horizontal position. We know, when it is in the latter, that it will continue to vibrate twice the length of time that it will do in the other. We are humbly of opinion, that the balance, with its spring in an isolated state, could be made to vibrate the same length of time in both positions. But who will be at the trouble and expense to make such experiments as may lead to this?

Mr. Earnshaw's pivots, with flat ends and shallow holes, should come very near to this object. About forty, or near to fifty years ago, endeavouring to come at this, we used to hollow out the ends of balance pivots.

In the interim between Tompion having left off his trials in attempting the horizontal 'scapement, and Graham having brought it to a state of perfection, M. Facio, a native of Geneva, having discovered the art of piercing holes in rubies, or any hard precious stone, came to Paris with this art as a secret, but not being well received, either by the Duke of Orleans, at that time Regent of France, or by the watch-makers there, he repaired to London with it about the year

OO, which was at that time a school where the art of watch-making was more cultivated than at Paris. He was admitted a member of the Royal Society; and, having entered into a kind of partnership with a native of France, who had been settled in London, whose name was Debaufre, they carried on the business of watch-jewelling. *Some of Debaufre's family, or name, were at this profession in London so late as* 1773. Facio's partner had at this time contrived a new 'scapement; it was a dead-beat one, which was the thing now sought for. The balance and balance-wheel holes of it were jewelled; the pallet was made of a diamond, formed from a very short cylinder E, Plate VIII. No. 45. of two-tenths of an inch in diameter, fixed on the verge or axis C D of the balance A B; the upper end of the cylinder was cut down nearly one-half of the diameter, and flanched to the lower end and opposite side, rounded off from the base left at top to the lower end of the flanch, resembling something like a cone bent and wanting a part of the top. Two flat balance wheels W W, having ratchet sort of teeth, were on the same arbor, the teeth of the one being opposite to the middle of the spaces in the other; the distance between these wheels was a little less than the diameter of the cylinder; the drop of the teeth in 'scaping falls on what was left of the upper base of the cylinder,—*the lower base being taken away in forming the pallet,*—and near to the edge formed from the flanch; here they rested during the time of the vibration of the balance. On the return, the tooth gets on the flanch, and passes over it; during which, giving impulse to the balance, and escaping at the lower end, a tooth of the other wheel drops opposite on the same base of the cylinder, and so on. A watch having this 'scapement, and bearing Debaufre's name, was put for trial into the hands of Sir Isaac Newton, who, on shewing it to *Sully*, in 1704, gave a very flattering account of its performance. It attracted Sully's notice very much, but thinking it by no means well executed, and not being quite satisfied with two wheels, it was thought that an improvement would be made, by having one wheel only, and two pallets, which was part of the scheme of the 'scapement he adopted for his marine time-keeper, made in 1721. Considering the genius that Sully was allowed to possess, this was by no means an improvement on Debaufre's 'scapement.

Although an Englishman, Sully's name was unknown to his countrymen, and would have remained so, had it not been for the accounts given of him by the French artists, in whom he excited an emulation and also inspiring them with a taste to acquire such a pre-eminence in their profession, as had been before unknown. Julic

PREMIUMS FOR FINDING THE LONGITUDE.

Le Roy, *who was intimately acquainted with Sully*, and Berthoud, are uncommonly lavish of their encomiums on him. Soon after he had completed his apprenticeship with Mr. Gretton, watchmaker in London, he went to Holland, Germany, and Austria, and, attracting the notice of several of the princes and nobility, he was much employed by them. Having seen, in the library of Prince Eugene, the *Memoirs of the Royal Academy of Sciences in Paris*, he eagerly acquired the French language, in order to read them. This excited in him a strong desire to see Paris, to which he repaired about the year 1713 or 1714, under the patronage, and in the suite of the Duke of Aremburg, at whose hotel he lodged, with a pension of 600 livres. He had not been long there, when our countryman, Law of Lauriston, under the authority of the Court of Versailles, got him engaged to establish a manufactory of clocks and watches. In consequence of this, he came twice to London; and having carried away a great number of workmen, and spent much money on tools and other articles, Law began to murmur, and the establishment in two years fell to the ground. This made him complain bitterly of his bad fortune to a friend; but, fortunately, a nobleman, to whom this was mentioned, feeling much for the disagreeable situation in which Sully was placed, sent him, *as a present*, some shares in the public funds,—value 12,000 livres,—which enabled him, for several years afterwards, to pursue very zealously his favourite scheme of making a marine time-keeper, to ascertain the longitude at sea. In this attempt he was not so successful, in his first trials, as he had led himself to expect. It was in general believed, however, that, had he lived, he would have been the first to have deservedly acquired one or other of the premiums which were before that time offered by four of the greatest maritime powers in Europe, to those who should produce a time-keeper, which could ascertain, to a certain extent, the longitude at sea. Philip the Third, who ascended the throne of Spain in 1591, was the first who proposed, in 1598, a reward of 1000 crowns for this invention.

The states of Holland soon after followed his example, and offered 100,000 florins. The British Parliament, in the reign of Queen Anne, voted £20,000 Sterling for the same purpose; and the Duke of Orleans, Regent of France, in 1716, promised, in name of the King, 100,000 livres. Sully may literally be said to have died a martyr to the cause in which he was engaged. Having got a false address to a person *who, it was said, was* occupied in the same pursuit with himself, he got so overheated, in his anxious and vain endeavour to find him out, that he died in a few days after, at Paris, in the month of October, 1728, and was buried, with great pomp, in the church of St. Sulpicius. In this church, some few years before his death, he constructed a remarkably long gnomon, or meridian line.

Sully having acted so conspicuous a part in the profession, no apology is deemed necessary for giving this short account of him.

It may be observed here, that Debaufre's 'scapement has this advantage, which is not in Graham's, that the impulse given is the same in every vibration, and the time of rest on both sides is the same, bearing mostly on the foot pivot end, a little on the sides of the pivots, but not wholly on the sides of the pivots as in Graham's. Having made one or two watches, to which this 'scapement was put, they were found to perform very well; and we would recommend it to the attention of 'scapement-makers. A little practice will make the execution of it very easy. The two thin steel wheels may at pleasure be placed at any distance from one another; their diameters should be as large as can be admitted between the potence foot and the verge collet. An agate, or any hard stone, for the pallet, whose height is half the spaces between the teeth, or a little less, is fixed on the verge or axis of the balance; the level of the base of the pallet on which the teeth rest, being a very little above that of the line of the balance-wheel pinion, the teeth must be a very little undercut, so that the points only may rest on the pallet. The verge should be placed more inward in the frame than in common contrate wheel movements, in order to give room for the balance wheels. The necessity of a contrate wheel movement for this 'scapement, is a trifling objection, which will wear away in spite of prejujudice.

In 1722, l'Abbè Hautefeuille, *who long before this had at Paris disputed in a process at law with Huygens, the right of the invention and application of the pendulum spring to the balance of a watch, Huygens being cast, was prevented from taking out a patent in France as he wished*, published a quarto pamphlet containing descriptions of three new 'scapements for watches. One of these was the anchor or recoiling 'scapement, on the verge of which was attached a small toothed segment of a circle or rack, working into a pinion which was the axis of the balance. The idea of a pinion being the axis of the balance, seems to have been taken from the 'scapement of Huygens, and is here contrived so as to make scarcely one revolution at every vibration. This 'scapement is the same as it came from the hands of Hautefeuille, without any improvement having been made upon it even to this day, although a patent was taken out for the same about twenty or near to thirty years ago, by some persons in Liverpool. The name of lever watches, which they received from the patentees, is that which is generally given to those having this 'scapement, which is the same that Berthoud has described in his *Essai sur l'Horlogerie*, published in 1763, see tom. ii. No. 1933, and Plate XXIII. Fig. 5. of which our figure is a copy, Plate VIII. No. 46. Berthoud, under certain modifications, introduced the principle of this 'scapement into some of his marine time-keepers. In this 'scapement of l'Abbè Hautefeuille, A is the 'scapement wheel, B the anchor pallets, having inclined planes, or made with such curves as are best suited to obtain isochronous oscillations from the balance: C D the balance, a, a pinion on whose arbor the balance is rivetted; b is the toothed rack which pitches in with the pinion, the rack is carried by the axis of the anchor pallets. In the drawing, the pinion appears to be the arbor of the 'scapement wheel as well as that of the balance; but this is done by way of concentrating the figure E, the counterpoise to the rack.

A very able and ingenious artist at Paris, M. Dutertre, who was zealous in his profession, and had considerable success in his pursuits, invented, in 1724, as is said, a new 'scapement, or, in our humble opinion, rather improved that of Dr. Hooke's, with two balances, which has already been described. The additions and improvements, however, which he made, were so great as to give him a sort of title to claim it as his own, and to render it, in the opinion of good judges, the best 'scapement by far that was known at that time. The additions which he made consisted in putting another wheel on the same arbor with the first, but it was considerably larger in diameter, having the same number of teeth with the other, and which formed the chief merit of his improvement of this 'scapement. The balance arbors at one place were made rather thicker than usual, for the purpose of having notches cut across them, and as deep as the centre. This part of the arbor became then a semi-cylinder. The larger wheel, which may be called that of *arrête*, or repose, is placed on its arbor, so as to correspond with the semi-cylinders and their notches, the points of whose teeth are made just to clear the bottom of the notches, alternately passing one of them, and resting on the semi-cylindrical part of the other.

The action of the two wheels shall now be explained. Let us suppose that one of the larger wheel teeth, after reposing on one of the semi-cylinders, is, on the return of the vibration of the balance, admitted to pass through the notch; after having passed, a tooth of the impulse wheel, falls on the corresponding pallet, gives impulse, carrying it on till it escapes, when another tooth of the wheel of repose falls on the other semi-cylinder, and rests there until the return of the vibration of the other balance, when it passes the notch in its turn, and the corresponding pallet presenting itself, is impelled by a tooth of the impulse wheel, and so on. Hooke's 'scapement had a small recoil; the aim of Dutertre was to make a dead beat one of it, in which he succeeded. There is a drawing of this 'scapement in Plate XIV. Fig 4. of Berthoud's *Histoire de la Mésure du Temps*. He says, " that the properties of this 'scapement are such, that sudden shocks do not sensibly derange the vibrations; that the pressure of the wheel teeth of arrête on the cylinders, corrects the impulse that the balance receives from the wheel work, which, on the motive force being even doubled, prevents the vibrations from being affected."

Plate IX. No. 47. represents this 'scapement having two balances, A B, toothed on their edges, and pitching in with one another; as constructed by Dutertre, they are placed outside of the potence plate, as well as the double ratchet toothed wheels, the three arbors being kept in their places by a cock to each. Upon one of the crosses of each balance are fixed a sort of pallet, D, and E, the arbors of the balances have each a notch out across them, so as to allow the points of the teeth of the larger ratchet wheel to escape. When the points of the teeth of the wheel of arrête, get in on the notches, they pass through instantly, and by this, the teeth of the impulse wheel get forward and impel either one or other of the pallets, D or E; in the scheme or figure, the tooth 5 of the wheel of arrête (or of rest) is seen to have escaped from the notch of the arbor of the balance A, and a tooth of the wheel of impulse is ready to come on, and impel the pallet D, meanwhile the tooth 5 will have got forward, and rests on the semi-cylindrical part of the arbor of the balance B; on the return of the balance, it passes through the notch, and gives the wheel of impulse liberty to strike the pallet E, and so on.

In plate XLI. Fig. 16. of the first volume of Thiout's work, is a drawing of this 'scapement modelled from that of a clock, described at page 101. He says, " Fig. 16. is a 'scapement of the Sieur Jean Baptiste Dutertre, which has only one pallet, on the axis of which is the fork. The two ratchets or wheels are on the same arbor; when the pallet escapes from the small ratchet, the larger one, which is called the ratchet or wheel of *arrête*, rests on the arbor of the pallet, and leaves the vibrations to be pretty free. On the pallet's returning to meet with the teeth of the small ratchet, the pallet arbor or cylinder being notched or cut across into the centre, allows the wheel of *arrête* to pass; and the wheel of impulsion, after getting a small recoil, gives new force to the vibrations; so that in two vibrations, only one of them is accelerated: hence it was thought, that the half of the vibration being *free*, and independent of the wheel-work and its inequalities, they would be more correct than others; but experience did not confirm this." This is, then, the duplex 'scapement, or the nearest possible approach to it.

It is more than fifty years since we saw a small spring clock having this 'scapement, made by a very ingenious clock-maker of this place, whose name was Robert Brackenrig. It may be supposed to have been made a very few years after Thiout's work was published.

In 1727, Peter le Roy gave an account of a 'scapement which he had made, having one pallet on the axis of the balance, and a notch below it, a wheel of *arrête*, and one of impulse, as described in the preceding 'scapement, so that one half of the vibrations were independent of the wheel work. Dutertre claimed the *pretended* invention of Le Roy; the latter, finding it not to answer his expectations, gave it up. That Dutertre made the one which is represented in plate XLI. of Thiout, we have no doubt; and there is unquestionable authority, that he brought Dr. Hooke's to the improved state which has just been mentioned. It is said that he had made a free or detached 'scapement; but no account whatever has been given of it.

The duplex 'scapement, as it is now called, was introduced into its native country about thirty years ago or more, under the name of Tyrers' 'scapment, *the name it is supposed of him who put the last hand to improve that, which came in a lineal descent from Dr. Hooke*. In place of the notch being made right across the arbor, as has been mentioned before, Tyrers' had a very small cylinder or roller, whose diameter was about .03 of an inch, *the diameter of the wheel of arrête being .51 or .52*, into which was made, in a longitudinal direction, a deep angular notch of 30 to 40 degrees. The cylinder was sometimes of steel, but most frequently of ruby. When the points of the teeth of the wheel of repose fall into the notch, they meet with a very small recoil by the balance, in what may be called the returning vibration. This goes so far as to make the tooth for a little to leave the notch, at the side opposite to that by which it came in. The balance, on returning, is now in the course of that vibration, when it is to receive impulse from the wheel, which takes place immediately on the tooth of the wheel of repose leaving the notch and the small cylinder, and as soon as the tooth of impulse escapes from the pallet, the next tooth of repose falls to rest on the small cylinder, and so on.

Plate IX. No. 49. represents the duplex 'scapement, W W being the wheel of arrête or repose, the bases of the teeth of the wheel of impulse are seen at *a b c*, black and triangular, and stand a little up perpendicular to the plane of the wheel of arrête, as represented in perspective of wheel, No. 53. both being formed out of the same piece of brass. A B is the pallet which receives impulse from the upright teeth *a b c*, &c. of the wheel; the roller is represented by a faint dotted circle on the arbor of the pallet, having a small angular notch in it.

Tyrers' 'scapement is much superior to that of the cylinder or horizontal one; it is almost independent of oil, requiring only a very little to the points of the wheel teeth of repose. It can carry a balance of much greater momentum, and, when well executed, performs most admirably. But there are in it so many circumstances or minutiæ to be attended to, that some of them may at times escape the eye of the most judicious and careful: the watch may stop, and yet the 'scapement be in every respect as complete as possible. This has often given the wearer cause to complain, and to suspect the qualities of his watch, and hence watch-makers have sometimes been induced to abandon this 'scapement, and adopt those of an inferior sort. The pallets of Tyrers were at first made very thin. We frequently urged the propriety of having them made much thicker, and were pleased to see that this was gradually adopted. Why should they not be made as thick as the pallet of a detached 'scapement? There is no 'scapement which requires to have the balance-wheel teeth more correctly cut, or the steady pins of the cock and potence more nicely fitted to their places in the potence plate than in this. The minutiæ alluded to, were, too much or too little drop of the impulse teeth on the pallet; the 'scapement not set quite so near to beat as might be; the balance rather heavy; or the points of the teeth of repose too much or too little in on the small cylinder. In a good sizeable pocket-watch, the wheels having fifteen teeth, the ratio of the diameter of the wheel of repose to that of impulse may be as .520 of an inch to .400, the cylinder .030. The angle of 'scapement will be 60 degrees, taking from the escape of the impulse tooth, to that of the tooth of repose falling on the cylinder, the balance passes 20 degrees of these before the impulse tooth gets again on the pallet, consequently it has only 40 degrees for the acting angle of the 'scapement. There is a variety of 'scapements in Berthoud's *Histoire*, which appeared in 1802, many of which are of very inferior note to that of Tyrers, and yet he has taken no notice of the latter. This is remarkable, as he surely must have seen it, considering the great number of them which had been made

A watch having a cylinder or horizontal 'scapement, not giving that performance that it ought to have done, arising from the cause of the cylinder wheel teeth, having somehow accidentally got a tendency to cut the cylinder so fast, that good performance could not possibly be obtained from it. We, therefore, thought it advisable to take this 'scapement altogether away from the watch, and substitute a duplex one in its place. With the cylinder 'scapement, the train was 18,000, and that to the duplex was made 18,200; yet, notwithstanding this additional quickness of train, the same balance, and its spring, kept the exact same time as they did before; which, in some degree, shows the superiority of the duplex over that of the cylinder 'scapement. The freedom and ease with which the balance-wheel gives impulse to the duplex pallet, and with such velocity or quickness of time, that less of the exertion of the pendulum spring was required to bring the pallet back to get a new impulse.

While Dutertre was engaged with Dr. Hooke's 'scapement, an artist in England, whose name is unknown, produced a 'scapement with the dead beat, which seems at that time to have been the great desideratum. Julien Le Roy having got one of these watches, showed it to Sully in November, 1727, and told him that it was a 'scapement very deserving of notice. Thiout mentions it as a 'scapement of M. Flamenville, having two pallets of repose, and says, that it much attracted the attention of the English watch-makers, who had made it for three or four years. (See page 108, Plate XLIII. Fig. 26. of his first volume.) With our workmen, it went by the name of the 'scapement with the tumbling pallets. The axis of the balance had two semi-cylindrical pallets, whose faces stood in the same plane or centre of the axis: the balance-wheel was the common crown-wheel one, the teeth of which got a very small hold of the face of the pallets. When dropping from the face of one pallet, a tooth on the opposite side dropped on the semi-cylindrical part of the other pallet, where it rested during the going and coming of the vibration; getting then on the face, it gave new impulse, escaping in its turn; the pallet on the opposite end of the verge received a tooth on the semi-cylindrical part, and so on. After having been laid aside for some time, it was of late years taken up by several, who, no doubt, must have thought well of it. Among these was Kendal, a man of no common talents; he transformed it into one having two crown-wheels on the same pinion arbor, the tops of the teeth of the one pointing to the middle of the spaces in the other, and with only one pallet, the diameter of the semi-cylinder being of any size. (See Plate IX. No. 50.) About thirty years ago, or more, we had some watches made, having tumbling pallets, and, after a few years trial, gave them up. The principle of the 'scapement is good, as long as the parts of it remain unimpaired, and the oil continues fresh; but the acting parts having such a small hold of one another, get soon altered, which causes a great deviation from the rate of time with which it first sets out. They cannot be expected to last long, unless with a diamond pallet, and a steel wheel of the hardest temper. Drawings of these two 'scapements being given, it becomes necessary to give a short explanation.

Plate IX. No. 1. is one view of the tumbling pallet 'scapement, where W W represents the crown-wheel, and A B the pallets. In No. 2. another view is given, where a tooth on the lower side of the wheel is seen, as escaping from the shaded or dark pallet B; at the same instant, a tooth on the upper side falls just in on the cylindrical part of the light semi-cylindrical pallet A, and here the time of rest commences; on its return, the face of the pallet presenting itself, gets, in its turn, new impulse, which is communicated to the balance, and so on. C D, No. 2. is a view of the bottom of the crown-wheel.

In Kendal's 'scapement, at K, No. 3. a few of the teeth of the two crown-wheels W W, are represented; a tooth of the wheel, on the right hand side, is seen just escaping from the face of the pallet *p p*, after having given impulse to it, and a tooth of the wheel on the left hand falls that instant on the semi-cylindrical part, and rests there until the return, when the face presenting itself, *it*, on that side, gets impulse in its turn, and so on.

The *free* or *detached 'scapement* is that in which the greater part of the vibrations of the balance is free and independent of the wheels, the balance-wheel being then locked; when unlocked, it gives impulse, which only takes place at every second vibration. In Mudge's detached 'scapement, the impulse is given at every vibration. The progress which has of late years been made in improving the detached 'scapement has been wonderful, when we consider, that half a century ago, the name of this 'scapement was unknown. The first rude draught of any thing like it, appears to be that of Thiout's, described at page 110 of the first volume of his Work, and shown in Plate XLIII. Fig. 80. which he calls, " a 'scapement of a watch, the half of whose vibrations appear to be independent of the wheel work during the time they are made." " The hook B, *or detent, as it would now be called*, detains the 'scapement wheel for a short while; see Plate X. No. 54. the balance, in returning, carries with it the pallet A, and consequently disengages the hook from the teeth of the 'scapement wheel, and leaves one of them at liberty to strike anew on the pallet, and so on. This 'scapement cannot go without a spiral or balance spring."

If the arm from the pallet arbor had a pin to work in the slit of one of the detent arms, it would be greatly improved. Although the drawing of this 'scapement, which was given in Nicholson's Journal, September 1806, is not exactly like the original, the principle of the 'scapement is, however, still the same.

Peter Le Roy's 'scapement is the next step that was made towards this invention. He contrived it in 1748, and, like Thiout's, it has hardly ever been made use of. Both of them have a great recoil to give to the wheel before it could be disengaged, and their arcs of free vibration are not of much extent. Berthoud informs us, that in 1754, he made a model of one, which he gave in to the Royal Academy of Sciences. Camus, on its being shown to him at that time, told him, that the late Dutertre had made and used such a 'scapement, having a long *detent*, and free vibrations. Nothing appears now to be known of the construction of Dutertre's, and Le Roy seems to have acknowledged the priority of it to the one he contrived in 1748. " My thought or invention," he says, " was not so new as I had imagined. Dutertre's sons, artists of considerable repute, shewed me very soon after, a model of a watch in this way by their late father, which the oldest Dutertre must still have. This model, very different from my construction, is, however, the same with respect to the end proposed."

The detached 'scapement in Le Roy's time-keeper, which was tried at sea in 1768, is very different from that of his in 1748.

Berthoud, in his *Traité des Horologes Marines*, published in 1773, has given, in No. 281, an account of the principle on which the model was made in 1754; and, in No. 971, a particular description of the parts composing it, which are represented in plate XIX. fig. 4. of that work. It may be somewhat interesting to lay before our readers what is contained in No. 281. " I composed," says he, " in 1754, a 'scapement upon a principle of which I made a model, in which the balance makes two vibrations in the time that one tooth only of the wheel escapes, that is to say, the time in which the balance goes and comes back on itself; and, at the return, the wheel escapes and restores, in one vibration, the motion that the regulator or balance had lost in two. The 'scapement wheel is of the ratchet sort, whose action remains suspended *(while the balance vibrates freely)* by an anchor or click, fixed to an axis carrying a lever with a deer's foot joint, the lever corresponding to a pin placed near the centre of the axis of the balance. When the balance retrogrades, the

t vibration being made, the pin which it carries turns the deer's-
ɔt joint a little back, and the balance continues freely its course, its
ɔerty not being disturbed during the whole of this vibration, but by
, very small and short resistance of the deer's-foot joint spring. When
the balance comes back on itself and makes the second vibration, the
same pin which it carries, raises the deer's-foot lever in such a way,
that the anchor which it carries unlocks the wheel, in order that it
may restore to the balance the force which it had lost in the first vibration. This effect is produced in the following manner:—On the
instant that the deer's-foot jointed lever is raised, the wheel turns and
acts upon the lever of impulsion, formed with a pallet of steel which
acts upon the wheel, and with another arm that acts on a steel roller
placed near the axis of the balance; and, in the same instant that
the wheel acts upon the lever of impulsion, the second arm, which
its axis carries, and which is the greatest, stays on the roller, and
the motion of the wheel is communicated to the balance, almost without loss and without friction, and by the least decomposition of force.
As soon as the wheel ceases to act on the lever of impulsion, the lever falls again, and presents itself to another tooth." " To render the
vibrations of the balance more free and independent of the wheel-
work," continues Berthoud, in No. 281, " and diminish as much as
possible the resistance it meets with at every vibration, the pin must
be placed very near the centre of the balance, so that the lever may
not be made to describe a greater course than that required to render the effect of the click perfectly sure, and while the balance turns
and makes its two vibrations, prevent only one tooth from escaping;
as otherwise, it would be dangerous, by the second's hand, which is
carried by its wheel, announcing more seconds or time than the balance by its motion would have measured. It was the dread of such
a defect that made me then give this 'scapement up, which, I confess, seems to be rather flattering; but it did not give to the mind
that security in its effect which is so necessary, particularly in marine time-keepers, the use of which is of too great consequence to
allow any thing in them suspicious to be hazarded."

The principle given here by Berthoud, is the same as that of the
detatched 'scapements now made, although the parts of the model are
more complex. This 'scapement had received a variety of modifications under his hands. In 1768 he had five marine time-keeper
planned out to have spring *detents* to their 'scapements, the liftin
spring being placed on the roller, or pallet, which received the iʇ
pulse. These were not finished till 1782. Subsequent impro
ments, made by the late Mr. Arnold and others, can hardly be c

sidered as differing very materially from those of Berthoud. This 'scapement in pocket-watches may sometimes come under such circumstances as have been noticed with Tyrer's, or the duplex; but no other can well be admitted into box-chronometers, whether it is made in the manner of Arnold's, or in that of Earnshaw's. In this 'scapement of Arnold's (see plate IX. No. 51.) that part of the face of the pallet, at the point or nearly so, on meeting the cycloidal curved tooth to give impulse, rolls down on this curve, for one-half of the angle, and in the other goes up; or it may be thus expressed,—the curve goes in on the pallet for the first part of the impulse, and comes out during the last. In making this curve too circular near the point of the tooth, as has been done by some, when the drop is on the nice side, the pallet has to turn a little way before the wheel can move forward, which has sometimes caused stopping; but where attention is given to the proper form of the teeth, this is not likely to happen.

In that of Earnshaw's (see No. 52.) the face of the pallet is considerably undercut. Here, the point of the tooth will slide up for the first part of the impulse, and down in the last; in the first part of its action, it seems to have little to do, and may acquire some velocity in order to overcome the part it has to perform in the last, which perhaps may be deemed a consideration, or property of some value. The face of the pallet being undercut, had, from experience, been found requisite, *as is said*, in order to prevent cutting or wearing. In Berthoud's box-chronometers, or time-keepers, the face of the pallet is made straight, or in a line to the centre. One of them, after twenty-eight years going, the greater part of which was from Europe to India, and in the Chinese seas, was put into our hands, and neither the face of the steel pallet, or that of the steel detent, had the least appearance of being any way marked. This was the more remarkable, as the wheel was uncommonly thin. It must have been made of very fine brass. The wheel had ten teeth; the ratio of the diameter to that of the roller or pallet was .530 to .340: the balance weighed 174 grains, and made two vibrations in a second. The balance was suspended by a short and very weak piece of pendulum spring wire, which had been broken by some accident before we got it. The length of the suspension spring required to be .9 of an inch, and so very delicate, that many were made before the chronometer could be brought any way near to time. It seemed to have more influence during the adjusting of it to time, than any spiral spring could possibly have. From being confined to a certain length, it gave a great deal more trouble in the operation, than otherwise it would have done.

The balance of a marine time-piece, when suspended in this way by a very delicate piece of pendulum spring wire, will admit of being much heavier than of that whose pivots run in bottomed holes, and rest or turn on the end in one of them; because all the friction which the pivots of the suspended balance have, is only on the edges of the friction rollers, and which is very inconsiderable. As here, each of the balance pivots turned between three rollers, which were more than one inch in diameter, and from them and the suspension spring perhaps arose that ease and freedom in the motion of the balance, in consequence of which the balance-wheel teeth had little to do when impelling the roller or pallet; this may have been one cause why the pallet face was not cut or marked. It may be observed, that it had the common spiral balance spring, and a compensation consisting of two laminæ, or blades of brass and steel pinned together and rivetted; and, in the moveable end was a screw, which, by its connection with an arm in which the curb pins were placed, served to regulate for mean time: three screws in the edge or rim of the balance were also used for this purpose.

When the diameter of the pallet roller has a considerable proportion to that of the wheel, the angle of 'scapement will be less, and the hold on the face of the pallet by the wheel-teeth will also be less; but the impulse given will be more direct, and the chance of stopping, from any counter-action by external motion, will also be greatly lessened. In this angle, more must be included than that which is made from the drop of the tooth to its escaping the pallet. The angle of 'scapement is included between the point where the tooth escapes from the main pallet or roller, and the point to which the lifting pallet comes in returning, after having passed the lifting spring. There can be no 'scaping, unless the lifting pallet has passed the lifting spring; it is then again ready to unlock the wheel. It is desirable that the unlocking of the wheel should be made with the least possible resistance to the vibration of the balance, which is attained by having the end of the lifting pallet as near to the centre of the balance as is consistent with its getting such a hold of the lifting spring, that, in its course, it can readily and easily bring out the detent from locking the wheel. The hold of the tooth on the detent should not be more than the hundredth part of an inch; in some cases this may be even too much: but, in doing this, the supplementary angle becomes greater, and increases the angle of 'scapement; and, therefore, it may be proper to have the lifting pallet a little longer. A little additional length will greatly reduce the angle of 'scapement, and not much increase the evil of a greater resistance to the vibrations of the balance.

In a box-chronometer, where the balance-wheel has twelve teeth, and the whole angle of 'scapement is to be 60 degrees, it is required to find the ratio of the diameter of the wheel to that of the roller. The supplementary angle being taken at 15°, the angle of impulse must then be 45°, which is rather wide as otherwise; but it will be less than this, when the thickness of the points of the teeth, and the spaces for drop and escape, are taken into computation. Now, 360°, being divided by 12, the number of the wheel-teeth, gives 30° for the quotient, and, when divided by 45, the number of degrees for the angle of impulse, the quotient will be 8°. The diameter of the wheel is supposed to be .6 of an inch, to find that of the roller, say, as 12 : 6 :: 8 : 4. Four-tenths of an inch is the diameter required for the roller, which will give somewhat less than 45° for the angle of impulse. The diameter of the roller may be found in another way, sufficiently near for practice. The diameter of the wheel is .6 of an inch, or .600; then say, as 113 : 355 : : .600 : 1.885, this last being divided by 12, the number of the wheel-teeth, gives for the quotient .157, the distance between the teeth. This distance, taken as a radius for the roller, would give 60° for the angle of impulse; about one-fourth more of this added, will give .200 for the radius, so that the angle may be about 45°.

Nothing should be overlooked which can contribute to make the balance unlock the wheel with the least possible resistance. When the wheel is locked by the extremity of the teeth, it must be easier unlocked than when the locking is at a less distance from the centre. The unlocking cannot be done easier than with such a wheel, for a detached 'scapement, as was contrived about twenty or five and twenty years ago by Owen Robinson, (see No. 53.) a very judicious 'scapement-maker in London, who worked long with the late Mr. Arnold. This wheel is like that for Tyrer's 'scapement. The long teeth of *arrêts* rest on the detent, and the upright teeth give impulse. It is evident that the unlocking with such teeth must be very easy, when compared with the teeth of those wheels which are made after the ordinary way.

Lest what has been said concerning the principle of a detached 'scapement may not be sufficient, we shall endeavour to describe the 'scapement itself, such as it is at present commonly made, so as to give an idea of it, and of the manner by which it acts. The balance-wheel of a pocket chronometer has frequently fifteen teeth, not very deep cut, and a little undercut on the face; a notch, cut in a round piece of flat steel or roller, which is thicker than the wheel, forms the face of the pallet. Sometimes, or rather frequently, a small piece of ruby or sapphire is inserted into the notch at the face of the pallet, for the wheel-teeth to act upon, so that no wearing may ensue. The ratio of the diameter of the wheel to that of the roller, is that of .425 to .175. When the wheel and roller are in their places, the wheel supposed to be locked, the roller must turn freely between two teeth, having only freedom to do so, and not much more. From the centre of the roller to the point of one of the teeth that next the last escaped, let a line be drawn at a tangent to this tooth ; on this line is placed the detent and lifting springs. The detent piece on which the wheel is locked, is a small bit of fine stone, either ruby or sapphire, set into steel, formed into a delicate spring, of such a length as to be equal to that of the distance of two or three spaces between the teeth, with a sole and a steady pin at one end of it, which must be fixed to the potence-plate by a screw. This is what is called the *detent spring*, the end of which goes within a little distance of the circle described by the extremity of the lifting pallet. On the left hand side of the detent spring, is attached another, called the *lifting spring*, which cannot be too delicate, but is made a little thicker towards the outer or lifting end than anywhere else. This end of the lifting spring projects a very little beyond that of the detent spring. On the arbor of the roller and balance, and placed near the roller, is twisted a short and thick steel socket, in which is set a bit of precious stone, the face of which is made flat, and nearly in a line with the centre; behind, it is chamfered on towards the point, and made rather thin than otherwise. This is called the *lifting pallet*. The length or height is made so as to unlock the wheel to the best advantage, that is, by only carrying the detent a short way beyond the unlocking. This excursion is to be confined to as small an angle as may be. Near to the detent piece is fixed a stud, in which is a screw to regulate or adjust the depth of the detent into the wheel-teeth. The point of the screw should be hardened, and have a part of the ruby detent to rest upon it, when the detent spring presses that way. In Earnshaw's way, the detent spring presses against the shoulder of the screw m. (See No. 52.) When the balance is at rest, the face of the lifting pallet n is very near to the outer side and end of the lifting spring. If the balance is brought a very little about to the left, the lifting pallet will pass the end of the lifting spring. On the balance being now turned towards the right, at the moment of the wheel being unlocked, the face or notch of the main pallet or roller presents itself to receive the point of one of the teeth, and is impelled by it with considerable force; meanwhile the detent falls again to its place, and locks the wheel. The balance having completed this vibration, returns; in the returning, the lifting pallet pushes the lifting spring easily aside, being no longer supported by the detent spring when turning in this direction,—that is, from the right to the left; the detent is again ready to be disengaged on the next return of the balance, and so on. The words *right* and *left*, in this description, apply to Arnold's plan of a detached 'scapement, and must be taken on the contrary sides, when applied to Earnshaw's plan. It is usual to make the bending part of the lifting spring as weak as possible; it should even be made to come to its place, at the end of the detent spring, with no more force than just to bring it there; the detent spring, besides being also very weak at the bending part, should have that force *only*, and no more, which will bring it to its banking or limits, and keep it there: the circular part of the detent nib being drawn from a point, that is the smallest matter eccentric from its centre of motion, will tend a little, by means of the wheel-teeth, to keep it to its place. When these springs happen to be a little stronger than what has been suggested, it will show a considerable difference (of loss) in the extent of the arcs of vibration of the balance.

Box-chronometers are commonly hung on gimbals, the plane of the dial being somewhat above that of the gimbal pivots; the brass box in which the chronometer is fixed may be about an inch and a half deep, and this, like a short pendulum, must make many and quick vibrations, when affected by external motion, from whatever cause; and whatever agitation the chronometer may meet with, must, of course, naturally affect the motion of the balance in *some degree*. In order to correct or prevent, as much as possible, the effect of external motion reaching the balance, it might be proposed to have the box, in which the chronometer is placed, as long or deep as could conveniently be adopted,—say, from eight to ten, twelve or more inches; this would then be something like having a greater length of pendulum, and consequently any vibrations made by the box would not only be slower, but fewer in number, and hence the balance would be less affected. Berthoud seems to have perceived the advantage of this, by having his marine time-keepers suspended or fixed in a long case or box, on account of the less number of vibrations it would make from any external motion that might take place. In one of his marine clocks, the brass case which contained it had a thick piece of lead fixed to the bottom inside, in order to make the clock hang steady on its gimbals; the case over all, from the bottom to the top of the glass, was about nine inches and a half in length, and the whole, when together, weighed sixteen pounds, three ounces and a half. The pivots of the gimbals were about three and a half, or four inches, or perhaps a little more below the plane of the dial, but, as thus placed, were in the plane of the balance, so that any pendulous motion the case might get, should be as slow as possible, and have the least effect on the balance. A pendulum may be so fitted up as to give as few vibrations, in a given time, as one of six times the length. Having the rod extended above and below the centre of motion, a weight of 130 grains being on the upper part of the rod, at seven inches above the centre of motion, and a ball of 480 grains, three inches and two-tenths of an inch below the centre, would require a minute to make fifty vibrations; a pendulum to do this in the ordinary way, would need to be fifty-six inches and a half in length. The weight of 130 grains being placed one inch and two-tenths above the centre of motion, the vibrations in a minute will be one hundred and sixty. The vibrations of a pendulum, one inch and a half in length, the depth or length of the box which usually contains our chronometers, ought to make above three hundred vibrations in a minute, which is six times the number that would be made, were they suspended properly in a deeper or longer case; and surely, when the agitation or the number of vibrations can be so much lessened, must not this also lessen its effect on the motion of the balance? Notwithstanding what has been said, it is surprising to observe with what steadiness marine time-keepers in gimbals maintain the horizontal position, even while the ship may be pitching or rolling with great force.

Our marine or box-chronometers are commonly turned upside down before they can be got at to wind up; and this motion of turning them, however little the influence it may have on the motion of the balance, yet it may be supposed to have some, which might be easily obviated, by making the winding up have place on the dial, the fusee square being made to come up as much above the surface, as just to allow freedom for the minute-hand to pass freely between the glass and the top of the fusee square, nor ought the hour-hand to be put concentric with the minute-hand: the custom of our artists doing so, has made any inconvenience attending it be overlooked. It is, however, obvious, that when the hour and minute-hands are passing together over the place where the second's circle and second's hand are, that this assemblage of all the hands, to say the least of it, must create a degree of confusion at this time, and give more trouble to an observer to take the time so accurately as he could wish to have it. Berthoud, Le Roy, and others of the French artists, always placed the hands of their chronometers separately, and from one another, for the reasons which have been stated, as well as for other views they had, regarding the drawing the calipers of the movement of these machines.

The detached 'scapement of Mudge was contrived more than sixty years ago, if we may reckon from the year 1766, when he showed it to Berthoud, who was then in London, and who informs us that it had been made a considerable time before. See Plate X. No. 55.

This 'scapement is composed of a wheel and pallets like those made for the dead beat 'scapement of a clock, only the wheel-teeth are not cut half the depth. On the verge or arbor of the pallets is placed an arm of some length, generally a little longer than that of the pallets. The end of this arm is formed into a fork-like shape. On the axis of the balance is a short pallet, whose acting end may be of a small circular form, having the sharp part of the angles blunted, coming a little way within the prongs of the fork, which alternately acts, and is acted upon. There is also on the axis of the balance a small roller, having a notch in it. On the end of the arm is attached a small steel piece or index, in a plane which may either be above or below the prongs of the fork; this index is on the outside of the roller, when the free part of the vibration is performing, and prevents the wheel-teeth from getting away from the place of rest. On the return of the balance, the index passes with the notch in the roller to the opposite side; meanwhile the short pallet gets into the fork, meeting with one of the prongs, pushes it on a very little way, and thus disengages the teeth of the wheel from the circular part of the pallet, where they rest during the free excursions of the balance. When disengaged, the teeth get upon the flanches of the pallet, and give impulse, which causes the opposite prong of the fork to come forward on the short pallet, and communicate impulse to it. There are two short pallets, and the prongs of the fork lie in different planes. The impulse in this 'scapement is given at every vibration; and it seems to have performed uncommonly well in the watch which he made for *her late Majesty Queen Charlotte*. It is by no means suited for the execution of ordinary workmen, as it requires more address than usually falls to their share. The late Mr. Emery was much taken up with it; and although he had a little success, and had the aid of a very excellent workman, yet he experienced considerable difficulties. It may be somewhat easier managed, by adopting Lepaute's mode of Graham's dead beat, which we have tried. Of late this principle of Mudge's has been adopted in many common pocket-watches.

The following is a description of the 'scapement, given nearly in Mr. Mudge's own words. A, the balance or pallet wheel: B and C, pallets similar to dead-beat pallets in clock-work, from the centre of which, at D, an arm projects, having the forked ends *a, b*. Upon the axis of the balance are the pallets *d* and *e*, which act and are acted upon alternately by the forked ends *a, b*, of the arm D. The pallets *e, d,* as well as the forked ends *a, b*, lie in different planes, viz. the pallet *d*, and the projection *a*, are in one plane; whilst the other pallet *e*, and the other projection *b*, are in another plane, as represented at 1. Upon the arm D, 1 and 2, is screwed the piece *f*, by means of which, and the roller *g*, the wheel is prevented from being unlocked when the forked ends *a, b*, and the pallets *d* and *e*, are disengaged. *This piece is left out in No. 55.*

In 1792, a very neat and ingenious sort of a detached 'scapement was contrived by the late Mr. Howell, founded on that of Kendal's, *in whose hands he had occasion frequently to see it*, in which the wheel-teeth rested on the semi-cylindrical part of the pallet, during a part of the going and returning vibrations of the balance, as has already been described in that of Kendal's.

In this of Howell's, after impulse is given on the face of the semi-cylinder, and just before the tooth is quit, a detent is presented to receive one of the wheel-teeth; this locks it, by which the action of the wheels is suspended during the greater part of the going and returning vibrations, the pallet being then free, and independent of the wheels. This 'scapement is composed of two crown wheels, A B, A B, Plate X. No. 56.; on the same pinion arbor *p p*, the points of the teeth of the one wheel being opposite to the middle of the spaces in the other. On the axis or verge of the balance R R, which stands quite close to that of the balance or crown wheels, is a semi-cylindrical pallet, whose diameter should be made according to the angle of the 'scapement required, which will also regulate the distance of the wheels from each other. The pallet is put near to the collet on which the balance is rivetted; a small arbor at *h*, having very fine or small pivots, is run in so as to stand parallel with that of the balance, and placed at some distance outside of the wheels; but where a line drawn from it, and passing at equal distances from or between the points of the wheel-teeth, when continued, shall fall in with the centre of the balance. On this arbor is fixed an arm *d d*, at the inner end of which is a small fork and index; on the verge or balance axis, and near the lower end, is a short pallet, and a roller connecting with the fork and index, in imitation of Mudge's, acting in the same way as has been described, but here only in the locking and unlocking part. Where the arm passes between the wheel-teeth, which may be at ninety degrees, or so, from where they act on the pallet, are fixed at d two detent pieces, one for each wheel; opposite to the inside arm, and in the same line with it, a part of it is prolonged beyond the small arbor at h, outside of it, with a small ball on the extreme end by way of counterpoise, near to where two screws $b\ b$, in fixed studs not represented, serve here as a banking. It may easily be conceived, that one of the wheels being locked, suppose that on the left, the balance, when returning from the left to the right, will, by means of the short pallet and forked arm, &c. carry the detent away; and, just as the point of the tooth is free, the face of the semi-cylinder is presented, to meet with a tooth of the same wheel and get impulse; but before this tooth has nearly escaped, the other detent is ready to receive a tooth of the opposite wheel, and so on. This 'scapement gives an impulse at every vibration, as is done in Mudge's. In the tenth volume of the *Transactions of the Society for the Encouragement of Arts, &c.* there is a description and drawing of this 'scapement. It may be observed, that were the semi-cylindrical pallet, either faced with a piece of precious stone, or made wholly so, the 'scapement would go on for a considerable time without falling off.

In the marine time-keepers which Mr. Mudge himself had made, the 'scapement is apparently on a very flattering principle, which he had suggested as the means of improvement many years before he put it in practice. Their good performance seems to have been unequalled; and it is singular that, notwithstanding the efforts of three or four of the best or ablest workmen that could be got to the establishment set up by Mr. Mudge, jun. in order to put this 'scapement of his father's to time-keepers, which they, the artists were employed to make, not one was ever produced that was at all equal to the originals. This 'scapement is, however, really very complex, elaborate, and of course expensive in making; yet, when once executed, it will be permanent in its effect, and require no after adjustment like the common detached one. After what has happened, it is not likely, however, that it will be again adopted.

The basis of it is, that of the curious old crown wheel and verge. In place of the verge being in one, having two pivots, and the balance rivetted on it, let us conceive that each of the pallets of the verge has an arbor and two pivots, and that the balance is on a double-kneed crank, having a pivot at the end of each knee, one of which may be called the foot pivot, the other, the balance pivot; the piece of steel from which this last is turned being in the collet on which the balance is rivetted. These pivots, and those of the pallet arbors, are in one upright line, coinciding and concentric with one another, having their motion, as it were, free and independent of each other, unless when, in their parts of the action of the 'scapement, the face of the pallets, in place of being flat, are hollow or a little curved, having a nib at the edge to lock the wheel by. On the lower end of the lower pallet arbor, is an arm, projecting nearly as far as the bending part of the crank knee, in which is fixed a pin that acts on the inner side, and near to the end of the arm, and is alternately acted upon: close by the arm, and on the pallet arbor, the inner end of a spiral spring is fixed; the outer end is in a stud, having a certain degree of tension or bending up *(in that direction which tends to bring the pallets down into the spaces of the teeth)* before fixing it in the stud. The upper pallet arbor has the same as has been described to the lower one, and a corresponding pin in the upper knee of the crank. It may easily be conceived, that the length of the crank knees ought to be such as to allow it to sweep round and behind the crown wheel, its boundary or banking being that of the crown-wheel arbor, or *its pinion arbor*. When the pallets are not raised up, and the wheel unlocked, the tendency of the spiral springs is to bring them down within the spaces of the crown-wheel teeth. Suppose the upper pallet raised up, and the wheel locked, the under one being in the reverse position, and the balance vibrating towards the right, the pin in the upper crank will of course meet with the small arm, and, carrying it on a little way, the wheel tooth gets disengaged; by this, the wheel getting forward, the lower pallet is raised up, and the wheel is again locked. In the interim, the upper arm being carried on a few degrees, by means of the momentum of the balance in vibrating, bends up the spiral still more than what was done by the wheel in raising up the pallet; the reaction of which, on the returning vibration, gives impulse, by means of the arm on the pin of the crank. The pin in the lower crank now getting forward, meets with the arm of the lower pallet arbor, carries it on, the wheel gets disengaged, and so on. This 'scapement cannot set itself off; for, before this can be effected, the plane of the balance must get some degree of external circular motion. The balance may be said to be free in that part of the vibration, after the pin of one crank has left its corresponding arm, till the pin of the other meets with *its* arm; this is, however, so momentary, that it has no claim to the title of a free or detached 'scapement, *as so called by a distinguished artist,*—a name which foreign artists will think rather an improper one. Berthoud says, it is one of the most ingenious *remontoir* 'scapements hitherto known. The balance had, on its arbor, two spirals or pendulum springs, for the purpose of obtaining the most isochronous vibrations. Something in this way had formerly been proposed by one of the Bernouillis. Drawings, and a more detailed description of this 'scapement, will be found in the work published by Mr Thomas Mudge, junior, entitled, "*A description, with plates, of the Time-Keeper invented by the late Mr. Thomas Mudge. By Thomas Mudge, his son. London, printed for the Author*, 1799." The compensation work in this, like every thing of Mudge's, is ingenious; though nothing of this kind can ever be equal to that of being in the balance itself. The train of wheels went contrary to the ordinary direction, and we have no satisfactory reason assigned for it.

The foregoing description of this 'scapement of Mudge's may perhaps be rendered more intelligible, by having recourse to the letters in Plate VI. Nos. 32, 33, which represent the 'scapement under different views, the letters referring to the same parts in both figures. A A, the balance-wheel ; B B, the balance, the verge or axis of which C C, is a crank : F, the pendulum spring, by means whereof the timekeeper is regulated : G, the pendulum spring stud, which is screwed on the cock : H, the pendulum spring, which is acted upon by the compensation pieces : I, the stud which is screwed on the upper plate : D, $a\ e\ k\ m$, and E, $b\ f\ i\ l$, are two compound pieces, which communicate the motion from the balance-wheel to the balance, and consist of the following parts, viz. the projections or pallets $l\ m$, which are acted upon by the teeth of the balance-wheel, and were made of black flint in the original time-keeper, but they may be made of ruby, sapphire, or other hard stone ; a and b, steel arms, which act upon the pins c, d of the balance crank ; e and f, the impelling springs which are attached to the arbors of the pallets at the inner ends, and to the studs g and h at the outer ends ; i and k, small screws which fix the pallets to the arbors by means of the clamps or pieces of steel D and E ; 1 and 2 are separate views of the pallets and their springs. Having mentioned all the parts of the 'scapement, we shall now attempt to describe its action.

When the balance-wheel *(as appears in No. 33.)* has raised the pallet l, this is kept from going any farther by the hook at the end of it, until the pin d, in the crank, meets the arm b ; for then the crank will carry on with itself the arm b to the end of its vibration, and at the same time, the tooth of the wheel will be disengaged from the above-mentioned hook at l. Afterwards, as the crank returns, the arm *b*, actuated by its spring *f*, will communicate an impulse to the crank, and soon after its crooked part will come to rest against one of the teeth of the wheel, which again raises the pallet *l*. With respect to the balance-wheel, as soon as its tooth is disengaged from the pallet *l*, by the means above stated, it raises the pallet *m*, which, on the returning vibration of the balance, is, by the pin *c*, acting on the arm *a*, carried on in a contrary direction, after the manner mentioned respecting the other pallet; and thus the springs attached to the two pallets, alternately give their auxiliary aid to the vibrations of the balance.

It may perhaps gratify the reader to have Berthoud's observations on this 'scapement.—" The assemblage of parts in this 'scapement may appear seducing; however it is to be dreaded, that a mechanism so complicated, and the action of whose parts is so delicate, cannot be easily put in practice; for it requires an extreme niceness of execution to make their effect sure and certain, such as the stop for the pallets, to make the axis of the pallets coincide exactly with that of the balance, the pallets of the *remontoir* increasing the friction of the regulator; two pivots of these pallets are constantly in action during each vibration, which comes to the same thing as if the balance had four pivots, &c."

" We shall observe, moreover, that the regulator of Mr. Mudge is composed of four spiral springs, two for the pallets, and two for the balance; and these ought to procure isochronism; for it is indispensably necessary, that, in a portable machine, the oscillations of unequal extent of the balance should be isochronous; now, if they are so, the mechanism of the *remontoir* is of no use, and, if they are not so, the watch will vary, *notwithstanding the remontoir*, when, from agitation or shocks, the balance shall describe greater or less arcs; and also when these arcs shall vary either by the friction of the pivots, or by a change of force in the spirals by heat or by cold." &c.

Although the balance in pocket-watches may be put tolerably near to the equilibrium, yet many circumstances contribute to make them go unequally in different positions, such as in hanging, laying, &c. which require time, and give a great deal of trouble before they can be completely corrected. In order to get the better of this, *Breguet*, an eminent watch-maker in Paris, contrived a 'scapement, which, with the pendulum spring stud, revolved round the centre of the balance once every minute. By this means, whether the balance was in equilibrium or not, the going of the watch was little affected by it, as every part of it was up and down in the course of a minute, which compensated any want of equilibrium in it. This contrivance is merely mentioned by Berthoud in his *Histoire*, as he did not think himself at liberty to give any description of it, since Breguet had a patent or *brevet d'invention* to make them. We have been informed that the same sort of thing had been made before by the late Mr. John Arnold, to whom Breguet had acknowledged having copied the invention from him.

Those who wish for farther information respecting 'scapements, may consult *Traité d'Horlogerie*, par M. Thiout. *Histoire de la Mésure du Temps*, par M. J. Berthoud. And *the Transactions of the Society for the encouragement of Arts, Commerce, &c.*

CHAPTER IX.

On Compensation Curbs, and Balances.

COMPENSATION against the effect of heat and cold in time-keepers, is certainly one of the greatest improvements that has been made. Without this, they would have been far from keeping time, and would have varied continually with the temperature of the atmosphere, so that no fixed or settled rate could have been obtained. The detached 'scapement will show this more than any other; for, if there is no compensation to it, the watch will vary nearly thirty seconds in twenty-four hours. The influence of oil in the cylinder 'scapement becomes in itself a sort of compensation, and the effect of changes of temperature is much less obvious in it than in the detached 'scapement. There is very great reason to believe, that Harrison was the first who applied a compensation; but there is no written documents to warrant us in ascribing to him the honour of the invention, to which, however, we think he has a just title. Some very imperfect hints thrown out by Martin Folkes, Esq. President of the Royal Society, about 1749, of Harrison having some mechanism of this sort to the three time-pieces made prior to a fourth, which gained the reward voted by Parliament; but as no description of this was ever published, the French artists have had it in their power to claim the priority. In Harrison's fourth machine, it is known that the compensation-piece was composed of laminae of brass and steel pinned and rivetted together in several places. Perhaps those in the three former differed little or nothing from this.

s

The first pocket-watch made in Europe with a compensation was by F. Berthoud. It was begun in 1763, finished the beginning of 1764, and was sold in London, in 1766, to Mr. Pinchbeck, for his Britannic Majesty King George the Third. The compensation was effected by laminæ of brass and steel pinned together, one end of which being fixed to the potence plate outside, the other acted on a short arm projecting from a moveable arbor,—a longer arm having the curb pins in it, which were made to move nearly in the circle of the outer coil of the spiral spring. It had a common crown-wheel and verge-scapement, and a going work in time of winding. The balance was so heavy as to set, *that is, if the balance was brought to rest by the finger, it would remain so, till set off by a circular motion,* being sixteen grains in weight, and the vibrations were four in a second. Mr. Kendal adopted this mode of compensation in some of his pocket-watches. See Fig. 4. Plate XVI. of Berthoud's *Histoire, &c.*

Mudge, some time before the year 1770, made a watch for Mr. Smeaton, in which the compensation was effected by two long slips of brass and steel soldered together; being afterwards dressed up, the united piece was coiled or turned up into a spiral, as close together on the coils as to be free, and no more. The inner end was fixed to a circular curbed toothed wheel; a short portion of the outer end had a sort of pivot formed on it, bent in the circle of the outer coil, and supported by a small stud fixed in the curb wheel, having freedom to move easily in a hole in this stud. At this end were the curb pins, between which the spiral or pendulum spring played; the effect of heat or cold on it was counteracted by the spiral compensation piece. The 'scapement of this watch was the cylindrical or horisontal one; and so long as the oil kept clean and fresh, the compensation might be useful to it. In 1774, we made one or two of the same sort of compensation-curb work for horisontal watches. At that time no better kind of 'scapement and compensation were much known, at least so far as came under what was then in the common practice.

Notwithstanding what has been already mentioned, it may be proper to observe, that an artificial compensation against the effects of heat and cold on the pendulum spring, can be of little or no use to a watch having the cylinder 'scapement, unless for a short time, while the oil is clean and fresh on the cylinder. From the nature of this 'scapement, and the oil which is requisite for it, it possesses in itself a kind of natural compensation, as we have mentioned before. This is quite otherwise with the free or detached 'scapement, which is more perfect and independent of oil; for the effect of heat and cold on the pendulum spring in it are so immediately obvious, as to show that it cannot do well without an artificial compensation to correct those effects.

For the trial of Le Roy's time-keeper in 1768, a voyage was undertaken on purpose, the particulars of which were published by M. Cassini and M. Le Roy, jointly in 1770, accompanied with drawings of that time-keeper. Le Roy, in the same volume, gives a compensation balance, which is pretty nearly like those of the present day, only the laminæ are pinned together, in place of the brass being melted on the steel, as is done by our artists. The compensation of Le Roy's time-keeper, however, was not of this kind. It consisted of two glass tube thermometers, bent nearly into the form of a parallelogram, with a small ball to each at one end; the other open, and filled partly with mercury, partly with spirit of wine: these were fixed to the axis of the balance opposite one another; the balls lay very near to the axis. It would appear that Le Roy had not thought of a metallic compensation, until the return of his time-keeper from the voyage. He had taken the idea of this from getting an account of Harrison's, which was sent to the Royal Academy, signed by Ludlam, who was one of the scientific gentlemen appointed by the Commissioners of t h Board of Longitude, to take Harrison's account of his time-keeper, previous to any part of the reward being paid to him.

In a Life of Peter Le Roy, the son of Julien, the method of compensation is erroneously ascribed to that artist's father, "to whom we are indebted," says the writer of the article, "for the method of compensating the effect of heat and cold on the balances of chronometers, by the unequal expansion of different metals. *This effect takes place chiefly on the pendulum spring, and a plain balance is very little affected,*—a discovery which has been brought by our English artists to a state of great perfection, although it had been laid aside by the inventor's son Peter."

It is difficult to understand how this mistake should have been committed; for the following account of the discovery, given by Peter Le Roy himself, is in direct contradiction to the preceding statement. But, to allow the reader to judge for himself, we shall give it in his own language.

Observation V.—*Sur la Compensation des Effets de la Chaleur et du Froid.*

" Selon la gazette du commerce, et la raport signé Ludlam, envoyé à l'academie, pour remedier aux irregularités produites dans les montres marines par la chaleur et par le froid, *M. Harrison se sert d'une barre composée de deux pièces minces de cuivre et d'acier de la longeur de deux pouces, rivées ensemble dans plusieurs endroits, fixées par un bout, et ayant de l'autre deux goupilles au travers desquelles passe le ressort du balancier. Si cette barre reste droit dans le tems temperé (comme le cuivre reçoit plus l'impression de la chaleur que l'acier,) le coté de cuivre deviendra convex au tems chaud, et le coté d'acier le sera au tems froid. Ainsi les goupilles fixent tour-a-tour les parties du ressort, selon les differens degrés de chaleur, et l'alongent ou le recourcissent; d'ou nait la compensation des effets du chaud et du froid.*

" Si j'avois connu cette ingenieuse methode avant d'avoir pensé à mes thermometres, je n'aurois vraisemblablement point hesité à en faire usage dans ma machine.

" J'ai balancé quelque tems si je ne devois pas lui donner la preference. J'ai même fait quelques essais dans cette vue. J'en parlerai bientôt, mais après y avoir pensé mûrement, et avoir mis à part, autant qu'il m'a été possible, ce penchant qui nous parle en faveur de nos productions, mes thermometres m'ont paru preferable," &c. &c. See *Memoir sur la meilleur Maniere du Mésurer le Tems en Mer*, pp. 55, 56, inserted at the end of *Voyage fait par ordre du Roi*, in 1768, *par éprouver les montres marines inventées* par M. Le Roy, &c. par M. Cassini, fils, Paris, 1770.

As must always be the case in the infancy of any branch of science, various methods are fallen on before it arrives at its most improved state. Berthoud, Arnold, and others, had recourse to different modes of compensation, before they arrived at the one which gave them complete satisfaction. The former, in his first machines, used small wires of brass and steel combined, nearly like the gridiron pendulum, to effect the purpose of compensation; to those of a later date was applied a straight piece, composed of laminæ of brass and steel pinned together, acting on the arm of a short lever. In the end of the other arm, which was long, the curb-pins were fixed. Even with those balances which were afterwards made, and composed of brass and steel pinned together, he adopted as a supplementary aid, tl straight compensation-piece, with the moveable arm and curb-pir Considering the talents he possessed, and the great experience wh be must have had, this seems a little curious; as, we think, where there is a complete compensation in the balance, it alone should be sufficient; and the curb pins would tend to disturb the pendulum spring rather than give any aid to the compensation. The more free the pendulum spring is, the chance is more in favour of good performance; and this is more likely to be the case, when the compensation balance is supposed to be fit and competent for what is required. In some of Arnold's balances, two pair of laminæ were placed parallel to the diametrical arms; on the middle of each of the combined laminæ was fixed a small wire, which came through the rim of the balance, outside of which, and on the end of the wires, a small ball was fixed to each. These balls were pushed out or drawn inwards by changes of temperature. The arguments given in favour of such balances, as those of Earnshaw's, which are turned first on the steel, and again on the brass, after being melted on the steel, are certainly very strong and convincing; indeed nothing can well be said against them: yet there appears to be a degree of softness in such a balance, that cannot exist so readily in those where the laminæ are set or turned up by hand. There is undoubtedly a great deal more trouble in making the last; and though it has been said, that they cannot be true or round, when made in this way, yet we have seen some of those done by Owen Robinson, as round and true as any turning could make them, and possessing a degree of stiffness that cannot be supposed to have place in the other: they have been even unscrewed, or taken to pieces, and again put together, without altering the rate of the chronometer. After all, we are not aware that chronometers, with the one balance, perform better than those with the other.

It may be observed, that on the rim of the turned balances, which is separated into two, there are small pieces of brass, made to slide backward and forward, according as it may be found requisite, when under the process of adjusting for heat and cold. In the other, this is done by screwing backward and forward the pieces of brass or gold, which turn spring tight on small tapped parts, formed at the outer end of the steel laminæ, and are bent or set in the same circle with them. Both balances have what are called mean-time screws, placed in the vertical line of the hanging position, which serve with other *minute operations* to adjust them to their rate of time. We have seen, and made compensation-balances with three arms, three compound-pieces, and three mean-time screws, which were stiff, and answered very well.

Plate X. No. 57, represents the compensation balance of Arnold; *a b* is a steel rim, on which three pieces are put so as to slide here and there, in order to adjust, in some degree, the equilibrium of the balance; *c c* are pieces of gold, which turn spring tight on the tapped parts formed from the ends of the steel laminæ; *e e*, are small screws put in through the compound laminæ, serving to adjust for small differences, as the mean-time screws, *d d*, do for greater portions of time, &c. No. 1. is a side view of the balance.

No. 58 represents Earnshaw's compensation balance; *d d*, are the brass pieces having a groove turned in them, by which they take in the compound rim of the balance, and can be made to slide back and forward on it; *c c* are screws which fix them to the rim, after the adjustment for heat and cold is completed; *a a* are the the screws which adjust to mean time. No. 1. is a side view of the balance.

A compensation balance of Berthoud's is represented in Plate X. No. 59. A B is a plain circle of the balance, from the inner part of which, a sort of contrate rim is formed, so as to receive at *a, b,* and *c*, the compound laminæ *e d, e d, e d*; the ends *e* of these laminæ are fixed upon the heels or parts reserved of the contrate rim at *a, b, c*, by the screws *e*. The ends that are free carry the compensation weights C, D, E. These weights or masses are fixed on the compound laminæ, each by a screw and two steady pins. By this disposition of the balance, when these masses are put of such a weight as to regulate the chronometer to time nearly, the balance being in equilibrium, if the compound laminæ are well executed, the balance will keep its state of equilibrium, although the masses recede from, or approach toward the centre of the balance by changes of temperature, and the effect of such a regulator will be as invariable as if the balance was a plain one. The plain circle of the balance carries three small pieces of brass or gold, *d, d, d*, which serve to regulate the chronometer to the nearest, in giving them more or less of weight.

Plate X. No. 60, represents the outside of the potence plate, B B, of the wheel-work frame; it carries the balance and mechanism for correcting the effect of heat and cold on the pendulum spring, 1, 2, 3, 4, the top parts of the pillars by which the frame is pinned together; C C represents a plain balance; but in this case it may be supposed to be a compound or compensation one. D, E, is the cock for the balance, and also for the lever, in which are put the curb pins for the spiral spring; the sole D is fixed to the potence plate; F being the cock for the arbor of the lever arms, which serve to move the curb pins, *f* is a part attached to the upper side of the small cock E, and carries the lower pivot of the balance. The double cock, D E, is seen in profile. D E is the first cock, which is attached to the potence plate, the end *e* receives the pivot *e* of the axis *d e*, of the lower curb pin arbor, the pivot *d* enters into the hole *d* of the second cock E, *d*; the arm *b*, or pallet of the curb pin lever *a b*, is that upon which the screw of the compound laminæ acts, the arm *a* carries the box or piece *e a*, in which it is slit at *a*, forming kind of pins for the spiral to play between. It is the motion of the part *a* which forms the compensation in rendering the spiral spring longer or shorter, the small part *f* of the cock receives the pivot of the balance. The axis of the balance passes through the hole of the axis *d e*, which is formed in the manner of a canon, above the piece *f*, which may have either a brass or a jewelled hole in it, should be placed either a diamond or ruby for the end of the balance pivot to work on; it will be the lowest when the watch is placed horizontally, the dial upward. *a b* is the lever or arm for the curb pins, and *b*, the one on which the screw *c* of the compound laminæ *d b* acts; G H is a cock with chops, between which the compound laminæ are fixed. *d b* is a small and delicate spring which constantly presses the arm *b* against the point of the screw *c*. The spiral spring must be placed quite near to the balance C C, and above it. The cock E lies above the spiral, so as the curb pins may come so far below as to take the spiral between them.

CHAPTER X.

On the Balance Spring of Watches and Chronometers, commonly called the pendulum spring.

THE invention and application of the spiral spring to the balance of a watch, is, by the foreign artists in general, ascribed to Huygens, while they admit the idea of a straight spring having been, long before this, applied by Dr. Hooke. It was in 1658 that Dr. Hooke observed the restorative force of springs, when he put one to the balance of a watch, and applied for a patent to secure his right of invention. The profits were to be divided between himself, Sir Robert Moray, Mr. Boyle, and Lord Brouncker. It was not carried into effect, in consequence of a quarrel between the parties, on account of a very unreasonable demand on the part of these gentlemen. Nor was it till 1674 that Huygens claimed the same discovery. Hooke charged Huygens with plagiarism, through the intervention of Mr. Oldenburgh, Secretary to the Royal Society, who communicated to him the registers of the Society when he was in England, and also corresponded with him upon the subject. In 1665, Sir Robert Moray requests Oldenburgh to tell Huygens that such watches had already been made in England, and to ask him, if he does not apply a spiral spring to the balance arbor? It may be asked, where had Sir Robert seen a spiral spring? The natural answer is, that he must have seen it in the hands of Dr. Hooke. The Doctor, however, had for long kept his invention tenaciously secret, under a sort of enigma, a practice which seems to have prevailed about that period with things —in this way, the letters of which were *c e i i i n o s s s t t u u*, that is, *ut tensio sic vis*, or the power of any spring is in the same proportion with the tension thereof.

As Montucla appears to be the only foreigner who allows the invention and application of the balance spiral spring to Dr. Hooke, we shall transcribe what he says on the subject, from his *Histoire des Mathématiques. Tome II. p. 468.*

"A detail of the inventions and of the new fancies of Dr. Hooke, would be extremely prolix; readers must have recourse to his numerous writings, which will justify the eulogium we have just now made him. We shall here confine ourselves to a mark of his sagacity: it is the application of the spring to regulate the motion of watches. This invention, so fortunate, and which is ordinarily ascribed to Huygens, appears to me to be legitimately claimed by Dr. Hooke. We actually find in the history of the Royal Society of London, (Part II. ch. 36.) among the titles of manuscripts presented to that Society, before it published its *Transactions*, we find what evidently concerns this application. Now this history appeared in 1668, several years before there was a question in France about any thing of the kind. Dr. Hooke says that he had made the discovery about the year 1660, (see Lectures on the Spring), and communicated it to Messrs Brouncker and Moray, as a specimen of some more inventions that he said he was in possession of, and which must give the solution of the famous problem regarding the longitude; but not being at one with these gentlemen, on the articles of agreement to be contracted between them, he would not disclose his secret, so kept it, and carried it away with him. We shall remark, that when Huygens published in 1674 this use of the spring, Hooke was very indignant at it. He raised a very sharp process against Mr. Oldenburgh, the Secretary to the Royal Society, accusing him of collusion, and of making known to learned foreigners, discoveries deposited in the registers of the Royal Society; but it was nowise necessary that Oldenburgh should commit this indiscretion, seeing that the invention of which we speak, transpired; for the book, quoted above, appeared in French, about the year 1699, and perhaps it was from it that Huygens and the Abbé Hautefeuille, who disputed this discovery in a court of law, took the first idea of it. Moreover, Huygens had already been several times in England, and it is to be presumed, that during his residence there, he would carefully get what information he could of all the inventions of the learned of the country. As to what Waller, in the life of Hooke, says, giving him also the right of the cycloid to render the motion of the pendulum perfectly equal, *that is not well founded*. There is nothing in the work that supports Waller, namely, the remarks of Hooke on the Machina Celestis of Hevelius, which favours the pretension, they having to do only with the circulating pendulum,* which indeed seems may be justly claimed for Hooke. It is true, among the titles of writings cited above, they touch at the application of the cycloid; but it is probable that this writing is from Huygens himself, who was a member of the Royal Society, and who was at London in 1668. Moreover, we are warranted to think that Hooke was not so profound a Mathematician as to make a discovery of this nature."

Being highly favoured, by a gentleman, a descendant of the noble family of Kincardine, (to whose father we had the pleasure of being introduced, at a convivial party in the year 1782,) with the perusal of a large collection of very valuable MS. letters, about to be deposited in the British Museum, which embrace a correspondence between Christian Huygens de Zulichem, the celebrated philosopher and astronomer, the Earl of Kincardine, Sir Robert Moray, Lord Brouncker and others, on a variety of useful and highly interesting subjects; the first of these letters is dated September 1657, and the latest in 1673. Among other subjects, illustrative of the spirit and character of the times, medicine, agriculture, draining of mines, and other mechanical inventions, are introduced by the respective writers. The letters relative to our subject were with Huygens in the years 1663, 64, and 65, concerning what they called *pendule* watches, which probably were no other than the old common watches, to which were applied a spiral spring to the balance, at that period a new invention; or the movement of these *pendule* watches might be such as that of Huygens, represented No. 44, Plate VIII.

Lord Brouncker, the Honourable Mr. Boyle, and Sir Robert Moray.

---

* The circulating pendulum was contrived by Hooke for the purpose of illustrating the motion of the planets, and for measuring small portions of time. It has of late years been introduced into steam-engines as a regulator for the fly.

ray, who were before this, say 1660, in terms with Dr. Hooke, to get a patent for *his* invention of the spiral spring and its application to the balance of a watch, but not willing to fulfil their engagement with him, on account of a very unreasonable clause which they wished to have inserted in Hooke's patent, with which he very indignantly refused to comply. The clause was, " *That if* after I had discovered my inventions about the finding the longitude by watches, or otherwise (though in themselves sufficient,) they, or any other person should find a way of improving my principles, he or they should have the benefit thereof, during the time of the patent, and not I !"

After having broken off from him, by the letters, they appear to have had a desire to have a share in this business with Huygens. Indeed the principal subject in the letters seems to be, whose name, or whose joint names, should be inserted in a patent proposed to be taken out in Holland, France, Spain, Sweden, and Denmark, what the amount of the share should be to Huygens, and what to them.

The Earl of Kincardine, by a letter of his to Huygens, appears to have had a watch on trial to ascertain longitude at sea, which hung by a ball and socket from the underside of the ship's deck, first tried in 1662; afterwards, being at the Hague, where he had occasionally been several times on this business, there seems to have been some *debates* between him and Huygens, as to which of their watches had the most likely means of doing the best; and also explaining some misunderstanding about terms, said to have formerly passed between them, regarding a patent intended to be taken out. About this time, it appears, by these letters, that several watch-makers had set to make up *pendule watches*, to ascertain the longitude at sea; among them, a Mr. East is mentioned to have put two springs to turn a pinion in his watch; *but in what manner, or for what purpose, it is not mentioned.* We shall take the liberty to notice, by way of an anecdote, that East was a watch-maker in Pall Mall, London, where there was a Tennis Court kept, which Charles the Second, when Prince of Wales, resorted to, and his stake frequently was an Edwardus East, as his Royal Highness called it, that is, a watch of East's making. From pendulum watches, the spiral or balance-spring has improperly got the name of the pendulum spring, which should rather be applied to the suspension spring of a clock pendulum.

On nothing does a chronometer depend so much, as the good quality of the pendulum spring. *Great, as the power of the rudder is in controlling and regulating the motions of a ship,* it is not more extraordinary than that of this spring in regulating the motions of a chronometer, *and we may be allowed to say, that it possesses something like invisible properties.* It may be set so as to make the machine go fast or slow, in any position required, while neither its length, nor the weight of the balance, are in any way altered. Le Roy thought that he had made a great discovery, and it must be granted to be one, when he found " that there is in every spring of a sufficient extent, a certain length where all the vibrations, long or short, great or small, are isochronous; that this length being found, if you shorten the spring, the great vibrations will be quicker than the small ones; if, on the contrary, it is lengthened, the small arcs will be performed in less time than the great ones."

Notwithstanding this condition of *sufficient extent*, the isochronous property will remain no longer than while the form of the spring is preserved as it originally was. Should the coils be more compressed or taken in, the long vibrations will now be slower than the short ones; and, on the contrary, if they are more let out or extended, the long vibrations will be faster than the short ones. A more general principle for obtaining the quality of isochronism may be applied, by making the spring act proportionally, in arithmetical progression, according to its tension. Every five degrees of tension should make an equilibrium, with a given force or weight, of ten grains; suppose, that is, 5, 10, 15, 20, &c. degrees of tension, should be balanced by 10, 20, 30, 40, &c. grains. To try small springs by this process, would require a very nice and delicate instrument. The circumstances of the properties of the spring, which have just now been mentioned, were well known to Hooke. In order to obtain these properties in pendulum springs for his time-keepers, Berthoud made them thicker, gradually, from the outer to the inner end; our old English way is the reverse of this. Whatever may be the form of the springs, whether flat or cylindrical, the best and most direct way is to try them in the time-keeper itself, by taking four hours going with the greatest force the main-spring can give, and then four hours with the least. It is of consequence to have these springs hard or well tempered.

" M. Frederick Houriet of Lodi, an artist equally praise-worthy, under the double view of instruction and of morality, is the first who used spherical balance springs; he has proved, in a memorial given in to the Institute of France, 9th of March, 1818, that this form gives the most perfect isochronism, if made with pendulum spring-wire, of equal dimensions, through the whole of its length, and consequently, the easier to execute a balance-spring of it." See *Manuel Chronométrique,* p. 90, by Antide Janvier, Paris, 1821.

We apprehend, that the sphere must have a spiral flat-bottomed groove cut round it, otherwise the wire cannot be regularly applied on it. Our cylindrical helical springs have done so well hitherto, that very few of our chronometer-makers, we suspect, will be induced to try spherical springs. M. Houriet made a very ingenious sort of tool, for trying the isochronism of balance-springs. No copy of it has hitherto been made; the only one to be seen, is the original, in the hands of M. M. Breguet. By tapering a spiral spring inwards properly, when it is wanted to be a flat helix, it ought to have the same effect as the cylindrical helix, made of pendulum spring wire, of an uniform breadth and thickness; but there is an uncertainty in the operation of tapering the wire; whereas, in the cylindrical helix, thus made, isochronism is likely to be more readily obtained, as experience hitherto has shown to be the case.

Those engaged in making and timeing of chronometers, must see many curious and interesting effects of the pendulum spring. For those, however, who may not have had an opportunity in that way, we shall give two examples. A pocket-chronometer (by one of the earliest and most eminent masters,) was found to go three minutes slow in 24 hours, when hanging, and when laying, kept near to time. The 'scapement had rather too much drop for the tooth on the pallet, which being set a little forward, to lessen the drop, it was now found to go three minutes slow in 24 hours, whether hanging or laying; so that, in the meantime, screws being put home a little, the chronometer was brought to time equally hanging or laying.

Another pocket-chronometer, made by a very capital artist, was found to lose five seconds in 12 hours in the hanging position, and to gain two seconds and a half in the same time when laying: it occurred to our mind, that the pendulum spring must be rather too short as otherwise, seeing that the long vibrations were the quickest. The face of the pallet was set a little back, so as the extent of the vibrations might be lessened; this had the desired effect; for in 12 hours hanging, it lost only half a second, and in the same time, laying, gained one second.

Let those who are curious for research in this subject, see Hooke's Lectures, *De Potentia Restitutiva*, or of Spring.—Eclaircissemens sur l'Invention, la Theorie, la Construction, et les Epreuves, &c. Et de Reponse à un Ecrit qui a pour titre: *Précis des Recherches faites en France pour la determination des Longitudes en Mer, par la Mesure Artificielle du Temps*. Nicholson's Philosophical Journal, vol. XIV. September, 1906.

CHAPTER XI.

On the Jewelling of Pivot Holes in Watches, Chronometers, and Clocks.

FROM the art of Jewelling the pivot holes, our chronometers may be said to have acquired a durability and character, which they would not otherwise have obtained. It must not be imagined, that there is any time-keeping principle or improvement in a jewelled hole more than in a brass one; and, notwithstanding what has been said in favour of the last, few will be hardy enough to run the hazard of having the balance and balance-wheel pivots to run in brass holes, especially where the machine is destined to be either a pocket or box-chronometer. It is very well known, that in a common verge watch, where the balance holes are jewelled, its motion will be kept up for a longer time than when it runs in brass holes. The friction at the balance holes cannot be supposed to be less than at those of the fusee; for, in the time of one fourth of a turn of the fusee, the balance must make more than what is equivalent to 9000 revolutions. Berthoud regretted much that he had not an opportunity of getting the pivot holes of his time-keepers jewelled; yet, from that versatility of genius which he possessed, he supplied admirably the want of this, in such a manner that very few could have equalled or attained. Some of the balances in his time-keepers were made to give six vibrations in a second, while others gave only one. His number *eight* made one vibration in a second, and was the one which gave the best performance of all those which he had constructed. It seems to have been a wonderful discovery, that jewelled holes wore down the pivots, and thickened the oil, after *they* had been used for upwards of an hundred years. How came this not to have been sooner observed, when so many were engaged in making chronometers, and that too in considerable numbers? That pivots, from a length of time, even with good oil, and with greater probability from bad oil, may have got, as it were, glued in their holes, there is little reason to doubt; but this never arose from particles wearing away from either the steel or the stone, by the friction of the pivot. Let any one try to whet a graver, *which requires some degree of force,* on a polished Scotch pebble, for instance, and they will find, that no exertion whatever will make the graver bite the stone, or the stone the graver; for where any effect of this kind takes place, it must be

* See page 179.

nearly mutual. The hardness of the Scotch pebble is well known to be much inferior to that of either the ruby or the sapphire. After being exposed to the air for a considerable time, oil gets viscid and thick, which arises, as has been observed by chemists, from the absorbing or attracting of oxygen. We suspect, that oil, from this cause *alone*, may become more glutinous at a jewelled hole than at a brass one. By its application to brass, it soon acquires a bluish-green tinge, as if something acted on it. This is owing to the metal becoming oxidated by the joint action of the oil and air. The oxide thus formed, combines with the oil, and forms a metallic soap, which is much less tenacious than that formed at a jewelled hole. By the continuation of this process, the hole in brass becomes wider, and the oil disappears, leaving the pivot and hole in a greater or less degree wasted; and, instead of the oil, we have the metallic soap, which has hitherto been considered as rust. To be convinced, however, that this is not the case, we need only attempt to wipe it off from the pivot, from which it easily parts, and which it would not do were it really rust. Oil, however, can have no action on the jewelled hole, and any change that is effected by the oil must be confined to the steel pivot, on which its action is so exceedingly slow, that a great length of time must elapse before the oil is decomposed and disappears; and hence what is called rust in a brass hole, is seldom or never met with in a jewelled hole. If a little Florence oil is put into a small phial, for about two tenths of an inch deep, and remain for a few years, it will become exceedingly viscid and glutinous, and will be intermixed with parts tinged with red of various shades. The same appearance is sometimes seen at jewelled pivot holes, and has been erroneously supposed to be produced by the operation of the pivot on the hole. It is singular that oil will act more forcibly on fine brass than on the common sort, or even on copper; a metallic soap, somewhat resembling verdigrease, will soon show itself on the former, while the latter will have no appearance of being injured. But we are not to infer from this, that copper holes would be preferable to those made in fine brass; for although the oil in this case would be more durable, from its acting more slowly on copper than on brass, yet the increase of friction from the copper, would more than counterbalance this advantage. It can hardly have escaped the eye, even of the most indifferent observer, that oil acts more readily and forcibly on new than on old work. On the former, it will frequently show itself in the course of 24 hours. Oil varies so much in its quality, that some will become so thick and viscid, in the course of a few months, as to stop the machine altogether. This has occured in the experience of a very celebrated artist, who informs us that "his regulator, which has been found to go to a greater degree of accuracy, *though not to a second in two months, as has been said of others,* than even that of Verona, as observed by the Astronomer Cagnoli, or that at Manheim, as observed by Mayer, was found to perform very indifferently, after being cleaned, and at the end of three or four months stopped altogether, which arose from the application of bad oil." We are of opinion, that where the pivots are small, and the revolution of the wheel quick, jewelled pivot holes are the best. It will not be an easy matter to do without oil or jewelled holes, particularly in pocket or box-chronometers, although astronomical clocks or regulators may be so constructed as not to require either, provided the expense for doing so is not spared.

OIL FOR WATCHES AND CLOCKS.

Being of essential advantage to have good oil, we shall give several methods of preparing it.

A Receipt to Deprive Oil of its Acid.

To four ounces of the best spermaceti oil, add four grains of *Kali aeratum,** in five ounces of distilled water, shake them well for a day or two, then pour the whole into a tumbler, covered by another, and when exposed to the light for three or four weeks, the pure oil will float on the top, to be skimmed off by a tea-spoon. This oil, it is said, neither dries nor turns green.

Oil may be prepared in the following manner:

Put a quantity of the best olive oil into a phial, with two or three times as much water, so as the phial may be about half full. Shake the phial briskly for a little time, turn the cork downwards and let most of the water flow out between the side of the cork and the neck of the phial. Thus the oil must be washed five or six times. After the last quantity of water has been drawn off, what remains is a mixture of water, oil, and mucilage. To separate these from each other, put the phial into hot water for three or four minutes, and most part of the water will fall to the bottom, which must be drawn off as before. The oil must then be poured into a smaller phial, which being nearly full, must be well corked, set in a cool place, and suffered

---

*Kali aeratum, ℞. Kali praeparati ʒ ss. Aqu. distillatae ʒ v. Ammon. praeparatae ʒ j. Dissolve the Kali in a water bath; add the ammonia, and when the effervescence has ceased, let the fluid chrystalise. Two drams are given as a Lithontriptic, in a pint of distilled water, twice a-day at St. Bartholomew's Hospital. (Pharmacopœia Chirurg.) From Cooper's Dictionary of Practical Surgery.

to stand for three or four months, or until the water shall have subsided, with the mucilage above it, and the oil perfectly transparent, swimming on the top of the mucilage. When *time* has thus completed the operation, the pure oil must be poured off into smaller phials, and kept in a cool place, well corked, to preserve it from the air. This, by Mr. E. Walker, of Lynn, dated 13th Nov. 1810. (See Nicholson's *Phil. Journ.*)

The fat or oil which is left in the pan after making calves-feet jelly, if taken and put into a jug or bowl, and allowed to remain for some months, what swims on the surface may be skimmed off, put into a small phial, and kept there for some time: this will be found to be a very fine kind of oil, at least it has the appearance of being so. A French chemist, of the name of Jodin, prepares an oil, adapted for the use of watch-makers; it resists the cold to a considerable degree, but in time will become green at pivot holes, like most other oils. Olive oil freezes at 38° or 36° of Fahrenheit's thermometer, but if put into an open glass phial, and exposed to the sun-shine for a little while, it will not be apt to freeze till the thermometer is down to 21°. "As the amount of friction, even in the best clocks, in a great measure depends upon the oil, with which the various parts are lubricated, the following information may be considered of some importance. Colonel Beaufoy states, that olive oil may be freed from its mucilage, merely by exposure to the rays of the sun for one or two years."

"Chevreul, an eminent French chemist, recommends another process for the same purpose. To effect this, he mixes seven parts of alcohol with one of oil, which must be heated in a flask almost to boiling; the lighter fluid is then decanted, and, on being suffered to cool, a little portion of fatty matter separates, which is to be removed. The alcoholic solution must be evaporated to one-fifth of its bulk, and the fluid part of the oil will be deposited colourless, tasteless, and free from smell." This oil seems much like what was called Arabian oil, lately (April 1825) exhibited in Edinburgh. The printed description given with it, gave neither name of an inventor, or any place of abode, a circumstance somewhat extraordinary, and unless a great quantity of it was to be taken, none could be purchased.

Of old, watch-makers were taught not to allow the small phial, which contained the olive oil, to stand *even* in the light, far less to be exposed to the rays of the sun, because this deprived it of its yellow colour, which was considered to be a quality of the goodness of the oil. And now, the moderns, by depriving it of that colour, say they improve it.

Oil extracted from poppy seeds, and properly prepared, will remain uncongealed at a very low temperature. Almond, walnut, and hasel-nut oil, if freed from the mucilage, with which these oils are frequently intermixed, may be tried for watches. It was formerly an object of inquiry, to know when a jar of Florence oil was in a frozen state, which sometimes took place in severe winters,—a portion of it remaining unfrozen was taken out for the use of watch-makers.

We are informed that M. Frederic Schmidt, of Stutgard, has discovered an oil for chronometers, &c. which will not freeze at minus 17 of Fahrenheit's thermometer; does not dry at ×212, and boils at 512; it is not affected by cold at upwards of 50 degrees below the freezing point. M. S. is of opinion, in which he is confirmed by experiments, that this oil will not be affected under the Poles.

The process of pouring the water off between the cork and neck of the phial, was found to have something in it awkward and clumsy; we therefore got a large phial of about 17 or 18 inches deep, two inches wide, made with a glass stopper at top, and another at the side and close on the bottom, to let the water out, which answered the purpose extremely well. Also a few long sort of phials, with ground glass stoppers to each. The tall phial and its stop-cock was found very convenient in the process of washing with water, and letting the water out occasionally, to give room for more fresh and clean water. Oil thus prepared, and afterwards carefully managed, will perhaps be found to be as good as can in *any other way* be obtained; some of it we prepared in this way, and applied to the pivots and holes of the clock in the Royal Observatory, Edinburgh. This clock was taken down to be cleaned about the beginning of the year 1825, after having gone nearly twelve years; the pivot holes had a little greenish and thick oil in them, but in the reservoirs, it was in some degree tolerably fresh and yellow. It is singular that the washing did not deprive it of its yellow colour.

How to preserve the Oil, by Making such Reservoirs, as to allow the greatest quantity to be put to the Pivots and Holes.

To have the pivot holes, so as to preserve the oil for the greatest length of time, with the greatest quantity possible, the following is what should be done, if a little more expense can be allowed: For those holes, where the pivot-ends do not go beyond the surface of the plates, fit, into a drill stock, a drill made so as to form something like a drop of fat, when dropt on a table, or such like surface, making the diameter of the artificial drop to be made by the drill near to four-tenths of an inch or so; in a thick piece of plate brass, make a round hole to receive the drill; the piece of brass must be fixed outside on the frame plates, so as the pivot hole shall be in the centre of the round hole, in order to guide the drill, which must be allowed to cut no farther down in the plate, than barely to come to the surface, which should be left to remain, particularly at the pivot hole. A kind of collet might be put on the drill to prevent it from sinking too deep. The drill has the cutting part concave as seen at D, Plate V; the inside of the pivot holes may be chamfered a little way by a tool, whose point should be a little on the obtuse side; pieces of hard steel must be screwed on, outside of the plates, so as to cover fully the sinks made by the concave drill, and against the pieces of steel, the pivot ends should occasionally bear; the shoulders of the pivots should be turned nearly away, leaving a sort of cone in their place; and near to the shoulder, or top end of the cone, with the point of a very nice graver, make a slight notch.

The shape of a drop of fat *(goutte de suif)* at the top of a pivot hole, was a thought or contrivance of that celebrated artist, the late Julian Le Roy, and a most beautiful idea it was: (It is to be regretted that it was not adopted in a clock, otherwise very nicely got up, and for public purposes.) Between the hard steel pieces and the top of the dome, formed by the concave drill, there should be a small degree of space; if they are too close, the oil will spread too much over them, and, if at a proper distance, the oil will be attracted to a point connected with the pivot ends, gradually draining the reservoirs to supply the waste at the pivot holes.

CHAPTER XII.

On the various sorts of Machinery for going in time of winding.

THE earliest machinery for going in time of winding, *is that contrived by Huygens, described page 138*, is the simplest and the best that has yet been produced, although upon the whole it may not be so convenient in its application. In the old thirty-hour clocks, the first wheel of the going part had on its arbor a fixed jagged pulley A, (See Plate IV. No. 22). On the arbor of the first wheel of the striking part was a moveable jagged pulley H, with click and ratchet to it. Over these, and through or under the pulleys of the counter weight *p*, and main weight P, went an endless cord, woven either of silk or cotton. Both parts of the clock were carried on by a single or main weight, and when winding it up, this was done by the striking pulley; by which means the weight acted constantly on the going part. This is a method which we adopted in some common regulators, and afterwards found it was the same that Berthoud had used in some of his. The moveable and winding up pulley with its ratchet, turned on a stud, having a click and spring, which were fixed to one of the plates, as was also the stud. The other pulley was on the arbor of the first wheel, and fixed to it. The only inconvenience and objection to this contrivance, particularly in eight-day clocks, arises from the wearing of the cord on the jagged parts of the pulleys, which produce a great deal of dust, and makes the clock get sooner dirty than it would do, if this was effected in a different way. In clocks which go a month, or six months, as some of Berthoud's did, this will be very much obviated, particularly with a fine and well woven silk cord.

There is a very ancient way of going while winding, which was long applied to the fusees in clocks and watches. On the inside of the great wheel is another wheel, whose teeth are cut to look inward to the centre, upon which acts a pinion of six, which runs in the bottom of the fusee, and is turned round with it. The fusee arbor is free within both the great wheel and the fusee; upon it is fixed the fusee ratchet, and a wheel with about half the number of teeth of those in the inward toothed wheel. It is evident, that if the fusee arbor is turned round, the wheel fixed on it, which acts also on the pinion of six, will by this make the pinion turn; and this again, acting on the inside wheel teeth, will apply as much force to it as the fusee requires in setting up. When wound up, the click in the great wheel, as in the ordinary way, stops the fusee by the ratchet from running back. This method takes six times longer of winding up than by the common way; and the great strain which is laid on the pinion and inside wheel teeth, soon destroys them. With a little more apparatus, a fusee of this kind can be made to wind up whichever way the arbor is turned; hence it got the name of the *drunken fusee*. (*See particulars of it in Thiout, Vol. II. p. 333. and Plate XXXVIII. Fig. 14.*)

A going in time of winding, of later application to clocks and regulators, consisted of an arbor within the frame, on which was a pin, and an arm inside with a nib and a deer's-foot joint; another arm on the outside, when pulled down, served to make the jointed nib rise and pass the third wheel teeth; a spring, acting on the pin, brought the nib in a contrary direction, to act on the third wheel teeth, by which it gave motion to the swing-wheel during the time of winding, and continued to do so until getting clear of the teeth.

The general method which is now adopted, both in clocks and

chronometers, consists of an auxiliary spring, ratchet, and detent. In clocks, two springs are sometimes used; being doubled round, are screwed by one end to the back of the auxiliary ratchet; the other end is made to act against the arms or crosses of the great wheel. On the opposite side is the click, which acts with the barrel-ratchet; and when the force of the weight is taken off by winding up, the force of the springs act on the great wheel, not being allowed to bring the auxiliary ratchet forward which they would do; but this is prevented by the detent, consisting of an arbor whose pivots run in the frame, and an arm acting against the face of the small teeth in the auxiliary ratchet.

When this method is applied to a clock or watch fusee, there is a circular and flat steel spring, screwed or made fast by one end to the inside of the great wheel, in the other end is a small hole, opposite to which is made a short and circular slit in the great wheel. A pin in the auxiliary ratchet is placed so as to correspond to the hole in the spring and slit in the great wheel, through both of which it comes; the slit gives range for the bending up of the spring. When the force of the main-spring does not act on the fusee, which is taken off when winding up, the auxiliary ratchet, and detent, which has a slender spring to keep it to its place, serve the same end as has been described for the clock.

The mechanism of this going in time of winding, was first exhibited by Harrison, in his time-keeper, when explaining its principles to the commissioners who were appointed to receive them. It has been said that he took the idea of it from having seen an analagous contrivance in an old kitchen jack, where it had been applied to keep the spit turning while the jack was winding up. *There has been a great deal of ingenuity displayed even in jack-making. It is singular, however, that it was never thought of the applying vanes or wings to the fly, which could have been set, so, as to regulate the velocity according to the greater or less weight with which the spit may be loaded; but simple as the setting of these wings would be, it might not be so easy to prevail upon the cook to take the trouble of either understanding or using them. The water-jack, which has been known in this country for more than seventy years, is very convenient in this respect, as it is easy to make the discharge of water at the cock to run full, half, or quarter, on the small kind of mill-wheel which drives the whole of the machinery belonging to it.*

A great many years ago, we contrived an easy way of making a going in time of winding for a clock, to several of which it was applied. The third wheel has a socket (*with a small shoulder*) nicely fitted to it, the hole being soundly and smoothly broached. That part of the third wheel pinion arbor which works in the socket, must also be carefully turned, and made as smooth as any pivot, so as to be free, easy, and without shake. The end of the socket, which is not in the wheel, should be smooth and flat; its diameter outside, about three-tenths of an inch, and to apply to a flat smooth steel shoulder formed on the pinion arbor. On the side of the wheel opposite that on which the socket shoulder is placed, let there be fixed a small steel pin, distant from the centre about three-tenths of an inch, the height of it being about one-tenth. Make a piece of brass so as to have a fine small ratchet wheel on it, of about four-tenths of an inch in diameter, with a sort of hoop or contrate wheel rim on one side of it, three-tenths and a half in diameter inside, the thickness being a little more than that of an ordinary contrate wheel of a watch, and the depth one-twentieth of an inch. The ratchet-wheel and hoop have a socket common to both, which is twisted on the third wheel-pinion arbor; this socket, on that side of the hoop inside, is the smallest matter lower than the edge of the hoop. On this part of the socket is fixed the inner end of a small and weak spiral spring, of two or three turns, the outer end having fixed to it a small stud, with a hole in it, that goes over the steel-pin of the third wheel, which works in a short circular opening in the ratchet-wheel or bottom of the hoop, of a sufficient range for the spiral-spring to keep the clock going during the time of winding up. The detent for the ratchet has one of the pivots of its arbor in the back frame-plate; the other runs in a small cock attached to the inside of this frame-plate, and sufficiently clear of the third wheel on that side. The edge of the hoop, when the socket is twisted home, should allow the third wheel to have freedom during the action of the spiral spring upon it. In applying this going in time of winding apparatus to a clock, it will easily be seen in which way the small ratchet-teeth must be cut, and also in which way the spiral-spring must exert itself. During the action of winding up, this allows the minute-hand to make a retrograde motion; but it resumes its place as soon as the weight is at liberty.

In the early part of the last century, a considerable intercourse was carried on between Holland and Port Seaton, by the ship-owners of Prestonpans, in East-Lothian. Among other imports, was old iron in hogsheads; and many of the articles were little worse for being used, as, by an old Dutch law, no iron work was allowed to be repaired. Among the things which came home, were some camp-jacks, of a very ingenious construction, and evidently of German origin. Two or three of them, one of which we have seen, are still in that neighbourhood. It was composed of the usual wheels and pinions, endless screw, and a small fly rather weighty. The frame, mounted on an upright stand, was about four feet or more in height. A thin and narrow iron bar, of four or five feet long, was attached to the stand, and could be made to slide up and down on it, nearly the whole four or five feet; one edge of it was toothed like a straight rack, and worked into the pinion of the first wheel, by means of a weight hung on a hook at the lower end of the bar; when the weight and bar came to the lowest point, it was easily moved up to the greatest height, when the jack was to be wound up. The pinion had a hollow socket, and could turn freely round the arbor of the first wheel; on the lower end of the socket was a ratchet, which worked on the first wheel where the click and spring were placed to act with the ratchet, which, by the hollow socket, allowed the pinion to turn freely backward when winding up; on the weight being allowed to act on the rack, all the wheels were made to turn the proper way, and so on. An idea occurred to us, that, in place of the rack moving, a machine might be made to go by its own weight, by means of a pinion turning down on the toothed edge of a fixed rack. A scheme shall be given for a box-chronometer of this construction, which supersedes the necessity of either fusée, barrel, spring, or chain. A contrivance of a similar kind has lately been communicated to the Society of Arts in Paris, by M. Isabelle, and is described in the *Bulletin de la Société d'Encouragement*, No. 52. The same method, which has been known for a considerable time, is used at Liege, by Hubert Sarton, who makes eight-day spring clocks on this plan.

On the arbor of the first or great wheel, is fixed what may be called the fusee-ratchet, working with the click and spring, which are on the auxiliary or going-ratchet; in the last is fixed a pin, which comes through the end of the auxiliary spring, and the circular notch in the great wheel, which is keyed on in the same way as in the case with a fusee; having also a detent and spring for the going-ratchet,—the whole forming the great wheel, and the mechanism for going in time of winding. On the great wheel-arbor, close to the main-ratchet, let a small bevelled wheel be fixed, of any small number of teeth, fully stronger than those in the great wheel, the back of the bevelled wheel lying against the main-ratchet. Indeed, both might be made from one and the same piece of brass. Supposing the diameter of the pillar-plate to be 2.25 inches, that of the great wheel would be 1.5 inch, and the number of the teeth 72; the bevelled wheel, being half an inch in diameter, would admit 24 teeth; and, if made a little thicker than the great wheel, the teeth would be sufficiently strong. Another bevelled wheel of the same diameter and number of teeth as the other, is fixed on a pinion arbor, *(a hole being made in the potence plate, to allow the bevelled wheels to pitch together,)* which is placed within the frame in a horizontal direction, in that line which passes through the centres of the great and second wheels; one of the pivots runs in a cock inside of the potence-plate, and placed near to the great wheel arbor; the other, which is a little beyond the pinion-head, runs in a cock fixed on the outside of the potence-plate. This pinion has sixteen leaves, of the same strength as the teeth of the bevelled wheels, and runs in with the edge of a toothed-rack; every revolution will be over the length of one inch on the rack, and equal to four hours, or one turn of the great wheel; the second wheel-pinion being 18. The length of rack, supposed to be 8 inches, would allow the time of going to be equal to 32 hours,— 8 inches, multiplied by 4, being equal to 32. Were the rack 12 inches long, it would admit the time of going to be 48 hours; or the diameter of the pinion might be increased from .333 to .500 parts of an inch, and the time of going would then be somewhat more than 30 hours. Let a slip of wood be made 15 inches long, five-eighths of an inch broad, and rather more than one-eighth thick; on one side of this, and close to the edge, let another slip of the same dimensions, but not quite so broad, be set on edge at a right angle to the side of the other. This will form a pattern to have two such cast in brass from it: after being dressed up, one is left plain, the other so as to have twelve inches of teeth made on one of the edges; the plain one is screwed to the inside of the case, and the other is screwed on to the plain one, having the toothed-edge on the right-hand side of the pinion, so as to make the second wheel and pinion turn the proper way. To the ring or cap which incloses the movement of the chronometer, are attached three pieces of brass, kneed up at each end; the distance from the ends is about two inches and a half, in which are holes made quite parallel to one another, and go on three steel rods, 15 inches long, and two-tenths of an inch in diameter, fixed in the lower and upper ends of the case, and parallel to one another, and near to the dial of the chronometer. The case may be either of wood or brass, having a door on one side, which serves the purpose of getting at the chronometer, either to observe the time, or to push it up after it is nearly run down. In the lower part of the cap, a recess may be made to receive any additional weight requisite to load the chronometer with, in order to give greater extent of vibration to the balance; the upper part of the case should, if necessary, be hung in gimbals, and the lower end loaded with lead to keep it steady.

A chronometer might be easily fitted up in this way to go eight days, by giving more length of rack, a greater weight to the bottom of the cap, more teeth to the bevelled wheel, which is on the horizontal pinion arbor, fewer to that which is on the arbor of the great wheel, and the second wheel pinion to make more revolutions for one turn of the great wheel. Suppose the great wheel 80, the second wheel pinion 16, one turn will be equal to five hours; the bevelled wheel, which is on it, *being* 16, will have a revolution also in five hours; the bevelled wheel which turns it, having 24 teeth, will make a revolution in seven hours and a half. The rack being 25.6 inches long, the pinion of 16, making a revolution on it in seven hours and a half, and $25.6 \times 7.5 = 192$, the number of hours in eight days. The length of the case, being thirty inches, could be no inconvenience where eight days going without winding is obtained. A similar, and we think a preferable, construction might be adopted, by having the chronometer fixed, and a weight hung to the lower end of the rack, *which, as in the case of a jack*, would keep up the motion required for the chronometer. This plan, however, of a moveable rack, would require a space for the rack to move in, equal to twice its length.

CHAPTER XIII.

On the Force of Main-Springs in Box-Chronometers, and how to Calculate it.

BOX-CHRONOMETERS, or marine time-keepers, being sometimes made to go eight days, without requiring to be again wound up; and, in order that these machines may run such a length of time, the motive force ought to be pretty strong; it becomes, therefore, a matter of some consideration, to obtain this force of such a quantity, as shall be little more than sufficiently adequate for the purpose, which must be obvious to every judicious mechanic; any thing beyond this being rather hurtful as otherwise:[*] while, at the same time, the mainspring should, as nearly as possible, retain its force with the great

[*] This restriction applies more properly to dead beat or cylinder 'scapements, th' to those of the detached kind, which are not in this respect quite so limited.

est degree of constancy and invariability. To have strength of main-spring, it must be either broad or thick; if broad, then the rubbing of the coils creates a great deal of friction, and the oil, on getting glutinous, adds still a little more to the resistance of the spring when the coils are unbending. On the other hand, when the spring is thick, it requires a barrel of a greater diameter, which takes up more room than could be wished; besides, thick springs are more apt to break than thin ones. Very few are aware of the difficulties attending the procuring of a good spring; if they are hard, this exposes them continually to the risk of breaking; if they are soft, they gradually relax, and in the end become good for nothing. Much depends on the part of the spring-maker, *and no small degree of care is required by him*, to have steel of the best quality selected, also carefully to hammer, harden, and temper it, and lastly, in being very attentive when coiling or turning it up. To obviate as much as possible the objections which have been mentioned, Mudge and Berthoud adopted the mode of having a double barrel in one, and a spring put into each, with an arbor common to both; by which means they obtained the force of a broad spring, without its concomitant defects. It may be observed, that neither of these celebrated artists thought of making, *what they did not approve of*, a time-piece to go eight days; and if the expedient of a double barrel was had recourse to, for the main-spring of a time-piece to go thirty hours only, it must be still more requisite, for that which is constructed to go eight days.

The force of main-spring in a box-chronometer, should depend on the extent of the arcs of vibration which the balance must describe, and however long or short these arcs may be, they ought nevertheless to be performed in the same space of time. Now, on that account, this force becomes limited, by the extent of those arcs that are found to be isochronal. Therefore, to determine this force of main-spring, make the chronometer go with different weights, making no use of a barrel, a main-spring, or a fusee; fit to the square of the fusee arbor, a short cylinder of wood or brass, about two inches or so in diameter, let one end of a fine piece of cord, or small gut, be fixed and wrapped three or four times round it, to the other end, *after being conducted over a small directing roller or pulley*, attach weights of different quantities, according as they may be found requisite to make the balance describe arcs of unequal extent, in order to come at those vibrations where the balance with the pendulum-spring are found to be most isochronal. Having obtained this

, calculate how much the balance ought to weigh, so as the nometer may be at time; consequently, diminish or increase the ght of the balance, regulating the chronometer wholly by the ight, and masses of the balance, without touching the pendulum-ring. Keeping the chronometer still going, adding to or taking way from the going weight the quantity requisite to make the balance describe the arcs, where it was found, that, even with unequal vibrations, they were isochronal. We have now the measure of the motive force, and may find what the force of the main-spring ought to be, so as that it may be made equal to the trial weight. To make such trials as those which have been mentioned, the frame of the chronometer must be fixed in a horizontal position, to a stand, contrived and adapted for this purpose. Suppose the amount of the trial weight was found to be equal to 30 Troy ounces, or 14,400 grains Troy, the radius of the short cylinder, including the semi-diameter of the cord being one inch, and let the fusee adjusting tool be fixed at six inches: then the weight on the adjusting tool, at a radius of six inches, will be five ounces, which is that required to be in equilibrium with the force of the main-spring, when adjusting it with the fusee, whose semi-diameter at bottom is one inch. A spring may now be made to accord as nearly as may be with the given force, and, if required, this may be increased or diminished by altering a little the diameter of the fusee, or by such like means, till such time as the spring draws the given weight on the adjusting tool, at the fixed radius. A main-spring being made, it may be known if it has the force required without making use of either the fusee or barrel in the frame. Fix the arbor of the barrel in the vise, and one end of a cord fixed to the barrel, and wrapped three or four times round it, to the other end put on weights till such time as they are in equilibrium with the barrel, the main-spring being bent up a turn, or a turn and a quarter. Assuming the semi-diameter of the bottom of the fusee at seven and a half-tenths of an inch, by calculation, may be found, according to the weights required to make equilibrium with the spring, what weight the adjusting tool will draw on a radius of six inches. For example, if a spring, when bent up a turn, makes equilibrium with 48 ounces at the end of the cord, the radius or semi-diameter of the fusee bottom given, is seven and a half-tenths of an inch, as the radius of the arm of the adjusting tool is six inches, or six tenths, what weight on it must the spring draw? Say, as 60 tenths is to 7.5 tenths, the radius of the fusee, so is 48 ounces the equilibrium at the fusee, to 6 ounces that the adjusting tool ought to

on a radius of 6 inches. Having the weight that the adjusting tool will carry, we may thence find the semi-diameter of the fusee by the following proportion: As 48 ounces is to 6 ounces, so is 60 tenths to 7.5 tenths for the radius or semi-diameter of the fusee. *Example 2d.* The diameter of a fusee being given, likewise the weight, which on the adjusting tool ought to be in equilibrium with the main-spring. To find what this force ought to be at the circumference of the barrel. If the spring draws 6 ounces on the adjusting tool, with a radius of six inches, and the diameter of the fusee at bottom is one inch and a half, equal to seven and a half-tenths of radius. To find the force of the spring on the circumference of the barrel, make the following proportion: As seven and a half-tenths is to sixty tenths, so is six ounces to forty-eight ounces, the force exerted at the circumference of the barrel, or what it is at the bottom of the fusee.

By following such a process as this, as was done by Berthoud, much time might be saved, and the ends required will be obtained with a greater degree of certainty and accuracy than could otherwise be acquired.

When the chronometer is at last completely finished, cleaned out, and put together, it may be satisfactory to put it again under trial: but, when fixed to the stand, the conducting pulley, the cord, and weights attached to the end of it, must *now* be put in an opposite direction, so as to oppose at pleasure the force of the main-spring with any quantity of weight, when trying and comparing the short vibrations of the balance with those of the long ones given by the natural force of the main-spring. We ought to make use of such methods as are simple and certain, without taking the trouble of putting the barrel and fusee into the frame, in order to guess at the force of the spring and diameter of the fusee, and we could then direct the spring-maker to produce springs which should have at once the force required, by giving him the *weight*, which being attached to a cord wrapped round the barrel, and fixed to its circumference, it should be in equilibrium when bent up one turn. Take, as a third *Example*: The force of a spring being given at the circumference of the barrel, and the diameter of the fusee being also given, to find how much this spring will draw on a radius of six inches, in order to estimate somewhat nearly from these data the weight and diameter of the balance. What is given may serve from practice by comparison, to find the weight and diameter of a balance, but it is too limited to be general. There are many other circumstances to be taken into consideration, such as the number of vibrations in a minute, &c. &c.

Suppose a spring, set up half a turn, makes equilibrium with forty ounces at the circumference of the barrel, and the fusee is one inch in diameter at the bottom, or the radius is equal to half an inch. We may find the weight it will draw, by the following proportion:
60 : 5 : : 40 : 3.33, which is equal to 3 6 16, or 1600 grains Troy. To find readily and surely the shape of a fusee and its diameter, a trial fusee must be used. If the trial fusee is one inch in diameter, and draws ten ounces, for example. In order that the fusee required may draw eight ounces, make the following proportion, 10 : 10 : : 8 : 8. The fusee required must be 8-tenths of an inch in diameter. If a spring must draw twelve ounces, and the trial fusee draws ten, 10 : 12 : : 10 : 12. The diameter of the fusee must be twelve-tenths of an inch, that is, one inch and two-tenths of an inch.

CHAPTER XIV.

On the Dividing and Cutting Engine, and on the Methods of Dividing Circles into various Numbers for the plates of Dividing and Wheel-Cutting Engines

AMONG the inventions in the Art of Horology, produced in this country, may be mentioned that of the wheel-dividing and cutting engines, which are said to have been invented by Dr. Hooke. In the preface to the fourth edition of *Derham's Artificial Clock-maker*, he remarks, that " the invention of cutting engines, (*which was Dr. Hooke's*) fusee engines, and others, were never thought of till towards the end of King Charles the Second's reign." It is well known that he contrived and used an endless screw and wheel for the purpose of dividing astronomical instruments, in 1664. The wheel-cutting engine was contrived by him in 1655. Sully carried over to Paris wheel-cutting engines, of British manufacture, which were much admired there, not only for their beauty and fanciful execution, but also for their utility. The French artists, however, unwillingly admit our claim to this invention; and, could they have brought forward documents to the contrary, it would most readily have been done. They maintain, that it could not have been invented and improved at the same time by any one man, an opinion in which we must agree with them.

A wheel-cutting engine, and one which could divide almost any number, by means of an endless screw and toothed wheel, was made about 70 years ago, by Hindley of York, which came afterwards into the possession of Mr. Smeaton, from whom we purchased it in the year 1786, As Hindley knew what had been done in this way by Dr. Hooke, this seems to have been made in imitation of his, with some additions and improvements, as it is evidently not copied from that which is described in Thiout's work, Vol. I. p. 53. Plate XXIII. Fig. 1. said to have been invented by M. P. Fardoil, watch-maker at Paris. Ramsden's dividing engine, for which he got a considerable premium from the Board of Longitude, was executed on this principle, the great merit of which consisted in having a more perfect screw than had hitherto been made. For a copious history of *Dividing Engines*, and a full account of the engines invented by Ramsden and Troughton, see the article GRADUATION, Vol. X. p. 352. of the *Edinburgh Encyclopædia*.

About the years 1778, or 1780, Mr. Smeaton (see the *Philosophical Transactions* for 1785,) gave into the Royal Society a paper, describing a very simple and ingenious method of dividing, contrived by Hindley, who, providing himself with a narrow strip or ribbon of very thin plate-brass, about three yards long; into this he pierced four hundred holes, less or more, according to the extent of the greatest number he meant to have on the engine-dividing plate; the equality of distance between the holes was kept by drilling, and opening them from two small holes in a hard piece of steel, shifting from one hole to the next, having a nice cylindrical steel pin to put through the steel and brass as he went along. After the holes were all drilled, and the strip of brass a little dressed up, he got a block of wood chucked on to the mandrel of a stout turning lathe, turning the edge of the block down to that diameter, that the strip of brass, when wrapped tightly round it, should have the two extreme holes to meet exactly, and form one hole, into which a pin being put, kept the ends together, and the whole fast to the wood. The face of the block being previously turned flat, and on it fixed the engine-plate, having a number of concentric circles traced upon it, to be severally divided. One end of a steel spring index was fixed to the lathe, in the other was a nice conical point of steel, tempered, applied so as to enter fairly and freely into the holes in the strip of brass; taking them step by step, the divisions, in going along, were marked off on the plate. The greatest number being first laid down, then before the next less could be laid on, the strip of brass was taken off, and the block turned down, so as to allow the holes in the extreme ends to meet for that number, and so on downwards to the smallest number.

A Method, showing how to Divide Circles on the Dividing Plate of a Wheel-Cutting Engine.

This is a method which we have used, and frequently practised with much satisfaction and success. Wheel-cutting engines are made having a few *common numbers only* laid down on the dividing plate. But should a number be wanted which is not on the engine-dividing plate, the following directions will enable any one to lay down on it the number required. Having a scale of equal parts very nicely divided, and by which every inch can be subdivided into a thousand, this, accompanied with a small beam compass, or a pair of very fine spring dividers, with such points as could take from the scale the two thousandth part of an inch, and with these to operate. For example: The circle described on the engine plate, is supposed to be two inches, and six-tenths of an inch in diameter, and the number eleven is required to be laid down on it. Then say, as 113 : 355 : : 26 : 81.68. The last term is the number of tenth parts, and decimal parts of a tenth contained in the circumference of the circle; this divided by eleven, the number to be laid on it, will give seven-tenths, and forty-two hundredths of a tenth, for the opening of the compasses to be taken from the scale of equal parts, to make one eleventh part of the circle. If the scale is accurate, and the measure of the parts accurately taken, the circle will be found to be so well divided as to answer all the purposes wanted. Suppose a wheel of 73 is wanted, and this number is not on the plate, a circle described on it is 5.75 inches in diameter, what opening should the compasses have, so as to take the seventy-third part of the circumference? As 113 : 355 : : 50.75 : 159.436. Divide this last term by 73, and the quotient will be 2.184 tenths for the opening of the compasses. The rule is equally applicable to even or odd numbers. Bisection of even numbers makes it a very easy matter to lay them down on any circle, without having recourse to the rule just given. The greater part of an odd number may likewise be done by bisection, as shown by Ferguson, in his *Select Exercises*, p. 38, from which the following is extracted.

To divide the Circumference of a Circle into any Given Number of Parts, whether Even or Odd.

As there are very uncommon and odd numbers of teeth in some of the wheels of astronomical clocks, and which consequently could not be cut by any common engine used by clock-makers for cutting the numbers of teeth in their clock wheels, I thought proper to show how to divide the circumference of a circle into any given odd or even number of parts, so as *that* number may be laid upon the dividing plate of a cutting engine. There is no odd number but from which, if a certain number be subtracted, there will remain an even number, easy to be subdivided. Thus, supposing the given number of equal divisions of a circle on the dividing plate to be 69, subtract 9, and there will remain 60. Every circle is supposed to contain 360 degrees; therefore say, as the given number of parts in the circle, which is 69, is to 360 degrees, so is 9 parts to the corresponding arc of the circle that will contain them; which arc, by the rule of three, will be found to be $46 \frac{54}{100}$. Therefore, by the line of cords on a common scale, or rather on a sector, set off $46 \frac{54}{100}$ (or $46 \frac{1}{2}$) degrees with your compasses in the periphery of the circle, and divide that arc or portion of the circle into 9 equal parts, and the rest of the circle into 60, and the whole of the circle will be divided into 69 equal parts, as was required. Again, suppose it were required to divide the circumference of a circle into 83 equal parts, subtract 8, and 80 will remain. Then, as 83 parts are to 360 degrees, so, *by the rule of proportion*, are 3 parts to 13 degrees, and one-hundredth part of a degree; which small fraction may be neglected. Therefore, by the line of chords, and compasses, set off 13 degrees in the periphery of the circle, and divide that portion or arc into 3 equal parts, and the rest into 80, and the thing will be done. The following is from the same work, p. 42, and may be useful to those engaged in large clock-work, or in mill-machinery. " Supposing the distance between the centres of two wheels, one of which is to turn the other, be given, that the number of teeth in one of these wheels is different from the number of teeth in the other, and it is required to make the diameter of these wheels in such proportion to one another, as their number of teeth are, so that the teeth in both wheels may be of equal size, and the spaces between them equal, that either of them may turn the other easily and freely: it is required to find their diameters. Here it is plain, that the distance between the centres of the wheels is equal to the sum of both their radii in the working parts of the teeth. Therefore, as the number of teeth in both wheels, taken together, is to the distance between their centres, taken in any kind of measure, as feet, inches, or parts of an inch, so is the number of teeth in either of the wheels to the radius or semi-diameter of that wheel, taken in the like measure, from the centre to the working part of any one of its teeth. Thus, suppose the two wheels must be of such sizes as to have the distance between their centres five inches; that one wheel is to have 75 teeth, and the other to have 33, and that the sizes of the teeth in both wheels is equal, so that either of them may turn the other, the sum of the teeth in both wheels is 108: Therefore say, as 108 is to five inches, so is 75 teeth to 3 $\frac{47}{100}$ inches; and as 108 is to 5 inches, so is 33 to 1 $\frac{53}{100}$, so that from the centre of the wheel of 75 teeth, to the working part of any tooth in it, is 3 inches and 47 hundredth parts of an inch; and from the centre of the wheel of 33 teeth, to the working part of either of its teeth, is 1 inch and 53 hundredth parts of an inch."

Having the diameter of a wheel, which is proposed to be cut into a given number of teeth, to find the thickness of a cutter suitable, so as to give the teeth and space in due proportion. For example:—A wheel of 4.8 inches in diameter is wanted to have 144 teeth cut on it; suppose the depth of the teeth to be one-tenth of an inch, then the diameter of the wheel, taken at the bottom of the teeth and spaces, will be 4.6 inches; and it is intended to have the teeth and spaces alike at the bottom, which will allow the teeth to be broader from the bottom upwards. To find the circumference of a diameter of 4.6 inches, say, as 113 is to 355, so is 4.6 to its circumference, which, in this case, will be 14.4513 inches. Reduce this to thousand parts, and we shall have 14451.3 to divide by 288, the number of teeth and spaces, the quotient will be 50.2 nearly, call it 50 thousandths of an inch, or half a tenth, which is the same thing, and this is what the thickness of the cutter ought to be.

By the same sort of scale of equal parts, as used in the division of circles, any given straight line may be divided into any required number. For example: A given straight line is 5.5 inches long, and it is proposed to divide it into ten equal parts 5.5÷10=5.5 tenths of an inch. Suppose a given straight line is equal in length to 6048, which is 6 inches and .048 of an inch, or 48 thousand parts of an inch more,—it is required to have this line divided into 24 equal parts: 6048 + 24, the quotient will be 252 thousand parts of an inch, or somewhat more than 2.5 tenths of an inch. This is a much neater, and a more accurate way than any proportional compasses can give, and is even easier in its operations; the calculation or operation of division may be considered as nothing. It is hardly possible to bring the centre piece of the proportional compasses accurately to its place at all times, admitting the marks or places to be correctly put on; besides, any repairs to the points of the compasses will put all out of order. For these reasons, we consider proportional compasses to be of little use, however ingenious they may appear to be.

The Honourable the Commissioners of the Board of Longitude, some years ago, deservedly awarded the sum of one hundred guineas to the late Mr. James Allan, watchmaker, London, (an ingenious master in the art of dividing mathematical and astronomical instruments,) for what they conceived to be his superior method of dividing.[*] Mr. Allan's method of cutting a very accurate screw for his dividing engine, appears to be neat and simple. We are, however, humbly of opinion, that a screw cut by a good engine, having an inclined plane or edge, would likely be as perfect, if not more so, than any that could be otherwise obtained.

The engine mentioned at page 221, made by the celebrated Henry Hindley, of York, about the year 1740 or 1741,[†] and sent to us by Mr. Smeaton, in May, 1786, along with a full description, and the principles of its construction, with which he seems to have taken a great deal of pains; and as it is done evidently by a masterly hand on subjects in mechanics, it is deemed interesting to preserve a copy, which follows:

"*Description of the method of the count-wheel work of Hindley's Engine.*

"The use of this is to form the different numbers for cutting the teeth of clock wheels, &c. and to make the requisite moves of the endless screw and wheel as readily as can be done by a common

---

[*] See Mr. Allan's method in vol. xxxiv. of Trans. Society of Arts, &c. 1816, or Smith's Mechanic, a valuable collection published at Liverpool, in 2 vols. 8vo.

[†] It may fairly be concluded that Hindley did not copy any thing from Fardoil, as his engine would appear to have been made before Thiout published the description of Fardoil's. Both may have taken the idea of the endless screw and wheel from Dr. Hooke.

dividing plate. As an appendage of the engine, No. 7 and 8 contain two sets of count-wheels, containing all the numbers that Hindley had in general use for clock-work, from 128 to 56, and the largest number 128, is upon the end of the endless screw in its place; and any other of the numbers being put upon the end of the arbor in the same manner, and the larger locking wheel slided till it engrain therewith, the smallest of the three winches being put upon the square of the arbor, there is nothing to do but to turn the handle till the wheel locks, and then lifting it out, turn again till it locks a second time; and then the main arbor of the engine will have turned round a quantity answerable to the space of one tooth of a wheel of the same number as that on the end of the screw arbor. The reason of which is as follows:—Suppose, for a moment, the locking wheel to have 360 teeth, the same as the great wheel, the locking wheel locks at a whole turn only. Suppose, for an easy calculation, the wheel required to be cut to be 36, then a turn of the endless screw will be the space for one tooth, but the number 36 being on, you must turn it round ten times to make the locking wheel go round once, if it was 360; but being only 180, as it really is, then the locking wheel must go two turns to make the screw go round ten times.

"It may seem that it would have been more ready to have had the locking wheel to have been really 360, and then one lock would produce the number. What was Mr. Hindley's reason for this, Mr. S. does not exactly know, as he never knew but that it was so till the engine came into his hands; but he supposes it to have been to avoid too fine teeth, or over heavy a locking wheel, as its weight lies on the lever by which the main endless screw is, by a spring, commanded into the teeth of the great wheel, and consequently, by a different distance from the centre of the lever, will counteract the spring in different degrees. Its being only 180, however, has some advantages, for every number will produce its double; thus 72 being put on by single locks, it will produce 144. Also, if you want an original number, or one there is not, put on the minute circle, or circle of 60, that is figured, to which there is a proper index to drop into the notches. The minutes in the whole circle are 21600; divide this number by the number wanted, and the quotient will be the number of minutes due to each; which, if above 60, divide by 60, and you will then have the number of turns of the screw, and parts to form each tooth; and the fraction remaining being distributed through the whole circle, all your teeth will be true within a minute. By counting thus, you may ruff cut a count wheel, which being obtained, all others of the same, or a double number, are easily cut: but if you never can count the double, and the number given is even, then you had better produce the half, because that will produce your number by single moves. If those count wheels are ever so coarsely cut, even by hand, yet if they are near enough to engrain with and turn round the locking wheel, its untruth signifies little, as every error of its angle will be lessened in the proportion of 360 to 1.

"If you want a high number, suppose 365; amongst the dividing plates No. 9, you will probably find the number 73, which, multiplied by 5, produces 365; and 360 multiplied by 73, produces 26280; and this divided by 365 gives 72. It therefore follows, if you put the plate 73 upon the arbor, and turn a whole turn, wanting one division, you will produce the number 365; and Mr. S. apprehends the other dividing plates will be found adapted to similar purposes. Mr. S. remembers, that, for the more ease in counting, Hindley had a couple of pointers that he could separate like a pair of compasses, and fix at any angle, which, turned round upon the centre of the arbor, and by a springing plate or staple, were stiff enough to keep any place to which they were set. The whole turns of the arbor were easily counted, and the pointers being separated to the number of minutes required at each move, you set the follower pointer to the minute to be cut, and pressing down the index, you moved the leader pointer to the index, then cutting your notch upon the wheel, you move the arbor, first the whole turns, if necessary, and then so much farther, that the follower pointer comes to the index, which press down, move the pointer, and cut as before. This apparatus, for want of use, appears to be lost, as it did not come to Mr. S. with the engine, but may be made afresh without much trouble.

CAUTIONS TO MR. REID.—"The great dividing wheel being setts entirely at liberty from the screw, the catch that holds it there is lashed fast with pack-thread,—before he undoes that, it will be well to introduce a bit of soft wood wedge, a card, or a bit of leather, between the main screw and wheel; then releasing the pack-thread and the catch, he will soon find, by pressing upon the lever near the catch, what will enable him to release the wedge; then setting a tooth of the wheel exactly corresponding to a notch of the screw, let it go gently into it. Without this precaution, (before he was aware of it) the catch being undone, and a tooth opposing a thread of the screw, the sudden flirt of the spring that lifts it upwards, might set a bruise upon the end of the tooth or the thread. If upon letting the screw fairly into the wheel, and putting on the smallest handle or winch which belongs to it, the screw either moves stifly, or there is a sensible shake between the wheel and the screw, he will find a screw against which the upper part of the frame of the main screw at the right hand end *stops*, by which he can adjust it, so as to be *just without* shake; and then if the screw turns easy and pleasant, all is right; if not, clear the teeth of the wheel from dust, with a middling hard brush, and also the screw, and give them a little goose-grease, (not what drips from them in roasting) but what is *rendered* from the internal fat cake, as the fat of sheep and bullocks are to make tallow. If the teeth of the wheel, or threads of the screw, should get any accidental bruise, the projecting parts should be taken off by a small scraper, or such like tool; the teeth of the wheel and screw, well cleaned with a brush and soap and water, and then ground together (not with emery), but with such stuff as the cock-founders ground their brass cocks with. For this purpose, the pulley No. 23, must be put upon the handle of the screw arbor, and fixed with the plate and screws; the less grinding the better, the rotation moderately quick, but must keep the engine wheel going quite round, and not forward and backward in any one place. As soon as it appears to go tolerably regular, no more grinding stuff must be put to it, but gradually wiped off and reduced, as it becomes finer and smoother; and when the wet is a little dried up, feed it gradually with oil, and when judged smooth with that, take off the pulley, give it a little goose-grease, turning the screw gently to make the wheel go round several times by hand. But if there are no palpable defects, it will be best not to meddle with it in the grinding way: small matters will remedy themselves.

" There was a part which was obliged to be taken off from the upper part of the engine, to suffer the lid of the packing to go down, which perhaps Mr. R. will not know what to make of without some directions: it consists of two steel plates, (see S. Plate IV.) both concentrated upon the same arbor, they slide against one another, and are held together by a screw, so that either of them may be pushed forwarder than the other. The arbor which is fixed is marked to its place where it goes. The use of those is to set either side or middle of the cutter to cut directly towards the centre of the wheel to be cut, which will be known and adjusted by bringing the joint or separation between the two plates, to the centre of the cutting arbor on which the wheel is screwed down and fixed; and when once fixed, will scarcely need an adjustment, without there is as at present occasion to take it off.

" If the engine had fallen to Mr Smeaton's lot, he would have put it into a complete general repair. Particularly, the cutter wheel is much worn, several of the teeth have been broken, and very roughly put in, so that it goes very coarsely in its pinion; he not only would have made a new wheel, but have reduced the number from 48 to 36, or rather 35; in which case, he would have shortened the handle, if he had found it necessary for motion. As to the cutter pinion, he believes it is the very same he saw in the engine in the year 1741; and therefore, though somewhat worn, must be quite hard; he therefore did not propose to change it, but to accommodate the teeth of the wheel thereto.

"The spring that lifts the lever of the endless screw, is perhaps too stunt, too stubborn, and too sudden; and, on the whole, is so injudiciously applied, that Mr. S. cannot suppose it the spring Hindley left in the engine at his death, which happened in the year 1771. Mr. S. therefore proposed to fix a new one in such a manner as to act more kindly and more equably. He also meant to make anew the compass pointers above described, for easy counting for original numbers, verniers, &c. for divided instruments."

Having a wheel for a clock requiring the number 105 to be cut on it, our clockmaker, though well acquainted with using Hindley's engine in the usual way with count wheels, and even with some of the plate wheels, was at a loss how to proceed in it, when we put him on the following process:—The endless screw wheel has 360 teeth, then divide this number by 105, and we have for quotient $3\frac{45}{105}$, or $\frac{15}{35}$, or $\frac{3}{7}$, or $\frac{1}{7}$. It may not be so easy to get a wheel of 105, but one of 70 or 42 may more readily be obtained, particularly 42, as it is quite a common number with clockmakers. A large plate wheel of 42 notches being made and fixed on the end of the endless screw arbor, if we turn this plate three times round, and 18 notches more, cut one tooth or space, this gone over 105 times, will give 105 teeth, and will be equal to 360, the number in the endless screw wheel. A plate wheel of 7 might readily be notched by hand, and 3 turns and 3 notches would equally produce the number 105.

There is almost no number but may be come at, by taking a process somewhat similar to the above. Take the number 115 for example, 366 divided by it has for quotient $3\frac{21}{115}$, or $\frac{3}{5}$. A plate wheel of 23 notches cut on it, thus turned round three times, taking 3 notches more, will produce 115.

Suppose a wheel was required to be cut into a number greater than 360; for example 735, which would be 15 more than the double of 360, a plate wheel having 49 notches, and taking 24 of these for every time a space is cut in the wheel, it will give the number of teeth required, as 720, the double of 360, being multiplied by 49, will give 35280, and this divided by 735 will give 48. It hardly occurs in practice, that wheels of such a high number as this are ever required; the case is given merely to show the great extent of numbers that can be cut by such an engine. It may be requisite to show how the numbers 48 and 49 were obtained. If we divide 720 by 15, we have 48 for quotient, and, by the rule of proportion, 49 is got. As 720 : 48 : : 735 : 49."

Though a detail of the properties of Hindley's engine has been given by Mr. Smeaton, yet what follows will perhaps show more at large the variety of numbers that may be cut by it.

With the combined assistance of the minute wheel, and the large wheel of 360, there may be cut a great many numbers between 3 and 21600; but as these very high numbers are seldom or never required, we shall content ourselves with marking down the majority of those under 600 teeth, though there is no doubt other intermediate numbers might easily be found by a little calculation, that could also be cut by this combination.

There are, however, some numbers which cannot be produced from the minute wheel, and the great wheel of 360, such as 420, 56, 42, 21, 14, 7, &c.; but these, with many others, can be got, by substituting instead of the minute wheel of 60, a wheel of 70. By this last, several numbers can be got, which are also produced by the wheel of 60; but we shall confine ourselves by stating some of those which the minute wheel cannot produce.

A very few plate wheels, (perhaps ten or a dozen) may be sufficient to give any number whatever, however odd or uncommon.

It is to be observed, that in the following tables, the first column indicates the number of entire turns and fractional parts of a turn of the endless screw, and these fractional parts are again expressed in the second column, by the number of 60th parts of a turn of the minute wheel, or 70th parts of a turn of the wheel of 70, over and above the number of entire turns of the endless screw. The third column points out the number of teeth cut.

TABLE I.

Turns and Fractions.	60th Parts.	Teeth.	Turns and Fractions.	60th Parts.	Teeth.
120	-	3	$4\frac{4}{5}$	48	75
90	-	4	$4\frac{1}{2}$	30	80
72	-	5	4	-	90
60	-	6	$3\frac{3}{4}$	45	96
45	-	8	$3\frac{3}{5}$	36	100
40	-	9	$3\frac{1}{3}$	20	108
36	-	10	3	-	120
30	-	12	$2\frac{2}{3}$	40	135
24	-	15	$2\frac{1}{2}$	30	144
$22\frac{1}{2}$	30	16	$2\frac{2}{5}$	24	150
20	-	18	$2\frac{1}{4}$	15	160
18	-	20	2	-	180
15	-	24	$1\frac{4}{5}$	48	200
$14\frac{2}{5}$	24	25	$1\frac{2}{3}$	40	216
$13\frac{1}{3}$	20	27	$1\frac{1}{2}$	30	240
12	-	30	$1\frac{1}{3}$	20	270
$11\frac{1}{4}$	15	32	$1\frac{1}{4}$	15	288
10	-	36	$1\frac{1}{5}$	12	300
9	-	40	1	-	360
8	-	45	$\frac{9}{10}$	54	400
$7\frac{1}{2}$	30	48	$\frac{5}{6}$	50	432
$7\frac{1}{5}$	12	50	$\frac{4}{5}$	48	450
$6\frac{2}{3}$	40	54	$\frac{3}{4}$	45	480
6	-	60	$\frac{2}{3}$	40	540
5	-	72	$\frac{3}{5}$	36	600

TABLE II.

Turns and Fractions.	70th Parts.	Teeth.
$51\frac{3}{7}$	30	7
$25\frac{5}{7}$	50	14
$17\frac{1}{7}$	10	21
$12\frac{6}{7}$	60	28
$10\frac{2}{7}$	20	35
$8\frac{4}{7}$	40	42
$6\frac{3}{7}$	30	56
$5\frac{5}{7}$	50	63
$5\frac{1}{7}$	10	70
$4\frac{2}{7}$	20	84
$3\frac{3}{7}$	30	105
$3\frac{3}{14}$	15	112
$2\frac{6}{7}$	60	126
$2\frac{4}{7}$	40	140
$2\frac{1}{7}$	10	168
$1\frac{5}{7}$	50	210
$1\frac{3}{5}$	42	225
$1\frac{3}{7}$	30	252
$1\frac{2}{7}$	20	280
$1\frac{1}{7}$	10	315
$1\frac{1}{14}$	5	336
$1\frac{1}{35}$	2	350
$\frac{6}{7}$	60	420
$\frac{5}{7}$	50	504
$\frac{24}{35}$	48	525
$\frac{9}{14}$	45	560

CHAPTER XV.

On Equation Clocks, Equation of Time, and Lunar Motions.

The first equation clock, which is a very ingenious contrivance to show both mean and apparent time, was made in London about 120 years ago. The following history of the invention is given by Berthoud:

"The most ancient equation clock," says he, "which has come to our knowledge, is that which was placed in the cabinet of Charles II.

King of Spain, and which is mentioned at the end of *The Artificial Rule of Time*, by Sully, (edition 1717,) who gives the following account of it, from an extract of a letter from the Rev. Father Kresa, of the Society of Jesus, written to Mr. Williamson, watchmaker of the cabinet of his Imperial Majesty, of the 9th January, 1715.

" What M. Baron Leibnitz says, in his remarks at the end of Sully's book,—that if a watch or clock did of itself make the reduction of *equal time* to *apparent*, it would be a very fine and convenient thing,—on this subject, I have to tell you, that from the years 1699 and 1700, there has been in the cabinet of King Charles II. of glorious memory, King of Spain, a clock, with a royal pendulum, (seconds pendulum,) made to go with weights, and not with springs, going four hundred days without requiring to be once wound up. I have, by order of his Majesty, and in his presence, seen and explained the instructions, which were sent from London with watches, which contained many curious things. I had orders to go every day to the palace, during several months, to observe the said clock, and compare it with the sun-dial; and, at that time, I remarked that it showed the equation of time, *equal* and *apparent*, exactly according to the tables of Flamstead,* which are found likewise in the Rodolphine Tables, &c."

Sully, at the end of the letter, of which an extract has just been given, makes the following remarks, page 9: " What the Rev. Father Kresa relates of the clock of the late King of Spain, is very true. It is more than twenty years since such clocks were made in London; and I believe that I am the first who applied this mechanism (for equation,) to a pocket-watch, twelve or fourteen years ago."

A very curious and excellent equation clock, (made by Mudge and Dutton,) and some *other things*, were left by the late General Clerk to the late Sir John Clerk, and entailed on the house of Pennycuick. *One of which* was a spring clock by the same makers, having a very ingenious sort of motion work, so contrived as to make the clock strike what may be called *Roman hours*. The General was of a studious disposition, and disliked hearing the long hours as they were struck in the ordinary way by common clocks. This spring clock stood in his library, or reading room; it had two bells, one of them larger than the other, having a tenor sound, the smaller one sounding sharp; one blow on the tenor bell was

---

* The earliest equation tables were calculated by our first Astronomer Royal, Mr. Flamstead, at Greenwich.

reckoned five, and one on the sharp bell was reckoned; one for example, when a long hour was to be struck, such as the twelve o'clock hour, two blows on the tenor bell made ten, and two on the sharp bell made two more, equal to twelve. One blow on the tenor bell and three on the sharp bell indicates the eight o'clock hour. One blow on the sharp bell and two on the tenor bell, or ten minus one, was the hour of nine. One blow on the tenor bell was the five o'clock hour, and in like manner the other hours were given. There is a clock made by Tompion, belonging to the Right Honourable the Earl of Moray, at the house of Donibristle, which strikes the hours somewhat in this way, by means of a sort of count wheel, so far as we remember.

A gentleman, somewhat like General Clerk, complained to his watchmaker, that he could not bear the *tick tack* noise which his spring-clock made, and wanted much to have it suppressed if possible; the 'scapement it had was of the crown wheel and verge kind: To obtain the end of preventing a noise being made, a piece of gut was put across the opening or sink made for the pallets of the verge, just at the part where the crown-wheel teeth dropped or fell on them, (it must be observed that the gut was stretched parallel to the line of the verge arbor,) which had the desired effect of taking the noise away; and what was very remarkable, after a great many years going, no wearing or mark of any kind was *visible* on the gut. We have put thin and hard steel springs, both on verge and anchor, or recoiling pallets, with pretty good effect, for softening down the noise made by the beats of the clock.

Description of Pennycuick House Equation Clock.

This clock goes a month, strikes the hour, and has a strike-silent piece. The 'scapement is made after that of John Harrison's, requiring no oil to the pallets; the pendulum is a gridiron compensation one, composed of five rods, three of which are steel, the other two of zinc, or some compound of zinc. On the dial are seen the hours, minutes, and seconds, and their hands. The minute hand keeps mean or equal time; the equation of time is given by a hand with a figure of the sun on it, keeping solar or unequal time, and shows at all times when the sun is on the meridian. Its difference from the minute hand is the equation of time. The age and phases of the moon are also represented, the days of the year, and of the month, the degrees of the ecliptic, and the signs of the zodiac, the rising, and setting of the sun, the length of the day, &c. The dial is a twelve inch arched one. Concentric with the arch, is a sort of ring-plate wheel of 365 teeth, making its revolution in a year, or 365 days. Its diameter is about 8 inches, and the breadth of the rim or ring 1½ inch nearly. On this ring-plate, at the outermost circles containing divisions, are laid down the days of the year; and on the space next within, are the names of the months, the days being numbered by the figures, 10, 20, &c. The next circles contain the 360 degrees of the ecliptic; the space within has the signs of the zodiac; and the numbers 10, 20, and 30, marked for the degrees in every sign, and corresponding with the days of the year and of the month, when the sun is in any of these signs. The innermost circles contain what may be called the divisions of the semi-diurnal arcs. On the space outside of this are marked the corresponding hour figures in Roman characters. This is what gives the time of the rising and setting of the sun, and the length of the day.

In the annual plate-ring are rivetted six small brass pillars, one inch and one-tenth of an inch in height, whose opposite ends are screwed by steel screws, and their heads sunk into a plain ring wheel neatly crossed into six arms, the diameter being five inches and three quarters of an inch, and the breadth of the rim three-eighths of an inch. The back of this plain ring is distant from the back of the annual plate-ring one inch and a quarter. The plain ring is at the centre, screwed on a brass socket, having a square hole in it. Within the frame of the clock movement, and at a perpendicular distance of six inches from the centre wheel holes, a steel arbor is run in, and at one end, prolonged about an inch and a half beyond the fore frame plate, somewhat like a stud. The pivot in the fore plate is of such a length and thickness as to allow a square on its outside. It is on this square that the equation ecliptic plate is put, and above it is put on the annual plain ring by means of its socket, with a square hole in it. That part of the arbor which is above the socket is round, and serves as a stud for the moon's age ring socket to revolve on it freely and easily. The moon's age ring turns within the annual plate ring, and is divided into 59 equal parts, numbered 3, 6, 9, and so on to 29¼. Its diameter is five inches and one-eighth; its breadth fully three-eighths of an inch, and it is connected with a plain wheel neatly crossed into six arms, of the same diameter and breadth of rim as the moon's age ring, having six small pillars, nearly an inch in height rivetted into it, and the moon's age ring screwed, at the opposite ends of three of them, by three sunk steel screws. This plain ring has a socket which runs or turns on the stud above the annual plain wheel; the face of the moon's age ring comes flush up with that of the annual plate-ring, and both come up to the back of the dial; in which an opening in the arch is made, in order to show a great part of what is on these rings. From the top of the arch, across the opening, and down in a straight direction, is stretched a very fine wire, serving as an index to the days of the year, the moon's age, &c. The annual plate-ring and the moon's age ring, move or turn from the right to the left hand, yet separately and independently of each other. On the inside shoulder of the socket of the moon's age ring is screwed a small bevelled wheel, having 37 teeth, and one inch in diameter, the use of which will be afterwards explained. In the dial is a circular opening of one inch and three quarters in diameter, a little below the opening in the arch: in this opening is exhibited the lunar globe of an inch and a quarter in diameter, made of brass, and silvered; one half of it is perpendicularly painted black, in order to give the phases the new and the full moon. On the arbor of the lunar globe are two wheels, one of 63 teeth, and about an inch in diameter, the other, a bevelled one of the same diameter, and with 37 teeth. Both are placed below the lunar globe; the wheel of 37 and the globe are fast on the arbor; the wheel of 63 being keyed spring-tight above the bevelled one. The arbor of the lunar globe is in the plane of the dial, or nearly so, and this bevelled wheel takes or pitches into that of the same number, which is screwed on the moon's age ring socket as before mentioned; and, by means of holes in the ring, the whole, that is, the globe, the bevelled wheels, and the moon's age ring, &c. can be made to turn together, when the moon is at any time setting to its proper age. The pivots of the lunar globe arbor run on cocks, which are screwed on to the back of the dial. Behind the globe, and at a little distance from it, is screwed on to the back of the dial, a sort of concave or hollow hemisphere of thin plate brass, painted inside of a sky-blue colour.

We shall now proceed to show how the moon's motion is produced. On the top of the month nut-socket, where it lies in the plane of the dial, is cut a right-handed double endless screw, working into a small brass wheel of 15 teeth, which is on the lower end of a long arbor, standing upright in a slit made in the dial. This slit is covered by a large circular silvered plate, on which are engraved the hours, minutes, and seconds; on the upper end of this long arbor, is a pinion of 8, which carries about the wheel of 63, and with it, at the same time, the bevelled wheels, globe, and moon's age ring. The pivots of the long upright arbor run in small cocks attached to the back of the dial. The month nut, or hour wheel socket, makes a revolution in twelve hours, carrying the hour hand. The revolution of the moon's age ring is made in 29 days, 12 hours, and 45 minutes. The wheel of 63 and 15 being multiplied together, the product is 945, and this divided by 8, the number of the pinion, gives 118.125 times six hours, which being reduced, gives the lunation, or a revolution of the moon's age ring as above, of 29 days, 12 hours, 45 minutes. The time of the revolution may be made out by another way. It is evident that one tooth of the small wheel of 15 is turned every six hours; of course the wheel will be made to have a revolution in 90 hours, and so will the pinion 8. Then, if we say, as 8 : 90 : : 63 : 708.75 hours, which is also equal to the given lunation of 29 days, 12 hours, 45 minutes. To produce the annual motion of the ring-plate wheel of 365 teeth, the month nut is cut into 42 teeth, and makes its revolution, as was said before, in 12 hours, and turns a wheel of 84, concentric with which is a pinion of 8, leading a wheel of 96, having concentric with it a pinion of 12, leading the wheel of 365, which is the plate-ring circle, having on it the days and months of the year, the degrees of the ecliptic, &c. turning once round in 365 days. Now, as $365 \times 96 \times 84 = 2943360$, this product, divided by that of $42 \times 8 \times 12 = 4032$, will give 730 times twelve hours, or 365 days. The pinion of 12 is put on a square, which comes in and through a small hole in the large silvered circular plate, the wheel of 96 is put on a round part of the arbor just below the pinion, and is keyed spring-tight on it; by means of a small key which fits the square, to turn the pinion, the annual wheel of 365 teeth can be set to any required day of the month, which can be done without disturbing any of the motion wheels. The setting of the moon's age ring is equally free as this from any disturbing cause. The diameter of the month nut wheel of 42 is one inch, and three and a half tenths of an inch; that of the wheel of 84 is 2.5 inches, and near to a tenth and a half more. The wheel of 96 is three inches, its pinion of 12 is .307 of an inch, the pinion of 8 is .316 of an inch in diameter.

The minute-pipe wheel of 56 teeth, and 1.8 inch in diameter, runs on the arbor of the centre wheel, carrying the minute hand. It turns in the common way the minute wheel m of the same number and diameter, whose centre lies nearly under that of the other, about .6 of an inch to the right of the middle line of the fore frame plate, and 1.7 inch from the centre of the minute-hand wheel. The arbor of the minute wheel has a pinion of 8, leading in the common way the hour wheel of 96, whose diameter is 3.25 inches, that of the pinion is .426 of an inch. This pinion of 8 is put on the arbor by means of a square, and with the minute wheel both are fast on the arbor. See Plate XI. No. 62. The upper side of the wheel may be distant from the lower face of the pinion about .7 of an inch, the lower side having a proper freedom from the fore plate. Two wheels, one a plain wheel of 38, the other a bevelled one of 38, having the same diameter 1.2 inch, are screwed together, and on a socket common to both; the flat wheel is the uppermost, and is pretty close to the back of the bevelled one, whose teeth look downwards; their socket turns on the minute-wheel pinion arbor, between the lower face of the pinion and the upper side of the minute wheel, having a proper end-shake between them; the back of the flat wheel of 38 is below the lower face of the pinion .4 of an inch. These wheels of 38 can be made to turn on the minute-pinion arbor, independent of it and the minute-wheel. The minute-wheel and pinion arbor extend a little way beyond and below the minute-wheel, perhaps one inch, and three or four-tenths more to the end of its pivot; it extends also beyond the face of the pinion more than .6 of an inch to the end of its pivot, which runs into a cock C screwed on the fore-frame plate. There is a part formed on the arbor of a flat circular shape, and whose thickness is rather more than that of the diameter of the arbor; in the middle of this a hole is tapped, into which is screwed a stud, standing at right angles to the arbor; a bevelled wheel of 38, and diameter 1.2 inch with its socket turns on this stud, which is placed on the arbor at that distance, so that the two bevelled wheels may fairly pitch into one another; the minute wheel is crossed into four, and through one of the cross openings, the bevelled wheel B, which is on the stud, gets to pitch with the bevelled wheel b, which is above the minute one. On the inside of the pillar plate is screwed a cock A, nearly 1.2 inch in height, and so that the middle part of the upper knee shall be opposite to the lower end and pivot of the minute pinion arbor. On one end of another arbor, in length about 2.1 inches, having a shoulder on it, is rivetted a bevelled wheel c of the same diameter and number of teeth as the others; another shoulder, of just a sufficient thickness, is made on this arbor at the back of the bevelled wheel; the rest of the arbor is nearly straight all the way to the shoulder of a pivot which is at this end; from this shoulder the arbor is squared down for about .6 or .7 of an inch, to receive the socket of a small wheel W of 32 teeth, which turns behind the pillar plate; this wheel is nearly one inch in diameter, and a cock K is screwed on the back of the pillar plate, in which the pivot of the wheel of 32 runs; a pin is put through the socket and square, to keep the wheel fast to its place on the arbor. When the shoulder at the back of the bevelled wheel bears on the outside of the kneed cock, which is on the inside of the pillar plate, the cock having a hole in it which allows the arbor to go through and to turn freely, then the pivot of the arbor will run in the cock which is at the back of the pillar plate. The inside bottom of the bevelled wheel, which is rivetted on the shoulder of this arbor, has the end of the arbor made flush with it, and a hole made in the end and centre of the arbor to receive the lower pivot of the minute pinion, in which it runs or turns; the bevelled wheel, which is on the stud, being supposed to be set as low down as it shall meet, and pitch properly with that which is at the end of the other arbor.

It will now be seen that the end-shake of these arbors, when combined, will lie between the minute-pinion cock on the fore plate, and that which is on the back of the pillar plate. Let us suppose, that the bevelled wheel, which is at the end of one of these arbors, remains stationary, and that the minute pinion and wheel are carried about by the minute-pipe wheel, which is on the arbor of the centre wheel; during a revolution of the minute-wheel and pinion, the bevelled wheel which turns on the stud, will be carried not only round with its stud, but is made to make another revolution by means of its turning round on the teeth of the bevelled wheel, which is stationary, causing the bevelled wheel, and the flat wheel connected with it, which are below the minute pinion, to make two revolutions in the hour; and as the flat wheel of 38 teeth turns the sun-hand wheel of 76 teeth, and 2.3 inches in diameter, this last must make its revolution in an hour. Its socket turns freely on that of the minute-pipe wheel, which carries the minute hand; between the sun-hand wheel and this minute-pipe wheel, is a slender spiral spring, the inner end of which is fixed to the lower end of the sun's-wheel socket, the outer end being fixed in a stud on the upper surface of the minute-hand wheel. This spring is for the purpose of keeping forward the sun hand to its place, notwithstanding any shake which may be among the teeth of those wheels concerned in the equation motion work. The sun's hand is of brass gilded, having the figure of the sun on it, at a little distance from the end which points to the minute divisions. The sun's hand lies between the hour and minute hands; the wheel of 76, which carries it, besides the motion of going once round in an hour, has at one time a small motion retrograde, at another a small motion progressive, according to the equation; and there are four times in the year when the minute and sun hands are nearly together. One half nearly of the sun wheel is crossed out on that side in which the sun's hand lies, in order that the equilibrium of the hand and wheel may be as nice as possible, whatever may be the position of the sun hand.

From the centre wheel hole on the fore frame plate, towards the left hand, and a little upwards, take, with a pair of compasses, a distance of 3.8 inches, and sweep an arch, and then from the centre of the hole in which the arbor runs, which carries the annual-plate wheel, take in the compasses an extent of 4.6 inches, and sweep another arch so as to intersect the first, the place of intersection will be that of an arbor having pivots, one of which runs into a cock screwed on the back of the pillar plate; the other runs into a cock screwed on the front of the fore-frame plate; a notch is made on the edge of each frame plate to admit the arbor to come to its place. On the end of this arbor, which is just behind the pillar plate, is fixed a rack, or segment of a circle, 5 inches radius, having 32 teeth cut on it, *cut from a number on the engine plate of* 318; the rack-teeth pitch into the small wheel of 32, which lies behind the pillar plate, and whose centre coincides with that of the minute-pinion arbor, as mentioned before. On the other end of this arbor, and beyond the fore-frame plate a very little, is fixed an arm of 4.5 inches long, having at the end of it a smooth hard steel pin, which bears on the edge of the annual-elliptic equation plate, being made to do so by means of a coil or two of watch main-spring not very strong, attached to the arbor, near to the inside of the fore-frame plate, the outer end being fixed to one of the pillars, or to a stud fixed for that purpose on the inside of the fore plate. The elliptic equation plate is a very irregular sort of a figure, as may be conceived in some degree by the description of its shape; its greatest length over all is 6.5 inches; the centre is 3.8 inches from the broadest end, and 2.7 inches from the narrowest; the nearest edge across the centre is about one inch, and the edge opposite is 1.8 inch; the greatest breadth of the broad end is near to 4 inches, that of the narrowest end is 2.8 inches. During the course of its annual revolution, the edge of the elliptic plate makes the arm which has the steel pin in it rise to various heights, and fall as variously to different depths. By this rising and falling, the rack which is at the opposite end of the arbor, is made to have a motion sometimes backward, and at other times forward, which it communicates to the small wheel of 32, behind the pillar plate, and of course to the bevelled wheel of 38 on the same arbor with it. This continually causes a small change of place to the bevelled wheel of 38, consequently a change of place to that which turns on the stud, and hence to the wheel carrying the sun hand. This change is what gives the equation, shown by the difference of time between the minute and sun hand. When the pin in the arm falls, the equation or sun hand goes forward, and when rising it goes backward. The greatest negative equation for 1815, on the third day of November, is 16 minutes, 14.9 seconds, which, added to the greatest positive equation for the same year on the 11th of February, being 14 minutes, 36.5 seconds, makes in all 30 minutes, 51.4 seconds; so that one tooth of the wheel of 32 may be nearly equivalent to one minute of equation. To trace properly a true figure to the equation plate, must be a very tedious and nice operation; for this purpose the rack, and all the wheels immediately connected with the equation, must be put into their places, as also all those which give motion to the annual plate, and to have a spring tight arm, having a sharp point to it, bearing on the face of the brass-plate, which is to be the elliptic one: the sharp point must lie so as to coincide with the side of the steel pin when bearing on the edge of the elliptic plate. The sun and minute hands being on, and the annual plate set to the 1st of January, the equation hand set to the equation for that day, then by setting forward the minute hand 12 or 24 hours, the equation hand may be changed to what it ought to be in the same time; so by going on step by step in this way, the figure of the equation or elliptic plate may be truly done. The rack must be artificially made to assist in this; and when the revolution is completely at the end, before taking out the rack and the equation wheels, marks must be made to one of those teeth, and likewise to its corresponding space in the other wheels, so that when they are again put into their places, they shall give such equation as was done when tracing for the elliptic plate.

Besides the days of the month, which are shown on the annual plate, there is a common month ring, having 31 figures engraved on it, placed as usual at the back of the dial. One of these figures is shifted every day through the whole ring when the month consists of 31 days, and two figures at the last are shifted at once when the month consists of 30 days, to bring the ring to the first day of the succeeding month; and at the 28th of February, four figures are shifted, so as to bring the ring to the first of March: by this means, the day of the month ring requires no shifting or correcting at these periods, as those in the common way do. To produce this motion, five short steel pins are placed in a circle, on the under side of the elliptic plate, whose radius may be about half an inch, and set at such a distance from one another as to correspond with the numbers of days between February and April, between April and June, between June and September, between September and November, and between November and February. This may be done by applying the elliptic plate on a cutting or dividing engine, having the number 365 on the dividing plate. When fixed on the engine, and set to the first point of the number, make a point for February on the elliptic plate, then count off 61 from the dividing plate, which will give the place for the pin on the 30th of April; another 61 will bring it to June 30th; 92 will give the 30th September; 61 the 30th November; and 90 more will bring it to the 28th of February, the point from which we set out. When the pins are put in the elliptic plate, that for February will require to be longer than the others, for a reason which will be explained when we come to show the use of these pins. The month wheel of 84 teeth, and whose diameter is 2.75 inches, has its centre on the left-hand side, distant from the central perpendicular line 1.4 inch, and from the centre hole in the fore-frame plate 2 inches. The month wheel, as usual, is turned about by the month nut. A long piece of brass forming two arms, each four inches in length, has a small arbor through the middle of the whole length of eight inches. The pivots of this arbor run into small cocks, attached to the front of the fore plate, keeping the long piece of brass very near to the plate: indeed a great part, particularly the end of the upper arm, and towards it, is sunk partly into the fore plate. This long piece of brass is placed so, that one of the arms shall come to the socket of the month wheel, and the other with its end nearly below the circle in which are the five pins, in the annual elliptic plate described as before. A spring is placed below this upper arm to keep it up, unless when any of the pins get on the end of the arm and press it down. The end of the arm is chamfered, or made so that any pin, when approaching it, gets easily on and presses it down gradually, by means of ascending the chamfered part; and, when past this, it meets with a flat and very narrow place, where it cannot remain longer than some time short of 24 hours, say 16 or 18 hours, or perhaps not so long. After having passed the flat part, it meets with a chamfered side opposite to that of the first. Besides that of freeing the pin, this is made for the purpose of more easily setting back or forward the annual plate.

The month wheel has its socket equally long on both sides, and quite straight, the length of each may be .6 or .7 of an inch. Two small brass pillars are rivetted on the upper side, and opposite one another, each at a distance from the centre of the wheel about .7 of an inch, (See No. 62. 2 and 3.) the height of the pillars from the wheel to the shoulder about half an inch; and from the shoulder of each pillar, a sort of straight pivot is prolonged about half an inch more; the diameter of these pivots about one-tenth of an inch, that of the pillar .2 of an inch. There is another socket which goes easily on the lower or under socket of the month wheel, which is rivetted in a rectangular piece of brass, about an inch long, and half an inch broad, or nearly so, say .4 of an inch. In this piece of brass, on the side opposite that of the socket, are also rivetted two small and straight brass pillars, about an inch in length, and the diameter about one-tenth of an inch. There are holes in the month wheel to allow these pillars to go easily back and forward in them; their places will be equally between the month-wheel socket and the pillars which are rivetted in the month wheel. The other ends of the small straight pillars are made fast, by two small steel screws, to a piece of brass, which is formed to correspond with two broad crosses of the month wheel. Only one of them is made to have at the end a segment of a circle, whose radius is nearly equal to that of the month wheel. On this segment three teeth are cut, equal in their spaces, and conform to those of the month ring. In the arms or crosses of the segment are three holes, one of which goes easily over or on the upper socket of the month wheel: the other two holes go easily on the small straight pivots, which have been already mentioned. This segment cannot be put on the ends of the small pillars, till the socket of the rectangular piece of brass is put on the lower socket of the month wheel, having previously made the pillars connected with it to pass through their holes in the month wheel. It will be easy to perceive, that when the segment is put on to its pillars, and a sufficient space left behind the month wheel and the rectangular piece of brass, its socket may be made to pump up and down on that of the month wheel, and at the same time carrying the segment back and forward with it: a pin in the month wheel stud keeps the month wheel socket always to its proper end-shake, notwithstanding any motion of the segment backward and forward. Below the rectangular piece on its socket, a small groove is turned out, for the purpose of a forked piece getting on it: this forked piece is formed on that end of the arm which lies along the fore plate, and on to the socket or centre of the month wheel.

From the preceding description, it is evident that when any of the elliptic plate pins come to press down that end of the upper arm which lies near and under them, the forked end will raise up the grooved socket, and the segment which is connected with it; hence the teeth of the segment will meet with pins which are at the back of the month ring, and by their means will turn the month ring. On the month wheel is fixed a pin, which, in common, shifts the day of the month ring; but in those months in which there are only 30 days, the pins in the elliptic plate, which press down the end of the arm, make the segment be pumped up only so far as to meet with one of the pins at the back of the month ring, which is a little longer than the other two; and one day being shifted by it, and another by the fixed pin in the month wheel, this makes the shifting from the 30th to the 1st day of the succeeding month.

The pin in the elliptic plate, for the month of February, being longer than the others, presses the end of the arm a little more down, consequently the pumping up of the segment must be to a greater height: by this means the three teeth on the segment get hold of the three pins on the back of the month ring; this, with the fixed pin in the month wheel, are ready to shift four teeth of the month ring, viz. from the 28th of February to the 1st of March; and by this very ingenious sort of mechanism, the month ring shows always the right day of the month, except on the 29th of February in leap years. It may be necessary to notice, that the fixed pin in the day of the month wheel must be placed at such a distance from the first tooth on the segment, as is equal to the space between the teeth on the segment: The month ring is not attached by rollers to the back of the dial in the usual way, but runs in four rollers, which are fixed on four brass studs on the fore-frame plate. This is for the conveniency of seeing more easily the operations of the segment with the month ring, when the segment is pumped up and down.

The construction of the month wheel, and the apparatus for shifting the month ring, will be better understood from No. 62, 2 and 3, where A, A, is the month wheel; B, B, two arms or crosses nearly similar to those of the month wheel, having a hole in the centre, which goes freely on the upper socket of the month wheel. On one of these arms is a segment of a circle, nearly of the same radius as that of the month wheel, having three teeth cut on it, like those of the month ring; $a, a,$ are two brass pillars rivetted on the upper side of the month wheel, the upper ends being formed into sort of pivots. On these and the month-wheel socket, the segment is made to move freely up and down. C is a rectangular piece of brass, into which a socket is rivetted, which moves up and down on the lower socket of the month wheel, having a groove turned out on it, receiving the forked end of the arm, which pumps it up and down; $b, b,$ are two small pillars, which are rivetted also into the rectangular piece of brass, having two holes in the month wheel, through which they pass easily up and down; the other ends of them go into the segment B B, and are screwed to it by means of two small screws. On one of the arms of the month wheel, is screwed a small knee'd sort of cock d, having a pin fixed in it, for turning the day of the month ring in the usual manner.

For an account of an equation clock by Henry Ward of Blandford, See *Trans. of the Society for Encouraging Arts, Manufactures, and Commerce. Vol. XXXII.* See also *Journal de Physique, Paris, par M. Abbé Rozier. Tom. XXXII. Part 1st*, for a description of a clock made by Robin of Paris going apparent time.

The following is a method that may be proposed to shift a day of the month ring, or a day of the month wheel, whose arbor carries a hand that will require no correcting except to February in leap years.

Take a wheel of 73 teeth, being the fifth part of 365, the number of days in a year; if a small star wheel of 5 is put on the arbor of a single threaded endless screw, working into the teeth of the wheel of 73, and one of the radii of the star wheel be turned every 24 hours, it is evident that five days will be required to move one tooth of the wheel of 73. Let a contrate web or rim be formed on one side of the wheel of 73; to a fixed stud, apply a double or jointed lever, one end of which is knee'd, the nib resting on the edge of the contrate rim, and occasionally falling into notches made in it. The other end, which is forked, takes in with a groove or notch, turned on the socket of a 24 hour wheel, with clockmakers commonly called the month wheel: on the knee'd end of the lever, falling into any of the notches, the forked end will rise and pump up the month wheel, which will take place at the end of the months having 30 days; the notch for the end of February is a little deeper, so as the month wheel may be pumped a little more up. In the month wheel which pumps up and down, there are four pins placed so as they may pitch in with four teeth of the month ring or wheel. The pins are of different heights; the longest is that which turns the month ring in ordinary; the next is a little shorter; these two take in with the ring when the month has 30 days, and turn it to the first day of the succeeding month; all the four take in with it at the end of February, and turn it from the 28th to the 1st of March: the last two pins are of the same height, and a little shorter than the shortest of the other two. The chief thing to be considered in this business, is the proportioning the distances of the notches in the contrate rim. There are seven months in the year consisting of 31 days each, four of 30 days each, and one, in common years, of 28 days. It will be found, when seeking for the proportions, that the screw must make 6.2 turns for each month of 31 days, for those of 30 days 6 turns, and for that of 28 days 5.6 turns. The number of turns required for the screw to make according to the respective months, being multiplied by the number of months, will give 73, the number of teeth in the wheel having the contrate rim on it, and which must make a revolution once in a year or twelve months. The number of turns which the screw must make in a year, is shown by the following operation: $6.2 \times 7 = 43.4$, $6 \times 4 = 24$, and $5.6 \times 1 = 5.6$. Now $43.4 + 24 + 5.6 = 73$, the number sought for. In setting off from the beginning of January, the nib of the knee'd piece will rest or be on the edge of the contrate rim until the 28th day of February; the screw in the meanwhile moving the wheel of 73, will bring the rim forward with a notch, into which the knee'd piece falling, the opposite or forked end of the jointed lever then pumps up the wheel with the four pins, and they turn the month ring from the 28th of February on to the 1st day of March. One side of the knee'd piece is bevelled, so as it may rise easily up again on the edge of the contrate rim, which moving forward, the nib keeps on the same plane, until the wheel of 73 has turned so far on as the 30th day of April: a notch at this time presents itself, and the knee'd piece drops into it; on being raised up, it keeps as before on the edge of the rim, until the 30th of June, when another notch comes; after which the knee'd piece will be on the rim until the 30th of September, and again from that to the 30th November. So that there is only five times in the year that the knee'd piece has to fall into the notches, whose distances are proportioned according to the number of turns the screw has to make during the intervening number of days. Two wheels of 24 hours each are required, one for turning the small star wheel, the other a pumping one for the month ring. The double or jointed lever would require a spring to press it not only into the notches, but also to keep it steady on the edge of the contrate rim. It may perhaps not be unnecessary to apply a jumper with a slender spring to the star wheel, to keep it in its place during the time when it is not turning, which is for the greater part of the 24 hours. In place of the pumping being made by the knee'd piece falling into notches, the same may be obtained by raised pieces, formed from the edge of the contrate rim, retaining planes for the nib to hold on; but this will give a contrary direction to the pumping, which any judicious workman can adapt to the plan of the motion he sets about. Seing the motion of the screw is so slow, the execution will require to be nicely done, so as to make the shifting at all times effectual.

Another way of shifting a day of the month ring right, except to February in leap years, may be done without the intervention of an annual wheel. Suppose the month ring to be turned by a pin in the month wheel in the usual way, when the month has 31 days, or even when it has 30 or 28 days. But in order to make the ring, on those months having 30 and 28 days, be turned to the first day of the succeeding month, the following, which is to be described, has been contrived. A star wheel of twelve radii and 3.7 inches in diameter, whose centre is 4.5 inches below that of the dial, concentric with it is a contrate rim or hoop 2.5 inches in diameter, and near to .3 of an inch deep. In the month wheel are four pins, equally distant from one another, so as to pitch equally and freely with the teeth of the month ring. The height of the first pin is about .3 of an inch, that of the second about .2 of an inch, and the next two .1 of an inch, or a very little higher. On the back of the month ring are three pins, the longest of which is near .4 of an inch in height, and placed near to the space which is opposite to the tooth for the 28th day; that is to say, on the left hand, when looking at the back of the ring, in the middle between the 28th and 29th tooth, the other two pins are about half of the height of the first, one of which is placed in the middle of the breadth of the ring, and below that space which is opposite the 30th tooth, the other is placed within a tenth of an inch to the outer edge of the ring, and under the middle of the space opposite the 31st tooth: one begins, the other terminates the motion of the star wheel at all times. The diameter of the month ring is about 8.6 inches, the breadth .7 of an inch, the breadth including the teeth .85 of an inch: These conditions, however, are not arbitrary. The lower edge of the ring is below the centre of the dial 3.1 inches. There is a long arm or double lever, whose centre of motion lies near to the fore-frame plate, and between the centre of the month wheel and that point, which is a tangent to the contrate rim on the star wheel, the whole length being 3.6 inches. That arm which comes to the centre of the month wheel, is forked at the end, and takes in with a groove in the month-wheel socket, and by a spring, which lies under it, the month wheel is made to pump up and down, requiring to have a thick month nut, unless the pin and segment, as described to the equation clock, were adopted. The other arm of the double lever has its end bent into a square hook or knee'd piece, whose nib rests always by means of the lever spring, on the edge or planes of the contrate rim, which is formed into steps and *notches with a plain bottom*. The steps are required only at the months having 30 days, and at February, having 28 days. The nib of the lever remains on the bottom or plane of the notches during the whole of the month, and the star wheel is then stationary; its motion takes place only at the time of shifting any of the twelve radii: when this happens at the end of the months having 31 days, the nib then moves along the plane or bottom of the notch. Above one of the radii, that which serves for the month February, a piece of brass is put, and prolonged a little beyond it; so that when the month-wheel pin comes to turn the ring from the 28th day, at that instant, the long pin on the ring meets with this piece of brass, and, carrying it on, makes the lever nib to rise up on one of the steps, where it remains for a while, and the month wheel being pumped up, all the four pins in it get engaged with the teeth of the month ring, and turn it forward to the first day of March; and, just about, or a little before the termination of the shifting, the outermost pin on the ring carries one of the radii (that in the line with the piece of brass,) so far on, as to make the nib to fall or drop from off the step into the plane of the succeeding notch, where it remains till the next shifting of the star wheel. When the month has 30 days, the pin in the middle of the month-ring's breadth is made, by means of the month-wheel pin shifting the ring, to push on one of the star-wheel radii; and this having a step here, the nib rises up on it, and remains so long as the ring is nearly shifted to the first day of the succeeding month. The pin on the outermost place on the ring always terminates the motion of the star wheel, and makes the nib fall when it happens to be on a step, there being no step to meet it when the month consists of 31 days. Not depending on very nice execution, this is perhaps the simplest and easiest way of making a shifting for the days of the month, requiring no correcting except in leap years.

The following are other two Methods for this purpose, which we used also to put in practice.

In one of these, the day of the month is shown by a hand from the centre of the dial, which makes two revolutions in 365 days, and points to two sets of circles of divisions near the outer edge of the dial. These divisions are made from the number 365 on the dividing plate, by taking them alternately, setting out from the twelve o'clock line on the inner circles of division, two 365th parts will be the first of January, and, continuing so on to the last day of June, will be 181 days, which will be short from the line or point set out from, by one division and a half; so that when the hand starts from the 30th of June, to the first of July, on the outer circles of divisions, it will then be half a division from the line set out from on beginning January; the 2d of July will be half a division beyond it; hence these last set of divisions will lie opposite the middle of the spaces of those divisions gone over in the first six months: by this means, the hand shows always to what day it is pointing, and also to what month. There is a small space between the two sets of divisions; the names of the first six months are on the inside of their circle of divisions, and those of the last six months are on the outside of theirs; the days are figured or numbered 10, 20, 30, or 31 and 28; the intermediate fives are distinguished by the division being prolonged a little outward on the outer divisions, and inward on the inner. To produce this motion for the hand, let a 24 hour wheel, having a pin in it, and near to its centre, taking into a ratchet or star wheel of 25, with a jumper and spring to press it on the ratchet-wheel teeth; concentric with the ratchet wheel is a pinion of 10, leading a wheel of 73, on whose socket is the day of the month hand, one of the star or ratchet-wheel teeth being turned every 24 hours, the jumper makes the hand to start daily over one of the divisions on the circles.

In the other method, the day of the month is shown on a moveable circle, whose revolution is made in 365 days. This circle should be as large in diameter as the square or circle of the dial, and its breadth fully 1.25 inch, and made to turn on rollers inside, or on the back of the dial. The inside edge of this plate or ring circle, is cut into 365 teeth, a pinion of 8, on whose arbor is a star wheel of eight radii, on which a jumper with a smart spring works; one of the radii of the star wheel, being turned daily by the month wheel, carries the circle on, by means of the jumper and spring, one 365th part of its revolution. On the annual circle are 365 divisions between circles, with the names of the months, numbered and figured much in the same way as in the former case; a small index, made from the opening in the dial, points to the divisions or days of the month; the pinion of 8 has one of its pivots run into the fore-frame plate; the pinion head pivot runs in the dial, so as to pitch the pinion with the teeth inside of the circle. The opening in the dial may be one fifth or sixth part of the circumference of the circle, in order to show the months coming on and going off. If the plate circle was made somewhat broader, the sun's equation and declination might be laid down on it.

There is no occasion to describe the common month-ring work, as it is well known to every clock maker.

Lunar Motion Work.

For a lunation consisting of 29 days and a half, let a twelve-hour wheel, with a pin near its centre, turn a tooth of a ratchet wheel of 59, having on its arbor a hand pointing to a circle divided into $29\frac{1}{2}$ for days, in which time the hand will make one revolution, and, in the interim, it shows the age of the moon. This, though not giving a lunation completely, is more commonly done by a large plate wheel having 118 ratchet teeth cut on its edge, and placed concentric with the circle of the arch of a clock dial; at which centre there is a stud, on this the plate-wheel socket turns, one of the ratchet teeth being turned every twelve hours by the pin in the twelve-hour wheel. Near to the edge of the plate wheel, is a circular space divided into twice $29\frac{1}{2}$ for the days of the moon's age; within the space are two full faces opposite one another, representing the moon, and coinciding nearly with the fifteenth divisions; a small index fixed at the top of the arch, pointing to the circle of divisions, shows the day of the moon's age.

On the line forming the upper side or square of the dial, coinciding with that of the diameter of the semi-circular opening in the arch of the dial, two semi-circular parts are formed from and above the line, whose diameters are equal to the moon faces, and as these, by the revolving of the moon plate, gradually emerge from or get behind the semi-circular parts, making the phases of the moon to be shown. It is usual to paint the ground of the moon plate a sky-blue, with a few stars of a gold or yellow colour on it.

A lunation of 29 days, 12 hours, 45 minutes, which is perhaps near enough for common ordinary purposes, may be given by a twelve-hour wheel, having, concentric with it, a lantern pinion of 4 leading a wheel of 45, on the axis of which is a pinion of 12 leading the moon plate, having 126 teeth cut on its edge. The pinion of 12 is keyed by means of its socket spring-tight on the wheel of 45, for the conveniency of setting occasionally the moon to the proper day of its age. The moon plate, with the opening in the arch, may be the same as before described, to show the age and phases.

Should greater accuracy, and a nearer approximation to a mean lunation be required, seeing it consists of 29 d. 12 h. 44 m. 2 s. 8283 dec., we refer to pages 66, 67, 68, 69, for the solution of a problem by *Camus*, to find the numbers of wheel teeth and pinion leaves that shall give a true lunation. And to pages 70, 71, and 72, for a lunation work by *Mudge*, that gives the time of a lunation extremely near; and also to pages 56 and 57, for the mode adopted by *Janvier* in his *Sphere Meuvante*, to find numbers for the wheels and pinions so as to get a lunation for it, which by him is said to consist of 29 d. 12 h. 44 m. 2 s. 52. $\frac{501}{583}$ th, assuming a true lunation to be 29 d. 12 h. 44 m. 2 s. 8283, and turning it into days and decimals of a day, we have 29.5305882905, &c. &c.; but as this number is great, and not very easily broken down into proper factors, let us take only as far as six of the decimal figures, and let it terminate at four instead of 8, which will give the lunation a very little in defect, and let us suppose a mover of 24 hours, we shall then have the fraction $\frac{1.000000}{29.530584}$ = $\frac{125000}{569133}$, which gives the eleven following quotients, viz. 29, 1, 1, 7, 1, 2, 14, 1, 1, 34, and from them forming alternate ratios in the manner which has formerly been shown: this done, if we take the seventh ratio $\frac{703}{20760}$, we shall obtain two pinions of 19 and 37, and two wheels of 120 and 173, which form a 24 hour mover, will give a lunation of 29 d. 12 h. 44 m. 2 s. 38975, which is only short of the true lunation $\frac{40935}{100000}$ of a second,—an error so small, as it would require above 67 days to amount to a second, and more than 11 years before it amounted to one minute.

On Time, and the Equation of Time.

A table of the equation of time becomes absolutely necessary for the practical artist when regulating his clock, whether he takes the sun's time from a sun-dial, a meridian line, or from a transit instrument. Time has always been measured and defined by the motions of the heavenly bodies, and particularly by the motion of the sun, as being the most regular in his *apparent* revolutions. An apparent day, however, or the interval between two successive transits of the sun's centre over the same meridian, is subject to continual variation, owing to the eccentricity of the earth's orbit, and obliquity of the ecliptic to the plane of the equator. These variations are inserted in a table, which is called a Table of the Equation of Time. The obliquity of the ecliptic is the angle made by the intersection of the equinoctial and ecliptic, or earth's orbit. At the beginning of the year 1815, this angle was 23° 27′ 46″.4, and which has been found to decrease about half a second annually, and at the end of the year 1825, it is 23° 27′ 41″.2. A mean day is the interval that would be observed between two successive transits of the sun's centre over the same meridian, if the earth's orbit was circular, and the sun always in the equinoctial. Thus, the intervals betwixt the transits would be all equal, such as are shown by an equal going clock, that counts 24 hours in a day, and 365 days, 5 hours, 48 minutes, 48 seconds in a year. A clock or watch thus set, is said to be adjusted to mean time.

The principal divisions of time, are the year and the day, which are measured by the apparent annual and diurnal revolutions of the sun. The day or the time which the sun appears to go round the earth, is divided by clocks and watches into hours, minutes, and seconds. The length of a tropical year, or the time the sun is in going from any point of the ecliptic to the same again, contains 365 days, 5 hours, 48 minutes, 48 seconds. And the siderial year, or the time which intervenes betwixt the conjunction of the sun, and any fixed star, to his next conjunction with the same star, contains 365 days, 6 hours, 9 minutes, 11.5 seconds. The difference betwixt the tropical and siderial year is occasioned by what is called the precession of the equinoxes, which is the falling back of the equinoctial points every year $50\frac{1}{4}$ seconds of a degree, or one degree in 72 years; so that in about 2160 years, these points change a whole sign in the zodiac.

Time is distinguished according to the manner of measuring the day, into *apparent*, *mean*, and *siderial*. Apparent time, also called *true Solar* and *Astronomical time*, is derived from the observations of the sun. Mean, or mean solar time, also called *equated time*, is a mean or average of apparent time, which is not always equal. Siderial time is shown by the diurnal revolution of the stars.

Mean time is deduced from apparent, by adding or subtracting the equation, as directed in the tables. A siderial day is the interval between two successive transits of a star over the same meridian, which interval is always uniform; for all the fixed stars make their revolutions in equal times, owing to their immense distance, and to the uniformity of the earth's diurnal rotation about its axis. The siderial day is shorter than the *mean solar day*, by 3 minutes, 56 seconds nearly. This difference arises from the sun's apparent annual motion from west to east, which leaves the star as it were behind. Thus, if the sun and a star be observed on any day, to pass the meridian at the same instant, the next day, when the star returns to the meridian, the sun will have advanced nearly a degree easterly; and as the earth's diurnal rotation on its axis is from west to east, the star will come to the meridian before the sun, and in the course of a year the star will have gained a day on the sun; that is, it will have passed the meridian 366 times, while the sun will have passed it only 365 times. Now, as the sun appears to perform his revolution of 360° in a year, or 365 days, 5 hours, 48 minutes, 48 seconds, he will describe 59′ 8″.3 of the ecliptic in a day, at a mean rate; and this space, reduced to time, is nearly equal to 3 minutes, 56 seconds, the excess of a mean solar day above a siderial day. Hence it appears, that the earth revolves 59′ 8″.3 more than once round its axis, or 360° 59′ 8″.3 in a mean solar day, and a complete revolution, or 360° in a siderial day; therefore, the length of a siderial day, in mean solar time, may be found by this proportion, as 360° 59′ 8″.3 : 360 : : $\overset{h.}{24}$: $\overset{h.}{23}$ $\overset{m.}{56}$ $\overset{s.}{4}$.1, the length of a siderial day in mean solar time, or the interval between two successive transits of a star over the same meridian.

From the above proportion results the following *general rule*, for converting siderial to mean time, and *vice versa*; as $\overset{h.}{24}$: $\overset{h.}{23}$ $\overset{m.}{56}$ $\overset{s.}{4}$.1 : : any portion of siderial time, to its equivalent in mean time; and as $\overset{h.}{23}$ $\overset{m.}{56}$ $\overset{s.}{4}$.1 : 24 : : any portion of mean time to its equivalent in siderial time. For *some neat Formulæ in this way, see Kelly's Spherics, page* 208, *Ed.* 4*th.*

The equation of time, or the difference between mean and apparent time, as already mentioned, arises from two causes, namely the obliquity of the ecliptic, and the eccentricity of the earth's orbit. The greatest part of the equation arises from the former of these causes, and is found, by converting the difference between the sun's longitude and his right ascension, as set down in the Nautical Almanack, into time. That part which arises from the latter of these causes, is obtained by converting what is called the *equation of the centre* into time. These two parts being added to, or subtracted from each other, according as they have like or unlike signs, from the absolute equation. By the *equation of the centre* is meant the difference between the sun's *true* and *mean anomaly*; these never being the same but when he is in perigee or apogee. *See this subject more at large in Lalandes' Astronomy, or any of the works on physical or practical Astronomy.*

Mean and *apparent* time, or the time shown by an equal going clock, and a true sun-dial, are never the same, except on four days of the year, and these are the 15th April, the 15th June, the 1st September, and the 24th December. From the 24th December to the 15th April, the clock will be before the sun; from the 15th April to 15th

June, the sun will be before the clock; from the 15th June to 1st September, the clock will again be before the sun; and from the 1st September to the 24th December, the sun will again be before the clock, and so on in the same order. See the following tables; or the equation in the Nautical Almanack with the daily differences, which are for noon at the Royal Observatory at Greenwich. These differences are convenient when using the equation at any place distant from the meridian of Greenwich. For example, the equation being wanted at Kingston, Jamaica, for the 6th December 1821, which at Greenwich, for the noon of that day, is 8 minutes, 42.5 seconds, and the daily difference is 25.8 seconds; Kingston is five hours, 7 minutes, and 2 seconds, in time west of Greenwich: Then say as 24 : 25.8 : : 5 7 2 : 5.5, which is subtractive from the equation, as it is on the decrease; this 5.5 seconds, then subtracted from 8 minutes, 42.5 seconds, the equation at Greenwich, gives 8 minutes 37 seconds, the equation at Kingston, and the equated time for that day there, will be 11 hours, 51 minutes, 23 seconds. From what has been done, the process is obvious when the longitude is east. A good deal of the foregoing on the equation of time, is from Carey's Elements of Astronomy, &c. and we shall take the same liberty with Mylne's Elementary Treatise on Astronomy, by copying from it the two following excellent tables.

TABLES OF THE EQUATION OF TIME.

1st, Arising from the Obliquity of the Ecliptic.

Dial Faster.	Dial Slower.	Dial Faster.	Dial Slower.
m. s.	m. s.	m. s.	m. s.
Mar. 21. 0 00	June 21. 0 00	Sept. 23. 0 00	Dec. 21. 0 00
25. 1 29	26. 1 48	28. 1 39	26. 1 48
30. 3 15	July 1. 3 32	Oct. 3. 3 15	31. 3 32
April 4. 4 46	7. 5 08	8. 4 46	Jan. 5. 5 08
9. 6 09	12. 6 35	13. 6 09	10. 6 35
14. 7 22	17. 7 48	18. 7 22	15. 7 48
19. 8 23	22. 8 45	23. 8 23	20. 8 45
24. 9 09	28. 9 26	28. 9 09	25. 9 26
30. 9 40	Aug. 2. 9 49	Nov. 2. 9 40	29. 9 49
May 5. 9 53	7. 9 53	7. 9 53	Feb. 3. 9 53
10. 9 49	12. 9 40	12. 9 49	8. 9 40
15. 9 26	17. 9 09	17. 9 26	13. 9 09
20. 8 45	22. 8 45	22. 8 45	18. 8 23
26. 7 48	28. 7 22	27. 7 48	23. 7 22
31. 6 35	Sept. 2. 6 09	Dec. 2. 6 35	28. 6 09
June 5. 5 08	7. 4 46	7. 5 08	Mar. 5. 4 46
10. 3 32	12. 3 15	12. 3 32	10. 3 15
16. 1 48	17. 1 39	17. 1 48	15. 1 39
			20. 0 00

2d, Arising from the inequality of the Sun's Motion.

Dial faster than Clock.		Dial slower than Clock.	
m. s.	m. s.	m. s.	m. s.
July 1. 0 00	Oct. 3. 7 43	Dec. 31. 0 00	Mar. 30. 7 43
7. 0 40	8. 7 42	Jan. 5. 0 41	April 4. 7 40
12. 1 19	13. 7 37	10. 1 22	9. 7 34
17. 1 57	18. 7 29	15. 2 02	14. 7 24
22. 2 35	23. 7 18	20. 2 41	19. 7 12
28. 3 12	28. 7 03	25. 3 19	24. 6 56
Aug. 2. 3 47	Nov. 2. 6 45	29. 3 56	30. 6 36
7. 4 21	7. 6 24	Feb. 3. 4 30	May 5. 6 14
12. 4 52	12. 5 39	8. 5 02	10. 5 50
17. 5 22	17. 5 32	13. 5 32	15. 5 22
22. 5 50	22. 5 02	18. 5 39	20. 4 52
28. 6 14	27. 4 30	23. 6 24	26. 4 21
Sept. 2. 6 36	Dec. 2. 3 56	28. 6 45	31. 3 47
7. 6 56	7. 3 19	Mar. 5. 7 03	June 5. 3 12
12. 7 12	12. 2 41	10. 7 18	10. 2 35
17. 7 24	17. 2 02	15. 7 29	16. 1 57
23. 7 34	21. 1 22	20. 7 37	21. 1 19
28. 7 40	26. 0 41	25. 7 42	26. 0 40

By comparing the two tables, it will appear that the difference between the clock and the dial is produced sometimes by one of the causes above mentioned only, but more commonly by both; that the effect of the one is often counterbalanced by the other; and that the action of both causes is sometimes combined. For example, the equation of time from the first cause, viz. the obliquity of the ecliptic, is on the 21st March, 0 minutes 0 seconds; but from the second cause, viz. the unequal motion of the sun, is 7 minutes 37 seconds. On the 5th May, the dial, by the first cause, is faster than the clock 9 minutes 53 seconds, and slower by the second cause, 6 minutes 14 seconds; therefore the difference between them is the true equation, viz. 3 minutes 39 seconds. On the 2d of November, the dial from the first cause is 9 minutes 40 seconds faster than the clock, and by the second cause, 6 minutes 45 seconds also faster; consequently the sums, when added, will give the true equation, viz. 16 minutes 25 seconds. By combining in this way the two parts of the equation, subtracting them when the dial is slower from the one cause, and faster from the other, and adding them when the dial is faster or slower from both causes, the true equation may be found for any day in the year, and in the foregoing tables for every fifth day of the year. But in order to save the time of the practical artist, we shall subjoin an extended equation table for every day in the year, calculated for the second year after leap year.

The following Tables give the time that a well-regulated clock or watch should be at, for every day of the year, when the sun's centre is on the meridian; and in place of a common equation Table, these give what may be called *Equated* Time, and will serve for ordinary purposes, through the greater part of the nineteenth century. Those who take in the Nautical Almanack will have no need of them.

TABLE OF MEAN TIME AT TRUE NOON.

Days.	JANUARY. H. M. S.	FEBRUARY. H. M. S.	MARCH. H. M. S.	APRIL. H. M. S.
1	0 3 49.3	0 13 57.3	0 12 43.3	0 4 4.9
2	0 4 17.6	0 14 5.1	0 12 31.1	0 3 16.7
3	0 4 45.7	0 14 12.0	0 12 18.6	0 3 28.6
4	0 5 13.5	0 14 18.1	0 12 5.7	0 3 10.6
5	0 5 40.9	0 14 23.5	0 11 52.3	0 2 52.8
6	0 6 7.7	0 14 28.0	0 11 38.4	0 2 35.2
7	0 6 34.1	0 14 31.7	0 11 24.1	0 2 17.8
8	0 7 0.0	0 14 34.6	0 11 9.3	0 2 0.6
9	0 7 25.4	0 14 36.5	0 10 54.2	0 1 43.6
10	0 7 50.1	0 14 37.7	0 10 38.7	0 1 26.8
11	0 8 14.3	0 14 38.1	0 10 22.8	0 1 10.3
12	0 8 37.9	0 14 37.9	0 10 6.6	0 0 54.1
13	0 9 0.9	0 14 36.8	0 9 50.1	0 0 38.1
14	0 9 23.3	0 14 34.9	0 9 33.3	0 0 22.4
15	0 9 44.9	0 14 32.1	0 9 16.3	0 0 7.1
16	0 10 5.8	0 14 28.7	0 8 50.9	11 59 52.1
17	0 10 26.0	0 14 24.4	0 8 41.3	11 59 37.4
18	0 10 45.5	0 14 19.6	0 8 23.5	11 59 23.0
19	0 11 4.3	0 14 14.1	0 8 5.5	11 59 9.1
20	0 11 22.4	0 14 7.8	0 7 47.3	11 58 55.6
21	0 11 39.7	0 14 0.7	0 7 29.0	11 58 42.5
22	0 11 56.2	0 13 53.1	0 7 10.6	11 58 29.8
23	0 12 11.9	0 13 44.9	0 6 52.1	11 58 17.5
24	0 12 26.7	0 13 36.0	0 6 33.5	11 58 5.7
25	0 12 60.7	0 13 26.7	0 6 14.8	11 57 54.4
26	0 12 54.0	0 13 16.1	0 5 56.1	11 57 43.7
27	0 13 6.5	0 13 6.2	0 5 37.4	11 57 33./
28	0 13 18.3	0 12 55.0	0 5 18.7	11 57 24.
29	0 13 29.3		0 5 0.1	11 57 14
30	0 13 39.4		0 4 41.6	11 57 l
31	0 13 48.8		0 4 23.2	

TABLE OF MEAN TIME AT TRUE NOON.

Days	MAY. H. M. S.	JUNE. H. M. S.	JULY. H. M. S.	AUGUST. H. M. S.
1	11 56 57.7	11 57 19.9	0 3 16.5	0 5 58.7
2	11 56 50.2	11 57 28.9	0 3 28.2	0 5 55.3
3	11 56 43.2	11 57 38.3	0 3 39.7	0 5 51.3
4	11 56 36.7	11 57 48.1	0 3 50.9	0 5 46.7
5	11 56 30.7	11 57 58.2	0 4 1.8	0 5 41.5
6	11 56 25.4	11 58 8.6	0 4 12.3	0 5 35.7
7	11 56 20.6	11 58 19.4	0 4 22.5	0 5 29.3
8	11 56 16.5	11 58 30.5	0 4 32.3	0 5 22.3
9	11 56 12.8	11 58 42.0	0 4 41.7	0 5 14.7
10	11 56 9.7	11 58 53.6	0 4 50.7	0 5 6.4
11	11 56 7.2	11 59 5.5	0 4 59.2	0 4 57.5
12	11 56 5.2	11 59 17.5	0 5 7.2	0 4 48.1
13	11 56 3.9	11 59 29.7	0 5 14.8	0 4 38.1
14	11 56 2.9	11 59 42.0	0 5 22.0	0 4 27.5
15	11 56 2.8	11 59 54.4	0 5 28.6	0 4 6.4
16	11 56 2.9	0 0 7.0	0 5 34.6	0 4 4.8
17	11 56 3.8	0 0 19.7	0 5 40.1	0 3 52.6
18	11 56 5.1	0 0 32.4	0 5 45.2	0 3 39.9
19	11 56 7.0	0 0 45.2	0 5 49.8	0 3 26.8
20	11 56 9.4	0 0 58.0	0 5 53.8	0 3 13.1
21	11 56 12.4	0 1 10.9	0 5 57.3	0 2 59.0
22	11 56 16.0	0 1 23.8	0 6 0.2	0 2 44.5
23	11 56 20.0	0 1 36.6	0 6 2.6	0 2 29.5
24	11 56 24.6	0 1 49.4	0 6 4.5	0 2 14.0
25	11 56 29.8	0 2 2.2	0 6 5.8	0 1 58.2
26	11 56 35.5	0 2 15.0	0 6 6.5	0 1 42.0
27	11 56 41.7	0 2 27.7	0 6 6.6	0 1 25.4
28	11 56 48.2	0 2 40.2	0 6 6.2	0 1 8.5
29	11 56 55.5	0 2 52.5	0 6 5.2	0 0 51.2
30	11 57 3.2	0 3 4.6	0 6 3.6	0 0 33.4
31	11 57 11.3		0 6 1 5	0 0 15.3

Y

TABLE OF MEAN TIME AT TRUE NOON.

Days	SEPTEMBER H. M. S.	OCTOBER H. M. S.	NOVEMBER H. M. S.	DECEMBER H. M. S.
1	11 59 57.1	11 49 47.4	11 43 45.1	11 49 10.3
2	11 59 38.6	11 49 28.5	11 43 44.1	11 49 33.2
3	11 59 19.7	11 49 9.9	11 43 43.3	11 49 56.7
4	11 59 0.5	11 48 51.6	11 43 44.3	11 50 20.8
5	11 58 41.0	11 48 33.7	11 43 45.6	11 50 45.5
6	11 58 21.3	11 48 16.0	11 43 47.7	11 51 10.6
7	11 58 1.4	11 47 58.7	11 43 50.6	11 51 36.2
8	11 57 41.3	11 47 41.9	11 43 54.3	11 52 2.4
9	11 57 20.9	11 47 25.5	11 43 58.9	11 52 29.1
10	11 57 0.3	11 47 9.4	11 44 4.4	11 52 56.2
11	11 56 39.6	11 46 53.8	11 44 10.7	11 53 23.6
12	11 56 18.8	11 46 38.6	11 44 17.8	11 53 51.4
13	11 55 57.8	11 46 23.9	11 44 25.7	11 54 19.6
14	11 55 36.8	11 46 9.7	11 44 34.5	11 54 48.1
15	11 55 15.7	11 45 56.2	11 44 44.1	11 55 17.0
16	11 54 54.5	11 45 43.2	11 44 54.6	11 55 46.1
17	11 54 33.3	11 45 30.7	11 45 6.0	11 56 15.4
18	11 54 12.2	11 45 18.8	11 45 18.2	11 56 44.9
19	11 53 51.1	11 45 7.5	11 45 31.3	11 57 14.7
20	11 53 30.0	11 44 56.9	11 45 45.2	11 57 44.7
21	11 53 9.0	11 44 47.0	11 45 59.9	11 58 14.7
22	11 52 48.1	11 44 37.7	11 46 15.5	11 58 44.8
23	11 52 27.3	11 44 29.2	11 46 31.9	11 59 14.9
24	11 52 6.7	11 44 21.4	11 46 49.1	11 59 45.0
25	11 51 46.2	11 44 14.3	11 47 7.1	0 0 15.1
26	11 51 25.8	11 44 7.8	11 47 25.8	0 0 45.2
27	11 51 5.6	11 44 2.0	11 47 45.2	0 1 15.1
28	11 50 45.7	11 43 57.0	11 48 5.4	0 1 44.8
29	11 50 26.0	11 43 52.8	11 48 26.3	0 2 14.3
30	11 50 6.6	11 43 49.4	11 48 48.0	0 2 43.7
31		11 43 46.8		0 3 13.0

A TABLE

Of the Acceleration of the fixed Stars, for 32 Days.

Days.	H.	M.	S.	Days.	H.	M.	S.
1	0	3	55.9	17	1	6	50.3
2	0	7	51.8	18	1	10	46.2
3	0	11	47.7	19	1	14	42.1
4	0	15	43.6	20	1	18	38.0
5	0	19	39.5	21	1	22	33.9
6	0	23	35.4	22	1	26	29.8
7	0	27	31.3	23	1	30	25.7
8	0	31	27.2	24	1	34	21.6
9	0	35	23.1	25	1	38	17.5
10	0	39	19.0	26	1	42	13.4
11	0	43	14.9	27	1	46	9.3
12	0	47	10.8	28	1	50	5.2
13	0	51	6.7	29	1	54	1.1
14	0	55	2.6	30	1	57	57.0
15	0	58	58.5	31	2	1	53.9
16	1	2	54.4	32	2	5	48.8

The stars will accelerate 3 minutes, 55.9 seconds, every 24 hours, on a clock keeping mean solar time; if a clock is made to keep siderial time, it will give the time marked in the Tables, according to the number of days. The sun's right ascension, as given in the Nautical Almanack, is the siderial time when the sun's centre is on the meridian. For example, on the 21st of March, 1825, a clock keeping siderial time should be set 0 hours, 2 minutes, 13.6 seconds, at the instant of the sun's centre being on the meridian.

Having mentioned to our ingenious friend, Mr. Scott, that he might take time, (though not very nicely) by fixing in any window shutter having a south exposure, a piece of brass with a small hole in it, to allow the sun's rays to come in to a dark room against a plummet line whose shadow would be seen on the opposite side of the room; by perseverance, he brought it by degrees to a very great nicety. We have known him take a transit of the sun by it to half a second—that is to say, there was only half a second of difference between the time taken by the sun's semi-diameter, in passing from the first limb to the sun's centre, and from the centre to the last limb. This must be allowed to be a great degree of precision. It is well known, that by any common meridian line, or sun-dial, that time cannot be taken nearer than to 8 or 10 seconds, if even so near. We shall give in his own words how the apparatus for this purpose is constructed.

Directions for fitting up a Substitute for a Transit Instrument.

" Having obtained, by some of the means usually resorted to, a correct meridian line; for which purpose there should be fixed in a temporary yet steady manner, and perfectly level, a piece of very flat and even deal-board about three feet long, in the window recess, and as near as may be in the line of that part of it where the instrument is intended to be erected: on this let the meridian line be carefully laid down.

" The next thing to provide is a piece of good steel-wire, about 3.5 inches long and .25 of an inch in diameter; one end of which should be forged either into a square adapted to a key, or else into a flat plate, that it may be turned by the finger and thumb. A very fine and equal screw is then to be formed upon the wire, after which, let it be put into a lathe, and about .4 of an inch of its point (or other end,) turned down into a cylinder, about .2 of an inch diameter; in the middle length of which let there be hollowed out a small groove about .02 of an inch in diameter, and about the same depth; this groove should be very well cleaned out and polished, as on it the plummet after described is hung.

" The next thing to procure, is a stout brass stud with a sole, either firmly rivetted on or cast in the solid; this stud should be at least 1.5 inch high above the sole, and .75 of an inch in breadth and thickness; it is then to be drilled at an equal distance from the top and sides, and carefully tapped so as accurately to fit the screw on the steel-wire: four holes for screw nails being now made in the sole, and the steel-wire screwed into the stud, the whole should be firmly fixed up in the suffit of the window, pretty near the sash, in such a manner, that the steel-wire screw may lie quite horizontally, and in a due east and west direction; and when equal portions of the screw are seen on each side of the stud, the plummet shall, after being hung on the groove, be perfectly co-incident with the meridian line drawn on the board.

"The plummet is thus formed.—Select as many of the smallest and blackest, yet stout horse hairs, as will be sufficient fully to reach from the top to the sole of the window, and having joined these together, by what are termed fisher's knots, (whereby the small ends may be closely cut off, without the risk of any of the knots slipping,) form upon one end a loop, which is to pass over the groove on the cylindrical part of the screw: on the other end a double or triple knot is to be cast: a short conical leaden plummet of two or three ounces weight is then to be bored down through its apex, .25 of an inch deep, by means of a fine heckle tooth, or some other small pointed instrument; the knotted end of the hair is then to be inserted, and the orifice of the hole gently beat round, so as closely to embrace the hair, taking care that it shall not be chafed or injured, lest it should be unable to support the weight of the plummet; this is perhaps the neatest way of doing it, but it requires address and management.

Another way, however, is to take a common pin, and after cutting off its point, turn it up into a hook a little bent backwards, that the centre of the hook may be in a line with the straight shank, and inserting the head and part of the shank into the hole in the plummet, close the lead round in the same manner as directed for the hair, and hang it by a loop similar to that made on the other end of the line. The plummet should be immersed in a small jar of water to promote its steadiness.

"A piece of well-seasoned wood, about five inches broad, three inches thick, and sufficiently long to reach from the floor to (within the thickness of a board placed on its top, for the double purpose of fixture, and preventing injury to) the ceiling, is now to be prepared; one edge and side of which should be planed quite straight and smooth, for the purpose of facilitating its being placed perfectly perpendicular: Take then three slips of hard wood, two of them about five feet long, so shaped, that when fixed to the post, they shall form a hollow dovetail groove; to receive the third, which should be about 18 or 20 inches long, and at least one inch broad on the upper or narrow surface, the lower surface and sides fitting spring-tight into the groove formed by the other two pieces, which are to be planted on the north side of the upright post, or that next to the observer, close to the straight planed edge, and reaching within a few inches of the floor. That this sliding piece may move easily, although tightly fitted to the groove, it should be well rubbed over with black lead: and it would not be amiss that it were made fully thicker than the pieces which form the groove, in order that its upper surface may be rather above the plane of the other two.

"The use of this sliding piece, (to which the sight or eye-piece is attached,) is, by being pushed down its groove, the sun may be seen through the eye piece, even at his greatest north declination; it moreover serves when any of the knots on the hair plummet should by accident intervene between the observer's eye and the sun's disc, to bring a straight part of the hair opposite to the sun by sliding it up or down little more than a quarter of an inch.

"The eye-piece is formed as follows:—A circular plate of brass, about two inches diameter, and .08 of an inch in thickness, terminates on one side in a sort of pillar about one inch long, all neatly dressed up and smoothed; in the centre of the plate is drilled a small hole, not exceeding .016 or .018 of an inch in diameter, and the burr well cleaned away; on that side of the plate destined to be farthest from the observer, the small hole is to be deeply and widely counter-sunk; yet leaving a small part of the original bore quite entire; two pretty thick slips of brass, undercut so as to form a dovetail, are then to be pinned or otherwise fixed on the counter-sunk side of the plate, at right angles to the line of the pillar, and so far separate on each side of the centre hole, as will be sufficient to admit a dovetail brass frame, hereafter to be described. At the other extremity of the pillar is formed a stout pivot, fitting into a socket; the pivot has a groove turned upon it, in which the end of a screw passing through the socket works, keeping it in its place, only admitting the eye-piece to turn on its axis, so as it may be made directly to face the sun whatever be his altitude.

"This socket constitutes a part of the remainder of the eye-piece whereby it is attached to the wooden slider; on the front or outside of the socket is prolonged or continued a pretty stout brass plate, either soldered on or cast in the solid, and this carries a hollow cylinder, which is made to turn, (and secured from coming off by a screw, nut, and washers,) on a strong pin or stud fixed by means of a sole to the sliding wood; this last part serves to turn up the eye-piece to be out of the way when not in use; and when let down for the purpose of making an observation, the bottom of the socket rests on the edge of the upright post, and keeps the pillar of the eye-piece always in a horizontal position.

"With regard to the brass frame, it should be in length about the diameter of the circular brass plate of the eye-piece, besides a prolongation formed to serve as a handle to push it up and down in the groove; its broader or under surface should be in width about .6 of an inch, and, consequently, the upper surface as much narrower as the slopped sides of the two pinned on dovetailed pieces, will naturally require it to be; in this upper surface is formed a hollow or recess, nearly the length and breadth of the frame, and of sufficient depth, having only a narrow rim below to receive and support a slip of the finest thin and equal crown glass of like size, and above it a spring-wire to keep it in its place, similar to the wires used for the ivory slips of microscopes, only a good deal stronger.

"This slip of glass is to be smoked by a lamp or candle, so that there shall be a gradual diminution of shade from one end to the other, commencing in the deepest, and ending in the slightest tinge; by these means, the sun may be viewed in all stages of his brilliancy, from that of his utmost splendour, to his being barely visible through thin clouds. And herein is a great advantage over using Claude Lorraine glasses, as in an instant all the intermediate shades between the lightest and very deepest may be obtained.

"All things being now prepared, the wooden post is to be set up at the distance of about 4 feet north of the plummet, observing that the smoothed side, bearing the dovetailed groove and eye-piece, is to be placed as before directed, and the straight edge brought just so near to the meridian line, that when the eye-piece is folded down, it, the meridian line, and the hair plummet shall be exactly in one plain.

"As to the mode of fixing the upright post, after being carefully set quite perpendicular and exactly in its proper place, the best way, is, by means of square-knee'd pieces of iron, screwed at top and bottom to the straight edge, the floor and ceiling, as well as on each side close to the straight edge, without otherwise attempting to confine the rest or remainder of the sides, or even the remote edge, except by fillets nailed to the floor and ceiling; that, should any cling or contraction take place in the upright post, the straight edge shall at all times maintain its perfect perpendicularity and first position.

"It may be necessary to observe, that in order to verify the true meridian position of the plummet and eye-piece, it would be as well to compare the result of several trials of it, with the time given by a good regulator or astronomical clock, allowing of course for the equation, and after being perfectly satisfied of its having been brought, by means of the adjusting screw which moves the plummet, precisely into the proper line, then remove the board on which the meridian was laid down, and endeavour to find some fixed mark or object, at the distance of 30 or 40 yards, with which the hole in the eye-piece and the hair co-incide; and this will, at all future times, serve as a mean of readjusting the instrument.

"With such an apparatus as above described, after a very little practice, the sun's meridian passage may easily be taken to at least within 2 seconds; and if the observer has much turn for accuracy, it may generally be done within even less than one. It is not, however, so well adapted for taking the meridian passage of the fixed stars; for besides the difficulty of throwing a sufficient light upon the hair, to cause it to be distinctly seen at night, the small hole in the eye-piece transmits so few rays from a star, even of the first magnitude, that it seems to dwindle into the obscurity of one of the sixth or seventh. But for observations of the sun, the smaller the hole, and the greater the distance between it and the hair plummet, so much more accuracy will be obtained in the observations. Nevertheless, should the hole be found inconveniently small, it can easily be a little widened by a small broach.

"*Note.*—In placing the smoked glass in the frame, the obscured side should be placed under, resting on the narrow rim, so that when the frame is put into the dovetail groove, there may be no risk of the coat of smoke being injured or rubbed off. J. S.

"*Edinburgh, November,* 1825."

CHAPTER XVI.

On Repeating Clocks and Watches.

To those who do not sleep well, nothing can be more convenient and useful than a repeater, whether it is in a watch, or in a small fixed clock. A history of this invention is given by Mr. Derham, in his *Artificial Clockmaker.* Berthoud, in his *Histoire,* has given the following account of it, which is taken chiefly from Derham:

"The art of measuring time," says Berthoud, "was again enriched with two fine and useful inventions, before the end of the seventeenth century. One was the equation clock; the other, which is the most precious, and of the most general utility, is that kind of striking which has been called repeating. It is of the most ingenious mechanism, and, when added to a clock, serves to make known at pleasure, at every instant of the day or night, without seeing the dial, the hour, and parts of the hour, which are pointed out by the hands of the clock. Both these inventions are due to the English artists."

" The clocks in question here," says Derham, " are those which, by means of a cord, when pulled, strike the hours, the quarters, and even some the minutes, at all times of the day and of the night. This striking, or repeating, was invented by a Mr. Barlow, towards the end of the reign of King Charles II. in 1676."

It is not mentioned by Derham whether Barlow was a watchmaker or not. We have heard it said by old watchmakers, that he was a clergyman. This seems in some measure confirmed, by his having applied to Tompion to make his repeating watch, when he was about to obtain a patent for the invention.

" This ingenious invention," continues Berthoud, " which had not been before thought of, made at the outset a great noise, and much engaged the attention of the London watchmakers. On the idea alone which each formed of it, they all set to work to try the same thing, but by very different ways; whence has arisen that great variety in the work of repeating motions, which was seen at this time in London.

" This discovery continued to be practised in chamber clocks until the reign of James II. It was then applied to pocket watches. But there arose disputes concerning the author of the invention, of which I shall simply relate the facts to the reader, leaving him to judge of it as he thinks proper."

Towards the end of the reign of James II., Mr. Barlow applied his invention to pocket watches, and employed the celebrated Tompion to make a watch of this kind according to his ideas; and, at that time, conjointly with the Lord Alleborne, Chief Justice, and some others, he endeavoured to obtain a patent for it.

Mr. Quare, an eminent watchmaker in London, had entertained the same notion some years before, but not having brought it to perfection, he thought no more of it until the noise excited by Mr. Barlow's patent awakened in him his former ideas. He set to work, and finished his mechanism. The fame of it spread abroad among the watchmakers, who solicited him to oppose Barlow's privilege to obtain a patent. They addressed themselves to the court; and a watch of the invention of each was brought before the King and his council. The King, after having made trial of them, gave the preference to that of Mr. Quare.

The difference between these two inventions is this:—The repetition in Mr. Barlow's watch was effected by pushing in two small pieces, one on each side of the watch-case, one of which repeated the hour, the other the quarters. Quare's watch repeated by means of one pin only, fixed in the pendant of the case, which, being pushed in, made the repetition of the hours and quarters, the same as is done at present, by pushing in once only the *pendant*, which carries this pin.

This invention of repeating the hours in small fixed clocks and in watches, was soon known and imitated in France; and these machines were very common in 1728, when the celebrated Julien Le Roy, was much occupied in their improvement. It was at this period that he made the repeating clock, of which a description is given at the end of *The Artificial Rule of Time*. This was made for the bed-chamber of Louis the Fifteenth of France.

The first repeaters, even those of Quare, as well as others, gave the number of the hour according to the length pushed in of the pendant, which was very inconvenient, by striking improper hours, when the pendant was not pushed home to the snail. This frequently caused mistakes in regard to the true hour, which ought to have been given. We have heard our predecessor, Mr. James Cowan of Edinburgh, who went to Paris in 1751, for improvement in his profession, *and who executed some pieces under Julien Le Roy*, say, that Le Roy introduced the mechanism into the repeater, which prevented the watch from striking any thing but the true hour. This, we think, was done to the repeating clock for Louis the Fifteenth's bed-chamber. In this construction, it struck none, unless the cord or pendant made the rack go fully home to the snail, when it struck the true hour, which was a very considerable improvement. The piece employed for this purpose is called the *all or nothing* piece. Considering the great talents which Julien Le Roy possessed, we have no reason to doubt of this improvement being his.

"Although the *repetition*," says Berthoud, "such as is now in practice, is a particular kind of striking, its mechanism differs totally from that of the striking clock. 1*st*, Because every time that it is made to repeat, the main repeating spring is wound up, whereas in the common striking part, the main-spring is wound up only once in eight days, fifteen days, or a month. 2*d*, In the repetition we must substitute for the count-wheel, which determines the number of blows that the hammer must strike, a contrivance wholly different. The first author of this ingenious mechanism, substituted for the count-wheel, a piece, to which, in regard to its form, he gave the name of the snail. The snail is a plain piece, divided into twelve parts, which is formed of steps, and they come gradually in from the circumference towards the centre. It makes a revolution in twelve hours. Each of the steps is formed by a portion of a circle. Every time that the clock is made to repeat the hour, the pulley which carries the cord is connected with and turns a pinion, which leads a rack, whose arm falls on one or other of the steps of the snail, on the cord being pulled, and regulates the number of blows which the hammer ought to give; as the snail advances only one step in an hour, it follows, that if it is wanted to be made to repeat at every instant in the hour, we shall have always the same number of blows of the hammer; whereas, in setting off the wheel work of an ordinary striking movement more than once in the hour, we should have a different hour. A count-wheel would then not be fit for a repetition. The mechanism of the repetition has a second snail, which bears four steps also in portions of a circle, to regulate the blows which the quarter hammers must give.

The count and hoop wheels, and locking plate of the old striking clocks, for regulating the number of blows of the hammer, and locking the wheel-work, was excellently contrived. It had only one inconvenience, for when set off by accident, it would prematurely strike the hour to come: this made it requisite to strike eleven hours before it could be brought again to the hour wanted. Had it not been for the invention of the repeater, these would have continued, and would have been still made in the modern clocks, the same as in the ancient ones. But the snail of the repeater showed that it could be adapted for regulating the number of blows for the hammer of a common striking clock, and has prevented the inconvenience of striking over a number of hours before the clock could be set to the right hour again.

"We owe to Julien Le Roy," continues Berthoud, "the suppressing of the bell in repeating watches, a change which has made these machines more simple, by rendering the movement larger, more solid, and less exposed to dust. These watches, which he called *raised brass edges*, are of a more handsome form. From the time of this celebrated artist, all the French repeaters have been made according to this model; but in England, where repeating watches were invented, they make them for the most part with a bell; and in Spain, this construction is still more preferred. In repeating watches without a bell, the hammers strike on brass pieces, either soldered or screwed to the case. Repeating watches with a bell, have also, *as well as those without one*, the property of being umb, that is to say, repeating at pleasure, without the hammers being allowed to strike on the bell or brass pieces."

This effect is produced after the pendant is pushed in, by putting the point of the fore finger on a small spring button that comes though the case. Being a little pressed in, it opposes a piece against the hammers, which prevents them from striking either a bell or the brass pieces inside of the case; by which means the blows for hours and quarters are *felt*, though they cannot now be easily heard. These kind of repeaters are found very convenient for those who are deaf, as during the dark of night they can feel the hour at a time when they cannot *see* it. These *sourdine or* dumb parts have been left off of late years; yet they are not without their advantages, as have been now shown.

The late Julien Le Roy had tried to render repeating watches more simple by suppressing the wheel-work which serves to regulate the intervals between the blows of the hammers, and also the main repeating spring. This celebrated artist succeeded in constructing new repeating movements, of which several have been made on this plan. But it appears that the public have not found them very convenient, so that this mode of constructing them has not been imitated.

The only one of this kind which we have seen of Julien Le Roy's, was a very good one, in the possession of John Rutherfurd, Esq. of Edgerston. Although they have not been copied, they certainly deserve to be so.

Repeaters have, of late, been made with springs in place of bells, (a very ingenious substitute, it must be allowed,) of Swiss invention, though they are as superfluous as bells. Considerable trouble is necessary in making and placing them. They ought never to be recommended, if it could be avoided; but we are often obliged to yield to the fashion of the day, even when it does not coincide with our own opinion. When three or more hammers are used to give the quarters, we then would admit springs in place of bells, as, when they are well tuned, they give a most beautiful chime for the quarters. Were bells introduced for this purpose, they would give a clumsy appearance to the watch. Julien Le Roy saw good reasons for setting aside the bell; and no plan of a repeater will ever be superior or equal to that of his, which Graham frequently adopted in many of his watches, though his repeating motions were different: Julien Le Roy's having what is called the *plain*, and Graham's th *stogden* motion, a most ingenious contrivance, requiring great judgment in planning, and nice execution in making it This motion well adapted for half quarters. Though we have hardly see

French repeater with it, yet it is not unknown to the foreign artists, as appears from Thiout's Work. *Tom. II. p. 367, Plate XXXVI. fig. 3. Paris,* 1741. This repeating motion must have got its name from the inventor. Upon inquiring after him when in London, in the year 1770, we learned, with much regret, that he had died a few months before, in a charity work-house, at a very advanced age. The name appears to be German; but whether he was a foreigner or Englishman, we have not been able to learn.

We shall now lay before our readers a complete description of the repeating movement and motion-work of clocks and watches, which we have taken principally from Berthoud's *Essai sur L'Horlogerie*.

Clocks that have a striking part, strike of themselves the hours, and some strike the hours and half hours; those having a repeating part, *strike the hours the same as other clocks, but the repeating part acts only on a cord connected with that particular portion of the work being pulled.* In repeating watches, when the pendant or pusher is forced home, one hammer strikes the hour, which the hands point to on the dial, and the quarters are struck by the blows of two hammers. We shall see by the description of a repeating clock, how this is produced; but before doing so, we shall give a general idea of this ingenious mechanism, which is nearly the same for a clock as for a watch.

In order to make a clock repeat the hour, (see Plate XII. No. 64.) the cord X is drawn, which is wound round the pulley P, fixed on the arbor of the first wheel of a particular wheel-work, the sole object of which is to regulate the intervals between each blow of the hammer. The arbor of this wheel has on it a hook, which takes hold of the inner end of the repeating main-spring, contained in the barrel R, No. 63. On this arbor is also a plain wheel G, having 15 pins in it, which serve to raise the hammers, twelve of them for the hours, and three for the quarters. The number of blows that the hour hammer strikes, depends on the greater or less course which the pin-wheel G is made to take when pulling the cord; and this course depends itself on the hour pointed at, by the hands on the dial. Thus, if the cord is drawn when it is twelve hours and three quarters, the pin-wheel is obliged to make an entire revolution; at this instant the repeating spring brings it back, in which course it makes the hammer give twelve blows for the hours, and then three for the quarters. To distinguish the quarters from the hours, a second hammer is added, which with the first, makes a double blow at each quarter.

It must now be shown by what means the course which the pin-wheel takes, is regulated on the cord being pulled, and how it is proportioned to the hour which the hands point to on the dial.

A wheel S, or minute wheel of the dial work, No. 65, has its arbor prolonged and outside of the back of the pillar plate. *In this case, and in common, the repeating work is put between the dial and fore plate of the frame.*[*] It carries the piece $s\ h$, No. 64, the pin of which C, turns the star wheel E, which takes twelve hours to go once round, and carries with it a piece L, called the hour snail, divided into twelve parts, tending to the centre of the star wheel. Each of these parts forms different depths, like as many steps, which gradually come nearer the centre, and which serve to regulate the number of the hours which the hammer must strike. For this purpose, the pulley P carries a pinion a, which pitches in with a portion of a wheel C, No. 64, called the *rack*. When the cord is pulled, and the rack is in consequence made to advance towards the snail, the arm b stops on such a step of the snail as it may meet with in its course; and, according to the depth of this step, the hammer strikes a greater or less number of blows. It will strike only one hour if the arm b of the rack is stopped on the step 1, the most distant one from the centre, as then the pin wheel getting only one of its pins engaged, the hammer strikes only one blow. If, on the contrary, the step 12, which is the deepest and nearest the centre, is met by the arm b in its course, which cannot get there until the pin wheel shall have made one turn, then the spring in the barrel bringing it back, will cause the hammer to give twelve blows.

It remains to be seen how the quarters are repeated. The piece s, No. 64, which turns the star wheel, and takes one hour to make a revolution, is carried by another snail h, *called the quarter snail,* formed by four divisions, making three paths or steps, on one of which, when the cord is pulled, the arm Q of a piece Q D, called the finger, places itself, and according as the step is nearer or farther from the centre of the snail, the end D of the finger finds itself more or less aside from the centre a of the pulley P, so that when the pull of the cord is finished, and the pulley returns by the force of the spring in the barrel, one of its four pins acts on this finger, namely, the one which it finds at a distance from the centre a, which answers to the elevation of the arm D, and this is what determines the blows for the quarters: Thus, when the finger is applied on the pin nearest

---

[*] This part of the repeating work, with the dial wheels, go under the general name of the motion work.

the centre of the pulley, the hour hammer strikes only the number of hours that the snail L, and the arm b of the rack have determined. If the finger is placed on the second pin, it does not stop the pulley till after the hour hammer has struck the hour, then a quarter, and so on for the three quarters. Having thus given an idea of the essential parts of a repeater, let us now proceed to a particular description of a repeating clock with an anchor 'scapement.

Plate XII. Nos. 63, 64, and 65, represent all the parts of a repeating clock seen in plan. No. 63 represents the wheels and pieces contained within the frame, or what are put between the two plates, with the exception of the anchor A, which is placed in this way, to show the 'scapement.

The wheels B, C, D, E, F, are those of the movement. B is the barrel which contains the clock main-spring. The great wheel is fixed to the bottom of the barrel B, and pitches into the pinion of the wheel C, which is the great intermediate wheel, D is the third or the centre or minute wheel. *Our workmen give the name of minute-wheel to what Berthoud gives the name of the returning-wheel; and what he calls the minute-wheel, obliges us to make it the centre or third wheel, in conformity to his language.* E, the fourth wheel, or that where the contrate wheel was usually placed. F the ratchet or 'scapement wheel. The centre wheel D makes a revolution in an hour. The pinion on which this wheel is fixed, has its pivot prolonged, which passes through the fore plate No. 65. This arbor or pivot enters spring tight into the cannon of the minute-pipe wheel m, seen in perspective figure 2, which makes also by this means a turn in an hour. This cannon carries the minute-hand; and its wheel m pitches into the returning or minute-wheel S, of the same number of teeth, and of the same diameter as the wheel m. The pinion of the wheel S makes twelve revolutions in the time that the hour-wheel C makes one. The wheel C, which is one of the dial wheels, takes then twelve hours to make one revolution, and is that which carries the hour hand.

It must be observed, with regard to these three wheels, C, m, S, which are called the dial wheels, that they are always the same, whether the clock is a striking one or a repeating one: their effect causing the hour or dial wheel C to make a revolution in the space of twelve hours. The wheels G, L, M, N, No. 64, and the fly V, form the wheel-work of the repeating part. The object of this wheel-work, as has already been mentioned, is to regulate the interval between each blow of the hammer. The ratchet R, and the pin wheel G, are fixed on the same arbor in common with the wheel L, within whose centre it freely turns. The spring R and the click c, are placed on the wheel L.

When the cord X, which is wound round the pulley P, No. 64, is pulled, the ratchet R, No. 63, fixed on the same arbor as the pulley, retrogrades, or goes backward, and the inclined planes of the teeth raise the end of the click at O. Then the repeating spring brings back the ratchet, whose teeth butt or stop against the end of the click, which carries about the wheel L, and the wheel work M, N, V: but while the ratchet R thus carries the wheel L, and while the pin wheel G, and the pulley P, which are fixed on the same arbor, turn also, the pins of the wheel G act on pieces m, n, No. 63, whose arbors prolonged carry the hammers l, m, No. 63. Each piece m, n, is pressed by a spring to bring forward the hammers, after the pins had made them rise up or go backward. The spring r is only seen, which acts on the piece m.; that which acts on the piece n is placed under the plate which carries the motion work, No. 64. The piece o serves to communicate the motion of that of m to the arbor or piece n, which carries the hour hammer.

The piece, (bascule,) or see-saw m x, No 63, is moveable on the arbor which carries the quarter hammer. On this arbor below m x, an arm like that of m moves, on which act the three pins placed on the under side of the wheel G. These three pins serve to raise the quarter hammer fixed on the arbor which carries the piece m. It is this hammer which the spring r presses. When the cord is pulled, the wheel G is made to go backward, the pins of which come to act on the back part of the arm m, which yields and comes from m to x. The small arm which is below for the quarters, makes the same motion; and when the repeating spring brings back the wheel G, a small spring, which acts on these pieces m, obliges them to get engaged between the spaces of the pins, and to present the right planes on which these pins act to raise the hammers.

The pulley P, No. 64, carries the pinion a, which pitches into the rack b C, the effect of which is, as has been said, to make the point b go upon the steps of the snail L, and determine the number of blows which the hour hammer must give.

The star wheel E, and the snail L, are fixed together by two screws. This star moves on a screw stud V, No. 64, attached to the piece T R, moveable itself in T. This piece forms, with the plate, a small frame, in which the star E and snail L turn. One of the radii or teeth of the star bears on the jumper Y, which is pressed by the spring g. When the pin C of the quarter snail turns the star-wheel, the jumper Y moves out, receding from V, the centre of the star, until the tooth of the star arrives at the angle of the jumper, which happens when it has made half of the way which it ought to do. Having escaped this angle, the inclined plane of the jumper pushes it behind, and makes it precipitately finish the other half; so that from the changing of one hour to another, that of the star and of the snail is done in an instant, which is when the minute-hand points to the 60th minute on the dial.

The jumper finishing thus in turning the star wheel, each tooth placed in *c* comes on the back of the pin *c*, and makes the *surprise i*, to which it is fixed advance. The surprise is a thin plate, adjusted on the quarter snail; it turns with it by means of the pin which comes through an opening made in the surprise: the advance which the star-wheel teeth causes the surprise to make, serves to prevent the arm Q of the finger from falling into the step 3, which would make the three quarters repeated when at the 60th minute. As soon as the star changes the hour, it then obliges the *surprise* to advance to receive the arm Q; so that if the cord is pulled at this instant, the hammer will strike the precise hour.

The arm Q and the finger are moveable on the same centre When we have drawn the cord, and when the pins of the pulley have freed or left the finger at liberty, then the spring *p* makes the arm Q fall on the quarter snail, and the finger D presents itself to one or other of the pins in the pulley. These two pieces can turn one on the other, and be moved separately. This serves in the case where the arm Q going to fall on the step A of the quarter snail, and the finger D being engaged in the pins of the pulley, this arm bends and yields to the pins of the pulley, which at this instant cause it to retrograde, or go backward; it is necessary that the pin for the present *in hold* can make the finger move separately from the piece Q. The spring B brings back the finger D as soon as the pin has retrograded, so that it may present itself to the pin which stops for the hour alone, or for the quarter, if the arm falls on the step 1, &c.

Having pointed out the most essential parts of the repetition, there remains only *one* of which an idea must be given, and which we shall endeavour to make the reader understand. This is the *all or nothing*, which has this property, that if the cord is not fully drawn, so as to make the arm *b* of the rack C press on the snail L, the hammer will not strike, so that by this ingenious mechanism the piece will repeat the exact hour; if otherwise, it will not repeat at all.

· We have seen, that when the cord X is pulled, the pin-wheel G oversets the piece *m* and makes it come to *s*; and that before the hammer can strike, a small spring must bring back the piece *m* to put in holding with the pins; after that, it is easy to see that if, in place of allowing the piece m to take its situation, it were made still more to be overset, the repeating spring bringing back the pin-wheel, the hammer would not strike while this piece remained over-set: this is precisely the effect that the piece TR (No. 64.) produces, which is on that account called the *all or nothing* piece. This is effected in the following manner: the piece m (No. 68.) carries a pin, which goes through the plate by the opening o; if we pull the cord, the pin-wheel causes the piece m to move, as we have just now described. The pin which it carries comes to press against the end o of the all or nothing piece, and sets it aside, so that the pin shall arrive at the extremity, which is a little inclined; but the spring d, tending to bring back the arm o, the inclined plane obliges the pin to describe still a small space which takes the arm m (No. 63.) entirely out of the reach of the pins, so that the hammer cannot strike unless the pin is disengaged from the end of the arm o. To effect this, the arm of the rack must come and press on the snail L, which moves on a stud V, fixed to the all or nothing piece TR. Now, in pressing the snail, the arm o of the pin is set aside, which, getting free, gives liberty to the arm m to present itself to the pins of the wheel G, and to the hammers, that of striking the hours and quarters given by the dial work and hands.

The ratchet R (No. 63.) is that of the click and ratchet work of the movement, o is the click, r the spring. The ratchet R is put on a square of the barrel arbor; this square being prolonged, serves to wind up the spring by means of a key; B is the barrel in which the spring or motive force for the repetition must be put; V is a screw called the eccentric or pivot-carrying piece; on the part which enters with force into the plate, a little out from the centre of the arbor of the screw, a hole is made for the pivot of the anchor A. In making this screw turn, the pivot of the arbor of the anchor is made to go farther or nearer the centre, and consequently the anchor itself, so that the points of the pallet take more or less in, according as it is required with the teeth of the 'scapement wheel. A, (No. 64.) is the cock of the scapement, it carries the silk thread or spring, to which the pendulum is suspended. One of the ends of the silk thread is attached to the arbor c, which is called *avance or retard*, (*fast or slow*;) the other end of this arbor goes through to the dial, and is squared to receive a small key. By this means we can turn the arbor c, to any side, so as to lengthen or shorten the silk thread, which serves to suspend the pendulum, whose length is changed by this method.

The anchor A, (No. 63.) is fixed on an arbor similar to that for a seconds pendulum. This arbor carries the fork T, which gives motion to the pendulum. The pivot which this arbor carries at the end where the fork is, enters into a hole made in the cock A.

1 represents in perspective the wheel D, whose revolution is performed in an hour; it is the arbor of it that carries the wheel m. (No. 65.) This wheel m is seen in perspective in 2, whose canon serves to carry the minute-hand; 3 represents in perspective the wheel S of (No. 65.) It is the arbor of this wheel prolonged, which passing to the motion work, carries the quarter snail 4 (No. 64.) The pinion of this wheel S, pitches into the hour-wheel seen in perspective 4; and it is on the socket of this wheel that the hour hand is adjusted or fixed.

It will be seen from the preceeding description, that the pieces of the repeating motion work are here placed on the back of the pillar plate. Placing them on the fore plate will make no difference.

We shall now proceed to describe a repeating watch, with a horizontal or cylindrical 'scapement of Graham's.

What has been said concerning the repetitions in pendulum clocks and the simple or plain watch, being once well understood, the reader will have no difficulty in comprehending the mechanism of a repeating watch, which is only on a small scale what the clock is on a great scale.

No. 66. of Plate XIII. represents the wheel-work of the movement and of the repetition, and all the pieces which are put within the frame plates. There is a distinction here between the wheels,—those of the movement, or which serve to measure the time, as the wheels B, C, D, E, F, and those of the repetition, which serve to regulate the interval between the blows of the hammer; such are the wheels a, b, c, d, e, f, whose assemblage is called the little wheel-work, or runners.

The spring of the movement is contained in the barrel A; B is the great or fusee wheel, C the centre or second wheel, whose arbor prolonged carries the canon pinion, on which the minute-hand is fitted and adjusted; D is the third wheel; E the fourth wheel; and F the cylinder 'scapement, or balance wheel. The fusee I is adjusted on the great wheel B, a spring-tight collet and pin keeping the wheel to its place on the fusee; the chain is wound round on the fusee, and holds likewise of the barrel. The hook O of the fusee serves to stop the hand, on the watch being full wound up, by the hook stopping against the end of the *guard de gut stop, (the name it got before the chain was put to the fusee; the modern name of it*

z 2

is the fusee stop,) c, (No. 67.) attached to the other plate: its effect is the same as in the plain watch. No. 66 represents the cylinder 'scapement, of which a description has already been given in page 227.

B is the balance fixed on the cylinder; F is the cylinder wheel, which is represented as tending to act on the cylinder, and cause vibrations to be made by the balance. None of the pieces are drawn here, such as the cock, slide-curb, and pendulum, or spiral spring, as they would have rather made the 'scapement part obscure. The wheel work or runners of the repetition, is composed of five wheels *a, b, c, d, e,* and the fly-pinion *f,* and of four other pinions. The effect of this wheel work is to regulate the interval between each blow of the hammer: so that if the first wheel *a* is made to have 42 teeth, the second *b* 36, the third *c* 33, the fourth *d* 30, and the fifth *e* 25; and moreover, if all the pinions into which these wheels pitch have six leaves or teeth, then in the time that the first wheel *a* makes a turn, the pinion *f* will make 4812¼ revolutions; but the ratchet R, which the first wheel *a* carries, is commonly divided into 24 parts, the half of which are afterwards taken away, in order that there may remain only 12 to strike 12 blows for the 12 hours. If then we divide 4812 by 24, we shall have the number of turns that the fifth pinion makes for each blow of the hammer, which gives 200¼ turns of the pinion *f* for one tooth of the ratchet R.

The first wheel *a,* or great wheel of the striking part, carries a click and a spring, on which acts a small ratchet, put under the ratchet wheel R, which forms click and ratchet work, like what has been seen in the first wheel of repetition, which has the same use; that is to say, when we push the pendant or pusher, the ratchet R retrogrades, without the wheel *a* turning; and the spring which is in the barrel B, (No. 67,) bringing back the ratchet R, on whose arbor *g,* the inner end of the spring is hooked; the small ratchet comes butt against the click, and turns the wheel *a*; and the ratchet R makes the hammer M to strike, whose arm *m* is engaged with the teeth of this ratchet.

The spring *r* attached to the plate (No. 67,) acts on the small part *n* of the arm *m,* (No. 66.) The effect of this spring is to press the arm *m* against the teeth of the ratchet, so that when we make the watch to repeat, the ratchet R retrogrades, and the spring *r* brings always back the arm *m,* in order that the teeth of the ratchet may make the hammer to strike. Let us now pass on to the description of the motion work.

No. 68 represents that part of a repeater which is called the dial or motion work. It is seen in the instant where the button or pendant is just pushed home to make it repeat. In first taking off the hands, and then the screw which fixes the dial of repeating watches, we will see the same mechanism that this figure represents. This is the kind of repeating motion work most generally adopted; it is solid and of easy execution. P is the ring or bow to which the pendant shank or pusher is attached, and this enters into the socket O of the watch-case, and moves within its whole length in tending towards the centre. It carries the piece p, which is of steel, and fixed in the pendant shank, both composing the pusher; the under side is filed flat. A plate of steel, fixed to the case inside, prevents it from turning round, and permits it to move lengthwise only. The end part of the steel in the pusher is formed so that it cannot come out of the case socket, this being also prevented by the small steel plate.

The end of the piece p acts on the heel t of the rack C C, whose centre of motion is at y, and at whose extremity c, is fixed one end of the chain S S. The other end keeps hold of the circumference of a pulley A, put by a square on the prolonged arbor of the first wheel of the runners. This chain passes over a second pulley B.

If then we push the pusher P, the end c of the rack will describe a certain space, and, by means of the chain s s, will cause the pulleys A B to turn. The ratchet R, (No. 66.) will also retrograde, until the arm b of the rack comes upon the snail L; then the main spring of the repetition bringing back the ratchet, and the pieces which it carries, the arm m will present itself to the teeth of the ratchet, and the hammer M will strike the hours, the number of which depends on the step of the snail, which is presented to the arm b.

In order to have a better idea of the effect and disposition of this repetition, it is only necessary to look at (No. 68.) where the rack y c is seen in perspective; the hour snail L, and the star wheel E; the pulleys A and B, the ratchet R, the wheel a, the part of raising m n of the hour hammer; these are the principal parts of a repetition, which are drawn as if they were in action.

The snail L is fixed to the star E by means of two screws; they both turn on the pivot formed from the screw V, carried by the all or nothing piece T R, moveable on its centre T; the all or nothing piece forms with the plate a sort of frame, in which the star and hour snail turn. Let us now see how the quarters are repeated.

Besides the hour hammer M, there is another hammer N, (No. 66.) whose arbor or pivot comes up within the motion work, and carries the piece 5 6, (No. 68.) The prolonged pivot of the hour or great hammer passes also within the motion work, and carries the small arm q: these pieces 5, 6, and q, serve to make the quarters strike by double blows. This is the effect of the quarter rack Q, which has teeth at the ends F and G, that act on the pieces q, 6, and cause the hammers to strike. This piece or rack Q, is carried about by the arm k, which the arbor of the ratchet R has on it, by a square above the pully A, in such a manner, that when the hours are repeated, the arm k acts on the pin G fixed in the quarter rack, and obliges it to turn and raise the arms q and 6, and consequently the hammers.

The number of quarters which the hammers must strike, is determined by the quarter snail N, according to the depth of the steps h, 1, 2, or 3, which it presents: the quarter rack Q, pressed by the spring D, retrogrades, and the teeth of the rack engage more or less with the arms q, 6, which get also a retrograde motion, and are brought back by the springs 10 and 9: The arm k, bringing back the quarter rack, its arm m acts on the extremity R of the all or nothing T R, the opening of which at a, traversing against a stud fixed to the plate, allows R to describe a small space: the arm m, coming to the extremity of R, this last pressed by the spring i at, is made to return into its place, so that the arm m rests on the end R, and by this the quarter rack cannot fall or retrograde, unless the all or nothing piece is pushed aside. The arm u, carried by the quarter rack, serves to overturn or set aside the raising piece m. (No. 66.) *which is moveable on the arbor of the hour hammer*, whose pin 1 comes up within the motion work; so that when even the hours and quarters are repeated, the quarter rack still continues to move a little way, and the arm u turns aside the raising piece m, by means of the pin 1, which comes within the motion-work, and by this it is put from having any holding with the ratchet R, so long as the all or nothing T R does not allow the quarter rack to retrograde or fall, which can only happen in the case when, having pushed home the pendant against the snail, the arm b of the rack C C presses the snail, and makes it describe a small space at the extremity R of the all or nothing: then the quarter rack will fall and disengage the backs or lifting pieces, and the hammers will strike hour and quarters, given by the snails L and N.

The great hammer carries a pin 3, (No. 68.) which comes up to the motion-work, through an opening marked 3, (No. 68.) the spring r acts on this pin, and causes the great hammer to strike. This hammer carries another pin 2, which passes also through to the motion-work by an opening 2, (No. 68); it is upon this that the small tail of the raising piece q acts, to make it give blows for the quarters: the small hammer has also a pin which passes through to the motion-work by the opening 4; it is upon this pin that the spring 7 presses, to cause the quarter hammer to strike. The spring S is the spring jumper, which acts on the star wheel E. 3 represents the canon pinion, and the quarter snail N, seen in perspective. The quarter snail N is rivetted on the canon pinion C, the end of which, D, carries the minute-hand; the snail N carries the surprise S, the effect of which is the same as that for the repeating clock, that is to say, when the pin O of the surprise shifts the place, or causes the star to advance, and the jumper having done turning it, one of the teeth of the star comes to touch the pin O, which is carried by the surprise, and causes the part of the surprise Z, (No. 68.) to advance; so that when the arm Q of the quarter rack falls on this part Z, and prevents it from falling on the step 3 of the snail, by this the piece repeats only the hour. The changing from one hour to another is by this way made in an instant, and the watch strikes the hour exactly as marked by the hands. The socket or canon of the canon pinion C D, 3, is slit, in order that it may move spring tight on the arbor of the second wheel, on which it enters with a degree of stiffness or friction slight enough to be able to turn easily the minute-hand to either side, by setting it back or forward according as it may be required, which sets also the hour-hand to the hours.

It is proper here to undeceive those who think that they injure their watches in setting the minute-hand backward. In order to convince one's self that there is nothing in this, it is sufficient to remark the position which the pieces must have in a repeating motion-work, when it has to repeat the hour, when the pendant or pusher has brought back and set aside all the pieces which communicate with the snails L, N; for at this time there is no communication or connection between the pieces of the movement and those of the motion-work, but that of the pin O of the snail or surprise, with the teeth of the star wheel E, which nothing can prevent from retrograding. If then the minute hand is made to make a complete turn backward, the pin O will also make one of the teeth of the star retrograde; and if the watch is made afterwards to repeat, it will strike always the hours and quarters as marked by the hands; but it must be observed, that if the hands were turned in the same instant that the watch is made to repeat, they would then be prevented. It is necessary therefore, before touching the hands of a repeating clock or watch, to wait till it has repeated the hour, so that all the pieces shall have taken their natural situations.

It is easy to conclude from this, that since, with a repeating watch we can set backward or forward the minute-hand, according as it may be required, we may, with much greater reason, do this in a plain watch where no obstacle is opposed to it.

As to the hour-hand of a repeating watch, it ought never to be turned, without that being done by the minute-hand alone; except in that case where the repeater does not strike the hour marked by the hour-hand, when it would be necessary to put it to the hour which the repeater strikes.

When the repeater gets of itself deranged, by the hour-hand not according with the hour which the watch strikes, it is a proof that the jumper S, or the pin O of the snail, do not produce the effect required.

The returning or minute wheel 5, of 40 teeth, is placed, and turns on the stud 12, (No. 68.) which is led by the canon pinion N, of 10 leaves; the minute wheel pinion of 12 leads the hour-wheel of 36, causing it to make a revolution in 12 hours, and the canon pinion makes 12 revolutions for one of the hour-wheel; it is the socket of the hour-wheel which carries the hour hand. The raising or lifting pieces *n*, (No. 66.) can only describe a small arc, which permits the ratchet R to retrograde; and so soon as the mover brings it back, the arm 1 of the raising piece draws the hammer M. 2 represents the under side of the all or nothing, with the two studs; one U as a centre on which it moves, and the other *n* on which the star and snail turn, the hole *e* of this piece allows the square of the fusee of the movement to come through, and lastly passing through the dial, serves for winding up the watch. W, (No. 68,) is the locking spring and bolt; this is what prevents the movement from opening out of the case.

Y is a small cock or bridge which keeps the rack to its place, and prevents it from getting away from the plate, permitting it to turn only on its own centre.

All the parts of the repetition or motion work which have been described, are placed on the back of the pillar plate, and are covered by the dial; so that between the plate (No. 68.) and the dial, there must be an interval to allow sufficient play for the motion work. It is for this purpose that a piece is destined, which is not represented here, and which is called the brass edge. This is a sort of circle or ring, into which the circumference or edge of the pillar plate is sunk a little way, with which it is kept fast, by means of keys, or griffs 13 and 14. The brass edge is covered by the dial, fixed on the brass edge, by means of a screw.

A repeater is made to strike the hour which it indicates the moment we press in the pendant; so that the machine must be contrived in such a way, that it may be easy to push in the pendant, and that the blows of the hammers may be the strongest possible. With respect to the first, that depends on two things, the given force of the spring, and the length of the pusher; that is to say, the space described, and the manner of making the pusher act on the rack. With regard to the last, the rack must be placed in such a manner, that the point of contact of the pusher follows the arc described by the rack, in such a way that the force shall not be decomposed, so that the action of the hand on the pusher shall be exerted wholly upon the rack.

With regard to the pusher, its length depends on the point where it acts on the rack, that is to say, according as farther or nearer the centre of motion. It is obvious, that if it acts near the centre, more force is required, and it will describe a less space, and *vice versa*. As to the force of the blow of the hammer, it is limited by the force of the repeating main-spring, and by the force that the runners require to move or keep them in motion; for it is clear that it is only the excess of the force of the spring over the resistance of these wheels that can be employed to raise the hammer. The number of blows of the hammer, for one revolution of the ratchet, determines again the force of the blow.

CHAPTER XVII.

On Thermometers, Pyrometers, and the expansive ratio of Metals, &c.

Before giving descriptions of compensation pendulums, it will be proper to take a review of Thermometers, their different scales, and corresponding degrees, because they are required, when making trials of the expansion of metals, by the application of heat to them, when placed for this purpose in a Pyrometer. We shall give an account of the result of such experiments as have been made in this way by sundry philosophers, leaving the artist to adopt any of them which he pleases. They will show what has progressively been done, and by getting a general knowledge of the relative expansion of metals, he will be better enabled to construct compensation pendulums, on such principles as may seem to him the best calculated to obtain the end required.

Fahrenheit's thermometer is used in Britain, at least it is the one in most general use. The space on the scale of it, between the freezing and boiling points, is divided into 180 degrees, beginning at the temperature produced by mixing snow and common salt together, which is 32 degrees below freezing; of course the freezing point is marked 32°, and the boiling point 212°. The thermometer known by the name of Reaumur's was in fact constructed by De Luc, and used in France before the revolution; it is still used in Italy, Spain, and in general throughout the most part of the continent of Europe, even in Russia where that of De Lisle's was contrived. The scale of Reaumur's between the freezing and boiling points, is divided into 80 degrees, the freezing point being marked zero or 0, and the boiling point 80°, consequently 180 degrees of Fahrenheit is equal to 80 degrees of Reaumur, or 18 of Fahrenheit is equal to 8 of Reaumur, or 9 of F. equal to 4 of R.; therefore $F = \dfrac{9 R}{4} + 32$. Then 2.25 degrees of Fahrenheit is equal to 1 degree of Reaumur. 27 degrees of Reaumur's thermometer, the height which Berthoud raised it to, in his experiments on the expansion of metals, will be found to be equivalent to 92°.75 of Fahrenheit; or $92.75° - 32 = 60.75$ degrees, the whole range of the difference of temperature made use of in his experiments. We believe that this was also the extent taken by Mr. Troughton with his superlative pyrometer; for these reasons, it may be proper to take the expansive ratios of brass and steel, as given either by Berthoud or Troughton, seeing their experiments did not go so far as boiling water, yet far enough to give such proportions sufficient to fit up a compensation pendulum. A pendulum may sometimes be exposed to a cold below the freezing point, and at other times to a greater degree of heat than 92.75° of Fahrenheit; a range of 60.75° should surely be enough for this purpose.

The thermometer of Celsius is used in Sweden. It has been used also in France since the Revolution, under the name of *thermomètre centigrade*. In it the space between the freezing and boiling point is divided into 100; the freezing point is marked zero, the boiling point 100. Consequently the degrees of Fahrenheit are to those of Celsius as $180 : 100 = 18 : 10 = 9 : 5$; that is, 9 degrees of Fahrenheit are equal to 5 of Celsius. Therefore to reduce the degrees of Celsius to those of Fahrenheit, we have $F = \dfrac{9 C}{5} + 32$, and 1.8 degree of Fahrenheit is equal to one degree of the centigrade thermometer. It may be observed, that it was the fertile genius of Dr. Hooke that suggested the freezing and boiling of water, as fixed points of temperature, to include a scale marked with the various degrees.

These being the principal thermometers now in use, the temperature indicated by any of them, may be reduced into the corresponding degrees of the others, by means of the following simple theorems, in which R signifies the degrees on Reaumur's scale, F those of Fahrenheit, and S those of Celsius or the Swedish thermometer.

1st, To convert the degrees of Reaumur into those of Fahrenheit.
$$\frac{R \times 9}{4} + 32 = F.$$

2d, To convert the degrees of Fahrenheit into those of Reaumur.
$$\left(\frac{F-32}{9}\right) \times 4 = R.$$

3d, To convert the Swedish degrees into those of Fahrenheit.
$$\frac{S \times 9}{5} + 32 = F.$$

4th, To convert Fahrenheit into Swedish. $\left(\frac{F-32}{9}\right) \times 5 = S.$

5th, To convert Swedish into those of Reaumur. $\frac{S \times 4}{5} = R.$

6th, To convert Reaumur's degrees into Swedish. $\frac{R \times 5}{4} = S.$

For those unacquainted with the algebraic expressions of arithmetical formulæ, it may be necessary to explain, in words, one or two of these theorems. Case 1st, Multiply the degrees of Reaumur by 9, divide the product by 4, and to the quotient add 32, the sum expresses the degree on the scale of Fahrenheit. Case 2d, From the degree of Fahrenheit subtract 32, multiply the remainder by 4, and divide the product by 9, the quotient is the degree according to the scale of Reaumur.

Self-registering thermometers have been contrived by several; for an account of one by the late Alexander Keith, Esq. of Ravelstone, *See Nicholson's Journal*, vol. iii. 4to. Series. *Or Edinburgh Philosophical Transactions*, vol. iv.

For the following on thermometer scales, we are indebted to our ingenious friend Mr. Scott.

" Although Fahrenheit's scale coincides in many instances with degrees on the centigrade and Reaumur, yet the only points which are characterised on Fahrenheit, which agree with points on the other scales, without fractional parts, are those of freezing and boiling water, as seen below.

	Fahrenheit.	Centigrade.	Reaumur.
" Freezing	32°	0	0
" Temperate	48	$8\frac{8}{9}$	$7\frac{1}{9}$
" Agreeable	64	$17\frac{7}{9}$	$14\frac{2}{9}$
" Very warm	80	$26\frac{6}{9}$	$21\frac{3}{9}$
" Blood heat	96	$35\frac{5}{9}$	$28\frac{4}{9}$
" Fever heat	112	$44\frac{4}{9}$	$35\frac{5}{9}$
" Water boils	212	100	80

" Therefore, if Fahrenheit is right in his scale of temperatures, there is a want in the other two, in as much as fractions of a degree are required to point out the most usual known temperatures. But, as Fahrenheit's scale commences at a degree of cold which seldom or never is known in Europe,—perhaps it would be better to make his scale begin at freezing with O, and ascend to 180° for boiling water, and the degrees below O or freezing, might be made negative, as is done in the others; freezing and boiling water being points with which we are familiar. (A sketch of the proposed improvement of Fahrenheit's scale, see Plate XIV.) It is done by simply deducting 32° from all the points of Fahrenheit's usual scale. Were such a one adopted, there is no doubt but it would soon supersede the present mode; it is both more natural, and agrees with the two extreme points, so well defined. For scales of the three thermometers, and the formulæ for reducing the degrees of one scale into those of another, six cases being given, with their solution, see Plate XIV.

Godfroi Wendelinus, or Vendelinus, Canon of Conde, in Flanders, who published a dissertation on the obliquity of the ecliptic in 1626, seems to have been the first who observed, that by changes of temperature, metals changed their lengths; and Muschenbrock appears to have been the first who made experiments with a machine which he called a pyrometer, to try the effects of heat and cold on various metals: an improved pyrometer was made soon afterwards by Mr. John Ellicott. See *Muschenbrock's Phil.* vol. I. p. 202. *Riccioli's Alm.* I. 109. *Weidler,* p. 457. *Gass. op.* Tome V. p. 525.

A curious fact is published by De Luc. A brass rod, which he used as a thermometer, became in summer *habitually* longer; that is to say, that after being for some time lengthened by heat, it did not contract by the application of cold to its former length, but continued somewhat longer. In winter the contrary phenomenon took place. After being contracted by cold, it did not return to its former length on the application of heat, but kept somewhat shorter. A leaden rod showed these effects in a greater degree. Glass has not this quality De Luc suspects this property, is inversely as the elasticity of bo dies. Glass is perfectly elastic, and lead is less elastic than brass. *Jour de Phys.* xviii. 369. The compound pendulum by Smeaton has a glass rod, and pendulums of this kind have been observed to do uncommonly well. Can this arise from the principle noticed by M. De Luc?

Dr. Ure, an eminent chemist, observed something of this kind to have taken taken place in zinc. See his Chemical Dictionary, article *Caloric*. If the experiment was pushed to a great length, this property might be perceived in other metals; it was found even in steel by Berthoud.

Zinc, from this cause, may be reckoned a metal unfit for a compensation pendulum. The zinc tube pendulum we found to do extremely well, as did also the zinc bar one contrived by Mr. Henry Ward, who was a man of very considerable talent. We shall give an extract of what he says on this matter in his pamphlet, published from the Transactions of the Society for the Encouragement of Arts, Manufactures, and Commerce, for the year 1807. "It has been the opinion of some mechanists, that zinc is an unfit substance for a compensation pendulum, because they have thought it too soft for the purpose, and that, after being heated or cooled to a considerable degree, it does not return to its original dimensions. If that was really the case, no doubt but it would be a general one, common to all metals in a greater or less degree; but from the experiments and observations I have made on zinc pendulums, I am fully satisfied there is no foundation whatever for such an opinion. Some time in the latter part of the last summer, I however noticed a circumstance that made me doubt the matter; for, when I first used any zinc pendulums, I could never bring the clock to keep the same rate for two days together, but that it was continually retarding, whether I used the lamp or not; and had I not before observed a similar effect on a lever pendulum, that was made of brass and steel, I should have ascribed the cause wholly to the softness of the zinc bar; but by constantly comparing its daily rate with one that had been going a longer time, I found that this retarding property gradually wore off, and in less than a month, would become quite settled to the rate that it would afterwards keep. By subsequent experiments with the lamp too, I have constantly found, that all the pendulums I have hitherto tried, kept precisely the same rate, both during the time they were heated (provided they were properly adjusted) and afterwards, as they had done before. The cause of this retardation appears to me to be, that the points of contact of the different pieces which compose the pendulum, are more closely connected after a little time than they were at first; that is, those points of contact do, by the weight of the ball, yield to each other in a small degree, until they get a broader bearing."

Tables of the Expansion of Metals.

FERGUSON's—Iron and Steel as 3.   ELLICOTT's—Gold - 73.
          Copper - 4½.   Silver - 103.
          Brass - - 5.   Brass - - 95.
          Tin - - 6.   Copper - 89.
          Lead - - 7.   Iron - - 60.
                                        Steel   - 56.
                                        Lead - 149.

The following is Smeaton's Table, showing how much a foot in length of each metal lengthens by an increase of heat, corresponding to 180 degrees of Fahrenheit's thermometer, or the difference between freezing and boiling. The unit is the 10,000th part of an inch.

White glass barometer tube	100.
Martial regulus of antimony	130.
Blistered steel	138.
Hard steel	147.
Iron	151.
Bismuth	167.
Copper, hammered	204.
Copper, 8 parts, mixed with tin, 1	218
Cast brass	225.
Brass, 16 parts, with tin, 1	229.
Brass wire, and speculum metal	232.
Spelter solder, vis. brass, 2 parts—zinc, 1	247.
Fine pewter	274.
Grain tin	298
Soft solder, vis. lead, 2—tin, 1	301.
Zinc, 8 parts—tin, 1, a little hammered	323.
Lead	344.
Zinc, or spelter	353.
Zinc, hammered half an inch per foot	373.

See *Phil. Trans.* vol. 48, Art. 79, p. 598; and for De Lu periments on Ramsden's pyrometer, see *Phil. Trans.* vol. 1st. Art. 20. p. 419—546.

General Roy's Table of Expansion.

In the pendulum of seconds, the quantity required to be added to or subtracted from the length, to cause a gain or loss of one minute per day, is 0.0545 of an inch at a medium, which does not differ from either extreme, more than the half of unity in the last figure. Hence the mean variation of length answering to one second, is 0.00098 of an inch. And by General Roy's experiments, in the 75th volume of the *Phil. Trans.* the expansions of five feet, of the under-mentioned substances, by a variation of temperature of 180 degrees of Fahrenheit, namely from 32 degrees to 212 degrees, are,

	Inch.
Rod of English plate brass	0.113568.
Ditto of steel	0.068684.
Prism of cast iron	0.066563.
Glass tube	0.046569.
Solid glass, and made long before	0.048472.

Expansion of mercury is said to be fifteen times that of iron. Hence, it is seen, that in a clock with a simple pendulum, having the rod of steel, every difference of temperature of four degrees will cause a variation of one second per day; that the variation with a brass rod is nearly twice as much, and, with a glass rod, not much more than half the quantity. The difference between the mean heights of the thermometer within, at the Royal Society's apartments, in summer and in winter, is about 25 degrees. Hence, the difference between the going of a clock with a simple pendulum, in winter and in summer, or in summer and in winter, will be about six seconds per day, or one minute in ten days.

The difference in length, in straight grained deal wood, is found to be very small, whence it is a general opinion, that in clocks of the common construction, in which the pendulum is without intermission connected with the train, and the parts of the 'scapement are oiled, the errors of expansion in such a pendulum are much less than those which arise from the unequal transmission of the maintaining power. See *Nicholson's Journal*, quarto series, vol. 1st, page 58, May, 1797.

"Lieutenant Henry Kater (now Captain Kater) makes the expansion of white deal, from the temperature of 186 to 49, to be 0.0205 for four feet, and, for one foot, to be 0.0040 parts of an inch. Deal is then to sinc as 49 to 353". This seems to have been unhammered zinc. From the trials we have made with wood there did not appear a possibility of getting such a result as could be depended on.

M. Berthoud made experiments with wood, but finding nothing that was satisfactory in his trials, has given us no account of them that could be of any service, otherwise they would have been given. His conclusion is, that wood is very unfit for a pendulum rod; he means, perhaps, for a complete or compensation pendulum.

Mr. Rittenhouse, a native of Switzerland, and a very able philosopher, now residing in America, says, " That there is no expansion in white deal." See in Dr. Ure's *Chemical Dictionary*, very neat and copious tables, not only of the expansion of solids, but also of liquids, from 32 to 212 degrees.

Before giving the table of expansion of metals by M. Berthoud, it may be proper to give his detail of the process he made in making these experiments on his pyrometer. Being an excellent workman as a watchmaker, an intelligent mechanic and philosopher, and at the same time zealous to find what were the materials proper for fitting up a compensation pendulum, we may have great confidence in the results he has given.

He says, " An abstract of the experiments which I made on the expansion of different bodies, No. 1687 of his *Essai sur l'horlogerie*. To make experiments on different metals, in order to deduce the proportion or ratios of their expansion, it is not enough to have constructed the instrument we have described, (meaning his pyrometer;) these experiments require an extreme precision, without which, it is astonishing to find such opposite results, although we think to have always operated in the same way. This is what I have found several times, for the same degrees of cold and heat, have not always given the same extensions. These were the difficulties which obliged me often to repeat the same experiments; and willing to avail myself of the cold of January 1760, I perceived, that in making these experiments, in the same way as in the preceding years, I found results very different, which I attributed particularly to the way by which the heat of the pan was introduced into the stove. *In the stove he placed his pyrometer and thermometer, and the rods of metal under trial*; for hitherto it was a pipe from the warming pan, which went up by the side of the rod of metal under trial, and as the thermometer was at a distance from it, it happened that the heat which impressed the rod, was not exactly that which impressed the thermometer; so that, according to the greater or less liveliness of the fire from the pan, and of the time which the experiment lasted, the rod and the thermometer were heated very differently.

" 1687. Here, then, are the changes which I made. *First*, I placed in the stove a plate, bent at the place where the heat which comes from the pipe of the pan, to impress the inside of the stove; this plate is bent in such a manner that the heat goes down again, and divides itself to get up equally in every part of the stove.

" 1688. *Secondly*, I placed the thermometer quite near the rod of metal, at the requisite distance, so as they do not touch one another; by this means, it happens that they are equally impressed by the same heat.

" *Note*. I applied on the same plate three thermometers of mercury, divided after the scale of Reaumur; the first with a cylindrical kind of ball, it rises to boiling water; the second has three branches, and goes to 39 degrees above freezing; the third has four cylindrical branches, and rises to 74° above freezing. They are made thus with several branches, in order to render them more or less sensible; and to compare them with rods of different thicknesses, so that a degree of heat acts with an equal advantage to dilate a rod of a given thickness, and dilate the mercury of one of the thermometers: so, when I examine in the stove the lengthening of a rod a little strong, to know the degree of temperature which makes it change, I see the thermometer which has the greatest quantity of mercury under the least surface; and when I have a small rod, I use the thermometer with two branches, which has less mercury under a greater surface, &c.

" 1689. *Thirdly*, To set out in a sure or certain way, with the same degree of cold, I made a cask of about 4 feet deep, and 9 inches in the base; I filled it with pounded ice, so, by placing in it the rods which I wanted to try, they took exactly the temperature of the ice.

" 1690. I made use of a more moderate and continued fire to give heat to the stove. I formerly used live coal or charcoal, now I make use of the peats which the tanners make up and sell for burning; this fire is mild, lasts a long while the same, and introduces itself by this means in an uniform manner, which imitates the gradual heat of the air. I did not use those peats which are of the same largeness of size, till they have been equally burned, so far as to smoke no more: I had particular attention that the time of the experiment was always of the same duration, in order to have exact results; and I can positively say they were so. For, having repeated several times the same experiments, I have always found the same results; in consequence, I have recommenced all my experiments, not only on those metals which I had observed, but even upon glass, gold, and silver, having got drawn a rod of gold and of silver, 40 inches in length each.

"M. Romilly, a very able watchmaker, was present at some of my experiments; having invited him to see them, he had the complaisance to procure for me the rods of gold and silver. By means of these experiments, I give here a complete and exact table of the expansion of all the metals which I tried, and I suppress all the experiments which I made during four preceding winters, with several substances compounded of lead, antimony, &c. being not sufficiently exact to have a place here.

17th March, 1760.

"1691. Having filled the cask with ice, I placed in it different rods, of the same length, that is to say, of 3 feet, 2 inches, 5 lines=461 lines, reckoning from the fixed point which keeps to the upper pillar of the pyrometer, to the point where they act against the rack; the breadth of these rods is 5 lines, and 3 lines thick; it must be remarked, that to each rod which I tried, I brought the thermometer to the freezing point, by covering it with pounded ice.

Experiment.

"1692. Having taken the rod of glass from the cask, and placed it on the pyrometer, the thermometer at zero, the hand or index of the pyrometer at 68 degrees of cold; having placed the stove and heated it, the thermometer rose to 27 degrees, and the index of the pyrometer to 6 degrees; so for 27 degrees of the thermometer, the index of the pyrometer has described or run over 62 divisions of the circle, that is to say, the glass rod has lengthened $\frac{62}{100}$ths of a line.

"1693. I took from the cask a rod of tempered steel, which had been brought back to a blue, that is to say, that it had the temper of springs, or nearly so; having placed it on the pyrometer, when the thermometer marked zero, and the index of the pyrometer 19 degrees of cold; by means of the stove, I made the thermometer rise to 27 degrees, the pyrometer to 58 of heat, the index of the pyrometer has described 77 divisions of the limb or arch of the circle, so the tempered steel rod has lengthened $\frac{77}{100}$ths of a line.

"1694. Likewise, having taken the rod of lead from out of the ice, and placed it on the pyrometer when the thermometer was at zero, and the index of the pyrometer at 91 degrees of cold, when the thermometer was raised to 27 degrees, the pyrometer marked 102 of heat; then, whilst the thermometer was raised to 27 degrees, the index of the pyrometer has described 193 divisions of the limb; that is, that the rod of lead has lengthened $\frac{193}{200}$ of a line in setting out, and being heated to 27 degrees of the thermometer of M. de Reaumur.

"1695. By a process perfectly similar, a rod of tin lengthened $\frac{160}{360}$; a rod of brass $\frac{121}{360}$; a rod of gold, quality 21 carats, wire drawn, and very hard, lengthened, $\frac{91}{360}$; the same rod brought back in the fire to soften it, lengthened $\frac{94}{360}$: the rod of steel being softened, lengthened $\frac{69}{360}$, which was found by two separate trials; a rod of iron hammered cold, lengthened $\frac{78}{360}$; the same rod softened, $\frac{75}{360}$; a rod of copper, $\frac{107}{360}$; a rod of metal, composed of lead, and with one-sixth part of antimony, $\frac{160}{360}$; a glass tube, four lines in diameter, $\frac{62}{360}$; a rod of silver wire drawn, $\frac{119}{360}$. These expansions are arranged in the following Table:

Berthoud's Table of the Proportion of the Expansion of Metals, &c.

"1695. Steel softened   -   -   -   -   69
        Iron ditto -   -   -   -   -   75
        Steel tempered   -   -   -   -   77
        Iron forged cold   -   -   -   78
        Gold softened   -   -   -   -   82
        Ditto wire drawn hard -   -   -   -   94
        Copper   -   -   -   -   107
        Silver wire drawn   -   -   -   -   119
        Brass -   -   -   -   -   -   121
        Tin   -   -   -   -   -   -   -   160
        Lead   -   -   -   -   -   -   -   193
        Glass -   -   -   -   -   -   62
        Mercury -   -   -   -   -   -   1235"

Berthoud, in his calculations, made use of the ratios of 74 for steel to 121 for brass. Some have made the expansion of platinum the same as glass.

"1697. All these rods were tried, without being loaded or charged with weights: Afterwards, wishing to know the change that the weight of a pendulum ball, or lens, would cause to the extension of the rods, I fixed to a rod of steel, a lentille of 35 lb., and found that the extension was sensibly the same, but the cold did not shorten the rod the same quantity that the heat had dilated it. I shall not relate these experiments here, because they did not appear to me to be exact enough.

"1698. I suppress also, to make short details of the experiments that I made on rods of wood of different kinds; suffice it to say, that wood is subject to very considerable alterations by heat and cold, by moisture and dryness, in so much, that it is very unfit to make pendulum rods of.

"1699. Although metals expand in all directions, we have considered their extension only in their length, because it is only this which we need; it matters very little whether a pendulum rod is thicker in summer than in winter; but it is not the same with regard to its length, as we shall see in the following chapter; moreover, if it is wanted to know how much a given metal rod becomes thicker or broader by such a degree of heat, it is only necessary to compare its extent to that of the same rod in our table, and the extension of the demanded dimension may easily be ascertained." See *Essai sur l'Horlogerie, par M. Berthoud. Tome second, Seconde Partie. No.* 1686. *Anno* 1763.

Late experiments made by Messrs. de Luc and Dalby. From the freezing point 32, to the boiling point of 212 of Fahrenheit's thermometer, the unit a 10,000th part of an inch,

The results were as follow:

Glass.	Platinum.	Blistered Steel.	Iron.	Brass wire.
.0083	.0087	.0112	.0126	.0194
	Zinc.	Hammered Zinc.	Mercury.	
	.0296	.0308	.1835	

If we take the expansive ratio of brass at 80, and steel at 49.575 as given by Mr. Troughton, then Mr. Smeaton's would be 80.55, and 47.912, and General Roy's would be 78.95, and 47.7. Mr. Troughton's pyrometer being so extremely nice or sensible in its operations, that the proportion of brass, 80, to steel, 49.575, may be the nearest and best we can fix on.

Some estimate may be formed of the advantages of a compensation pendulum, by comparing the going of a clock, which had one of Ellicott's construction, with that which had none, as shown in a letter from Mr. Bliss at Oxford, dated 12th July 1752, to Mr. Short in London, who says, " I find, upon examining my book, that the greatest difference in the going of the clock, between the coldest weather of the two last winters, and the hottest weather of the two last summers, is no more than one second a day; and this was occasioned by the levers being made too short, of which I advised Mr. Ellicott above a year since: whereas a clock with a simple pendulum with a brass rod, made by Mr. Graham, and which belongs to Dr. Bradley, in the coldest weather lost above fifteen seconds per day, and in the warmest gained above thirteen seconds per day, and went very near the equal time in temperate weather." It is plain that Mr. Bliss must have meant *gained* in the coldest weather, and *lost* in the hottest, otherwise there would be no analogy with the effect of the temperature in summer and in winter on the brass rod of the pendulum. The pendulum ball resting by its lower edge on the regulating nut, as they usually do, the expansion of the lead in it upwards, *surely*, could not operate so much against the brass rod as to make the clock go fast in summer, nor its contraction downwards, so much as to make it go so very slow in winter. Perhaps this may have been the case agreeably to Mr. Bliss' account of the matter. See *Description of Two Methods, &c.* by John Ellicott, F. R. S. published 1753.

Graham was the first who thought of making a pendulum rod that should counteract the effects of heat and cold, by a combination of rods or wires of different metals, such as brass, silver, steel, &c. but had never put it in execution, thinking they would not be effectual enough in their operations: this was about the year 1715. It occured to him at that time, that Mercury, from its great expansion by heat, would be more adequate to the end he was in pursuit of. Having made a pendulum on this principle, it was applied to a clock, and set agoing. In the *Philosophical Transactions, No.* 392, it is described in a paper which was given into the Royal Society, 1726. He says, "The clock was kept constantly going without having either the pendulum or the hands altered, from the 9th of June, 1722, to the 14th of November, 1725, being three years and four months." Somewhile previous to 1726, Harrison, living at Barrow, in Lincolnshire, was engaged in making experiments on brass and steel rods, when he produced what is now called the Gridiron Pendulum. See Ellicott's pamphlet, already quoted. For a very extensive table of the dilatation of solids by heat, see *Dr. Ure's Chemical Dictionary.*

CHAPTER XVIII.

On Compensation Pendulums.

Compensation pendulums are those which are constructed to counteract the effect of heat and cold in lengthening or shortening a pendulum rod.

Graham's Mercurial Pendulum.

The mercurial pendulum invented by Graham, having been the first that was applied to a clock, for the purpose of compensation, we shall begin with the description of it, taking the others nearly in the order of their invention. This pendulum consists of a steel rod, at the lower end it carries a large glass jar filled with mercury, so that the expansion or contraction of the rod may be counteracted by the opposite expansion or contraction of the mercury. To make this pendulum in the way which has hitherto been adopted, is attended with considerable trouble, from the nature of the material. The construction of such a pendulum must always be troublesome, because any addition to, or abstraction of the mercury from the hollow cylinder or glass jar, to bring about the compensation, will cause a change of place with the index point on the graduated arch or index plate, if such a thing is used. A pendulum which will remedy this, shall be afterwards described; in the mean time, we shall proceed to give a more detailed description of such as have been commonly made.

The length of the pendulum over all, from the bottom of the sole to the upper end of the pendulum spring, is about 43.95 inches; the inside bottom of the jar .6 of an inch from the under side of the sole, the height of the column of mercury in the jar, about 7.47 inches. From the upper end of the pendulum spring, take a length of 39.2 inches on the pendulum downwards, then 43.95 inches—39.2 +.6, will give that part of the column of mercury, below the centre of oscillation, equal to 4.15 inches, and that above the centre 3.32 inches. The height of the jar outside 7.8 inches, inside, 7.6 inches; mean diameter inside, 2.018 inches, weight 7.5 ounces. Although it would be still better to have it of a less weight, yet it is doubtful if it would then be strong enough to support such a column of quicksilver. The weight of the stirrup or jar frame, 1 lb. 6 ounces; if we take 2.55 ounces from the brass sole, and from the top, 3.45 ounces, making 6 ounces in all, leaving for weight of the stirrup 1 lb. The clock when set a-going, (with the pendulum the same length as before,) after taking this quantity of weight from the stirrup, went slow, at the rate of 46 seconds in 24 hours, and when shortened by setting up the regulating nut, it was found to be .15 of an inch less than the former length.

The length of the stirrup bars outside, including sole and part of the top, 8.125 inches; breadth from outside of the bars, 3.25 inches; thickness of the pendulum rod and stirrup bars, 0.136 of an inch; breadth 0.384 of an inch; thickness of the sole outside, 0.515 of an inch; length from bottom of the sole to the upper side of the jar cover, 8.187 inches; jar bottom sunk into the sole near to 0.25 inch; from upper side of jar cover, to under side of stirrup top 1.25 inch; height of stirrup top from flat part of pendulum rod, 1.75 inch;

thickness of the flat, 0.220 inch; diameter of the regulating screw, 0.278 inch; that of the nut, 1.156 inch. The screw contains 36.25 turns in an inch, the nut divided into 30 prime divisions, each being equal to one second a day, the prime divisors subdivided into four.

	inches.
Length of stirrup bars inside - - -	8.05
Thickness of sole outside - - - -	0.515
Length of stirrup top - - - -	1.75
From the stirrup top to the upper end of pendulum spring	33.465
Length of the pendulum over all - - -	43.800
Length of pendulum spring - - -	.625
Breadth of the double laminae, including .164, the space between them, each laminæ .168 - -	.500
Thickness of ditto - - - -	.007

	lb.	oz.	dr.
Weight of quicksilver in the jar - -	11	12	5.35
Ditto of the stirrup frame - -	1	0	0
Pendulum rod and spring, regulating nut, jar, cover, &c.	0	13	0
Jar - - - -	0	7	8
Total weight of pendulum - -	14	0	13.35

Before the pendulum was altered, the rate of the clock showed, that the compensation was not sufficiently effective, although the height of the column of mercury was nearly 7.5 inches, the jar being about full, allowed no more to be put in: reducing the weight of the jar-frame or stirrup, required the rod to be shortened, as has been stated, .15 of an inch; whether this is enough, remains to be determined. The daily rate for a month or six weeks, was 0.1 second slow when the temperature was from 36 degrees to 40 degrees of Fahrenheit's thermometer, and got gradually slower as the height of the thermometer increased; between 60 and 66 degrees, the daily loss was from 0.37 to 0.45 second; for about two weeks, when the weather was extremely cold, the thermometer at the freezing point and under, the clock showed a tendency of rather gaining.

Of late years, the mercurial pendulum has been adopted in some astronomical clocks, and on the whole, seems to have answered very well. The author of the *Elements of Clock and Watch Work* thought, that it was not fit for this purpose, being too quick in its operations of expansion and contraction; but if the cover is well fitted to the top of the jar, we can venture to say, from the resultance made by glass to changes of temperature, that the operations will be too slow; and, for this reason, it is proposed to make such a pendulum, with a thicker rod, and stirrup bars, that they may not take heat and cold too readily. A steel jar would perhaps answer the end as well as any other contrivance; but some would object to this, on account of the danger of magnetism; but even a jar of this kind, from its being made thin, (for it would be heavy were it as thick as the glass one,) would be easily effected by changes of temperature, and mercury being still more susceptible of these changes, the operations of counteracting the effects of them might be too sudden. But perhaps, if the glass jar had an external coating of tinfoil, similar to the lining of the Leyden Phial, or some other coating, the irradiations of heat from the polished surface of the glass would be lessened, and the operations of the change of temperature might be sufficiently quick without being too rapid. It is of the greatest importance that a pendulum rod should, with the smallest quantity of matter, be as stiff and inflexible as possible; and although it was proposed to have thicker bars and rods, let us suppose the same quantity of matter is taken as before, but under a circular in place of a rectangular surface,—it must, in this form, require more time to get heated and cooled, which is the end we now attempt to gain. The sides of the parallelogram were .384, and .136 of an inch, the product of which two numbers, gives .052224 of an inch for the area or superficies of the parallelogram. To find the diameter of a cylindrical rod, whose circumference should contain a superficies equal to that of the parallelogram, divide .052224 by .7854, and extract the square root of the quotient, which will give .258 of an inch, very nearly as the diameter of the rods, for $.258^s \times .7854 = .0522793656$.

Let the improved jar-frame, or stirrup, therefore, be composed of two round steel rods, .258 of an inch in diameter, and 8.85 inches in length, from shoulder to shoulder, at each of which pivots are formed; those for the upper ends should be a quarter of an inch long, and about .190 of an inch in diameter, tapped so as to screw firm into the upper brass cross piece, the distance from the centres of the tapped holes in the traverse or cross piece requires to be 2.8 inches, in order to give freedom for the jar between the rods; the length of the cross piece over all should be 3.3 inches, and its breadth at the places where the rods are screwed in .450 of an inch. At the middle, a circular part is formed, .5 of an inch in diameter, in the centre of which a hole is tapped, by which the regulating screw may raise or lower the jar-frame without changing the place of the index point. The cross piece may be either brass or steel, though the latter is perhaps preferable: the pivots on the lower end of the rods may be of the same diameter as those on the upper end, but a little longer, and tapped a little way in on the ends, when well fitted into the lugs of the brass sole, on which the jar rests, and sunk a little way down into it: nuts are screwed on to the ends of the pivots, and sunk into the lower side of the brass sole; care must be taken to have the distance between the centres of the holes in the sole the same as in the cross piece, so as to make the rods stand parallel to each other. To go outside of the frame just now described, another is made to which is attached the pendulum rod, the regulating nut, and lower sole, in which is fixed the small steel index, which cannot change its place after being properly adjusted to it. The upper cross piece for this may be of the same thickness as the former, and in length not less than 4 inches; a hole is tapped near to each of the ends, and their centres are distant from one another 3.56 inches nearly, and are wide enough to allow a round steel rod of .23 of an inch in diameter to pass freely through: the length of these rods, from the lower side of the cross piece to the upper side of lower sole, is nearly 10.6 inches. The lower sole may be a brass wheel, crossed into four, the centre part being large enough to have a hole tapped, so as to fix the steel index in it; the diameter of the wheel is the same as the length of the upper cross piece, which is 4 inches, and the thickness .25 of an inch, or a little more: this sole, in which the index is fixed, serves also as a resting part for the pendulum, when it happens to be taken from its place. The upper end of the rods is formed into a sort of double shouldered screw, the tapped part is a little more than a quarter of an inch long, and something less in diameter; the length of the plain and tapped part of the screw is about .7 of an inch, and when screwed into the upper cross piece, it bends to it; the lower end of the pendulum rod, which is formed something like an inverted and compressed Λ, having lugs or soles, through which the screws for fixing it pass. The regulating screw has an untapped or plain part, which turns freely in a hole, in the middle of the upper cross piece, formed in the same way as the upper cross piece for the jar-frame; the nut or head of the regulating screw is shaped so as to lie under the hollow of the Λ, at the lower end of the pendulum rod, and on the upper side of the cross piece; the lower ends of the rods of the outside frame are gently tapered, and fitted into holes in the brass wheel, through the edge of which are put pins to fix them and the wheel together; this outside frame has no part in the compensation: the brass cover for the jar has the lugs hollowed out a very little, so as to come in on the rods of the jar-frame; the ends of the upper traverse of which, as well as the lugs of the jar sole, are hollowed, and take in with a part of the rods of the outside frame, along which, the jar frame is moved up and down. The height of the glass jar outside is about 8 inches, and its weight and other dimensions nearly the same as those stated for the former pendulum, and the diameter of the rod and λ part is .258 of an inch.

A view of the improved mercurial pendulum is given in Plate XV. No. 69. $a\,b$ is the pendulum rod, $c\,c$, $d\,d$, the stirrup or frame, within is the frame for the jar $e\,f$, and $h\,h$ are the soles for the jar and for the pendulum; g is the index which serves to show by the graduated plate, fixed to inside of the clock-case, the number of degrees and minutes swung out by the pendulum, S the regulating screw, and i, the jar cover.

Philosophers seem not to be agreed respecting the expansion of mercury, in comparison with that of other metals, some making it 15 times, others 16 times greater than that of iron.

In regard to the column of mercury for a mercurial pendulum, something depends on its diameter as well as height; suppose the length of steel to be 43 inches, and the column of mercury 7.5 inches in height, and 2 inches in diameter, which were the dimensions used in a pendulum brought nearly to its state of compensation, we may then find how many times the expansion of this column is contained in the 43 inches. Say, as 43 inches is to 74, the expansive ratio of steel, so is 7.5 inches of mercury to its expansion for compensating steel.

Length of steel 43 inches	log.	1.6334685
Ratio 74	log.	1.8692317
		3.5027002
Height of column of mercury 7.5 inches	log.	0.8750613
Ratio, 424.26	log.	2.6276369
		3.5027002

By this process, it appears that the expansion of mercury is not quite 5.75 times that of steel. A pendulum, whose vibrations are three or four degrees on each side of the point of rest, will require a column less in height than that which vibrates only one degree; hence it is a very nice matter to give precise rules for making a mercurial pendulum that shall at once be at the point of perfect compensation.

If the steel rod $a\,b$, and rods of the jar frame of a mercurial pendulum, are lengthened by heat, the jar *e f*, containing the mercury, will, from this cause, be let lower down, and the centre of oscillation be carried farther from the point of suspension; but the heat which lengthens the rod will at the same time expand the mercury upwards, and by this means the centre of oscillation is kept always at the same distance from the point of suspension. When the rods are contracted or shortened by cold, the mercury will also be contracted by it, and hence the lengthening or shortening of the pendulum rod, by heat or cold, is compensated by equal and opposite expansions or contractions of the mercury.

The mercurial pendulum at the clock in the Royal Observatory of Edinburgh, had (after two adjustments being made for compensation,) about 87600 grains Troy in the glass jar, say, 15lb. 2os. 10dwt. Troy, (about 12¼ lb. avoirdupois.) The height of the column of mercury about 7.4 inches, and diameter about 2.037 inches.

Gridiron Pendulum.

M. Lalande,* on taking notice of clocks fitted for the use of astronomers, says, " Pendulum rods which consist only of a single bar of iron, will lengthen about one-fifth of a line, *nearly the* .0178 *of an English inch*, for 30° of Reaumur's thermometer, so that being regulated in summer, the clock will gain in winter 20 seconds a day." It is then important for astronomers to have the pendulum rod composed in such a way as to correct this expansion and contraction of metals; several methods for this purpose will be found in books just now quoted; see that of the *Gridiron*, contrived by Harrison about the year 1726, and which is, without doubt, the best of all those that have been proposed. Graham made up one of them, in 1740, for the Earl of Macclesfield; most of the clocks for astronomers are fitted up on this principle. M. Lepaute, M. Berthoud, M. Robin, and M. Janvier, at Paris, have made a great number of them, and they answer the end in the most complete manner.

The gridiron pendulum is composed of nine round rods, five of which are made of steel, and four of brass, and is represented, No. 70, Plate XV. where the steel rods are distinguished from the brass ones by a darker shade. As it somewhat resembles the common gridiron in appearance, it hence probably received its present name. Not many years after this was produced, the French artists contrived a variety of compensation pendulums, but the gridiron seems to be the one now generally adopted by them. The first pendulum of this kind which

* M. Lalande lost an excellent astronomical clock, by allowing it to go ten years without cleaning, or even giving it fresh oil.

we made was nearly 40 years ago; and knowing that Mr. Cumming had some practice in this way, he was applied to, and very obligingly sent a drawing, and the different lengths for the brass and steel rods, which, on being tried for some years afterwards, was found, on the whole, to be tolerably correct; but not quite so accurate in the compensation as could have been wished. From an abstract of the going of a clock with this pendulum, it appeared, that, during the temperature from 46 to 48 degrees of Fahrenheit's thermometer, it kept mean time. A temperature ten degrees lower, made the clock gain at the rate of nearly half a second in a day, and 10 degrees higher, (that is about 58°) made the clock lose about as much.

The lengths of the rods were, outside steel rods from pin to pin, 29.5 inches; middle steel rod from upper end of the pendulum spring to the pin at the lower end, 31.5 inches; inside rods from pin to pin, 24.5 inches; from the pinning of the lower end of the outside steel rods to the centre of the ball, five inches; making in all 90.25 inches of steel, to be compensated by the brass. Outside brass rods from pin to pin, 26.87 inches; inside ditto, 22.25 inches, being in all 49.12 inches of brass. The length which the brass ought to have, may thus be found by the inverse rule of proportion. As 90.25 inches, is to 74, the number for the expansion of steel, according to Berthoud, so is 121 that of the expansion for brass, to the length of brass required; that is $90.25 \times 74 \div 121 = 49.4$ inches the length required. Although the deficiency of brass here is very little, yet, to remedy the compensation, a greater number of inches, both of brass and steel, must be taken, before this pendulum can be made complete. A description of such a one shall now be given.

The length of the outside steel rods from pin to pin, in the uppermost and lowermost traverses or brass cross pieces, a, b, c, d, is 36 inches, the next or innermost steel rods, from their pinning in the second uppermost traverse m, to that in the second lowermost n, is 35 inches; the steel centre rod from the pinning of it, in the third lowermost traverse o, to the upper end of the pendulum spring, is 37.625 inches, or 37 inches and $\frac{5}{8}$ of an inch, the centre c of the ball below the pinning of the outside steel rods and index rod, is 3.94 inches; the outermost brass rods from their pinning in the uppermost traverse to that in the second lowermost, is the smallest quantity possible less than 35.5 inches; the innermost brass rods from their pinning in the second uppermost traverse to the third lowest one, is 34.5 inches. The whole length of the steel is then 112.568 inches, and that of the brass 71 inches. The diameter of the rods about one quarter of an inch, the brass rods a little more in diameter than the steel; the proportions may be as 25 is to 28. The distance from the centres of the two outside steel rods is 2.5 inches; the rods are placed equi-distant from one another, only there is a little more space left between the two brass rods nearest the middle steel rod, in order to give room for the fork to come in and clip the middle steel rod. The two outside steel rods are prolonged below their pinning in the lowest traverse, as seen below *c d*, about 5 or 6 inches within the ball, in order to keep it properly flat in the plane in which the pendulum should swing. In the middle of the lowest traverse *c d*, is pinned a steel rod *e f*, somewhat more than a quarter of an inch in diameter, and about nine inches long; this rod goes through the diameter of the ball, equal portions being round it; the lower end *f* is formed into a taper and sharp point as an index for the degree plate, fixed to the inside back of the case, and for four inches or so below the upper end; it is tapped at that part which lies near to the centre of the ball. A thin cross piece of brass is fixed to the inside of the ball before filling it with lead, the lowest side of which is in a line across the centre horizontally; the ends of the two outer steel rods and the centre or inner rod, pass easily through this cross piece of brass: a hollow tube comes up within the ball as far as the under side of the inside cross piece, on the end of which, where the cross piece and ball rest, is fixed within it a tapped nut, which screws upon the tapped part of the index rod. On the lower end of the tube is soldered a sort of flat conical head *h*, milled on the edge outside, whose diameter may be an inch, or an inch and a quarter. On the upper surface of this nut are traced two circles, in order to put divisons between them and figures, so as to correspond with the turns of the screw in an inch. A small steel index *c* is screwed on to the lower part of the ball to point at these divisions; the lower end of the tube is a little below the edge of the ball, that it may rest freely on the upper end of the tube. The total length, from the upper end *g* of the pendulum spring to the index point *f*, is 47.75 inches, a length of radius which will require the length of a degree on the degree plate, to be .833142 of an inch. The distance from the upper end of the pendulum spring to the centre of the ball is 42.5 inches very nearly, so that the centre of the ball is about 3.3 inches below the centre of oscillation. The lowermost traverse *c d*, may be about half an inch thick, and its length and breadth such as to give it sufficient strength to receive the outside steel rods, and the centre or index rod; the uppermost traverse *a b* is nearly of the same dimensions; the second lowermost traverse *n*, and the second uppermost, *m*, are nearly of the same size, and almost equal to that of the uppermost and lowermost, only they are a little shorter, having in their ends a sort of half hole, through which, in the second lowermost traverse, the outer steel rods pass easily, and through these, in the uppermost traverse, the outside brass rods freely pass. This traverse is of course a little shorter than the second lowermost; in the second lowermost traverse is pinned the ends of the outermost brass rods; and in the second uppermost traverse are pinned those of the innermost steel and brass rods; in the third lowest traverse is pinned the innermost brass rods, and the centre steel rod; the dimensions of this are nearly the same as the second uppermost and lowermost, only shorter, having a half hole at the ends, through which the inner steel rods pass freely. There is a hole in each of the two uppermost traverses, through which the centre rod passes freely. Towards the lower ends of the centre steel rod, and those of the innermost brass rods, are two sets of holes, by which the third or upper of the lower traverses can be moved or shifted up three or six inches, should the compensation be found in excess. It would be convenient, when shifting, to have a piece similar to this traverse, and three spare pins; this piece being like a half of the traverse, it may then be applied to the three rods, and pinned, but not to the place where the shifting is to be made. This piece will prevent the rods shifting away from one another, and will allow the traverse to be moved, and fixed to the intended place.

Two thin pieces of brass, pq, rs, must be provided, having nine holes in them, so that all the rods can move easily through them; the two outermost being kept rather a little tighter than the others; these pieces are intended to prevent tremulous motion in the rods or pendulum, and are put at the same distance from the upper and lower traverses, as seen No. 70. The pendulum ball is composed of two frustums of equal cones, the greater diameter is seven inches, the lesser four inches, and the height half an inch, giving by calculation, 24.3474 cubic inches, the weight of which in lead is 9.997 lb. The ball, when filled with lead, together with the outside brass shells and inside cross piece, weighed 10 lb. 8 oz. The weight of the brass and steel rods, traverse pieces, pendulum spring, and top piece, &c., was 5 lb. 13 oz.; in all 16 lb. 5 oz. The clock to which this pendulum was put was a month one, and was kept going by a weight of 7 lb. 7 oz. We cannot help thinking, that this pendulum appears to be better fitted up than either Cumming's or Berthoud's.

The third lowest traverse being shifted up three inches, there will then be this quantity less for brass and steel than has been before stated, the steel will be $36 + 35 + 37.628 + 3.94 - 3 = 109.568$ inches, and the longest brass rods may be taken at 35.49 + 34.5 — 3 = 66.99. Their lengths and expansive ratios may be given thus:

Steel 109.568 inches,	- - -	log.	2.0396838
Ratio 74,	- - - -	log.	1.8692317
			3.9089155
Brass 66.99 inches,	- - -	log.	1.8260100
Ratio 121,	- - - -	log.	2.0827854
			3.9087954

The difference in excess of compensation is here extremely little, and is on the side of the steel rods, being scarcely an inch too much. In taking into account the length of the rods, those on one side along with the centre rod are only taken; those on the other side serve as a kind of counterpoise, for giving an appearance of uniformity to the pendulum, and for preventing the weight of the pendulum ball from bending the rods which it would do were they all on one side. The manner of compensation may be thus explained: The steel rods go downwards when expanded by heat, and the brass rods from the like cause, go upwards, and thus counteract the effect of heat on the length of the pendulum. A degree of cold will contract or shorten the steel rods; this will tend to bring the ball of the pendulum up; but the brass rods contracting at the same time, allow the ball to go downwards, by which the effect of cold on the length of the pendulum is counteracted; so that whatever the temperature is, the centre of oscillation keeps always at an equal distance from the point of suspension, and hence the length of the pendulum is constantly and invariably the same. The comparative lengths of brass and steel rods may be computed by any other expansive ratio than those of Berthoud, which we have used, such as those by Smeaton, or by that ingenious artist Troughton. Their differences will vary a little from Berthoud, but they will be very trifling. It will require long experience to know which are the best founded, as the going of astronomical clocks may be affected by other causes which have no connection with the compensation of the pendulum rod.

A considerable time after the gridiron pendulum was produced, some adopted zinc rods in place of brass, and from their greater expansibility, fewer were required, three of steel and two of zinc being sufficient for the compensation; but such of them as we have seen appeared to have the zinc rods of a greater length than they should have been, according to the comparative expansions of zinc and steel,

They had also a large cavity in the upper part of the ball for lodging the lower traverse, which took away much of the momentum or force of the ball; and the holes for shifting, being at the upper ends of the rods, rendered it very inconvenient to adjust the compensation.

The following lengths should answer very well for a pendulum of this kind: The length from pin to pin, in the upper and lower traverses of the two outside steel rods, should be 27 inches, and 5 or 6 inches more beyond the lower traverse, to go within the ball, for the same purpose that was mentioned for one having brass rods; from the pin, in the lower end of the middle steel rod, which is in a traverse just above the lower one, to the upper end of the pendulum spring, should be 36.75 inches; from the pin in lower end of the middle rod to the centre of the ball, 4.75 inches, making in all 68.5 inches of steel. The diameter of the steel rods should be .25 of an inch. In the upper traverse is a hole, through which the middle steel rod must freely pass. The length of the zinc rods, from the pin in the upper traverse to that in the upper of the lower traverses, is 25.34 inches, and their diameter .27 or .28 of an inch or upwards: there may be holes put near the lower ends of the middle and zinc rods, for adjusting the compensation, like those in the brass rods; the ends of the upper and lower traverses must have half holes, taking in with the outside steel rods, pieces for preventing tremulous motion, and the manner of fitting up the pendulum ball and regulating nut, &c. as has already been described for the gridiron pendulum. The lengths and expansive ratios may be put thus:

Steel, 68.5 inches - - -	log.	1.8356906
Smeaton's ratio for steel 138 - -	log.	2.1998791
		3.9755697
Zinc, 25.34 inches - - -	log.	1.4038609
Do. for Zinc, .373 - - -	log.	2.5717088
		3.9755697

Pendulum balls composed of two equal frustums of cones, an edge view of section of one of them is seen at S, No. 78, Plate XVI.

In this pendulum, as in the gridiron one, the steel rods, when heated, go downwards, and the zinc rods upwards; it is the reverse when cold takes place. The zinc, which is used in these pendulums, must always be understood to be that which is hammered half an inch per foot; when hammering a bar or rod of zinc, it is necessary to have it very hot to prevent it flying or breaking; hammering makes it have more expansibility, but whether it expands as much as Ward makes it, remains to be determined.

Ellicott's Pendulum.

Not many years after Harrison's pendulum was known, Mr. Ellicott, and some of the French artists, contrived compensation pendulums in different ways, most of them having the ball adjustable by levers, which can never be equal to those in which the expansion and contraction act by contact in the direct line of the pendulum rod. Mr. Ellicott was a very ingenious artist of the old school, as appears from several of his works; and his pendulum evinces great ingenuity in its construction.

Ellicott's pendulum, shown in Plate XV. 71. consisted of two bars, one of which $a\,b$ was of brass, and the other of iron or steel. Mr. Cumming conceived, that where there were two bars only, a flexure and unequal bearing would take place, and, therefore, an exact compensation could not be effected. To remedy this, he constructed the pendulum with two steel bars, and one bar of brass, as shown in No. 3. Into the lower end of the brass bar $a\,b$, No. 1. was let one half of the diameter of a small steel roller r, the other half being let into a moveable brass piece, having two short arms 1, 2. These arms, by the levers $m\,o\,2$, $n\,o\,1$, moving round $o\,o$ as fulcra, make the roller press equally on the lower end of the brass bar. The steel roller marked r, has a fillet raised up on each end, for the purpose of keeping this part of the brass bar at an equal distance from the steel bars. The length of the brass bar $a\,b$ should be 39.25 inches from the upper end which is square, to the lower end which is rounded; its breadth three quarters of an inch, and its thickness at least one-eighth of an inch. The steel bars are in length, from the upper square ends to the centre of the ball, nearly where the short arms of the levers act on the moveable brass piece, about 39.75 inches; and the bars are left broader here, so as to be about one inch and a quarter; and this breadth is prolonged below the end of the brass bar three quarters of an inch or more. The thickness of the steel bars is one-tenth of an inch, and their breadth three quarters. The back steel bar has no opening in it; but the front bar has one, which is represented in the drawing at A, No. 2. In order to see the action of the levers on both arms of the moveable brass piece, a cavity $s\,s$, 71, is left for this purpose in the ball. A piece of glass is inserted in the opening, so as to prevent dust from getting into this part of the pendulum. This broad part of the steel bars serves as a kind of frame, on which are screwed two pieces of brass of the same figure as the steel bars, to connect them with that steel part of the lower end of the pendulum rod which goes through the ball, on which is a nut and screw, and a strong double spring *s s* in 71, for the purpose of taking off somewhat of the weight of the ball, according as it bears too much or too little on the short arms of the levers. The levers are shown at 71 and No. 1; the screws and lower end of the pendulum rod the nut N, and double spring S S, in 71. The use of the nut and screw is to adjust the strength of the spring, as they have nothing to do in the regulation of the pendulum for time to the clock, which is done by an apparatus for this purpose at top connected with the pendulum spring. In the brass pieces which are screwed on to the broad part of the steel bars, the pivots *o o* of the levers turn. There is a piece of brass put on at top, formed so as to interpose a little way down between the brass bar and the steel ones, keeping them at a proper distance from one another. The sides near to the square ends of the bars and this piece of brass are firmly pinned or screwed together. It is in this piece of brass that the lower end of the pendulum spring is fixed; the upper end being fixed to a piece, which is moveable up and down in a fixed frame by a nut and screw. The pendulum is lengthened or shortened according as the pendulum spring is let out or brought within that part of the frame through which the spring passes. The bars of the pendulum are connected by four or five screws, equal spaces being taken for their places between the centre of the ball and the square or upper end of the bars. The back bar is tapped to receive the screws, which go through holes made in the front steel bar, to let them easily pass. On the shank or body of the screws are fitted hollow cylinders, either of brass or steel, and of such a length, that when the screws are put home there shall be no pinching of the front steel bar by the head of the screws. Rectangular openings are made in the brass bar, for the hollow cylinders to come through, whose length may be about equal to twice the diameter of the cylinders, and so that the brass bar may easily move on them, by any small motion they may have in contracting or expanding. On each of these cylinders is put two loose brass collets or washers, one between each steel bar and the brass bar, to keep them free of each other. Their thickness should be at least .04 of an inch, so as to allow the air to pass freely between them. The small hollow cylinders, through which the screws pass when connecting the bars, should go easily into the front steel bar, the lower base bearing on the inside of the back steel bar. The upper base should be above the surface of the front bar, fully more than the thickness of strong writing paper, so that when the screw is put home, the shoulder of it may not pinch the bar. The edges of all the bars should be chamfered off from each side, so as to form an angle in the middle plane of their thickness, for the purpose of giving them a lighter appearance, and making them less susceptible of the resistance of the air. The diameter of the pendulum ball may be seven inches and a half, and its thickness, at the centre, about two inches and a quarter. In the edges, and in the line of the diameter horizontally across, are placed two long and stout screws $g\ g$, 71, whose heads have graduated circles on them, and are near the edge of the ball, and an index $i\ i$ to each. The inner ends of the screws shown at $s\ s$, are turned of such a shape, so as to apply by one point only on the long arms of the levers $m\ n$, as seen in 71. The front shell of the pendulum ball is fixed on by four screws. It has been objected by some, that, from the weight of the ball, the brass rods in a compensation pendulum are compressed, and the steel rods stretched; a matter of no moment whatever in our opinion. This may, however, in some degree, be remedied in Ellicott's pendulum, by making the brass bar of such a length, as to come through and below the lower edge of the ball, in place of the steel part, which was common to both steel bars, as has just now been described. This part of the brass bar is tapped, having on it the nut and strong double spring, which takes off a part of the weight, as has been noticed. A certain portion of the weight of the ball, will, in this case, bear on the brass bar; supposing it one-third of the weight, the remaining two-thirds will be carried jointly by the steel bars. Although the brass bar is here carried through the ball, it is easy to put a piece to it, moveable on a pivot in the middle of the bar, having two lugs applying to the edges of the bar, on which the short arms of the levers $m\ n$, may act, as was the case in the other by the moveable brass piece.

Things being in this situation, let us suppose that the bars composing the pendulum rod are lengthened by heat, and that the brass lengthens more than the same length of steel does; then the brass bar $a\ b$, by its excess of expansion, will press down the short ends of the levers $m\ n$, at b, and consequently raise up the ball, which, by the screws $s\ s$, rest on the long arms $m\ n$, of the levers; and, provided the ends of the screws press on the levers at a proper distance from the centres $o\ o$, the ball will be always kept at the same distance from the point of suspension, notwithstanding any alteration the rod of the pendulum may experience from heat or cold. What this distance ought to be may very nearly be determined, if the difference of the expansion between brass and steel is known; for the proportion which the shorter arms of the levers ought to bear to the longer ones, will always be as the excess of the expansion is to the whole expansion of the steel. Instead of the brass heads of the screws being placed near the outer edge of the ball, they may be more advantageously placed within the ball, at the distance of about an inch and a quarter from the edge, as shown in 71.

See *Phil. Trans.* 1751, p. 479, and a pamphlet which Mr. Ellicott published in London in 1753. For an account of the improvement made upon it by Mr. A. Cumming, see his *Elements of Clock and Watchmaking*, p. 107.

Smeaton's Pendulum.

Mr. Smeaton's compensation pendulum (Plate XV. 72.) consists of a glass rod A B, half an inch or more in diameter, and 45.5 inches long. To the upper end is fixed the pendulum spring; to the lower a screw *s*, and regulating nut *n*. A brass tube or ring *m*, of an inch or so in length, is put to move easily on the lower end of the rod, having a fillet at each end, one bearing on the regulating nut, the other supporting the zinc, iron, and lead tubes, which compose what may be called the pendulum ball. The zinc cylinder or tube is 12¼ inches in length, ¼th of an inch thick, and fits easily on the glass rod, the lower end resting on the upper fillet of the brass ring. On the zinc tube is put another of iron, 12 inches long, and ¼th of an inch thick, easily moveable on the zinc tube, with a kind of bottom to it, in which is a hole for the glass rod to go freely through. The bottom is uppermost, and rests on the upper end of the zinc tube. The lower end of the iron tube has a fillet on its outside, on which rests a leaden tube of 12 inches long, and ¼th of an inch thick, and which goes easily over on the iron tube. The outside diameter of the leaden tube will be nearly two inches. Although this pendulum will not be thought elegant in appearance, yet it is said to have answered the purpose of compensation very well. A section of the rod and tubes is shown at S.

As glass does not suffer much expansion or contraction from heat or cold, it will be the more easily compensated. The glass rod AB of this pendulum being supposed to lengthen in a small degree by heat, is compensated by a zinc tube of twelve inches and a quarter long, whose lower end resting on the lower end of the glass rod, would be carried down by the lengthening of the glass rod, but the same cause which produces this, will make the zinc tube expand upwards, which will carry up the iron and leaden tubes. The iron tube has in this case its expansion downwards, and the leaden tube compensates this by having its expansion upwards.

Reid's Pendulums.

This compensation pendulum (Plate XVI. 74.) is composed of a zinc tube A B, and three steel rods, *ab*, *cd*, *ef*. In order to obtain a proper tube, the zinc must be very gently fused into a bar about an inch square, and 24.25 inches long, and the mould into which it is poured should be upright, or nearly so. Let this be very carefully hammered to half an inch per foot, meanwhile keeping it pretty warm to prevent cracking or breaking. After this operation, a hole is pierced straight through the bar, from end to end, and opened up by means of a clean cutting broach, until it is .450 of an inch, or so, in diameter. The outside may be turned down till it is .7 of an inch, or less. The length should be 25.34 inches, the same as the zinc rods were taken at. The steel rods must be a quarter of an inch in diameter; the length, from pin to pin, in the upper and lower traverses of the two outside steel rods, *c d*, *ef*, 27 inches, five or six inches more being prolonged to go within the ball. In the middle of the lower traverse *m n*, is pinned a steel rod *g h*, somewhat more than a quarter of an inch in diameter, and nine inches long, which comes through the centre of the ball, which is fitted up in the same way in every respect as was described for the gridiron pendulum. The steel centre rod *a b*, goes up inside of the zinc tube, from a pin in the lower end of it, which is in a traverse a very little above the lower one, its length, including the pendulum spring, is 36.75 inches; from the pin in the lower end of the centre rod, to the centre of the ball, 4.75 inches. A hole in the upper traverse *o p* allows the centre rod to pass freely through. The lower end of the tube rests on the traverse *g f*, in which the centre rod is pinned. The upper traverse bears on the upper end, both traverses having a part turned from them, about one-tenth of an inch in height, and of such a diameter as to go into the ends of the tube, for the purpose of keeping it to its proper place. The distance from the centre of the holes in the upper and lower traverses, about 1.25 inch, which will be enough to make the two outside steel rods stand clear of the zinc tube. A thin piece of brass, with three holes in it for the outside steel rods and tube, might be put half way between the ends of the tube, to prevent any bending, or tremulous motion, a thing, however, not likely to take place. It would be proper to have a few holes in the tube, for the purpose of admitting air more freely to the centre rod.

The centre steel rod $a\,b$, when lengthened by heat, will make the lower end B of the zinc tube, (which is supported by the lower end b of the steel rod $a\,b$,) descend with it; but the same cause which lengthens the steel rod $a\,b$ downwards will expand the zinc tube A B upwards, and this will carry up the two outside steel rods with which the ball of the pendulum is connected: their expansion downwards, as well as that of the centre rod, is compensated by the upward expansion of the zinc tube. The length of the steel rods and of the zinc tube, has been shown to be in proportion to their expansive ratios.

It is about fifteen years since we contrived and made this kind of compensation pendulum, which seems to do very well. The following is of another kind, but we never had it put in execution, although there is no doubt but it would serve the purpose extremely well, notwithstanding the risk arising from the brittleness of the glass.

Provide a white glass tube, AB, Plate XVI. 75, whose outside diameter is ⅞ths of an inch, its inside diameter ⅝ths, and its length 54 inches. Such a tube may be supposed equal in strength to a solid glass rod, and will be considerably lighter. Make a zinc tube DE, from a square bar, hammered, &c. in the same way as has just now been directed, its length being 16.3 inches, and its inside diameter ⅞ths of an inch, or as much more as will allow it to move freely up and down on the outside of the glass tube. If the thickness of the zinc tube is ⅛th of an inch, it ought to answer very well; if it is somewhat thicker, it may answer even better. There must be a core of brass fitted to each end of the glass tube, ground gently into the glass, and fixed in by some of the lime cements. To make the fixing more secure, a hole might be bored through the tube and core, about half an inch from each end of the tube, and a copper pin put through them. The core in the lower end must have a small cylindrical piece, or wire formed from it of .3 or .4 of an inch in diameter, stretching 1.5 inch beyond the end of the glass tube, and tapped for the nut inside of the zinc tube to work upon. The regulating nut D should be under the pendulum ball c, yet a little free of it, as it would be difficult to get at it, were it placed near the lower end of the rod. The core at the upper end has also a part of the brass, a little way above the end of the tube, for the purpose of fixing in the pendulum spring. The zinc tube goes up to the centre of the ball, which rests on the end of it; the lower end, having the tapped nut in it, bears on the regulating screw. The nut may be either soldered into the tube or not, provided it is fast there. As both the glass rod and zinc tube are round, and go through the ball, it will be requisite to have something to keep the ball to its proper swinging position. For this purpose, let a brass tube of an inch and a half in length, be fitted *strongly* spring tight on the glass rod, and put on above the upper edge of the ball. To the lower end of the brass tube or socket is fixed a traverse piece, into which are fixed two steel rods, a quarter of an inch in diameter, and six inches long. These go within the ball, in the same manner as the lower ends of the outside steel rods in the gridiron pendulum. The distance between the holes in the traverse should be 3 inches, that is, each rod should be distant outside 1.5 inch from the centre of the glass tube. When the traverse with the spring tube is once set, so that the ball may have its proper position, it cannot be easily altered. The length taken for the zinc tube is rather in excess for the compensation of the glass rod, and should it be found so, the tube can readily be shortened. 8 is also a section of the ball of the zinc tube pendulum, glass tube pendulum, and wooden rod pendulum.

The glass tube having a length of 54 inches, will, when expanded by heat, carry down with it the zinc tube, whose lower end rests on that of the glass tube. The centre of the ball of the pendulum, resting on the upper end of the zinc tube, will expand upwards from the same cause which lengthens the glass tube, and, by this means, carry the ball of the pendulum up, and keep the centre of oscillation always at the same distance from the point of suspension. The length of the glass tube rod, and its expansive ratio, will be found to be in just proportion to the length of the zinc tube and its expansive ratio.

As the glass rod is not very fit for the pendulum fork to work on, the following apparatus is proposed, and has been found in other cases to answer the end as well as could be wished. See Plate XV. 73.

A A is a hollow cylinder of brass 1.5 inch long, which fits the glass rod rather more than spring tight. It is made a little thin near the ends, and at the middle it is left thick, having the appearance of a brass ring, a, a, a, a, formed on the cylinder, into which are fixed two pivots p, p, a piece of brass not very thick, .3 of an inch broad, being bent up nearly in a bow form, as at B, B, having a small hole at each end, b, b, to receive the pivots p, p. One of the ends must be screwed on, in order to get the pivots more conveniently into their holes. At the end or middle of the bow is a solid or round knob of brass C, in which is a hole tapped to receive the screw D, the head of which is milled on the edge and sunk on the outside, to receive the round flat piece of brass E, which snaps easily in like a barrel cover, and is not left so tight but that it may be easily turned round in its place, without any risk of coming out, and supposed to have no shake outwards. Into the piece E is fixed a piece of brass, having a hole in it to receive the pin of the crutch. Two views of this piece are seen at F F. When these pieces are all combined to act in their places, it can easily be seen, that, by turning the milled head of the screw D, holding the piece F in its front view position, the crutch pin will be made to move out or in, according as the screw D is turned, by which the clock will be set on beat, to a degree of nicety which is not easily obtained by bending the fork or crutch shank.

There are other modes of putting a clock on beat, but they generally consist of an apparatus for that purpose, carried by the crutch or fork, which is a load on the cock pivot. The one which has been described, has the advantage of being supported by the pendulum rod.

Troughton's Tubular Pendulum.

Mr. Edward Troughton's tubular pendulum, is a very neat and ingenious one, in every respect worthy of that celebrated artist, to whom science is so much indebted for the great perfection to which he has brought the dividing of astronomical instruments. Having a good opinion of the pendulum, we shall give it a place here. See Plate XVI. 76.

This pendulum, Mr. Troughton says, in his description, is, " drawn to a scale of one-eighth of the real dimensions, exhibits the shape of the whole instrument, in which the parts of action being completely concealed from view, it appears, excepting the usual suspension spring, to be made of solid brass. This figure gives a front view of the pendulum. The form of the bob is used more on account of its being easy to make, and sightly, than from any other considerations; it is made of one piece of brass, about 7 inches diameter, 2.5 thick at the centre, and weighs about 15 lbs. avoirdupoise: the front and back surfaces are spherical, with a thick edge or cylindrical part between them. The apparent rod is a tube of brass, reaching from the bob nearly to the top. This contains another tube and five wires in its belly, so disposed as to produce altogether (like the nine-bar gridiron of Harrison) three expansions of steel downwards, and two of brass upwards; whose lengths being inversely proportioned to their dilatation, when properly combined, destroy the whole effect that either metal would have singly. The small visible part of the rod near the top, is a brass tube, whose use is to cover the upper end of the middle wire, which is here single, and otherwise unsupported.

" Reckoning from the top, the first action is downwards, and consists of the spring, a short wire 0.2 diameter, and a long wire 0.1 diameter; these all of steel, firmly connected, reach down within an inch of the centre of the bob, and occupy the middle line of the whole apparatus. To the lower end of the middle branch is fastened the lower end of the interior brass tube, 0.6 in diameter, which terminates a little short of the top of the exterior tube, and produces the first dilatation upwards. From the top of the interior tube depend two wires 0.1 diameter, whose situation is in a line at right angles to the swing of the pendulum, and reach somewhat lower than the attached tube itself, which they pass through without touching, and effect the second expansion downwards. The second action upwards is gained by the exterior tube, whose internal diameter just allows the interior tube to pass freely through it; its bottom is connected with the lower ends of the last described wires. To complete the connection, a second pair of wires of the same diameter as the former, and occupying a position at right angles to them, act downwards, reaching a little below the exterior tube, having also passed through the interior one without touching either. The lower ends of these wires are fastened to a short cylindrical piece of brass, of the same diameter as the exterior tube, to which the bob is suspended by its centre.

"No 1. is a full size section of the rod, in which the three concentric circles are designed to represent the two tubes; and the rectangular position of the two pair of wires round the middle one, are shown by the five small circles. By copying this arrangement, from the elegant construction of your own half seconds pendulum, (*Phil. Journal* for August 1799,) I avoided much trouble, which must have occured to me, unless, indeed, I had been impelled on the same idea, by the difficulty of contriving the five wires to act all in a row, with sufficient freedom and in so small a space.

"No. 2. explains the part which closes the upper end of the interior tube: the two small circles are the two wires which depend from it, and the three large circles show the holes in it, through which the middle and other pair of wires pass.

"No. 3. is designed to explain the part which stops up the bottom of the interior tube; the small circle in the centre is where the middle wire is fastened to it; the others the holes for the other four wires to pass through. No. 4. is the part which closes the upper end of the external tube; the large circle in the centre is the place where the brass covering for the upper part of the middle wire is inserted; and the two small circles denote the fastening for the wires of the last expansion. No. 5. represents the bottom of the exterior tube, in which the small circles show the fastening places for the wires of the second expansion, and the larger ones the holes for the other pair of wires to pass through. "No. 6. is a cylindrical piece of brass, which shows how the lower ends of the wires of the last expansion are fastened to it, and the hole in the middle is that whereby it is pinned to the centre of the bob. The fastening of the upper ends of the two pair of wires is done by screwing them into the pieces which stop up the ends of the tubes: but at the lower ends they are all fixed as represented by No. 6. I have only to add to this description, that the pieces represented in Nos. 5. and 6. have each a jointed motion, by means of which the fellow wires of each pair would be equally stretched, although they were not exactly of the same length.

"In the apparatus thus connected, the middle wire will be stretched by the weight of the whole; the interior tube will support at its top the whole except the middle wire; the second pair of wires will be stretched by all except the middle wire and interior tube; the exterior tube supports at its top the weight of the second pair of wires and the bob; and the second pair of wires are stretched by the weight of the bob only.

"The first pendulum which I made of the tubular kind, had only three steel wires, and one tube above the bob; that is two expansions down and one up; and the quantity which one of brass falls short, to correct two of steel, was compensated for by extending those branches of the rod below the bob, and bringing up an external tube to which the bob was affixed. There is an awkwardness in this construction, owing to the rod reaching about 13 inches below the lower edge of the bob, otherwise it is not inferior to the one first described."

J.H.

Ward's Pendulum.

The rod of this pendulum consists of two flat bars of steel, and one of zinc, connected together by three screws, as shown in Plate XVI. 77. No. 1. No. 2. is a side view of the pendulum rod when the bars are together; "*hh, ii,*" says Mr. Ward, "are two flat rods or bars of iron, about an eighth of an inch thick; *kk* is a bar of zinc interposed between them, and is nearly a quarter of an inch thick. The corners of the iron bars are bevelled off, that they may meet with less resistance from the air; and it likewise gives them a much lighter appearance. These bars are kept together by three screws, *l, l, l,* which pass through oblong holes in *h h* and *k k*, and screw into *i i.* The bar *h h* is connected to the one *k k* by the screw *m*, which is called the adjusting screw. This screw is tapped into *h h*, and passes barely through *k k*; but that part of the screw which enters *k k* has its threads turned off. The bar *i i* has a shoulder at its upper end, turned at right angles, and bears at the top of the zinc bar *k k*, and is supported by it. It is necessary to have several holes for the screw *m*, in order to adjust the compensation. Nos. 3. 4. 5. are a side view of each bar separately. No. 6. shows the flat side of the zinc bar. No. 1. is a front view of the pendulum rod when screwed together. The letters have the same reference to the different figures."

The front steel bar being lengthened by heat, and having its expansion downwards, will carry along with it the zinc bar, whose lower end is supported by a screw in the front bar; the zinc bar in this case will have its expansion upwards, and carry up the back steel bar, whose upper end rests by means of a knee on the upper end of the zinc bar. The pendulum ball hangs to the lower part of the back steel bar, which has its expansion downwards; but the two expansions downwards of the steel bars are compensated by the upward expansion of the zinc bar.

Mr. Ward's pendulum must be allowed to be a very excellent one, as it possesses the advantage of permitting the compensation to be readily and easily altered. The description which has been given of it in the Transactions of the Society for the Encouragement of Arts, &c. for the year 1807, and in the pamphlet which Mr. Ward published at Blandford in 1808, contain sufficient details to enable any common clockmaker to copy it. We have only to add, that there should be a spare screw, for shifting the compensation, and that the screws connecting the two steel bars and the zinc one should never on any account be moved. It will be found of great advantage to have a spare screw, which may be put into that place which is supposed requisite to correct the compensation; and then release the one supposed to be, where the compensation is thought too much or too little. Our experience with it soon led us to this contrivance. Having made one of these pendulums, we shall now give an account of its dimensions, &c. The distance from the upper part of the pendulum spring to the centre of the ball, is 40.75 inches; and to the lower end of the front steel bar, 2 feet 11.5 inches. From the upper end of the zinc bar, where the back bar of steel rests or hangs on, to the centre of the ball, is 2 feet 6.25 inches. The steel bars are forged from cast steel, and annealed; their breadth is three quarters of an inch, and their thickness about one-tenth of an inch. The length of the zinc bar is 24.6 inches; and its thickness a little more than two-tenths of an inch. The centre of the ball hangs on the end of the tube of the regulating nut, where it was tapped, to work on its corresponding screw, made near the lower part of the back bar, formed here into a round rod, the lower end of which is a point, or index, to a graduated plate fixed to the back of the case, and 5.25 inches below the centre of the ball. The weight of the ball is 18 lb.

2 oz.; that of the zinc and steel bars, nut, pendulum spring, and connecting screws, 2 lb. 13¼ oz.; weighing in all nearly 16 lb. In making up steel bars or rods for any compensation pendulum, it is proper to heat or blue them after they are finished, which will dispel whatever magnetism they may have acquired in working them up. The zinc bar of this pendulum, when brought near to the length of compensation, was about 21 inches. Taking the length of steel to be compensated by this at 61.75 inches, we may find what the compensation of the zinc should be, if the steel is rightly taken at 138.

Steel in inches 61.75 - - - log. 1.7906370
Ratio 138 - - - - - log. 2.1398791

3.9305161

Zinc in inches 21 - - - log. 1.3222193
Ratio 405.7 - - - - log. 2.6082968

3.9305161

The expansive ratio here is greater than 373, as given by Mr. Smeaton; but is not equal to 420, as given by Mr. Ward, from trials made with his pendulum.

The three zinc pendulums which have been described, have each their peculiar properties. The zinc rods of the gridiron one are very troublesome to make; but they are more exposed to the air or to changes of temperature, are easy to adjust by means of the shortest traverse, and the sets of holes which are in them and the centre rod. When this pendulum is well executed, it is perhaps the best of the three. The one with the zinc tube is the strongest, the bearing on it being more firm and direct than in either of the other two, only it has no means for adjusting the compensation, unless by shortening the tube from time to time, according as the excess of its compensation is shown. Something might be contrived to adjust it, without taking it from its place, but this would be too complicated; so that the shortening of the tube by degrees is rather the better way. Ward's is much more easily made than the other two. Those who use gridiron pendulums should have a half traverse, with three pins on it, similar to the shortest one in the pendulum, which will be found very convenient, when it is necessary, to shift for compensation. The half traverse and pins should be put into the holes, where the traverse in shifting is not to come. This will keep the pendulum rods in their places, and serve in the same way as the spare screw proposed for Ward's pendulum.

Rhomboidal Compensation Pendulum.

A great many years ago, an old clock was put into our hands, which had been made in this country, having a pendulum of this kind, consisting of seven or eight lozenges or rhombi, with diagonal bars to each, so as to make a sort of compensation to the pendulum rod. It will readily be seen, that when heat should elongate the sides of the rhombi, it will also elongate the diagonal bars, and cause their ends to press against the internal and horizontal angles of the lozenges; by this, the distance between the vertical angles will be kept invariably the same, and the centre of oscillation will be kept constantly so. The effect of cold on the rhombi or lozenges will be in the reverse order; and if there is a due proportion between the length of their sides and that of the diagonal bars, it is likely to compensate the effects of heat and cold on the pendulum. We shall hazard a proportion: say, for the length of the diagonal bars about six inches, and the distance between the vertical angles about five inches and six-tenths of an inch, the number of lozenges being seven: experience alone can best determine what these measures and number should be. A compensation pendulum rod of this kind was certainly an ingenious contrivance; the idea, *we presume*, seems to have been taken from the form of the tongs used by the Hollanders, when taking any live piece of burning coal or charcoal to light their tobacco pipes with. A great objection, however, to this kind of pendulum rod, is, that there are too many points of oblique bearing in it.

Some of the French artists have lately proposed to have one lozenge only, which would surely be unsightly, from the great length that the diagonal bar must have, and the clock-case much distorted to contain such a pendulum. For more on this subject, see the Appendix to the ninety-second volume of the Monthly Review, or *tome* xii. *Archives des Découvertes*.

On the Wooden Pendulum Rod.

The wooden pendulum rod does not come under the class of those which have just now been described; nor can it be supposed equal to any metallic compensation one. Having a good opinion of it, however, we put to trial one of them made of a very fine piece of straight-grained deal, that, for the purpose of seasoning, had been kept for five years near a parlour fire, which was almost constantly lighted throughout the whole year. The rod, when dressed up and fitted to the ball, and the pendulum spring put to it, was well var-

On the upper end of the screw, the lower edge of the pendulum ball rests; and when moved up or down by the screw, the nuts *a, a*, are screwed against the brass piece *b* 2, in order to keep all fast.

The advantages which this pendulum possesses, are very obvious. The whole of the momentum of the ball is so near the centre, that it maintains a very steady motion; and should any lengthening or shortening of the rod and steel wires take place, this will in some degree be compensated by the ball. Should they lengthen, the same cause will make the centre of the ball get upwards, the edge meanwhile resting on the end of the regulating screw, and *vice versa*. A piece of flat brass is fitted and pinned into the upper part of the rod C C, as seen in the drawing. In front of the rectangular hole made in this piece of brass to receive the crutch pin, a part of the wood is taken away, in order that the crutch with its pin may get as near as may be to the piece of brass. The piece of brass in which the lower end of the pendulum spring is, is fitted to the top of the rod, having two pins through it, to make it fast there. The upper end is fixed to a piece of brass, which goes on a steel arbor, having pivots to rest on a cock, and turn freely on it, so that the pendulum may take its plumb-line when hung on.

It has been observed by some cabinet-makers, that from drawers, whose sides and bottom were of cedar, there issued effluvia, that inspissated the oil at the locks, and thickened it so much, that the locks became of no use till they were taken off and cleaned.

Pendulum rods have sometimes been made of cedar wood, and are objectionable on this account, as the oil at the pivot holes of the clock becomes thickened by it. Perhaps if pendulum rods of cedar were strongly varnished, this might deprive the wood of this inspissating quality.

It is of the utmost importance to have the pendulums of clocks well fixed at the point of their suspension; and the cock to which they are suspended should, at the same time, be strong and firmly fixed to the wall of the place where the clock stands. This requires to be particularly attended to in turret clocks, and still more so in clocks intended for astronomical purposes. These last ought to be placed upon an iron bracket, strongly fixed to as massy a stone pier as can possibly be got into the place where the clock is to stand. We have had an instance of a pendulum which was so well fixed up, that there did not appear a possibility of its being made any firmer, or that the motion of the pendulum could in the least affect the cock and suspension, yet the arc of its vibration was a little increased, after having made considerable exertions to put farther home the screws,

&c. concerned with the fixtures of the cock and the suspension of the pendulum. The arc of vibration did not exceed two degrees on each side of the point of rest, so that its motion, or centrifugal force, could not be very great at the point of suspension; yet small as this force was, it is clear that it was sufficiently great to affect the cock there, as this cause made the arc of vibration of less extent than when the suspension was afterwards more firmly fixed. We have suspended the pendulum on a strong brass cock, which was either rivetted or screwed to an iron plate. This iron plate was screwed firmly to the wall, the back of the clock-case being between the plate and the wall, and sometimes a notch was left in the pillar plate to receive the end of the brass cock, by which means the clock frame, and the pendulum suspension were made to keep together as nearly as possible; and when every thing here was so far adjusted, a strong screw with a square head was put through the cock, binding it and the pendulum top-piece firmly together. Another way is, to have two brass supports screwed on to a very strong seat board. These supports may be about one inch broad and half an inch thick, and in height about six inches more or less, according to the height of the bending of the pendulum spring above the seat board. Each support has a strong and broad sole, and these soles have a stout steady pin to go into the seat board, which is screwed from underneath the seat board, by a strong iron or steel screw, fast to the upper side. The supports at the top incline a little towards each other, and a thick and broad piece of plate brass is screwed to them behind, so as to connect them firmly together. The upper ends of the supports are made level, and parallel with the soles and seat board. Across these ends is made a triangular notch, to receive the pivots of a piece of steel, to which the pendulum is suspended. By means of these pivots the pendulum turns, so as to hang freely in a vertical position. The distance between the ends of the brass supports at the top need not be more than two inches, while at the bottom the distance may be four inches, or not quite so much, the inclination being about ten degrees or so from the perpendicular. The piece of steel should not be less than half an inch thick at the middle, where it should be circular, and about three quarters of an inch broad. In the middle is a hole of about three-tenths of an inch in diameter: the two conical arbors are formed from the circular part, so as to be in a line with the diameter of the hole. The pivots of these arbors, which turn in the triangular notches, may be about three-twentieths of an inch thick. In the hole, which is three-tenths of an inch wide, is fitted a steel pivot, having a shoulder on the under side, which comes so far beyond the upper side as to admit a stout brass collet to be pinned on it, and against the upper flat side of the circular part, besides a sort of screw head on the end, with a slit in it, by which a screw-driver can turn it about, so that the pendulum ball may be made to stand in the plane in which it ought to swing. From the shoulder, below the circular part of the steel piece, to the lower end, may be an inch long. To this the pendulum spring is fixed. This, in some respects, is a very convenient mode of suspension, but we do not think it so strong and so firm as the other.

When the astronomical clock, formerly mentioned, which goes six weeks without winding up, was planned, care was taken to have the weight kept at as great a distance as possible from the pendulum ball, as we conceived that the attraction of the weight would disturb the vibrations of the pendulum. This idea, which appeared to us new, had occurred, we have been told, long before to several very able artists and amateurs, such as Graham, Harrison, Lord Macclesfield, Sir George Shuckburgh, Troughton, and others. In the course of our trials with the clock, the arc of the vibrations of the pendulum, when the weight came as far down as the ball, was observed to suffer a sensible diminution, and this was imputed to their mutual attraction. Upon mentioning this afterwards to one or two persons, supposed to be competent to judge in an affair of this kind, they entertained some doubts respecting this explanation of the fact, and thought it might probably arise from some motion communicated to the air by the swinging of the pendulum. Without making any experiments in order to examine the action of the air on the motion of the pendulum, an account of the fact, which was ascribed solely to attraction, was published in Nicholson's *Phil. Jour.* Oct. 1812, vol. xxxiii. octavo series. Soon after this, Mr. Ezekiel Walker of Lynn, in a paper published in the same Journal, endeavoured to show, that the cause of this disturbance of the pendulum, (which he says had been known to him 30 years before,) arose from the motion of the air communicated by the weight to the pendulum, which is certainly did, as we soon afterwards found from one or two experiments, which did not occupy much time. In a paper of Mr. Walker's, in Nicholson's *Phil. Jour.* for May 1802, vol. ii. octavo series, p. 76, entitled, "Methods for diminishing the irregularities of Time-pieces, arising from differences in the arc of vibration of the Pendulum," he has assigned several causes for the changes that take place in the arcs of vibration, and proposed different methods to prevent them. But no notice whatever is taken of the motion communicated to the air by the pendulum. M. Berthoud mentions, in the first volume of his *Essai*, published in

1763, No. 648, that the air put in motion by the vibrations of the pendulum, acts against the weight of the clock, so as to set it in motion; and that this will in its turn gradually diminish the motion of the pendulum until it stops it altogether. This takes place more readily when the weight hangs by a single line than when it is suspended by a pulley and double line. This fact, it must be confessed, had either been overlooked by us, or had entirely escaped our memory. Month clocks, from stopping frequently, have long been very troublesome to clockmakers, who no doubt assigned for it a different cause from the true one. In the old month clocks, the weights are very large and heavy, and the momentum of the pendulum very small, so that they were extremely liable to be stopped. But in clocks where the pendulum has even a considerable momentum, this agitation of the air will be sufficient to stop them altogether.

Having been called upon to examine a good astronomical regulator of Graham's, which had stopped, and which belonged to a nobleman in the neighbourhood of Edinburgh, we informed the man who was sent to put it in order, that he would find the weight opposite to the pendulum ball; which was actually found to be the case. In general, all month clocks will be observed to stop under similar circumstances.

CHAPTER XIX.

Sympathy, or Mutual Action of the Pendulums of Clocks.

It is now nearly a century since it was known, nay, it is much longer, for this was known even to Huygens, and has been observed by many since his time, that when two clocks are set agoing on the same shelf, they will disturb each other;—that the pendulum of the one will stop that of the other; and that the pendulum which was stopped will, after a while, resume its vibrations, and in its turn stop that of the other clock, as was observed by the late Mr. John Ellicott. When two clocks are placed near one another, whose cases are very slightly fixed, or when they stand on the thin boards of a floor, it has been long known that they will affect a little the motions of each other's pendulum. Mr. Ellicott observed, that two clocks resting against the same rail, which agreed to a second for several days, varied 1′ 36″ in 24 hours when separated. The slower having a longer pendulum, set the other in motion in 16½ minutes, and stopped itself in 36½ minutes. It never could have been supposed, however, that when very strong fixtures were made, it was possible for any thing of this kind to take place. About ten years ago, in a room where astronomical clocks were placed under trial, two strong deal planks were firmly nailed to a tolerably stout brick wall or partition, the ends of the planks being jambed between the adjoining partitions. The planks were 6 feet long, 6 inches broad, and 1$\frac{1}{4}$ths of an inch thick. One of them was placed behind the suspension, and the other behind the balls of the pendulums. The pendulums were suspended on strong massy cocks, partly of brass and partly of iron, which, with the backs of the cases, (one of which was of very hard oak,) were firmly screwed to the upper plank, the middle of the cases to the lower one, the bottoms being free and independent of the floor. Two clocks, whose pendulums were nearly of equal length and weight, and whose suspensions were distant from each other about two feet, kept so unaccountably close together for the greater part of twelve months, as to become a matter of considerable surprise. When the cold weather commenced in November, they made a small deviation from one another for a few days, and then resumed the same uniformity which they had before. An account of this was published in Mr. Tilloch's Philosophical Magazine, where the observations of M. de Luc, which seem to have been a very near approach to the cause, were inserted by way of reply. The pendulum which was at one of the clocks, was of Ward's kind. On its being taken away, a gridiron one was put in its place ; but with this, which was longer than Ward's, the clocks could never be brought to the same time as before. Their arcs of vibration continually varied, and no satisfactory going could be obtained from them, although we were well aware that they were competent to have given a very different performance. The gridiron pendulum clock was one of the best possible in its execution, and had one of the best recoiling 'scapements we have ever seen or made. The clock was taken from its case, to have a 'scapement of a different kind put to it. In the meanwhile, the pendulum being left hanging in its place, was observed to be in motion, which was at first imputed to some shaking of the house. On being stopped, it got again into motion, and upon observing it narrowly, it was found not to be in such a direction as any shaking of the house could produce, swinging quite in time with the pendulum of the going clock, the two pendulums mutually receding and approaching each other. The cure was instantly obvious ; and after the upper plank was sawed through between the clocks, the pendulum became in a little while dead and still. The arc in which it vibrated was about twelve minutes of a degree on each side of the point of rest, which was nearly about the greatest extent of variation in the arcs of the two pendulums. It would be impossible to make two clocks go closely together, in any other situation than the one which has been mentioned.

After the plank was cut through, the going clock was observed to be losing nearly at the rate of a second and a half a day ; and if the clock which kept so long in unison with it had been tried under the same circumstances, it is probable that the rate would have been found to be fast. The rate they had for a period of eight or nine months or more, when they went close together, did not exceed two-tenths of a second fast a-day, and this may have been a mean of the natural rate of each pendulum, if it may be so expressed ; that is, suppose one clock was going slow 1.5 second per day, the other fast 1.7 second, there will be two-tenths of a second left for the acceleration of both, which seems to be the only way of explaining this phenomenon.

Subsequent trials with these two clocks, in still more detached situations, have given rise to an idea, that it is probable and seemingly possible, that two clocks, fixed as these were, where the pendulums affected each other, could be made to keep a rate of time much nearer than any clock singly could do. It is the opinion of an eminent foreign artist, that a few clocks, placed in this way, would communicate the motion of their pendulums to each other, till they came all at last to beat at the same instant.—We entertain no doubt of this opinion.

CHAPTER XX.

On Turret Clocks.

We have frequently seen turret clocks put up in places where no advantage was taken of the length of fall for the weights, which either did not descend through the whole height, or, if they did, the ropes had a second re-winding, as it were, on the barrel. Hindley, who was certainly a man of genius, and whose turret clocks were perhaps unequalled in regard to their execution, though defective, from no advantage being taken of the fall, made them all with barrels of a small diameter, and of such a length as to admit almost any number of turns, so that they could be placed in any situation, whether with propriety or not. We shall therefore lay down such rules, that a clockmaker may fit up a turret clock suited to any given fall for the weights.

Suppose that the height of fall for the weights is 25 feet, and that the clock is required to go eight days without being wound up, and with a single line to the weight, that is, with no pulley for the weight to hang on,—we may allow 12 inches for what the weight will take. This reduces the length of fall to 24 feet; allowing 16 turns of the barrel to give 8 days going, and dividing the 24 feet of fall by 16, we shall have, for length of the rope, 18 inches, for one turn of the barrel. To find the diameter of the barrel, we say, as 355 for the circumference is to a diameter of 113, so is the circumference 18 inches of the barrel to its required diameter, which will be found to be 5.73 inches nearly. But this diameter would be too large, since the diameter of the rope must be taken into account; for the true diameter, or that which is necessary to run out the fall, must be taken at the centre of the rope when wound round the barrel. Allowing the diameter of the rope to be half an inch, then taking this from 5.73 inches, we shall have for the proper diameter of the barrel 5.23 inches. Having now obtained the diameter of the barrel, its length, between the ends, may easily be found. Sixteen turns of the barrel, the number wanted to produce eight days going, and a rope of half an inch in diameter, will require eight inches; but as the coils of the rope cannot lie quite close to each other, we may allow, for freedom, one inch and a quarter; consequently, if the barrel is made 9.25 inches in length between the ends, it will be sufficiently long. For the striking part, a rope of half an inch in diameter will be strong enough; and, as one of a considerably smaller diameter, even one-half, would suit the going part, the going barrel may be made shorter. If the clock should be made to go by a double line and pulley, then the diameter of the barrels will require to be the double of 5.23 inches, or 10.46 inches. Or if the fall is only 13 or 14 feet, then the barrels of 5.23 inches in diameter would do, by means of a pulley. The diameter of the pulley will in part lessen the length of the fall, and in place of 12 inches, we may now deduct 16 inches, or so, from the fall, on account of the length taken up by the weight and pulley; but this trifling circumstance requires little accommodation on the part of the clockmaker. Taking then the diameter of the barrel at 10.46 inches, in order to ascertain what diameter the barrel ends and the great wheel ought to have, the rope being half an inch in diameter, twice this added to the barrel's diameter will make it 11.46 inches, but, for the sake of even numbers, let it be taken at 11 inches and a half for the diameter of the plain barrel end; an additional inch, or 12.5 inches in diameter for the barrel ratchet end ought to do, unless when the barrel ratchet is put on the barrel end, and within its diameter, as is sometimes done, in order to have the great wheel of a less diameter than it otherwise would be, when the barrel ratchet end is done in the usual way. The centre of motion of the ratchet and click need not be more distant from the top of the ratchet than half an inch, or at most .6 of an inch, and .75 of an inch more than this for the breadth of the wheel rim, including the teeth. The semidiameter of the barrel ratchet end is 6.25 inches; to this being added .6 of an inch, and .75 of an inch, we shall have, for the semidiameter of the great wheel 7.6 inches, or its diameter 15.2 inches. The diameter of the great wheel being thus obtained, we may get the circumference by saying, as 113 is to 355, so is 15.2 to the circumference required, which is found to be 47.75 inches; this divided by 240, the double of the number of the teeth proposed to be put into the great wheel of the going part, we have for the breadth of each tooth and each space 0.199 of an inch, or nearly .2 of an inch. It is perhaps advisable to have the space a very small degree less than what is here given; the teeth will then be somewhat more than .2 of an inch in breadth. By taking small temporary segments of thin brass, having the same radii as the wheel, and cutting them from the proposed number on the cutting engine, they will lead us to form an idea of the strength that the teeth may have. Indeed, this, and calculation together, ought to go hand in hand, and is the way that any ingenious clockmaker ought to adopt, if his object is to have the best possible contrivance in the construction of any piece of work in which he may be engaged.

As it is of consequence to have length of pendulum, it should be adopted when the clock is in such a situation as to allow its being applied. We recommend one of 20 feet 5 inches in length, which would have almost as much dominion over the clock as those made by Hindley of 52 feet 4 inches, and could be more easily made. The wheels 72, 60, and 24, the pinions 12 and 10, give 24 vibrations in a minute, each oscillation being equal to two seconds and a half.

If it is proposed to have the pendulum of such a length as to swing 30 beats in a minute, the swing wheel having 30 teeth, and the pinions 10 each; then the numbers for the teeth of the second and third wheels will be 60 and 50, and the length of the pendulum 156.8 inches; where twenty feet or upwards, for length of fall, and strength of clock can be obtained, a shorter pendulum than this should never be adopted. The diameter of the second wheel may be made half of that of the great wheel, or even a little less; however, we may safely take it at the half, viz. 7.6 inches, as it is to be cut into half the number of teeth, and being considerably thinner than the great wheel, the teeth will, notwithstanding this, be sufficiently strong for the force exerted on them. The third wheel having 50 teeth, and the force exerted on them being considerably less than that on the second wheel, we may obtain the diameter of the third wheel, by first taking the proportion of 60 to 50, and then making the diameter somewhat less than the first proportion would give, because, were the teeth cut on this diameter as given, they would be as strong as those of the second wheel. We then say, as 60 teeth is to its diameter of 7.6 inches, so is 50 teeth to the diameter required, which is found to be six inches. Taking six inches in the compasses, and applying them to the legs of any sector that has a line of equal parts, both legs of the sector being extended till the points of the compasses fall exactly on 50, set the compasses to the number 45, which will give a distance suitable for the diameter of the third wheel. This will be found to be 5.5 inches nearly, and if the swing wheel is made five inches in diameter, it will do very well; it ought to be made pretty thick, so as the teeth may have a broad bearing on the pallets, and if two small holes are drilled through near to their points, making equal portions or spaces there, these will contribute much to keep a good quantity of oil on them for a considerable time.

The barrels both in the going and striking parts being made equal in diameter, and each performing a revolution in 12 hours, we now proceed to make out proper numbers for the striking part, and diameters for the great wheel, the pin wheel, and the tumbler wheel; this last we shall also make use of as a fly wheel. The diameter of the barrels being equal, the great wheels may also be equal, and the diameter of the striking great wheel will be 15.2 inches. The number of blows which the hammer must make in 12 hours, can be obtained by a very simple rule. The first blow 1, being added to the last blow 12, will make 13, and 13 multiplied by 6, half of the number 12, will give 78 for the number of blows required during one revolution of the great wheel and barrel. The great wheel of the striking part will require to have rather stronger teeth than those of the great wheel of the going part, because there is a stronger rope and a heavier weight applied against them, in order to raise as much weight of hammer as may be, so as to bring a sufficient sound from the clock bell. The pin wheel pinion being 10, and the wheel 64, having eight lifting pins in it for the hammer tail, the number of teeth in the great wheel which will be necessary, so that one turn of it may produce 78 blows, may be either 98 or 100.

Suppose we take 98 for the number of teeth, 98 divided by 10, the number in the pin-wheel pinion, the quotient will be 9.8, which, multiplied by 8, the number of pins in the pin wheel, will give 78.4 for the number of blows for one revolution of the great wheel. If the great wheel should have 100 teeth, this, divided by 10, will give 10, and this again mutiplied by 8, will give 80 for the number of blows during one turn of the barrel; either of these numbers for the teeth of the striking great wheel would do very well. If we take 98, and as the pin wheel is to have 64 teeth, we may find a proper diameter for it, so that the teeth may be nearly about the same size as those of the great wheel. Say as 98, the number of teeth in the great wheel, is to 15.2 inches, its diameter, so is 64, the number of teeth required in the pin wheel, to a diameter required for it, which will be found to be 9.9 inches.

The pin wheel, having 64 teeth, and 8 lifting pins in it, the tumbler wheel pinion, which makes one revolution for every blow of the hammer, must have 8 teeth or leaves in it. The diameter of the tumbler wheel must be considerably smaller than that of the pin wheel, and this will depend on the number of teeth it ought to have, on the number of leaves in the fly pinion, and on the number of the revolutions which the fly pinion is to make for every blow of the hammer. The less the number of revolutions given to the fly pinion during one blow of the hammer, the less will the striking part be under the influence of oil. But few turns in the fly, require it to be considerably extended in the wings or vanes, and this demands some ingenuity and address in the clockmaker to carry them out, so that they shall be conveniently clear of every part of the clock. When the arms of the fly are extended, the wings or vanes can be considerably diminished in surface; and a little weight may be given them, so that when once the fly is set in motion it will not easily stop. The construction of the fly, and of the fly pinion, has hitherto been injudicious. The flys commonly applied to turret clocks were too heavy, the wings or vanes were too broad, they made too many revolutions, and the fly pinion was not so properly sized as it might be: for it must be considered that it acts not merely as being driven, but it must sometimes act as a leader. For although the tumbler wheel, or fly wheel, which turns the fly pinion, acts as a driver, yet, from the nature and application of the fly pinion, and fly to regulate the velocity of the striking, the fly pinion, from the acceleration which it will acquire, must sometimes act as a leader, so that the size of the fly pinion ought to be a mean between the size of a leader and that of being driven. If the pinion is made too large, or the size of a leader, the wheel teeth in driving it would be apt to butt on the pinion; and if made too nicely, to be driven, it could hardly ever act as a leader, as here the pinion would butt on the wheel teeth; this then, is the reason of keeping it to the mean size of the two, which will be found to have a good effect. The arms of the fly may be about 26 inches in length.

The number of the revolutions of the fly pinion for one blow of the hammer is not arbitrary; in some clocks the fly may make twenty revolutions, in some more and in some less. When the revolutions are few, and the acceleration of the fly fit to carry forward in a small degree the striking, it may appear to strike faster towards the end of a long hour, but it will require a nice ear to perceive it. We have made the fly pinion to have only four turns for one blow of the hammer, which answered extremely well, so that the tumbler wheel will require 40 teeth, supposing the fly pinion to have 10. If we take the ratio of the pin wheel of 64 to its diameter 9.9 inches, then the tumbler wheel of 40 would have its diameter 6.25 inches, the teeth would then be of the same size or strength with those of the pin wheel; but this is not requisite, as they will bear to be considerably diminished in size, and if the diameter of the tumbler wheel is nearly 5.5 inches, the teeth will be sufficiently strong. In this striking part there is no fly wheel and pinion.

The locking of the striking part of turret clocks requires safe and good mechanism. That which Hindley used is very ingenious, and was adopted in the clock made for St. Andrew's Church in Edinburgh; yet, from foulness of oil or dirt, it is liable to misgive, and in attempting to rectify it, the ignorance or carelessness of workmen is apt to increase the evil. The nicety of this locking lies in the pins of the count-wheel, whose office is to raise up the locking-lifter, and pass it at the same time. The locking which is here proposed, is by means of two pins or detents on the fly pinion arbor, one of which is for locking on, and the other is a detainer while the striking is on warning. In this motion work, we have a rack, having teeth on the inside as well as on the outside; the tumbler raises the rack by means of the inside teeth, the rack-catch acts by those on the outside, and is concentric with the hour lifting arm, or that which discharges the striking; but both move freely and independently of each other. When the rack is on the lifting of the last tooth by the tumbler, a pin which is in the rack carries forward the end of a lever or arm. Concentric with this arm, and fixed with it, another arm presents itself (at the same instant when the pin in the rack has carried the arm forward) to a pin or detent on the fly pinion arbor, and here the striking is locked. The pin in the minute wheel, on raising up the hour lifting arm, raises at the same time the rack catch, and consequently allows the rack to fall, and the pin from the fly pinion arbor, which before this was locked, gets disengaged; and here the striking would go improperly on, but another arm, which is connected with the hour lifting arm, presents itself to the other detent on the fly pinion arbor, and detains it till such time as the lifting arm drops off from the pin in the minute wheel, and then the striking being at liberty goes on, and is again locked when the pin in the rack is made to move one of the locking arms forward. This locking is sure and safe, and very easily executed. It was contrived for one of the clocks at Annan.

The pins of the pin-wheel ought to be pretty stout, and one half of their diameters should be cut away, so as to allow the hammer tail to drop off freely, causing as little loss as possible of the force of the weight. Some have made very slender pins, and strengthened them by their opposite ends being fixed in a small circular rim or ring over them; but small pins are apt to tear and wear away the acting part of the hammer tail. The hammer tail may be so constructed that it begins to raise the hammer head when the lever by which it acts is at its maximum length, the head having then a more horizontal position than when it is afterwards raised up. The principle laid down here of the striking, &c. was adopted and put in execution in the two turret clocks which we made for the royal burgh of Annan, and which are not equalled by any turret clock in the island. The frames of these clocks are so constructed, and the wheels so disposed, that any wheel can be separately lifted out of the frame, without either taking it to pieces, or removing any of the other wheels.

The diameters of the wheels and the length of the barrels being determined, we may thence fix upon the length and breadth of the clock frame, which is proposed to be rectangular, and the wheels lying all nearly in a horizontal position, making it of such dimensions as not to pinch any part of the work, nor yet to have a superabundance of room. Beginning, then, with the going part:—The great wheel being 15.2 inches in diameter, and having 120 teeth, and the pinion which it drives 10, we know that the distance of their centres will be 8.061, or 8.1 inches nearly. We also know, that in the case of the second wheel of 7.6 inches in diameter, and 60 teeth driving the third wheel pinion of 10, the distance of their centres must be 4.273 inches. In like manner, we get the distance of the centres of the third wheel, and swing-wheel. The diameter of the third wheel is 5.500 inches; the swing-wheel pinion being 10, we have for the distance of their centres, 3.158 inches. By taking these distances, and adding them together, with the semi-diameters of the great and swing-wheels, we shall have the space that would be required to contain the going part.

	Inches.
From the centre of the great wheel to that of the second wheel	8.081
From the centre of the second wheel to that of the third wheel	4.273
From the centre of the third wheel to that of the swing wheel	3.158
The semi-diameter of the swing wheel,	2.5
The semi-diameter of the great wheel,	7.6
	25.612

So that it requires 2 feet, 1 inch, 6 tenths, and a very little more, to contain the going part.

By proceeding in the same manner, we shall find the distance of the centres of the wheels in the striking part to be as follows:

	Inches.
From the centre of the great wheel to that of the pin wheel,	8.1875
From the centre of the pin wheel to that of the tumbler wheel,	5.6815
From the centre of the tumbler wheel to that of the fly pinion,	3.2544
Semi-diameter of tumbler wheel,	2.75
Ditto of the great wheel,	7.6
	27.4734
To which add the space required for the going part,	25.612
Gives for Inches,	53.0854

The length, then, required to contain the going and striking parts, is about 4 feet 5 inches, being the inside length of the frame.

The width inside of the frame, depends on the length of the barrels, the thickness of the ends, and of the great wheels, &c. The striking barrel being the longest, we must take the length given for it, which was determined to be 9.25 inches between the ends. Allow one quarter of an inch or so for the thickness of the plain end, and half an inch for that of the ratchet end, and about 3-4ths of an inch or so for the thickness of the great wheel, these being 1.5 inch, which, added to the length of the barrel, makes 10.75 inches. The pin wheel is supposed to run behind the great wheel, having a proper freedom between them, the pins for lifting the hammer tail being on the opposite side of the pin wheel, and the plain barrel end having a sufficient freedom of the front bar of the clock frame. We shall call this freedom about .3 of an inch, and as much for the freedom of pin wheel and great wheel; the thickness of the pin wheel about .4 of an inch, or a very little more; the height of the pins from the surface of the pin wheel about .6 or .7 of an inch.

	Inches
The length of the barrel, with its additions, was,	10.75
Freedom of plain barrel end,	.3
Ditto of great and pin wheels,	.3
Thickness of pin wheel,	.45
Height of pin wheel pins,	.7
And take the distance of their tops from the side bar of the frame at	1.25
Inches,	13.75

By this it appears that the distance between the bars of the frame inside, will require to be 13.75 inches. The side bars, one on each side of the frame, are of forged iron, above four inches in breadth, and .4 of an inch thick, having at the ends a sort of thickness left there, so as to form a shoulder, and beyond the shoulders are tenons, not quite so thick nor so broad as the bars themselves; these tenons, about 4.5 or 5 inches long, are fitted into a rectangular hole, in the cast iron part of the frame, which compose the ends of it. The ends of the tenons are sometimes formed into two screws, each having nuts to bind them against the shoulders, and with the cast iron ends: or having sometimes slits in them to receive a strong iron wedge to bind the shoulders; either of them will do very well. The length from shoulder to shoulder of the side bars need not be quite so much as that which has been allowed for containing the going and striking wheels. If this length is 4 feet 4 inches, it will be sufficient; the space given by the cast-iron frame ends will more than compensate what has been deducted from the calculated length. The cast-iron ends are composed of two sorts of pillars, connected by a rectangular bar, near 5 inches broad, and about half an inch thick; the length of the rectangular bar such as to allow the side bars, when the tenons are into the square part of the pillars, and in the rectangular hole which is made there to receive the tenons, that the inside of the side bars shall be only distant from one another 13.75 inches. The middle part of the pillars is a square of about 3 inches, and 6 inches long; the upper and lower ends of the pillars are turned into such a figure or shape, as the taste or fancy of the artist may suggest. The middle of the rectangular hole which receives the tenons, may be distant from the lower end of the pillar about 12 inches; the top of the upper end may be equally distant. This frame, if constructed in the manner which has been directed, will be found to be strong, firm, and stiff, and very handy and convenient, while going

pinion of four will lead about the snail wheel and snail, having a common socket; the wheel having 48 teeth and 7 inches in diameter, and turning on a stud in the back bar; the rack is also on a stud here. The pivot required to have a lanthorn pinion formed on the end of it, for a wheel of 48 teeth, and 7 inches diameter, would be rather too thick; so that by keeping the pivot of a moderate size, or sufficiently thick to have a hole in it to receive the prong of a pinion of 6, and the snail wheel 72, may be a better way than that which we first proposed. The hour lifting arm and the detaining one may be formed or not from one and the same piece, and fixed on an arbor which lies above the great wheel, whose pivots must run in cocks attached to the main frame; cocks are also required for the hammer, the verge, and pendulum. The length of the pendulum which we have proposed for this clock, may be thought by some rather inconveniently long, which is a matter that can very easily be got the better of, by assuming any other lengths, say 6, 7, or 8 feet: either of these lengths will perhaps have dominion enough over the clock; but these will require other sets of numbers for the second and third wheels, allowing the pinions to remain 10 each, and the swing wheel to have 30 teeth. The second wheel having 75 teeth, the third wheel 60, the pinions 10 each, and the swing wheel 30, the vibrations in a minute are 45, the length of pendulum required is 5 feet 9.7 inches. If the third wheel of this set be made 70, all others remaining the same, the vibrations in a minute will be 42, and the length of the pendulum 6 feet 8 inches; 40 vibrations in a minute would require the wheels to be too disproportionate in numbers, unless we were to make one of the pinions 12 in place of 10; the wheels in this case would be 75 and 64. In the other they would have been 80 and 50. The length of pendulum is 7 feet 4.2 inches; the vibrations in a minute 38; the pinions 10 each, and the swing wheel 30. The wheels are 75 and 64, the length of pendulum 8 feet, 1.73 inches. Wheels 80, 72, and 30, and pinions of 12, will give 40 vibrations in a minute.

It is certainly not requisite to give any more examples of constructing turret clocks. The one which has been given is sufficient to enable any intelligent artist to proceed in this way, whether with clocks going eight days, or with those which require daily winding up. There are often great objections made against the trouble of daily winding up a turret clock, but when this trouble can be submitted to, a clock of this sort is decidedly preferable to those which go eight days. Turret clocks which strike quarters are sometimes made, some of which are done by a quarter rack and snail, and others by a count wheel. For the description of a thirty-hour clock of this kind, put up in the town-house of Paris in the year 1782, we refer to Berthoud's *Histoire de la Mésure du Temps par les Horloges*. This is perhaps one of the finest public clocks in Europe. It was constructed with much care and expense, and is the only one which has enamelled dials, one of which is above 9 feet in diameter.

Although not in its proper place, we may here remark, that where four sets of dials and dial work are required, it would hardly be safe to trust them to a strong tight collet behind the minute wheel. We would therefore propose, that the pivot of the second wheel pinion be squared down, and a little longer beyond the fore bar than what was proposed for the square of the spring; this is for the particular reason of getting easily at a bolt pin when at any time setting the hands. On this square of the pinion let the squared socket of a plain wheel be very well fitted. This wheel is about 3.6 inches in diameter, and in thickness about one-fourth of an inch. The minute wheel must have a sink in it, so as to receive the plain wheel, but the sink must be more extended in diameter, to admit a skeleton sort of a rim of a wheel with forty teeth cut inside of it. This rim must fit well the inside of the sink in the minute wheel, and be fixed to it, either by soft solder, or some other means. The minute wheel, in this case of the sink in it, will require to be thicker than in the case of the spring collet. A bolt may be lodged under a dovetail slit made in the plain wheel; in this slit, and lying close to the sink, the bolt can be made to move out or in to the inside teeth on the minute wheel; on the end opposite that of the locking end of the bolt, is fixed a stout round pin or knob, for the finger to pull out when occasionally setting the hands; this pin serves also for a stout spring to push the bolt into its place between the inside teeth.

In fitting up the dial work immediately behind the dials, it may be recommended to adopt that which was contrived and put in practice in the different dial-works of St. Andrew's church clock: on the minute arbor, just by the lower end of the hour wheel socket, is a loose steel washer, which lies close to the fore plate of the dial work frame; and should the wind press the hour hand and hour wheel socket down, it affects no other part, but only presses the washer against the plate. Inside of the dial-work frame, and on the minute arbor, are washers to prevent any binding on the ends of the hour-wheel socket.

In the town clock at Paris, the revolutions of the fly striking the hour, are eight for every blow of the hammer; the fly of the quarter part makes four revolutions for every quarter hammer blow, there

2 D

being ten lifting pins on each side of the great wheel, making 20 lifts, the amount of the quarter blows in an hour. The wings or vanes of the flys in this clock are pretty broad and long, and can be set to take more or less hold of the air. The fly of Hindley's clock, in the Orphan Hospital, Edinburgh, makes 4.57 turns for every blow of the hammer; but, from the imperfect construction of the clock, no adequate weight of hammer can be raised; and hence a sufficiency of sound cannot be obtained from the bell. It has been said that the weight of the hammer for this purpose should be 5 pounds weight for every 100 pounds in the bell. Turret clocks in general must either have their bells too large for this proportion, or the clocks have not been made to raise a heavy enough hammer. The arm of the hammer, when at rest, should hardly make an angle of elevation above 20 degrees, or 24 at most; and in order to get as much mass of matter in the hammer head, the tail by which it is raised should be pretty long, and give a rise from the bell as little as possible. But this distance of rise from the bell must depend, among other things, on the length of the arm, and on the angle or length raised by the pin wheel and hammer tail.

It was formerly proposed to fix on the fore bar the small dial, to which the minute hand is set at, when setting those of the principal dials; but it matters not whether a dial is fixed and the minute hand is moveable, or the minute hand is fixed and the dial moveable. Suppose that, by means of three small and short brass pillars, fixed inside of the bevelled wheel, we now screw on the tops of them a light round dial, having the minute divisions and figures on it, and the minute index fixed on the fore bar, we can here make the bevelled wheel be turned about till the minute index points to the proper minute. This mode will, besides, allow us to have more conveniently three sets of dial work, that is, two by the bevelled wheels, whose arbors are laid horizontal, and the third by connecting it with the socket of the first or front bevelled wheel.

Where turret clocks are of a large size, and have very heavy weights applied to the barrels, they require much force and strength to wind them up. In order to remedy this, an apparatus of the same nature as that which is commonly applied to cranes has been used. This consists of a wheel, with rather strong and coarse teeth, fixed on the barrel end, opposite to that where the great wheel or pinion of any number, on whose arbor a square to receive the winding up key is attached to the clock frame, by means of a cock so as to pitch with the wheel on the barrel end; and by this means a considerable weight can be raised with ease, requiring much exertion, but more time than when the winding up is performed by the barrel arbor. The clock in the town-house of Paris is wound up in this manner, which is represented in the drawing of Vick's clock, Plate I. 1. The size of the wheels and strength of teeth, may be regulated according to the weight to be wound up. The weight of the going part is in all cases light, when compared with that which is necessary for the striking part, in most of these clocks. Besides the advantage of winding up a heavy weight with ease, this method has another, which is, that the barrel arbor pivots can be used, either in conducting the hands, discharging the quarter or striking parts, or turning count wheels, &c. The old way of the division of the hours striking by the count wheels and locking plate, and locking on the hoop wheel, does not yield in ingenuity to any thing which has been since introduced in its place by modern clockmakers. The only great objection to the old way, was the trouble of making the clock strike a round of eleven hours or so, when the striking of the hour not corresponding with the hands, took place from any accidental discharge. It may not be out of its place to observe here, that the application of the cord or rope for the weight should be on that side of the barrel which lies next to the pinion into which the great wheel acts, especially in turret clocks, as this relieves the barrel pivots of a great degree of friction, which they would otherwise undergo were the course of the rope and weight on the opposite side.

If the barrel is made the same diameter with that of the great wheel, the action of the weight or moving force, may be applied wholly or nearly so on the pinion, by which means the friction on the barrel pivots will be almost nothing or nearly annihilated. It is but justice to the memory of Julien Le Roy to say, that he seems to have been the first who takes notice of this. (See the new edition of Sully's *Règle Artificielle du Temps, par Le Roy*, p. 340. Paris, 1737.) And Professor Ludlam, in his correspondence about the Greenwich clock in 1779, recommends it to the attention of Mr. Holmes. See the diagram, Plate XIV. Let B be the barrel, and as large in diameter as the great wheel, C its centre, A is the pinion which the great wheel acts on. Suppose the line or cord to part from the barrel at A, and to go downwards; in this case the whole weight will rest on the leaves of the pinion, and none of it on the centre C. Secondly, Suppose the line to part from the barrel, on the opposite side at D, to go upwards, and turning round a pulley to have the same weight hung upon it; in this case the very same force or weight, will act upon the leaves of the pinion as before, but *double* that weight will rest upon or press the centre C. In both cases the pinion is turned the same way, and with exactly the same force. In the former, the centre C has no pressure from the weight; in the latter, the pivots press the pivot holes with double the weight hung on.

Although we have taken an eight-day turret clock by way of an example, we however by no means recommend them. Clocks which require to be wound up every day, are much better, and have greatly the advantage; any that we have made, were all of the latter kind. The fine clock in the Hotel de Ville at Paris, that of St. Paul's, and of the Horse Guards in London; the Town Clock, and that of St. Andrew's Church, Edinburgh, and almost all public clocks of character, require to be wound up every day. It is to be regretted that modern architects, when planning out a church or any building, where it is known that it is to have, or must have a clock, that they take this matter so little into consideration. Height or length of fall for the clock weights, and sounding boards for the bells, were much attended to when building spires for the ancient churches. An instance of this is seen in Sir Christopher Wren's architecture of the great Cathedral Church of St. Paul's, where the fall for the clock weights allow of such a force, as by a stroke of the hammer it can make a bell of 11,474 lb. be heard at a distance of two and twenty miles. We heard it at Windsor Castle in the month of June, 1773: the day was still and calm; and attending to try if the clock could be heard when striking the twelve o'clock hour at noon, (which we did hear,) the sound that came through the air, was not like that of a bell, but had a low, dull, and feeble tone barely perceivable.

We have heard a story of a sentinel when on duty at Windsor Castle in the night time: it was alleged that he had been off during the time of his being on guard, for which he was brought to trial by a court martial, for neglect of duty. He stated in his defence, that he heard St. Paul's clock strike thirteen at midnight, which was corroborated by others who heard the same number; by this he was acquitted. A little ticklishness in the locking of the striking part may have caused this to take place.

At the time when the public clock for the Royal Hospital at Greenwich was about to be made, Mr. John Smeaton, civil engineer, and the Reverend William Ludlam, professor of mathematics in the university of Cambridge, having taken a warm interest in the construction of it, *as will appear by their letters on that occasion,** strongly recommended that it should be made to go only thirty hours. They

* For these letters, see APPENDIX (A.)

were both well known in their time as very competent to give the best of directions in this affair; yet their advice was over-ruled by a majority of the commissioners. Mr. Smeaton was at the time one of them, but was left in the minority. It was humorously observed by Mr. Ludlam, that it was grudging shoe-leather to serve a good purpose. It may be supposed that many of the gallant old tars or invalids in the hospital, would, for a mere trifle of tobacco, have gone every morning up to the cupola, and wound up the clock.

CHAPTER XXI.

On the Method of fitting up Astronomical Clocks.

Although the example of calculation which we have given for the different parts of a turret clock, is applicable to any clock; yet, in order to make the calculation more familiar and easy, we shall apply it to an astronomical clock, intended to go 32 days without winding up, performing the computation in the most rigid manner, as these clocks ought to be made as perfect as possible in all their parts.

From the inside bottom of the intended case to the under side of the seat board, is supposed to be 4 feet 10.7 inches, the seat board one inch thick, and the distance from the upper side of it to the centre of the dial 3.125 inches, or 3⅛ inches. From these, to obtain a proper diameter for the barrel, which is to have sixteen turns on it, we propose that the length taken up by the pulley and weight shall not exceed 6 inches, and that the weight shall be about 10lb. or perhaps even less. Four feet 10.7 inches diminished by 6 inches, will be 4 feet 4.7 inches, and this doubled will be 8 feet 9.4 inches; which divided by 16, the number of turns proposed for the barrel, we shall have 1054 tenths of inches, which divided by 16, will give 65.875 tenths for one turn round the barrel. From this to find the diameter of the barrel, say as 355 is to 113 so is 65.875 to the diameter required, which will be found to be 2.0968 inches. The diameter given here for the barrel must be lessened by a diameter of the gut. The diameter of the gut, which we had 24 years at a month clock, and which carried a weight of 24lbs. was .045 of an inch; it might have even supported it much longer, but a different weight was afterwards hung on. It is very thick gut at .080 of an inch, and .060 of an inch is about the diameter of common sized gut, which we shall take for our estimate in the diameter of the barrel; then 2.0968 inches minus .060 of an inch, will give for the true diameter of the barrel 2.0368 inches. The diameter might be kept even a little larger than this, since the cutting of the screw upon the barrel for the gut to ride in will lessen it a little. The depth of the screw cannot be much more or less than .020 of an inch, at which we shall take it; 2.0368.+020 will then make the diameter of the barrel 2.0568 inches.

It is more than 40 years ago since we proposed that the trade in general should adopt, for all their work, gages having inches and the lowest subdivisions of an inch marked on them. Had this been done, it would have made all the communications between the different branches of the art extremely simple and easy; and yet however simple this may appear, it has never been done. It must be observed, that every branch, such as movement-maker, enameller, glass-maker, spring-maker, verge-maker, &c. have all their own gages, not one of which corresponds with that of his neighbour's, and all these gages have numbers applied to them. On what these numbers are founded, it would puzzle very much both the makers and owners of the gages to tell.

To get the length of the barrel between the ends, let us take the diameter of the gut at .080 of an inch, in order to allow freedom between the turns on winding round the barrel. This .080 multiplied by 16, the number of turns proposed, will give 1.28 inch, or very near 1 inch and $\frac{7}{25}$ths of an inch for the length of the barrel between the ends. The barrel, or great wheel, making a revolution in 48 hours, we must see what the number of teeth for it, and the second wheel pinion which it drives, ought to be, and likewise the number of teeth for the second wheel, and that of the centre pinion, so that this last shall make 48 turns for one of the great wheel. Let us assume 24 for the number of the second wheel pinion, and 20 for that of the centre pinion. If we take 6 times 24 for the number of the great wheel teeth, and 8 times 20 for the number of teeth in the second wheel, then the centre pinion will be turned 48 times round for once of the great wheel, as $6 \times 8 = 48$. Having assumed the pinions to be 24 and 20, these multiplied into one another, and the product multiplied by 48, the last product will be such a number, as when divided by a number for one wheel, the quotient will be a number for another wheel, $24 \times 20 = 480 \times 48 = 23040$, which divided by 144, the number for one wheel, the quotient will be 160 for the number of teeth of the other wheel. Or if we take 25 for the number of the second wheel pinion, and 20 for the other, these multiplied together, and the product again by 48, will give such a number, as when divided by 150, the number for one wheel, the quotient will be 160 for the number of the other wheel, $25 \times 20 = 500 \times 48 = 24000 \div 150 = 160$. The numbers for the teeth of these wheels may be obtained in the same way which we make use of to find the numbers of the teeth of the wheels for clock and watch movements. If we take 26 for the second wheel pinion, and 20 for the centre pinion, and multiply them into one another, and if the product is again multiplied by 48, the number of turns of the centre pinion for one of the great wheel, we shall have a number which being subdivided till there is no remainder, the divisors will form such sets of numbers as may be given for the teeth of the two wheels. Thus 26 × 20 = 520 × 48 = 24960, the divisors of which will be seven 2's, one 3, one 5, and 13, which give the numbers 156 and 160 for the wheels. For the subject of our astronomical clock, we shall adopt the number 144 for the great wheel, and 160 for the second wheel, and its pinion 24, and 20 for the centre wheel. The object is to have as high numbered wheels and pinions as can be conveniently got in. The diameter of the great wheel is assumed to be such, as will allow the teeth proposed for it to have strength enough to bear the exertion put on them, which we shall take at 3.520, and for that of the second wheel 3.300. In other words, there are 3.5 inches, and .020 parts more of an inch, for the one, and 3.3 inches for the other. The pinions for the third and swing wheels are to be 16 each, the number of teeth for the centre wheel 128, and for the third wheel 120. For the sake of saving trouble to those who may be inclined to make such a clock, we shall give the diameters of the wheels and pinions, and the distance of their centres.

	Teeth.	Diameter.	Distance of Centres.	Pinion.	Diameter.
The great wheel	144	3.520	2.0217	24	.614
Second wheel	160	3.300	1.830	20	.4372
Centre wheel	128	2.600	1.4372	16	.3493
Third wheel	120	2.300	1.280	16	.329
Swing wheel	30	2.000			
Wheel concentric with the second ditto	20	.7,436	1.522		
Wheel carrying the hour hand	60	2.0325			

The wheel of 20 is concentric with the second wheel, which making three revolutions in 24 hours, carries the hour-hand wheel of 60 once round in that time. The hour circle will have the 24 hours marked on it, that is, from 1 to 24, being intended for a siderial time clock. There is no other dial-work than the wheels of 20 and 60, which will require to have the hour-hand turned about by itself, (this cannot be considered as inconvenient by those who wish to have the most perfect mechanism for the dial work) when at any time the clock is set by the minute hand. From the centre of the dial to the centre of the hours and seconds circles, is 2.5 inches to each. The centre of the great wheel is on a line below the centre of the dial about 1 inch, and to the left of the perpendicular line, in the centre of the dial, 2.9 inches. The centre of the third wheel is also to the left of this line, a little more than half an inch, say .519 of an inch. The 'scapement we would propose to be the same as those which we have made to astronomical clocks, after the principle of that of Mudge's time-keepers; only the pallets might be made longer, and the springs of course a little stronger. The angle of 'scapement might be reduced to 15 minutes on each side of the point of rest, and yet the pendulum may be made to vibrate about 1.5 degrees on each side. The unlocking here would be as near the lowest point as possible, or when the pendulum had its maximum of force; or the 'scapement which we think preferable. See page 207, &c. and Plate VIII. 42. Nos. 1 and 2.

CHAPTER XXII.

On Church Bells and Gongs.

It is still a point undetermined, whether the common shape of the bell, or that which is called the dish form, chiefly used for house clocks, is the best. The great expense which attends experiments on bell founding, will probably keep this long undecided.

Bells are said to have been invented by Paulinus, bishop of Nola in Campagnia, about the year 400; first known in France, 550; first used by the Greek empire, 864; were introduced into monasteries in the seventh or eighth century. Pope Stephen III. fixed three bells in a tower on St. Peter's in Rome. In the churches in Europe they were introduced and became general in 900. They were first introduced into Switzerland, 1020. The first tuneable set in England was hung up in Croyland Abbey, in Lincolnshire, 960. The custom of christening or blessing bells is very ancient, (which probably took place at their first introduction to churches); it was expressly prohibited by Charlemagne in 789. In some places this custom came as far down as 1030.

They were observed to be heard farther when placed on plains than on hills, and still farther in valleys than on plains; the reason of which will not be very difficult to explain, if it be considered that the higher the sonorous body is, the rarer is the medium; consequently, the less proper vehicle it is to convey the sound to a distance; from a like cause, they are well heard in foggy weather. Nankin, in China, was anciently famous for the largeness of its bells; but their enormous weight brought down the tower, and the bells have ever since lain on the ground. One of these bells is twelve English feet high, the diameter seven and a half, and its circumference twenty-three; its figure almost cylindrical, except for a small swelling in the middle; and the thickness of the metal about the edges seven inches. From the dimensions of this bell, its weight is computed at 50,000 lb. which is more than double the weight of that at Erfurt, said by Father Kircher to be the greatest bell in the world. But others assert that the bells at Moscow are vastly larger; that given to the cathedral by Boris Godona weighed 288,000 lbs. Even this, however, is exceeded by the bell which was cast by the order of the Empress Anne, the weight of which is 432,000 lbs.; its circumference at the bottom more than twenty yards, its height nineteen feet, and its thickness twenty-three inches. How diminutive, in comparison of this most stupendous bell, are the largest in England! the greatest bell in Christ College, Oxford, weighing only 17,000 lbs. that at St. Paul's, London, 11,474, and *Great Tom* of Lincoln, 10,845 lbs. See *Imperial Encyclopædia*.

" The great bell in the Kremlin, Moscow, (which must be that cast by the order of the Empress Anne,) the circumference obtained was sixty-seven feet and four inches, which allows a diameter of twenty-two feet, five inches, and one-third of an inch. The perpendicular height, from the top of the bell, corresponds exactly with the statement made by *Hanway*, namely, 21 feet four inches and a half. In the stoutest part, that which should have received the blow of the hammer, its thickness equalled twenty-three inches. The weight of this enormous mass of metal has been computed to be 443,772 lbs. which, if valued at three shillings per pound, amounts to £66,565. 16s. laying unemployed, and of no use to any one." " In the belfry of St. Ivan, Church of St. Nicolas, in the Kremlin at Moscow, there is a bell suspended beneath others, though of less size, which is enormous. It is forty feet nine inches in circumference, sixteen inches and a half thick, and its weight more than fifty-seven tons, 3551 Russian poods, or 127,836 lbs." See *Clarke's Travels*.

The bell in the metropolitan church at Rouen, is said to be eleven feet in diameter, and thirteen feet high. The great bell at Erfurt, mentioned by Kircher in his *Musurgia Universalis*, weighs only

25,000 lbs. It may be said *only*, when compared to a bell in China, said to be in diameter thirteen feet and a half, forty-two feet in circumference, twelve feet and a half in height, and weighs 120,000 lbs. or above fifty tons. "The brass bell in Strasburg weighs ten tons; the other, which is of silver, weighs above two." See *Dr. Moore's Travels.*

In 1752, the old clock in York Minster was rendered useless by age, and being removed, another was made and put up by Henry Hindley of York, at the expense of about £300. This clock is said to be very finely executed. The diameter of the largest (of a ring of twelve bells,) in York Minster, was five feet nine and a half inches, and was 59 cwt.

In 1765, they were taken down as untuneable, and were replaced, in the same year, by a set of ten bells, cast by Messrs Lester and Pack, bell-founders, Whitechapel. They are of the same weight and size as those which they cast for Bow Church in London in the year 1762. Any difference is at least too trifling to notice. The weight and sizes below are what were given for the set in York Minster.

	Cwt.	qrs.	lbs.		Feet.	inches.
1st,	8	3	7	Diameters	2	8¼
2d,	9	1	5	- - -	2	9¼
3d,	10	1	22	- - -	3	0
4th,	12	2	21	- - -	3	2¾
5th,	13	2	22	- - -	3	5
6th,	16	0	4	- - -	3	7¾
7th,	21	0	23	- - -	4	0¼
8th,	26	0	13	- - -	4	3½
9th,	33	2	16	- - -	4	9¼
10th,	53	0	25	- - -	5	5

June 4, 1762, being his Majesty's birth-day, (that of our late and much lamented Sovereign,) who then entered into the 25th year of his age, the same was observed with the usual demonstrations of joy. In the morning of that day, the famous new bells at Bow-church, the finest in England, were rung for the first time.

It may be added, to what has been said of the weight of the great bell in the Cathedral of St. Paul's, London, that the clapper of it is 180lbs; the diameter ten feet, and is the bell on which the clock strikes the hours; the quarters are struck on two lesser bells underneath. The length of the pendulum 14 feet, the weight of the ball 112 lb. The length of the minute hand is eight feet, its weight

75 lbs; the length of the hour hand five feet five inches, its weight 44 lbs. The length of the hour figures, two feet two and a half inches; the circumference of the dial fifty-seven feet, which is fully eighteen feet in diameter.

The great bell in St. Giles' Cathedral, Edinburgh, was cast by Messrs. Pack and Chapman, Whitechapel, weighs 25 cwt. and was put up about the year 1776. The bell in Heriot's Hospital, and the one in St. Cuthbert's church, are much about the same weight and size, each weighing 8 cwt. 2 quarters, and two feet eight inches in diameter.

In St. Andrew's church, there is a ring of eight bells; the largest is about 15 cwt., the smallest 6 cwt., cast by the Whitechapel bell founders. There was no little ingenuity displayed in hanging them, so as they could be rung without interfering with one another, considering the smallness of the space in which they are hung.

Of late, (1824,) we are informed, that a bell of 18,808 lbs. weight was found in one of the valleys of the Jura mountains in Switzerland; but how it came there, seems to be unknown.

The Gong.

We believe some attempts have been made in Europe to make such a sounding instrument as the Chinese gong, but without success; it being a sort of bell metal not so hard as clock bells, but perhaps somewhat near to the hardness which church bells have, and, being cast into the shape in which they come to us, the great secret in giving them that strong degree of tone may lay in the hammering them (after being cast,) a little here and there. But this cannot be done with safety, unless both anvil and hammer, and gong likewise, are hammered, when under a very considerable degree of heat, nearly to that under which they would be seen, when in a very dark place, having the colour of a dark red. And such a process as this must be attended with much difficulty and labour, so much so, as to have deterred our artists (even if they thought of such a thing,) from trying it. A Chinese gong would break into pieces, by applying the hammer to it when in a cold state. Experiments have been made, where the human body has stood the temperature of 240° for some minutes, in an apartment heated on purpose; this may show how far it is practicable to hammer a gong in a very warm place.

The gong which Mr. Ludlam had in his possession, may have been raised up by the hammer, (as he thinks, and he was pretty well qualified to judge of this) from a flat sheet of metal. Any of them, however, that we have had an opportunity of seeing, were flat at bottom, without any raised up part, and had all the appearance of having evidently been cast, by the sand-marks that were seen upon them, notwithstanding the application of the hammer, as the impressions made by it were seen, here and there, done seemingly to stiffen the gong, and give it tone. In China, gongs are consecrated to religious purposes, and strictly prohibited from being taken out of the country; so those which come here, must either be smuggled away, or clandestinely obtained. Farther on this subject, see Appendix (A.) *Ludlam's Letters.*

CHAPTER XXIII.

On Clock Chimes and Bell Music, mode of pricking Barrels, construction of Organ Clocks, &c.

Chime, in its general meaning, is applied to the sounding of bels such as change-ringing by church bells, or the striking quarters of the hour by a clock on two or more bells, or to tunes played by a clock on a series of nine, twelve, or sixteen bells, tuned to their respective notes on the scale. Clocks that play tunes on bells are called musical clocks; when quarters are chimed or struck by the clock itself, for example, on six, or on eight bells in octave, it is called a quarter clock, and sometimes a chime clock; and when the quarters are struck by a string being pulled, it is called a pull quarter or a repeating clock, whether the quarters are struck on six or eight bells, or whether they are given by a double blow on the hour-bell, as in the repeating watch. A time-piece, or going part, and having no hour striking part, but having a repeating part, is by some called a silent pull.

Various ways may be adopted for pricking tunes on the music barrels of clocks. The earlier mode of doing this was by taking a piece of writing paper of such a size as to cover exactly the surface of the barrel, and in a direction perpendicular to the axis of the barrel, to draw as many lines parallel to one another as there were notes in the tune to be laid down on the barrel, the lines being equidistant, and corresponding perfectly with the hammer tails as they stood in the hammer frame. They were marked at each end with the letters or notes they were to represent in the gamut or scale of music; and, according to the number of bars in the tune, as many spaces were made by lines drawn equidistant and parallel to each other, intersecting the others at right angles. The junction of the ends of the paper, when applied round the barrel, represented one of these bar lines. The length or breadth of the spaces (which might be either squares or parallelograms) contained between the bar and note lines, was again divided on the note lines into as many parts or spaces as the number of crotchets in a bar, and for notes of lesser value a less space was taken. While the paper was lying on a table, the notes in the tune proposed to be laid on the barrel were marked by a black ink dot on their respective lines, and in the same order as the bars of the music lay. After this was done, the paper was pasted on the barrel: the note lines now appeared like so many circles traced round the circumference of the barrel, while the bar lines lay longitudinally on the surface of it. By this means the black ink dots were transferred and marked on the barrel by a punch or finger drill. This mode might answer very well where large barrels were used, and only one tune laid on; but in smaller work, and where several tunes were to be put on the same barrel, it is neither sufficiently neat nor accurate.

We are not acquainted with the method adopted by those workmen in London, who practise the pricking of music on clock barrels; but having had occasion to construct some musical clocks above thirty years ago, and having no opportunity of getting the music pricked on the barrels by any professional person, it became necessary to contrive some method for this purpose. One way consisted in applying the barrel concentric with the arbor of a wheel-cutting engine, whose dividing part consisted of an endless screw and wheel; and having fixed other apparatus on the engine for this purpose, different numbers of turns of the endless screw were taken for the longer or shorter notes, and the tunes were as accurately put on the barrel as could be wished. Another way consisted in placing the barrel and its train of wheel work and regulating fly in the frame. A force was applied to turn the barrel, wheel work, and fly round in the order of lifting the music hammer tails, and an apparatus was used to mark the dots on the barrel. The fly made 360 revolutions for one turn of the barrel; or, should this be thought too quick a train, it might be made by altering the numbers of the wheel teeth to make 250 or 260 revolutions for one turn of the barrel; the train or revolutions of the fly being fixed, were made use of in the same way as the endless screw in the former way, by taking a greater or a smaller number of turns of the fly for the longer or the shorter notes. Knowing the number of bars in the tune, and the crotchets in a bar, by calculation, the number of turns of the fly was obtained (and parts of a turn if necessary) that a crotchet required, so that the tune might go round the barrel, leaving a small space for locking and running; this was all that was required to be known: quavers and semiquavers came to have their proportion according to the value of the crotchet. Although the process of putting tunes on barrels answered very well by both these methods, yet it was rather tedious, and attended with some trouble and embarrassment in the operation; and a more simple and easier method of doing this was afterwards contrived and adopted, by which we could lay on a tune with the greatest accuracy and expedition in nearly ten minutes.

Although bell music is not of a favourite kind, yet for the benefit of such clockmakers as may be disposed to construct music clocks, and have not the opportunity of getting the music pricked on the barrel by those whose profession it is to do this sort of work, we shall give a description of the tool and its apparatus, which will be found very well adapted for this purpose, and also of the manner of using it.

Having a good strong turn-bench, such as those used by clockmakers for their larger sort of work, to the standards or heads of it let there be attached supports on each side; to the supports on the side nearest the workman, let there be fixed a straight cylindrical rod A B, Plate XVII. 79, about ten or twelve inches long, and in diameter a quarter of an inch, or even three-tenths of an inch. A spring socket CD must be made for this rod to slide easily and steadily along it, somewhat like the socket which slides on the upright stalk or rod of a watchmaker's glass stand. In the thick and strong part of this socket E is fixed a steel arm EFG, bent into a curve, which lies over and above the music barrel when in the turn bench, as shown in 89, at EFG. The steel rod AB may at pleasure be placed at any distance from the barrel, about an inch or rather more, and should stand parallel to the barrel arbor MN, and nearly in the same plane with it, but rather a little above this than otherwise. On the outer end of the curved arm is fixed a flat piece of steel G, a little more than half an inch long, in breadth not quite so much, and about one-tenth of an inch thick. The lower and front edges of this flat piece of steel should be neatly and smoothly rounded off, so as to allow it to come easily and freely into the notches $a, b, a,$ &c. which are on the edge of a thin brass scale, whose use will come afterwards to be explained. To the supports attached to the turn-bench heads, and on the opposite side to that where the round steel rod is placed, let these be fixed a slip of brass XY, about ten or twelve inches long, an inch and a half broad, and nearly a tenth of an inch thick; the inner edge of which must be made to stand parallel with the barrel, and the flat side to stand nearly in a plane between the upper surface of the barrel and its centre, the edge being placed so as to stand clear of the tops of the teeth of a high numbered wheel WW screwed on to the end of the barrel. Near the ends of this slip of brass, slits are made, through which screws e, e, pass, which screw it to the upper side of the supports; the slits serving to allow it to be moved a little occasionally lengthwise when required. On the upper side of the slip of brass is fixed another, but not quite so thick, the length being about that of the barrel, and breadth one inch and three quarters. On the inner edge of this are made as many notches a, b, c, &c. as there are hammers, bells, or notes to be used in the tune or tunes to be marked on the barrel. These notches are equidistant, and the middle of them should correspond to the middle or line of the hammer tails; their width being such as to admit the flat steel piece G on the end of the curved arm EFG; the depth of them cut on the edge of the brass should be about one quarter of an inch. The edge of this piece of brass, or music scale as it may be called, must also stand parallel with the barrel, and at a little distance from it, not nearer than three-tenths of an inch, so that the flat steel piece on the end of the curved arm may have room to get in a little way, and to pass through at the same time to a certain degree of depth. On the upper side of this brass slip, the letters of the scale of music or gamut are marked to those notches which correspond with the hammer tails, and hammers intended to strike on the bells the notes so marked; but in an inverted order to the usual way in which they are marked in the scales of music, the lower notes being on the right hand side, and as they rise going to the left. This is done to suit the way in which the bells are commonly, though not necessarily, placed in music clocks, see 81; it is in the power of a clockmaker, of any ingenuity, to contrive the barrel to turn any way he thinks proper, and place the bells to stand in the order of the music scale, if there is any advantage to be derived from it. In the curved arm E F G, 80, is fixed a punch f, having a very fine and sharp conical point, at the distance of four inches or so from the centre of the sliding socket, and not quite an inch from the outer end of the flat steel piece; the punch, when applied to the barrel, should stand upright, and directly over the centre of it. This apparatus being all adjusted, as we have directed, it is evident that when the curved arm is raised up a little way, the socket can then be made to slide easily along the steel rod, and by this means bring the outer end of the flat steel piece very readily into any notch required; and the point of the punch is brought at the same time with the greatest precision to the place of the note on the barrel, leaving the flat steel piece for the time in the notch. The point of the punch touching or resting on the barrel, a stroke from a very small hammer on the top of it will cause the point to make a pretty deep mark or conical hole on the surface of the barrel.

It now remains to be shown how the time or the lengths of the different notes are determined. Long or slow, short or quick notes, such as the minum and demi-semi-quaver, are not well suited to bell-music, and, of course, are seldom introduced into tunes chosen for it; the crotchet, quaver, and semiquaver, forming the greatest part of the composition: the minum and demi-semi-quaver may, however, be brought in at some parts. It may be unnecessary to state, what is pretty generally known, the proportional value of the notes to one another; suffice it to say, that a minum is equal to two crotchets, a crotchet to two quavers, a quaver to two semi-quavers, and a semi-quaver to two demi-semi-quavers. The time in which the barrel turns, after striking or lifting a hammer-tail, to strike any note on a bell, must be in the same proportion with the notes, according to their respective character. Let a wheel of 250 teeth, for example, be fixed on the end of the barrel, and let both be placed in the turn-bench, with the apparatus which has been described. To the turn-bench is now attached a steel or brass spring, having a knee or bending at one end, so that it may fall into the spaces of the wheel teeth.

The tune proposed to be laid on the barrel, contains 20 bars of three crotchets each, being 60 crotchets in all: if 250, the number of the wheel teeth, is divided by 60, the number of the crotchets, we shall have four for the quotient, and ten for the remainder; showing that we may take four teeth spaces for every crotchet, ten, the remaining part of it, serving as a run for locking, and the other part for a run at unlocking for a tune to be played. Now, as a crotchet is equal to four spaces, a quaver must be equal to two, and a semi-quaver equal to one. Suppose the first note, in the tune proposed, is F. 79; the curved arm is brought to the left hand, and the flat steel piece put into that notch; the punch is then made to mark the barrel; and this being a semi-quaver, or the fourth part of a crotchet, the spring index is shifted into the next space of the wheel teeth, and the curved arm moved to the next note, which is G, on the left hand, and the flat steel piece being put into the notch corresponding to G, the punch is made to mark it on the barrel. This being a semi-quaver also, the spring is shifted into the next space, and the curved arm moved to note A on the left; the steel piece is put into the corresponding notch, and the punch marks this on the barrel. A is here equal to a quaver and a half; therefore the spring index must be moved over three, or into the third space, and the curved arm moved to the next note, being B, on the left hand; the steel piece being put into this notch, the note is marked on the barrel; and as it is a semi-quaver, one space is taken for it, and the arm moved to G. This being marked, and as it is a quaver, two spaces are taken, and so on. When crotchets are marked, four spaces are taken after marking them. In the tune which we have used, nine bells or notes are all that are required; and three more, or a dozen, would give such a compass as to take in almost any tune that might be required. In place of the spring index, it would be better to have a single threaded endless screw to work into the wheel teeth, one turn of which would be equal to a tooth or space. The arbor of the screw being squared on one end, and a small handle for turning it being put on, there would be less danger of making mistakes with the screw than with the index. On the arbor of the screw there might also be put a hand or index to point to a circular space or dial of eight or ten divisions. This would give room to make parts of a turn, where great nicety is wanted. After one tune is laid on the barrel, either it or the music scale must be shifted a short space when the next one is to be put on. To shift the music scale is perhaps the preferable way of the two; and the spaces for shifting should be marked on the top of one of the supports, and close by one end of the long slip of brass; or they might be marked on a short line drawn longitudinally on the surface of the barrel at or towards one of the ends of it; or by taking both methods, the one would serve as a check on the other. The length of shifting depends on the distance between the hammer tails, and the number of tunes to be put upon the barrel. For example, if the distance between the hammer tails is four-tenths of an inch, and it is proposed to put eight tunes on the barrel, then if we divide four-tenths by eight, we shall have half a tenth for the length, or space to shift for each tune; and this is taking advantage of the whole space between the hammer tails, a circumstance which is frequently overlooked; for where the shifts have been confined to a less space for shifting than might have been got, so much room is lost. The distance between the hammer tails depends on their number, and on the length of the barrel. We have made the distance a quarter of an inch, where the number of hammers were eleven, and the length of barrel about three inches and a quarter, the number of tunes put on the barrel seven, the spaces for shifting were three hundred parts of an inch or thereabouts, and where the clock of itself shifted the tune. When the hammer tails are thin, a number of tunes could be made to have their shifts in a very short distance between the tails; the diameter of the lifting pins must also be taken into account, being of some consideration where the spaces for shifting are extremely limited. Although we have taken the number of the wheel teeth for dividing the notes at

250, yet either a greater or a less number may be assumed; all that is required, is, to proportion the number of turns of the endless screw, and parts of a turn, to the number of bars in the tune, to the notes in each bar, and to have the tunes to go nearly round the barrel, so that a small part of a revolution of it, after the tune is played over, may be left for what is called locking and running. If the dividing wheel was taken at 128 teeth, and the tune being supposed to have 20 bars, each bar having three crotchets, as in the former example, 128 teeth divided by 60, the number of crotchets, the quotient would be two, and the remainder would be eight; so that each crotchet would require two teeth or turns of the endless screw, a quaver one turn, and a semiquaver half a turn, and the remaining eight teeth would serve for locking and running. When the tunes are all marked on the barrel, each mark must be drilled to obtain holes for the lifting pins to be driven into them. Great care should be taken to have a stiff and excellent drill, so as to run no risk of breaking, which would occasion a great deal of trouble; and it should be of such a temper, and well and judiciously whetted up, so that it may drill all the holes without requiring to be once sharpened: the object here is to have all the holes of the same width, so that the lifting pins may be all of the same diameter. The holes being drilled, and the barrel polished, a number of pins should be prepared into lengths of half an inch or so each, and a very little tapered at one end. The stronger and harder the brass wire for the pins is, so much the better; some of the best kind of pins used in the female dress are very fit for this purpose. In placing the pins in the holes, if they should be found too long for knocking in by the hammer, they should be shortened by the cutting plyers before the hammer is applied, which will prevent bending, and allow the pins to have a more secure hold of the barrel rim. After all the pins are put in, they must now be shortened to an equal and proper length or height. For this purpose, prepare a hard cylindrical steel collet, having a hole in its centre sufficiently wide to allow it to be put readily on the pins; the lower end of it hollowed, the upper end rounded, and the height of the collet about one-twentieth of an inch or a little more; the height depending on the size of the barrel and the diameter of the pins. The collet being placed on a pin, the cutting plyers are applied to cut the pin just over by the rounded end; a small touch of a file takes away the burr made by cutting, and as the hardness of the collet prevents the file from taking any more away from the height of one pin than from another, they must all be of an equal height. This operation being finished, the small burrs made on the top of the pins by the file must be taken off; this is done by a piece of steel wire, about six or seven inches long. The end where it is twirled about by the fore finger and thumb, should, for the length of an inch or so, be made into an octangular form, for the more readily turning it round backward and forward. On the face or point of the other end, two notches are made across each other, which may be either angular or round at bottom; the latter may be the better of the two, if rightly executed, and should be made with the round edge of a flat file, whose thickness should not be more than the diameter of the pins. The point where the notches are cut should be hardened, and the inside and bottom of the notches polished, so that a sharpness may be given to take away the burrs easily from the top of the pins.

The shape of the hammer tail is such as is represented at 81. a form which makes the hammer easy enough to be drawn, and the nib of the tail takes little or no room when falling; and should two pins or notes succeed each other rapidly, the nib or point of the hammer tail will not be interrupted by the succeeding pin. In the first musical clocks, and even in those made long afterwards, the bells were all placed on one strong iron bell stud, the opposite end of which was supported by what may be called an auxiliary stud, which occasioned a crampness that prevented the bells, when they were struck by the hammers, from vibrating, or giving out that full tone which they might have otherwise been made to produce; and the improvement made on this, as well as on the quarter bell studs afterwards, was effected by placing each bell separately on its own bell stud, which was made of well-hammered brass, having some degree of elasticity. The sweetness given to the tone of the bells by this method was truly surprising. The bells in this kind of music may be sounding at the time that a succeeding note is struck out and sounding too, which may not be so pleasant to a very nice ear. This can be prevented by having a double set of hammers, and having every tune pinned twice over on the barrel, one set of the hammers having the heads of buff leather, or having a brass head with a piece of cloth sewed over it. These, when they strike the bell, will damp the sound of the note which is last struck. The buff hammer should fall on the bell to be damped, at the same instant that the brass hammer strikes the succeeding note on its bell. This improvement, however, must greatly increase the expence on such a clock; but the effect of buff or cloth hammers is so striking, that the additional price ought not to be grudged.

In Plate XVII. 81. A A is a circle representing an end view of a clock music barrel, and a few of the lifting pins. The dart shows the direction in which it turns. The letters *a, a, a, a,* represent a section or end view of a brass piece thus shaped. The length depends on that of the barrel, and the number of hammers to be let into this brass piece, which is called the hammer frame, the length of it being sometimes three or four inches, sometimes ten or twelve. The flat part of the hammer tails fills up the thick part of the hammer frame, into which slits are made to receive the hammers. Near to the outer and lower angular part at *a* of the frame, a hole *h* is made through the whole length of it, not drilled, but ploughed, *as the workmen call it*, and this is done before any slits are made in it for the hammers. A wire is put through this hole, and through corresponding holes in the flat part of the hammer tails. This wire is their centre of motion, and the holes in them are made so as to have freedom on it, and the flat part of the hammer tails are also made to have freedom in the slits made to receive them. On the under side of the hammer frame at *b*, the hammer springs *c, c,* are screwed, one for each hammer, acting on that part of the hammer tail just where it comes out of the thick part of the hammer frame. When the pins in the barrel raise up any hammer by the nib, and carrying it away from the bell, at the instant the pin quits the nib, the spring *c, c,* by its returning force, makes the hammer head give a blow on the bell to elicit the sound. To prevent any jarring in the bell by the hammer head resting or touching it after having given the blow, each hammer has a counter-spring acting near the lower end of the shank, and inside of it. All the counter-springs are made to project from one slip of well-hammered brass, and screwed on the top of three kneed brass cocks, fixed to the upper side of the brass frame. *d d* is a view of the side of one of the cocks; and *e e* an edge view of one of the counter-springs. *f f* is a side view of one of the bell studs, which are also screwed on the upper side of the hammer frame: an edge view is seen at *f f*, 81. *g, g, g, g,* are edge views of the bells. *g, g,* 92. is a side view of one of them as fixed to its stud. In some musical clocks, in place of the barrel being made to shift for change of tune, the hammer frame is made to shift, carrying with it all the hammers and bells. The change or shifts of the barrel is either done by the hand or by the clock itself. The mechanism for this commonly consists of a wheel fixed on a steel arbor, on the square of which a hand is put, which points to the name or number of the tune marked on a small dial, at which the barrel for the moment stands. The diameter of this wheel is about one inch and a half, and sometimes more or less. The rim is a strong and thick hoop or contrate form, having as many steps on it as there are tunes set on the barrel, the height of the steps being equal to the space from one tune to another. On these steps rests the kneed end of a double lever about four inches long, whose centre of motion is in the middle, and is either upon strong pivots run into a kind of frame, or upon a stout pin, which goes through the lever and the brass stud in which the lever moves. The other end of the lever bears on the end of one of the pivots of the music barrel, which is pressed against it by means of a pretty smart steel spring, acting against the end of the opposite pivot. Concentric with the hoop-wheel, and fixed on the same arbor, is a star-wheel of a number according with the steps on the hoop-wheel, a jumper with a pretty strong spring, works into the star-wheel, by which means the barrel is kept always to its place, by the lever bearing at one place on every step. Although the Figures which have been given to represent the hammer frame, hammers, springs, and counter-springs, bell studs, and bells of music striking, are not exactly like those which are commonly made to strike quarters in clocks, yet they are equally well calculated for the purpose: only the nibs of the hammer tails need not be so far from their centre of motion, being less confined by the pins in the quarter barrel, which are fewer in number than those on a music barrel. A quarter barrel need not be much in diameter, if five quarters are only to be put on it. If ten is intended to be put on, then the diameter should be double that of the other.

After having described the method of laying down the tunes on a music clock barrel, it may be thought unnecessary to explain the method of putting on the quarters of a clock quarter or chime barrel. But, simple as it is, we conceive it will be both interesting to the general reader, and acceptable to workmen who may not be in the habit of contriving for themselves, or who may not have had an opportunity of seeing it executed by others.

Quarters are commonly struck on a set of eight bells, from G to G in octave, or they may be numbered 1, 2, 3, &c. on to 8. The quarter barrel may have eight circles faintly turned on it, so as to correspond to the quarter hammer tails. Five, and sometimes ten quarters, are put on the barrel; we shall, however, in this instance, only lay five on the barrel. Take a wheel cut into 50 teeth not rounded off, and screwed temporarily on the end of the barrel; provide an index, and a piece of brass bent so as to apply to the barrel when in the turn bench, in the manner of a straight edge, and the index spring tight in the teeth; take a point, and make a slight trace across the circle, which corresponds to high G or No. 1, then move the index a tooth, in the direction the quarter barrel turns when moved by the wheel work; make a trace across the circle intended for the second hammer, and so on. When the eighth circle has been marked, move the index two teeth or three spaces, and trace here for the first hammer of the succeeding quarter, and so on till the whole is completed; the barrel may then be drilled and pinned accordingly. Should the intervals between the quarters be thought too little for locking, the wheel in place of 50, may be cut 55, and this will allow three teeth in place of two for the intervals, the hammers will be then a little quicker in their succession to one another. G, A, B, C, D, E, F, G, may also be represented by the figures, 1, 2, 3, 4, 5, 6, 7, and 8. No. 1 being the high G, and 8 the low G. The changes given in the following set of chimes or quarters, will exhibit how to proceed in putting them on the barrel, after what has been already said. It will save trouble even to a good reader of music, but much more so to those who cannot read it, to have the straight edge piece of brass, numbered from the bells, 1, 2, 3, 4, 5, &c. so as to correspond with the faint traces on the quarter barrel, or with the hammer tails; let the notes of the chimes have *their number* marked as in the example given here, in the order they stand in the gamut; by this means the notes can very quickly be transferred to the barrel.

A set of Chimes for Clock Quarters; the barrel making two revolutions in the hour.

With the number of 8 bells and hammers for the quarters of a chime or quarter clock, a great variety may be produced; and where it may be preferred to have the chime or quarter barrel to make one revolution for the ten quarters which are given in the course of every hour, we shall give a specimen of a set of chimes which may be put on such a barrel. The wheel put on for this must have 100 teeth, taking the same steps as with the wheel of 50.

A set of Chimes for Clock Quarter Barrels, which make one revolution in an hour.

Organ Clocks.

That music which is produced by clocks with organ barrels, must be greatly preferable to that of bells, and the apparatus for marking the tunes on clock barrels is equally suited to do the same on barrels intended by machinery to work or to sound the pipes of an organ; the difference consisting in marking off on the barrel the spaces of the longer and shorter notes, as in place of pins they have staples or bridges of various lengths, according to the length of the note, or the time which the pipe should be allowed to sound it: The very short notes are by pins of different thicknesses. When an organ part is put to a clock, considerable power or force of weight or spring is required; small as the organ may be, or its wind-chest, some force is required to work the bellows, so as to keep the wind-chest full and no more. To work the bellows, that is, to move the lower board of them up and down, on the inside of which is an air valve that opens on the board being moved downwards, and on the motion upwards it shuts, and the air being then compressed, it is forced into the wind-chest by a communication between them for that purpose, and is ready to give sound to any of the organ pipes the moment when any of their valves should open. This operation with the bellows, though of a different shape, is just the same as with the common bellows when blowing up a fire. The bellows is worked by means of a short crank fixed on one end of the arbor of an endless screw, which works into a trundle of a high numbered pinion, which is on the end of the organ barrel, and nearly of the same diameter with it. On the other end of the endless screw arbor is fixed a small jagged pulley, over which is put an endless silken cord, which being continued, goes round another jagged pulley on the end of a pinion arbor of one of the quick running or fly wheels in the organ train. These wheels are regulated by a fly, by which the velocity of the organ barrel in turning, is brought to keep the time required for the music. The wheels, on being impelled by the moving power, which is considerable, (being greater than that used in bell music), communicate their motion by means of the endless cord, and turn the organ barrel. The pins, bridges, or staples, on the barrel turning, act on the tails of levers nearly similar in form to the hammer tails of the bell musical clock, only they are a little longer, and equally moveable on a centre or wire. The other arms of these levers are in an opposite direction, and are about the same length as those which are lifted by the staples on the barrel when turning, and are a little broad and flattish towards the end, where the under side (on the opposite ends rising) press down on the upper ends of the slender rods, whose lower ends then, by this means open the valves of the organ pipes, and the sound is prolonged according as the lift is pins or bridges. What has been described constitutes the chief machinery in an organ clock. Many ways may be contrived to set the organ barrel in motion, and at the same time while playing, and at the end of a tune, to make the clock of itself shift the barrel from one tune to another.

By experience, when making up an organ clock, we found the making of the bellows to be rather a nice piece of business; if the leather is on the thick side, it requires a great force to work them and turn the organ barrel at the same time; the bellows leather should be of the thinest and finest kid, such as that of which ladies gloves are made; by this means the force necessary to work them will be greatly lessened, though still considerable, as it consisted of two large barrels, three inches and a half in diameter, and near to two inches broad, each containing a pretty powerful spring; the two fusees, on one arbor, were in diameter at the base, near to two inches and a half. In the organ train of wheels, the numbers of the wheel teeth were 80, 70, 60, and 16, the pinions 16, 14, 12 and 4 threads to the endless screw, on whose upper end the wings of a fly were put, the fly wheel of 16 worked into the screw; the wheels, barrels, and fusees were contained in a double frame, composed of three plates. It may easily be conceived, by having so great a force, that the first or great wheel would require to be thick, and to have strong teeth, the leaves of the first pinion of course to be also strong. The double frame, with the wheel work for driving the organ barrel, was fixed in the upper part of the clock-case; the organ barrel, bellows, wind-chest, &c. were placed in the lower part. The clock, a spring one, struck the hour, and the quarters were struck by a double blow, the pendulum 15 inches in length, the whole got up in an elaborate manner, yet we trust not injudiciously so.

Musical Springs.

Within these few years a new species of music by steel springs has been invented at Geneva. From the smallness of the machinery which plays the music, it is very surprising and curious, as it has been put into rings, seals, watches, and snuff boxes. Two ways are used to lift the ends of the springs which give the different notes; one is by a very small barrel, the other by a plate wheel. The last being more adapted to take up little room, is chiefly used in watches. The space for the springs falling, after being bent up, is short. A double set of springs for giving the same notes is made, without which the beauty of the music could not be produced. The number of springs varies, for the most part, from sixteen to twenty-four, or upwards. Those springs which are lifted by the barrel pins are straight, while those which are lifted by the pins in the plate wheel have a sort of part projecting from the end at one side; and this side edge of the spring lying over the top of the pins is taken away so as to clear them. The projecting part at the end of each spring corresponds with its own lifting pin. As the pins are on both sides of the plate-wheel, this allows a greater variety of notes than the barrel can perhaps admit. The springs on the upper and under sides of the plate-wheel are sometimes sixteen or seventeen on each side. On the plate-wheel are traced 16 or 17 concentric circles, for the pins to meet their corresponding notes in the springs whose ends, come each to their corresponding circle both above and under the plate-wheel. An apparatus on a small scale being made like that which has been described, will serve to put or mark the places for the notes both on the barrel and the plate-wheel; the only difference is, that the barrel will require to be marked by a curved arm sliding on a steel rod. The concentric circles on the plate-wheel, must have short and faint traces across them: This is regulated by a thin straight edge laid in an oblique direction across the circles, and the intersections are afterwards marked by a point. The springs may be easily tuned to their respective notes, as the least thinning or shortening them will make a very sensible alteration on the tone. *The tongue of a steel trump, or Jew's harp, shows, in some degree, what may be done in this way by steel springs.* The train which regulates this very minute musical machinery, as may very easily be conceived, must be composed of a few very small wheels, the motive force being proportionably small. It must be a great effort of patience and ingenuity to make them play two or more tunes. However beautiful and ingenious the machinery of these small contrivances is, they can only be considered as toys for amusing children. A spiral steel spring has been lately introduced into clocks, in place of bells.

TABLE OF PRIME NUMBERS UP TO 10,000.

7727	7933	8147	8317	8539	8713	8893	—	9283	9461	9649	9833
7741	7937	8161	8329	8543	8719	—	9103	9293	9463	9661	9839
7753	7949	8167	8353	8563	8731	8923	9109	—	9467	9677	9851
7757	7951	8171	8363	8573	8737	8929	9127	9311	9473	9679	9857
7759	7963	8179	8369	8581	8741	8933	9133	9319	9479	9689	9859
7789	7993	8191	8377	8597	8747	8941	9137	9328	9491	9697	9871
7793	—	—	8387	8599	8753	8951	9151	9337	9497	—	9883
—	8009	8209	8389	—	8761	8963	9157	9341	—	9719	9887
7817	8011	8219	—	8609	8779	8969	9161	9343	9511	9721	—
7823	8017	8221	8419	8623	8783	8971	9173	9349	9521	9733	9901
7829	8039	8231	8423	8627	—	8999	9181	9371	9533	9739	9907
7841	8053	8233	8429	8629	8803	—	9187	9377	9539	9743	9923
7853	8059	8237	8431	8641	8807	9001	9199	9391	9547	9749	9929
7867	8069	8243	8443	8647	8819	9007	—	9399	9551	9767	9931
7873	8081	8263	8447	8663	8821	9011	9203	—	9587	9769	9941
7877	8087	8269	8461	8669	8831	9013	9209	9403	—	9781	9949
7879	8089	8273	8467	8677	8837	9027	9221	9413	9601	9787	9967
7883	8093	8287	—	8681	8839	9041	9227	9419	9613	9791	9973
—	—	8291	8501	8689	8849	9043	9239	9421	9619	—	10001
7901	8101	8293	8513	8693	8861	9049	9241	9431	9623	9803
7907	8111	8297	8521	8699	8863	9059	9257	9433	9629	9811
7917	8117	—	8527	—	8867	9067	9277	9437	9631	9817
7927	8123	8311	8537	8707	8887	9091	9281	9439	9643	9829

APPENDIX.

(A.)

Edinburgh, 4th Feb. 1788.—The following are copies of Letters given me by my good friend Mr. JOHN HOLMES, watchmaker, London, for information on the subject of Turret Clocks, and were sent as *such* to him, by his ingenious friends, Mr. JOHN SMEATON, engineer, and the Rev. WM. LUDLAM, Professor of Mathematics, Cambridge. T. R.

From Mr. John Smeaton to Mr. John Holmes.

Ansthorpe, 5th July, 1779.

DEAR BROTHER H.

I congratulate you on your contract with the Board at Greenwich Hospital, so much to your credit; and doubt not but you will give satisfaction, only wish you had had a little more money, for though, I think, you may save yourself, yet I would have wished you to have had an adequate recompence for the invention, care, and attendance that must be necessary in such an undertaking. When I mentioned giving my opinion, I did not mean to give you a plan; for that never being put to me, I never absolutely fixed upon; I only think in general, that the plan commonly used by Father Hindley, for many years past, was elegant and commodious, in giving liberty of length for the barrels, without inelegantly lengthening the pinion arbors; but as, especially in his latter days, he got into many schemes, that appear to me to be much more cost than worship, my meaning was merely to chalk out the outlines, in order to weed out those things, that create much trouble and difficulty, and mean little; and to mark out those things on which a good performance, so as to give satisfaction to the public eye and ear, depends; and I am glad to see, both by your proposal and what you farther say upon it, that your ideas and that of the town artists, are very correspondent in the outset with my own; and as you are pleased to say, you shall not stick a spoke till you have heard from me, I shall give you my notions in the rough, as they run, that this great work may suffer no hinderance by me; and perhaps it may be saving of time to say, that I never saw any work of Hindley's that, upon the whole, gave my mind so much satisfaction, as that executed for Bishop Thorpe. *1stly*, A clock with minute hands, two dials, and to go eight days, in so exposed a situation, should not only be made stout and able, but so contrived as to go through thick and thin; that is, aim it rather to keep going tolerably with very different powers, than framed for accurate measure of time, when a pound or two too little shall make it stop entirely. *2dly*, On this view I totally reject the idea of going with two wheels, which distorts every proportion, and puts every thing in distress, and all this to save a very trifle of friction, which Mr. Harrison very justly observes, that in clock-work (even intended for an accurate measure of time) means nothing, provided it is always equal. The proposition here seems to be, not to make the clock go with the least weight possible, but to make it bear as much as possible, without a total derangement of the time; for this reason, *3dly*, I would not wish the pendulum to be longer than to beat 30 per minute, but would give it an heavy ball to swing out well, with a deep 'scapement, and to admit the angle of vibration without banking, to be fully double, when the clock is clean with all its movements on, and in calm weather, to what will let it 'scape. I say a ball, for, in this case, I should prefer a sphere to a lens, that it might take the more air, and bear the more weight; which figure is also subject to the least change from accidental currents of air. Hindley's suspension and application of the crutch I think exceeds all I have seen. *4th*, For the reasons above, the teeth of the swing-wheel should be deep, and that the weight and pressure may not produce an unreasonable beat in the pallets, I would advise the working part to be at least one inch in thickness; and that the activity of the main weight may not be curbed by the sluggishness of the swing-wheel, I would not allow it above 30 teeth; so that allowing about half an inch to a tooth, it will be about five inches diameter. As to the 'scapement, I would neither make it dead, nor with the common recoil with planes, but with curved pallets, so that the extreme of the recoil should be dead, and this, I think, was somewhat near what father Hindley ultimately came into. *5th*, According to the above, the swing-wheel will go round once in two minutes; and if in other two wheels the turns be taken, 6 × 5 will make the minute wheel go round in an hour; and if this is driven 8 turns by the barrel wheel, the barrel will come out 9 inches diameter; or if 7 turns near upon 8 inches, which perhaps may be more commodious, on account of winding up easy, without any purchase but a common handle, this will give you coarse pitches, with high numbered pinions, and keep the wheels of very moderate size; and as you will have but 24 turns of the barrel in one case, and 27¼ths in the other, this will give you an inch to a cord, and keep the strength of your work, or the strength of your cord, if but one-third of an inch in diameter; and in public works appearances are to be regarded. If the angles of the minute spindle are considerable, I should prefer wheels to the universal joint. Be very careful to make the teeth of the dial work fit as close as possible, otherwise I think the continual agitation of the wind will produce too much wear in that part. 6*th*, Respecting the dial work, I would not only balance the hands very nicely as to weight outside, but also observe to proportion the quantity of surface in proportion to the distance from the centre, so that the power of the *wind* shall be in equal balance both frontways and edgeways; the balancing parts being painted black upon black ground, will either not be seen or not regarded. I would not use a cock socket, but let the hour hand be hung upon a socket of at least 3 feet length, bored truly, and the minute spindle turned, and nicely fitted thereto; this will throw the wheel work so far from the face that a man can get between, and oil the outward bearing of the hour hand; and, if thought necessary, a cap can be contrived to hold oil; the long socket can be made to admit oil to the spindle through holes in the socket. 7*thly*, I would conduct the striking part upon the same principles; but as you will be obliged to strike upon the second wheel, I would take as many blows as convenient in the time of it, (suppose 8) in order to get an high numbered pinion, which, I think, is here material; and then 6½ turns will bring you about to the same calculation in respect to the barrel as the watch part. I would not, to save a running wheel, have the fly of a large diameter, and would make it as heavy as possible, so as not to offend the ear, by too sensible a difference in the pauses between the 1st and 2d, and that between the 2d and 3d, and subsequent blows; the advantage of this towards continuing the motion with as little loss of power as possible is obvious. 8*th*, In respect to the pinions, I would make them either in the compound way of Mr. Hindley, or cut out of the solid, as they come cheapest. If made of iron, they are sufficiently lasting, if well figured, nor would I be at any cost to render my work *perpetual*, for you see clocks may be melted* as well as worn out. Brass wheels I think very sufficient,

---

* In allusion to the Greenwich Hospital clock, which was so, in consequence of a part of the building being burned 2d January, 1709.

nor would I use any bell metal, except for bushing the swing wheel, and verge pivot holes. I would content myself with making a sound substantial piece of work, strong and able to go through its business without complaining. I am, &c. J. S.—P. S. Respecting the necessary weight of the hammer, and height to which it should be raised, I believe friend Ludlam will be your best adviser. I speak in positive terms, to avoid unnecessary words, but I don't expect you to take any thing from me on this subject that is contrary to your own judgment. I have seen much trouble taken to do harm, which I would wish you to avoid.

The Rev. William Ludlam, Professor of Mathematics in Cambridge University, to Mr. J. Holmes.

DEAR SIR, July 1, 1779.

I chuse to answer you now, though I must do it hastily and imperfectly, rather than by delay, to make it of little use.

A turret clock, with a minute hand, is difficult to make in any way so as to be safe. The snow in winter will freeze in large lumps upon the minute hand, and then the eddy winds will whisk it round every way. Mr. Hindley had very good reasons for putting his dial within side of the church at York. It is safer to do with an hour hand only; if that may not be, contrive, if possible, to sink the dial plate within some bold moulding, or place it in any recess that is proper, shade the hands all you may from the wind, and do not make the *heart*, at end of the minute hand, bigger than necessary, to be readily seen. The hands must be balanced within, not without; for that adds to the power of the wind, and is unsightly. The dial wheels should be large to resist the force of the wind trying to turn the hands. The dial wheels cannot be too large. The purchase which a long minute hand has over the teeth of a small minute wheel, frequently gives the wind power to strip the teeth all round. The socket work is often made of gun barrels; beware of iron in the socket work of the hands, it is sure to rust and set all fast; and when the scaffolds are struck, perhaps you cannot come at the hands. Sometimes it is possible to make the *middle* of the dial plate take out, so as to come at the hands from within; when this can be done it is very convenient. It is a very great advantage to have a 13 foot pendulum; from many trials, I am sure no short pendulum will go well; nothing can make a 9 inch pendulum go as well as one of three feet, nor one of 3 feet equal to a 13 feet; though the advantage of the latter over the second sort, is not quite so great as the advantage of the second sort over the first, especially within doors; but the advantage of a 13 foot in a turret, or without doors, over a 3 foot is very great. I am of Mr. Hindley's mind, 52 feet would be better still. I will endeavour to expound the doctrine on which this maxim is founded. 1*st*, It is desirable that the clock's force on the pendulum ball should be but small in comparison of gravity's force; yet the clock's force must be adequate to all the impediments to the motion of the pendulum. 2*d*, Both the clock's force and that of the impediments will vary; but the less the variable part of the clock's force is, to the whole of the clock's force impressed on the ball, the better. Compute now the force with which the weight acts upon the pendulum rod at a given distance from the point of suspension; suppose 6 inches, and the proportion of the clock's force there to its force on the ball will be, as the length of the pendulum to that given distance; with a long pendulum, therefore, you may apply a greater weight to the clock barrel, (than with a short pendulum) and yet keep the clock's force on the ball the same. Now, the greater the weight on the barrel, the less will be the proportion *which* the variable part of the clock's force (arising from change of friction,) be to the whole force. The absolute friction, or absolute variable force, is a little increased by the increase of weight, but the proportion of its variations to the whole is lessened. In clocks so exposed and so neglected as turret clocks commonly are, you must lay on a great weight to drag the clock through fair weather and foul weather, and yet you must not (as Mr. Mudge would say,) make the auxiliary force too great, or as Harrison (by a very significant metaphor expressed it,) give the clock (that is the clock weight through the uncertain intervention of the wheels,) the dominion over the pendulum. From what I have said, you will see that the weight of the ball ought to be 50 or 60 pounds. As to shape, I think some resistance of the air far from being of disservice; the worst forms are those where the matter in the ball is spread out wide, and distant from the axis of the pendulum rod, and I think a globe the best form. It is of the utmost consequence to have the axis of the rod pass through the centre of gravity of the ball, otherwise the action of the clock will generate a rotatory motion of the ball round the axis of the pendulum rod, as well as a vibratory motion. This is best guarded against by making the ball a sphere. If the ball, by any accident, gets this rotatory motion, it will subside sooner in this case, than when the matter of the ball is spread out sideways. The gridiron pendulums are in this respect inconvenient things. It is no small difficulty to determine in what way to make the rod; if of iron, it will vary with heat and cold; even in this case it should not be a single bar, but a frame. A frame like that (See Plate XIX. Fig. R) was used by Eayre, of Kettering. The pin of the crutch took hold of the cross bar PR at the top. The several bars of the frame were rivetted at the joinings. A single rod of 13 feet will either be very weak or very heavy. The framed rods of T. Eayre were light and yet stiff; whether a wooden rod could be put together in some such way, I know not. I would have the tail or flat of the crutch, steel, and hard, to be clipt by two fine screws of steel, also hard: no oil to be interposed. Here I must refer you to paragraph 86 and 87 of my Astronomical Observations; I prefer this to the jointed crutch of Mr. Hindley in small clocks, and much more in turret clocks. If you think the hardened steel parts will rust, you may set an agate, ground flat with parallel sides, for the screws to bear against. The force of the clock has a strong tendency to twist the jointed crutch of Mr. Hindley; and the parts of it, from their shape, have very little tendency to resist that twist. There is difficulty in providing a proper spring; two springs are used to prevent the twisting of the rod; but no two springs can be made so alike in temper and thickness as to bend exactly alike. If a single spring is used, care should be taken that it be not thicker on the one edge than the other. I think a spring for a 13 foot pendulum should be about ¼ inch broad, by about 3 inches in the working part; should be pinched very tight in the pendulum rod, and also very tight in the cock; in both cases between parts or cheeks filed perfectly flat. And the cock, if it can be, should be screwed or bolted to a rock as big as the Hospital; by no means to what is loose or weak, or liable to warp or twist with the change of weather. Provision should be made to catch the pendulum in case the spring should break. See my observations, par. 89. As to 'scapements, by all means make it to retreat. I have four clocks in the house,—three with dead seconds, one retreat; none of them keep time, fair or foul, like the last. This kind of 'scapement gages the pendulum, the dead seconds leaves it at liberty. The church clock of Sheffield was made dead seconds, the pendulum 13 feet. When the work was worn smooth, the pendulum increased its swing a foot on each side. Harrison rejects the dead seconds in all cases with the utmost indignation; but it does the worst in clocks exposed to weather. The common 'scapement, taking in seven teeth, (the whole number being 30) is a good one; but the face of the leading pallet should not be a plane, but be rounded off, whilst the face of the driving pallet is an exact plane, and then the retreat on each pallet may be made equal. In these pallets, the tooth does not escape till the pendulum has ascended 3 degrees; of course a great weight is required. You may make a very good 'scapement by making the pallets take over 10 teeth, and the pendulum to escape at 1¼ degree. In this case, half the former weight will have an equal force on the pendulum ball, when all other circumstances are the same. I have sent a drawing of this, with the construction according to my book, pat. 124, and have just set out a large clock for a gentleman's kitchen on this construction. It is also executed by a workman here. See Fig. 1. Plate XIX. The greater fall you can obtain for your weight, the better, and especially the more turns you can allow for your first wheel, and the lighter you can (in consequence,) make the weight. If you have many turns of the line on the barrel, you may want length for the barrel. Two ways are used for this. One, which is called a double frame, the lower part of the frame wider than the upper part. See Fig. 2. The one frame behind the other. The arbor of the great wheel comes through the first frame, and has a square like as far a winding key, but on this square is put the ratch-wheel; the end of the square is hollow, and receives the pivot of the barrel arbor, and admits the barrel head to bear against the ratch-wheel, and the barrel head carries the click. The other end of the barrel arbor goes through the second frame, and has a square for the winding key. I like this the best, Fig. 3. Donnisthorpe, of Birmingham, (the best maker of church clocks I know,) made an excellent clock for Deritend chapel in Birmingham, in this manner. That man and his affairs are strangely disordered; if he could be set right he would be a most useful hand. I suppose you know that it is of consequence on which side of the barrel the line comes down, especially if the barrel be large. Let B be the barrel, &c. *For what is similar to this part of Mr. Ludlam's letter, see page* 408, *and Diagram, Plate XIV.*

I think I have now done with the watch part. It is often very advisable to have the watch part and striking part in separate frames, especially if there be quarters. That the striking may be regularly discharged without fail, you know by the example of the York clock. A very large frame is seldom strong. Two smaller frames are in many cases both cheaper and stronger, and the strength of the framing is much increased by diagonal braces or crosses in Mr. Smeaton's manner. This is far preferable to the depending on the shoulders of the tenons only. It is a good method to make the hammer heavy, but to let the weight in a great measure rest on the joint pin or arbor on which it (the hammer,) turns. Mr. Hindley did so at York; by this means the weight to be raised by the clock is not too much; the quantity of matter in the hammer-head considerable, and the blow is made so slow and leisurely, that time is given to waken thoroughly a large bell.

In large work there should always be a double locking, in Mr Hindley's manner. The principal locking detent should be strong, the locking piece bear it down with a good force, while an hook holds it up, which hook is removed in order to set the clock a striking. The clock at Deritend, in Birmingham, is in this way.* I do not think the repeating way so safe as the locking plate, carried on by a pinion. The worst is where the locking plate hath 78 ratch teeth, and is carried on by a pallet. I have known it fail through foulness of the work. Clocks of this sort should go fair or foul.

There are great diversities in making the pinions. The lantern pinion in parts, after Mr. Hindley's fashion, is troublesome to make. I have seen them put on an arbor filed into 5 sides, and followed by a screw: but the screw is very apt to set, that is to bend the arbor when it is forced up; sometimes the pinions are put on a square and pinned, sometimes made out of the solid, sometimes all steel, sometimes iron case-hardened. W. L.

P. S. I have seen turret clocks, where many hands and much load has been on the dial work, have a barrel and weight to keep the hands pressing forward with great force, which weight was wound up when the clock weight was. It was in circumstances where I do believe the clock could not have carried forward the great load of dial work. I cannot see the disadvantage of three wheels more than two, so much as you seem to account it. In the watch part, let the wheels and pinions be of a large diameter, well toothed, sized, and pitched, (yet the wheels light,) the pivots rather small, the frame stiff, and not encumbered with the running of the wheels in the striking part, (especially if quarters,) a frame behind, if you want length of barrel, and then 3 wheels will not hurt. By all means make the pendulum rod of wood. It may be flat, two, or even three inches broad, and one thick. The regulating ball may be above the fixed ball in two parts, and pinch the flat between the parts, and slide up and down. The regulating ball will have the most effect when in the middle. See my book, par. 165.

---

* In this case the pin that raises the detent must both raise it, and also pass it in the time of making the last stroke. When the detent is raised, the hook will catch and hold it up, but unless the pin passes the detent, it cannot drop down again when the hook is removed for striking.

From the Rev. William Ludlam, to Mr. Holmes.

30th Aug. 1779.

When I proposed to balance the hands from within, I did it only to lessen the surface on which the wind acts, and its influence on the hands. Mr Smeaton very judiciously proposes to make the action of the wind balance itself, and so have no effect to turn the hands round. Nor did I consider the danger of the hands getting loose on the square by their own weight, nor their tendency to twist the rod. I come over entirely to your opinion of balancing the hands without, and think Mr Smeaton's proposal should by all means be adopted. The long socket proposed by Mr. Smeaton, for the arbor of the hand, will support the rod, and, by touching all the way, there will be no danger of galling or biting; but then the metal in contact should not be iron against iron; they will rust and set fast; what think you of brass against bell-metal of a proper composition that is not too hard? You must, in this case, by all means, cut asunder the rod as soon as it comes out of the socket, and join the parts with Hooke's joint. Indeed such a joint is necessary, in whatever way you proceed; without it, if the clock-frame settles, or the building warps, the hands will be set fast; nor can the dial-plate, and the socket spoken of, be set so true to the work in the clock-frame, as that all shall be free. This allowing the rod to bend in that place, the two parts of the rod making a very obtuse angle, remedies all this danger. I speak here of the long rod coming from the clock-frame, and carrying the minute hand, or the rod conducting the minute hand; for you speak of this rod as turning round in an hour and a half. I suppose you will adopt the toothed rim of the contrate wheels, not at right angles to their planes, but making an angle of 135 degrees, (the supplement of 45° to 180°) as in Fig. 1. Plate XVIII. These sort of contrate wheels tooth together far more kindly than the common sort, (as in watches) when the two wheels are of a size. Where the contrate wheel turns a pinion, and only one or two leaves of that pinion at a time are engaged in the teeth of the contrate wheel, then the common way, as in watches, does very well. The danger and mischief of the parts of a machine biting or galling each other is very great, especially when the parts bear with great force on each other; and, with respect to the swing-wheel, it should be $\frac{1}{4}$ths of an inch broad at the webb. Old Harrison made the swing-wheel of the clock belonging to Trinity College, in Cambridge, as much or more; but the webb was but about 1/10th of an inch thick (when seen flatwise.) He also gave a very odd shape to the teeth of the wheel, Fig. 2, in order that the teeth might roll upon the pallets and not slide; because, by rolling, they would tear up (and that with a purchase) any matter that might glue the teeth and pallet together, and also to make the retreat equal on each tooth; see my quarto book, Art. 197. The pallet frame was brass, the pallets steel, and screwed in as you see. That part of the pallet frame of a light colour, is about ¼ inch thick, the end that holds the pallets full ⅜ths. Pray, show Mr. Kendall this curiosity. I am confident (with Mr. Smeaton's leave) that you cannot make a church-clock go so well with a 3 feet pendulum as with one of 13 feet; for you cannot lay that force upon the wheels necessary for foul-weather-work, and the neglect of the parish sexton, and yet keep a sufficient dominion of the pendulum over the wheels, unless it be much more than 3 feet; because the force of the swing-wheel upon the ball, (supposing the fashion of the escapement the same, that is the pallets and swing-wheel similar) is diminished in proportion of the length of the longer pendulum to the length of the shorter. I had not computed the swing of the pendulum when I wrote. The chord of 3 degrees on a radius of 39.2 is 2.05 inches, and on a radius of 13 feet, 0.8 inches, is only 8.2, so that if you take the common escapement, and drop off at three degrees, and swing 4 or 4¼ degrees, the pendulum will not have too much motion. I perfectly agree with Mr. Smeaton in desiring the pendulum should move 20 inches or near for the escapement, and have room for 20 inches more for vibration. The cycloidal cheeks are not of great use, as cycloids; but in large clocks they govern the spring, prevent it from bending irregularly or suddenly in weak places, which often occasions it to break in those places. Fig. 3. are the cheeks of Trinity College clock, Cambridge. The pendulum is 6 feet 4 inches long, escapes at 4.5 inches, or 3° 24'. Whether Harrison's cycloidal cheeks are brass or iron, I forget, but I think brass, very thick and strong, and very firmly fixed, and I believe their form circular, from a radius of five inches. In some instances he used a circle of four inches radius. By all means make provision to catch the pendulum, if the spring should break. I agree with Mr. Smeaton, that a cylindrical rod of 2 inches diameter, or more, is preferable to any framed one. If you suspend the weight by a single line, the rope will untwist, if by a double line and pulley, as in an eight-day clock, the force of twisting in the line will often twist the two lines together into one; especially when the weight has descended a great distance from the upper works, from whence the lines come down. In these cases I have put an arm to the weight, with a wheel at the end; which wheel, by the twisting of the line, bears against a smooth wall, and so stop the twisting. Consider of this. At all adventures, it will be proper to put somewhat to receive the weight if it should fall. Nothing better than a great stone upon a wool-sack. Perhaps Dr. Hooke's rope and arm had better be employed to guide the weight to the wool-sack, than to catch it. I am afraid the sudden jerk would break the safety-rope, and toss the weight to a great distance. If the weight be stone or cast iron, the stone at the bottom should have a bed of sand upon it; or rather you should substitute a box of sand instead of the stone. If stone dash against stone, or against cast iron, it will certainly fly into fragments, and that may be mischievous. Malt dust is very elastic, and yet solid; but will not the mice eat it? Is saw-dust not better? In the following figures, neither the proportion nor the arrangement of the parts is regarded. The drawings are intended to show only the manner in which they act on each other. The arrows in the wheels show which way they turn. Fig. 4. is the manner of locking and unlocking the great clock at York. A is the count-wheel which determines the number of strokes, and goes once round in 78 strokes. (*La Roue de compte.*) B is the detent wheel which goes once round in one stroke. (*La Roue d'Etoteau.*) D is the detent—d is the locking piece rivetted or screwed to the detent; e is a like piece screwed to the webb of the wheel B. The surface where these two meet is sloped pretty much, and the wheel pressing with great force, (by reason of the weight required to raise the hammer,) the detent D is pressed downward with so great a force, that the watch-part would not have force sufficient to raise it up, as is done in common; and were the slope of the parts d and e lessened, or were they square, the force of the wheel B might drive the detent upwards, and the clock not lock safe. H is an hook (*le crochet*) which holds up the detent when raised; the end of the detent D, which presses on the hook, presses (in the York clock) with but about the fourth of its force at d; the bearing parts are nearly square, and the hooks easily drawn back. K is the arm of the hook. L is the great loaded lever raised by the clock; having a weight at the end of the longer arm, and a nag's head N, at the end of the shorter arm, which, in lifting, passes the end K of the arm of the hook, and gets underneath it (as here drawn). The work is then charged, or, on the warning, when the lever is let go, it raises the hook, but the tail K and the nag's head part asunder at the point opposite to p, and the hook returns to its proper position of rest. In the meantime the detent D drops down, the piece d falls below e, the clock strikes. At the last blow, a pin q, in the count-wheel, lays hold of the talon, or nib of the other arm F of the detent, raises the arm D, and the hook H being now ready to receive it, gives way to let it pass, and then hooks it up, so that the piece e meets the piece d, and the clock is locked up. But the pin q must both raise the detent to the full height of the hook, and also pass the nib F in the time of the last blow; for, if the pin q is not clear of F, the detent cannot drop at the next hour.

This work can never miss, if the nag's head N (*le pied de Biche*),[*] does not stick, and its spring be sufficient to return to its place. Levering or coal-weighing the hook from under the detent, (by the purchase of the weight at the end of the lever) is a cooler motion, and far more certain than jogging it off by a pendulum, which hangs close to the hook. This pendulum is drawn back by the clock, and being let go, presses beyond its place of rest, gives the hook a blow, or a jog on the elbow, and so knocks it off its hold. If the blow is weak, it may not jog it off; if the pendulum is drawn a great way, it may continue its vibrations and jog it off a second time, and, at the short hour of one, may discharge the clock again. When this piece goes by a spring, it is called a flirt (*le detent à fauvet*). Whether you use a loaded lever, or a jogging pendulum, you have the whole hour to do it in, (but of this more hereafter). Mr. Hindley had but a quarter of an hour, (for the quarter part was discharged by the watch part), and therefore he was obliged to employ every minute of time. Fig. 5. is a repeating part having this property, that it is discharged without lifting against the striking weight of the clock. At the last blow the rack raises the arm L of the detent, by which means the striking is stopped. At discharging, one arm of the lifting piece H gets under the arm K of the detent, so that when the (*le crochet*) gathering piece G is lifted out of the rack C, the detent cannot fall although the rack falls. This makes warning. When the lifting piece falls back, the clock strikes. But observe: The ends of the pieces, K and H, must be so formed, that if the striking weight should be down in striking, and the arm K be fallen, that then the lifting piece H

---

[*] If a joint is of such a sort, that the two parts, when in their constant and regular position, make nearly a right line, I would then call it a deer's foot joint, *pied de Biche*. When these parts, at the regular position, make an obtuse angle, such as the head of an horse, I would then call it a nag's head joint, *tête de cheval*.

may raise it up, and not stop against it; for this would stop the watch part. Fig. 6. Plate XIX. is a new way of raising the vertival, (in French, *la bascule*) or arm that raises the hammer. Here the wheel has only 4 pins, A is the vertival in the common way, B is the vertival in the new way, *b* is the section the contrary way. This vertival ought to be of such a shape as to pass the arbor of the wheel, though not so drawn. In both cases, the pin will slide upon the vertival. In the former case, the quantity of sliding is the sum of the versed sines of the arch described by the lifting pin, and of the arch described by the end of the vertival; in the latter case, the quantity of *sliding* is the difference of those two versed sines, and therefore less by double the lesser of those versed sines. In the former case, the pin wheel and vertival turn contrary ways. In the latter the same way. In the former case, exactness in fitting the centres is not necessary; in the latter, a little wearing in the centres will much alter the height to which the hammer is raised. In the latter case, the pins should not be round, but flat pieces screwed to the wheel. Even in the case of pins, it is best to make them only half round, so that the vertival drops off from an edge. York clock is so. Fig. 7. regards the manner of lifting in the watch part for discharging the striking part. When you lift by a pin in the common way, you can lift only for half a revolution of the lifting-wheel, that is in common cases for half an hour. You must therefore be idle for half an hour, and of necessity you must do an hour's duty in half an hour's time, and therefore, while you do work, must labour twice as hard as is necessary, if you take the whole hour. Besides, it is not proper to have the duty so unequal; it is best to be at all times nearly equal. Lift it therefore from a two-hour wheel, with two pins; but if you lift in common with the lever A, Fig. 7. you cannot with two pins lift the whole hour, or through an entire semicircle; but in the new way before mentioned, with the lever B, you may lift through an entire semicircle, or for the whole hour. If the centre of B could be placed within the circumference of the wheel, you might lift for $\frac{1}{4}$ths of a revolution of the wheel or more. What has been written, are thoughts as they occurred, with little or no reference to yours. I will now speak to yours. Your wheels are of a noble size, and the numbers high; but I cannot clearly understand your design. There are 156 strokes of the striking part in 24 hours, and 1248 in 8 days. There are $45\frac{1}{4}$ strokes in one turn of the great wheel, and consequently $27\frac{1}{4}$ turns of the line upon the barrel. But the watch part does not correspond to this; for, suppose you have a

3 foot pendulum, to which you seem inclined, then your great wheel goes round in 4 hours, or 6 times in a day, or 48 in eight days; but with a 13 foot pendulum, the great wheel goes once round in 8 hours, or 24 turns in 8 days, which corresponds well enough. I am clear for a 13 foot pendulum. As to the escapement, the point lies between the common escapement that I sent (where the wheels have double force; and the clock will go with almost half the weight necessary in the common 'scapement.) This depends upon the care in keeping the clock, and its being exposed to weather. If neglected and suffered to go dry, if the wind, rain, and snow are let in upon the work, you must have as much weight as may be, but if not, the latter escapement will lessen the friction and load on the wheels; yet I doubt if it will give vibration enough. I perceive your dial-work goes off from the second wheel, whose period is 90 minutes. Your contrate wheels must be one larger than the other; yet make the webb where they tooth in form of figure 1. I suppose you will have a sliding plate, with one or two setting screws upon the second wheel, to set the hands occasionally. Take care that this plate may be easily released, and fixed firm, perhaps it turns some other wheel in an hour, or which is preferable, two hours and two turns, and the sliding is on this other wheel; for I cannot see how a wheel turning in 1¼ hour can carry the pins that discharge the striking part. With regard to the hammer, I scarce know what to say, nor indeed have I sufficiently considered whether the duty upon the striking pins is such as will require so great a weight as 170 lb. But you must not overload the clock. If your bell be a free bell, and willing to speak, a little matter will fetch the full tone out of it. If stiff and hide bound, do what you will, the tone will soon decay, and a wooden bell be as good.

- - - - - - - -
- - - - - - - -
- - - - - - - -

- - The best bell, the best peal of bells in the world, are in this very town, and yet they never regarded them. They undertook (what is impossible) to cast two bells, one of which should be an 8ve and 4th, the other an 8ve and 5th, or 12th, to the tenor at St. Mary's, Cambridge, which is D in the modern opera pitch. They did send two things they called bells; but neither ringers, singers, nor the professor of music at Cambridge, have been able to determine what note they speak; the general sentiment is, that they speak no note at all. I think it a pity to be at great expence and deface the cupola only for a temporary station for the clock. Surely for a while they might afford shoe-leather for a man to go and wind it up twice a-week. Excuse my writing in this rambling and desultory manner. To keep method and order, I must make half a dozen of copies. I find one enough; it will serve to suggest and bring all things to your mind, so that nothing may fall out, but what you have considered, and that is all I pretend to do.—I am yours.

WILLIAM LUDLAM.

The Rev. William Ludlam to Mr. J. Holmes.

DEAR SIR,   11th September, 1779.

When I wrote to you about a fortnight ago, I was just going a journey. Two things have occurred since, which I send you postpaid, to balance your franks. I am always entertained and obliged to you for accounts of mechanical undertakings; pray regard not the postage, nor, if it gives you trouble, seek for franks. I think your great clock should be kept going while winding it up; not merely to prevent loss of time, but to prevent the swing wheel from going backwards, through the friction of the barrel; and the consequent danger of the pallets pitching upon the points of the teeth. The common way, with a driver and shutter before the square, may do very well. The other two ways, one by a spring, the other by a pinion, &c. between the barrel and great wheel, you know very well. Instead of steel, you might have agate pallets; they may be set in, or screwed in a brass frame, many ways. Harrison, you know, used diamond pallets. Mudge, in an eight-day clock, applied pallets made of flint; but agate is harder, is not a stone of great value, and is not so hard but it may be easily wrought into a proper form, and highly polished.—Yours, &c.

WILLIAM LUDLAM.

Mr. J. Holmes to the Rev. William Ludlam.

DEAR SIR,   London, 17th August, 1779.

I really can't find words sufficient to express my grateful thanks to you for your very kind letter of the 1st of last month; you have therein communicated to me so many useful and ingenious things, that if I do not avail myself sufficiently of them in the Greenwich Hospital clock, it will be my own fault. I beg you will accept of my most sincere thanks for this very great and obliging favour, which I should not have been so long of transmitting to you, but that several things intervened, which I hope will plead my excuse. Mr. Smeaton had wrote me word, after I had wrote to you. He had thought very much on the subject. I was willing, therefore, of receiving his ideas before I made up my own mind, which he obligingly gave me in a full sheet. It turned out also that his business was likely to bring him to town, which it did, and he went with me to see the place, and only left us last week. I have the pleasure to inform you, that in almost all the great points, your ideas and his agreed. He read your letter with great pleasure, and found several ingenious things entirely new to him; he begged his best compliments to you and family. Having taken up so much of your time with this preamble, I shall now beg leave to mention some part of your letter, as also Mr. S's. and what passed in conversation, and to beg your farther assistance in some matters yet unsettled. The clock movement is in great forwardness, and I will annex to this the numbers and sizes of the wheels. I think you will smile when you find I have got 4 wheels into the train of the watch part; but this arose from necessity; the clock stands very much above the dials, which are opposite to each other; so that if the rods to the dial-work had been carried by a wheel, to go round in an hour, the contrate wheels must have been very small; I have therefore chose that wheel to go round in an hour and a half. I have adopted the double frame, after Mr. Hindley's, most of which is cast-iron, as also his pinions with the leaves let in; and, as far as I could prevail, (for I must work with other person's tools,) I shall have all the wheels and bearing parts considerably larger than common. Here Mr. S. carries the matter so far as to wish the swing-wheel one inch thick; the inconveniency arising from the change of tenacity of oil, he thinks of little consequence, compared with the danger of the parts biting one another; of this he is so much afraid in his practice, that in a new mill-wheel we have put in at Deptford water-works, our gudgeons are above 8 inches, and those of our old wheel only $2\frac{1}{4}$ inches; the large one wears perfectly smooth, and keeps its oily matter; whereas the small one, having so few bearing parts, presses out the oily matter, and is constantly getting dry, and wearing into rings. I shall take care, however, to keep my wheels as light as I can, by arming the crosses diagonally from the teeth to the bottom, so that they may have sufficient strength to support them. I now beg leave to come to your letter, and I hope you will excuse me, when I take the freedom of differing from you, and which, unluckily, will be in the first part of it, where you propose the hands to be balanced within; now, in this case, the minute hand is very liable to get loose on its square, as it will always be dragging, and it will be necessary to give it a large square to prevent it. It will also, when pressed by the wind, have nothing on the opposite side to take off that force, whereas a balance on the outside will in part prevent it. St. Paul's clock used to have no outward balance to the hand, so that when the hand got a little past 12, it would fall a minute or two at a time; it has been lately altered, and there is now to the minute hand, on the opposite end, a round ball, at about one-third of the length of the minute hand. Mr. S. proposes that the balance to the minute hand should be made as thick as it conveniently can, so, that it may present to the wind, when it blows parallel to the dial, near as much surface as the hand itself: He also proposes that the arbor of it should be fitted into a well-bored socket, and touch all the length, and that this socket should have holes in it, at convenient distances, to put in the oil. If you wish to read his letter, I will send you a copy of it; but part of this proposal was in conversation. Mr. S's. ideas are the same as yours, for the pendulum ball to be a sphere, and the 'scapement a retreat; but he thinks a short pendulum might be made to go well, by giving it an equal dominion over the main force; the principal part he differs in, is its vibration; if I calculated right, the 'scapement you have favoured me with, which 'scapes at $1\frac{1}{2}$, will only move a 13 foot pendulum ball from 'scapement to 'scapement 7.8 inches, whereas he seems to wish it to go to the extent of 20 inches, and room for 20 inches more of vibrations, and thinks the cycloidal difference will be small, compared with the advantage arising from the great dominion such a pendulum would have; for my own part, I am wishful of being in the mean, and think the common 'scapement may perhaps be best; but of this, I am very desirous of your further opinion. He likes very much Mr. Eayre's frame for the rod, but thinks a cylindrical rod of about 2 inches diameter would be more likely to keep straight than any framed one. The full explanation you have favoured me with, of the necessity of the pendulum having a great dominion over the main force, was so strongly impressed upon me, by your very sensible though short publication, after Mr. Harrison's communication, that I have made every use of it my practice would allow, and I now thank you for being more particular on that subject. Your observations on the lines drawing on that side next the pinion, though so ingenious and obvious when told, were entirely new to both Mr. S. and myself; but I shall tire you with repeating your observations; will therefore again thank you for them, and proceed to those I wish more particularly explained. Your reasons for the bell being struck by a heavy hammer resting on its joint, are so conclusive, that I only wish I could adopt that matter to your particular ideas of this case; our bell is nearly 12 cwt. 3 qrs. and our utmost fall for single line 55 feet. I have, therefore, by sketch and calculation, endeavoured to come at how this matter will stand to the abilities of the clock. Suppose a hammer 30lb., and that the centre of gravity of it is placed one foot from its joint, on an arm elevated 45°, that this hammer is drawn 5.7 inches, rising 3 inches perpendicular, it will require a weight of 170 lb. to be a balance to it, or the same hammer elevated 50° to be drawn 3.84 inches, rising 2 inches perpendicular, a weight 113 lb.: now, as the weight must be considerably larger to put all in motion, I am much afraid the first of these will be too much for the clock: how far the second will fetch the full tone out of the bell, I am no judge, and will therefore be particularly obliged by your opinion, not on my sketch, but on any you think will be best. Mr. Thwaites says, he thinks a hammer of 18 lb. lifted 4 inches, will do, and the weight 1 cwt. 1 qr.; but I have had no opportunity of seeing him since I had his letter, and do not know whether he means 4 inches perpendicular, but believe he means drawn 4 inches. Having mentioned the fall 55 feet, I will beg leave to give you the particulars and my ideas of the matter. The clock is intended to be put up in the new cupola, and a convenient place to be built for it; but till that is done, it is to be placed in the present cupola, near over the painted hall: here it will stand between the inner and outward dome; the lines must come through the painted roof of the inner cupola, and proceed down the side of a cylindrical part under, and so be carried into the corner, where there is a very convenient place for the weights to fall; but we can't get the 55 feet without cutting through about 3 feet of (I believe) stone work, for the weights to pass through, but I think can get about 46 feet without it. I should never have ventured to have proposed this place, fearing these lines would be too much an eye-sore in this building; my original intention was to have proposed the weights to have been within the two cupolas, where we can get near 18 feet, and I should then have proposed the clock being wound while in this place twice a-week; but I found this idea would not please, and this place was mentioned to me. I have since consulted Mr. S., and being wishful of avoiding this deformity, proposed still to keep the weights between the cupoles, and to put the axis in peritrochio to each; if so, Mr. S. proposed to lay under the weight a large flat stone, well bedded in some springy matter, to catch the weight, if it falls; and I should also add Dr. Hooke's rope and arm to the weight: but I believe the great weight this will require will frighten me, for people are frequently under it, and the inner roof is but slight; therefore think I shall content myself with such part of the 46 feet as will be necessary, and put a double line to it at first. There is only one part I will farther trouble you about. Mr. S. nor myself can't remember what was Mr. Hindley's double locking you mention; your description of it would therefore be very serviceable to me. I must now beg pardon for this long letter. I shall esteem any observations you please to make, a singular favour, and shall be particularly obliged to you for your farther instructions on the three following heads,— the 'scapement and pendulum, the hammer, and double locking.—I am, Sir, with the greatest deference and respect, &c.

J. HOLMES.

From Mr. John Holmes to the Rev. W. Ludlam.

DEAR SIR, London, 15th September, 1779.

I received your favours of the 28th of last month and 11th of this, and for which I return you my most sincere thanks: I am very sorry you should think of paying the postage of your last letters; this affair is wholly mine. Your reading my letters is doing me a great favour, and every line you write a singular service; your letters are so full, your drawings and descriptions so clear, that I have now little to trouble you with; but first, I will endeavour to set some matters clear, that I have been short or mistaken in my last letter. My intention, from the first, was to have a 13 foot pendulum; I had never any intention of a shorter; and, in consequence of this, the clock is raised about 16 or 18 feet above the dials; the two rods therefore coming down from the clock to the two dials, make an angle of near 80 degrees to one another, and these two rods have each a contrate wheel with teeth standing in the manner you describe, both which are turned by a contrate wheel in the clock; we found it necessary to enlarge the contrate wheel in the clock, otherwise these two wheels would have been very small; this, therefore, was the reason why the contrate wheel in the clock goes round in an hour and a half; but these two wheels being $\frac{2}{3}$ds of the size of the contrate wheel in the clock, will now run free of one another, be a good size, and go round in an hour each, and, as these rods are long, I propose a Hooke's joint to each: at the bottom of each of these rods will be another contrate wheel, toothed to the proper angle, and which will turn others to carry the hands. Had I been acquainted with the whole you favoured me with in your letter of the 28th last, I would undoubtedly have endeavoured to make the second wheel in the clock, on which the contrate wheel is, go round in two hours instead of an hour and a half. It would have saved us a wheel, which must be to set the hands by and unlock the clock; this wheel I intend to go round in two hours, and lift the lifting piece in the judicious manner you describe, bearing its load the whole hour; as this wheel is out of the train, it will be a small burthen to the clock. The pallet frame you describe has been long used by Thwaites, I be believe, ever since he made a clock, under Harrison's directions, for the Foundling Hospital. I had some thoughts of agate pallets, but found they would be an extra charge of three guineas, and, as I undertook to make this clock for £120, a moderate price for a good one in the common way, I think it needless to lay out a fourth or fifth part of my profit in them, and especially, as I propose to give more vibration to the pendulum than common, I am desirous of trying steel pallets first, and can add agate ones afterwards. The unlocking you have favoured me with is so very safe, that I propose to use it, also the manner of drawing the hammer, which is greatly eased of the friction in the common way; this I find is in a clock made by Thwaites, under directions of the late Mr. Ellicott, for the London Hospital. Nothing perplexes me so much as the bell; - - -

- - The case at present stands thus; he has got a bell by him, weight 12 cwt. 2 qrs. 21 lb. 2¼ inches in the sound bore, and I think about 3 feet and a half diameter, which he says is a very good bell. Mr. Green, who succeeds the late Mr. Romily, the small bell-founder, was so obliging as to go with me to hear it; he says it is a very good toned bell; he has also another bell of a larger size, and 1 cwt. 2 qr. 0 lb. heavier; on striking this bell, I found a lesser blow would bring the sound better out, than out of the other, and I was informed it was because the bell was more spread. This struck me, and on conversing with some of my friends, I am fully convinced that a bell, as commonly made for a peal, is not the fittest for a clock to strike on, and is what you call a tight bound bell. My ideas, therefore are, that if we have a bell of this weight, it must be larger, or if of this size lighter, the bell being then thinner, will be easier put into vibration by the power of the clock; the difficulty with me is what directions to give. It is a matter we can't easily make experiments on, so far as I can judge; if the same sized bell had 2 cwt. or 3 cwt. less metal in it, the blow the clock will strike would be much better spread. Also, that the same effect would be, if the bell was to be enlarged in that proportion, and have the same weight as this has. I will be extremely obliged to you for your opinion on this matter, before I speak again to the founder. I am well aware, if a bell is made in the manner I propose, it would pitch much farther; but I see no objection to this; all that we want is, to have a bell that will be best heard with the blow we can give. The way I calculated in my last letter, the weight of the clock, was by multiplying the weight of the hammer, by its perpendicular rise, and that by the number of blows in 8 days; the product of this multiplication, I divided by the fall which gives the weight that will be a balance to the hammer. Two things I have been informed of, the first of which I think will be of use, and the last, if not, can do no harm, viz. that by hammering, hardening, and smoothing the face of the hammer, and filing the part of the bell where it is struck on, we shall bring out a better tone at first than otherwise we should, if we left these in the rough. As I am informed, the oftener a bell is struck, the better it is heard, owing to the touching parts getting smoother and harder. The other, that if the hammer head is narrow and thin, and very long, it will strike a better blow, than if spread in breadth or thickness: how far this may be the case, I can't guess. One would think the same matter, with the same fall, would produce the same effect; there may be something in the matter laying behind the touching part, and pressing more directly upon it. Several trades, as caulkers, pewterers, &c. use very long hammer heads, perhaps for this reason. I shall now conclude, with my sincerest thanks for your very great and kind assistance in this matter; you have not only done me the most essential service, but given me the most heartfelt pleasure, in thinking I have in some shape, some merit, or you would not have taken so much pains to serve me. If your time will admit you to give me your opinion about the bell soon, pray do.—I am, &c. J. HOLMES.

The Rev. W. Ludlam, to Mr. John Holmes.

DEAR SIR, Sept. 24, 1779.

I am sorry that it is not in my power to give you the information I wish relating to bell-founding. I saw a great deal of it in the time of the late Mr. Thomas Eayre, of Kettering, a man who had a true taste for it, and spared no expense to make improvements; much of the tone depends on minute circumstances in the shape; and Mr. Eayre had crooks or forms cut on thin boards, carefully taken from the inside and outside of all the good bells he could find. This county and Northampton abound with the best bells I ever heard, cast by Hugh Watts, of Leicester, between 1630 and 1640. Ringers in general, who are commonly constituted the judges of bells, (and as such are fee'd by the bell-founder) regard neither tune nor tone. The hanging of the bell is all they regard, that they may show their dexterity in change-ringing. That shape of a bell that is best for tone, (a long one) is not the best for hanging or ringing; so tone is utterly disregarded,—to please the ringers and get money, is all. In my opinion, the thinner the bell and deeper the tone the better, provided it is not what they call shelly, that is like a thin shell, such a tone as the fragments of a broken Florence flask will give. A deep tone always suggests the idea of a great bell, is more grave, and better suited to the slow strokes of a church clock, and is heard farther. The clock at St. Clement Danes, in your neighbourhood, strikes the hour twice, once on the great bell in peal, and again on its octave or 12th, I know not which; listen to them and you will perceive which is most agreeable and best heard. The son of Mr Thomas Eayre, who was a good bell-founder, cast a dish bell, of five or six hundred weight, for the church clock at Boston, in Lincolnshire. Mr Thomas Eayre, very early in life, made a curious chime for Sir T. Wentworth, afterwards Lord Malton, and father of the Marquis of Rockingham, which had 13 dish bells, the biggest about two hundred weight. This is at Harrowden, near Kettering.

— — — — — —
— — — — — —
— — — — — —

I cannot help thinking a bell of 5 or 6 hundred weight, of the dish form, might be cast far fitter for your purpose than one of the church form. But who shall do it? Who has had any experience of bells of this form? It must also be observed, that small differences in the form, in the shape or thickness of the sound-bole of a church bell, will make great difference in the tone. All I can say is, it is not the weight of metal, but somewhat resulting from the shape of the bell, that gives both freedom and depth of tone, as I can prove by many instances. What that shape is that makes a bell so willing to speak, is a question which a good bell-founder ought to be able to answer. It is a known and undoubted fact, that a bell speaks much better when both the clapper and the bell is hammer-hardened, and when they are worked in to touch each other in many points. I had mentioned this, but I supposed you would make the hammer-head of cast iron. I think also the shape of the hammer you mention is of some advantage. Mr. Thomas Eayre used to make his chime hammers of the shape you mention. If you make the clock to unlock by a nag's-head-joint, &c. in Mr. Hindley's way, then observe, that if the clock be turned backwards, (that is, if the lifting pins be turned backwards) after the nag's-head is got under the hook of the detent, (which I call warning) you will then not only draw back the hook of the detent, but may keep it drawn back, and so the clock continue to strike till it is down. Indeed, to play this perverse trick, you must set the clock back, at the very nick of time just after warning, and you must set the clock back only a very little. A blot is no blot till it is hit, and yet I have known the veriest fool of a parish clerk, without the least design, stumble on such a nicety as this, and put all into confusion. I must now beg the favour of Mr Kendall to resolve me a few questions. What number of watches he had made by order of the Board of Longitude, &c.? The first I know was an exact copy of Harrison's, or as Mr Short phrased it, parts like parts, &c. After I sealed this, I recollected that above 40 years ago, Thomas Eayre made a large turret clock, with quarters, for Lady E. Germain, (now Lord G. Germain's) at Drayton, near Thropton, Northamptonshire, all the bells of which are dish bells, of a large size, I know not their weight, I suppose the biggest four hundred weight; they are heard a great way. I am, &c.

W. LUDLAM.

From the Rev. William Ludlam to Mr. John Holmes.

DEAR SIR, January 10, 1780.

Many things have occurred to me, since I wrote, about the proper form of a sounding body, to be struck by the clock hammer instead of a bell in the common form, of those made to be rung, and, of course, struck with a clapper. I am persuaded a shape might be contrived, that would give a strong, deep, clear, and lasting note, a note as perfectly uniform and musical, as the deep pipe of an organ,

APPENDIX, (A. & B.).

wild,) and that with so light a load on the clock wheels, as by no one to require very strong, or very large work, nor an heavy weight. or this, I suppose the hammer to have much matter in it, yet suppose the weight of that matter to rest very much on the arbor r axis of the hammer.) All this I am confident may be; but who will be at the expense of making trials, to explore this unknown region in the land of bell-founding? who will pay for journeys to visit that great dish, eight hundred weight, very deep, but wild bell, I mentioned at Boston, or those lesser ones (of 200 lb.) at Lord Rockingham's near Kettering? Now, as this cannot be, I mean to fill up my paper with an account of some curiosities in that way, which I have actually seen. There is an instrument brought from the East Indies, I think, from China, called a gon or gong, made of hammered brass, about 16 inches over. The drawing is a section of it. See Plate XVIII. Fig. T. What I call the sides, A A, are about 4 inches deep, and seem to supply the office of the sides of a drum, while the flat part, B B, answers to the stretched parchment; only there is a raised part in the middle, to stiffen it; on this raised part you beat, with a ball of pack-thread of 4 or 5 inches diameter, fastened to the end of a stick. The brass at a mean is about $\frac{1}{4}$ of an inch thick, but unequal. The whole form being manifestly raised out of a flat plate by the hammer. The tone is amazingly deep, clear, and sonorous. The note of that I saw, and had sometime in my possession, was F, an octave below the F-fa-let cliff in the bass: where that is, any musician can tell. Has Captain Maxwell seen any such thing? they are often to be found in India shops. N. B. The gong is above an 8ve below the deepest church bell known. Provide now a good clear clock bell of 4 or 5 inches diameter; provide a cylinder of thin tin, see Fig. S, about 2½ diameter, and 7 or 8 inches long, with a bottom soldered in it; provide a round flat cork to fit it, to make an occasional bottom. Having put the cork a little way in, set the bell, Fig. M, on its crown, mouth upwards, hold the cylinder horizontally, with the mouth very near the edge of the bell, a very little above it; strike the bell; if you find the sound not altered, push in the false bottom. At some place where the cylinder is of a proper depth, suitable to the tone of the bell, the sound will be increased. Cut the cylinder in this length, and i will do better without the cork. There is some nicety and uncertaint in finding a cylinder of a proper length; how far the diameter affe it I know not; but when circumstances are right, the sound is m wonderfully augmented: insomuch, that when the sound of the ked bell can no longer be heard, bring the cylinder to it, and will so revive and magnify the dying sound, that it may be p heard. This was accidentally discovered by T. Eayre, who having a number of brass shells for clock weights, and a number of clock bells, lying on his board together, observed this effect in an high degree, from the accidental position of one of them. It is not to be doubted but that the ancients used brasen vessels in some such way to augment the voice of the actors in their theatres, which were so monstrous large, the actor could not otherwise be heard. Now, my idea is to have a vast great gong, and I would so augment the sound with tin or brasen vessels, that it should shake the college walls from end to end. At the same time, I would have the sound so deep, clear, and melodious, that *Lord Sandwich* himself should acknowledge its place in the gamut, or scale of musical sounds. This is my Utopian idea. I doubt not but a flat sheet of bell-metal would give a great sound. All kind of metals, marble, &c. in this shape always give a great and free sound.

Yours, &c. WILLIAM LUDLAM.

(B.)

Dutertre's Clock 'Scapement, referred to at page 238, Plate IX. 48.

A B is the wheel of *arrêté*, or repose; C D the wheel of impulse; both having the same number of teeth, but differing greatly in their diameters. E is the pallet seen on its arbor, in which is a notch, to allow the teeth of the wheel of *arrêté* to pass; at the instant of this taking place, the teeth of the lesser wheel give impulse to the pallet, and, having escaped it, a tooth of the larger wheel falls on the circular part of the pallet arbor.

(C.)

Arnold's detached 'scapement, referred to, page 245, Plate IX. 51.

51. is a detached 'scapement, as made by the late Mr. Arnold, and by his son, the present Mr. Arnold, for box-chronometers. The 'scapement or balance-wheel A, having twelve teeth, is calculated to have a train of 14,400, and, by the seconds hand, half a second will be marked at every step by it, on the seconds circle of the dial. The acting part or face of the tooth, is partly in the form of a cycloidal curve, and stands above the plane of the wheel, as represented in the

edge view given of it; in the plane, the shaded or dark part of the tooth may be supposed either the upper end or top, or a section of it; the other two sides are flat, or bounded by right lines, the longest of which forms an angle with the cycloidal curve, and on this angle the wheel is locked by the spring detent C D, in which is set a small bit of fine stone, either of ruby or sapphire, for the purpose of the wheel being locked on it. This bit of stone may be supposed to be put into the spring detent, so as to stand near the point of the adjusting screw *b*, or nearly where the letter *a* is. It is by the screw *b* that the detent piece can be made to have more or less hold of the angle on the tooth. The end of the detent stone piece must be of such a length or height as to be quite free from the inside bottom of the wheel; R is the main pallet or roller, having an opening or notch in it, on one side of it, the right hand one being what is called the face of the pallet, in which is set a piece of precious stone, as seen at *e*. It is on it that the curved part of the tooth acts. As represented in the figure, the tooth 1. has carried the pallet so far on, by a distance equal to that between tooth 2. and the point of the adjusting screw. Concentric with the main pallet R, is a small lifting pallet *d*, whose use is to unlock the wheel, by pressing on the side end of the lifting spring D, and, carrying it so far inwards, takes the detent and its spring along with it; the detent piece of stone, by this means, getting free of the angle of the tooth at *a*, the wheel gets forward, and the tooth 1. gives impulse to the main pallet R. During the first part of the impulse, and before the impelling tooth gets so far on as is here represented, or it may not take place till the tooth gets a little farther on, the end of the lifting spring parts with the lifting pallet *d*, leaving the detent and its spring at liberty; the detent then, by means of its spring, comes quickly to its place at *a*, and, before tooth 1. has escaped, is ready to receive tooth 3. and lock it. On the balance returning from the vibration given by this impulse, the pallet *d*, meeting with the end of the delicate lifting spring, carries it so far outwards, and then parts with it to complete its vibration on this side. It is evident that the point of the adjusting screw opposes the detent being carried that way, although the lifting spring is not, and yet it is at the same time connected with the detent spring; but extends so far beyond the end of the detent spring, that the lifting pallet *d*, whether going or returning, cannot touch it, but cannot pass either way without meeting with the sides at the end of the lifting spring, and working on it. The detent spring is screwed to one of the frame plates, by the paume, or sole, near to which it is made very thin and weak; and at this place, the centre of motion of the detent piece may be supposed to lie. The lifting spring is pinned by one end to the side of the detent spring, which may be called the outside of it. It is easy to perceive that the unlocking is made, by carrying the detent spring inwards, or towards the centre of the wheel. When this takes place, the cycloidal part of the tooth falls (not on the point but a little within it,) on the blunted edge, or nearly so, of the face of the pallet; having given impulse, and escaping, the wheel is again locked, and so on. The wheel is unlocked at every alternate vibration of the balance, or 7200 times in an hour, or 120 times in a minute; hence half seconds are marked on the dial by the seconds hand. The diameter of the main pallet R, may be made at the option of the 'scapement maker in any proportion to that of the wheel; but it must always stand, when the wheel is locked, free between the teeth; and the impulse given by the wheel to it, will be so much the more direct the less the difference of the diameters. And in this, experience is the best test; but it requires long and reiterated trials.

(D.)

Earnshaw's detached 'scapement, referred to page 245,
Plate IX. 52.

52. shows the detached 'scapement made by Mr. Earnshaw for his box-chronometers. The balance wheel, A B C D, is plain, or flat, made of steel, and sometimes of brass, the teeth have somewhat of the ratchet form, and are considerably undercut on the face; the number of teeth being 12,* and calculated so as to give half seconds, by the steps of the seconds hand on the seconds circle, in the same way as has been mentioned in Arnold's. The steel roller or main pallet M S K has an opening in it, the face of which is also much undercut, having a piece of some fine stone, such as hard ruby or sapphire set into it, as seen at *l h*, for the purpose of making the points of the teeth work smoothly on it, and preventing any wearing from their constant action. A stud G is fixed to the potence plate, and to this stud the detent spring F F is screwed, and made very slender and weak near the stud. It is by the yielding at this place, that any motion can be given to the detent on which the wheel is locked; and here is its centre of motion. The tooth D of the wheel is supposed to be locked on a flat side of the stone detent, which is fixed in a thick part of the detent spring, by means of which it presses against the inside of the head of the adjusting screw *m*, which works in a fixed stud *a* P; so that

---

* In the specification he states 13 teeth for the balance wheel, (while 12 teeth is given in the Plate) and 18,000 for the train. We have shown at page 26, that a train of 18,000, with a balance wheel of 13, is not easily to be obtained.

when it is screwed into this stud, the detent will have less hold of the tooth, and *vice versa*. Y is a delicate spring attached to the inner side of the detent spring, and which is called the lifting spring. The end of the detent spring is bent a very little, so that the free end of the lifting spring may bear only on the inward bent point at *o*. Concentric with the main pallet, is the small lifting pallet *n*, which is flat on the face, or lifting side, and tapered or rounded off on the opposite side. Its position in the figure represents it coming with its face against the lifting spring, which it would carry away with it; but this cannot have place, without taking along with it the detent spring, and consequently the detent is carried out from locking a tooth of the wheel at D. By this time the main pallet has got so far forward, as to be in the way of receiving impulse from the tooth B, and before it can escape, the lifting pallet parts with the end of the lifting spring, and leaves the detent and detent-spring immediately to resume their place. The detent will then be ready to receive the tooth C, by which the wheel is again locked. The balance having performed this vibration, by the impulse given, returns, and with it the lifting pallet *n*, the tapered side of which will press the lifting spring inwards, but cannot carry the detent spring with it, this being prevented by the inside part of the head of the adjusting screw *m*; after passing the lifting spring, it goes along with the vibration of the balance, on whose return the face of it will again meet with the lifting spring; unlocking then takes place, and so on. The unlocking here is performed by carrying the detent outward from the centre of the wheel, which is locked by the extreme points of the teeth. Mr. Earnshaw gives as a rule for making the inclination of the faces of the teeth, and main pallet, that they should be in a line drawn from the points of the teeth, as a tangent to a circle whose diameter is half of that of the wheel; and the same rule is used for the face of the pallet, which is shown by the dotted lines and circle in the figure. As the detent stone-piece on which the tooth D is locked, being set into that side of the detent spring, lying undermost in the figure, it cannot therefore be well represented here. The points or dots at the letters *k* and *a*, show the relative positions of being locked and unlocked. The flat part of the stone detent goes a very little way in, as at *k*, to receive the point of the tooth A, on the opposite side of the wheel, when locking is supposed; and at unlocking the dot at *a*, may be supposed to be the utmost extent of the detent, when carried out by the detent, and lifting springs at that time. The detent spring lies above, and clear of the wheel, and the detent stone-piece, may be either a semi-cylinder or an angular piece. A flat side is however, in either way, requisite for the tooth of the wheel to lock on it, and the height or length of this stone should be a little below the under side of the wheel, so that the teeth may at all times have a sure hold on it. Mr. Earnshaw has stated that he makes the diameter of his roller or pallet larger than that of Arnold's, which will no doubt allow the teeth of the wheel to give a more direct impulse to it. The diameter of the roller, however, if carried too far, would lessen the hold of the teeth on the pallet. Where a wheel of 12 teeth is used, it will give scope for getting in a pallet of considerable length. If the drawings in the specifications be correct, the proportion between the diameter of the balance wheel and of the roller, seems to be the same, or nearly the same, in Arnold's and Earnshaw's 'scapements.

(E.)

Owen Robinson's detached 'scapement, referred to page 247, Plate IX. 53.

53. is a view of Owen Robinson's free, or detached 'scapement, where the unlocking should be easier effected than it is done either in Arnold's or Earnshaw's. AB, AB is a view of the balance wheel, both in plane, and edgeways, being somewhat similar to the wheel in the duplex 'scapement; that is, the upright teeth are those which give impulse to the pallet, while the long teeth in the plane of the wheel are those which lock on the detent. R is the roller or pallet, the acting face of which may be supposed to have a piece of fine stone inserted there, as in the two former 'scapements; $d, s,$ the detent spring, screwed to the potence plate, and made rather weaker at a place between s and the sole, than anywhere else. It is at this place only where it will readily bend, or yield, which becomes a centre of motion to the detent. At the thick part $d,$ the stone for the detent is inserted; the white part at d may be supposed the upper end of it, and a tooth of the wheel locked on the flat side, next the centre of the roller; $l\ l$ is the lifting spring attached to the inside of the detent spring. A part of both these springs lying under the roller, cannot properly be represented. The extreme, or free end of the lifting spring, goes a little beyond that of the detent spring, so that the lifting pallet can never pass, without touching it, but while passing, it never can touch the end of the detent spring. The lifting pallet is not easily seen, but is of the same form as that in 52, where the adjusting screw and stud is the same, as may be supposed for 53, though not drawn there. The face of the lifting pallet, is just on the eve of touching the lifting spring; carrying it on a little way, would unlock

the wheel, and the pallet face being brought to a part where its edge, as seen in the figure, would be ready to receive impulse from one of the upright teeth. The action of this 'scapement is quite the same as that of the others. The great difference of radius in the diameter of the wheel of impulse, and of the locking wheel, causes this to press with less force on the detent, than those which have been mentioned; the unlocking is outwards, or receding from the extremities of the points of the teeth, and when locked, the roller stands free between the teeth of impulse.

(F.)

P. Le Roy's Marine Timekeeper, referred to, pages 238 and 256, Plate XI. 61.

61. is a perspective view of the balance, the compensation, and other parts connected with it, in M. P. Le Roy's marine timekeeper, tried by order of the King of France, in a voyage on board the Lively frigate in the year 1768. From its good performance, a prize was awarded to him by the Royal Academy of Sciences. The balance, or regulator, VVVV, of this timekeeper was steel; it was four inches in diameter, weighed five ounces, and was fixed on an arbor AA, about five inches long. A brass frame or mounting, s, s, s, s, s, s, to which the movement is fixed, keeps the balance horizontally suspended by the upper end of its arbor, by means of F, a very fine harpsichord wire, to which it is attached; the length of the wire is three inches or so, forming one vertical right line with the axis. The movement cannot well be seen here, being behind the upper part of the brass mounting; the dark shade is part of the dial. The timekeeper goes 30 hours, and has no equalising for the main-spring, by means of a fusee; the balance-wheel is a star of six radii, or teeth, and extremely light; it gives impulse to a pallet on the upper side of the rim of the balance at every alternate vibration; and the 'scapement is a free or detached one. In order that the balance may turn freely on its axis, each of its pivots is retained, with proper play, between four rollers turning freely in two small frames cc, cc, one for the lower pivot, fixed to the under part of the brass mounting; the upper pivot runs in the uppermost frame, fixed to the brass mounting also, at a little distance from the lower end of the harpsichord or suspending wire. The whole is arranged with the necessary precautions, so that the wire and the axis of the balance may form always one vertical right line. The balance, thus suspended, would

make vibrations, each of which would take about 20 seconds of time, by means of the elasticity of the wire of suspension. Two spiral springs s s, s s, like those which serve as main-springs to common watches, are adjusted to the lower end of the balance arbor, by means of their collets or virrels, like what the spiral or pendulum springs have in ordinary watches, and are placed opposite each other in a centre of equilibrium absolutely at rest, so as to cause the vibrations to be made in half a second. The sliding cocks d d, serve to adjust, to any position, the pendulum springs, whose outer ends are fixed to these cocks. To regulate the timekeeper, there is placed, near to the lower end of the balance arbor, a small plain circular crossed wheel G G, on the upper side of which, and diametrically opposite, two studs are fixed, through which the two screws s G, s G, pass in such a manner, that turning them by the hand will make them come equally nearer to, or farther from the arbor. These screws, by their mass, which can be diminished at pleasure, according to the exigency of the case, can be made to describe a great space, and allow the machine to be regulated in the nicest manner. If the effects of heat and cold were of short duration, the inconveniences that have been exposed might be neglected; but as the machine may be placed so as to undergo such trials of temperature for six months at a time, it is obvious that the vibrations of different extent of the regulator, having then no longer the isochronism required, the causes which might be able to vary the largeness of the vibrations, would considerably alter the regularity of the timekeeper.

"Convinced of the principle," says Le Roy, "that I have just established, to compensate the effect of different temperatures on my machine, I took quite a new way. I adapted to the balance several small bars of brass and steel, disposed in such a manner, that, by their lengthening in heat, or shortening in cold, they were brought nearer to or farther from its centre; two considerable parts of its mass, placed each at the extremity of a lever, and diametrically opposite."* By the calculation which I had made of it, it appeared that the whole mass of the balance approached to or receded from the centre of the balance about $\frac{1}{74}$th of a line, to compensate a variation in heat, which would have produced one second out of 15 in an hour in the going of the watch. The inconvenience of the preceding method made me soon give it up; the play of the levers or bars, and the want of solidity of the balance, produced errors greater than those which I wanted to compensate. This made me have recourse to a

* This method, or something like it, was once used by the late Mr. Arnold.

method which afterwards answered my utmost expectations; it consists in the application to the balance of two small thermometers, $tt, tt; tt, tt$, made each of a glass tube, bent and open at one end, and having a ball at the other.

"These thermometers, composed of mercury and spirit of wine, would have formed each an exact parallelogram, if the upper side, which carries the ball wherein the spirit of wine is contained, and partly on this side of it, had not been a little inclined. Both these thermometers are adjusted firmly to the axis of the balance, and in opposition to each other, in such a manner that the axes of their tubes, and that of the balance, meet in the same plane; which intersects the balls in the middle. It must be understood, previous to explaining this compensation, that the mercury fills the lower side of the tube, and about half way up the side parts of it. It will be easily conceived how this construction produces the compensation required. The thermometers, making part of the regulator, or balance, when the spirit of wine, by its expansion, pushes a part of the mercury of the outer branch of the tube t, t, towards that which is near the axis, of motion; a portion of the mercury, as part of the mass of the regulator, passes then from its circumference towards its centre. At the mean of temperature, for example, the mercury occupies the tubes half way up in each side; whereas, in extreme cold, when the thermometer of Reaumur is —15°, or that of Fahrenheit 33.75° below the freezing point, or —1.75°, the outward branch of the tube is filled with mercury, whilst its inward corresponding branch is empty; and as the mass of the balance resists, in the ratio of the square of its distance from the centre, there evidently follows from this a compensation. If the chronometer goes slow, from a loss in the elasticity of the springs, and from the expansion of the balance by too great a heat, it is compensated by less weight or mass at the circumference of the regulator; and, vice versa, in the passage to cold, this effect is so much the more sure, as there is no shake or play to be apprehended here. Besides the expansion of the spirit of wine by heat, and its contraction by cold, are constant effects, as have been found by experience with thermometers of this liquor, which had lost nothing of their exactness at the end of thirty years. From the calculation made for these thermometers, it was found necessary to have them in the form represented here, by bringing the balls near to the centre of the balance, in order to diminish that resistance of the air to its motion, which it would have experienced, had the balls been placed at, or near the circumference."

61. Nos. 1. and 2. are more distinct views of the thermometers employed by Le Roy in the compensation of his time-keeper.

(G.)

Month Clocks, referred to, page 36.

In clocks going a month or upwards, the first and second wheels should be on the left side of the frame, in order that the cord should lead off from the barrel, on that side next the first pinion. An eight-day clock should have the barrel on the right hand side, for the like reason. We have made an eight-day clock, with two wheels transmitting their force to the centre pinion; in this case, the barrel was put to the left side; the great wheel here was 96, the second 90, its pinion 30, the centre pinion 24; $96 \times 90 \div 30 \times 24 = 12$, the number of hours for one turn of the barrel. In a clock going a month or more, it is indispensable to have two wheels to transmit the force to the centre pinion, though not so in an eight-day one. In whichever way the hour-hand is carried about, it may not be amiss to have a counterpoise to the minute hand; the spring to the minute pipe-wheel is commonly put on by a round hole, and sometimes by a square hole, fitted on a square made to the outside of the fore pivot of the centre pinion; for common clocks, this may perhaps serve well enough. The kind of spring we have made to some clocks, had a socket underneath, the depth or height about one-tenth of an inch nearly; this was fitted to a part of the pivot outside, and a very little twisting on it made it hold surprisingly fast; the minute pipe, on one end, had a plain or flat sort of a wheel, in diameter an inch or more, against which the spring pressed when the minute hand was by its collet pinned down; a spring-kind of socket was put on the minute pipe, from which an arm projected in a direction opposite to that of the minute hand, having at its end such a weight, so as it could be made in equipoise with that of the minute hand. By this means, the minute hand could be set pleasantly, and with the greatest precision.

INDEX.

A.

	Page
Acceleration of the fixed stars, table of	323
Alarm time-piece described	174
Alexander, Father, his description of ancient clocks	2
Allan, James, his method of dividing	289
Almond oil	273
Andrew's, St. Church, clock 'scapement of	212
Anchor pallet, Hooke's invention of	184
Apparent time	315
Arabian oil	272
Astronomical clock, Kinfauns Castle	195
Edinburgh Institution	196
new detached 'scapement for	207
pendulum of, remarks on	137
method of fitting up	405
gut for, diameter of	406
diameter of wheels, pinions, number of teeth and leaves for	407
dial for sidereal hours	ib.
'scapements for	408

B.

Balance clock, first known in France	6
Balance weight and diameter of	228
experiment on	230
effect of increasing diameter of	231
compensation	257
Ball of pendulum, remarks on weight of	160
Barlow, inventor of repeating clocks	329
Beat, numbers of in a seconds clock	12
common watch	ib.
Bells, church, in Europe	408
in Nankin, China	409
in Moscow	ib.
in Erfurt	ib.
in Christ church, Oxford	ib.
in St. Paul's, London	ib.
in Lincoln	ib.
in Edinburgh	ib.
diameters of	410
music	412
pricking barrels for	413
Berthoud on Vick's claim to the invention of clocks	5
his pitching tool for lunation work	101
his experiments on suspensions of pendulum	131
his tables for the expansion of metals	355
his pyrometrical experiments	352

	Page
Books referred to in history of Horology	4 & 6
Bürgen, or Byrgius, his application of pendulum to a clock	179
Box or marine chronometer, description of	240
Box chronometer, going by its own weight	273
Bradley, Mr. his opinion of pendulums in different latitudes	122
Brahe, Tycho, notice of	181
Briguet, his 'scapement	236
Bruhl, Count, his new calculation of numbers for lunation work	72

C

Camus, his work on mechanics referred to	17
his examples for finding numbers for the teeth of wheels	81
Canon pinions in dial wheel work	31
Celsus, his thermometer	346
Centigrade thermometer	ib
Charles V. of France, a clock in his palace	2
Chevereul, his method of preparing oil	272
Chime bells	412
Chronometers box, examples on	40
description of	ib
method of going by its own weight	278
method of calculating the force of mainspring	222
force of mainsprings in	230
Circle, to divide the circumference of	287
Clock making, history of	1
Clock, Vick's	2
Wallingford's	ib
Gerbert's	ib.
first in Westminster Hall	4
St. Mary's, Oxford	ib
month	34
and watches, winding of	ib.
six months	36
36 days	36 and App.
spring	37
repeating	41 & 328
striking parts of	41
quarter parts of	46
music, parts of	48
Mudge's description of	70
regulation of, to keep mean time	152
or watch, method of setting	153
striking part of described	174
apparatus for going in time of winding	274

INDEX.

	Page.
Clock, equation	295
Pennycuick-House, description of	297
turret work	349
Clement, William, his clock and improvements	184
Clepsydra, tooth wheels applied to	1
Compensation curbs and balances for time-keepers,	257
Mudge	258
Le Roy, description of	259 and App.
Berthoud	260
Arnold	261 and App.
pendulums	267
Cumming, his mode of applying 'scapement to the pendulum	135
Curbs, compensation	257
Cylinders, hollow, dimensions of, examples on	160
ruby, advantages of	232
D.	
Dauthiau, his clock and orrery	46
Debaufre, his 'scapement, description of	234
improved by Sully	ib.
De Luc and Dalby's experiments on expansion of metals	356
Derham, his artificial clockmaker noticed	4
his description of a clock in Hampton Court	ib.
pocket watch	ib.
Depthening tool, Ridley's notice of	119
Detached 'scapement, description of	242
Diagram for easing friction of turret clock barrel pivots	403
Diameter of wheels and pinions, examples on	114
Berthoud's rule for	116
Hatton's rule for	ib.
Dial, sun, first set up at Rome	5
wheels, to compute numbers for	31
wheels, nature of, used in the Stogden repeating motion	83
Drawing off 'scapements, manner of	189
Duplex 'scapement or Tyrer's	239
Dutch old striking clocks, going and striking parts	183
Dutertre's watch 'scapement, improvement of Hooke's	226
description 237 and App.
by Berthoud	238
by Thiout	ib.
E.	
East, Edward, biographical anecdote	266
Ellicott's tables for the expansion of metals	350
Engine cutting and dividing	284
by Hindley	285
wheel cutting, to divide circles on the dividing plate of	286
Hindley's description of, by Smeaton	289

	Page.
Equation clock, historical notice of	295
at Pennycuick House	297
of time	314
Examples on wheel teeth and pinion leaves	12
vibrations in an hour	13
swing wheel teeth	ib.
finding the numbers for the wheel teeth of a clock or watch	14
for watch movement makers	18
canon pinion	32
finding the time a clock or watch will go before winding	33
month clocks	34
six month clocks	35
36 day clocks	36
movement of flat watches	38
hor. chronometers	40
clock repeaters	41
striking part of clocks	42
watch mounting trains	44
quarter part of clocks	46
music of chime parts	47
music part of clocks	48
vibrations of the pendulum	140
calculating the motive forces of watch balances	229-230
of calculating force of mainsprings	280
of cutting teeth on a wheel	288
of cutting odd number of teeth by Hindley's cutting engine	293
of applying equation of time	317
for finding compensation to a pendulum	367
Experiments on the balance of a watch	232
Berthoud's pyrometrical	353
Expansion of metals	348
tables for, by Ferguson	350
by Ellicott	ib.
by Smeaton	ib.
by General Roy	351
by Berthoud	355
by De Luc & Dalby	356
F.	
Facio, Monsieur, his discovery of piercing holes in rubies, &c.	233
Fahrenheit's thermometer	346
proposed improvement on	347
Falling bodies, laws of	121, 125
Ferguson, James, his description of wheels, &c.	70
his tables for the expansion of metals	350
Force of main-springs	280
Fraser, Dr. his opinion on the history of the striking parts of clocks	176
G.	
Galileo, his observations on falling bodies	121
his discovery of the pendulum	177

INDEX.

	Page
Galileo, his son, applied the pendulum to a clock	178
Gerbert, biographical notice of	2
horologium of	ib.
hydraulic organs made by	3
Georgian, numbers for	78
Dr. Pearson's tables for	ib.
Glass jar for mercurial pendulums, rules for	168
Godfroi, Wendelinus, discovered expansibility of metals	348
Gong, description of the	411
Graham, George, notice of	49
his Jamaica astronomical clock, description of	122
his dead beat 'scapement	186
improved by Le Paute	ib.
his hollow cylinder 'scapement, improvement on Tompion's	226
Gray, Lord, his astronomical clock described	195
Gravity, centre of, in a pendulum	127
Gridiron pendulum, remarks on	128
Gunter's scale, use of, in taking diameters of large wheels	114

H.

Haley, C. his patent for a re-winder	218
Harrison's clock pallets, origin of	192
'scapements, whose pallets require no oil	204
Harris, Richard, his clock for St. Paul's	178
Hautefeuille's lever 'scapement	236
described by Berthoud	237
Hazel nut oil	273
Hindley, of York, his mode of applying pendulums to turret clocks	137
Hindley, his wheel cutting engine, described by Smeaton	289
History of remontoir 'scapement	213
History of the pendulum and its application	177
Historical account of orreries	49
Homberger on invention of clocks	5 & 176
Hooke, Robert, his invention of anchor pallets	184
biographical notice of	185
his new 'scapement for watches, origin of the duplex	225
Horizontal 'scapement of Graham	226
Horology, definition of	1
history of	ib.
Horological definitions of Smith noticed	185
Horologium of Gerbert	2
Houriet, M. Fred. of Locle	267
Howell, his detached 'scapement	252
Hull, cylinder 'scapement maker, London	228
Hutton, Dr. James, his opinion on the hardness of gun flints	217
Huygens, his clock, description of	181
remarks on	183
his original letters	265

I

India, method of striking the hour in some parts of	173

	Page
Instrument, transit, substitute for	324
Italy, striking clocks used in	4

J.

Jacks, Dutch, description of	276-277
Janvier, notices of, and of his works	49
his wheel work of sphere mouvant	74
Jewelling of pivot holes	269
Jewelled and brass holes compared	270
Jodin, his method to prepare oil	272
Jupiter's satellites, numbers for	75

K.

Kater, Captain, his experiments on the pendulum	124
on expansion of wood	351
Kincardine's, Earl of, MS. letters	265
Kress, Father, his account of an equation clock	296
Knife-edge pendulum suspender, remarks on	132
description of	ib.

L.

Lead, melted, rule for filling a vessel with	109
Length of pendulum, effects of on time-keeping of a clock	137
examples on, to find the number of vibrations	140
table to regulate	147
Lepaute improves Graham's dead-beat 'scapement	186
his 'scapement, description of	187
his attempts at simplicity in machinery	219
Lever, definition of	82
wheels and pinions of	83
remarks on	84-86
'scapement	237
Logarithms, use of, in computing lengths of pendulums	143
Longitude, first premiums for finding the	235
Ludlam, his calculations for lengthening of a pendulum	148
Lunar motion work	313
Lunation, numbers for	66
an inverted	80
method of finding	313-314

M.

Machinery for going in time of winding	274
old method	ib
new method	275
of clocks and watches, general description of	7
Main-spring, force of, in box chronometers	280
Marine chronometers described	249
Mean time	315
at true noon, table	330
Mercurial pendulum, remarks on	129

2 H

INDEX.

	Page
pansion and contraction of	348
Ferguson's tables of	350
Ellicott's ditto	ib.
Smeaton's	ib.
General Roy's	351
Berthoud	355
De Luc and Dalby	356
Berthoud's experiments on	352
ry pace pendulum, length of	152
tes and degrees to set off on a pendulum index plate	154
th clocks, examples on	34
six, clocks	35
ring, day of, mode of shifting	308–311
tion work and movement of repeat-clocks, description of	332
work, Stogden, of a watch 33 &	333
description of	339
Muschenbroeck invented the pyrometer	348
Mudge, his clock for showing the moon's age	70
his letter on lunation numbers	72
his detached 'scapement described	192 & 251
his spring pallet ditto	253
his spring pallet 'scapement, Berthoud's opinion on	256
Music and chime parts	47
part of clocks	48
barrel, mode of pricking	416
bells	419
hammers	ib.
Musical springs in snuff boxes, &c.	425

N.

New detached 'scapement for regulators	207
Newton, Sir Isaac, his opinion on pendulums in different latitudes	123
Numbers for teeth of wheels	14
for orreries and planetariums	49
planetary	54
for tropical year	57
for siderial year	59
odd, example of cutting on Hindley's dividing engine	293

O.

Oil to keep at crown wheel teeth	206
for watches	271
receipt to deprive, of its acid	ib.
prepared	ib.
neats' feet	272
prepared by Chevreul	ib.
Arabian	ib.
poppy seed	ib.
almond	273
walnut	ib.
hazel	ib.
Fred. Schmidt, of Stutgard	ib.
method of preserving, at pivot holes	ib.
method of washing	ib.
Organs, hydraulic	3

Organ clocks, description of machinery in	423
Orreries, numbers for	49
first made in Britain by Graham	ib.
wheels and pinions of	ib.
Oscillation, centre of, in a pendulum	127
Oxford, clock first set up at St. Mary's	4

P.

Pacificus, his horologia	2
Pearson, Dr. notice of his mechanical and astronomical observations	51
his table for revolutions of Jupiter's satellites	76
Pendulum, motion of	121
length of, in different latitudes	122
wooden rod, remarks on	128
gridiron	ib.
ball or bob of, described	130
effects of atmosphere on motion of	131
for siderial time	149
rules for touching when fast or slow	150
table of loss of, according to arc of vibration	153
index plate to set off minutes and degrees on	154
tables of lengths of, their vibrations, the numbers for teeth of wheels and pinions	157
ball, weight of, in proportion to moving force	159
lenticular, rules for and examples on	164
frustum of a cone, ditto ditto	166
sphere or globe, ditto, ditto	167
mercurial glass jar, ditto, ditto	168
discovery of, remarks on	177
spring of a watch, invented by Hooke	264
description of	265
isochronism of	267
compensation	357
Graham's mercurial	357
Reid's ditto	360
wooden rod	363
gridiron, Harrison's	364
Smeaton's	372
examples for finding compensation to	367
Ellicott's	369
Reid's zinc tube compensation	373
glass compensation	374
Troughton's tubular	371
Ward's	37
rhomboida	3
wooden rod	
suspension of	3
Pennington's sector tool described	1
Pennycuick House equation clock described	
Pinions and wheels, description of	
Pinion leaves, examples for finding canon, in dial work	

INDEX.

	Page
Pinions, diameter of	99
and examples on	114
directions for gauging	101
sizing, rules for	117
Pitchings of wheels and pinions	89
corollaries on	92
Pitching tool of Berthoud	101
Geneva	ib.
sliding scale of	111
by M. Le Cerf, notice of	120
Pivot holes, jewelling of	269
Planetarium, numbers for	49
Planetary numbers, tables of	73
Poppy seed oil	272
Prime numbers, table of	426
Proportional compasses noticed	289
Pyrometer	345

Q.

Quarters, mode of pricking	421
clock, chimes for	422–423

R.

Ratios alternate, examples of	32
Re-winding of clock or watch, examples on	33
Re-winders described	213
Repeaters, clock, description of	41
Repeating train of watches	44
Remontoir, notice of	135
'scapement of St. Andrew's church	213
Regulators detached, 'scapements for	196
Recoiling and dead-beat 'scapement	168
Repeating clock, description of	328
noticed	328
and watches	ib.
movement and motion-work	333
watch, dumb	332
Reaumur's thermometer	346
Reservoirs for oil at pivot holes	273
Ridley's sector depthening tool	119
Rittenhouse, his observations on air affecting pendulums	131
Ring-day of the month, mode of shifting	308–311
Romans, Horologia of	2
Rome, sun-dial at	5
time measured by water at	ib.
Roy, Julien Le, his time-keeper described	App. F. 458
Robison, Professor, his history of Hooke's inventions referred to	185
Roy, General, his table of expansion of metals	351

S

'Scapement, Cumming's, as applied to pendulums	135
of a clock described	172
detached, Mudge's	192–251
of a clock whose pallets require no oil	204
Hooke's old do. for watches	224
new for watches	225
Tompion's for watches	226

	Page
'Scapement, Graham's improvement of	226
cylinder	227
Debaufre	234
Hantefeuille	236
duplex, or Tyrer's	239
Flamenville	241
with the tumbling pallets	ib.
Kendal's	ib.
free or detached	242
Peter Le Roy's	243
Berthoud's	ib.
Arnold's App. C. &	244
Earnshaw's App. D. &	245
Howell's	252
spring pallet, Mudge's	253
revolving by Breguet	256
for Astronomical clock	408
Schmidt, M. of Stutgard, his oil	273
Scrymgeour, Mr. of Glasgow, his rewinder to a chronometer	219
Sector pitching tool	102
tables for	107
use of in giving sizes of wheels	109
Setting clock or watch, method of	153
Sidereal time, pendulum for	149
noticed	315
Sizing pinions, rule for	117
Smeaton's pallets for 'scapement of Greenwich clock	212
his tables for expansion of metals	350
Snail, description of	330
Spring clocks	37
Spring, balance of watches and chronometers	262
Spring, straight, Hooke's	263
Spring, spiral, properties of	266
balance, properties of	267
main, force of	281
musical, in snuff-boxes, &c.	425
Stars fixed, table of the acceleration of	323
Stogden, repeating motion-work	33
Sully, biographical notice of	234
his account of an equation clock	296
Substitute for a transit instrument	324
Sun-dials, use of by ancients	5

T

Table 1. Of the periodical revolutions	73
2. of the wheel-work in Antide Janvier's sphere mouvante	74
3. of the wheel-work of the revolutions of Jupiter's satellites	75
4. Of the wheel-work of the different motions, and revolutions of the moon	ib.
5. Of numbers calculated by Dr. Pearson to produce the revolutions of Jupiter's satellites from a mover of 24 hours	76
— Do. do. from a mover of 7 days	77
Table 1. For the sector, pinions of 6 leaves	107
2. of 7 do.	107

INDEX.

	Page
ble 3. For the sector pinions of 8 do.	108
4. of 10 do.	ib.
5. of 12 do.	ib.
For length of pendulum in different latitudes	123
the alteration necessary when gaining or losing	147
Of length of pendulum, their vibration in a minute, and the numbers for the teeth of each wheel to produce them	157
Of the trains of watches, chronometers, &c. or their beats in an hour, with the numbers for the wheels and pinions	159
Of various sizes of clock-weights and bells, their solidity, and weight necessary to fill them	171
for dividing and cutting teeth	295
of equation of time	318
of mean time at true noon	320
of the acceleration of fixed stars	323
of the expansion of metals, Ferguson's	350
Ellicott's	ib.
Smeaton's	ib.
General Roy	351
Berthoud	355
De Luc & Dalby	356
of prime numbers, up to 10,000	420
Temperature, effects of, on pendulum springs	133
Thermometers	345
Fahrenheit's	346
Reaumur's	ib.
Celsus, or thermometer Centigrade	346
Fahrenheit's, proposed alteration on	347
Thirty-six day clocks	36
Time, equation of	314
apparent	315
mean	ib.
sidereal	ib.
Tompion's watch 'scapement, solid cylinder	226
Trajan's column	4
Trains, examples on finding	21
for watches, chronometers tables of	159
Transit instrument, substitute for	324
Tyrer's 'scapement or duplex	239
Turret-clock	389
diameter of barrel of	390
length of pendulum of	391
numbers for wheels of	ib.
revolutions of fly pinion of	394
locking of striking part of	ib.
size of wheels	396
of frame	ib.
dial-wheels for 2, 3, & 4, dials	398
diameter of dial wheels of	399
Turret-clock of town-house of Paris	401

Turret-clocks, weight of hammer of	402
crane for winding up	ib.
30 hour preferable to 8 days	404
space necessary for	ib.
Smeaton, Ludlam, and Holmes, their letters on	App. A. 429
V.	
Vibrations, Numbers of in an hour, examples on	13
of pendulum in Jamaica and London	122
table of, in different latitudes	123
Phipps' observations on	124
Kater, Captain, experiments on	ib.
Warren's observations on	ib.
Le Roy, remarks on	129
examples to find number of	140
Vick, Henry, his ancient clock	2
general description of	8
W	
Walker of Lynn, his method of preparing oil	271
Walnut oil	273
Watches flat	28
repeating train	44
Watch finishers, hints to	211
Watches, historical remarks on	221
verge 'scapement, movement for	219
pendulum springs, collet of	222
imperfections of, remarks on	ib.
repeating, Quare's	329
Barlow's	ib.
balances	228
method of calculating their force	229
examples of	230
experiment on	ib.
Water clocks	1
Watt, James, his opinion of the hardness of flint, &c.	217
Wheels and pinions, general description of	7
Wheels and pinions of orreries	49
Wheel work of Janvier's sphere mouvante	74
to imitate the motion of Jupiter's satellites	75
annual revolutions of the earth	76
of the motion of the moon	75
numbers for, by Dr. Pearson	76
Wheels and pinions, pitchings of	89
Wheel teeth, shape of	96
problems on	94
Wheels and pinions, finding proportional sizes	104
rules for sizing	118
Winding, going in time of	274
Wood, expansion of	351
Wooden rod pendulum, remarks on	128

LIST OF WORKS,

REFERRED TO IN THIS TREATISE.

Horological Disquisitions. By J. Smith, Clockmaker, London, 1694.

The Artificial Clockmaker. By W. D. F, R. S. (William Derham, D. D.) London, 1696. The Fourth Edition, London, 1734.

A Description of Two Methods, by which the Irregularities in the Motion of a Clock, arising from the influence of heat and cold upon the rod of the pendulum, may be prevented. By John Ellicott, F. R. S. Read at the Royal Society, 4th June, 1752. Two plates. London, 1753.

The Elements of Clock and Watchwork, adapted to practice; in Two Essays. By Alexander Cumming, Member of the Philosophical Society, Edinburgh. 16 plates, London, 1766.

An Introduction to the Mechanical part of Clock and Watchwork, in two Parts. By Thomas Hatton, Watchmaker. 18 plates. London, 1773.

Astronomical Observations, made in St. John's College, Cambridge, in the years 1767 and 1768, with an account of several Astronomical Instruments. By the Rev. Mr. Ludlam. 8 Plates. Quarto. Cambridge, 1769.

A Description, with Plates, of the Time-keeper invented by the late Mr. Thomas Mudge. To which is prefixed, a Narrative by Thomas Mudge, his son, of measures taken to give effect to the invention since the reward bestowed upon it by the House of Commons in the year 1793. A republication of a Tract, by the late Mr. Mudge, on the Improvement of Time-keepers. And a series of Letters written by him to his Excellency Count Bruhl, between the years 1773 and 1787.

A Treatise on Mechanics, Theoretical, Practical, and Descriptive, by Olinthus Gregory, A.M. of the Royal Military Academy, Woolwich. London, 1807.

Whewall's Elementary Treatise on Mechanics, with Plates. 8vo. Cambridge, 1819. *An excellent work.*

Description abrégée d'une Horloge d'une nouvelle invention pour la juste Mesure du Temps en Mer, avec le jugement de l'Académie Royale des Sciences sur cette invention. Et une Dissertation sur la nature des tentatives pour la decouverte des Longitudes dans la Navigation, et sur l'usage des Horloges, pour la Mesure du Temps en Mer. Par Henry Sully, Horloger de S. A. S. Monseigneur le Duc D'Orleans. 3 Plates. Paris, 1726.

L'Art de Conduire et de Régler les Pendules et les Montres, à l'usage de ceux qui n'ont aucune connoissance d'Horlogerie. Paris, 1759. 4 Plates.—A Fourth edition, 5 plates. Par F. Berthoud, Mecanicien de la Marine, Membre de l'Institut de France, et de la Société Royale de Londres, Membre de la Legion d'Honneur. Paris, 1811.

Traité general des Horloges. Par le R. P. Dom. Jacques Alexandre, Religieux Benedictin de la Congregation de St. Maur. Ouvrage enriché de figures. Paris, 1734.

Regle Artificielle du Temps, traité de la division naturelle et artificielle du Temps, des Horloges et des Montres de différentes constructions, de la maniere de les connoitre, et de les regler avec justesse. Par M. Henry Sully, Horloger de Monseigneur Le Duc d'Orleans. De la Societé des Arts. Nouvelle edition, corrigée et augmentée de quelques Memoires sur l'Horlogerie, par M. Julien Le Roy, de la même Societé. Paris, 1737. The first edition was published at Vienna in 1714, and translated into various languages.

Traité de l'Horlogerie, Mécanique et Pratique, approuvé par l'Academie Royale des Sciences. Par Thiout l'ainé, maitre horloger à Paris, demeurant Quay Pelletier, Horloger Ordinaire de S. M. C. la Reine Douairière d'Espagne, et de S. A. S. Monseigneur le Duc d'Orleans. With 91 plates. Two vols. 4to. Paris, 1741.

Essai sur l'Horlogerie, dans lequel on traite de cet Art relativement à l'usage civile, à l'astronomie, et à la navigation, en etablissant des principes confirmés par l'experience. Dédié aux artistes, et aux amateurs. Par M. Ferdinand Berthoud, Horloger. With 38 plates. 2 vols. 4to. Paris, 1763.

Les Echappemens à Repos, comparés aux Echappemens à recueil, avec une memoire sur une montre de nouvelle construction, &c. suivi de quelques réflexions sur l'etat présent de l'horlogerie, sur la police des maîtres horlogers de Paris, et sur la nature de leur statuts. Par Jean Jodin, *Horloger à-Saint-Germain-en-Laye.* Paris, 1766.

Traité d'Horlogerie, contenant tout ce qui est nécessaire pour bien connoitre, et pour régler les pendules et les montres. La Déscription des pièces d'horlogerie les plus utiles, des répétitions, des équations, des pendules à une roue, &c. celle de nouvel échappement, un Traité des engrénages, avec plusieurs Tables, et xvii Planches en Taille-douce: Augmenté de la description d'une nouvelle pendule Policamératique. Par M. J. A. Lepaute, horloger du Roi. 1 vol. 4to. 17 Plates. Paris, 1767.

Voyage faite par ordre du Roi en 1768, pour éprouver les montres marines, inventées par M. Le Roy. Par M. Cassini, Fils. Avec le memoir sur la meilleure manière de mesurer le tems en mer, qui a remporté le prix double, au jugement de l'Academie Royale des Sciences. Co tenant la description de la montre à longitudes, presentée à sa Maje le 5 Aout 1766. Par M. Le Roy l'ainé, Horloger du Roi. 4to. containing 6 Plates, and a Chart. Paris, 1770.

Traité des Horloges Marines, contenant la théorie, la construction, la main-d'oeuvre de ces machines, et la manière de les éprouver, pour parvenir par leur moyen à la rectification des cartes marines, et à la détermination des Longitudes en Mer; dédié à sa Majesté, et publié par ses ordres. Par M. Ferdinand Berthoud, horloger mécanicien du Roi, et de la Marine, ayant l'inspection de la construction des horloges marines. Membre de la Société Royale de Londres. 27 Plates. 4to. Paris, 1773.

Eclaircissemens sur l'invention, la théorie, la construction, et les épreuves des nouvelles machines proposées en France, pour la détermination des Longitudes en Mer, par le Mésure du Temps; servant de suite à l'Essai sur l'Horlogerie et au Traité des Horloges Marines, et de Réponse à un Ecrit qui a pour titre; " Précis des Recherches faites en France, pour la détermination des Longitudes en Mer par la Mésure Artificièlle du Temps." Par F. Berthoud. Quarto. Paris, 1773.

Les Longitudes par la Mesure du Temps, ou Methode pour Déterminer les Longitudes en mer, avec le secours des Horloges Marines; suivi du Recueil des Tables nécessaires au Pilote, pour réduire les observations relative à la longitude et à la latitude. Par M. F. Berthoud. 4to. 1 Plate. Paris, 1775.

De la Mesure du Temps, ou Supplément au Traité du Horloges Marines, et à l'Essai sur l'Horlogerie, contenant les principes de construction, d'execution, et d'épreuves des Petites Horloges à Longitude; et l'application des mêmes principes des construction, &c. aux Montres de poche, ainsi que plusieurs constructions d'Horloges Astronomique, &c. Publié par ordre du Roi. Par M. F. Berthoud. 11 Plates. Quarto. Paris, 1787.

Traité des Montres à Longitudes, contenant la construction, la description, et tous les details de main-d'œuvres de ces machines; leurs dimensions, la manière de les éprouver, &c. suivi, 1°. Du mémoire instructif sur le travail des Horloges et des Montres à Longitude. 2°. De la description du deux Horloges Astronomiques. 3°. De Essai sur une methode simple de conserver le rapport des poids et des mésures, et d'etablir une mesure universelle et perpétuelle. Par M. F. Berthoud. 6 Plates. Quarto. Paris, 1792.

Suite du Traité des Montres à Longitudes, contenant, 1°. La construction des Montres verticales portatives, et celle des Horloges horisontales, pour servir dans le plus longues traversées. 2°. La description et les épreuves des petites horloges horisontales plus simples et plus portatives. 2 Plates. Quarto. Par F. Berthoud, l'An V. de la Republique (1797, vieux style) Paris.

De la Mesure du Temps par les Horloges dans l'usage civil, ou l'exposition des motifs qui doivent faire adopter dans l'usage de la mésure du temps par les Horloges, le temps egal, appellé *Temps Moyen;* au lieu du temps variable du soleil, appellé *Temps vrai ou apparent.* Par Ferdinand Berthoud, Membre de l'Institut National. Paris. Fructidor l'An V. de la Republique, 1797.

Histoire de la Mesure du Temps, par les Horloges. Par Ferdinand Berthoud, Mécanicien de la Marine, Membre de l'Institut National de France, et de la Société Royale de Londres. Paris. De l'Imprimerie de la République, An X. (1802.) 23 Plates. 4to. Two volumes.

Supplément au Traité des Montres à Longitudes, suivi de la notice des recherches de l'auteur depuis 1752 jusqu'au 1807. Par Ferdinand Berthoud, Mécanicien de la Marine, Membre de l'Institut National de France, et de la Société Royale de Londres, Membre de la Legion d'Honneur. Quarto. Paris, 1807

Des Révolutions des Corps Célestes par le Mécanistne des Rouages. Par Antide Janvier. 8 Plates. Quarto. Paris, 1812.

Manuel Chronométrique, ou Précis de ce qui concerne le temps, ses divisions, ses mesures, leurs usages, etc. Publié par Antide Janvier, Horloger Ordinaire du Roi, de l'Academie des Sciences de Besançon, de la Société R. Acad. de l'Athenée, des Arts, etc. Five Plates. 12mo. Paris, 1821.

Cours de Mathematique, Troisième Partie, Elémens de Mechanique Statique. Tome second. Par M. Camus, de l'Academie Royale des Sciences, de la Société Royale de Londres, Examinateur des Ingenieurs et du corps Royale de l'Artillerie, Professeur et Secretaire perpétuel de l'Academie Royale d'Architecture, et Honoraire de l'Academie de Marine. Paris. 1767.

Horlogerie Pratique, à l'usage des apprentis et des amateurs. Par M. Vigniaux, Horloger de Toulouse. Thick octavo, with 12 Plates. A Toulouse, 1788.

Essai sur les Montres aux repetitions, par François Crespe de Genève, &c. Genève. An. XII. 1804.

A work in German, by John George Hartmanns, watchmaker to the University of Halle. Octavo, with Plates, published at Halle, 1756.

In German, a good deal has been published by John Henry Morrice Poppe, in a pamphlet of 90 pages, entitled (in English,) " Essay of a History on the Rise and Progress of the Theory and Practice of Clockmaking, at Gottingen," 1797, and a larger work at Leipzig, 1801.

For a copious List of Authors, see *Gregory's Mechanics.*

FINIS.

LIST OF PLATES.

	Page
PLATE I—1. Vick's ancient clock,	8 to 12
2. Mudge's lunation	70
3. Ditto, ditto	70
4. Ditto, ditto	70
5. Camus' motion of the earth	60
II.—6. Principle of the lever	82
7. Ditto, ditto	86
8. Ditto, ditto	83
9. Ditto, ditto	ib.
10. Ditto, ditto	91
11. Ditto, ditto	92
II. (A.)—Fig. 1. Manner of tracing cyclodial curves, for teeth of wheels and leaves of pinions	94
2. Ditto, ditto	ib.
3. Ditto, ditto	ib.
4. Ditto, ditto	ib.
5. Ditto, ditto	ib.
III.—12. Lines, Triangles, &c.	121
13. Ditto, ditto	124
14. Ditto, ditto	125
15. Ditto, ditto	125
16. Ditto, ditto	125
17. Crown-wheel and verge 'scapement	172
18. Horizontal 'scapement	226
IV.—19. Alarm clock	174
20. Dial of ditto	174
21. C. Huygens de Zulichem's clock	181
No. Y. Ditto, cyclodial cheeks	182
22. Ditto, going in time of winding	183 & 274
23. Anchor 'scapement	184
24. Graham's dead-beat ditto	191
25. Recoil ditto	188
26. Dead-beat ditto	188

PLATE V.—27. Lepaute's 'scapement . . . 187
  28. Harrison's ditto . . . 205
  29. Parts of ditto . . . 205
  30. Parts of ditto . . . 205
  31. Crown-wheel, with the teeth formed to keep the oil at them . . . 206
  D. Form of drill, for making a hollow for oil reservoir at pivot holes . . 274

VI.—32. Mudge's re-winding 'scapement . 255
  33. Ditto, ditto . . . 255
  Nos. 1 & 2. Parts of ditto . 255
  34. Clock detached 'scapement . . 201
  Nos. 1 & 2. Parts of ditto . . 201
  35. Clock-spring pallet 'scapement . 196
  36. Parts of ditto . . . 197

VII.—37. Pennington's sector . . . 102
  38. Part of ditto . . . ib.
  39. Ditto, ditto . . . ib.
  40. Ditto, ditto . . . ib.
  41. Double Pulley . . . 138

VIII.—42. Reid's gravitating 'scapement . 207
  Nos. 1 & 2. Parts of ditto . . 208
  43. Movement with verge 'scapement . 220
  44. C. Huygens' movement . . . 225
  45. Debaufre's 'scapement . . . 234
  46. Hautefeuille's 'scapement . . 237

IX.—47. Dutertre's 'scapement . . 238
  48. Clock duplex ditto   238 and App. B. 453
  49. Watch ditto, ditto . . . 240
  50. Tumbling pallet ditto . . . 242
  Nos. 1, 2 & 3. Parts of ditto . . 242
  51. Arnold's detached ditto 245 and App. C. 453
  52. Earnshaw's ditto 245 and App. D. 455
  53. Robinson's ditto 247 and App. E. 457

X.—54. Thiout's detached 'scapement . . 242
  55. Mudge's ditto . . . 252
  Nos. 1. & 2. Parts of ditto . ib.
  56. Howell's ditto . . . ib.
  57. Arnold's compensation balance . . 262
  No. 1. Edge view of ditto . . ib.

LIST OF PLATES. 475

		Page
PLATE X. cont^d—58. Earnshaw's compensation balance		262
No. 1. Edge view of ditto	.	ib.
59. Berthoud's compensation balance	.	ib.
60. Ditto, ditto	.	ib.
D. and E. Parts of ditto	.	ib.

XI.—61. Le Roy's marine time-keeper 259 and App. F. 458
Nos. 1. & 2. two thermometers App. (F.) 459
62. Pennycuick House equation clock, equation wheels, &c. of Nos. 1. 2. and 3. . 301

XII.—63. Pull repeating clock 333
64. Different view . . . . ib.
65. Ditto, ditto 334
Nos. 1. 2. 3. & 4. Parts of ditto . . 339

XIII.—66. Repeating watch . . . 339
67. Different view . . 340
68. Ditto, ditto . . . 341
Nos. 1. 2. 3. 4. 5. & 6. Parts of ditto . 343

XIV.——Fahrenheit's thermometer . 347
proposed alteration on ditto . ib.
scale, &c. . . ib.
Celsius' centigrade thermometer . ib.
Reaumur's ditto . . ib.
Formulæ . . . ib.
S. Steel piece of Hindley's dividing engine 292
Diagram . . . 403

XV.—69. Reid's mercurial pendulum . . 362
70. Gridiron ditto . . . 363
71. Ellicott's ditto 369
Nos. 1. 2. & 3. Parts of ditto . . ib.
72. Smeaton's ditto . . . 372
73. Reid's piece for putting on pendulums, to assist in putting them on beat . . 375

XVI.—74. Reid's zinc tube pendulum . . 373
75. glass rod and zinc tube ditto . 374
76. Troughton's pendulum . . 376
Nos. 1. 2. 3. 4. 5. & 6. Parts of ditto . 377
77. Ward's zinc rod pendulum . . 378
Nos. 1. 2. 3. 4. 5. & 6. Parts of ditto . ib.
78. Reid's wooden rod pendulum . . 383
S. Section of a pendulum ball, consisting of frustums of two equal cones . . . 368

LIST OF PLATES.

Page

PLATE XVII.—79. Music barrel, with apparatus for pricking 414
80. Side view of the apparatus for pricking 415
81. End view of the bells, barrel, hammers, &c. 419
82. Set of music bells, fixed on their studs, &c. 420
83. Brass scale of music, and gamut . 415
84. Ditto, ditto . . . *ib.*

XVIII. and XIX.—Turret clock work, connected with Smeaton, Ludlam, and Holmes's letters . . . App. (A.) 429

O-1/13